PENGUIN BOOKS

TANK

Patrick Wright was born in 1951 and educated at the University of Kent and Simon Fraser University in Canada. A professor of modern cultural studies at Nottingham Trent University, Wright has also written *On Living in an Old Country, A Journey Through Ruins,* and *The Village That Died for England.*

International Acclaim
for Patrick Wright and *Tank*

"[A] wide-ranging and lively history . . . Wright has assembled a prodigious saga. . . .This witty, trenchant and engaging chronicle of the tank and its century is, indeed, something more instructive and astonishing than anything H.G. Wells ever dreamed of."
—Chris Lehman, *The Washington Post*

"Wright's book is an excellent military history . . . written in a lively prose and with a wealth of unfamiliar detail."
—Gordon A. Craig, *The New York Review of Books*

"Wright liberates military history from the military experts' blinkered view . . . we should all be deeply grateful that he has done us the favor of pouring so much into this rich, fascinating, definitive book."
—Bruce McCall, *The New York Times Book Review*

"Wright's exhaustive research offers a treasure trove of facts usually eclipsed in conventional military or technical histories . . . Wright brings vital social and microhistorical data to military history and fleshes out the story of one of the twentieth century's most powerful, destructive and highly symbolic creations."
—*Publishers Weekly*

"Particularly delightful for readers interested in military history, but Wright's witty prose and careful cultural analysis will also appeal to general readers." —*Kirkus Reviews*

D1488001

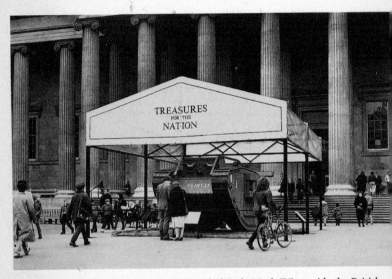

The restored First World War tank 'Flirt II' (female Mark IV) outside the British Museum, London, during the National Heritage Memorial Foundation's exhibition of its works, *Treasures for the Nation* (1989).

TANK

The Progress of
a Monstrous War Machine

PATRICK WRIGHT

PENGUIN BOOKS

PENGUIN BOOKS
Published by the Penguin Group
Penguin Putnam Inc., 375 Hudson Street,
New York, New York 10014, U.S.A.
Penguin Books Ltd, 80 Strand, London WC2R 0RL, England
Penguin Books Australia Ltd, 250 Camberwell Road,
Camberwell, Victoria 3124, Australia
Penguin Books Canada Ltd, 10 Alcorn Avenue,
Toronto, Ontario, Canada M4V 3B2
Penguin Books India (P) Ltd, 11 Community Centre,
Panchsheel Park, New Delhi – 110 017, India
Penguin Books (N.Z.) Ltd, Cnr Rosedale and Airborne Roads,
Albany, Auckland, New Zealand
Penguin Books (South Africa) (Pty) Ltd, 24 Sturdee Avenue,
Rosebank, Johannesburg 2196, South Africa

Penguin Books Ltd, Registered Offices:
Harmondsworth, Middlesex, England

First published in Great Britain by Faber and Faber Limited 2000
First published in the United States of America by Viking Penguin,
a member of Penguin Putnam Inc. 2002
Published in Penguin Books 2003

1 3 5 7 9 10 8 6 4 2

ISBN 0-670-03070-8 (hc.)
ISBN 0 14 20.0191 0 (pbk.)
CIP data available

Printed in the United States of America

Contents

List of Illustrations

Pictures in text

TANK

'Don't be too painstaking in putting in every rivet. Leave something to the imagination and try and develop the art of suggestion.'

Terence Cuneo, *Tanks and How to Draw Them*, London, 1943

1

The Heaviness of an Age

'Behold now Behemoth, which I made with thee.' It was with these words, spoken out of a whirlwind, that God chose to remind a rebellious Job of the barely imaginable power he had dared to question.

Literal-minded readers of the Book of Job may imagine that the vast grass-eating monster pictured lying 'under the shady trees, in the covert of the reed, and fens' is really a hippopotamus or a water buffalo, just as the awe-inspiring Leviathan ('Shall not one be cast down even at the sight of him?') that God invokes next is plainly a whale. Yet this Behemoth cannot be reduced even to the most formidable of ordinary creatures. His bones are like bars of iron and he 'pierceth through snares' with his nose. He has a tail as vast as a cedar and unearthly power lodged in the 'navel of his belly'. He 'drinketh up' the entire River Jordan at a single unhurried gulp. As 'the chief of the ways of God', Behemoth has the whole of Creation at his service: 'mountains bring him forth food . . . The shady trees cover him with their shadow; the willows of the brook compass him about.'

Confronted with this overwhelming manifestation of divine force, Job can only put his hand over his complaining mouth and 'repent in dust and ashes'. And no sooner has he done so than Behemoth becomes the guarantor of a divine promise: submit to the power of the Lord and things will get better, as they were indeed to do for Job, who is said to have lived on to the ripe old age of a hundred and forty, generously landed, blessed with beautiful daughters and prosperous sons.

The tank has been compared to Behemoth many times during its history, and for good reason. It too is a monstrous presence that compels by show as well as by the more conventional force hidden in its belly. It is a spellbinding contrivance that leaves onlookers in no doubt where they stand, even if it rarely offers a better life to the crushed and overawed.

Job's Behemoth testified to the might of God, but by the early nineteen-nineties, when I first took notice of it, the tank was an emblem of secular state power, crawling chaotically through the wreckage of the Cold War while the global television audience looked on. Disorientated by recent events, it was a savage compound of fact and fiction: a practical weapon but also a terrifying emblem of the very history that was unravelling all around it. For many soldiers and military historians, the symbolic life of the tank is merely a sideshow, a secondary reflection of this weapon's true capabilities. Yet, as technically ignorant civilians have often been well placed to grasp, the power of this war machine is inseparable from its potency as an idea and image. The tank is indeed a Behemoth of the modern age and, for one brilliant moment in 1989, the man who confronted it seemed braver than Job.

Bodies heaped up at a hospital, crushed bicycles, the Goddess of Democracy toppled and broken . . . Many pictures emerged from Tiananmen Square over those tumultuous weeks, but the one that came to speak for them all dates from 5 June, a day or so after the massacre, when the People's Liberation Army were securing lines of supply into the reoccupied square. As part of this operation a column of Norinco Type 69/59 main battle tanks set off down the Avenue of Eternal Peace, 'rolling', as tanks do in reality as well as in their attendant journalistic cliché, into the encounter that would be captured by nervous Western photographers and cameramen crouching on the balconies of the old Beijing Hotel.

Kate Adie reported the event that night on the BBC's *Nine O'Clock News*. 'Just after midday the tanks rolled out of the square. A lone young man stood in front of the first one. The tank faltered; came to a stop . . .' And there the man stayed, squared off against a 40-ton state war machine that sat there, dominating the tarmac with an evenly distributed ground pressure of a little over 0.8 kg per square centimetre. The leading tank veered to the right, but the man stepped into its way. It turned to the left, but he moved to obstruct it again, all the time shouting and gesturing for it to withdraw. He climbed up on to the thing, attempting to speak to the men inside. Eventually the tank commander emerged to reply to the tiny figure, who was by this time back on the ground. Later the man cycled off, returning to intercept the column again some hundred and twenty yards further down the road.

The photographs of this perilous mechanical ballet appeared on the front pages the next day. Some tried to bring the heroic figure as close as possible, while others stressed his vulnerability, showing him tiny and remote in the eerie void of Changan Avenue, with a long column of tanks, perhaps as many as twenty updated descendants of the first Soviet T-54s supplied to China in the 1950s, stretching away in front of him, and a burned-out bus at the side of the road. The man's stance varied with every click of the shutter: his two bags shifted from one hand to the other; in some pictures he gesticulated; in others he stood with arms at his side, apparently passive.

Three years later, when writing about this instantly globalized image for the *Guardian,* I talked to some of the people who had been involved in its initial capture.[1] As Kate Adie remembered, the most striking thing about the confrontation was that it wasn't actually a single moment. The man was there for some time, persisting and engaging the tank soldiers in conversation. 'It was an extraordinarily purposeful but mundane way of doing things . . . It seemed impromptu. There he was with his little plastic bag – such a human touch, as if he had been shopping.' Despite the contrast between the man and those menacing machines, it had seemed remarkably unheroic at the time: here was 'Little Mr Ordinary' in a drama that looked all the more remarkable because 'the Chinese people are not known for individualistic behaviour'.

Photographer Stuart Franklin, who works with the Magnum agency, was on a balcony higher up the Beijing Hotel, one with a better angle than had been available to the BBC. Most Western photographers and reporters missed the event, having booked into the Sheraton, where you could get hamburgers rather than just noodles, but Franklin remembered sharing his vantage point with the American photographer Charlie Cole, who was working for *Newsweek,* and also a writer from *Vanity Fair.* Speaking from another far-flung hotel room, this time in Quito, Ecuador, he confirmed that his picture has been widely used: indeed, he even had multiple copies in his rucksack in Ecuador, emblazoned on American 'Fruit of the Loom' T-shirts. He had watched the column of tanks forming up behind a group of soldiers and then starting to move slowly down Changan Avenue. He had seen the student coming out to talk with the tank commander, an encounter that may have gone on for as long as five minutes, until the man was dragged away, presumably by friends. *Vanity Fair*'s correspondent had quickly declared this to be the key symbolic moment of the whole Tiananmen Square story, but Franklin had hardly seen the point at the time. He had not thought of it as 'a strong moment or photo', and he still didn't think much of his picture, preferring other less well-known images that he had taken in Tiananmen Square over previous days. 'The guy isn't even gesticulating,' he declared with the mild despair of a professional who finds one of his lesser works – little more than a grainy, ill-composed snap – selected by history and elevated far above the others. He dismissed the picture as 'a bit of a reach really', far too dependent on what people were prepared to read into it. Not a photograph then, but 'a symbol' of the kind that hadn't been seen since Czechoslovakia in 1968: 'all that stuff about man against the machine, and war becoming more and more mechanized . . . You can go off into desperate vagaries, really.'

Charlie Cole also remembered the event from a hotel room, this one in Bangkok. He and other occupants of the Beijing Hotel had spent the previous night lying on the floor, with gunfire blazing around them, and bullets ricocheting off the hotel wall. He recalled the emptiness of the street, remarking that only a short time previously soldiers had opened fire on people crowding there. When the man appeared in front of the tank, 'there was no doubt in my mind that he was going to be killed. They'd shot so many others, and I was certain he'd die.' He remembers hoping that the young man would run, and also shaking and trying to hold his breath while he took the last few pictures on his reel. Reaching for comparison, he likened the experience to deer-hunting – to the 'buck fever' that induces trembling just as the trigger has to be squeezed.

It was Charlie Cole's photograph that went on to win the World Press Award, a fact he described as 'a bit of an embarrassment', doubting that his was better than anyone else's, and smiling at Stuart Franklin's suggestion that it must have been more stylishly cropped. He too reckoned the event should be recognized as 'an incredible action not an incredible picture'. In his view, this was one of the few occasions when television had the edge on still photography. Indeed, for many people the photographs had probably only served to confirm the memory of the television pictures, which were able to show the tension building up in a way that no single image could do. So one image recedes into another in the hall of mirrors that is global media coverage.

The third man on that remembered balcony of the Beijing Hotel was T. D. Allman, the American writer whose long feature article eventually appeared in the October 1989 issue of *Vanity Fair*, several months after the events in Tiananmen Square had been concentrated into that single image of an unarmed man stopping tanks.[2] Allman set the encounter against a background of cacophonous ferment in the square, with blaring government loudspeakers suppressing the softer sound of a million voices speaking 'individually and freely', while, somewhere far away on the other side of the square, someone played Beethoven's 'Ode to Joy' through a tinny megaphone. Although he had been in no position to break the word at the time, Allman put himself back on that tenth-floor balcony at the Beijing Hotel as the prophetic first observer of one of the twentieth century's most telling moments: '"Tank Man," I silently called to him, craning out over the balcony, "the whole world will revere you because you're stopping the tanks with your right hand."' Yet it had been the object this man held in his left hand – 'a small valise, a shopping bag perhaps' – that had made him a 'true exemplar of Beijing's heroism. For weeks now, the people of Beijing have been stopping tanks with their right hands, while going about the daily business of life carrying bags – with vegetables, or laundry, or democracy posters in them – in their left hands.'

By visiting this seizure on the machinery of the communist state, 'Tank Man' had also proved that time is now spatial not linear: 'Tiananmen Square in its hour of freedom was not just an outpost of democracy in an autocratic land. It belonged to a new millennium, in which human dreams and hopes, as much as video images, span continents and cultures instantly . . . one had only to look at Tiananmen Square to know: their time was our time. People looked at their TV screens and realized: those people are us.' The cameras had shown a small man, 'Little Mr Ordinary' as Kate Adie called him, standing up to a large tank, but Allman took this diminutive figure and pumped him up until he was immense: 'so much bigger than the tank that, even when you were standing on a balcony on the tenth floor, you looked up to him'. Earlier, Allman had seen Deng's machines at work elsewhere in Tiananmen Square: armoured personnel carriers, hanging back when the demonstrators were still strong, but then roaring down Changan Avenue when they were safe – 'safe even from someone throwing a stone' – and shooting at people just for fun. 'Then, with the bodies still lying around, the APCs danced. They gyrated. They swivelled. They turned pirouettes. They flaunted themselves . . .' Such was the grotesque masquerade that Tank Man had momentarily stopped. By standing up to the tank he had broken, and momentarily even reversed its mesmerism – surprising that unyielding instrument of totalitarian rule with a fleeting glimpse of the democratic future that would one day consign it to the scrapyard.

To begin with, Tank Man was entirely anonymous: a heroic Everyman of the democracy movement, name, whereabouts and subsequent fate unknown. But this was more than the Western press could bear. On 18 June 1989 an article in the *Sunday Express* identified the 'brave Chinese student seen by millions on TV', as Wang Weilin, nineteen-year-old son of a Peking factory worker. Alfred Lee reported that Wang had been identified by friends who saw him in a line of shaven-headed dissidents paraded on state TV: he was said to have been arrested by secret police less than two miles from

Changan Avenue, and to have been charged as 'a counter-revolutionary, a traitor, a political hooligan', and with 'attempting to subvert members of the People's Liberation Army'. The wavering tank commander was also reported to have been demoted for 'bringing disgrace and world-wide loss of face to the People's Army by halting his tanks'.

And that was about the extent of it. Amnesty International conceded that the evidence was speculative and 'very thin'. In June 1990 Jiang Zemin, the general secretary of the Chinese Communist Party, told American journalist Barbara Walters that Wang was 'I think never killed', but failed to say what had happened to him. A pro-Chinese newspaper in Hong Kong later denied that Wang had ever even been arrested, but there was considerable speculation in the West that the unknown hero had been shot shortly after the event that brought such humiliation to the People's Liberation Army. As a spokesman for Amnesty International pointed out, things like that were happening on the street at that time, sometimes without any authorization from senior officers. The *Sunday Express* quoted one of Wang's friends as saying: 'We fear he has been killed. He is the one person the authorities could never bring before a People's Court. He's a hero. If Wang was publicly executed, he would become a martyr and there would be a world outcry.' More recently, the Hong Kong-based Information Centre for Human Rights and Democracy Movement in China, has stated, on the evidence of an internal Chinese government document, that Tank Man had never been found, and that the name Wang Weilin may have been invented by friends in order to shield him.[3]

Whatever they have or have not done with the anonymous hero who came to be known as Wang Weilin, the Chinese authorities could not suppress the image he had given to the world. Deng Xiaoping was not at all conciliatory. On 9 June 1989 he gave a speech of thanks to the Martial Law Units who had suppressed the uprising, commending the People's Army as 'a great wall of iron and steel of the party and state'.[4] Yet the Chinese authorities would also make a half-hearted attempt to claim 'the scene recorded on videotape', as proof of the moderation with which the People's Liberation Army had set out to restore order. Anyone with any common sense could see that the tanks could have moved on if they wanted too: 'this lone scoundrel could never have stopped them'.[5] So the scene actually 'flies in the face of Western propaganda. It proves that our soldiers exercised the highest degree of restraint.'

Such claims did nothing to discourage the Chinese opposition, which had taken the highly condensed image to heart. Dr Wang Hao, who, by

1992, was training as an investment analyst in London, spoke of the new vision of Chinese youth that Wang Weilin had given to the Chinese people. While Wang embodied the old virtues of self-sacrifice and civilian courage, he also offered a new 'James Bond kind of image', which showed the individual triumphing against apparently insuperable odds. Wang Weilin's stand offered an alternative to the mass-based imagery of official propaganda, which, as Dr Wang remembered from his own schooldays, favoured the idea of the 'human wave' pouring on, regardless of the machine guns and tanks with which the capitalist enemy sought to repel it. Wang Weilin was a new kind of hero, and certainly not an industrious cog in the machine or a 'rustless screw', in the phrase applied to one propaganda hero of the fifties.

Tank Man's image has been subject to much interpretation in the West too. For military observers it reveals little other than the heavy-handed incompetence of the People's Liberation Army when it comes to engagements of the type known, in post-Cold War parlance, as 'Operations other than War'. Thus the eminent military historian Sir John Keegan informed me that Tank Man's stand had very little military significance: after characterizing it as a 'poetic image', which revealed 'the impersonal armed might of the army lined up against the unvanquished human spirit', Keegan broke off, rather as Stuart Franklin had done, saying dismissively: 'You can write the words yourself.' Some newspapers had certainly been doing that all along. Tantalized by the image of this man, who is universally known and yet almost completely obscure, newspapers have felt obliged to augment the story. One report confirmed Wang's status as a student by putting books in his bag; and there were diverse variations of the words he is said to have shouted at the tanks, from the simple 'Go away' of the *Sunday Express* to the more elaborate 'Go back, turn around, stop killing my people,' quoted by *Today* a week or so later.

Meanwhile leaders all over the world hailed this unknown hero. President Bush commended his courage, as did diverse cultural figures, from the senior rock star Neil Young to the composer and humanist Sir Michael Tippett. In Britain, it was Neil Kinnock, then leader of the Labour Party, who was generally reckoned to have spoken for Parliament, remarking: 'The memory of one unarmed young man standing in front of a column of tanks in Peking will remain with the British people long after the present leadership in China and what they stand for has been forgotten.' His claim would soon be corroborated by Wim Wenders, whose film *Until the End of the World* (1991) envisioned Tiananmen Square in the year 1999, complete with a golden monument of the man who faced up to the tanks. France's

President Mitterrand was forthright too: on the night of 5 June, he told the cameras that 'a regime reduced to firing on its youth has no future'.

If Tank Man's stand could immediately be grasped as one of the great global images of the twentieth century, this was partly because the Western imagination was already primed to receive it as such. Here was a representative Individual taking a uniquely heroic stand against a weapon that was itself far more than just a grinding thing of steel. By 1989 the tank was instantly recognizable as a spellbinding symbol of the crushing, all-powerful state monolith. The plastic shopping bag may have tilted the image towards consumerism, but Wang Weilin's stand was never just an unexpected incident on China's road to the shopping mall. The separation of military and civilian spheres is one of the defining characteristics of the modern nation state and, against that background, China's transgression was immediately identified as a classic human rights image: the perfect enactment of a sharply polarized drama already rehearsed through many previous incidents in which the apparently powerless citizen had been squared off against the rolling armour of dictators, juntas, and totalitarian regimes.

In Greece, the image stirred memories of the CIA-backed junta that drove tanks into Syntagma (Constitution) Square in Athens during the Colonels' Coup of 21 April 1967, and which later used armoured vehicles to break into Athens Polytechnic, where hundreds of striking students were slaughtered on 17 November 1973. Viewers in Chile are more likely to have recalled the tanks that were on the streets of Santiago on 11 September 1973, flattening Salvador Allende's elected Popular Unity government in what one over-involved American witness called a 'close to perfect' coup,[6] and heralding the installation of General Pinochet's seventeen-year dictatorship. But the most recent of these globally observed rehearsals had been enacted only three years previously in the Philippines, during the ESDA revolution that brought down Ferdinand Marcos's regime. Early in 1986, Marcos had rejected the results of a general election in which, despite extensive rigging, he had been defeated by Cory Aquino; and so, on 23 February, a coup was launched by a small pro-Aquino faction of the army. Marcos's armoured vehicles duly clattered out into the streets of Manila, only to find themselves surrounded by a human barricade of unarmed civilians who, encouraged by Cardinal Sin's radio appeal, had finally broken with the cowed habits of martial law and who, as the celebratory websites of 'people power' attest to this day, were not inclined to overestimate the difference between an armoured personnel carrier and the more brutal sounding 'tanks' of preferred description.

In this confrontation, the tank-stopper was not a single individual like Wang Weilin, but a virtuous collective of spell-busting civilians: priests with rosaries; nuns who knelt in the road holding up crucifixes and praying to the Virgin Mary; children and other courageous demonstrators who further defined the cause by climbing up on to those monstrous creatures of state to soften Marcos's often-bribed soldiers with free gifts of flowers, food and cigarettes. Carnage had loomed, but though Marcos warned his rebellious subjects: 'you are very vulnerable to artillery attack and tank attack',[7] he did not give his impatient General Fabian Ver the expected order to open fire, and the invincible metal of his dictatorship melted away: his machines turned to grey jelly by this festive assertion of 'people power' and, altogether less visible in the visual snapshot that defined world perceptions of this transition, a pronounced shift in American allegiance.[8]

The memory of Filipino 'people power' was certainly stirred by Tiananmen, but there were older precedents too. In that instantly eternalized moment on Beijing's Avenue of Eternal Peace, Tank Man had carried off the magical operation that failed so memorably in the Czech writer Bohumil Hrabal's *A Close Watch on the Trains*. The tank-stopper in this novella of 1965 was a circus hypnotist rather than a crucifix-bearing nun. This fellow was considered a feckless fraud by his townsfolk and yet, as Hitler's tanks advanced towards Prague, it had been he alone who set out to 'hold them back by the force of suggestion':

He went striding along the high road with his eyes fixed on the leading tank, the spearhead of that entire motorised army. In this tank, waist deep in the cabin, stood an officer of the Reich, with a black beret with the death's-head badge and the crossed bones on his head, and my grandfather kept on going steadily forward, straight towards this tank, with his hands stretched out, and his eyes spraying towards the Germans the thought: 'Turn round and go back!'

And really, that first tank halted. The whole army stood still. Grandfather touched the leading tank with his outstretched fingers, and kept pouring out towards it the same suggestion: 'Turn round and . . .' And then the lieutenant gave a signal with his pennant, and the tank changed its mind and moved forward, but Grandfather never budged, and the tank ran over him and crushed his head, and after that there was nothing standing in the way of the German Army.[9]

Hitler's invading tanks had given way to Soviet machines by the time Hrabal's story was first published in 1965, and not just for the people of Czechoslovakia. These symbols of 'liberating' Soviet power had made a forceful appearance at the beginning of the Korean War, decked in leaves and pouring into South Korea with the North Korean People's Army in June

1950. Yet by 1989, when Tank Man made his stand in Tiananmen Square, the picture also confirmed everything that the West had learned about communism through more than four decades of tank-written history in Eastern Europe. Indeed, for millions of viewers, those machines in Changan Avenue were surely made of the same symbolic stuff as the 'Iron Curtain' that Winston Churchill had seen rolling across the continent of Europe shortly after the Second World War, and first named in a speech given at Fulton, Missouri, on 5 March 1946. Soviet and American tanks had confronted each other in a tense and closely observed two-day stand-off at Berlin's Checkpoint Charlie in October 1961 (the novelist Uwe Johnson describes gun barrels actually protruding over the border[10]); and, three years later, the mere sight of Soviet tanks assembling for a May Day parade in Berlin is said to have been enough to provoke Frederick Forsyth, then a Reuters correspondent in Berlin, into informing the West that World War Three was imminent.[11]

It was, however, the subjected and unarmed citizen who had faced the Soviet tank most dramatically: on the streets in the East Berlin uprising of 17 June 1953, in Hungary 1956 and, as Stuart Franklin remarked, in Prague 1968, when demonstrators put flowers in gun barrels and opened their shirts to these rolling emblems of Soviet power. By re-enacting this contest between heroic citizens and merciless totalitarian tanks, Wang Weilin dramatized a brutal truth about Chinese Communism; yet if the sight of his stand against that armoured column was immediately grasped as one of the great images of the age, this was because he did so in a manner that reinforced the West in its own most unyielding certainties: he had produced an image that the CIA would hardly have dared to invent.

The sight of this lone man would satisfy the anti-communist imagination, but it would also turn up in books of anarchist and radical persuasion, an ambient snap of the unsubdued subject standing out against the ever more total power of the state.[12] Philosophers around the world fell upon the image of Tiananmen, unravelling and recombining its elements to convert it into a sign of the spiritual and political condition of our times. For the Italian literary theorist Giorgio Agamben, Tiananmen was emphatically not just the latest reprise of the familiar struggle between communism and democracy. Far from being a straightforward case of 'Power' against 'the People', Tiananmen was the herald of a new kind of 'non-State', which interested Agamben precisely because it had 'nothing to do with the simple affirmation of the social in opposition to the State that has often found expression in the protest movements of recent years'.[13] For him, Tiananmen revealed the 'insurmountable disjunction' between the state and a 'coming community' that 'does not possess any identity to vindicate nor any bond of belonging for which to seek recognition' and which, for precisely that reason, could neither be co-opted nor tolerated by the state. The Chinese protesters could not be martialled either as 'the people' seeking to exercise power over the state, or under the flag of state-endorsed 'human rights'. As Agamben prophesied, 'Wherever these singularities peacefully demonstrate their being in common there will be a Tiananmen, and, sooner or later, the tanks will appear.'

By 1992 Amnesty International had adopted the image and was reprinting it in fund-raising advertisements to mark the third anniversary of the Tiananmen Square massacre. Yet some human rights activists were already wary of seeing the events of Tiananmen Square only through this polarizing lens. Robbie Barnett, who helped set up 'June 4th China Support' to assist refugees from the democracy movement, observed that while the struggle enacted in Tiananmen Square over those fifty days in 1989 had indeed been intensely iconographic, the symbolic drama at its core was actually more complex than was suggested by this isolated picture of one brave prisoner of conscience holding out against the totalitarian oppressor.

Tiananmen Square has been the site of what the critic Wu Hung has described as 'a war of monuments'[14] since at least 1919 when students from Beijing University came out to protest against the Treaty of Versailles, which ceded Chinese territory to the Japanese. In 1949 Mao came to Tiananmen to declare the founding of the People's Republic of China; and the communist regime has since sought to remake this vast imperial square in its own image. Yet the place had remained a focus of opposition as people came to reinterpret its monuments and use them to 'refresh their memories of previous struggles and sacrifices'. The student movement of 1989 was squarely in that ongoing tradition.

Barnett also wondered whether this highly individualized image of Wang Weilin standing up to the evil tank might not appear to corroborate a Western perception of China that was actually challenged by the events of 1989. Until that time it had been customary to view the communist system as a strong and stable state that would gradually loosen as the West traded with it. This approach, developed in the USA during the sixties, was inclined to avoid open condemnation of the regime in China, preferring to confine its criticism to individual cases of human rights abuses. The image was also revealing about the way the Western media handled international news. Knowledgeable specialist journalists were increasingly being replaced by roving celebrity reporters who scooped up 'action' wherever they found it. Meanwhile, television's appetite for personal witnesses and 'spectacle' remained insatiable and some people who had been rash enough to provide soundbites from the front line had already incurred lengthy jail sentences as a result. From this perspective, Tank Man was the star interviewee who got away.

Most important of all, however, Barnett hoped the image of Wang Weilin would not deflect people from asking the fundamental question about the democracy movement in China: was it only a student movement, or had it achieved a genuine integration with workers in the city and the countryside? It may have been the emergence of exactly this sort of wider support that convinced Chinese leaders that the movement had to be suppressed. The first tents to be crushed were those of the Worker's Autonomous Federation, and the first people arrested were workers too. From this perspective the true heroes of the event were the ordinary citizens of Peking who came out to defend the students and bore the brunt of the military response. What would have happened, Barnett wondered, if the democracy movement had produced an image that was not so immediately graspable on the West's own terms: a non-heroic image, say, or one in which the protest was more collective, or that included those ordinary workers? Would the West have been willing to read it?

These questions were understood by Li Lu, who had been in charge of the students' congress in Tiananmen Square. 'We feel so fortunate to have that image,' he told me from Columbia University in New York, adding that it belonged not to the West, not even just to the student movement, but to China as a whole. In Li's eyes, Tank Man was neither an individualistic figure nor a hero of superhuman proportions. Instead, he was a representative of his generation and its hopes: 'I feel so attached to this image, and I can assure you that all the people in that place share the attachment.'

But though Li was proud of Wang Weilin, he was also troubled by the way the momentarily arrested tank had been interpreted in the West. If the tank is a faceless emblem of totalitarian state power, then it takes a positive effort to imagine the driver as anything but a dehumanized automaton, dosed up on dogma and ideology – like the Chinese pilots of the 1960s, who are said to have read the Thoughts of Chairman Mao in order to learn how to fly an aeroplane.[15]

As Li pointed out, we can indeed conceive this image as the stand of a lone hero pitched against the brutal force of the armoured communist state, but only if we overlook the heroism of the tank commander who refused to drive on, as so many had done in the massacre of the day before. It was the tank commander's action that made all the difference to Li, demonstrating that the democracy movement could raise a sympathetic response not just among workers, but in the People's Liberation Army too. Li couldn't be sure, but he liked to think that both men were about the same age. It was the participation of the tank commander (or perhaps just the driver) that widened the image, bringing it away from the student movement, and making it the idealistic icon of the young generation as a whole.

Li Lu was interested to hear about the gold monument in Wim Wenders' film of the year 1999, but he preferred his own mind's eye to any cinema. 'I can see it now,' he said, peering into a Tiananmen Square where the Goddess of Democracy is back in place, this time made of more substantial stuff than the temporary materials used first time round. Behind that he saw a rather different new statue – golden perhaps and dedicated not just to Wang Weilin but also to the idealized tank commander who wouldn't run him over. It was only once the tank commander had been reinstated that Li was content to embrace that image as the primary icon of a revolution that would, he was quite sure, one day prevail.

Tank Man's stand was quickly adopted by CNN, incorporated into a tightly edited frieze of world events that was repeated endlessly to prove that CNN was number one when it came to global news coverage. The image has since found many other ways of careering around the world – speaking a harsh truth about the Chinese government, and, like so many Cold War images before it, marshalling complex events into a simple opposition between good and evil. It became one of the touchstones whereby Western leaders demonstrate their loyalty to democratic principles, a yardstick of integrity that showed up cynics and renegades for what they were – whether they were 'realists' like Henry Kissinger, whose patience with protesting students seems to have expired during the Vietnam War, or Edward Heath, the former British prime minister who visited China shortly afterwards and expressed the view that the problems of maintaining order in such a country were not exactly to be sniffed at; or more conventional fellow-travellers like the author Dr Han Suyin, who was soon telling a *Sunday Telegraph* reporter that the students would have been sensible to pull out of the square earlier, and suggesting that their struggle had been bank-rolled from Taiwan.[16] The same polarized measure has been applied to *The Gate of Heavenly Peace*, a film made in the USA that tried to take a wider view of the democracy movement in Tiananmen Square, and which was reviled for its efforts in the most vehement terms from both sides – by the Chinese authorities, and also by former activists who used their own kind of tank-logic to condemn the film's makers as Beijing collaborators of the worst sort.

Once created, Tank Man's image was soon being brought to bear on political situations elsewhere. In March 1990, thanks to the Tibet Information Network, of which Robbie Barnett was a founder member, news reached the outside world that the Chinese had stationed four 'tanks' outside the Jokhang temple, the Dalai Lama's Winter Palace in the central square of the ancient Tibetan quarter of Lhasa. These reports, in which Chinese tanks were lined up against 'the heart of the spiritual world of Tibetan Buddhism', were ridiculed by the authorities in Beijing, but then the pictures started emerging. As Barnett pointed out, 'For pure weight of symbolism, nothing can be much heavier than the tank,'[17] and this latest Chinese outrage was rendered all the more symbolic by the fact that it occurred on the tenth anniversary of the central government's First Symposium on Work in Tibet, which had admitted and condemned 'the excesses of ultra-leftism' previously visited upon Tibet, thereby initiating the period of liberalization that those armoured vehicles in front of the Jokhang temple now brought to an end.

Tibetan culture is intensely iconographic by tradition, and Barnett proceeded to weave those Chinese machines into an ingenious symbolic drama that threw the People's Liberation Army back on to the defensive. The Chinese may not have known it, but they had been lured into 'an arena rich in symbolism where, step by step, the ideology of Chinese liberalisation was stripped of value and exposed as rhetoric'.[18] They may have been all powerful on the street, but they were losing the battle against Tibetan iconography: 'a struggle over symbols in which they were constantly caught on the defensive'. Deprived of all disguise, their power was now revealed as the armoured monster that it was. The final irony was that this confrontation took place at the end of the Tibetan New Year festivities which, in that year of 1990, marked the inauguration of the Year of the Iron Horse. So the 'tanks' in front of the Johkang temple only confirmed the prophecies of the traditional Tibetan calendar.

In 1993 Wang Weilin's stand was to turn up in an unexpected connection in the USA. 'I'm the kind of guy that'll stand in front of a tank. You can run over me but I'll be back on one of the tracks . . .' Depending on your movie or perhaps your comic strip, those might have been the words of Wang Weilin, but they were actually uttered by David Koresh, leader of the Branch Davidians at Waco, speaking to the FBI through a specially provided video camera shortly before the final onslaught in April 1993. And then, as is suggested in William Gazecki's film *Waco: The Rules of Engagement*, the tanks went in, filling the place with CS gas, knocking holes in the structure to open it up to the wind, and setting off the conflagration that engulfed both the compound and many of its inhabitants.[19] In the end, Koresh may not have stood in front of the tanks, but it appears that one of his Branch Davidians, the late James Riddle, certainly did, and also that it was here, in Texas rather than Beijing, that the tank failed to stop. If Gazecki is right, Riddle lost a large portion of his right side, and became so caught up in the tracks that the tank itself was briefly immobilized.

On the eight anniversary of the conflict in Tiananmen Square, 4 June 1997, Senator Daniel Patrick Moynihan told the US Senate that the photograph of 'one lone Chinese individual – Wang Weilin – confronting a column of eighteen PLA tanks is both a tribute to the courage of the Chinese people and a fitting emblem for a regime that believes it can crush ideas with 120-millimetre guns and hold back the tide of history with bayonets'.[20] By then, the thought of Tank Man had moved on from the video promoting Michael Jackson's 'Earth Song', in which the megalomaniac pop star chanted 'What about Us?', while magically healing all the world's wounds: restoring the forests, bringing the dead back to life and throwing an advancing tank into reverse. Indeed, the migrant image was now hovering over Hong Kong, shaping the diplomacy of that industrious territory's return to China from the moment it was announced that more than 4,000 soldiers of the People's Liberation Army would be crossing the border in a convoy of 400 vehicles, including twenty-one armoured personnel carriers.

This was immediately condemned as 'completely inappropriate' by the British Governor of Hong Kong, Chris Patten. According to an Associated Press reporter, Patten remarked that while China had the right to send in its army, the 'most unfortunate' method it had chosen sent 'a very bad signal to Hong Kong and the rest of the world'. The same reporter observed that the presence of British troops had largely been seen as benign, and suggested that 'younger people have probably never even seen a real armoured vehicle except on television in 1989 when the Chinese Army was crushing democracy rallies in Beijing'.[21] On 29 June, British Foreign Secretary Robin Cook was reported to have challenged the Chinese not to deploy armoured cars in the streets of the territory. The British press surveyed 'the military build up' with one thought in mind. 'Here come the Tanks' as Simon Winchester's report was headed in the *Sunday Telegraph*, which duly printed the picture of Tank Man standing firm on the front page. The size of the military deployment showed the 'urgency' with which 'Sinicisation, or the patriotic re-education of Hong Kong would proceed'. 'Four thousand troops will stream in at dawn on Tuesday, by land, by sea and air, in a steady cavalcade of armoured cars, helicopters and naval vessels.'[22] The memory of Tiananmen Square seems also to have leant over the shoulder of the *Guardian*'s correspondent, Andrew Higgins, placing 'armoured personnel carriers' before helicopters and ships in his list of the hardware the Chinese were preparing to bring into Hong Kong on the following day.

Some Western reporters conceded that China's 196-strong advance guard had been unarmed and impeccably behaved; and the pro-Beijing press reported that Chinese troops had undergone special 'image training', including sing-alongs and lessons in correct posture, which certainly meant not driving your tank over lone demonstrators. Yet it was the human rights image from Tiananmen Square that governed perceptions – even in those organs of the Western press that were more inclined to remember that the tanks hadn't actually crushed Wang Weilin, and to conclude that, in the longer term, Hong Kong might also have an arresting influence on Chinese communism. That was the anticipation of *The Economist*, which featured yet another drawing of Wang Weilin on the cover, standing in front of the tank fitted with braces and a bag of dollars, looking altogether more like a banker than an aspiring consumer caught by surprise on his way home from the supermarket.

So communist China came to Hong Kong, unbending in its anti-imperialist rhetoric of succession but considerably more yielding in the image its army offered the world – its soldiers arrived in open trucks, apparently unarmed as they drove in through the rain. The tanks of Tiananmen Square may not since have materialized on the streets of Hong Kong but, having presided over the handover, the thought of Wang Weilin continued to roll forward. Indeed, he soon emerged as a leading contender in *Time* magazine's ongoing poll of 'the Person of the Century': identified as 'The Unknown Rebel', he was listed among the twenty people who have 'helped define the political and social fabric of our times' – an inspiring figure placed alongside more conventional candidates such as Einstein (the eventual winner), Mao Zedong, Margaret Thatcher and Adolf Hitler as 'the Unknown Soldier of a new Republic of the Image'.[23] The image had become a cliché by June 1998, when Clinton visited Beijing, seeking 'constructive engagement' with Jiang Zemin's China but also speaking out against human rights abuses. It was in order to review the troops of the People's Liberation Army that Clinton went to Tiananmen Square on

Saturday 27th, but the by now inevitable comparison was made by the *Guardian*'s cartoonist Steve Bell, who showed Clinton as Wang Weilin – crossed with Superman and, some years before Monica Lewinsky appeared on the scene, bravely opening his coat to the column of advancing tanks. [24]

Mobility, Protection and Firepower – that, as countless military advocates have explained, is the novel combination with which the tank transformed the modern battlefield. Yet 'poetics' are also central to this story, as the episode in Tiananmen Square demonstrated despite Sir John Keegan's warning to the contrary. The monster that came crawling out of the Cold War was by no means just a practical instrument of warfare. It was also attended by its own mythic cult – a miasmic afterlife, which has lifted the machine from its customary motor pools and battlefields and relaunched it as a phantom of the modern imagination. It is that symbolic drama, rather than just the instrumental history of powerpacks, gun tubes and deployments, that I have set out to investigate in this book. It is one that precedes the tank as well as following it, and it is here approached in a spirit of exorcism rather than celebration.

In its collusion with the camera and the reporter's breathless witnessing phrase, the tank has told much of the truth about its violent century. It has impressed its shape on the emergent and contrary phenomenon known as 'people power', yet it has also served as a hardener of thought and a spectacular stand-in for understanding – one that is all too likely to be in attendance as global affairs are converted into a tightly managed 'slideshow' of moments captured by roving reporters, or those frisson-hunting travel writers for whom distant war is a chance to jump up on to one of these advancing machines, and charge heroically into the dawn of somebody or other's grim little new era. [25]

Nations have long been defined by their creeds, languages and literatures, but in modern times they've come to be known by their tanks too. In January 1996 the then Prime Minister of India, P. V. Narasimha Rao, climbed into a 56.5-ton trial Arjun tank and dedicated the new machine, named after a mythical Hindu warrior, to his country. There was much argument about the effectiveness of India's first 'indigenous' tank, and also the propriety of symbolically commissioning a new weapon, as Rao did, without clearance from the Army General Staff. [26] Yet it is not just in India that the tank has entered the character of nations. The same pact between nationalism and military technology has attended the development of the latest generation everywhere: the Abrams M1 (USA), the Merkava (Israel), the Challenger

(UK), the Leclerc (France), the Leopard (Germany), the Mitsubishi Type 90 (Japan), the T-95 (Russia), even the unrealized Gorilla (Poland). The tank has ploughed its way into common parlance as a figure of speech, applied to athletes and business manoeuvres alike. All over the world, it has inspired and horrified the citizenry as well as taxing them.

It has also placed its own testing demands on civilian politicians. Thus, for example, the variety of Conservative politics introduced into Britain by Margaret Thatcher was not always appreciated by British tank veterans of the Second World War. On gathering that Thatcher's successors were planning to reduce the state pensions awarded to war veterans, one of these soon-to-be-impoverished elders, Tony Heath, recalled how a fellow crew member had died next to him in the Battle of Bremen and hurled his memory back against the 'pernicious' Thatcherite mantra: 'There is no such thing as society.'[27] Similar outrage would be expressed when it emerged that a charity called 'Friends of War Memorials' was considering a scheme that would attract private businesses to sponsor the conservation of war memorials: as the disgusted secretary of the Birmingham British Legion remarked, 'I never saw tanks rolling through the desert painted with the words "sponsored by Typhoo Tea".'[28] This was an acute remark for anyone who remembered that the tanks that 'brewed up' in the North African campaign certainly did not do so in order to produce a drink – but it was still insufficiently sharp to cut through Lady Thatcher's defences. She had passed her own tank test triumphantly at Fallingbostel on the North German plain in September 1986. One of the most enduring photographs of her entire period in power shows the 'Iron Lady' riding around in a Challenger from the Royal Hussars (Prince of Wales's Own) Regiment, wearing curious goggles and draped in pale cloth that seemed to tilt haute couture in the vague direction of Lawrence of Arabia.

No liberal politician failed the tank test more decisively than Mike Dukakis, who stood unsuccessfully for the Democrats against Bush in the US presidential election of 1988. Determined to prove that their candidate was not just a soft liberal, the Democratic campaign team took Dukakis to the General Dynamics Plant at Sterling Heights, Michigan, stuck a combat helmet on his head and sent him out in front of the cameras in an Abrams M1A1. The manoeuvre backfired horribly. Peering out from under his helmet and waving at the cameras as if he was enjoying a fairground ride, Dukakis looked absurd: the bleeding-heart liberal revealed as nodding doll. The image was a gift to George Bush, a true battle-hardened veteran, who promptly announced that Dukakis could not fool American voters or 'the

Soviet leadership by knocking American defence for ten years and then riding around in a TANK for ten minutes'.[29] Bush made mocking reference to the same fiasco in his first public debate with Dukakis ('I wanted to hitchhike a ride home in his tank with him')[30] and, by 18 October, the Republican campaign team had incorporated the image into a television advertisement of their own, which would be screened countless times over the course of the election. The defining image of the entire election, it showed news footage of Governor Dukakis's disastrous photo-opportunity, while an announcer stressed his alleged weakness on defence: 'He even criticized our rescue mission to Grenada and our strike on Libya. And now he wants to be our commander-in-chief . . . America can't afford the risk.'[31] And America didn't.

PART I

It Was an Actual Fact

PW: You've got an eye for hideous military technology, these curious death-dealing constructions. What is a tank to you as you see one coming up the street?

KURT VONNEGUT: It is astonishing and utterly irresistible and . . . I never had to fight one so I have no idea . . . but, my God, they are magnificently designed and a British invention, I believe.

From an interview for BBC Radio Three's *Night Waves*, 22 September 1997

Trials in tank defence: a tank in a hole, Bermicourt, 10 February 1918, 3rd Australian Tunnelling Company.

Do not expect a work of the classic canon,
Take binoculars to these nests of camouflage -
Spy out what is half-there . . .
Wyndham Lewis, 'One-Way Song', 1933

2

A Monster is Evolved

On 20 March 1838 John George sat down with his son in Saint Blazey, Cornwall, and wrote a petition to the House of Commons. The pair announced themselves the sole inventors of a 'modern steam war chariot' that would prove 'very destructive in case of war'.[1] Their machine 'would break the enemy's line in whatever position it might be placed, and at the same time carry destruction into the ranks wherever it came into contact with them'. This coke-burning chariot would be operated by three men, and its sides were to be armoured against 'muskett and grape shot'. When the scythes and iron beaters were fixed for battle, each machine would cut an opening in enemy ranks of twenty-three feet wide, confounding the conventional logic of war and spreading panic as it did so: 'the more the enemy are in number the more certain is their destruction'. Nothing in the traditional arsenal would be able to withstand a modern steam war chariot as it moved forward to 'penetrate the densest lines, the firmest cahorts and the most compact squadrons with as much certainty as a cannon ball would pass through a partition of paste board'. In case Members of Parliament were merely amused by these claims, the Cornish engineers asked them to imagine how a recent engagement might have turned out had their invention been available to the enemy: 'a steam carriage, carefully equipped and directed would have broken through the hollow squares on the field of Waterloo, opened a passage for napolion's cavalry and changed the face of the battle – as well as the fate of nations'.

All this might have seemed worth the price of a journey to London; but though John George and Son offered to bring a demonstration model up to Westminster, their inventive mixture of poetry and engineering was never to be tried. A copy of their petition eventually found its way into the archives of the National Army Museum in London, but the machine itself disappeared into the oblivion in which even the vaguest prehistory would not be recognized until eighty years later. The modern steam war chariot was just one of many 'tentative and inconclusive incarnations' through which, according to Major Bertram Clough Williams-Ellis, the tank had passed by the time its historical moment finally came on the Western Front in September 1916.[2]

The First World War was fought over a new and unexpectedly static geography of battle. As Winston Churchill was quick to grasp, the rifle and machine gun meant that a rush could be beaten back in a very short distance. Hostile armies were now able to entrench right up against one another and the outcome, as Churchill wrote to Asquith in January 1915, was 'a short range instead of a long range war as was expected'. The question to be solved was not 'the long attack over a carefully prepared glacis of former times, but the actual getting across of 100 or 200 yards of open space and wire entanglements'.[3] The tank was developed as the machine that would cut across this immobilized geography, making a decisive break with what one of its officers, Brevet Colonel J. F. C. Fuller, called the new 'trinity of trench, machine gun and wire'.[4]

The tanks of the Great War were certainly novel contrivances but, as most of the pioneers themselves repeatedly stressed, they did not issue from any singular act of invention. Towards the end of 1919, a Royal Commission on Awards for Inventors considered the claims of twelve ostensible inventors of the tank, distributing £18,000 between six of them.[5] But the Crown's case against these awards had been strong; it was simply not possible to say that 'this or that man invented the tank'. As First Lord of the Admiralty, Winston Churchill had secured the conditions under which a variety of people could contribute to the experimental 'landship' project, but the conception behind the tank was, as he told the commission, actually one of 'extreme antiquity'. No one paused to remember John George and son of Saint Blazey, but many other previous if also inconclusive incarnations were cited at the time: Boadicea's chariots, the Roman testudo, Hannibal's elephants, the belfry of medieval siege operations, and the 'living tank' familiar to everyone as the medieval knight in armour.[6] The Scots had used protected 'war carts' against the English, Leonardo de Vinci had sketched a plan for secured and covered chariots, and Simon Stevin was thought actually to have constructed two wind-blown 'landships' – fully rigged battleships on wheels – for the Prince of Orange in the late sixteenth century. Napoleon's interest in Cugnot's plans for a steam-powered 'Automobile of War' was also registered, and the nineteenth-century examples included a number of heavy agricultural machines such as the American Batter and Holt tractors, both of which used caterpillar tracks. By 1915, the three mechanical constituents – bullet-proof armour, the internal combustion engine and caterpillar tracks – were at hand, and it was their combination around the unexpectedly static circumstances of the Western Front that gave practical realization to this long-rehearsed but still frankly fantastic idea.

In admitting that no single inventor created the tank out of nothing, the pioneers were not being unduly modest about their own place in what Churchill called 'the chain of causation'.[7] If they weren't simple inventors, this was only because they were the prophets and technicians of a larger process in which evolution, mechanical tinkering and the emergence of a new *Zeitgeist* were combined. Colonel J. F. C. Fuller, the chief general staff officer and tactician with the early Tank Corps, described the 'evolution of the caterpillar track' as 'the fourth phase in the evolution of the battle car', and placed it in the vanguard of a wider evolution that was transforming the entire basis of warfare.[8] Convinced that, 'one can predict certain events in war as surely as Darwin could in life directly he grasped the principles of evolution',[9] Fuller theorized the tank as a clairvoyant vehicle, which made it possible to win a modern war without going through the carnage that was engulfing so many traditional infantrymen on the Western Front: carrying the future within its bizarrely geometric frame, the tank was a life-saving device which would hasten the evolution of war from the old, 'muscular' phase to a new 'mechanized' and scientific one. The same point would be made by Sir Ernest Dunlop Swinton, the founder and commander of the emerging Tank Corps and one of the 'inventors' who did receive an award. He described the modern tank more pragmatically as 'the result of evolution' which has progressed 'through intermediate stages, as mechanical science has grown'.[10]

According to Major Clough Williams-Ellis, the tank was 'in the air' of the new century and it certainly wasn't just experimental engineers who could grasp its essential features.[11] Artists, writers and poets were also there from the start. In a famous example of literary prophecy, H. G. Wells had caught a glimpse of the looming machine eleven years before the outbreak of war. In a story first published by the *Strand Magazine* in 1903 – and hastily reprinted just after the tanks had first gone into action on the Somme as 'a prophecy fulfilled' and 'the most startling case on record in which the vision of a fiction-writer has "come true" in actual fact' – Wells had shown 'Land Ironclads' emerging from behind a wood to shatter the 'idyllic calm' of an entrenched battleground and to initiate 'a new form of warfare' as they did so.[12] Named after iron ships of the kind that had first proved their superiority in the American Civil War, these sinister war machines were slung around with sealed rifle-cabins, each one equipped with a rapid-fire automatic rifle and an 'advanced' camera obscura sighting system, and they sailed forward on huge pedrail wheels hung with 'elephant-like feet'. Immune to counter-fire, they advanced on Wells's horrified war correspondent 'like large and clumsy black insects' crawling over 'amazed and disordered trenches' that couldn't hold them back.

Wells's 'Land Ironclads' were creatures of fantasy, but the initial ideas that inspired the actual development of the tank were scarcely less fantastic. Shortly after the outbreak of war in 1914 the Royal Navy Air Service had taken to using armoured touring cars to mount hit-and-run raids against German cavalry and to protect naval planes based on the French and Belgian coast. These road-based armoured car squadrons had attracted a number of affluent adventurers such as the Duke of Westminster into their buccaneering ranks, but by the end of the year they had been hemmed in by trenches, a development that encouraged speculation about mobile artillery and trench-crossing machinery. Set up under the Director of Naval Construction in February 1915, the Admiralty Landships Committee submitted one hopeful vision after another to empirical testing. One of the first sightings took place over a dinner table at Murray's Club in London. Sir Albert Stern, a City banker who was to become Secretary to the Landships Committee, recalls the evening when he and another fellow sat down to hear Major Hetherington of the Admiralty's Armoured Car Division outline his proposal for a landship consisting of 'a sort of Crystal Palace body'[13] mounted on three wheels, 'each as big as the Great Wheel at Earls Court'.[14] Hetherington's garguantuan machine would have a length of one hundred feet and weigh three hundred tons, and no doubt it would roll straight through the Rhine to the amazement of a quickly defeated Germany. This 'fantastic idea', which Stern describes as 'much the same' as that of H. G. Wells, was put to Winston Churchill over a dinner arranged for this purpose by the Duke of Westminster, and six scaled-down 'Big Wheel Landships' were actually commissioned shortly afterwards. But no amount of tinkering could make Hetherington's idea work, and the first effective prototypes only emerged after the next evolutionary leap (actually an ordinary personnel change) had softened up those 'Big Wheels', replacing them with an 'endless chain' or 'Creeping Grip' which could be wrapped around the body of an entirely recast tank in the form of caterpillar tracks.

The idea that was first put to the War Office at about the same time seemed no less fantastic than Hetherington's 'Big Wheel Landship'. It came from Ernest Swinton, then a Major who was well known as 'Ole-Luk-Oie', the author of pre-war military adventure stories of the kind that ensured that 'blasted anarchists' received the proper 'biffing' that was their due.[15] In 1914 Lord Kitchener had bowed to mounting national pressure for news from the blacked-out Western Front and sent Swinton to France as Official Observer – or 'Eyewitness' as he was dubbed – with the British Expeditionary Force. Swinton's job was to produce uplifting reports ('Eye-wash' as they came to be called by some), which would be censored, at first by Lord Kitchener himself, and then distributed to newspapers for publication alongside the drier official dispatches. As this colourist travelled around in the entrenched war zone, he saw siege warfare being re-established under modern conditions and recognized the urgent need for 'machine gun destroyers' to be developed. To begin with, Swinton imagined the machine gun destroyer as 'a self-propelling climbing block-house or rifle bullet-proof cupola'.[16] But, as he wrote, the really decisive moment of vision came on 19 October 1914 when he was driving from General Headquarters in St Omer to Calais. 'Bowling along' in his car, he was ruminating on the machine that might break through the immobilized front. Just as the *phare* at Calais came into view, the lights went on in his mind. He remembered a report he had once read on the Californian Holt tractor, and knew immediately that the answer must lie with the caterpillar track. Swinton expressed his claim to be the originator of this idea with characteristic literary verve, but his conveniently dated sudden flash of illumination can hardly have impressed Rear-Admiral Sir Murray Sueter, then the Director of the Admiralty Air Department, whose Air and Armoured Car Officers were experimenting with caterpillar tracks at the beginning of 1915. Sueter had known about caterpillar tracks before the war: indeed, he had helped devise the tracks that were used on Captain Robert Falcon Scott's Antarctic sledge.[17]

Swinton's proposals fell on deaf ears at the War Office, where 'rigid non-receptivity and complacent omniscience' were very much the order of the day.[18] In February 1915 a Holt tractor was tested at Shoeburyness, but the War Office was unimpressed and did nothing. The idea that a fiction-writing war correspondent – a member of the 'happy thought brigade' – might come up with a significant military idea was plainly beyond credit and it wasn't until June 1915, when Field Marshal Sir John French wrote from France demanding that the War Office carry out research into Swinton's idea, that reluctant attention was granted and the Landships Committee was reformed as a joint Naval and Military body.[19] Swinton didn't doubt the significance of his eventual meeting with its Chairman, Sir Albert Stern. Looking back in the early thirties, he described it as 'the meeting of Stanley and Livingstone in the forest of the Dark Continent over again'.[20] That is not how it seemed to the 'obstructionists' at the War Office who refused to attend trials or, for a while, to allocate even 'a single man' to the new arm: it is said that sixty women immediately volunteered when a 'necessarily tentative and unofficial' approach was made to Mrs Pankhurst, but the Admiralty took on the cost of the project, and their offer was not taken up.[21]

Here the pace of this much-told story quickens.[22] The Big Wheel idea has failed, as have various attempts to make the pedrail work – including one that involved fitting 'elephant's feet' in apparent tribute to H. G. Wells. The committee has received some specially extended caterpillar tracks from the makers of the Bullock tractor in Chicago, and these have been sent to the factory of William Foster and Co., a manufacturer of agricultural implements in Lincoln, where they are received by managing director William Tritton and a specially appointed engineer named Walter Wilson. The first prototype emerges from Tritton's factory a month later. Dubbed the 'Number 1 Lincoln machine', it only serves to demonstrate the inadequacy of the American tracks. Wilson and Tritton retreat to a room in Lincoln's White Hart Hotel and burn the midnight oil until they've come up with an improved design. The next prototype, in which the new tracks are fitted beneath a similar box-like body, is found to work when it is tested in September 1915. However, it also turns out to be too small for the recently declared requirements of the Western Front. Wilson and Tritton consequently enlarge the tracks and the tank arrives at its characteristically rhomboid and famously 'lozenge-like' shape as it is fitted inside them. The new design is first materialized in wood – the result being dubbed 'HMS Centipede' – and the working model known as 'Mother' is produced soon afterwards.

For the first people who saw it, the tank was a noisy machine in a secluded English garden. The first organized sightings took place in pastoral and sometimes classically aristocratic settings. Late in September 1915, HMS Centipede was taken to the experimental ground of the Trench Warfare Department at Wembley Park. 'Guarded by sentries and screened off in an enclosure such as might have sheltered a coker-nut shy or the fat lady at a fair,' the wooden model was shown to a collection of officers from the Admiralty Landships Committee, the Ministry of Munitions, General Headquarters in France, General Staff and other such bodies.[23] By December, when Mother itself was put on display, the setting had been changed.

The experimental ground at Wembley Park was now considered insufficiently secret, and a 'lonely field within a mile of Lincoln Cathedral' was chosen instead.[24] Late in January, both Mother and the discarded earlier prototype were taken by night to Hatfield Park for a series of demonstrations on a specially designed 'steeple chase course' built over the edge of Lord Salisbury's private golf course.[25] There were simulated trenches, and also a swamp made by damming a stream. Parked under tarpaulins at the edge of a nearby plantation, the tanks were described as 'motor pumps' in an attempt to dampen the curiosity of interested motorists. But these 'shapeless masses' also gained the tanks more lasting designations. Mother was found to resemble 'a gigantic canvas-covered sow with a sucking pig alongside her'. And it was on that day they were dubbed 'Little Willie' and 'Big Willie'.[26]

The first demonstration took place on 29 January 1916. Asquith was unable to attend the next one on 2 February, but the spectators did include Lloyd George, Chancellor Reginald McKenna, and A. J. Balfour, who had replaced Churchill as First Lord of the Admiralty. In Swinton's words, 'it was a striking scene when the signal was given and a species of gigantic cubist steel slug slid out of its lair and proceeded to rear its grey bulk over the bright-yellow clay of the enemy parapet, before the assemblage of Cabinet Ministers and highly placed sailors and soldiers collected under the trees'.[27] The Secretary of State for War, Lord Kitchener, remained sceptical and stubborn in his already stated belief that the tank was little more than 'a pretty mechanical toy', but other observers, including Lieutenant General Sir William R. Robertson, Chief of the Imperial General Staff, were persuaded by the sight of Mother crossing a trench nine feet wide. Balfour, who is said to have demonstrated 'an almost childlike pleasure' in the new machine, was taken for a ride. And on 8 February, a special trial was arranged so that the interested King could enjoy the same experience. By the 11th, a request for tanks had been received from France. A hundred machines were ordered shortly afterwards, their production to be overseen by an interdepartmental supply committee set up under Stern's chairmanship.

Swinton was ordered to raise and command the Tank Detachment, which would eventually take the novel weapon to France as the Heavy Section of the Machine Gun Corps. Granted the temporary rank of colonel, he set about raising a force of six companies intended to have twenty-five tanks each. He recruited the majority of his men from the Midlands and the North of England, with the active assistance of the editor of the *Motor Cycle*, considered an appropriate magazine in which to advertise for men who, even if they were not all to be of short stature, would benefit from experience of motoring or mechanical engineering.[28] Such was the emphasis on secrecy that the recruits had little idea what they were joining even after their initial interview. They were not much enlightened, as one recalls, when they arrived at a camp called Siberia at Bisley, to be informed that their job would be to 'drive an armed caterpillar which could go through and over anything and knock down trees'.[29] Perplexity was part of the tank soldier's initial experience during the early years: late in 1916, recruits were still being lured in by advertisements seeking men who could drive 'light cars', and then arriving at camp to find that the vehicles in question actually weighed 28 tons.[30]

Further demonstrations followed later that year, but not before Colonel Swinton had moved the Heavy Section from its insufficiently secluded base at Siberia Camp near Bisley, to a 'magnificent wooded domain' in Suffolk's big shoot country. This fifteen-square-mile stretch of remote heathland between Elveden and Culford was taken over from the estates of Lord Iveagh, Lord Cadogan and the Duke of Grafton, swept clear of inhabitants at a few days' notice and redesignated the Elveden Explosives Area.[31]

Sealed off by three rows of plantations and guarded by 450 members of the Royal Defence Corps, the Elveden Explosives Area was, in Major Bertram Clough Williams-Ellis's words, soon 'more ringed about than was the palace of the Sleeping Beauty, more zealously guarded than the Paradise of a Shah'.[32] A well was sunk and three battalions of Pioneers from the Home Defence Force were brought in to replicate a mile-and-a-half-wide strip of the Western Front, complete with no man's land, shell craters, wire entanglements, dugouts and a full set of both German and British trench systems. Local supply officers were astonished when a million sandbags were ordered, along with barbed wire by the mile. Mother came first, but by the end of June 1916, more tanks had arrived from Lincoln – adorned with the words 'With Care to Petrograd', written in Russian script in order to sustain the pretence that these new weapons were actually mobile water-tanks built to suit conditions in that roadless country.[33] Recalling his initial encounter with a tank twenty years after the war, one recruit to the 'Hush-hush Corps' described going for a run through the apparently deserted woods on his second evening at the Elveden Explosives Area in early September 1916: 'Suddenly round the bend in a lane I heard a grinding and a grunting, and a few seconds later I was confronted by the awful apparition of a Mark I Tank with its weird wheeled tail. I drew up, petrified, wondering whether this was another manifestation of the concussion which had caused me to be invalided home from France.'[34]

One of the first men to arrive at the Elveden Explosives Area was the well-known artist Solomon J. Solomon, a Royal Academician who was then associated with the Royal Engineers. Brought in to devise camouflage schemes for the tanks, Solomon features as an exotic figure in a number of the veterans' memoirs. Swinton portrays him as a formal and traditional-looking man on a horse, riding to work in the 'open-air studio' where a permanent detachment of men waited with tons of specially allocated paint to execute his designs.[35] According to the anonymous 'Tank Major', the 'open-air studio' was actually a local barn that had been quickly converted for the use of this 'famous artist'.[36] Basil L. Q. Henriques recalls Solomon arriving and commandeering Mother when she was still the only tank at Elveden, and working on her for 'a good part of the day during which he painted her with as much care and trouble as if he were covering a canvas for the Royal Academy. I can see him now standing away from the tank with one eye closed and holding his brush at arm's length between the delicate touches that he painted on to her.'[37] The final effect was 'a kind of jolly landscape in green against a pink sunset sky' and the crews, when they eventually received their own tanks to work on, were ordered to copy Solomon's design. This they did, 'with great care, but with little skill'. Many hours of 'precious time' were spent in this decorative activity and 'we were all rather proud of our achievements'. Unfortunately, however, Solomon's design didn't appear entirely suited to conditions on the Somme. It can be seen on some of the tanks that were filmed in France; but, though it looks particularly resplendent on a tank named as HMLS 'Oh I Say!', there was no great future in it.[38] As Henriques continues, 'It makes one's blood boil at the time we wasted, for no sooner had we disembarked in France than a black-and-white artist appeared on the scene, and we were immediately ordered to paint over our landscape with a bold pattern of brown, broken by broad black lines.'[39]

Veterans of the Heavy Section had their fun with the memory of this Jewish artist – known for his society portraits and for his large figurative canvases on mythical and allegorical themes – who turned up one day in the summer of 1916 to paint the tanks. In reality, however, Solomon J. Solomon was not nearly so disengaged or otherworldly as the tank men liked to imply. His involvement with camouflage dated back to 1914, when the War Office had arranged trials at Woolwich dockyards to test his idea of using painted canvas to disguise trenches from aerial view.[40] Before going to the Elveden Explosives Area, he been busy on the Western Front, visiting the more advanced French camouflage atelier at Amiens (where he found a number of artists with whom he had been a student at the Ecole des Beaux-Arts in Paris) and then setting up his own camouflage workshop in a barn at Poperinge, Belgium. Solomon had become adept at fitting tin observation posts into the apexes of haystacks, using raffia and painted cloth to ensure their invisibility. He had devised a form of camouflage netting that could be threaded with grass, hay, seaweed or anything else that might give it a textured surface, and that was to be much used throughout the war. He had also pioneered a method of 'tree blendage' – first tried on some willow trees on the Ypres salient – which replaced real trees with mock ones constructed around a steel core and suitable, despite their deceptive slenderness, for use as gunnery observation posts. His experiments in this latter project had involved theatrical scene painters and excursions, made by permission of the King, into Windsor Great Park in search of old willows. Although he was unpaid (indeed, he insisted on paying his own expenses rather than submitting to direct military control), Solomon had received a temporary commission as Lieutenant Colonel from General Haig in December 1915. By May 1916, when he arrived at the Elveden Explosives Area, Solomon was as experienced as anyone could have been in the emerging art of camouflage, and his retrospectively written diary of those times shows just how considered his apparently whimsical approach to the tank actually was. Solomon was quick to identify a consequence of the tank's famous rhomboid shape that had previously gone unremarked. The fundamental problem, as he saw it, was 'as far as possible to hide the machine on its way to its objective, while it was within the range of artillery fire'. Camouflage painting might be effective under some conditions and 'silhouettes of perforated zinc' would also help to hide the angles of the new machine; however, the tank was 'so constructed that under its belly was a square, black shadow, impossible to efface, except by some form of screen'. If a painting by John Singer Sargent is to be believed, this shaded area would come to be appreciated by tank crews as a cool place in which to rest and play cards.[41] But Solomon was concerned that, whatever might be done to make the upper part of the tank disappear against some backgrounds, 'this black hole would be conspicuous, as all black shadows are, in a landscape for miles'. He consequently concluded that 'smoke and mist was [the tank's] best safeguard'.

Solomon's work may have come to seem absurd to the tank crews who were soon to drown his pink sunsets in the mud of the Somme, but he and Swinton had at least tried to anticipate this problem. After a short initial stay in Thetford, in which he could only sketch his designs on two small wooden models because no real tanks were yet available, Solomon went to France to seek out information about the 'local colour' of the scene in which the tanks would first be used: 'it was important to know whether the first tanks would be used in flat country or hilly. Their camouflage treatment would be designed accordingly.'[42] On arriving at GHQ, however, Solomon couldn't persuade the generals to disclose their intentions. Frustrated by what he saw as their all-too-typical obstructionism ('if things are to be purposely and not blindly done, some one has to be trusted'), he returned none the wiser to the Elveden Explosives Area, and took up his brushes.[43]

Solomon had six men to assist him with the fetching and carrying, and others to help tone the big canvas covers he planned for the tanks. Initially he stayed in Thetford's Bull Hotel, but he soon transferred to rooms above Lord Iveagh's stables where the Heavy Section's mess was based. When I tried to take a look at this site, I was apprehended by an estate worker who couldn't stop raising his eyebrows about the 'unbelievable' scenes going on in the nearby house, an exotic orientalist pile in which Stanley Kubrick was then secretly filming *Eyes Wide Shut*. But Solomon remembered the atmosphere as being distinctly 'light-headed' for different reasons connected to the fact that the caterer had formerly been head butler at the Senior Army and Navy Club, and was 'renowned for his cocktails'.[44] While the 'younger bloods' of the Heavy Section teamed up with airmen from the nearby Thetford aerodrome to do 'full justice' to this fellow's concoctions, Solomon got up early to sketch the designs that he and his men would paint on the tanks. On 12 May 1916 he writes that he had painted three tanks himself, and on the 17th a further four: 'I had to take off my tunic and put on overalls, just like an ordinary house painter.'[45] He reports on the loss of prestige he suffered in the mess because he insisted on painting with his own hand instead of just ordering subordinates to exercise his designs. On hearing that Solomon had visited the area before the war to paint portraits of the Cadogans at nearby Culford House, one thoroughly 'dandified' staff secretary was withering about the change of circumstance that saw him now reduced to 'painting tanks'.[46] Solomon's status problems were not helped by the fact that initially at least he was 'forced to ride a push-bike' to work, although things started to look up when he organized the pony on which Swinton chose to remember him and got it accustomed to 'going among hideous snorting tanks'.[47]

On 21 July Lloyd George, who was now Secretary of State for War, came along to inspect the progress of the war machine that might help to break through the fatal deadlock of the ongoing Battle of the Somme. Wearing the flowing cloak that also distinguished his visits to the Front,[48] he watched as the roar of twenty-five tanks shattered the peace of their tranquil setting. Machine and sylvan background were normally protected from each other by a rule forbidding stunts. But this could be waived on special occasions. On the visit of Colonel Estienne, the man in charge of France's experimental tanks, one of the machines was permitted to turn on its incongruously tranquil surroundings and knock down a tree twenty-six inches thick.[49]

These demonstrations were the first carefully limited breaches in a veil of secrecy that was otherwise kept firmly in place. Locals had certainly wondered as mines were exploded to create shell craters and acetylene flares whitened the night sky around Elveden: some speculated that the military were tunnelling through to Germany. Yet the fact that the tanks entered the war without losing their vital 'element of surprise' guaranteed much praise for the workers of both William Foster's in Lincoln and the Metropolitan Carriage, Wagon and Finance Company, at Wednesbury, Birmingham, where tanks later went into production. As was stressed in the accounts that appeared shortly after the Armistice, William Foster and Company's workers had known almost everything about the machines they were making, but as true John Bulls – and they would be praised in precisely these terms – they never breathed a word. The diligence with which they and the Birmingham workers toiled day and night, forfeiting holidays to ensure a maximum supply of tanks to the front, was contrasted with the strike-bound record of other war industries; and their loyal silence was set off against the rumoured loose talk of the women who nearly betrayed everything with their wagging tongues. Swinton recalls a London actress who knew too much and had to be frightened into silence, and also a lot of unsubstantiated talk of 'women spies'. A 'Fraulein Doktor' was said to have tried to betray the secret to a German technical officer who wouldn't believe what he heard, and a similar rumour accused the hapless 'so-called Javanese dancer' Mata Hari of the same treachery.[50]

As fantasy became reality, the need for secrecy increased, necessitating certain adjustments to the vocabulary of the tank. Early names such as 'landship' and 'land cruiser' had become 'tell tale' now that this precipitate of the *Zeitgeist* was actually in production. The new vocabulary was designed to uphold secrecy, but it also enhanced the new weapon with a bumptious kind of imaginative effect. It was at this point, as Swinton wrote during the war, that the word 'tanks' came to be 'invested with a romantic meaning of which it can never be deprived'.[51] The name 'tank' could be squared with the diversionary story being put about that the new machines were actually mobile water tanks being built to a mad Russian design. It had the additional advantage of being less clumsy than considered alternatives such as 'reservoir', 'cistern', 'container' or 'receptacle'. The same need for secrecy informed the differentiation of the tanks into 'males' and 'females' – the males carrying 6-pounder guns and doing the heavy work while the females, designed to accompany the males as loyal 'consorts', were equipped with 'man-killing' machine guns. Swinton claimed to have chosen these gendered designations because they involved 'short and familiar words that gave nothing away and, being based on a biological analogy, were unlikely to be forgotten'.[52]

Years after the war, Basil Henriques would look back on the training he and his fellows in the Heavy Section had undergone at Elveden as 'one huge game . . . we used to look for trees to knock down . . . we pictured ourselves slowly wending our way to Berlin over beautiful parkland such as we were now practising on'.[53] That was not how Swinton thought of it, although he was the first to admit that the training had been rudimentary at best. He issued the men of the Heavy Section with 'Tank Tips', a 'child's guide to knowledge', which opened as follows:

Remember your orders.
Shoot quick
Shoot low. A miss which throws dust in the enemy's eyes is better than one which whistles in his ear.
Shoot cunning.[54]

They rehearsed the 'art of manoeuvring together' but, with the Battle of the Somme proceeding with terrible losses, there was no time for training in combined operations with infantry, and some of the drivers are said to have arrived in France with little more than an hour's worth of practice behind them.

C Company was the first of four scheduled companies to embark for France. Half its machines were loaded on to trains at night while a German Zeppelin floated blindly overhead; and on 13 August, the men sat down among the pine trees after a final parade, lit their pipes, and listened as Swinton reiterated what he called 'the Tank idea', and reminded these 'pioneers of a new form in warfare' that they were 'going forth to battle with the express and special object of helping their unprotected comrades of the infantry'.[55]

The companies of the Heavy Section were 'self-contained and unattached',[56] practically disconnected from their supposed parent, the Machine Gun Corps (which was itself, in the words of its own founder, 'merely an improvisation to meet immediate and urgent needs'[57]); and, to begin with, Swinton's pioneers found themselves rather adrift in France. Running tanks was dirty work, and their dishevelment was duly noted by barking professional officers who expected the 'smartness and precision of a Military Tournament turn'.[58] This response caused lasting resentment among the proud if not clean-cut members of the new force. But if their first days in France seemed 'an almost comically complete nightmare', this was because they were also expected to perform like ragamuffin members of an exotic fairground troup.

The arriving tank companies of the Heavy Section assembled at Yvrench, near Abbeville. Visiting the training centre here at the end of August, Swinton was horrified to find his tanks being treated as 'a new kind of toy'.[59] There were frequent displays, with French and British officers coming from miles around to see the 'antics of the Tanks' – performances that were of no tactical value whatsoever. In one account of these demonstrations, a British officer orders a tank commander into manoeuvres whose only purpose is to widen the eyes of incredulous French officers who have never before seen such an 'elephant-tortoise'.[60] So the tanks were set to work, pressing boulders into the ground or crushing them like chestnuts, crashing through walls, and, of course, breaking down trees 'as easily as one breaks a match between one's fingers'.

By the time they moved up to The Loop, where they were concentrated before proceeding to the points from which they would go into battle with General Rawlinson's Fourth Army, the first tank crews were regarded as 'the star variety-turn of the Western Front'.[61] They found to their dismay that it was to be 'Roses, roses all the way'. Williams-Ellis quotes one tank commander saying bitterly: 'It rather reminded me of Hampstead Heath. When we got there we found that the Infantry Brigades had been notified that the Tanks were to perform daily from 9 to 10 and from 2 to 3 and every officer within a large radius and an enormous member of the Staff came to inspect us. We were an object of interest to everyone. This did not help one's work.' Basil Henriques recalled a certain amount of ineffectual training in gas-mask drill and pigeons, but between this, as he writes, 'we were for ever showing off, not to the men with whom we were to fight, but to the "brass-hats" from H.Q., who found us a highly amusing diversion'.[62]

Swinton objected to 'these "stunts" and frequent exhibitions, which were wearing out both the machines and the personnel', and also displacing the serious consideration that should have been given to finding ways of using tanks alongside infantry. But complaining didn't always help, as was discovered by Lieutenant Colonel John Brough, the first commander of the Heavy Section in France. He too protested against the constant round of demonstrations, and was promptly removed from his position on orders from GHQ, obliging the Heavy Section to come to terms with a new commander two weeks before it went into battle.

3

Big Joke

The result of inexpressible terror long and inexplicably endured is . . . a plethora of very un-modern superstitions, talismans, wonders, miracles, relics, legends and rumours.

Paul Fussell[1]

On 15 September 1916 the Heavy Section of the Machine Gun Corps went into action in the Battle of the Somme. Forty-nine machines were available for the attack, but some broke down, or sank into craters and collapsing dugouts. Others lost their direction and one is said to have failed because its driver refused to plough down a narrow sunken road full of dead bodies.[2] Rather than being used in the concentration that Swinton had advocated from the earliest days, the thirty-six tanks that did reach their starting points were directed against strong points in 'driblets' or 'penny packets' of two and three.[3] The results of those first engagements were modest. A tank named 'Crème de Menthe' took the heavily manned sugar factory at Courcelette. Another advanced on the village of Martinpuich, reputedly to a chorus of 'Mercy! Mercy!' sung by a hundred horrified German soldiers. Various tanks 'enfiladed' trenches successfully or took large numbers of prisoners, but the popular triumph belonged to Lieutenant Hastie, whose tank Dinnaken went on to take Flers. As an airman announced in a famous wireless message: 'Tank seen in main street Flers going on with a large number of troops following it.'[4] Enhanced by the press, this soon read: 'A Tank is walking up the High Street of Flers with the British Army cheering behind.' The tank was also said to be flying a piece of paper on which was written: 'GREAT HUN DEFEAT. SPECIAL!'[5]

Fantasy becomes reality, but it doesn't immediately become prosaic in the process. When those huge lozenge-shaped objects first loomed into view on the front, they were greeted with a convulsion. The tank that advanced on Martinpuich, was watched by an official cameraman, Lieutenant Geoffrey H. Malins:

For the life of me I could not take my eyes off it. The thing – I really do not know how else to describe it – ambled forward, with slow, jerky, uncertain movements . . . It waddled, it ambled, it jolted, it rolled – well it did everything in turn and nothing long or wrong. And, most remarkable of all, this weird-looking creature with a metal hide performed tricks which almost made one doubt the evidence of one's senses . . .

It came to a crater. Down went its nose; a slight dip, and a clinging, crawling motion, and it came up merrily on the other side. And all the time as it slowly advanced, it breathed and belched forth tongues of flame, its nostrils seemed to breath death and destruction, and the Huns, terrified by its appearance, were mown down like corn falling to the reaper's sickle.

Presently it stopped. The humming ceased. The spell was broken. We looked at one another, and then we laughed. How we laughed! Officers and men were doubled up with mirth as they watched the acrobatic antics of this mechanical marvel – this Wellsian wonder.[6]

That laughter was recorded by many witnesses. Stephen Foot, who first saw tanks at a place called the Green Dump on 13 September, noted that 'the predominant emotion excited in anyone seeing them for the first time was a feeling of hilarity. One wanted to laugh . . . standing still they were funny, moving along they were a scream.'[7] And the laughter had many constituents: 'pride in a British invention, anticipation as to what the tank might achieve, amusement at the horror these great machines would strike in the heart of the enemy . . .' Here was monstrous unreality itself, conscripted as a life-saving device for an infantry that was already horribly familiar with the carnage of General Haig's offensives and couldn't now believe its luck. As manufacturers William Foster and Company recounted in a celebratory book published after the war, the tank quickly became 'the new topic', spreading 'a smile throughout the land' and giving the Tommy 'a new peg on which to hang his chaff'.[8] Reminded of pantomime animals, British soldiers dubbed the tank 'Old Mother Hubbard' and laughed at it: 'there she was groanin' and gruntin' along, pokin' her nose here and there', as a wounded soldier recalled for Clough Williams-Ellis.[9] And by all accounts they laughed again as they imagined the enemy – who had, in John Buchan's words, always prided himself on 'the superior merit' of his own 'fighting "machine"' – quaking in his well-organized boots and crying out 'Kamerad! Kamerad!' as the tank bore down on him.[10] In the jaunty and victorious estimate of William Foster and Company, the tank 'terrified the German to his wit's end, while equally and appositely it cheered, delighted and amused the troops who found themselves in its company'.

Captain D. G. Browne, who joined the Heavy Section after these first appearances, also understood the appeal of the old Mark I tank:

Its shape, unlike that of any other example of man's handiwork, its deliberate but at times curiously active and disconcerting movements, its obvious weight and power, even the two ports, like lidded eyes which ornament the front of the cab, combine irresistibly (as all journalists will testify) to suggest some huge prehistorical animal – some giant sloth or toad. Indeed, to visit a training-ground in the evening when some dozens of these creatures are rolling home to their stalls or hangars is, for all the world, like being at a Zoo during the Pleistocene Age. The striking pattern of colours with which the machines were painted in the early days only aided the illusion. The British soldier, whose great merit it is to see the comic side of everything, could not fail to be exhilarated by these gorgeous monsters.[11]

The impressions recorded by soldiers who saw those first tanks as they went into action reveal that this laughter was mixed with awe, and perhaps a little slow to build too. On 11 September 1916 a certain Captain Foxell, who was serving with the Royal Engineers, noted the coming of the tank: 'In evening saw a new horror of war arrive – an armoured "caterpillar".' Describing the still untested tank as 'a fearful looking article manned by desperadoes', he noted that 'hopes are built upon its action. It seems to move slowly with considerable noise and smoke'.[12] J. H. Price, an NCO with the Fifth Battalion of the Shropshire Light Infantry, described a general coming up the night before the attack (on 14 September) to brief the troops as they took up positions close to Delville Wood. When he remarked that 'we would have the help of three tanks', Price asked: 'Did the General think we would be running short of water?' He was soon to see one of these engines of war 'spitting bullets from the top of it. We had never seen anything like it before, and I think it attracted more of our attention than the enemy. It certainly looked a monster and it is a job for me to explain its shape, and I can only say it had huge caterpillar tracks and a large wheel behind. It went forward rather slowly and I should think it must have struck terror in many of the enemy.'

Captain D. H. Pegler, a battery sergeant major with the RFA, recorded his recollections after the event on September 18, 1916.

I have forgotten the 'Land Crabs' – the great armoured cars that took part in the battle of the fifteenth – some are lying on their backs, mangled masses of twisted and broken iron, others are back in their repairing yards, all are more or less crocked, but Gad the execution they did was awful. It struck me as I saw them from the corner of Leuze Wood how symbolic of all war they were. Then one saw them creeping along at about four miles an hour, taking all obstacles as they came, spluttering death with all their guns, enfilading each trench as they came to it – and crushing beneath them our own dead and dying as they passed. I saw one body on a concrete parapet over which one had passed. This body was just a splash of blood and clothing about two feet wide and perhaps an inch thick. An hour before this thing had been a thinking breathing man, with life before him and loved ones awaiting him probably somewhere in Scotland, for he was a kiltie.

Nothing stops these cars, trees bend and break, boulders are pressed into the earth. One had been hit by a large shell and the petrol tank pierced. She lay on her side in flames, a picture of hopelessness but every gun on her uppermost side still working with dogged determination. The firing gradually slackened and she lay silent, the gallant little crew burned to death each man at his gun.[13]

The Revd Canon C. Lomax, chaplain with the 151st Infantry Brigade, had only heard of the new weapon. 'The tanks were a great success. I did not see them in action but our men were full of them. They certainly put the wind up the Bosche. His favourite strong places were as nothing and they crossed trenches with ease.'[14]

Tank laughter became a subject for speculation among the five independent war correspondents who, under an arrangement proposed by the Newspaper Proprietors' Association, had taken up positions on the front after Swinton's withdrawal as official 'Eyewitness'.[15] For the *Daily Mail*'s William Beach Thomas, the soldiers' guffaws seemed to imply a dismissal of the new machines. Indeed, they were connected to the infantryman's assumption that tanks were 'a jest, a cause of cheerfulness; possibly faithful creatures, but no rival to the bayonet'.[16] Philip Gibbs, the Liberal journalist and pro-suffragette novelist who worked as special correspondent for the *Daily Chronicle* and *Daily Telegraph*, noticed the same chronic outbursts – in his account of the exploits of the tank known as Crème de Menthe British infantrymen were laughing 'even when bullets caught them in the throat' – and conjectured more deeply on their psychological origins some years after the war.[17] He compared the mirth that greeted the tank on the Western Front with the ribaldry of the *Decameron*, laughter ringing out in the midst of plague:

I am not strong enough in the science of psychology to understand the origin of laughter and to get in touch with the mainstreams of gaiety. The sharp contrast between normal ethics and an abnormality of action provides a grotesque point of view arousing ironical mirth. It is probable also that surroundings of enormous tragedy stimulate the sense of humour of the individual, so that any small, ridiculous thing assumes the proportion of monstrous absurdity. It is also likely – certain I think – that laughter is an escape from terror, a liberation of the soul by mental explosion, from the prison walls of despair and brooding.[18]

A similar trench humour was found among German soldiers, although not necessarily one that was provoked by the approaching British tank. It was on this side of no man's land, however, that a young soldier called Wilhelm Reich realized that this laughter was itself a form of armour. Looking back in the 1930s, he wrote: 'I, like most others, experienced the war as a machine, which, once set in motion, works senselessly according to its rules.'[19] And again: 'One developed a gallows humour, protecting oneself from the thought of one's own death. One armored oneself. This humanization the German warmongers called "front experience". By using it to promote war enthusiasm, they reversed its meaning.' In this sense, perhaps, those who laughed at tanks had themselves already become like tanks: the armoured self apprehended its own image and roared.

The 'mental explosion' that greeted the tanks may also have been triggered by the new weapon's promised reformation of war.[20] If it was possible to break through the stinking void of no man's land, restoring movement where an apparently endless immobility ruled and bringing back the prospect of a decisive 'offensive' that wasn't just another bloodbath, then where indeed did the limits of the new machine lie?

Onlooking soldiers gave the tank all sorts of nicknames, but their humour, threaded as it was with hope, also carried over into fantastic stories that stretched the capabilities of the tank to ludicrous extremes. For some, the tank was like one of the comic and imaginary 'Terrible Machines' of war drawn by William Heath Robinson in 1914–15: indeed, one 'agriculturally minded' major wrote from France to this famous cartoonist, proposing that he draw 'a new Terrible Machine – a tank with an enormous Self Binder attached, which mows down Bosches, ties them up and throws them out in bundles of ten'.[21] The same frantic spirit animated Private C. E. Dukes of the Bedfordshire Regiment who, in a letter written to his fiancée from the front, went far beyond anything Heath Robinson was prepared to dream up:

They can do up prisoners in bundles like straw-binders, and, in addition, have an adaptation of a printing machine which enables them to catch the Huns, fold, count, and deliver them in quires, every thirteenth man being thrown out a little further than the others. The Tanks can truss refractory prisoners like fowls prepared for cooking, while their equipment renders it possible for them to charge into a crowd of Huns, and by shooting out spokes like porcupine quills, carry off an opponent on each. Though 'stuck up', the prisoners are, needless to say, by no means proud of their position.

They can chew up barbed wire and turn it into munitions. As they run they slash their tails and clear away trees, horses, howitzers, and anything else in the vicinity. They turn over on their backs and catch live shells in their caterpillar feet, and they can easily be adapted as submarines; in fact, most of them crossed the Channel in this guise. They loop the loop, travel forwards, sideways and backwards, not only with equal speed, but at the same time. They spin round like a top, only far more quickly, dig themselves in, bury themselves, scoop out a tunnel, and come out again ten miles away in half an hour. [22]

In reality, the tank certainly did come to owe a lot to the printing machine. H. G. Wells may have mistaken some of the new machine's technical details, but it was with clairvoyant insight that he had brought his 'Land Ironclads' into the public eye through the stunned prose of an onlooking war correspondent. Based with their censors at a small chateau in Tatingham near General Headquarters at St Omer, the five 'special' correspondents were uniquely placed to project an idea of the new machines into the wider national imagination at home, traumatized as it was by the terrible slaughter being suffered by British infantrymen in the Battle of the Somme. [23] For weeks past these journalists had, in the words of Brigadier General C. D. Baker-Carr, the founder of the Machine Gun Corps who went on to command the First Tank Brigade, been 'confined to writing solely of "the roar of the barrage", "the calm heroism of our gallant men", the mud and the ruined villages. This sort of stuff is all very well two or three times, but, after a while, it begins to pall.' [24] So the tank was 'a perfect God-Send', and, as Clough Williams-Ellis recalled, the correspondents 'threw up their hats' in unbounded delight.

Leaving measured prose to General Haig's official Somme dispatches, they rushed to adorn the new machines with fantastic devices of their own. In their coinage the tanks became Behemoths, Juggernauts, elephantine tractors and anything else that came to mind. They 'ransacked their dictionaries for octosyllables in which to describe the new "All British" destroyer of Germans . . . It was "Diplodocus Galumphant", it was "Polychromatic Toad". It was a "flat-footed monster" which performed the most astonishing feats of agility as it advanced, spouting flames from every side.' [25] The impact of the correspondents' descriptions was only increased by the absence of literal images of the new machine. Neither photographs nor accurate drawings were allowed into circulation until a full two months after the first written reports had been printed, and the first public impressions of the tank were therefore conjured in words alone. Illustrated journals such as *Punch*, the *Weekly Dispatch* and the *Illustrated London News* had been able to print entirely fantastic line drawings that showed tanks as the strange creatures that seemed to emerge from the war correspondents' prose.[26] Many of these drawings, including the first one produced by Heath Robinson, assumed the tank was mounted on saw-toothed wheels, and at least one postcard imagined it had a pincer-like 'Hun-catcher' on the front.[27] Desperate to keep up with the war correspondents, the magazines also reviewed the prehistory of the tank and featured drawings of 'Tanks of Other Days', such as the medieval belfry.[28] It was not until 22 November that the *Daily Mirror* was able to print its famous (and exorbitantly expensive) front-page photograph of a camouflaged tank going into action; and by this time the actual image was subordinate to the fanciful cult that had preceded its delayed appearance: it could only be used to illustrate, confirm and justify the extravagant vocabulary of the war correspondents. The *Illustrated London News* followed a few days later, but here too the newly permitted photographic images were surrounded by quotations from the correspondents who had already set the scene.[29] The moving pictures came later, with *The Battle of the Ancre*, a tank-starring film that was screened in 107 cinemas in London alone and seen by an estimated 20 million people in all.[30]

The press reports had started to appear in newspapers immediately after the tanks first went into action on 15 September, and the growing contrast between the prose of the 'official' dispatch and that of the special correspondents is easily traced in *The Times*. On 16 September the dispatch from GHQ made passing mention of 'a new type of heavily armoured car' which had proved of 'considerable utility' in battle. By the 18th, *The Times*'s special correspondent was offering a more vivid account of the story. The new 'fortresses on wheels' – which correspondent Percy Robinson claimed to have seen with his own eyes – were of an 'extraordinary and ungainly shape' and readers were asked to imagine them 'thrusting themselves with all their spines out, like the hedgehogs into a nest of snakes'. By the 19th, the official dispatch had quickened slightly, stressing the 'indescribable demoralisation' that the tanks were producing in enemy ranks. But Robinson was back on the 21st: by this time he had seen tanks 'trundling' about in previously impossible terrain and 'sitting down' on enemy trenches like 'huge tame pachyderms'. As he said, 'It is difficult to speak of the things quite seriously, because they are so preposterous, so unlike anything that ever was on earth before.'

Lord Northcliffe's *Times* may have felt obliged to bury its amusement under this respectable sigh of wonder, but the *Daily Mail* knew no such inhibition, and William Beach Thomas's report on the camouflaged tanks that he had seen gathering for the attack on the night of 14 September was considerably less restrained:

A gibbous moon and brilliant stars, shining in an almost frosty night, lit with fantastic shadows and crescent patches of light the earth-craters and parapet ridges of the bare highland; and as the night yielded to the dawn, the colours on the backs of the monsters shifted like a chameleon's . . .

They looked like blind creatures emerging from the primeval slime. To watch one crawling round a battered wood in the half-light was to think of 'the Jabberwock with eyes of flame' who

> Came whiffling round the tulgey wood
> And burbled as it came . . .

With ludicrous serenity they wobbled across the gridiron fields and shook themselves as if the bullets were flies that bit just deep enough to deserve a flick. Those who had inspected these saurias in their alfresco stalls beforehand or followed their lethargic course over impossible roads in the moonlight gasped with humorous wonder at the prodigy. Munchausen (sic) never approached the stories imagined for them by soldiers. But their pet name will always be 'Tanks' and they were chiefly regarded as a practical joke. Whales, Boojums, Dreadnoughts, slugs, snarks – never were creatures that so tempted the gift of nicknaming. They were said to live on trees and houses and jump like grass hoppers or kangaroos.[31]

Thomas surrendered the tank's crew to his sense of humour as well. Like their machines, the men of the tank were a comic species apart: 'it is a pity the Tanks were not invented in the time of the Little Picts. They are made for tough little men, who can stow themselves away anywhere.' He felt honoured to have been inside one of these 'humourous Juggernauts', to 'enter their cribbed cabin and talk with the little men, wearing their padded leather helmets, who inhabited them'. Since the tanks were whales as well as 'jaundiced Batrachians', their crews, predictably, were also 'Jonahs', cramped up inside their monster and 'seeking the obscurity of the latest camouflage'.[32]

Philip Gibbs was also pleased to exceed the 'dull' description of the official Somme dispatch and to offer his readers some indication of the 'rich and rare qualities which belong to these extraordinary vehicles'. In a famous article called 'The Coming of the Tanks' he writes as one who has just heard the word. The jealously guarded secret has just been vouchsafed to him by an officer of the Heavy Section on the front:

'Like prehistoric monsters. You know, the old Ichthyosaurus,' said the officer. I told him he was pulling my leg.

'But it's a fact, man!' He breathed hard and laughed in a queer way some enormous comicality.

'They eat up houses and put the refuse under their bellies. Walk right over 'em!'

I knew this man was a truthful and simple soul, and yet could not believe.

'They knock down trees like match-sticks,' he said, staring at me with shining eyes. 'They go clean through a wood!'

'And anything else?' I asked, enjoying what I thought was a new sense of humour.

'Everything else,' he said earnestly. 'They take ditches like kangaroos. They simply love shell craters! Laugh at 'em.'

It appeared, also, that they were proof against rifle-bullets, machine-gun bullets, bombs, shell splinters. Just shrugged their shoulders and passed on. Nothing but a direct hit from a fair-sized shell could do them any harm.

'But what's the name of these mythical monsters?' I asked, not believing a word of it.

He said, 'Hush!' Other people said 'Hush! . . . Hush!' when the subject was alluded to in a remote way. And since then I have heard that one name for them is the 'Hush-hush'. But their real name is Tanks.

For they are real, and I have seen them, and walked round them, and got inside their bodies, and looked at their mysterious organs, and watched their monstrous movements . . .

I came across a herd of them in a field, and like the countryman who first saw a giraffe, said 'Hell . . . I don't believe it.' Then I sat down on the grass and laughed until the tears came into my eyes (in war one has a funny sense of humour). For they were monstrously comical, like toads of vast size emerging from the primeval slime in the twilight of the world's dawn.[33]

Gibbs enjoyed these 'weird and wonderful armoured monsters'. He wrote of 'queer low-squatting things moving slowly in the creeping mists', and in the evening he followed the tank crews back to their 'lair, where the dark forms of their machines looked very beast-like among their camp-fires, which flickered with a ruddy glare on their mud-cased flanks, so that it seemed a nightmare to me, with the flash of shell-fire etching the outlines of the trees about them'.[34]

Such was the power of the tank imagery launched by the war correspondents that, by 1917, an imaginative young woman writing a letter to her fiancé at the front would only have to see an upended insect struggling on her desk for the heavy thought to press its way into her sentences: 'a little armoured-car insect is lying on its back trying to get up . . . poor little tank'.[35] Yet these fanciful descriptions were themselves misshapen creatures of circumstance. While Gibbs emphasized the 'humour and fantasy' of the new machines, his descriptions were like those of the other special correspondents in owing their metaphorical exuberance as much to the demands of official secrecy as to any more intrinsic beast-like qualities of the tank. The five correspondents lived and worked with the censors specially assigned to them, and while the most whimsical flights of fancy would get through, neither the crews nor the tanks nor the rudimentary tactics governing their first movements, could be reported in actual detail. The war correspondents used fantastic imagery to mask this secrecy: full of noisy imaginative effect, their descriptions were built up around a silent core of things that could not be said. As Gibbs himself wrote after the war: 'The vagueness of our descriptions was owing to the censorship which forbade, wisely enough, any technical and exact definition, so we had to compare [the tanks] to giant toads, mammoths and prehistoric animals of all kinds.'[36]

The Bible and other literary sources were mined for arresting metaphors, and the pounded historical sites of the Western Front also offered imagery of a suitably displaced kind. As Gibbs watched two tanks advance on the ruins of a monastery at Eaucourt-l'Abbaye, he wondered if the ghosts of any ancient monks were there to see that 'modern warfare has brought back the mediaeval dragon-myth, and made it real, and more terrible than superstition. They were the Tanks which came.'[37] Predictably enough, Gibbs's dragons 'breathed out smoke and fire', killing men by rolling on them in ditches and 'hurling invisible bolts' at them. If the tank had the propensity to cause dragons to walk the earth, it also prompted new movement in the fossil-beds and natural history museums. A tactician like J. F. C. Fuller would later describe the tank in progressive evolutionary terms, but out in the blood-soaked mud of the Somme evolution itself seemed to have gone spiralling off in reverse. For soldiers and war correspondents alike, this anticking machine was an ecstatic throwback to prehistoric times; and the Battle of the Somme was hardly the time to indulge second thoughts about the form in which this manifestation of the *Zeitgeist* was casting the twentieth century's once optimistic dream of reason.

The tank triumphed as an exuberant metaphor before it had been proven as a military machine; and it is easy enough to sympathize with the tank soldiers' irritation at the laughter that attended their first awkward endeavours on the Western Front. While the war correspondents chortled and coined evocative phrases for the benefit of a British public that had good reason to celebrate any apparent 'wonder weapon' that promised a victorious end to the slaughter on the Somme, the tank crews were discovering the reality of their primitive machines under far from congenial circumstances. Suddenly 'pitch-forked from the calm, almost academic, atmosphere of a training camp in England into the ear-splitting, nerve-racking tornado of the front line', they had minimal experience of military procedure as it was in this army of divisions and brigades, and could neither read aerial photographs nor understand the 'jargon of warfare' in which they were addressed.[38]

Crouching inside 'Behemoth' in their leather helmets and chain visors, they were exposed to unimagined extremes of noise, smoke and heat from the sometimes red-hot engine – a 'near pandemonium' in which 'a language of pantomime was perfected. One hit a man to catch his attention and then conveyed one's meaning by gesticulation.'[39] Enemy fire brought red-hot splinters of 'bullet-splash', which would pour in through the gun port and sighting slits or come sparking off the inside of the tank's metal hull – each strike 'for all the world like a miniature catherine wheel', as one tankman remembered it.[40] The facial burns caused by 'bullet splash' may have been reduced a little by the issuing of special chain-mail visors. Yet those inside this 'pocket hell'[41] also risked wholesale incineration, especially the commander and driver who, in the early Mark I models, sat with petrol tanks on either side of them in the front of the cab.

To the extent that they communicated at all, the tank crews did so by squeezing carrier pigeons out through a hole in a gun sponson, by brandishing a shovel through the manhole, or by frantically waving coloured discs in the air. Their navigation systems were even more primitive. Each landship had a compass, and a periscope that was liable to be shot off in the early stages of any engagement. The two portholes or sighting slits at the front might appear to wink engagingly at war correspondents, but they were no joke to the men who had to navigate through them. Vision was highly restricted at the best of times, and when enemy fire necessitated the closure of the portholes, the crew could only peer out of tiny holes the size of a pea. In those early operations on the Somme the tank crews lacked the benefit of preliminary reconnaissance work, of the sort for which the Tank Corps later became well known. But even when tapes were laid over previously scouted ground for the tanks to follow, it was frequently necessary for a commander to get out of the tank in the middle of a battle to guide his disorientated 'mastodon' by hand, thereby running the double risk of being shot by the enemy, or of being crushed by his own machine at the slightest slip.[42]

Onlookers may have appreciated the apparently autonomous 'waddling' movements of the miraculous tanks, but the men inside knew that it took great effort and, in the case of the Mark I, perhaps as long as ten minutes, to persuade one of these purblind vehicles to change direction:[43] first the wheels at the back had to be raised, then one caterpillar had to be locked and, if the gears got stuck (which they often did at this stage), the tank would be left revolving on its axis until they were released. The war correspondents told of 'motor-monsters' ploughing effortlessly through the deepest woods, but the tanks that tried any such thing were likely to find themselves stuck in a hellish scene with desperate German soldiers crawling up to pull the guns down, trying to ignite the tank's petrol or to force bombs into the exhaust pipe.

Basil Henriques commanded what appears to have been the first tank to fire in action, and his description of the experience reveals the insult of Beach Thomas's joke about 'little Picts'. Writing twenty years after the event, Henriques, who was actually a tall man of six feet three inches, declared that 'the physical, mental and nervous exhaustion' of that first experience of warfare 'still haunts me and fills me with horror'.[44] His 'female' tank was one of three that set off with the village of Morval as their objective. Exhausted before they started (and not just by those endless displays of meaningless 'showing off'), they had advanced over heavily cratered land, trying to follow the route of a railway line. The periscope was soon enough shot off. Then the sighting prisms were shattered and armour-piercing bullets started to break through the supposedly impregnable armour. The driver and a gunner were hit, and, with fire now pouring in through the broken front flap, Henriques directed his tank back to the British line, where he climbed out with blood pouring from splinter wounds to his legs and face, and found himself en route for an ophthalmic hospital back in London. In his company alone, one officer 'went mad' and shot his engine in an endeavour to make it go faster. Another was overwhelmed by a sense of failure and shot himself, while two others – including Henriques himself – suffered nervous breakdowns of a kind. As for Colonel Swinton's insistence that the tank was the infantryman's friend, Henriques was quickly disabused of this illusion too: once in action the tanks drew such concentrated fire from the enemy that the infantry quickly learned to hate the very sight of them.

The faltering manoeuvres of 15 September were followed by others, although 'work on the tanks was hampered by the multitude of visitors who came to see these novelties now that the secret was disclosed'.[45] Ten days later there was an attack on Thiépval, in which the men in one female tank managed to clear out a trench before running out of petrol. Two tank crews also distinguished themselves attacking a strong point near Beaumont Hamel, in the Battle of Ancre on 13 November: an achievement that bore little resemblance to the irresistible 'advance of the tanks' that would be claimed in British cinemas a few months later.

While the men of the Heavy Section struggled on through the Battle of the Somme, their miraculous machines were breaking into popular songs back home. A comic number called 'The Tanks that Broke the Ranks' was being advertised for British pantomime performances over Christmas 1916.[46] Set to the tune of 'The Man who Broke the Bank in Monte Carlo', it is a jaunty number with a catchy chorus – 'And the tanks went on / and they strolled along / with their independent air . . .' – and a full rehearsal of tank clichés. The new machines do the 'caterpillar crawl' across no man's land, pushing through walls and 'pulling trees up by the roots'. The advancing tanks terrorize the enemy. 'Huns' peer out of their trenches in horror ('here comes the British navy sailing on the land'), and are not consoled by the Kaiser and his generals who want to believe the new weapon is only 'a motor-omnibus'. Eventually one of these unstoppable machines captures a ginger-haired Hun colonel and carries him off for 'a joy-ride around Picardy'.

The 'star variety-turn of the Western Front' also conquered the London stage. It found a role in *Vanity Fair*, a revue that opened at London's Gaiety Theatre on 6 November 1916, and showed the still secret wonder weapon interrupting a poolside romance involving a frog, a beetle and a dragon-fly. At an opportune moment, the sixteen Palace Girls wound their way onstage disguised as 'His Majesty's Landship "Tanko"': a 'weird and wonderful' caterpillar-like monster that bristled with guns and was 'commanded' by the twenty-two-year-old French singer and 'speciality' (i.e. erotic) dancer Mlle Regine Flory, who sang Max Darewski's song 'The Tanko' while the Palace girls threw off their carapace and danced along ('I will teach the Kaiser & Co., we know how to win, / When they see us dance the Tanko right into Berlin . . .').[47]

It was this sort of stuff that affronted Siegfried Sassoon, whose poem 'Blighters', dated 4 February 1917, struck back so memorably against those who had converted the 'dear old tank' into a frolicking variety act:

> The House is crammed; tier beyond tier they grin
> And cackle at the Show, while prancing ranks
> Of harlots shrill the chorus, drunk with din;

We're sure the Kaiser loves our dear old Tanks!
I'd like to see a Tank come down the stalls,
Lurching to rag-time tunes, or 'Home, sweet Home'
And there'd be no more jokes in Music-halls
To mock the riddled corpses round Bapaume.[48]

The men of the Heavy Section had an additional reason for objecting to this onlooking cult of the tank, for in building unrealistic hopes it placed disappointment in the wings, and thereby threatened to recoil on their own struggle to turn painted and theatrical metal boxes into effective weapons. As the newspaperman Philip Gibbs himself pointed out, the desperate rush of excitement that had initially greeted the tanks quickly dissipated: 'After the first great surprise, the exaltation of spirits caused by these new motor monsters, there followed a disappointment in the public mind and even among our soldiers.'[49] The men of the Heavy Section came to regret the excessive symbolism of the tank and blamed the press for their embarrassment. As an unforgiving Capt. D. G. Browne, MC, would later recall:

an immense amount of nonsense was talked and written about the first appearance of the tanks in the field. The newspapers, as was to be expected, excelled themselves in absurdity. Any lie was good enough for them. The war correspondents, in their safe and comfortable chateau in the valley of the Ternoise, ransacked Scripture and zoology for suitable similes. There is a story of those halfpenny strategists, Messrs Gibbs and Beach Thomas, tossing up a coin (no doubt a halfpenny) to decide who should use the word Behemoth.[50]

Disgusted by the knighthoods awarded after the war to correspondents such as Gibbs and Beach Thomas, Browne dismissed them as purveyors of 'ignorant flapdoodle', which had only served to humiliate the early tank crews. Few people had seen the new machines in successful action, but 'tens of thousands had seen tanks lying derelict in the Somme mud or holding up traffic through mechanical breakdowns on important thoroughfares'. Exaggerated claims made in ill-informed newspapers may have inspired readers in Britain, but on the front they only brought down ridicule upon 'men who had done wonders in circumstances inconceivable to the writers'. Indeed, the men of the Heavy Section 'got more chaff than any unit except the London Scottish'. Meanwhile, 'people at home, who believe anything they read in print and have the Press they deserve, naturally expected miracles of machines which pushed down houses on battlefields, where, in fact, no house had been standing for months'.

In Captain Browne's view, the things that could not be said for reasons of secrecy were exactly what had to be understood if the tank was to be seen as more than a miracle or diverting joke. Instead of grasping that tanks were governed by tactical considerations, people preferred to 'read more or less worthless books in which these machines figure occasionally as comic and semi-animate monsters moving capriciously here and there without method or principle'.[51] Captain Clough Williams-Ellis also condemned the press commentary that had greeted the first appearance of the tanks in September 1916: 'This lavish praise had spread a gloom over the Tank Corps: they had been unmercifully twitted by unfeeling gunners and infantrymen who knew the real facts. The newspapers had succeeded in making their intercourse with any but battalions fresh from England an unbearable round of facile jest . . .'[52]

Swinton eventually made the same point in the opening of his autobiography, defending the trials of flesh and blood from this upstart and usurping image: 'To me, against this overwhelming background of mortal anguish, the minor picturesque feature about which some have rhapsodized, made but slight appeal.'[53] Over and again, the war correspondents were reprimanded for turning the ordeals of the Heavy Section into light amusement for that other, increasingly polarized nation that stayed at home. Some, like the anonymous 'Tank Major' who teamed up with adventure story writer Eric Wood to produce a book called *Tank Tales* in 1919, eventually acknowledged the difficulties imposed on the war correspondents by the censor:

Perhaps the Censor was to blame, but the fact remains that amongst the innumerable newspaper articles which described the advent of the Tanks, there was not a single one which discussed, soberly and with intelligence, the military meaning of this new weapon of warfare . . . The secret was too well kept, and the idea of their grotesque nature came uppermost and held the popular imagination.[54]

Many of the veteran chroniclers, however, didn't bother themselves with the extenuating circumstances; indeed, after the war, it became entirely routine for Tank Corps veterans to take a passing swipe at the sensationalizing war correspondents. J. F. C. Fuller singled out the title of one of Philip Gibbs's volumes of collected dispatches to dismiss the 'so called "Realities of War" frequently described by shell shocked war correspondents' before proceeding with his own altogether more rigorous account of what the tank really amounted to.

Confronted with this accusation while still in France, the correspondents did the decent thing and apologized. Beach Thomas wrote that 'possibly

the humour has been overdone', conceding that, far from just armouring
the weapon against the loss of its secret, the whimsical imagery that he and
his fellow correspondents had built up around the tank might have become
an additional burden on the Tank Corps.[55] Philip Gibbs also acknowledged
the problem: 'One could write all this fantastically and make a queer tale of
it. The truth is fantastic, but one must write it soberly, because they were
British boys who gave their lives . . .'[56] So he apologized too, without ever
quite cancelling the jauntiness of those first reports with his retrospective
expression of contrition:

They are a little sensitive, these young men, to the comic descriptions we used to
give of them when they were first seen, and when our words had to camouflage
their real shape and structure. 'Look here,' said one of their officers, 'don't go calling the Tanks obscene monsters or ichthyosauris or prehistoric toads. It seems to
make a joke of what, after all, is no joke . . .

  'Let us take the Tanks seriously, for inside their steel walls are the bodies and
souls of men who are going out into battle with no light-heartedness, for it is a
grim and deadly business, but with ideals of duty and endeavour which lead them
to stern and terrible adventures, to enormous fatigues of the body and spirit, and
to many ugly places where, unless they have luck, they may be ditched forever.'[57]

4

Breaking the Line (the War Artist's Dilemma)

As one veteran came to see it, the tank was the 'abnormal factor' that was necessary if one side was to gain the advantage and put a decisive end to the grinding and deadlocked warfare of attrition.[1] In its less precise publicity cult, this was to say that the tank broke over the static geography of trench warfare with all the force of a freakish sea crashing over land. Marine imagery was everywhere, and only partly because the tank was an Admiralty innovation: a 'landship' that brought the tactics of naval engagement on to land. The commander of the tank was a 'skipper', his men formed a 'crew', and much of the tank's equipment had naval origins too: the 6-pounder guns, the sponsons in which they were mounted, the specially demagnetized compass . . . Those who served in tanks repeatedly used nautical metaphors to describe the experience: Clough Williams-Ellis quotes from a Sergeant Littledale, who describes a tank 'raising herself to the incline, like a ship rising on a wave', adding: 'We were to sail over stranger seas than man had ever crossed.'[2] The early accounts appreciated the tanks as 'Land Dreadnoughts', emphasizing the sea-sickness that afflicted their crews and relishing the nautical movements with which they 'plunge and swing as they make their way over "earth billows" and "earth troughs" shaped by high-explosive shells'.[3] Popular novelists were quick to amplify on this nautical theme: F. S. Brereton's adventure story, *The Armoured-car Scouts* (1918), included a chapter on 'A Naval Land Battle' in which the 'British naval armoured-car detachment' advance, handling their 'monstrous steel-clad wagons' as if they were 'ships at sea'.[4] J. F. C. Fuller may have considered himself more 'scientific' in approach, but he too would imagine this potent weapon converting ground into 'a solid sea, as easily traversable in all directions as ice is by a skater'.[5]

As an emblem of broader developments that were 'in the air', the tank shared aspects of its imagery with the literary and artistic movements of the time. The marine analogy found ambient echoes along the fringes of Bloomsbury, where Imagist poets articulated their own transformational works by means of an elemental vocabulary in which land and sea kept giving way to one another. Leaves torn by storm from plane trees in Meck-lenburgh Square, where H. D. (Hilda Doolittle) lived in the early years of the war, were never more likely to be glimpsed through the window as green stones sinking through water. In the same sudden poetic, mountainous pine forests were liable to be raked with wind until they crested as phallic waves beating in towards nymphs on a rocky shore. If the tank was a landship or, like the prototype which was fitted with 'lobster claws' to cut wire, a monster from the deep, its battlefield also resembled the transformative geography of H. D.'s *Sea Garden* (1916): static but unstable, a land of suffocating immobility where every trace of moisture summoned up wild prospects, forgotten gods and the roaring sea.[6] Like those taut Imagist poems, the tank was a machine of sudden conversion that broke up habituated perspectives to outline new and fluid possibilities for the first time. Like those poems again, its unexpected movements suggested a deep structural change in the world.

This coincidence between the tank and the cultural avant-garde may seem entirely accidental, but it was widely perceived at the time and became a persistent feature of the new weapon's progress through the war. Gertrude Stein remembered standing with Picasso on the Boulevard Raspail in Paris during the early days of the war; a camouflaged truck went by and Picasso immediately hailed it as an outcome of Cubism. In fact, she claimed in the nineteen-thirties, the entire 'composition' of the Great War had been Cubist: a new and decentred form of battle that apparently had 'neither a beginning nor an end'.[7] The historian Stephen Kern has since extended Stein's metaphor of 'the Cubist War', connecting it to the transformations of both time and space that took place on the Western Front. He considers such developments as the war's fragmentation of time into the endless flux of life in the trenches and the synchronized, homogeneous time in which engagements were planned; its heightened distinction between day and night; and its apparent disconnection of history into a single cataclysmic differentiation of Then (i.e. before the war) from Now. He also cites its mockery of civilization's evolutionary and progressive ideals, the sense of helplessness that it visited on combatants, its confusion of the traditional 'line of battle' and its removal of the point of command from anywhere near the battlefront.[8]

In some respects the tank seems to cut against all this. The major achievement of the tanks would be to restore the traditional perspectives of the decisive breakthrough to the bewildered and, in Kern's analogy, 'Cubist' geography of modern battle: they put the commander back at the head of his troops and, for many, revived the lost romance of battle. The same argument applies to the activities of the British tank's main camoufleur. If Solomon J. Solomon felt at every step 'thwarted in the development of his ideas', this was certainly not because he was a Cubist. Like Giron de Scevola, the fashionable Parisian portrait painter who is said to have worn his white kid gloves even while heading the French camouflage endeavour, Solomon was a stickler for the realist figure. In a text book written for budding artists before the war, he had acknowledged the 'extraordinary insights' of 'born experimentalists like Monet and Sorolla y Bastida', but he left no doubt that the modern 'reaction against sentimentality' had been altogether too violent and inclined to exaggeration.[9] Urging his reader to distrust the 'over strange', Solomon concluded that 'there are few things more depressing than the sight that meets one on the walls of some continental exhibitions, where the decadent spirit of revolt – anarchy is the better word – excites the would-be famous to make little fireworks of their own with their private and special box of matches, on the chance that the fermenting critics may be impressed by the glare . . .'

Previous commentators have expressed surprise that an artist of such traditional persuasion should have become a leading camoufleur. As Olga Phillips wrote in the thirties, 'In effect, as it was said, he aimed at making aerodromes look like lakes and gas-emplacements look like cabbage fields, and for one who hated "the modern art" impositions, this was a great achievement.'[10] But for Solomon himself there was no discrepancy here. In what he saw as his major achievement, namely his detection of German camouflage from aerial photographs, it was precisely his old-fashioned knowledge of traditional perspective that enabled him to triumph over the manipulated appearances of modern war. As he wrote, the coming of aerial reconnaissance meant that '"the other side of the hill" no longer existed, and Art alone could screen men and intentions where natural cover failed'.[11] From now on, intelligence would be 'largely made up of the results of a fight between the camera and the camoufleur'.[12]

Working with a new kind of magic lantern called a 'radiographer', Solomon studied aerial photographs taken from behind the German line in Flanders and quickly became convinced that German camouflage was already so good that 'only the trained eye and mind' of an artist could see through its deceptions.[13] The powerful electric lights of the radiographer enabled Solomon to study the play of light and shade in his photographs with sufficient precision to detect the tell-tale signs of art replacing nature in the 'hollow landscape' down below.[14] As he stared down on the German-held village of St Pierre Capelle he saw a house without a shadow and deduced from this that an artificial field must extend out from its eaves. Studying minute variations in the shadows cast by stooks in a series of fields, he deduced that they were fakes planted on the gently sloping and therefore shadowless sides of a series of huge 'undulating hangars'. With his trained eye, Solomon could see through the 'modelled fudge' down below.[15] Far from being Cubist, his deciphering of German camouflage was a triumph of classical perspective over modern deception. Even so, however, it was more than the 'brass hats' could bring themselves to believe in. For them Solomon was just a 'troublesome lunatic' with crazy ideas, and his warnings were inadequately heeded.

Yet while the triumph of the tank may seem to cut against the grain of Kern's deeper Cubist analogy, a superficial kinship between the tank and modern movements such as Futurism and Cubism has nevertheless been claimed since the earliest days. Marinetti was thinking of tramcars when he talked about caressing the breasts of 'snorting machines', and the slow crawling tank was scarcely illustrative of 'the beauty of speed'. Yet the tank was violently anti-traditional, and easily reconciled with Marinetti's Futurist insistence that art should offer a machine-like 'assault on the forces of the unknown'.[16]

Some of the cameramen who filmed the early tanks saw them in a decidedly Modernist way: closing in on the machine to frame it as a bizarre assemblage of geometrical planes that all seem to move off in different directions at once, contrasting the sliding movement of the tank's hull with the circular motion of the tracks surrounding it, and using primitive 'subjective camera' techniques to look out as if through the all-consuming monster's very own eye. After the war, Wyndham Lewis built up his 'soldier of humour' around a convulsive trench laughter just like that which had greeted the tank's early appearances on the Western Front: his 'wild body' may look like a 'visi-gothic fighting-machine', but it is actually a laughing machine, and laughter is the most profound of its 'mysterious spasms'.[17] Lewis's world is full of rivets and armour that entirely obscure the old characteristics of individual personality, and the anti-pastoral tank would have served him at least as well as his chosen locomotive when it came to finding a machine that would 'put out of business all the craftsmen who grew fat on the classic scene'.[18]

Among the generation that fought the Great War, it quickly became conventional to describe the tank in terms borrowed from the European avant-garde. In the autobiography that he published in the early thirties, Swinton looked back on Mother as a 'gigantic cubist steel slug',[19] but the analogy was decidedly second-hand by then: indeed, it can can be traced right back to September 1916, when the tanks first went into action. A ludicrous Futurist 'Ode to the Tank' ('Crash . . . Rattle' etc.) was published in the *Tank Corps Journal* in May 1920,[20] and before that, in 1917, there were 'Futurist colour-designs' on the sides of a vividly imagined wrecked landship in Percy F. Westerman's adventure story *To the Fore With the Tanks!*[21] H. G. Wells had made the same connection after watching 'Land Ironclads' demonstrated in October 1916. In an article written that same month, he invoked the name of England's then best known Futurist or Cubist painter as he tried to describe what it was like to travel in a tank:

Only Mr C. R. W. Nevinson could do justice to the interior of a Tank. You see a hand gripping something; you see the eyes and forehead of an engineer's face; you perceive that an overall blueishness beyond the engine is the back of another man. "Don't hold that," says some one. "It is too hot. Hold on to that." The engines roar, so loudly that I doubt whether one could hear guns without; the floor begins to slope, and slopes until one seems to be at forty-five degrees or thereabouts; and then the whole concern swings up, and sways and slants the other way. You have crossed a bank. You heel sideways. Through the door, which has been left open, you see the little group of engineers, staff officers and naval men receding and falling away behind you. You straighten up and go uphill. You halt and begin to rotate. Through the open door, the green field with its red walls, rows of worksheds and forests of chimneys in the background, begins a steady processional movement. The group of engineers and officers and naval men appears at the other side of the door and further off. Then comes a sprint down-hill.

You descend and stretch your legs.[22]

There was good reason why C. R. W. Nevinson should have come to mind in October 1916. The newspapers at that time were full of him, either condemning him as a fraudulent opportunist or hailing him as the one British artist whose reputation had justly been made by the war. A Futurist and sometime 'automobilist' who had collaborated with Marinetti before the war, he had gone out to France to drive a motor ambulance with the Red Cross in 1914, thus becoming one of the first to make his excursion into what the critic P. G. Konody now described as 'the Futurist paradise of modern warfare'.[23] Nevinson's paintings and drawings of the war were being exhibited in Leicester Square, at exactly the time when the tanks went into their first much reported actions in France. Held in the Hogarth Room of the Leicester Gallery, the exhibition ran through September and October 1916 and was both well attended and widely discussed. It confirmed Nevinson's fame as the 'soldier-cubist', an artist who worked by 'clinching the appearance of Nature with a discreet application of the principles of Cubism'.[24]

In the catalogue to his exhibition, Nevinson insisted that 'it is impossible to express the scientific and mechanical spirit of this twentieth-century war with the languishing or obsolete symbolism of Mediaeval and Classical art'. For Sir Claude Phillips, writing a few months earlier, Nevinson's war pictures had finally proved the Cubist technique justified; 'has he not through its cold, calculated violence, its cruel, metallic, angularity, expressed something of the awful unconsciousness of Fate controlling yet ignoring the tragic destinies of man?'[25] Nevinson had previously exhibited La Mitrailleuse, his famous painting of a dehumanized machine gunner, above the following statement: 'Man made the machine in his own image. The machine has retaliated by re-making man in its own image.' Commentators on the new exhibition were now quick to link the 'geometrical convention' that Nevinson had acquired from Cubism with the much discussed appearance of the tank. For C. Lewis Hinds, writing in the Daily Chronicle at the height of the tank drama, Nevinson 'is artist, a fighting artist, who has rampaged, like a "Tank", through all the modern movements . . . Out of Cubism he has brought to birth a curious geometrical formula, sharp and glittering like a sword, which is admirably suited to his vision of this scientific, mechanical war.'[26]

But it was in the pacifist and socialist pages of the Ploughshare, a Quaker magazine with a small circulation of about 1,000, that a direct connection between Nevinson's art and the tank was spelt out most explicitly. Nevinson's war pictures were first mentioned in the November issue. Having visited the exhibition in Leicester Square, an unnamed correspondent wrote in to remark that where old artists used to invest their battles with 'romantic glamour', Nevinson's subjects 'have the glamour . . . of some unknown and diabolic sphere': with Nevinson, 'the covering is off'. This prompted William Loftus Hare, the Ploughshare's most active editor (the other one, Hubert W. Peet, was just beginning a period of detention as a conscientious objector), to write a larger review of his own. In an article published in December 1916 as 'Art and the Tank', he describes how Nevinson shows man becoming 'just a tender to the machine'. In this war, as Nevinson is said to reveal, men are no longer personalities; they have been squeezed through an 'Easter Island' mould and given 'an equal shape, size and value'. Looking at Nevinson's remarkable 'A Column on the March', William Loftus Hare saw:[27]

a human 'Tank', a mechanical monster whose fuel is flesh and whose lubricant is blood; we see it as the triumphant achievement of science without sympathy, of power without love; we see also its purpose. It is not mere blind Destiny, as General Hamilton thinks, which urges this scaley 'caterpillar' to drag its loathsome body over all lands, all homes, all hearts, to the destruction of everything human. No; this reptile Tank, symbolised by Nevinson's 'Column on the March', is designed in every part, be it of bone and sinew or blade and gun, to serve one purpose well known to its designers and to us: to conquer the markets of the world for competing dynasties of capitalism – for profit!

On 16 November 1916, the *New Age* dismissed the modern 'geometric convention' that Nevinson brought to bear on the appearance of war as self-indulgent opportunism, reminiscent perhaps of the rhetorical excesses of the war correspondents. It scolded him for stressing the special effects of war: 'Kill war with truth; don't play with its lights.' Not all war artists succumbed to the light show, but even the drawings of a traditionalist among the official war artists like Muirhead Bone were threatened with a distinctly modern kind of disturbance by the moving geometry of the tank. The *Times Literary Supplement* declared that Bone 'had not allowed the novelty of his subject matter to affect his treatment. There he differs from Mr Nevinson . . . He draws the Western Front, he draws a tank even, as if he were drawing the streets of London or a windmill, or an old ship in a harbour.'[28] But in fact, Bone's famous drawing of a tank was only achieved at some risk to the conventions of the classical scene. As C. E. Montague remarked, 'Thanks to the imaginative power of the artist, the "Tank" is here seen not as the British soldier sees it – a friendly giant with lovably droll tricks of gait and texture – but as it must look to a threatened enemy, the very embodiment of momentum irresistibly grinding its way towards its prey.' For Montague, the tank burst through Bone's normal restraint to make the spectator feel like 'a crushed worm'.[29] John Cournos saw the same thing happening in Bone's image. 'Only once does he get out of his own skin, as it were, and that is when he draws an advancing "tank" as if it were a blind antediluvian monster crawling ruthlessly to the destruction of all that should dare to oppose it.'[30] But in fact, Bone appears to have improvised his own robustly English way of capturing the astonishing appearance of the tank without having to become a Cubist. Eric Kennington, another official war artist, remembers being there to help him hold the line:

Bone drew it (in 1916) on two sheets in a gale of wind and rain. While I held a raincoat over his board. He first completed the left-half, then made two lines on the new sheet to make top and base of tank. Then he drew the right hand half. When assembled the two halves fitted exactly making one picture – which surprised me but not Bone.[31]

Kennington had come up with his own unillusioned definition of the tank by the time he recorded that awkward collaboration during the Second World War: 'They are male monsters. The jolly feminine names chalked or painted on them won't fit. I imagine the embodiment of what is left of man when all his culture is removed and then add strength and combativeness a thousand-fold. The result is the tank.'[32]

As for Nevinson, he mounted a second exhibition at the Leicester Gallery in March 1918. One picture showed a dead British soldier lying in a trench and was censored at the last minute by the military authorities, suggesting, once again, that the presence of a bare fact of war was more likely to worry the censor than the most heightened imaginative treatment. To begin with, the offending picture appeared in the exhibition with the censor's tape running across it. But after a few days it was reported that Nevinson had taken it down and replaced it with a picture showing a camouflaged tank rising up out of the swamp-like filth to be silhouetted against a nauseating off-white sky.[33] By the time Nevinson got round to it, the jolly 'pink' of Solomon's famous sunset design had become a blood-red streak smeared over the foul bulk of the mud-coloured tank. The joke was also over in France by then, and the tank's contribution to Cubism was beginning to look different too: figured not in camouflage paint, or in zany modern 'waddling' effects, but in a transformation of tactics that opened up a new and mobile warfare of 'area' on the other side of a broken, if not entirely 'classic', line.

5

Raising the Heavy Branch at Bermicourt

For a sense of the atmosphere in which this difficult transformation was brought about, we are indebted to an anonymously printed memoir called *H.Q. Tanks,* written by a staff officer of unusually refined sensibility. Its author, the Hon. Evan Edwards Charteris, had been a temporary captain with the Tank Corps Command in London since August 1916; and in July 1917, at the age of fifty-three, he was transferred to France to take up what he called 'a sort of nondescript post as historian to the Tank Corps'.[1] In his younger days Charteris had been a lieutenant in the Coldstream Guards, but his real passion was the fine arts. A collector and usefully connected friend to artists, including the London-based American John Singer Sargent, this old-Etonian bachelor was 'a sybarite, an eclectic and an epicurean'; and his immaculate, far from avant-garde taste was evident in every picture and piece of furniture in the 'exquisite' Mayfair maisonette that was his London home.[2]

Captain Charteris travelled to France with two senior officers, and had ample time during the journey to run his detached connoisseur's eye across the pair of them. Lieutenant Colonel Sir John Keane impressed him only as 'an old soldier of a rather enlightened type, with bushy eyebrows, a feature which in the early stages of the war was certainly associated with military advancement'. Lieutenant Colonel G. B. Matthew-Lannowe, who was senior staff officer with the Tank Corps at Wool in Dorset, seemed representative of 'all that is most unsympathetic in the way of War Office mentality'. A 'disciplinarian of the old school', Matthew-Lannowe was rigid and 'quite uneducated' outside soldiering – the kind of colonel who 'thinks martial law a remedy for strikes, shooting a cure for discontent, and bayonets the panacea for all social ills'.

Having arrived late in Boulogne, the three men drove through the night for two hours. The turning for Bermicourt is easily missed. But this did not deter Lieutenant Colonel Matthew-Lannowe who, being convinced that 'everything can be done by order', barked a last-minute instruction at the driver, causing him to swerve suddenly and land them all in the ditch. A passing lorry eventually dragged their car out and, at about 1 a.m., they finally pulled up at Bermicourt Château, which had 'a very dismantled appearance'. The Quartermaster General of the Tank Corps in France, Colonel T. D. Uzielli, emerged in his pyjamas and, with the help of an electric torch, ushered them into a building that seemed bare of furniture and 'totally unlived in'. Captain Charteris appraised Uzielli – whom he would later describe as 'a dark, short, well-appointed little man, Greek, I imagine by origin, Levantine in method, with much of the ingratiating technique of an Oriental . . .' and then, having been informed that the rest of the staff were encamped at Poperinge in Flanders as they prepared to launch tanks into the Third Battle of Ypres, he retired to 'a most admirable and sheeted bed, comfortable beyond the dreams of campaigning'. Perhaps, as he lay there in the billeted château that was now 'H.Q. Tanks', his mind wandered back to more habitual scenes – like the day in January 1907 when he had joined a royal shooting party at Chatsworth and been photographed alongside King Edward and other society guns, including Lady Desborough and the Duke of Devonshire.[3] Perhaps, in anticipation of the makeshift quarters that he himself would be sleeping in before long, he dreamed of aboriginal teepees of the kind that appear beneath the great crags and waterfalls of Yosemite Valley on the canvases of Thomas Hill, the nineteenth-century Californian artist who had numbered Charteris among his clients.

The Heavy Section was already being expanded and re-established as a Corps in its own right by the time the Battle of the Somme finally ground to a halt in November 1916, leaving half a million British soldiers dead. Colonel Swinton had gone the way of Lieutenant Colonel John Brough before him, removed by a military establishment that was suspicious of mavericks and much inclined to mutter about discipline and proper staff college qualifications. However 1,000 tanks had been ordered: in that matter at least, the fabled 'obstructionists' at the War Office had been over-ridden.

So it was that the Elveden Explosives Area was abandoned for a larger administrative headquarters and training centre at Wool in Dorset; and the Heavy Section in France – the 'Fighting Side', as it came to be known – was put on a more permanent basis too. Now commanded by Lieutenant Colonel H. J. Elles, an engineer and formerly the staff officer at GHQ who had been responsible for liaising with the first tank companies when they arrived at Yvrench, the tank force withdrew from the Somme and moved to Bermicourt, a small village just north of the Hesdin-St Pol road, where it entered a period of growth and reorganization.

The new establishment may have started with three Nissen huts, but it soon overwhelmed not just Bermicourt's already unoccupied château and its grounds, but the surrounding neighbourhood too. With the first four battalions being created from the residue of the original Heavy Section companies in outlying villages, Bermicourt quickly found itself the capital of what one tank soldier remembered as 'a small state' shaped like a pentagon and devoted entirely to British tanks.[4] Along with the usual blizzard of military tents and duckboards, there were acres of hangars, vast steel sheds, stalls for tanks ('like the old elephant stables of Carthage'),[5] and countless huts for a staff of 1,200 officers and men. Workshops soon covered over twenty-seven acres by the railway line at Erin and a special compound was built to house hundreds of Chinese labourers, members of the 51st Chinese Labour Company who feature as 'coolies' and 'jabbering chinks' in Charteris's unofficial portrait of *H.Q. Tanks*, and are additionally commended for their 'extraordinary aptitude for transporting heavy weights'.[6] The adjutant of the Central Workshops at Teneur was an enterprising and widely travelled former Shell oilman called Captain Stephen Foot, who thought nothing of reviving the region's timber industry to meet the requirements of this massive expansion.[7]

There was overspill far beyond Bermicourt too: the main depot at Treport; a coastal gunnery school among the 'gimcrack villas of Merlimont'[8] near Etaples; the driving school at Wailly not far from Arras, where captured German trenches were turned into a practice battleground for tanks with the help of more colonial labour – this time provided by Lushai hillmen, remembered by Charteris, as 'bright-eyed, velvet-footed creatures', who scuttled around among the trenches 'with the staccato activity of poultry', and who fought their own fatal set battles with unexploded bombs pulled from the mud.[9]

To visit Bermicourt now is to find a small and far from dismantled château in wooded parkland with a fine courtyard of farm buildings, and an avenue of tall trees along the silent drive. Placid obscurity has long since been reinstated, and the only indication of history's distant visit is a stone plinth bearing a small bronze replica of a First World War tank. Bermicourt is a castle in name alone, and it is not surprising that one British tank officer should have mocked the pretensions of this unfortified 'château of the normal Versailles type', observing with a literal-minded snort that 'château' seemed to be the French word for 'house'.

That was the typically sharp judgement of the thirty-eight-year-old Brevet Colonel J. F. C. Fuller, who had come to Bermicourt on 26 December 1916, to take up his duties as General Staff Officer to the tank force that was now known as the Heavy Branch of the Machine Gun Corps. Arriving at 'about tea-time' in what was already shaping up to be the coldest winter ever recorded in that part of France, he had stepped into the one-room-deep building and found Colonel Hugh Elles, who stood in front of an improvised wood-burning stove in the former drawing room and volunteered that 'this show badly wants pulling together; it's all so new that one hardly knows which way to turn'.[10]

Charteris would look back on Elles as an 'immensely popular figure . . . one of the paladins of the war, modernized and adjusted to the conditions of the hour': a man of charm as well as a natural leader, he was 'precociously successful and admirably good looking, reasonably vain of his appearance, but quite modest as to his attainments'.[11] Fuller was somewhat more specific about the panache of this 'universally loved' man. In his view, Elles was the personal embodiment of *esprit de cocarde*, by which he meant the flair, élan, and 'indefinable manliness' that became the spirit of the new force: 'To both officers and men he was what Henry IV of France had been to his soldiers: boyish and reckless in danger; perhaps a better soldier than a strategist, yet one who could profit from the co-operation of his advisers . . .'[12] A boyish thirty-six-year-old in 1916, but, as another senior colleague wrote of Elles, 'a grave, middle-aged man' by November 1918.[13]

Fuller was already acquainted with Captain T. J. Uzielli, the Quartermaster General who had recommended his appointment: he would describe him as '"King of the Grocers". . . business-like, and an administrator from boot to crown'.[14] He may have felt more inspired by the two officers who were to work under him in the 'Great Brotherhood'[15] that was the emerging Tank Corps. Captain Gifford Le Q. Martel, a sapper who had previously designed the mock Western Front at Elveden, came to be known as 'The Slosher' on account of his prowess as a boxer: wherever he was encamped Martel would improvise a ring in which he would fight all comers.[16] A man of 'desperate bravery', Martel had 'a deep, hoarse laugh', which he used to propel hideously Gothic stories of his encounters in the trenches: one characteristic tableau, well remembered in the officers' mess at Bermicourt, featured a group of Tommies discovered frying bacon on the fire from a burning enemy dugout, quite unperturbed by the cries of the German soldiers who were 'frizzling' below.[17] Captain F. E. Hotblack DSO, MC, was a former brewer who, as the notoriously 'fearless' intelligence officer with the tanks, used to 'go about a good deal' – reconnoitring all over the front on silent india-rubber soles.[18] An 'artistic' and unusually self-contained man, he had been decorated and fêted for his remarkable bravery during the Battle of the Ancre: finding that snow had covered the tapes laid to guide the advancing tanks he had, in his own understated words, 'led the tank forward, on foot, to its objective, taking what cover I could in shell holes half full of mud and ice' – an act for which the London press celebrated him as 'The Teacher of the Tank'.[19] Valiant but 'impossible to know', Captain 'Boots' Hotblack was one of the Heavy Branch's sheerest heroes. He would come back from the most formidable night excursions, curl up in the Bermicourt office and go to sleep without a word, leaving news of his exploits to trickle through a few days later.[20]

A man of ideas more than action, Fuller nevertheless brought his own searching and, when it came to his chosen enemies, quite merciless perspective with him. As an adjutant in the pre-war territorial army, Fuller had become known as a specialist in training and tactics. He had spent the first half of 1915 in Tunbridge Wells as a frustrated staff officer with General du Cane's Second Army. This 'penal servitude' had involved him in drawing up ludicrous plans to force-march all the sheep in Sussex, Kent and Surrey to Salisbury Plain in the event of a German invasion;[21] and when he fell out with du Cane, he was ordered to join the VIIth Corps, then part of the Third Army in France. In this role he had studied the Western Front and applied his critical faculties to the reform of the British trench system, which had grown 'like Topsy' and was, in his view, both irrationally laid out and lamentably detached from any offensive strategy.[22] Long concerned with 'the tactics of penetration', Fuller had watched the Battle of the Somme from its first day, and seen it become a 'veritable Moloch' and 'shambles'.[23] It was during this 'grim and grinding agony',[24] that a sapper called Captain F. H. E. Townsend had showed him a 'Manuscript in Red Ink', which identified the absurdity of the disposition of German forces, spread out as they were along a front that was five hundred miles long but only five miles deep, and suggested that victory would be guaranteed if only it were possible to penetrate a section of this front 'in a space of a few hours'.[25]

By the end of August, Fuller and Townshend had heard 'strange rumours of some new weapon of war' and got permission to attend a demonstration at Yvrench. As Fuller later recalled, they got there to be reminded of 'Epsom Down on a Derby morning. There were scores and scores of cars there and hundreds and hundreds of spectators both English and French. Everyone was talking and chatting, when slowly came into sight the first tank I ever saw. Not a monster, but a very graceful machine, with beautiful lines, lozenge-shaped, but with two clumsy-looking wheels behind it.' Others may have laughed and insisted that trees be pushed down, but Fuller and Townshend saw a very different promise: mindful of 'the Manuscript in Red Ink', they recognized the tank as 'the unknown x in the equation of victory'. After that fleeting glimpse of things to come, Fuller returned his mind to the improvement of dugouts, which should, he was convinced, have not one but two exits leading into different trench systems, so that they could then become 'offensive posts of resistance' rather than bunkers of 'passive defence'.[26] He was ready to go when, in the middle of December, the call came from the Heavy Branch.

Swept by waves of frenzied reorganization and planning, Bermicourt was the site of its own endless battle between the 'ultra-military' point of view as represented by Uzielli, and the 'business' outlook of men like Colonel F. Searle, the anti-bureaucratic and highly efficient Chief Engineer who only wanted to get things done. 'Flaming rows' were more or less contained in the officers' mess, which had its own distinctive atmosphere, thanks partly to the dry wit of its unofficial president and *arbiter elegantiarum*, the exquisite Captain Charteris, who also managed to ensure that 'strange little packets' kept arriving from Paris and London – filled with beech-nut bacon, rose-leaf honey and other 'rare exotic condiments'.[27] When an enemy shell burst into the driving school kitchen, it was Charteris's style to describe it 'dissipating' the cook along with his culinary implements.[28] Battles would be 'sanguinary' rather than just plain 'bloody'; and, as time went on, there would be much chuckling about the speed at which the Commander of the 2nd Tank Brigade, Brigadier General A. Courage DSO, MC, would keep talking, despite the fact that he had lost half his jaw to a German bullet, and was still coming to terms with an uncomfortable porcelain chin.

On reading *H.Q. Tanks* shortly after the war, one veteran detected 'a blasé indifference to good and evil', a streak of malice reminiscent of 'the Whistler-Oscar Wilde coterie' and a disconcerting combination of 'intellectual brilliancy and an almost entire lack of emotion'.[29] Captain the Hon. Evan Charteris was certainly an incongruous figure at Bermicourt: an aristocratic oddball right down to his 'animal-hide overcoat', he stepped through the war with the stylish detachment of a classically minded aesthete who found himself strolling through an exhibition of lurid post-impressionist works in a picture gallery. But despite its author's aestheticizing tendencies, *H.Q. Tanks* was, as this same veteran freely admitted, 'permeated with the well-remembered atmosphere'.

Bermicourt's much observed 'sardonic chuckle' could be defensive as well as cruel; indeed, it could be helpless, incredulous, exasperated and outraged. In simpler variations it reflected what Basil Henriques described as 'that curious steel-plate armour, which, as the war advanced seemed to grow round one's heart, so that one scarcely felt the pain of sorrow'. It also served to maintain the nerve of those whose responsibility was to abstract the terrible stuff of battles in which tank soldiers were incinerated or literally blasted to pieces, and turn it into a tactical idea that might yield better results next time.

Yet there was another reason why Bermicourt's dry and disbelieving snort was good for morale in this young and experimental force. It gave expression to widely shared exasperation at 'the stupidity and lack of imagination of GHQ',[30] and of a British High Command that offered 'the absolute negation of a guiding mind'.[31] Elles himself used to tell his Brigade Commander, Brigadier Baker-Carr: 'Fighting the Germans is a joke compared with fighting the British,'[32] and the officers of the Heavy Branch seem to have derived much of their own sense of solidarity from viewing the command structure above them as a second front. Countless sarcastic jibes were fired at the hidebound traditionalists at GHQ: old men who, refusing to heed the advice of Swinton and others, had used the new tanks in driblets rather than mass and frittered away their secret for the sake of a few modest local results; who had taken a mobile weapon and treated it as if it were a Martello tower; who ordered tanks to be employed in the most inappropriate conditions imaginable, and then turned round and dismissed them as useless; who viewed some of the most brilliant tank pioneers as dangerous buccaneers to be replaced as soon as possible by ignorant 'duds' who at least had a proper staff college background. This contempt was concentrated on GHQ, but it was easily extended both to the Tank Supply Committee in England, judged to be stubbornly and wrongly insistent on its own superior knowledge when it came to matters of design and delivery, and also to some of the men appointed to senior positions in the War Office's non-fighting side of the emerging Tank Corps. Thus Lieutenant Colonel Matthew-Lannowe was nick-named 'Potsdam' on account of his block-headed 'Prussian' outlook, whereas Major General Sir J. E. Capper, Director General of Tanks at the War Office, had to make do, thanks to the intervention of Captain Charteris, with the designation 'Stone Age'.[33] As for the horse, Colonel Mark Dillon named that old-fashioned creature 'the social difficulty', explaining that 'cavalry has always been the high-class thing to be in', and that War Office officials were 'horse-minded' and no doubt blinkered too.[34]

Fuller fitted into this impatient climate perfectly: besides being the Heavy Branch's chief tactician, he became its leading philosopher; the prophet of its hopes and the rationalizer of its most unyielding prejudices. Undoubtedly eccentric, as any true 'brain' must be, he was nonetheless a representative figure even in the extremism with which he raised the Heavy Branch's outlook into 'theoretical' expression, converting its feud with GHQ and the War Office into a full-scale crusade against the unintelligent conservatism of a dead military epoch. Colonel Dillon, who served as a reconnaissance officer with the Heavy Branch, remembered Fuller as 'the only bloke who knew what he was doing', and a man whose clarity of purpose contrasted starkly with the inconstant bumbling of GHQ. Similar views were expressed by Stephen Foot ('the brains behind it all were Fuller's);[35] and also by Brigadier Baker-Carr, who came to Bermicourt as Commanding Officer of C Battalion, and considered it 'impossible to overestimate' the importance of Fuller's contribution to the emerging tank force: 'His grasp of essential factors and disregard for tradition, in conjunction with an almost uncanny foresight, proved of paramount importance in working out the best methods of employing tanks in battle.' In H.Q. Tanks, Charteris provides a sketch of this 'GSO 1 and brain' as he was perceived in the officer's mess:

A little man, with a bald head, and a sharp face and a nose of Napoleonic cast, his general appearance, stature, and feature earning him the title of Boney. He stood out at once as a totally unconventional soldier, prolific in ideas, fluent in expression, at daggers drawn with received opinion, authority, and tradition. In the mess his attacks on the red-tabbed hierarchy were viewed in the spirit of a rat hunt: a spirit he responded to with much vivacity, and no little wit. But he could talk amusingly and paradoxically on any subject. His specialities were Eastern religions, about which he could be bewildering, spiritualism, occultism, military history and the theory of war. His knowledge of literature was wide enough to enable him to condemn most of what was good; on the other hand he was a great reader of Shakespeare, whom he admired and understood from an angle of his own, and had dabbled in philosophy, of which he could handle a few elementary statements to the complete confounding and obfuscation of the mess.[36]

'An inexhaustible writer', Fuller would sit in his 'brain barn' churning out 'reams on reams about training, plans of campaign, organization, and schemes for the use of tanks'. And in the evening he would launch into arguments that 'raged over hours' and often ended with the more conventional Colonel Elles, who plainly found his senior staff officer infernally clever, saying, '"No, Boney, you are wrong"; "You are wrong, Boney," an assertion which he had difficulty in supporting.' Charteris found no reason to regret his ignorance when Fuller pressed him to look through the works of his favourite poet, Aleister Crowley, but he concluded that Fuller was 'an invaluable element both from a military and social point of view': no administrator or commander, but 'just what a staff officer ought to be, evolving sound ideas and leaving their execution to others'.

Esprit de tank

As a 'brain' Fuller seems to have been licensed to enter all sorts of military proceedings from an unexpected angle of his own. Happy to find that the tanks were based so close to the site of Agincourt ('no bad place for the Headquarters of the modern knights in armour'),[37] he lectured some of Hotblack's reconnaissance officers on the ancient historical associations of the countryside in selected areas of the front, telling how the Franks had been overridden by the Romans who, in turn went down to the Hun (a barbarian, undoubtedly, but 'extremely robust') and comparing the 'blue-faces' who now decried the tank with the blustering fools who had railed against the bow and arrow at the time of the Battle of Crécy. And if any of the assembled men thought he was wandering off into 'fiction' at the expense of 'hard, solid fact', they should grasp that 'a general idea of topography' might be of real use. Boredom was a major problem of war, and knowledge of the history of your whereabouts made it a more interesting place to be, encouraging vigilance and observation too.

But Fuller's main responsibility in those early days was different. While Hotblack was equipping his historically informed trainees with tree irons and leading them up 'very tall smooth-barked beech trees' to demonstrate the 'great advantage of gaining height in order to observe';[38] and while Elles was fighting it out with a military establishment that had seen tanks floundering around on the Somme, and now appeared reluctant to prioritize the production of improved new machines, Fuller was taking steps to create a disciplined and effective force: devising tactics and logistical systems, but also creating the 'spirit of association' that came to be known as 'esprit de tank'.

On his first day after arriving at Bermicourt, Fuller drove round the Heavy Branch area, visiting the four tank battalions as they were being formed in various nearby villages, and drew his own abrupt conclusion: 'I had never seen such a band of brigands in my life.'[39] Enquiring further, he discovered that recruitment had been open to the whole army in France, and that the new arm had offered an escape route to 'every disgruntled man or "impossible" soldier' in the field. The men themselves might say that it was 'the spirit of adventure' rather than any grievance that had called them to the tanks,[40] but Fuller saw every variety of malcontent and misfit, and a bewildering array of backgrounds too: 'There were cavalrymen, infantrymen and gunners; A.S.C. men, sappers and actually a sailor, though how he had found his way to Bermicourt I cannot say. There were men in trousers, men in puttees, men in trench boots and men in kilts. There was every type of cap badge and deficiency in cap badges: the men looked exactly what they were – the down-and-outs of bawling Sergeants and unfriendly Corporals.'[41]

Very few of the recruits were trained soldiers. There was a music hall proprietor; a Scottish baker; a plebeian-looking auctioneer, said once to have been the Mayor of Cromer, who was often puce with drink. The Equipment Officer in C Battalion was the best known bee-keeper in Wales, while the Engineer Officer came from Birmingham's Hillman Car Company. The Medical Officer had previously spent two years with Shackleton at the South Pole, and the two Reconnaissance Officers, including Clough Williams-Ellis, were architects.[42] The assistant technical adviser at the workshops, Major Green, had previously managed motor buses in New York and had 'a good touch of the gutter about him'.[43] Somewhere in this unorthodox military improvisation there was also a Signals Officer called Lieutenant Colonel Molesworth – an acrobat whose pre-war achievements in the communications field included rigging up the electrical apparatus that had enabled some 'thought readers' known as the Smithsons to deceive their London audiences. And that was just the officers.

After the war, Brigadier General Hugh Elles would explain that the Tank Corps had been primarily and, indeed, peculiarly, 'a citizen force' with no more than 2 or 3 per cent of the 20,000 or so men who composed it being professional soldiers, and virtually its entire administrative and engineering staff hailing from civilian life.[44] This meant that as the units were built up, they were based, 'not on any old-time tradition of a parent regiment, but each one very much around the personality of its own commanding officer'. As for the morale of the Tank Corps, he and Fuller were agreed that this was squarely founded on the idea of the tank as 'a weapon for saving the lives of infantry'. This was the rock on which 'esprit de tank' was founded: namely, that the new arm existed to save the lives of the infantry, who were not lucky enough to have 'an inch or two of armour-plating between them and the enemy's bullets'.[45] And it lent an urgency to proceedings that is easily underestimated by latter-day historians who now condemn the pioneers for hugely overestimating the capabilities of their primitive machines.

Citizens, brigands or a bit of both . . . Fuller was charged with taking these men and forging an efficient fighting force in less than three months, and he plainly relished the opportunity. Having 'metaphorically burnt the King's Regulations' in the belief that there had 'obviously been too much of that book in their lives', he applied his own, firm but, in many respects, also unusually enlightened approach to training. His first measures were hygienic. Convinced that 'cheerfulness and comfort' were prerequisites if these desperadoes were to be remoralized and then forged into a new force, Fuller informed Uzielli: 'They must be bathed and scrubbed and cleaned up, and not until then can I set to work.' So baths and a laundry were opened at Blangy – with twenty washerwomen and an auxiliary force of locally appointed women ironers and menders: 'Thus the roots of discipline were dug into the only soil which will fertilise them; not the desire for reward or fear of punishment, but instead – personal comfort and cleanliness. Soap was our starting-point.' And along with soap came mobile canteens ('the mechanical *vivandières* of the Tank Corps'), cinemas, which were soon established at the depot in Merlimont and elsewhere; a rest camp at Erin, and another one among the sand dunes at Merlimont, where men who had been in action, or were unwell, could recuperate over fourteen-day periods. Fuller also entered a protracted battle with the War Office to secure adequate levels of pay for NCOs and the men, convinced that 'uncertainty of pay means uncertainty of *moral*'.[46] Then came insignia and uniforms, crucial to a training regimen that sought to create pride, smartness and prestige; and through that, the unorthodox but undisputably disciplined morale that came to be known as 'esprit de tank'. Each battalion was equipped with its own coloured shoulder strap, and a Corps badge was chosen to replace the Heavy Section's informally adopted skull and crossbones. The first version proposed had been drawn up in England, but Fuller and his fellow officers objected ('it resembled a sword fish ramming the stern of a whale'), and produced their own, assisted by Fuller, who turned out, fortuitously, to be skilled in the drawing of symbolic devices.

With the men cleaned up and equipped, Fuller set about 'moralizing' them, instructing the officers, and organizing the force so that the 'maximum tactical power might be developed'. All this was to be done in a few weeks, since the tanks had to be ready for action almost immediately. Eschewing mindless square-bashing, Fuller derived new forms of drill, using sports to encourage group solidarity and allowing intense competition to develop between individual tank crews. He also devised a series of lectures in which words (his own) served as 'the high tension wires of the spirit'.[47] He gave four to each company, 'on *discipline,* moral, leadership and *esprit de corps*'. Delivered in barns lit only by a few candles, these addresses were, as Fuller admitted, 'quite unconventional' and made no reference at all to pre-existing rules and regulations.

Fuller relished the fact that his force began as such a chaotic troop. Training the men was made all the easier by the absence of accumulated regimental convention in their minds to impede new understanding. The officers were more difficult, since they were 'better educated and consequently less receptive to new ideas'. They had, in other words, to be 'de-educated' before they could be re-educated. But the necessary results were obtained, thanks largely to the fact that the officers came from many different arms and included many temporary soldiers whose minds had not been 'permanently spoilt' by military tradition.

So the new tank crews played team games, drilled and thought up names for the machines that would eventually materialize, causing Martel to suggest some form of regulation to avoid early choices such as 'One-eyed Jonah', 'Autogophaster', or 'We're all in it', which he considered likely to give the Heavy Branch a bad name. And while they did so, Fuller concerned himself with working out an appropriate organization and tactics. The regime that emerged was a 'ceaselessly changing improvisation'.[48] As Fuller himself recalled, his views of organization were unorthodox and 'cut right across both those which I found and those which had been proposed'. Refusing to use 'as pro forma an existing unit organization', he worked out a system based on 'what I was presumptuous enough to call "scientific" lines'.[49]

In late February 1917, Fuller issued the document that he would later call 'the first training manual of its kind'. The tactics outlined in 'Training Note No. 16' were not entirely without precedent. Swinton had produced his 'Note on the Employment of Tanks' in February 1916; and, in November 1916, Martel had drawn up an 'astonishingly futuristic essay' called 'A Tank Army', which imagined fleets of amphibious 'Destroyer Tanks', 'Battle Tanks' and 'Torpedo Tanks' sallying out from a 'Tank Base' to operate not as 'adjuncts to the infantry', but as an all-tank force with the apparent autonomy of warships at sea.[50] But Fuller, who later claimed not to have read Martel's paper until March, dismissed earlier attempts to give tank soldiers practical guidance as 'a few platitudinous notes'. In his manual, the tank was neither a miracle nor a joke, but a 'mobile fortress' that could serve the infantry well as a primarily offensive weapon, the use of which should be governed by surprise. His recommendation that the artillery bombardment preceding any attack should be limited to forty-eight hours displeased the braided gentlemen at GHQ, who consequently ordered that the Note be withdrawn from circulation, thereby depriving other military units of an opportunity to learn about tank tactics. Fuller also restated the old Heavy Section belief that tanks should be used in mass, 'in echelon and with strong reserves'.[51]

Such was the theory that the newly trained men of the Heavy Branch prepared to put into practice in the Allied offensive of Spring 1917. In February, the First Brigade started preparing for operations to be carried out with the Third Army in the area of Arras. Plans involved considerable staff work concerned with supply and other logistical questions; and close preliminary reconnaissance was carried out under Clough Williams-Ellis, who was all the more effective, thanks to his artistic ability, when it came to sketching the terrain in question.[52] Owing to the dithering of those whom Fuller dubbed the 'real enemy', i.e. the old men lurking behind the line at GHQ and the War Office, there were acute problems of supply. Improved Mark IV tanks had failed to arrive as scheduled, and it is said that, at the beginning of March, there was not a single machine in France that was in any condition to fight.[53] Forty tanks of the Mark I and II types had been scraped together by the time fighting began in April: many of them were old training vehicles shipped out from England, and none were proof against armour-piercing bullets. Divided into packets for use against strong points by different corps of the Third Army, the tanks were additionally blighted by bad weather, which conspired with the preliminary artillery bombardment to immobilize them. So once again, the fabled 'wonder weapon' was to be seen floundering around in the mud and failing even to arrive at its allotted starting point in time. Three tanks successfully advanced on the village of Monchy-le-Preux. But local successes were insufficient to calm the rage of the Australian troops who suffered huge losses, and blamed the tanks and their over-optimistic staff.[54]

It took faith as well as the 'discerning eyes' of a committed enthusiast like Colonel Fuller to see much future in the tank as it performed through the Battle of Arras. He would look back on this time as a period of 'unceasing struggle against the present, and unending striving towards the future'.[55] Partly for reasons of self-preservation the Heavy Branch was forced into 'a revolutionary groove'; and its futuristic conceptions endowed the new corps with 'abnormal virility' and determination to overcome opposition. Plagued by problems of supply and inconstant military command, the tank force pressed on towards 'a transfiguration of war' that would make the slaughters of the ongoing Western Front unnecessary, and reveal the culpable error of the elderly generals who carried on as if 'human tonnage' was all that a twentieth-century army could throw into battle.[56]

Some tanks proved reasonably useful adjuncts in the June assault on Messines Ridge, the operation that opened the British campaign in Flanders, and owed its primary success to the work of engineers who tunnelled under German positions and detonated nineteen massive charges on the morning of the attack. The main offensive began some six weeks later; and all three brigades of the Tank Corps (as the Heavy Branch had been renamed at the beginning of July), were to serve with the Fifth Army in what became the Third Battle of Ypres. This order tested the sardonic humour of the officers at Bermicourt to the limit – they were 'absolutely astounded'[57] to hear that their tanks and crews were to be deployed in conditions they knew to be utterly inappropriate. The idea behind Haig's summer offensive in Belgium was to take the Channel ports of Ostend and Zeebrugge, then being used by German submarines. Yet much of the Ypres salient was itself below sea level, consisting of reclaimed swamp land dependent on a drainage system that had been untended and under attack for two years: the result was 'a thin crust of soil, beneath which lay a bottomless sea of mud and water'. And these already severe difficulties would be aggravated by the sixteen-day preliminary bombardment – the longest the British Army had ever conducted – which devastated the roads and ensured, even without the torrential rain that fell on the day of the assault (July 31), that the ground 'consisted of nothing but a series of overlapping shell craters, half full of yellow, slimy water'. Elles and his officers drew up 'swamp maps', showing the condition of the ground in which tanks were expected to fight, but these were dismissed as 'ridiculous' by General Sir Hubert Gough's staff. J. F. C. Fuller recalled inspecting the ground on the third day of the battle, and finding it quite shattered and covered with a two-foot-deep layer of slush: 'On my return, my General, Hugh Elles, asked me: "How are things going?", to which I replied, "Look at me!" – I was plastered with mud from head to foot.'[58] If unwounded men drowned in their hundreds, then what chance had a 28-ton 'landship'? None at all, according to Captain D. G. Browne MC, of G Battalion: 'The tanks were sent by scores, and then by hundreds, to drown ineffectually in a morass, and the whole existence of the corps was imperilled by this misusage.'[59]

Among the men who managed to manoeuvre their tanks into the positions from which they would launch into battle at sunrise on 31 July was a gunner called Ernest Beall: 'We were understandably grim. There was no wise-cracks, no leg-pulls, no laughter.' Poised on the brink of battle, Beall watched as the enemy fired green 'Crème de Menthe' flares into the sky, and found himself thinking, sympathetically, of the English socialist Robert Blatchford and his (highly patriotic) argument with war patriotism: 'I wouldn't raise a finger in the defence of my country . . . my country! Why, I haven't a stick or yard of land to call my own.' And then they set off into the unknown, 'virtually encased in a metal box' with mud squirming in through every hole in the tank's armour: 'It was like sausage meat of fantastic shapes and sizes.'[60]

For many of the tank crews, the Third Battle of Ypres was unspeakably ghastly. Numerous machines got bogged down in the 'slimy pulp'[61] of no man's land, leaving their men floundering around in the mud as they struggled to shift their ditched and water-logged machines under the most concentrated fire. Others were trapped as they tried to advance through defiles swept by artillery fire: as many as eighteen tanks were destroyed near Hooge, shelled one after the other, as they approached a strong point called 'Clapham Junction', creating a surreal landscape that came to be known as 'the Tank Graveyard' (perhaps the first of many in twentieth-century history). One of the defining pictures of the horrors of Passchendaele was provided by a tank engineer ordered to make his way up the road towards Poelcappelle and demolish a number of wrecked tanks that were blocking the entrance to the village:

I left St Julien in the dark, having been informed that our guns were not going to fire. I waded up the road, which was swimming in a foot or two of slush, frequently I would stumble into a shell-hole hidden by the mud. The road was a complete shambles and strewn with debris, broken vehicles, dead and dying horses and men. I must have passed hundreds of them as well as bits of men and animals littered everwhere. As I neared Poelcappelle our guns started to fire: at once the Germans replied, pouring shells on and around the road, the flashes of the bursting shells were all round me. I cannot describe what it felt like, the nearest approach of a picture I can give is that it was like standing in the centre of the flame of a gigantic Primus stove. As I neared the derelict tanks, the scene became truly appalling: wounded men lay drowned in the mud, others were stumbling and falling through exhaustion, others crawled and rested themselves up against the dead to raise themselves a little above the slush. On reaching the tanks I found them surrounded by the dead and dying; men had crawled to them for what shelter they would afford.

The nearest tank was a female, her left sponson doors were open, out of these protruded four pairs of legs, exhausted and wounded men had sought refuge in this machine and dead and dying lay in a jumbled heap inside.[62]

There were heroic moments in the chaos of Flanders, like the stand of the crew of a tank called Fray Bentos, who endured seventy-two hours ditched beyond the line and, through British misapprehension, under heavy attack from both sides. And there was much excitement after the night of 17–18 August, when a company of twelve specially selected tanks, led by Major Broome of G Battalion and assisted by the reconnaissance work of Captain Clough Williams-Ellis, assaulted some pillboxes near St Julien under a smoke barrage, successfully securing a 500-yard advance over a 1,000-yard front, with casualties of only twenty-nine.[63] That operation – the 'Cockcroft action'[64] – was so successful that, according to one of its participants, Captain D. G. Browne MC, even Mr Beach Thomas of the *Daily Mail* had 'felt impelled to leave the seclusion of the Ternoise Valley to gather copy among our tents at Lovie'.[65] Yet, with that exception, the Third Battle of Ypres remained a 'ghastly failure'[66] for the tanks – one that, had its losses not been so gruesome, might have seemed to justify the mockery of the onlooking infantryman who once came across a tank that had fallen into a river and asked: 'Wot yer arter, mates? U-boats?'[67] The officers of the Tank Corps attributed the failure to the 'ostrich-like attitude' of GHQ and with all the more irritation as it became clear that, having been so inappropriately ordered into operations in 'that dissolving world',[68] the tanks were, once again, to be blamed for the failure. As Brigadier Baker-Carr concluded, 'If the first submarine had been tested on Salisbury Plain, the results would not have been encouraging.'[69]

The decisive operation that finally gave the Tank Corps its long-demanded 'fair trial'[70] took place in November 1917. Claimed as a concentrated tank raid by Fuller (he later described himself pointing at a wall map and saying, 'Well, why not here?'),[71] the Battle of Cambrai was conducted according to a tactical idea that Brigadier General Elles was inclined to trace all the way back to Swinton's recommendations of 1915.[72] Prepared over many weeks by Elles and General Sir Julian Byng, commander of the Third Army, the attack may have been designed to exploit improved artillery techniques;[73] yet it also fulfilled many of the Tank Corps's criteria for a successful operation. Occurring on the most peaceful section of the line, it would maximize the element of surprise; it would use tanks in mass as a principal weapon rather than as a mere adjunct to the infantry, and employ them on firm chalk ground that had not been pulverized by a preliminary artillery barrage.

Fuller drew up detailed instructions, determined to make the engagement into a 'clockwork battle' by ensuring that it was as closely governed by its drill as any ceremonial parade. An advanced headquarters was opened in a shell-blasted cabaret in the main street of Albert, where Captain Charteris strove to maintain standards in the mess despite the rats and shifty servants that nibbled the food and drained the bottles at night. Extensive reconnaissance was carried out by Elles, Hotblack, Martel, and Williams-Ellis; and Byng's infantry units were trained alongside the tanks, assisted by a platoon drill that Fuller was proud to have derived from one described by Xenophon and said to have been originated by the Persian King Cyrus at about 500 BC. Being more than twelve feet across, the trenches of the Hindenburg Line were too wide for the Mark IV tank, so the machines were equipped with vast 'fascines', large rolls of brushwood compressed and tied with tank-pulled chains by those industrious Chinese labourers in Searle's Central Workshops. These were to be dropped into trenches, marked with flags, and then used as bridges.

Surprise was not lost, despite the 'dreadful noise'[74] made by the tanks as they manoeuvred into position; and on the morning of the 19th, Elles issued a special order announcing that the approaching battle would provide the Tank Corps with 'the chance for which it has been waiting for many months – to operate on good going in the van of the battle'. Having commended the 'judgement and pluck' of the tank crews, he made the famous announcement: 'I propose leading the attack of the centre division' – an exemplary expression of 'esprit de tank', which would almost certainly have been forbidden had Elles declared his intention any earlier. That evening Elles, Uzielli, Fuller and the 'exquisite' Captain Charteris dined and drank champagne in their infested Albert cabaret; and the next morning Elles stepped into his flag tank Hilda and, with his pipe in his mouth and the Tank Corps colours flying from his ash staff (its bands of red, brown and green silk were said, by Fuller, to symbolize blood, mud and the green fields beyond), led well over three hundred tanks through the mist and into the operation that, for the Tank Corps, was 'the consummation of two years of struggle and disappointment'. Elles is said to have ridden through much of the battle with his head and shoulders thrust up through the hatch, while kicking his gunners in the ribs to indicate targets.[75] He survived, and through less exceptional good fortune than preserved a tank commander called Chaddock, whose vehicle was hit by an artillery shell that decapitated the driver, flinging his head on to the section commander's knee, killed or wounded the two right-side gunners, and then passed through the tank without exploding.[76]

The Tank Corps suffered considerable losses. One German field gunner at Flesquières was reputed – at least, in Arthur Conan Doyle's account of the battle – to have knocked out sixteen tanks single-handedly (a figure the Tank Corps and its friends would later question, disgusted to find this fabled enemy gunner commended in General Haig's official dispatch). Overall, however, the breakthrough was a huge success: the typical experience was described by section commander Captain D. E. Hickey, who reached the German trench to find German soldiers trying to give up their rifles through the front porthole, and massing around the victorious tank and calling out their surrender in a clamorous manner that reminded him, or so he would claim years later, of a scene at Las Palmas when a fleet of little boats filled with local vendors surged around a visiting ocean liner as they tried to sell their wares.[77] In one day the supposedly impregnable Hindenburg trench system was overwhelmed over a frontage of seven miles, and eight thousand terrified and 'half-stupefied'[78] prisoners were taken. For losses of about 4,000 the British forces had achieved a penetration comparable, as Fuller was quick to point out, to that which had taken three months and countless deaths at the Third Battle of Ypres. British church bells sounded in celebration on 21 November, and Fuller, at least, was in no doubt that 'they tolled out an old tactics and rang in a new . . . the epoch of the mechanical engineer'.[79]

The Battle of Cambrai became one of the 'purple patches' of the war. Elles's heroic act of leadership was widely celebrated at home – in newspapers and also, thanks to its impression of clean-cut courage, in advertisements for shaving cream. In December the 'Admiral of the Tank Fleet' would find a photograph of his wife and children printed in the *Tatler*.[80] Even in this moment of triumph, however, the Tank Corps's battle with the press didn't let up. It was widely reported that, on the eve of battle, General Hugh Elles had come up with a variation of Nelson's signal at the Battle of Trafalgar, and informed his tank soldiers: 'England expects every tank to do its damnedest.' Elles is said to have been 'very angry' at this, partly because he considered 'it would be impertinent on his part to parody Nelson's celebrated message'.[81] In the Tank Corps memoirs this suggestion was variously denounced as an 'impudent lie' dreamed up by some 'illiterate scavenger of Fleet Street';[82] and as a 'spurious fosterling' that Elles 'hated the worse, the more he perceived its popularity'.[83] Fuller's view of the London press may be indicated by the fact that the newspaper cutting he chose to save came from a Salonica-based British publication called the *Balkan News*, which, on 24 November, quoted the view recently expressed by the German General von Ardenne. Writing in the *Berliner Tageblatt* on 14 November after visiting the Flanders Front, he had argued that 'the role of tanks is as good as played out, our artillery mows them down. The original terror they inspired has vanished . . .' The general should plainly have thought again in the light of Cambrai: 'Prisoners say that the first thing they knew of the attack was when out of the mist they saw the tanks advancing upon them, smashing down the wire, crawling over the trenches . . . The Germans were aghast and dazed . . .'[84]

Impressive as the breakthrough was, however, the Battle of Cambrai was to be no more than 'a brilliant but disappointing fragment' in the war.[85] No reserves had been held back to consolidate the breakthrough, and nothing came of the cavalry, which had been waiting for most of the year for an opportunity to pass 'through the gap' in a blaze of nineteenth-century glory and which, according to Browne, never tired of talking of 'speed and dash and initiative'.[86] The horsemen arrived late and, with the exception of a small Canadian squadron, simply 'sat down behind a hill', and then returned to the British line, blocking the road along which urgently needed supplies were being brought for the tanks.[87] This was too much for Brigadier Baker-Carr, who suspected the incompetent hand of GHQ and concluded that 'the one great chance in the War for mounted men came and went on 20th November, 1917, never to recur'. In short, the triumphant advance was followed by a confused 'mêlée', with battle-worn tanks and their exhausted crews being moved about and formed into composite units to mount ramshackle attacks on villages and woods, in which many died for little if any gain. Then, at the end of the month, the Germans counter-attacked, using storm troops and low-flying bombers, and the advances of 20 November were lost. But the Tank Corps felt vindicated all the same. Years afterwards Major General F. E. Hotblack, DSO, MC, recalled how, in the wake of Cambrai, the German High Command issued instructions to all units informing them: 'If they keep their heads the German infantry have nothing to fear from hostile tanks.' Hotblack claimed to have asked a 'corpulent' German prisoner what he and his fellows had made of that advice:

'He asked, "What does it weigh, your tank?"

"About 30 tons," I said.

"What difference shall it to me make if I shall keep my head or not, if the thirty tons are on my stomach?" '[88]

6

Banking on the Tank

May all thy plates be sheathed in gold
Old Ironsides! And may every bank
Its acreage of cheques unfold
And wish thee God-speed, patriot tank.
A. Saunders, 'Wolverhampton's Tank', 1918.[1]

On 22 September 1916, when the first wave of tank fever was raging throughout Britain, the *Daily Express* urged: 'Why not show one of the "Tanks" on the Horse Guards Parade? Let the people see them.' In the event it was not until over a year later, in the midst of frantic celebrations following the Tank Corps's advance at Cambrai, that the triumphant new machine actually went on display in London.[2]

On Monday, 26 November 1917, *The Times* announced that visitors would find the whole of Trafalgar Square turned into 'an advertising centre for the War Bond Campaign'. A large poster stretched across the front of the National Gallery showed how the nation's purchase of War Bonds was rising; while others, drawn by cartoonist Bert Thomas, issued their exhortations from hoardings around the square's fountains ('Tank You', as one poster said). Among the 'souvenirs' on display were a Russian howitzer, a flame-thrower, a Turkish mountain gun, and a machine gun salvaged from a Zeppelin shot down over England. Yet these assembled spoils of war were merely the sideshow. This week, *The Times* promised, people could come and see for themselves as the much fabled tank launched 'a vigorous offensive against the enemy' on the home front.

Destined for service in France, Tank 130 – 'a real tank of the latest type' – would first be putting in a fortnight raising funds for the war effort. Complete with armour and guns', it would be open for business as 'the most novel bank ever established'. The outside exhibition was free to all comers, but 'a peep at the interior of Behemoth comes only to those who are ready to lend money to the country'. Investors who attended the 'Tank bank' would be duly astonished to see how cramped was the space inside these 'amazing landships'. As they peered 'inside the monster' they would also discover that an adjustment had been made for the purposes of the new campaign. Instead of the little leather-helmeted 'Picts' of William Beach Thomas's description, they would find two 'women officials' sitting at an 'improvised table' ready to sell them War Bonds and Certificates specially stamped with the words 'British Tanks W.S.A'.

The body responsible for the Trafalgar Square Tank Bank, the National War Savings Committee, was established early in 1916 to help meet the escalating cost of the war. The great loan of July 1915 had raised some £600 million, but even this unprecedented sum was only enough to fund the war for a few months. Asquith's Chancellor of the Exchequer, Reginald McKenna, had introduced stringent increases in taxation, raised loans from the United States and levied a new tax designed to harvest the controversial 'excess profits' made by companies thriving on the war effort. Throughout 1916, the remaining daily shortfall of between 3 and 4 million pounds was made up mostly by appeal to financial institutions and a conventional range of investors that, in the estimate of the National War Savings Committee's Publicity Director, George A. Sutton, was 'perhaps 350,000 strong'.[3] By the end of 1917, with the cost of war running as high as ever and the national debt approaching £6,000,000,0000, it was an urgent priority to widen the appeal far beyond people who 'have a banking account and employ a stockbroker'.

The National War Savings Committee set out to raise a new mass of small investors by projecting the war as a truly national affair. In a letter written for the committee's use McKenna's successor as Chancellor of the Exchequer, Andrew Bonar Law, had urged the public to recognize that: 'This war is a struggle not between armies, alone, but between nations.' As the man with special responsibility for 'selling campaigns',[4] Sutton would reiterate the point: 'Beyond, infinitely beyond, all former wars, the Great War was the affair of the whole people, not merely that of a ruling class and a professional Army.'[5] Fortunately, there were three factors that helped the committee establish the cost of the war as a burden to be shared by the whole nation. Compulsory military service had 'brought home to all the fact that nothing less than the nation in arms was force enough to beat the foe'. The recent extension of the franchise ('especially to women'), had been accepted with 'marvellously little opposition', proving that the nation was willing to recognize 'the brotherhood and sisterhood of service'. Finally, but perhaps most important of all, the paradoxical prosperity of the war had not just created 'war profiteers'. It had also brought previously unimaginable wage increases to a wide range of workers: agricultural labourers, railwaymen, seamen, and miners had all seen their pay rise substantially, and women were now earning sums that would have seemed utterly impossible a few years before . . . In short, there was working-class money in the country, and Sutton only had to run his eye over the vast sums deposited with the twelve major joint-stock banks to know that it was 'awaiting investment' in the war.

A number of loan schemes were devised with this new small investor in mind. Introduced at the end of February 1916, War Savings Certificates cost 15s. 6d. each and could be redeemed five years later for one pound. Their purchase was organized through a national network of War Savings Committees and the many thousands of War Savings Associations set up under them in factories, offices, schools and localities. The National War Savings Committee serviced this movement with a monthly journal called *War Savings,* which set out to rally 'the might of the mite'.[6] It came up with 'symbols' to brand its cause, including the swastika and the silver bullet, and it sold over a million suitably adorned paper bags to shopkeepers. It also fielded a fleet of specially converted 'Cinemotors' – lorries fitted with projectors that took propaganda films out on the road. The Women's Auxiliary Committee for War Savings issued a 'Women's Manifesto' against extravagance and persuaded eminent women such as Ellen Terry and Lady Curzon to canvass in Onslow Gardens and assist as 'prominent social helpers' at fund-raising events.[7]

Designed to foster continuous weekly borrowing, the National War Bonds scheme was launched with an inaugural rally at the Royal Albert Hall on 22 October 1917. The new bonds were made available through post offices, and investors were encouraged to buy them in fractions through their Savings Association. It was in search of a 'novel kind of advertising' to help 'popularise' the new bonds, that the National War Savings Committee came up with the idea of the Tank bank.[8] In the words of H. Holford Bottomley, an authority on salesmanship who served as Special Publicity Director with the National War Savings Committee, the tank had 'captured the imagination of the man in the street like no other device of modern warfare', and its forceful symbolism was quickly harnessed to the new cause.[9]

The first Trafalgar Square Tank Bank opened only sixteen days after the idea had first been conceived.[10] Newspapers reported a continuous procession of visitors through the day. Lloyd George and Bonar Law turned up to buy bonds at the tank, and a whole flotilla of public figures (carefully primed by telegram the Saturday before) also sailed by to do their duty. Among the investors, there were wounded soldiers, 'men wearing the silver badge of service', artisans and, as *The Times* was careful to point out, 'representatives of all classes of the community'. A protocol emerged within the first week. At the first day's opening, the Mayor of Westminster addressed the crowd from the plinth of Nelson's Column, but it was soon found more effective for speakers to address the queuing crowds from on top of the tank itself. For the first day or so, the women inside the tank were reported to have been actually selling bonds but, as the queues grew, a speedier arrangement was introduced: bonds and certificates would be bought at a specially erected 'application hut' and investors would only go to the tank to have their receipts stamped. As part of these refinements, on Tuesday the tank was moved to a new position between Nelson's Column and the National Gallery, and 'its mobility was demonstrated to an admiring crowd'.[11]

Even before the first week had ended, an official of the National War Savings Committee was remarking that 'the tank has captured the hearts of the public'. Takings on the first day had only amounted to £8,000, but by the end of the week the daily rate of investment had risen to over £150,000. Early in the second week it was confidently declared that the tank would have exceeded its million-pound target before it had to depart for the battle front. By this time the first freelance hawkers had arrived on the scene, some of whom would later be said to have 'amassed quite appreciable fortunes' by selling tank souvenirs: brooches, postcards, tank money-boxes made of china, even tank handbags and teapots.[12] Tank 130 had also been joined by a 'consort'. Dubbed the 'wandering tank', Tank 113 would 'waddle' along previously announced routes to collect large donations from company offices, causing 'great interest' and 'cessation of traffic' as it went. On Wednesday, 5 November, for example, this peripatetic monster travelled to Holborn Bars to collect a cheque for £628,000 worth of bonds from the Prudential Assurance Company. There were a couple of unexpected stoppages along the crowded route; but though the tank killed a dog and caused a number of taxis to shy as it 'wobbled back' to Trafalgar Square, the journey was otherwise reported to have been 'without incident'.[13]

Meanwhile 'The Tankland of Trafalgar Square' echoed not just with music by the Band of the Coldstream Guards but with resounding speeches and the patriotic cheers that frequently interrupted them. Father Bernard Vaughan, an elderly Jesuit highly esteemed for his work with London's poor, mounted the tank in cassock and skullcap to deliver himself of a 'racy and stirring' speech that stressed 'the patriotic duty of citizens to supply our boys in blue and khaki with the means to carry the war to a successful conclusion'.[14] His animated gestures were captured on a Spanish newsreel, so the tragedy of war can still be seen in the jowl-quivering flourish with which this former advocate of Christian Socialism and 'the Worker's Right to Live', drew his plea to a close: 'If the lions at the base of the Nelson Monument could roar out their thoughts they would say, "Listen to this appeal today. Never was one so patriotic or so democratic made on this national rallying ground." '[15] The Castrol motor lubricants mogul Sir Charles Wakefield amused the crowd by writing a cheque on his secretary's back and then he too held forth from on top of the tank: 'Why is this Tank here not in France today? Because it is providing a great asset to the government in the National Bonds campaign. We can find yet another use for this Tank as symbolizing qualities which we must all develop if we are to carry on.'[16] Patriotic exhortations like this were interspersed with processions, variety and entertainment. On Wednesday the 28th, the tank was attended by 430 clerical staff, mostly women, from Martin's Tobacco Stores in Piccadilly. Mr Martin had presented each with a £1 War Savings Certificate and 'as quickly as each person handed in his or her book at the Tank door, the official stamp was affixed'.[17] At the end of that first week, the music hall entertainer George Robey brought along a large contingent of 'theatrical performers' to buy bonds. He himself put in a little time as a 'bank clerk' selling bonds, while the much-loved Miss Madge Titheradge recited Alfred Noyes's 'The Song of England' from the top of the tank.

The days of the second week were shared out between the British nations in a spirit of competitive patriotism that would feature prominently throughout the Tank Bank campaign. Ireland's day was carried off with 'Celtic entrain' on the Wednesday, with the band of the Coldstream Guards playing Irish airs. Lady Londonderry described the tank as 'a broth of a tank', while Miss Ada Forrest sang 'There is a Land' and Lady Carson handed out sprigs of shamrock to subscribers. On Scottish Day the sprigs were of heather and the responsibility for their distribution fell to the Duchess of Sutherland – a lady who was duly photographed on top of the tank together with her little kilted son. Mrs Lloyd George was unable to attend as originally planned on Welsh Day, but the Westminster Singers gave a recital of Welsh songs, and a touch of colour was lent to the scene by girls dressed in 'cloaks and quaint Welsh hats'. Mr Martin Harvey recited a 'Hymn of Love for England' and Miss Brackenbury, a campaigner with the Women's Auxiliary Committee, spoke up for the sterling and also – as she promised the Kaiser would soon be finding out – winning qualities of the British housewife.

The fortnight closed with another theatrical Saturday. Eighty girls from the beauty choruses of the two Grossmith and Laurillard shows playing at the Shaftesbury and Gaiety theatres marched down to Trafalgar Square. Led by Miss Julia James, who was to recite from the tank at midday, they carried a tempting placard asking: 'Who will follow us?' Billy Merson, a well-known variety performer, appeared on top of the tank in 'quaint nautical rig' and 'amused the public with his antics'. Mary Balfour sang 'Land of Hope and Glory' and Martin Harvey was back to repeat his 'Hymn of Love for England'. At the end of the day members of the National War Savings Committee thanked the 'girls from the banks and post offices' who had staffed the campaign and then led the assembled crowd into the National Anthem. In two weeks some three and a half million pounds had been raised for the nation.

After a slow start, the Tank bank in Trafalgar Square had greatly exceeded expectations. On the Friday of its first week a letter had appeared in *The Times* praising the 'prolific monster' and urging the government to 'make more use of this most effective of all types of advertisement' rather than dissipating so much of its energy on 'thousands of posters whose multiplicity and sameness defeat the purpose of their originators'.[18] The correspondent suggested that a Tank bank campaign should be extended throughout the country, and the National War Savings Committee was evidently of the same mind. When, at the end of its fortnight, Tank 130 left Trafalgar Square, it was bound not for the Western Front as had originally been announced, but for St Pancras Station where it would catch a train to Sheffield. Here it would 'waddle into position' in Fitzalan Square and be ready to attract the 'close attention of thousands of munition workers' when it opened for business on the following Monday morning.[19] Brought back from among the damaged machines in France, two other tanks were put into service in Liverpool and Cardiff and a series of simultaneous 'provincial campaigns' were launched at the beginning of December. The second stops were made a week later at Manchester, Leeds and Bristol, and the campaign was joined in Portsmouth by Egbert, a fourth tank that, having been 'badly battered' in 'active service' at Cambrai, justified its own welcoming slogan on the Town Hall: 'Every patriotic citizen should visit the battle-scarred war tank.'[20]

Over the months to come, Tank banks would be held in 168 towns throughout England, Scotland and Wales. The National War Savings Committee deliberately set out to foster 'inter-urban' competition; and towns are said to have vied with each other with 'a keenness that one would have scarcely credited'.[21] According to *War Savings*, 'municipal rivalry' was of the essence of war saving, and the newspapers kept the nation watching as the record for the highest total figure raised in a week passed from one large city to the next as the tanks travelled the country: from Liverpool (£2 million) to Manchester (£4.5 million) to Birmingham (£6.6 million). When the average sum raised per head of population was calculated, smaller cities such as Newcastle and Bradford rose to the top with extraordinary figures of some £14 per head.[22]

By the beginning of 1918 every provincial Tank Week was being organized according to a tried and tested formula. One of the National War Savings Committee's 'Tank Organizers' would arrive in the town a week or so before the tank itself was due, equipped with skeleton poster forms and ideas for publicity stunts that had already proved successful elsewhere. The Mayor was encouraged to form a special 'Tank Committee' and detailed 'Notes and Suggestions' were circulated to assist such committees in their preparations for the week ahead.[23] Since the tanks had come from France and were considerably 'war battered', their procession from the railway yard should be planned to take place at a maximum speed of only one mile per hour. The tank weighed some 27 tons and could easily damage roads, so the Borough Engineer should be consulted about the route of its procession, taking special care to avoid tramway systems, culverts, bridges and other 'weak spots'. A site was to be chosen in a 'populous and commercial centre', and on arrival the tank was to be barricaded into an enclosure with clearly marked 'Way In' and 'Way Out' signs. There should be a bandstand and facilities for temporary sales counters to be set up, and between six and twelve feet of clearance had to be allowed on either side of the tank so that investors could pass by easily: bonds on one side, certificates on the other.

The 'Notes and Suggestions' recommended that 'any means that presents itself for making the scene attractive should be adopted': the barricades would look well painted white and festooned with patriotic bunting; and in towns where the Tank bank was held in a roadway, it had been found that 'a sprinkling of sand in the enclosure has a great effect'. Special publicity effects would also be worked out in advance: searchlight displays, pigeon post, a 'telephonic canvass' of big firms to be conducted on the last day, the distribution of different coloured paper discs to different localities within the area so that residents could compete to cover more of the tank than their neighbours. As the organiser of the Newcastle tank stressed in a surviving report, special care was taken when drawing up a roster of speakers to 'make it representative of all shades of political thought'. Newcastle being 'a large Munitions area', a number of Labour speakers were 'prevailed upon to give their services'.[24]

The tank would normally arrive by train over the weekend and be ready to open on Monday morning. As the National War Savings Committee learned from an internal report, it was impossible 'verbally to reproduce the extraordinary atmosphere of enthusiasm' created by the travelling tanks.[25] H. Holford Bottomley recalls how the arrival of the tank was often turned into the occasion for a sham fight.[26] The town would be 'thrown into a state of defence' with sandbag entrenchments from which members of the local volunteer regiment would 'fire' at the approaching tank. The Mayor and other civic dignitaries would preside over the official opening ceremony at about midday on the Monday, and the event was 'invariably attended by a huge crowd'. Enthusiasm rose through the week, and 'Saturday at the Tank usually resembled the scene at a pre-war Cup Final'. Indeed, as H. Holford Bottomley concluded, 'it speaks volumes for the efficiency of the provincial police that no casualties occurred in the closing ceremony, when dense crowds insisted on escorting the Tank to the station'.

In Bristol, where Tank No. 119 was set up on College Green for six days from 17 December, the event was 'slow to move' but 'ultimately successful': it raised an investment of just under £1.5 million in bonds and certificates, thanks partly to an immense indicator above the Hippodrome music hall. In Birmingham the tank arrived at Hockley Station and was taken to Victoria Square 'amid great enthusiasm' with a marching band and a detachment of the Warwickshire Regiment. At Wolverhampton, the procession that led the tank up to its allotted space in the Wholesale Market was 'memorable and animated', with mounted police, the Women's Volunteer Reserve and a regimental fife and drum band leading the way: 'rarely, if ever have we seen a crowd of such dimensions as was assembled in the open market, and the immediate vicinity of the Town Hall'.[27] There were processions to the tank from 'various works' in the area and the cast of the Empire's current show performed the National War Bond Song, Herman Darewski's 'Tommy Over There'. Improvising a Black Country approach to the notorious futurism of the tank, a local reporter imagined an ancient 'worker in iron' named Ezra standing in astonished contemplation of the tank with his old friend Anuk, an equally superannuated 'worker in coal':

"E's the rummiest cratur ever I set eyes on . . ."[28] At the end of the week, 'Ole Bill' moved off in the appointed style, exploding the detonators that had been attached to its tracks for special effect and crushing its barricade into splinters, which were eagerly gathered up as souvenirs.

In Manchester, the city of Free Trade, the tank was said to look 'rusty and dull' as it stood in Albert Square, surrounded by the 'statues of great men who have been at the head and front of national causes to which Manchester was devoted'. The *Manchester Guardian* declared the tank a grim sight, made grimmer by dull winter skies and the driving winds of a snowstorm; its reporter remarked how strange it was to see the statues of Albert Square, and in particular the John Bright monument, plastered with appeals urging people to lend their money to the state. But even this disenchanted commentator recognized that the tank – a 'forbidding monster' – was offering a 'sound investment' and expected business to be brisk. There had been sixty voluntary helpers at Liverpool's tank, but such was demand in Manchester that the clerical work of issuing bonds and certificates was quickly transferred to the ground floor of the nearby Town Hall while the original 'application hut' – small and like the one first used in Trafalgar Square – was reserved for purely administrative purposes.

At the beginning of its Tank week in January 1918, Glasgow claimed to be the first city to have witnessed a moving demonstration of the tank's extraordinary capabilities: 'other towns and cities have had to be content with a stationary view'.[29] The tank Julian made its 'official entry' into the city at about ten o'clock on the morning of Monday, 14 January and then performed over a specially prepared obstacle course. As the *Glasgow Herald* reported:

Many historic scenes have been enacted in Glasgow Green, but none has touched the popular imagination more immediately than the first thrilling sight of the strange machine which has played such a great role in the desperate battles of France. Everyone in the city is familiar with the Tank by description, illustration, or cinematograph representation, but when it appeared on view the first sensation was of surprise at its uncouth proportions, its quaint waddling movement, and the sense of destructive power it conveyed.

Noting that there was no cheering as the tank proved its wire-crushing and trench-crossing capacities, the *Herald* conjectured that the impression made by the 'monstrous toad' was simply too great: 'the capacity for demonstration was evidently lost in the satisfaction of an intense curiosity'. After going through its paces on the Green, the tank crawled through crowded streets to George Square where it ground to a halt beside the City

Chambers. As usual, two 'lady attendants' were inside the tank to stamp bonds and certificates and as it sat there, brilliantly lit up with lines of 'vari-coloured electric lights' while a snow-storm raged around it, the tank was said to compose 'a very picturesque tableau'.

The Glasgow Tank bank was opened by the Lord Provost, who appealed especially for investments from the city's munitions workers. Bert Thomas's cartoons were on display again while entertainment was provided by the Glasgow Co-operative Baking Society's Silver Band and also by members of the variety company then playing *Dick Whittington* at the Alhambra. Many speakers held forth from the top of the tank through the week, including the Food Commissioner for the West of Scotland, Mr Gideon Murray, who exhorted the crowd to 'feed that great bulging monster the Tank'. The Mayor of Birmingham sent up a fraternal challenge urging Glasgow to beat his city's record, and among the telegrams that arrived at the City Chambers was one that read: 'Tank Glasgow – Teesside Scots warn Glesca' folks Middlesbrough will subscribe far more per head to tank than Glesca'.' There was some concern that the Glasgow tank was receiving large corporate investments that would have gone through the clearing banks in other towns, but the total was what mattered and the Glasgow tank was declared to have broken all records, bringing in some £16 million in all. So triumphant was the tank by this time that even that most famous opponent of the war, George Bernard Shaw, had felt obliged to submit. On 7 January, the intransigent sixty-one-year-old dramatist had written to Ellen Terry describing how he danced 'like a tank'.[30]

With the provincial tours producing such spectacular yields, the results of the initial Tank bank in Trafalgar Square quickly came to seem paltry. In mitigation, George Sutton pointed out that 'the competitive spirit had not then been kindled' and recommended that 'London should have another chance of beating the magnificent "record" which Glasgow has established'. The replay, which brought six tanks into London, took place during a special 'boost' week that was promoted as 'Business Men's Week'. Organized by the members of the Aldwych Club at the request of the National War Savings Committee, this nationwide campaign was launched on 4 March 1918 with the widely publicized aim of raising a minimum of £100,000,0000, and thereby staving off the prospect of another War Loan. As George Sutton announced, each town had been given 'a definite task'. Depending on the extent of its population, it would be targeted to raise the cost of a Super Dreadnought, a cruiser, a destroyer, an aircraft or a tank.

Held at the Connaught Rooms in London, the inaugural luncheon for Business Men's Week was the first major function of its kind since the introduction of food rationing, and the meal was reported to have been of the 'simplest possible character'. Some of the assembled dignitaries may have eyed their boiled turbot and potatoes in dismay, but there was no shortage of red meat in the speeches. Chancellor Bonar Law confessed that at first he had doubted it would be possible to raise significant sums through War Bonds and Certificates. He now recognized his error, and was glad that Business Men's Week would be conducted on the principles that had already worked so well for the National War Savings Committee: 'We're enlisting in our aid the patriotic rivalry between one part of the country and another.' Proposing the toast, the Hun-hating press baron Lord Northcliffe welcomed Business Men's Week as a revival of the ancient system in which 'every part of the land offered its contribution to the King' in order that he could then lead the nation into vigorous and whole-hearted war.

Business Men's Week brought a second Tank bank into Trafalgar Square. This time it was the battle-scarred Egbert that took up position between Nelson's Column and the portico of the National Gallery, which was entirely covered by a painting of the Spanish Armada bearing down on England's white cliffs ('Once again our country is threatened. Are your War Bonds helping the fight?'). The first Trafalgar Square Tank bank had been wired up to the telephone, but the second one featured a 'tank pigeon post'. Subscriptions of more than £10,000 could be forwarded by pigeon to Trafalgar Square and, as a souvenir, the investor could keep the cylinder used to attach his subscription to the bird's leg. The public figures who addressed the crowds 'from the top of the tank' included Anthony Hope, author of *The Prisoner of Zenda*, and the pro-war suffragette Mrs Fawcett. Coming across Egbert, bathed in artificial light while the enraptured masses queued up to pay tribute, the American Imagist poet John Gould Fletcher remembered the genial, less frantically focused Trafalgar Square of four years earlier: 'Then there were lights for all; now only the tank has lights.'[31] The sight of Father Bernard Vaughan ranting from the top of 'Behemoth' prompted him to observe, 'I confidently expect that prayers for the success of the next Tank war bank campaign will be offered in our churches. The Tank, in fact, is now an Institution.' The time had come for those thinkers who had been ruminating on the need for a new religion (ironically, Fletcher included H. G. Wells in his list) to throw their philosophy books into the Thames and buy a newspaper, which would quickly convince them that the 'New God' had already arrived.

While Egbert was knocking the stuffing out of this Arkansas-born poet in Trafalgar Square ('He is already the Archetype of the new dispensation'), a second tank was stationed outside the Royal Exchange to encourage business men to 'Go over the top of the City tank'. Throughout the week four wandering tanks – Ole Bill, Nelson, Julian and Drake – went the rounds of the London boroughs, 'searching' the city for investors and stirring up the 'competitive spirit' that had animated the provincial campaigns. Speakers bellowed encouragement from the top of the tank in places like Deptford, Bermondsey, East Ham and Bow; and spectacular touches of local colour were often added too. In Hackney's Mare Street the tank stood close to a shop 'camouflaged' to look like a communications trench. At St Pancras a bombed taxi was displayed next to the tank as 'a specimen of German Kultur'.

By March 1918 *War Savings* could pronounce confidently on the success of the Tank bank campaign: 'There has been no more popular appeal to investors, large and small, than the Tank. This mysterious engine of war has excited the imagination and the curiosity of everybody. Coming as it did out of the trenches direct to the homes of British people, it touched the hearts of those whose part it was to remain in Blighty.' Many large corporate investments came in through the Tank banks, but the campaign also reached the 'small investors' to whom it was addressed. After the first week of the initial Trafalgar Square Tank bank it was declared that 90 per cent of the applicants had not 'hitherto invested in War Loans of any kind',[32] and that an 'altogether new public' had been found: 'the large majority of those who have come from a distance have been unacquainted with the value of the investment and have known nothing about filling up the forms'.[33] At many Tank banks prosperous individuals and firms, such as Fenwick's in Newcastle, bought saving certificates and then redistributed them free among working-class subscribers. And yet the press, which plainly understood the aims of the campaign, was also careful to portray small investors who needed no such incentive. At the first Trafalgar Square Tank bank, *The Times* singled out a soldier who turned up with two little children and a bag of halfpennies and old farthings with which he bought them a certificate each. The tank that visited Southwark during Business Men's Week was said to have made its first sale – two £5 bonds – to 'a ratcatcher named Dalton'. Another investor was reported to have turned up shortly afterwards in odd boots and an old cap: 'To the Inspector of police on duty he said, "Do you think I haven't got any 'dough'?" He at once produced £60 in gold and bought War Bonds to that amount.' Succeeding where previous government appeals had failed, the travelling tanks flushed out so much hidden working-class gold that *War Savings* dubbed them 'vacuum cleaners' for precious metal.[34] In Birmingham a rustic cowman was said to have turned up with £75 in sovereigns and half-sovereigns that had been buried under bricks and boards in his cottage for thirty years. In Newcastle an old lady produced £500 in gold and then went home for more. The Edinburgh tank attracted gold pieces, Jubilee coins, two-guinea coins, while in Maesteg, South Wales, a man paid over £200 in gold coins.

Wounded soldiers and deaf-mutes were counted in among the small investors at the tank and there were also mourners who, in the words of the *Glamorgan Free Press,* arrived with 'a distant vision of some lonely cairn in France or Flanders' whose 'noisy sides' they wished to deck with 'Imperial Security – not only flowers'.[35] *The Times* spared a few lines for an old man who bought £100 worth of savings certificates at the first Trafalgar Square tank: '"This is all I can do to help," he said, "but I do it willingly in memory of four boys of mine who have given all they could – their lives"'.[36] Two days later the same paper recorded the arrival of 'ten young women each of whom had lost her lover in the war and had brought her savings to buy a war bond in order, as they said "to help other girls to get their sweethearts back quickly"'.[37] The National War Savings Committee also circulated the story of a poor woman who came to the tank in Preston with all the money she could raise: a half-crown, which was too small a sum to buy either a bond or a certificate, but which she nevertheless 'insisted on the tank having – not a loan but a gift'. Some better-off investors gathered round this patriotic figure to complete the fleeting cameo: clubbing together they bought her certificates 'so that she could play her part in the week'. As the *Glamorgan Free Press* spelt out, 'She was a symbol of our spirit.'[38]

From the beginning, the Tank banks were noted for the extraordinary compulsion they exercised over the young. Children were among the smallest of small investors, but though their pooled savings scarcely added up to a pittance, their attendance at the tank was a vital part of the spectacle. In Porth, South Wales, four or five thousand children were filed down to see the 'new mighty and romantic instrument of warfare'.[39] In Portsmouth it was reported that 'the juvenile portion of the population gather round the enclosure in considerable numbers' and that 'the muzzles of the 6-pounders, the jagged holes caused by shell and bullet, and the general war-battered appearance of the tank appeal vividly to their imaginations'.[40] In Edinburgh school children were released for the day to follow the tank

Julian as it crawled up from the goods station in Leith Walk to the Mound next to Princes Street. Their interest in the 'caterpillar method of progression' was reported to have been intense.

The Tank banks are said to have raised a total of £300,000,000[41] – a remarkable figure, even allowing for a good measure of propagandistic inflation. Yet, in the words of the *South Wales Evening Press,* the campaign was a spectacular success as well as a financial one.[42] Indeed, at home just as on the Western Front, the symbolic associations of the tank seemed quickly to have exceeded its more practical utility. For the salesman H. Holford Bottomley, it was marvellous to think that for many investors the symbolic value of the tank stamp would come to seem greater than the monetary value of the bond or certificate on which it was impressed: it was doubtful, as he ventured to suggest shortly after the war, 'whether many investors will ever part with their stamped receipts', and the gain to the state would be considerable.[43]

'Persons of discernment' associated with Mrs C. R. Buxton's war-doubting *Cambridge Magazine* may, 'until quite recently', have imagined that a right policy 'only required formulation' to be adopted, and that 'when once the path to happiness had been discovered it would only be a matter of regulating the queue'.[44] However, as this university publication felt obliged to admit in the spring of 1918, the Sunday papers had changed all that. Together with the war, they had enthroned 'the mechanism of publicity' as the 'determining factor in almost all affairs of moment'. Financially impoverished, the cause of Peace and Internationalism had 'failed entirely to secure publicity, except, as it were, on the Poet's Page.'

For the National War Savings Committee, which, in a characteristic act of 'Bonar Lawlessness',[45] had withdrawn its advertisements from the *Cambridge Magazine* precisely because of its 'Internationalist' habit of excerpting the German press and other foreign publications, the tank was certainly an unrivalled instrument of publicity. According to *War Savings,* its aura had proved irresistible:

As an advertising medium the Tank can claim to be the cheapest and most effective method so far devised to popularise the saving and lending movement. Unlike most advertisements of this kind, it has not grown stale. The people still love its unwieldy bulk; vaguely cajoling its officers for permission to get inside its riveted walls; standing for hours before it in wondering reverie and eager for tales of its prowess and its powers.[46]

Bonar Law was also impressed by the spellbinding power of the committee's travelling tanks and the ease with which they extracted money from a new public. As Chancellor of the Exchequer, he knew that in finance as well as publicity, 'appearance is reality'. Credit, as he announced at the launch of Business Men's Week, depends 'not merely on what things are, but on what people think they are'. The Tank banks had already proved his point decisively. And, with growing public objection to Lloyd George's continuation of the war, it was time for the National War Savings Committee's tanks to demonstrate that they had other capabilities beside fund-raising. The Chairman of the National War Savings Committee, Mr Kindersley, had been emphasizing the connection between patriotism and war savings for some time before the idea of the Tank bank was first conceived. Speaking at the Shire Hall in Gloucester on 20 October 1917, he had observed as follows: 'In one of his speeches General Smuts has remarked that under the stress of great difficulties practically everything broke down, and all that was left were the simple human feelings of loyalty, comradeship to one's fellows, and of patriotism which would bear them through almost any strain. It was upon these simple human feelings that this great movement of War Savings was founded.'[47] The tank was adopted by the National War Savings Committee not as a futurist instrument of *dérèglement*, but rather as a 'patriot tank' – a mechanical emblem of exactly those stripped-down, steely feelings of loyalty and fellowship. Whether it was Balfour praising the 'enlightened patriotism' of working-class investors in Edinburgh or the Lord Provost of Glasgow announcing how the Tank bank had shown the patriotism of his city developed to 'an extraordinary extent', this was the message that boomed out from on top of the tank all round the country.

To begin with, tank patriotism was associated with thrift and self-denial.[48] To buy bonds was to put the defence of the nation before the 'artificial prosperity' that Lloyd George, at the launch of the War Bond scheme, had identified as 'one of the greatest perils of war'.[49] It was in this context that the tank was declared emblematic of essentially British values. For Miss Brackenbury the tank was like the British character: 'rather slow to move, somewhat heavy, but sure'.[50] For Sir Charles Wakefield, it was a symbol of what the British character must become if the war was to be won: 'We must, like the tanks at Cambrai, ride ruthlessly, not over trenches and "pill-boxes", but over our natural and normal desires. We must crush with all the force of a triumphant tank the impulse to spend our spare cash on what, in peace-time, would be harmless indulgences.' By January 1918, *War Savings* had squeezed the tank's many patriotic associations into a predictably shaped nutshell: 'The tank is in the ascendancy. It is almost a personality. Indeed, one must speak about it as "he" or "she". It is cheered as it rolls along the streets, and carries in itself the expression of the people of England, of their "will to win".'[51]

The publicists of the Tank bank campaign took these patriotic values and tried to extend them to as broad a public as possible. Even during Business Men's Week George Sutton was careful to be as inclusive as he could, remarking that 'the term business men today includes nearly all civilians, shopkeepers no less than the heads of great firms and many women, so that the appeal will be a very wide one'.[52] Yet, as every demagogue knows, patriotic solidarity is often at its tightest when the forces that threaten it are also vividly imagined, and few of the speakers who sought to enthuse the crowds from on top of the tank were content merely to eulogize those positive and 'simple human feelings' of comradeship mentioned by Mr Kindersley. There was also an enemy to denounce, and not just the appalling Hun either. The most passionate rabble-rousers among those who spoke from the tank found enemies at home, and they weren't just thinking about extravagance or the self-indulgent spending of war profiteers.

The master of this idiom was Horatio Bottomley, the crooked stump orator and editor of the popular paper *John Bull*, who toured the country ranting about 'Germhuny', insisting that 'we must go on killing and killing', and pocketing the proceeds as he went. Bottomley singled out British citizens of German extraction for special persecution and demanded that the word 'neutrality' be 'struck from the vocabularies of civilization'. He denounced Keir Hardie, Ramsay MacDonald and other members of the anti-war faction in the Labour Party as 'traitors within our own gates', and could see no reason at all why conscientious objectors and pacifists should not be given 'the bullet in the early morning at the Tower'.[53] *John Bull* was full of pictures of tanks – advertising Meccano or 'Daisy Tablets', said to be used by scores of tank soldiers to relieve 'Battle Headache'. When it came to the Tank bank campaign, however, Bottomley missed his opportunity. Early in the campaign, he recommended that tanks should be used to issue Premium Bonds: 'London itself wouldn't be big enough to hold the people who would flock in for certificates.'[54] Yet his enthusiasm waned over the following weeks. Apparently convinced that the government would do better seizing the millions of unclaimed money lying in British banks, he referred to the Tank bank campaign as 'Tank Tosh' – mere 'clowning'; that was 'making us the laughing stock of Germany'.[55] His observation was supported by a correspondent who had seen the tank at Chiswick Green:

'Overhead, in rough weather, some of our airmen were performing a number of tricks – risking their lives to attract a few hundred pounds; and I never saw a more unlikely crowd, so far as money is concerned.'[56]

Perhaps the National War Savings Committee had crossed the editor of *John Bull*, for many speakers of Bottomley's super-patriotic kind were invited to use the tank as a platform from which to fire their jingoistic salvoes against enemies at home. One of the first British public figures to be denounced from the top of the tank was the elderly Lord Lansdowne, a former head of the Foreign Office who, in November 1917, had published a letter in the *Daily Telegraph* arguing against 'wanton prolongation' of the war and renewing his year-old plea that a compromise peace should be negotiated with Germany.[57] This proposal may have been considered sympathetically in the officers' mess at Bermicourt (J. F. C. Fuller certainly came to see it as preferable to the continuation of Haig's fatal frontal assaults[58]), but it was reviled on the home front. Lansdowne's proposal was regularly blasted and flattened during the Tank bank campaign – frequently enough to establish that the National War Savings Committee's battle against pacifism was not just a matter of withdrawing its advertisements from high-minded publications like the *Cambridge Magazine*.

Bonar Law's speech at the launch of Business Men's Week included the following utterance: 'I think this peace talk, this pacifist talk, is froth on the surface, and you can always be sure of this, that there are no silent pacifists; that every pacifist is vocal.' A far less restrained version of this patriotic accusation was bellowed out from the top of the travelling tanks. As George Robey snarled from the St Pancras tank during Business Men's Week: 'We will put those who talk about peace in the front line to dig trenches for old gentlemen like me to shoot from.' The same enemy was assailed by Mr Havelock Wilson, the President of the National Union of Sailors and Firemen, who came to the Trafalgar Square tank with some torpedoed amputee sailors as his visual aids. His was one of the more 'stirring' speeches of the day and he was 'frequently interrupted' by the cheering crowd as he roared that 'Lord Lansdowne must not for a moment believe that British seamen would ever forget German crimes on the High Seas . . .'[59]

The National War Savings Committee drove its war machine into battle against a considerably more radical strain of pacifism in Glasgow a few weeks later. A few days before Julian was brought into the city, the General Finance Committee of the Corporation of Glasgow had proposed a scheme that would enable the corporation to purchase War Bonds and Certificates worth £250,000, which could then be sold on to employees who could only afford to pay small instalments. This proposal was strongly backed by most members, but there was vociferous opposition from left-wingers associated with the 'unofficial movement' causing considerable industrial unrest at the time. Baillie Wheatley moved disapproval of the Finance Committee's minute on the grounds that when the conscription of men was introduced the government should also have 'started conscripting the necessary money-power'.[60] Invoking the approaching Tank bank, he remarked:

When they wanted men they did not send tanks round Calton and Cowcaddens districts asking the names and addresses of man-power to be put in the Tank. They sent them through the post a King's command telling them that unless they presented themselves at Sauchiehall Lane at a certain time, they would use all the civil and military power of the State to see that the State's necessity was complied with. Why should they regard wealth as more sacred than human life?

Another member of the 'unofficial' left was happy to support this objection to a War Savings scheme that sought to raise money from the working class when the bosses had not yet been taxed into the ground. Mr Emmanuel Shinwell felt that 'the test of patriotism' should be whether people were 'prepared, not to lend to the government, but to give to the government what they could afford'. This class warrior went on to claim that, unlike so many workers who had already given their all, 'the wealthy members of the community were not prepared to sacrifice their lives'. Outraged cries of 'Question' went up at this point, but Shinwell persisted with his attack on the idle rich: 'So far as he could ascertain they had not shown any undue haste to do so, nor had they shown undue haste to do service to the State by offering their accumulations of money.' The Glasgow objection was crushed by 64 votes to 8, and it left Treasurer Barrie 'more and more convinced than ever that the opponents of this minute were not the true representatives of labour in the city' – a point that must soon have seemed doubly vindicated by the record levels of investment achieved by the Glasgow Tank bank. But it was not just in Glasgow that tank Julian was sent to grind its way over the parapet of entrenched proletarian objection.

'Hard are the blows he has aimed at the fighting front, and many a Welsh boy knows him as a friend in need.' Thus declaimed the *Glamorgan Free Press* on 27 May 1918, as it prepared its readers for the metal column that was about to tour the mining districts of South Wales. Five tank organizers had been sent to arrange this late tour and the eagerly anticipated Julian attracted 'lusty cheers' in Pontypridd and Victoria Square, Aberdare, while a 'dispatch' tank – a full-sized replica named Julian Junior – was impressing schoolchildren at Tonypandy and Abercynon. Lent 'joyous harmony' by silver bands and male voice choirs, the South Wales tank tour advanced down roads made 'resplendent with bunting' and through fairgrounds and fields full of gaily dressed children. Over a period of two months, and despite fears that Julian would prove too heavy for the old bridges of the Rhondda Valley, the tour visited forty-seven towns in all, aided by Lady Howard, who was photographed in Llanelli, stamping certificates from her station deep within Julian's bowels.[61] On 7 June it was announced that Merthyr Tank bank had taken over £1 million, an average of £13 per head of the population and a record for South Wales. According to the *Cardiff Times,* 'scenes such as had never before been witnessed in the ancient borough greeted this announcement' when it was made from the top of the tank.

Yet the victory of the South Wales campaign was not to be counted in money alone. The war had brought limited 'Extravagance' or 'artificial prosperity' to the people of the Rhondda Valley, and the enemy that concerned this particular tank operation was identified in the National War Savings Committee's newsletter, the *Silver Bullet*:

Here and there in the valleys lined with rows of miners' dwellings there exists some feeling against the policy of ending the war by force of arms, a feeling that naturally affects the situation. When our speakers have explained that there is no more practical means of ending the war than contributing to its cost, it is confidently expected that this drag on the movement will be removed.[62]

This was mildly put. The South Wales campaign was reported in papers that carried news of colliery strikes next to lists of men killed or missing in what some people evidently considered to be a bosses' war. On 30 May 1918, the *Caerphilly Journal* carried a carefully written article that tried to defuse a potentially explosive argument circulating in the valleys. It was being said that by lending to the state a person is only 'lengthening, or helping to lengthen the war'. To the 'organized worker' this argument must be 'demonstrably unsound'. He knows, after all, that the 'stinginess' of bosses is 'fatal to good work' and, just like a factory, an army needs to be properly equipped if it is to do its job. 'Certainly no trade unionist could justify an attitude of indifference in this most serious of all enterprises . . .' Indeed, 'those who abstain from buying War Bonds are as much assisting the enemy as those who withhold any other form of service'.[63]

This anti-pacifist line had been forcefully stated at the opening of the

South Wales tank tour. At the inaugural rally, held in the Palladium at Pontypridd, a prearranged string of speakers stressed that they, as wage earners, knew the pacifist argument to be false. Fifty thousand miners had already gone to war from South Wales, and the pacifists should ask the Russians, and in particular Mr Trotsky, what they thought of treaties with Germany. Denouncing pacifists as cowards, a miners' agent declared himself proud of the men of Wales. As far as he was concerned, those who argued from public platforms that it was not 'in the best interest of the workers' that they should lend money to the state should be 'in another institution not far off'.

So the proven symbolic force of the tank was used to drive a wedge between true patriotism and the more or less revolutionary militancy of workers opposed to what they saw as an imperial bosses' war. When the inhabitants of Porth invested £87,000, the *Caerphilly Journal* was quick to point out that Porth was a 'so called centre of pacifism . . . It's a libel and an exposed one.' The National War Savings Committee did everything it could to ensure that tank patriotism was perceived as the polar opposite of working-class militancy, but another possibility can still be detected in the records. An 'extraordinary scene' took place at the Merthyr Tank bank, and it was not the wholehearted welcome accorded to Sergeant T. Collins, VC, a local war hero who was persuaded to get up and address the crowd from on top of the tank.[64] Instead it involved a certain Mr Woodcock, the manager of a Merthyr brewery. As the *South Wales Evening Press* reported, Mr Woodcock was on his way to the bank with the week's takings, when he was seized by two soldiers. These men were quickly joined by a score of patriotic civilians who hustled their captive into the tank enclosure and insisted that he invest the lot in War Bonds. This was not among the 'selling' techniques advocated by the National War Savings Committee's travelling tank organizers, and nor was it exported to Australia, where a tank tour was initiated (to 'tremendous enthusiasm') in September 1918.[65] But it does suggest a combination that the South Wales tank campaign was hardly designed to explore: namely, that left-wing political militancy and tank patriotism could actually go hand in hand.[66]

7

Moral Victory

Horatio Bottomley, the super-patriotic rabble-rouser and conman, turned up at Bermicourt wearing a tin hat and 'looking like a Dutch cheese covered up with a soup plate'.[1] George Bernard Shaw expressed a 'boy-like glee' at the tanks and, having been taken for a ride, had to be discouraged from trying to tip the driver as if he had been in a taxi.[2] There was 'momentary awkwardness' during the visit of HRH the Duchess of Argyll: the Princess was 'so overcome by the sight of a tank climbing a five-foot bank that she lapsed into her native tongue and exclaimed, *'Gott, wie Kolossal es ist.'*[3] The American artist John Singer Sargent passed through late, in July 1918. Arranged through the good auspices of his friend Captain the Hon. Evan Charteris, his visit included 'a joy ride in a Tank up and down slopes, and over trenches and looping the loop generally'.[4]

In the early months, displays at the Central Workshops near Bermicourt had become too much of an 'Earl's Court affair' and visitors are said to have been restricted, 'first to two days per week without lunch, then to one day, and finally forbidden altogether'.[5] Yet exceptions seem to have been the rule, both before and after tanks triumphed at the Battle of Cambrai. On 7 July 1917 the 2nd Battalion mounted a special display for the visiting British monarch. At the appointed time tanks emerged from their wooded hiding places to push over trees and chase the scribbling journalists back into their bestiary of clichés, where they found the usual moth-eaten collection of elephants, Leviathans and other such routinely abominable monsters. In a spectacular final turn designed to prove the miracle of the new weapon, a tank commanded by 'a cheery little subaltern called Haseler', soon to be killed in action, dropped over the sheer fifteen-foot front of an ammunition dump – an impressive feat, even if, unknown to the King, it did leave some of the crew unconscious inside the tank.[6] Visiting the tanks after the liberation of Messines Ridge, the grateful Queen of Belgium is said to have enjoyed a ride in a specially carpeted tank, although her husband, King Albert, was less pleased by the dirt and heat of the accompanying machine in which he insisted, quite unexpectedly, on travelling too.

And the monarchs and VIPs were only the sideshow. Soldiers and politicians of 'all races came in turn to see tanks – Chinese, Japs, Americans, Serbians, Russians, Italians, French, Belgians, Dutch, Swedes'.[7] The visit of a Chinese general and his staff prompted much low amusement among the British tank soldiers. Taken round by Charteris, this nameless fellow insisted on being addressed as if he understood English, which he did not; but the 'coolies' who had been specially trained to perform as a tank crew failed to keep up appearances even if the General managed. They climbed into their demonstration machine at the appointed time, but were so nervous at the thought of performing before their Commander-in-Chief that they couldn't get the thing to work: 'There followed an ominous pause, succeeded by the strangest sounds from within the tank. To us, ignorant of Chinese, it was the chattering of apes, accompanied by the violent jerking of levers, the racing of the engine and the absence of any sign of movement on the part of the tank.' Colonel J. F. C. Fuller identified a different set of aliens at a demonstration in February 1918. The Rolls-Royces duly arrived and disgorged the Commander-in-Chief and his generals from GHQ, who proceeded to watch as some specially lengthened (and potentially troop-carrying) Mark IVs were put through their antics. Fuller gazed at these old men contemptuously in turn: 'They reminded me of the heathen gods assembled to watch the entry of the new Christian era. They felt it was better than their own epoch and left determined to destroy it.'[8] In the annals of Bermicourt, that would go down as a typical example of 'Boney's' sayings.

Despite the ignorant excesses of visiting VIPs, war correspondents, dancing girls and rabble-rousing tank-bank patriots, the Tank Corps's complaints about the spectacular imagery built up around their machines were actually futile – little better than accusing water of being wet. From the outset, the tank was an enemy of sober truth, and the pioneers had known it all along.

When H. G. Wells saw tanks demonstrated at Birmingham's Metropolitan Carriage, Wagon and Finance Company in October 1916, he offered some quaint epithets of his own. Careful to leave no doubt that these were indeed his 'Land Ironclads' made real, this former pacifist who had developed a remarkable appetite for the war, went into competition with the special correspondents and described the tanks as 'slugs with spirit', 'active snails', and 'jokes by Heath Robinson'.[9] One might expect this from a man who clearly saw himself as the 'author' (if not exactly the inventor) of the tank, but there can be no doubt that, despite their many repudiations, the members of the Heavy Section also participated in the metaphorical convulsion. Even Mr

Eustace Tennyson d'Eyncourt, the practically-minded engineer who was Director of Naval Construction and Chairman of the Admiralty Landships Committee, resorted to fantastic coinage. Straining to describe an early tank trial in Hatfield Park, he reported to Winston Churchill that the prototype had astonished its audience and charged through wire entanglements 'like a rhinoceros through a field of corn'. [10] He also made the prehistoric connection, declaring that the tank 'looks rather like a great antediluvian monster, especially when it comes out of boggy ground'. [11] None of the veterans who wrote about the tank were entirely untouched by its appearance, and many of their accounts take a frankly literary approach to their subject. When it comes to the secret domain of the Elveden Explosives Area, Swinton's autobiographical history goes over directly into the fictional mode of his previous incarnation as Ole-Luk-Oie; and the early issues of the post-war *Tank Corps Journal* are full of real-life adventure stories in which veterans offer highly stylized narratives of their wartime experience.

If ever there was a solid barrier between the practical deployment of tanks and the fictional conventions of the boys' adventure story, it was tank soldiers themselves who helped to push it down. Escott Lynn's *Tommy of the Tanks*, [12] published in November 1919, was dedicated to the Tank Corps's Lieutenant Colonel F. H. Fernie, DSO, as 'a slight acknowledgement of his kindness in giving the author very valuable assistance on the working of the tanks during the last months of the war'. And even in cases where such direct co-operation was not possible, the most romanticized fictional treatments still turn out to have been curiously true to life. Percy F. Westerman published his adventure story *To the Fore with the Tanks* in 1917. This book was full of 'lucky bounders', traitors and young heroes who 'are all firmly determined to have a slap at Kaiser Bill's grey-coated Huns'. Westerman recycled the phraseology of the war correspondents to come up with the predictable 'mechanical mastodons' and 'gigantic tortoises': in his own Venetian contribution to the genre, he describes a tank straddling a trench as being 'like a steel Bridge of Sighs, across a canal of liquid mud with grey-coated Huns in place of gondolas'. [13] Westerman's heroes are infantrymen who become fascinated by a 'wrecked landship' around which they also fight with extraordinary courage. Having distinguished themselves in this episode, they are recruited into the tank service where they go on to fight even more heroically, flushing out a traitor bent on selling the secret of the tank to the Hun, and winning much deserved medals. Westerman had no trouble fitting the tank into the pre-existing conventions of the boy's adventure story: indeed, since the tank makes its first unanticipated appearance over eighty pages into his book, it is conceivable that this is what he did quite literally, fitting the new machine into a story that was already under way when the tanks made their dramatic debut in France.

Clichés abound, and yet the mood of excitement in which Westerman's fictional infantrymen join the tanks is actually very similar to that described by some early veterans of the Heavy Branch. Major W. H. L. Watson, DSO, DCM, who entered the force from a motor-cyclists' battalion, remembered the inspiring affect of the new machine: 'we imagined potentialities. They were coloured with the romance that had long ago departed from the war . . .'[14] Captain Richard Haigh, MC, who joined the tanks in late 1916, was equally moved.

TANKS! To the uninitiated – as we were in those days when we returned to the Somme, too late to see the tanks make their first dramatic entrance – the name conjures up a picture of an iron monster, breathing fire and exhaling bullets and shells, hurling itself against the enemy, unassailable by man and impervious to the most deadly engines of war; sublime, indeed, in its expression of indomitable power and resolution.[15]

It was 'this picture' of the tank that attracted infantrymen like Haigh to join the Heavy Section and, for him just as for Westerman's fictional soldiers, there was a wrecked landship in the centre of the frame: 'On the Somme we had seen a derelict tank, wrecked, despoiled of her guns, and forsaken in No Man's Land. We had swarmed around and over her, wild with curiosity, much as the Lilliputians must have swarmed around the prostrate Gulliver. Our imagination was fired.'

Haigh and his fellow recruits knew the dangers of going over the top as infantrymen, but 'above all, the new monster had our imaginations in thrall. Here were novelty and wonderful developments.'[16] Paul Fussell has described the deep imprint that the experience of the Great War would leave on the post-war cultural imagination, yet the story of the tank also reveals the enduring power of romantic conventions – essential to what Samuel Hynes has called 'the war in the head'[17] – that were carried into the fighting from the world before.

Fussell has condemned former war correspondent John Buchan for the 'impudent romancing' with which he described the exploits of the Tank Corps to American readers in 1919.[18] The fatuity of Buchan's account – in which the tank crews take to their task 'with the zest of boys on holiday' – is certainly breathtaking, but it would be mistaken to conclude that Buchan wouldn't have dared to write so flippantly for a readership closer to home.

Indeed, even at his most impudent, Buchan seems to have been in line with the Tank Corps's own view of its achievements. At the beginning of 1920 the *Tank Corps Journal* (a periodical that a few months earlier had reprinted H. G. Wells's 'The Land Ironclads' so that fact could once again be compared with founding fiction) quoted with approval Buchan's judgement that 'The Tank Corps was one of the miracles of the war, and its history was bound to be one of the best romances.'[19] And in that same year some Tank Corps veterans would be assisting Buchan as he set out, once again, to harmonize the story of the tank with the enthusiasm of adolescent boys. Entitled *The Long Road to Victory*, the John Buchan Annual for 1920 was addressed to the boys of Britain and it told the story of Cambrai in the romantic words of men who had actually been there.[20] It was in this volume that the much decorated tank hero Major Frederick Elliot Hotblack, DSO, MC, chose to publish his account of that celebrated victory.

It is the hour before dawn and the tank crews are waiting in their silent machines, which an ingenious Quartermaster has managed to load up with illicit supplies of raisins, lemons, chocolate and rum (these tanks must have struck some young readers as the ultimate schoolboy's tuck-box). Hotblack's heroic major gazes up at the sky – 'The blue and the gold vault holds that time-old witchery which is always new' – and muses on the ways of a Creator who has made the heavens like this 'when, after all, any old sky would have done', and who then goes on to tolerate 'this filthy slaughter'. The major's 'pointless musings' on the contrast between the heavens and the equally endless bloodbath stretched out beneath them are interrupted by a German star-shell, which soars up and bursts against those special skies, 'paling all the stars with its garish efficiency'.[21] With its geometric reconstellation of nature's cosmic attractions, the exploding star-shell marks the point where the tanks roar into life, beginning the day's 'show' (a word the war correspondents were properly reprimanded for using[22]) with its equally dramatic reconstellation of war.

Far from being confined to onlooking infantrymen, sniggering journalists and musical theatre audiences in London, the hilarity of the tank was well appreciated within the new arm itself. Indeed, a sense of the machine's comic propensities was a vital part of what came to be known as 'esprit de tank'.[23] The more scientifically minded officers of the Heavy Branch may have been irritated to hear of songs like Fred Curran's 'The Tanks that Broke the Ranks', or Mlle Regine Flory's exotic dance 'The Tanko', but this didn't prevent the men from pasting posters of their favourite starlets on to the front of their machines, or from naming them in the same spirit. 'Early

Bird' and 'Jail Bird' were named after the comic sketches mounted by Fred Karno, the hugely popular king of slapstick comedy.[24] (Another was called 'Charlie Chaplin'.) Nor, for that matter, did it prevent them from adapting a famous song by Clifford Grey to produce their own 'Tank Song', the text of which was printed on the 1918 Christmas card from the Central Workshops in France.

> In a gargantuan mechanical contrivance,
> A masterpiece of metallurgique skill.
> Disgorging from inflammatory intestines,
> Unwelcome souvenirs for Kaiser Bill.
> A little hell for those who are inside it,
> A greater hell for Huns on either flank.
> In a ponderous tintinnabulating monster,
> In other words, A TANK.

Veterans of the early engagements on the Somme returned as instructors to the Tank Corps base at Bovington full of fantastically enhanced or 'lyrical' stories in which their machines were literally dripping with the molten lead of enemy bullets, and the uproarious anecdote seems always to have had a place alongside heroic exaggerations like this.[25] There was the one about the wig at Cambrai: a tank ended up at the bottom of a river after a bridge collapsed, but the crew survived with only the loss of one member's wig. Great amusement followed as this fellow pursued his claim for compensation through an official bureaucracy that didn't know whether to categorize his loss under the heading of 'Field Equipment', 'Loss of a Limb', 'Medical Comfort', 'Clothing', 'Personal Effects' or 'Special Tank Stores'.[26] The same anecdotal humour turns up in an anonymous Tank Corps officer's retrospective account of the nocturnal visit he had to pay to the German wire, just before Cambrai, in order to establish how audible the preparatory movements of the tanks might be to the enemy. He discovered that while the machines themselves were inaudible, their crews were most definitely not; the 'steel bodies of the Tanks gave a bell-like resonance to the human voice, and faintly across the intervening 2,000 yards came: "Lock your diff., you — fool!" "Mind that — tree," etc.'[27] The Tank Corps's magazines were also full of desperate jokes. Published from Hazeley Camp near Winchester, the *Whippet* was the magazine of No. 24 Tank Corps and one of its articles imagined Samuel Pepys being taken for a ride in a 'Tanque' ('Much did I wonder at the foolishness of the driver who kept not on the good hard road, but made the Tanque to leap a ditch, and so upon the fields, having but small regard for the Hedges').[28] The cover of this short-lived journal showed a silhouetted tank crew riding out on giant snail – perhaps the 'active' one that H. G. Wells had seen in that Birmingham demonstration in October 1916.

Such was the ground on which a rapprochement would eventually be struck between the spectacle of the tanks as they were perceived at home and their military reality in France. In London, the symbolic occasion was called 'Harry Tate's Matinée', a fundraising event for the Tank Corps Prisoner of War Fund, which was held at the Hippodrome on 7 November 1918. With the support of General Elles and other senior officers of the Tank Corps, Harry Tate enacted a sketch entitled 'Motoring', and there were also performances by Billy Merson and George Robey, both of whom had done their bit for the Tank bank campaign. Whatever these performances consisted of, no one will have dissented from the point most forcibly emphasized in A. A. Milne's contribution to the programme. Tank poems from this period tend to clank along with noisy disregard for the edicts of free verse, and Milne's rhyming ditty is no exception. The future creator of *Winnie the Pooh* insisted that, while the 'grim mechanical tanks' may indeed deserve 'thanks' for their 'pranks', no one should forget that the real heroes were 'the wonderful men of the ranks'.

It might be assumed that the tank only lived by fantasy in the early stages of its development, before it possessed any proven capabilities as a weapon – that the better it functioned, the less reliant it would be on mythology and contrived symbolism. Yet the relation between the tank and its own imaginative impact was never as limited as that. From the very beginning the pioneers of the Tank Corps had been concerned less with cancelling the wild and untutored cult of the tank as perceived by onlookers than with harnessing the spellbinding power of their machine alongside its more conventional capabilities as a weapon. A writer of adventure stories such as Captain F. S. Brereton, author of *The Armoured-car Scouts: A Tale of the Campaign in the Caucasus* (1918), might enjoy imagining the response of dastardly Turks and primitive Kurdish tribesman as they watched the approach of 'these curious devices' ('"What means this strange movement?"'), but exactly this sort of confusion was calculated as a vital part of the tank's power in all arenas.[29]

As early as January 1915 Churchill had stressed the 'moral effect' of the experiments he wanted the military authorities to support, and Lord Cavan was among the first to remark, after one of the early demonstrations, that the tank would surely be 'a fat legacy to moral'.[30] Captain D. G. Browne insisted that the psychological impact of the tank could be sustained long after the initial 'element of surprise' had gone: 'the moral effect, all proverbs about familiarity to the contrary, is still and will always remain the chief asset of the tank as a weapon . . . And this moral influence works both ways: it helps the attacker as much as it demoralizes the attacked. The tank is terrifying, or inspiring and rather ludicrous, according to whether it is against you or for you.'[31] Williams-Ellis was insightful on the same theme. Speculating about the future of the tank in 1919, he ventured to suggest that it would prove especially useful in 'minor wars' and occasions of civil unrest when the 'moral import' of its appearance could be expected to ensure 'as much avoidance of bloodshed as is compatible with the bringing of our opponents to reason'.[32]

For Swinton, the 'moral effect' and its associated 'element of surprise' had always been a vital part of the tank idea.[33] The early list of 'Tank Tips' prepared for trainee crews at Elveden included the injunction: 'Shoot the enemy while they are rubbing their eyes,' and it was with that end in mind that considerations of an artistic and psychological kind found their place alongside more conventional questions of firepower and engineering.[34] Disguise may have been the main purpose of the camouflage artists who, in the preparations for Cambrai, covered the tanks assembled in a village with 'camouflage clothes' painted over with bricks and tiles; and of the members of the Maori Unit of the 2nd Anzac Corps who are said to have provided the 2nd Tank Battalion with 'expert help' of a similar kind.[35]

Yet the decoration of the tank was never just a matter of disguising or hiding the machine. It also included an element of deliberate and assertive display, intended to create a sense of confusion and uncertainty as to what the approaching machine might be able to do. In 1917 Mr Ev Tong Sen of the Federal Council of the Malay States offered the British government £6,000 for the purchase of a tank and, in proudly announced tribute to oriental custom, a large eye was painted on each side of the tank's bow before it went into action.[36] When eight tanks were being prepared for participation in the Battle of Gaza, Swinton had wondered how to maintain 'the moral effect of the tanks on the occasion of their final appearance, even though the Turks might have been aware of their existence'. He recommended that the tanks might regain the vital element of surprise if they were adorned with minatory texts from the Koran and painted over, as some actually were, with 'frightful faces' of 'Djinns or Afrits'. Swinton confesses that his primitive 'conception of the enemy mentality' was 'based more on recollections of the *Arabian Nights* than knowledge of the Modern Turk'.[37]

The terrifying impact of the tank was exploited more practically through the months from Cambrai to the end of the war. It was counted as a factor during the German spring offensive, when Allied tanks were expected to hide in hedges and other such places, and then emerge like 'savage rabbits' to make sudden counter-attacks. It attended the new elongated Mark V tanks, used successfully with the Australian Corps in the battle of Hamel; and it supported British contempt for the 'very ponderous' German tank when it was eventually fielded – a crude metal box containing an officer and eighteen men 'packed like a sardine tin' as *The Times* scoffed on 6 May 1918. It was found particularly effective on 8 August 1918, the first day of the Battle of Amiens, in which the British Tank Corps proved beyond doubt that 'iron mechanically moved' is an 'economiser of life'. On that day, Sir Henry Rawlinson's Fourth Army deployed over 400 British tanks alongside French, Canadian and Australian Corps. The rapid advance caused chaos and panic among the enemy. This was the real moment of defeat – the 'black day' of the German army, as Marshal Ludendorff would write in his memoirs. A somewhat more elaborate conclusion was drawn by the official commission set up by the German government to review the defeat after the war. The tanks at Cambrai had certainly taken German troops by surprise: 'They were rather at a loss what to do when confronted by the new weapon which suddenly advanced against them on a broad front in the morning mist and dealt without difficulty with the very well-constructed positions and the most powerful obstacles.'[38] However, 'tank fright' had receded after new systems of tank defence were organized. According to this commission, the 'turning point of the war' had been the French use of tanks, aided by early morning mist as much as by the absence of artillery preparation, in General Foch's counter-attack in the Battle of Soissons on 18 July 1918. Defensive measures were adopted once again, but 'tank fright' reappeared as the German defences became thinner, and the soldiers increasingly overworked and exhausted. 'The moral effect of the tanks was then often surprisingly great.'

Shortly after the advance at Amiens, *The Times* gloated that German officers were complaining of the humiliation of trying to surrender to such an 'ungentlemanly' thing as a tank: approaching these advancing machines to give themselves up, they were reduced to chasing after them 'as if they had been 'buses, hailing them to stop and take them on board'. Such reports were certainly not lost on the Tank Corps. During the last months of the war J. F. C. Fuller's publication *Weekly Tank Notes*, carried quotations from the German press to demonstrate how profoundly allied tanks were eroding the morale of the weakening German Army. It quoted from General von Ardenne, who had admitted that 'an attack by tanks has something appalling and demonical about it', and it rejoiced in the captured documents and statements from prisoners revealed that the German infantry had been '"hearing tanks" in sectors where there have certainly been no tanks for them to hear'.[39] As for the German policy of not developing tanks until very late in the war, *Weekly Tank Notes* gave the final word to a captured company commander who said: 'I consider the Tanks a most magnificent weapon and cannot understand why we have none to speak of.'[40] Present-day historians who are inclined to view the coming of the tank as a minor and largely inconsequential episode in the overall history of the Great War will recognize that Fuller had his own purposes in selecting that quotation; and yet such was the symbolic potency of the tank that, nine years after the war, the German novelist Arnold Zweig would deliver the same verdict, describing the German troops of the Great War as 'grey haggard men, without tanks'.[41]

PART II

In the Church of Mechanization

Tank light from War window by Ward & Hughes at St Mary's, Swaffham Prior.

8

Bringing it All Back Home

The image

One Easter Sunday in the nineteen-nineties I attended a family communion service in Swaffham Prior, a small Cambridgeshire village, which lies under a vast sky at the edge of the fens. Hallelujahs filled the air and the little medieval church of St Mary was a vision in white. Easter lilies prevailed among the flowers; the young organist was wearing his cricket flannels; and voluminous quantities of bleached white fabric hung from the two young girls in the choir, one of whom eventually clambered into the loft above a carved oak rood screen to boost the congregation's singing with a silver cornet.

Hymn 78 was full of 'strife that is o'er' and 'the battle won', and the lesson from Isaiah counselled us not to dwell on days gone by. When the time came to pray, most of the congregation bent their knees in the old-fashioned way, getting down on to hassocks embroidered by the Women's Institute. Some of the more dilatory worshippers let their eyes drift idly up patched stone pillars towards the roof. But I was more taken by the stained-glass windows, many of which had been made by the same late Victorian company, Ward & Hughes, and fitted in the early years of the twentieth century. A light in the south aisle was devoted entirely to cherubs, while another, dated 1914, showed the whole of creation – exemplified by walruses, burning volcanoes, a Chinaman and a void-defying owl – rising up into a 'Hymn of Praise' to the Lord.

The windows in the north aisle had been installed only a few years later. Their pictorial scenes were framed by the same Gothic-revival canopy work, but no attempt at formal constancy could disguise the fact that something terrible had happened in the interval. It was not a cherub or a host of singing angels that hovered in the top rose light, but a cigar-shaped Zeppelin wedged up against a starlit sky. Below that was a howitzer taking aim at a distant fort, and a bugler whose call to war was illustrated with a line from Handel's *Israel in Egypt*: 'The Lord is a man of war.' The window was packed with weapons, but none seemed more incongruous than the tank –

a looming rhomboid phantom with a couple of large cart-like wheels trailing behind as it rose out of the mud to bear down invincibly on the infernal Huns who were spraying scarlet liquid fire over helpless Tommies in the adjacent window. This silvery mass certainly glowed, but hardly with the whitened light of Easter – more like the glimmer of a smeared lunette above an old public lavatory, or the sluggish gleam of a fish turning in a muddy pool.

In accordance with medieval precedent, every image in these unexpected lights was accompanied by a quotation from the Bible. Women working among gleaming gold shells in a munitions factory were urged on with a line from Ecclesiastes: 'Whatsoever thy hand findeth to do, do it with thy might.' A German submarine minelayer, shown caught in the snake-like hawser of a steel net, was mocked with the words of Amos: 'Though they be hid from my sight in the bottom of the sea thence will I command the serpent and he shall bite them.' Yet the tank seemed unrivalled in this connection too. Its legend was lifted from the Second Book of Samuel, a passage concerned with the terrifying sons of Belial: 'But the man that shall touch them must be fenced with iron.'

Perhaps in 1919, when these painfully literal war memorial windows were installed, it was hoped that their texts would provide some consolation, demonstrating that the Bible at least remained unshaken and could accommodate even the most technological of twentieth-century horrors. Yet those ancient lines of truth had actually been twisted in strange and surreal directions as they were yoked to the machinery of modern war. Fixed in that glassy, technological frieze, the tank and its dangling legend seemed to have less in common with the saints and cherubs across the nave than with jingoistic comic strips and war-mongering newspapers.

The glass Behemoths that can still be found barging into angels in the windows of scattered British churches belong to a time when the memory of the Great War was a raw wound: a volatile compound of shock, grief and rage that had yet to be wrapped in the stately dressing of Armistice Day, the official ceremony on which historians of remembrance are inclined to dwell.[1] Some are almost mute expressions of bereavement, like those that can be seen in the window installed in 1918 at Nocton, just south of Lincoln, by the parents of Leslie Halkes Wray, killed in action as the driver of tank Ella during the Battle of Cambrai.

Other tank-bearing memorial windows are considerable works of art, like the somewhat later ones, dedicated in 1922, in the north transept of St Andrew's, a Scottish Presbyterian (now United Reformed) church at the junction of Finchley Road and Frognal Lane in north-west London. Created by Douglas Strachan, a major Scottish stained-glass artist, who also produced the Scottish National War Memorial window in Edinburgh Castle, these windows make a better job of enfolding the horrors of war in a redeeming biblical narrative. The first light shows the Sacrifice of War in its primitive Old Testament form, represented by Abraham's intended slaughter of his son and the savagery of Miriam and her pitiless dancing women. In the second, Strachan pictures war transformed in the spirit of Christ, its sacrifices invested with mystery and sublimity, and its 'unbridled passion' subordinated to 'discipline' and faith. The tank takes its place in this redeeming story, a processional and by now sacramental engine attended by soldiers as it rolls through the Apocalypse towards the numinous light of the Day of the Lord.

It is a less transfigured tank that appears in the windows of St Mary's, Swaffham Prior. Like the other hardware featured in this modern arsenal of a window, Swaffham Prior's glass tank rises up as a literal reality of modern warfare, accurate right down to its rivets and only weakly tethered to the scriptural legend accompanying it.

Known, if at all, for having two churches in a single churchyard, this remote Cambridgeshire village had lost twenty-three men in the war and, as happened all over the country, the work of memorialization was organized by a pillar of the community who had earlier done his bit to encourage local recruitment. Swaffham Prior's agonizing memorial windows were the work of Mr Charles Peter Allix, an elderly High Anglican squire who counted the restoration of St Mary's Church, which had been ongoing since the 1870s, as the major work of his life. Allix recognized the war as a calamitous interruption. There could be no more windows like those he had installed in the south aisle of St Mary's shortly before the outbreak of war – optimistic and feathery works, featuring owls as well as cherubs.[2] And yet, in its own uniquely dreadful way, the conflict did enable him to complete the restoration of the church. Having declared, in spring 1919, his intention to commission two memorial windows in the north aisle of St Mary's, Allix was happy when his much-encouraged parishioners, who had originally thought of erecting a cross in the churchyard, agreed to cover the cost of a third window – this one to be a portrayal not of war but of the final Peace in which Christ wipes away all tears – and also to mount their proposed memorial cross inside the church, where it still stands beneath the windows.

Allix's idea was to show the latest weapons in the first of his two windows, while devoting most of the second to attempts that were made to 'mitigate' the war's horror: field kitchens, Red Cross nurses, YMCA huts, military chaplains and, to mark the alliance with America, the Statue of Liberty. In designing the windows, Squire Allix seems to have started off with newscuttings and photographs of the war and its 'newest inventions'. The tank, an early Mark I that Allix described as 'a locomotive, iron-armoured battery', appears to have been copied from the famous first photograph for which the *Daily Mirror* paid so much in 1916. If local memory is correct, sketches for the various lights were exhibited in the billiard room at Allix's mansion and parishioners, bereaved or otherwise, were invited to join members of his family in searching the Bible for the quotations that would eventually accompany each image.

Ward & Hughes was a leading firm of Gothic-revival stained-glass painters, but Allix's unusually literal, even photographic, memorial windows have not been fêted as great works of art. Old guidebooks pronounce them 'most curious' and the present church leaflet even uses the word 'appalling'. Similar misgivings were expressed in the national press shortly after the windows were dedicated. A correspondent for the *Daily Sketch* judged Swaffham Prior's unusually 'realistic' war memorial windows to be a 'flagrant' sin against good taste. Believing that church windows should show redemption rather than raising infernal horrors to a lurid glow just a few yards from the altar, this reporter was only a little relieved to find that the windows were of painted rather than stained glass and could not, so he mistakenly thought, be expected to last for many centuries.

Swaffham Prior's war windows speak of unanimity, but their installation was attended by considerable discord. To establish his memorial, Allix had to overcome a long-running feud between High and Low Church interests in the village. He also had to break through parish distrust of his vicar, who is remembered to this day as an abusive 'consoler' of poor widows and also of young boys in the choir (local hostility to the Revd Lawrence Fisher was such that one farmer would even crucify a large and symbolic fish by the roadside). Partly as a result of this bad feeling, a large congregation attended the Baptist Chapel of Zion; and these non-conformists greatly resented the suggestion that the village's war memorial should be incorporated into the fabric of Fisher and Allix's refurbished High Church establishment across the road.

Squire Allix had these disconcerting antagonisms in mind when the newly installed windows were dedicated at a special service held on 21 December 1919. In his address Allix spoke movingly of the village's losses,

and denounced the 'greed and ferocity' of the Germans with their 'diabolical' flame-throwers. He also went out of his way to argue that St Mary's
was the most appropriate place for the memorial, claiming that it was not
just 'the best house in the parish' but the nationally established 'House of
God' – 'call it Church or Chapel' – which belonged to 'all who take Christ
as their leader'. Squire Allix had been able to override local dissent, sufficiently at least, to squeeze his tank into St Mary's. Yet, as he raised his eyes
beyond the confines of his fractious parish, he had to acknowledge that the
social fabric of the wider nation was also ripped and torn. There too, the
order of the day was not solidarity, concord and unanimous respect for the
dead, but violent bank robbery in the cities, murder and assassination in
Ireland, and deep political strife in the industrial areas: 'classes are at present in a state of something like antagonism one to another. This must be
ended.' It was essential, so this elderly squire insisted, that 'Capital and
Labour must become friends'. Only then could the harmonious and pasto-
rally imagined 'Peace' in the third and last of Swaffham Prior's memorial
windows be achieved; only then could the terrible losses of the war be vindicated, and the 'fruits of victory' be justly reaped.

Yet these disorders were beyond the solutions of any one parish. The
painted-glass windows in Swaffham Prior may have brought the image of
the wonder weapon home from the Western Front, but the conflicts
described by Squire Allix had already proved sufficient to draw the actual
tank – not just an image but the brutish thing itself – through the nation's
various theatres of remembrance and out into the square and street where
there was neither redeeming cherub nor feathery angel to be seen.

The memory

Many of Britain's tanks were eventually brought back from France and elsewhere, and taken to the Tank Corps's headquarters at Bovington Camp in
Dorset, where they were lined up along a minor road leading across the
heath to T. E. Lawrence's cottage at Cloud's Hill. Yet the tank that came
home from the war was far more than a battered metal box on a Dorset-
bound train. It was also a heroic image of power, a dance, a podium, and a
popular song. It was a mechanical film star, a fund-raising device, a string
of gruesome jokes, and an argument about the limits of experimentation in
art. For the homecoming soldiers of the Tank Corps, the tank was a freakish
memory – heavy, exotic and still moving – to be parked, often with considerable difficulty, somewhere in the back of the demobilized mind.

Captain Clough Williams-Ellis, the former reconnaissance officer, sat down with his wife Amabel to write the first book about the Tanks Corps. Having concluded that the tank evolved in Britain because it is 'a weapon peculiarly suited to the British temperament', he resumed his activities as an architect and became, as time went on, a steely defender of the native British landscape against modern encroachments: a campaigner for whom 'protection' was now to be achieved by means of town and country planning and the green belt.[3] Basil Henriques, who had gone into action in the first tank to fire on the enemy, reverted to his life as a social worker in the East End of London, happy to exchange 'esprit de tank' for the improving male community of the Jewish boys' clubs he had worked with before the war, and to trade the metal of his tank for the moral truth with which he now sought to armour his fellowship of lads against the corrupting attractions of the street, on which many of them had, perforce, grown up.[4] Wilfred Bion, who had served in Flanders with the 5th Battalion, trained as a doctor and then went on to practise as a Kleinian psychoanalyst, latterly in California. His anti-heroic memoirs betray no interest whatsoever in the cod-psychoanalytic potency of the tank, with its male and female versions, its 'Mothering' qualities and its promise of 'penetration with security'; yet Bion did go on to elaborate a theory of the self in which the idea of 'the container' featured prominently.[5]

The great majority of veterans had to reconcile their memories of tank warfare with altogether more ordinary lives. Their stories are likely to have been closer to that of Private W. L. M. Francis, MM, who, like Bion, served with the 5th Battalion of the Tank Corps and then discovered that, while a returning soldier may go back to where he came from, he can never, as the American novelist Thomas Wolfe pointed out, really go home.

'Mac' Francis was nearly ninety-nine when I met him, sitting by the fireside in a small bungalow in Oswestry and testing his memories against time and intervening mythology alike. He well remembered how history had pulled him – an uncomplicated lad from a devout Methodist family – out of that small market town on the Welsh border, and thrust him into a war very different from anything the correspondents and recruiters had described.

As the eldest son of Oswestry's leading grocer, Francis had been excused duty for a few months, but he was soon ordered to Shrewsbury barracks where he reported to a colonel who turned out to be on the lookout for recruits with some mechanical knowledge. Private Francis's training opened at Grove Park in London, but it was only after moving to Bovington Camp in Dorset that he saw tanks for the first time. As he watched these novel contrivances 'crawling up and down sandbanks and knocking down trees', he wondered, 'what the Bloody Hell I had come for'. It was, as he explained in a soft Welsh accent, 'the first time anyone from Oswestry had seen anything like it' and, without doubt, 'one of the biggest shocks of my life'.

Francis became a gunner in a 'female' tank, equipped with four Lewis machine guns. His driver was a former chauffeur from Scotland, Barney Gallagher, with whom he remained lifelong friends. He was twenty years old when they shipped out from Southampton to Le Havre, and first went into action during the Third Battle of Ypres, on 31 July 1917. The night before, he was shown a 'plan' mapped out in sand on the ground. He remembered the names of farms and villages like St Julien, and the pill-boxes that were identified as his target. It all 'sounded so easy', but any such expectation had disintegrated by the time they got their tank Enchantress to its appointed 'jumping off place' and, in the parlance that still came so naturally, went 'over the top'.

Francis paused here, mustering his resources beside a gas fire that also supported a bar of Bourneville chocolate, the doctor's telephone number, and a leatherbound volume of his favourite poet, Robert Burns. Young Francis's provincial outlook had already suffered terrible assaults during his descent into the trenches. He had been disconcerted to walk past a house in Le Havre and see a woman displaying herself stark naked in the window, and beckoning lewdly at the passing soldiers. He had been horrified by the lice and by the unremittingly filthy language of the Western Front. He had seen terrible slaughter while on guard duty in Oosthoek wood: a German plane had spotted candles and bombed a company of exhausted men, camped there on the way back from three weeks in the trenches.[6]

But even against this background, words could hardly describe the experience of driving in a tank across no man's land. There had been torrential rain, and constant artillery bombardment had broken up the watercourses as well as churning up the ground. 'It was Hell,' said Francis, adding that 'not one of the people who have described Flanders has overdone it'. The pulverized corpses of mules and horses seemed to be everywhere, and there were countless dead soldiers too, many of whom had been there for months – fragmented or half-buried with putrefying arms and legs sticking up. There didn't seem to be so many Germans, but Francis was still haunted by the sight of many corpses wearing kilts. As for those gruesome accounts of tanks driving over dead bodies, flattening them as they lay on trench parapets, or squashing them into the mud. Francis confirmed that his Enchantress did just that. 'We had to,' since there was no question of steering one of those primitive machines to avoid them. They had ploughed on through 'bodies, horses, machine guns, barbed wire, duckboards . . . everything mucked up, like a big farm churn has come and churned it up'.

'They might as well have put a tank on the ocean,' said Francis, rocking in his chair as he remembered how the Enchantress dipped and slid about in that putrid mire 'like a boat on a very windy sea'. Having got far enough to find their target villages in 'total ruin', they then sank into a deep shell crater. Francis remembered getting out to shift the unditching bar in an unsuccessful attempt to get the machine moving again. At that moment a shell landed nearby, covering him from head to toe in slime. The mud, he repeats was 'absolutely horrible – I can still smell it'.

He and his fellows were stuck there from 6 a.m. to 5 p.m., under constant bombardment. Eventually they struggled back through that repulsive mire to the British line: 'It felt like a mile, but could have been 500 yards.' After straining to squeeze the still vivid horror of that experience into ordinary words, Francis seemed to give up and drift away, volunteering that his father had been the best tea blender in the Oswestry region – an apparent diversion that was actually his way of emphasizing that he knew what he was talking about when he described the rough brew he received on returning to the British lines as 'the best cup of tea I've ever had in my life'. As for their ditched and sinking tank Enchantress, when the Salvage Corps reached it a few nights later, only the top foot or two remained visible above the slime.

Like many veterans, Francis was familiar with the exhaustion of loyal women. 'My people get fed up with it to the back teeth,' he said, joining his daughter as she laughed at the exasperation his compulsive, much-told war stories used to provoke in his late wife. As with every other serving soldier, Francis had only partial glimpses of the war, and he was still wondering how these fragments fitted into the overall picture. 'Can that be true?' he asked repeatedly of his own deeply scored recollections – as if confirmation could only come from somebody who hadn't been there. Yet the First World War had always remained 'the thing in my life', and on other points he was still holding the line. He clearly remembered the officer who poked his head into the Enchantress, just before the Battle of Cambrai, and communicated the famous message from Hugh Elles: 'England expects that every tank this day will do its damnedest.' Some veterans may later have insisted this story was just another insulting myth cooked up by war correspondents; but Francis was convinced of its truth, not least because he remembered his Scottish driver, Barney Gallagher, objecting that it should have been 'Britain' not 'England' that did the expecting. As the veterans have died off, it has become easier for smart revisionist historians to rehabilitate the reputation of Haig and the other generals who oversaw the slaughter from various châteaux behind the lines. But Francis insisted that no one should have ordered soldiers, on either side, to fight in the mud of Flanders: 'It was a death trap.'

The infantry had stopped laughing at tanks by the time Francis arrived on the scene, though not because they were impressed by their usefulness. 'Cursing, yes,' he recalled, and not just when the tanks broke down and blocked roads. Tanks were targeted by German artillery, and infantrymen had quickly learned the disadvantages of going anywhere near them. There were torrents of abuse from the British side as the tanks manoeuvred through woods – 'we were always in woods' – or broke the line and headed out into no man's land. One or two intellectual officers at Bermicourt might have imagined that these clumsy movements heralded a coming transformation of warfare, but the Signals Corps only stamped and swore as they saw their cables, which came in 'hundreds and thousands' and were often placed at considerable risk, being tangled and severed.

There were some things that Francis was still reluctant to speak about. He would have preferred to stay 'off the record' about the moment, during the Battle of Cambrai, when one of his fellow Lewis gunners in the Enchantress saw a column of German prisoners being marched back towards the British line, and machine-gunned them. He had also chosen to keep quiet when approached by a man curious to know exactly how his father had died in that same celebrated tank advance. Francis professed ignorance, although he knew very well that, like so many others, the poor fellow had been 'roasted alive' after his tank was hit by a shell: 'There's nothing worse than a tank going on fire, I tell you. Hopeless, hopeless.'

Having come home, Francis ran the family grocer's shop in Oswestry's Cross Street for half a century before he sold the building in 1970; and here he was, a quarter of a century after that, with the unsettling stench of Passchendaele still burning in his nose. 'I put myself into it,' he explained, adding that he had tried to serve the chapel and to advance the Liberal cause too, although gently, since most of his customers were staunch Conservatives. 'Nature is merciful,' he concluded, pulling himself back into his bungalow and explaining that he generally found himself predisposed to dwell upon the lighter side of things. Even so, he had hardly passed a day without thinking of the war, and he had never forgotten the two-minute silence, not since it was introduced on the first Armistice Day, 11 November 1919. Francis had his own memorials with which to fill that annual crack in time, including one that he called 'the worst sight I've ever seen in my life'. He had glimpsed it from the Enchantress as they passed a chalk quarry during the first stages of the advance at Cambrai: two soldiers, a Briton and a German, both dead but still propped up, one against the other, triangulated by their own bayonets.

The monument

No one who visited the British Museum in the last weeks of 1989 will have missed the sight of a First World War tank, a renovated female Mark IV called Flirt II. This prize exhibit was standing smack in front of the main entrance, under a plastic canopy emblazoned: 'Treasures for the Nation', the title of an exhibition devoted to the work of the National Heritage Memorial Foundation. Thought to be the last surviving tank from the Battle of Cambrai, Flirt II was still polarizing onlookers. A passing installation artist, Richard Wentworth, noted its formal qualities as a remarkable, even paradoxically beautiful sculptural object; but there was also at least one humanist scholar who, having passed Flirt II on the way to the British Museum's Reading Room, objected that, especially in the year of Tiananmen Square, a tank was surely the last thing that should be honoured as part of the cultural heritage. Be that as it may, this was certainly not the first time a statutory body had tried to make a monument of a First World War tank.

There were a lot of light-hearted jokes about the civilian uses to which tanks might be converted at the end of the Great War, from trouser presses to fairground Big Wheels with seats attached to their tracks. Nobody tried the suggestion made by William Heath Robinson, who sketched one such pacified machine, fitted with seats and converted into a London bus ('When Peace is Declared; Using up the old war tanks as motor busses'). But 265 of the tanks repatriated from the Western Front were dispatched into a new kind of service as town trophies. The Army Council gave these 'war-battered' hulks to the National War Savings Committee for presentation to towns of over ten thousand people that could claim 'conspicuous achievements' in the purchase of bonds and certificates.[7] When this scheme was first announced, the National War Savings Committee drew up a 'Memorandum of Suggestions for the Receipt of a Presentation Tank', stressing that these relics provided 'an exceptional opportunity for propaganda' for the War Savings movement and promising that a dedication plate would be provided, which might be inscribed with the names of the dignitaries who had served on the local war savings committee. In April, the National War Savings Committee's fortnightly bulletin, the *Silver Bullet*, had waxed lyrical about the 'war-weary monsters' that were now coming home 'to rest in civic splendour and meditate upon the bygone toils in France'.[8] In the interests of 'spectacle', it was suggested that a procession should accompany the presentation tank to its prepared resting place, which should be chosen carefully since the tank crew would be instructed to immobilize the tank once it was in place, frustrating any would-be insurrectionists by removing 'a portion of the machinery by which the tank is driven and also the wedges of the guns'.[9]

These municipal trophies were not always popular with Tank Corps veterans, who knew that tanks had been fiery coffins rather than just funny money boxes. And the National War Savings Committee also felt obliged to acknowledge that while tanks had, by 'a combination of chances', acquired a 'peculiar association' with the savings movement in this country, there were people who 'objected that this perpetuates a memory of the war through days when thoughts turn eagerly to peace'.[10] The committee's 265 presentation tanks would override this complaint and remind the public that, in its association with war savings, 'the world's most recent engine of destruction' had been converted into 'one of its first advocates for reconstruction'. Instead of standing for 'the feverish expenditure of war', the tank now represented 'careful economy' and offered 'a mute reminder of the fact that to squander money now is to weaken all our purpose in Peace'. Savings, in other words, would continue, even if it was now a matter of the Victory Loan rather than War Bonds and Certificates.

When he stepped up to hand over Berwick's tank, General Ernest Swinton, the former Commander of the Heavy Section, reminisced about the secrecy that had surrounded their manufacture: 'I lied like ten troopers,' he said. The intended moral of these unlikely monuments was spelt out more effectively by Sir Auckland Geddes, President of the Board of Trade, who, in August 1919, attended the presentation of Basingstoke's tank in order to draw out 'the Lesson of the Tank' for the benefit of the assembled crowd.[11] The tank, he said, was 'a memorial of the great war', a 'dumb teacher' which, 'for one who cannot talk is most loquacious'. It stood there as a reminder that 'liberty has to be fought for and struggled for with blood and tears'. But the most important thing taught by the 'metal monster' was 'the great lesson of national unity':

So let me say this, when any in Basingstoke is tempted to say, 'I and my class matter in the State,' let him come and sit beside this Tank and let the lesson it has to teach sink deep into his mind – each individual, each class needs the help of all if it is to conquer. We have seen examples of folly before now. The world has heard capital, wealth and social power say, 'The State – I am the State,' and the boasters perished. We have heard armies say, 'The State – I am the State,' and the army perished. We have heard Kings say, 'The State – it is I,' and the king perished. We have heard Labour say, 'The State – we are the State,' and Labour perished. In this country for many generations we have had a better way: we have said that we are all the State and we elect our rulers. We make no great changes till a majority is convinced that such a change is right. Then we make it, and England has not perished, but has grown strong and great. So let this old Tank speak to us of the English way of ordered co-operation, discipline, and respect for law.

So the homecoming tank added another role to its repertoire: that of public moralist. The machine that had entered the war as a shocking transgressor or 'Cubist slug', emerged as a rusty-faced old buffer of a distinctly English kind. Through the twenties and early thirties, it would sit in demobilized glory on a pedestal by the town hall or among the herbaceous borders of the municipal park, advocating self-denial and 'personal service for the State',[12] and dispensing other home truths for the benefit of a younger generation that might otherwise be seduced into class warfare.

The bloody thing itself

However loquacious they may have been, static memorial tanks were not adequate to all the requirements of the time. On 25 January 1919, the *Glasgow Herald* featured a drawing of a tank dressed up as Old Mother Hubbard and walking out of the town with a 'Goodbye-e!' and a caption explaining that there had been 'Nothing weak about our Victory Savings Week'. Glasgow had raised record sums for the Tank bank campaign in January 1918 and, at the special request of Glasgow Corporation, an exceptional second Tank Week was held a year later. The National War Bonds scheme had been due to close, but bonds were kept on sale for a further seven days in order to allow the final fund-raising jamboree that was to be Glasgow Victory Week. Two heavy tanks, named 'Haig' and 'Beatty' after the chief commanders of the recent war effort, were brought in by rail, and raised 'a good deal of public attention' as they proceeded, in consort with a lighter Whippet, through the streets to Glasgow Green where they demonstrated their 'military powers' in a simulated attack – advancing over mocked-up shell craters and barbed wire to crush the parapet of an enemy trench.[13] The tanks were then stationed outside the City Chambers in George Square, although the organizing committee, which had 'a true instinct in regard to the value of publicity', also arranged 'a short tour of the streets', which would 'visibly announce the presence and proclaim the mission in the City'.

Glasgow's second Tank bank campaign took place before the dust of war had settled. The *Glasgow Herald* reported it alongside General Haig's final dispatch, which commended the bravery of the Tank Corps while also promising that the infantry and cavalry would remain fundamental to the army of the future. Men were still being demobilized, and pouring back into the city in desperate pursuit of work, and the correspondence columns were filled with discussion about the kind of war memorial that might be appropriate for Glasgow. There was also unsettling news from overseas. Civil war and chaos loomed in Russia (the paper included an erroneous story claiming that Lenin had been arrested by Trotsky, who had made himself dictator), and there was ferment in Germany too, with revolution breaking out in Munich, Bremen, Hamburg and many other cities, including Berlin where, despite General Command Lüttwitz's eventual employment of captured British tanks,[14] it was by no means certain that the Spartacist uprising had been snuffed out by the misreported murder of its leaders Karl Liebknecht and Rosa Luxemburg. The edition of the *Glasgow Herald* that described the cavorting of tanks Haig and Beatty on Glasgow Green at the beginning of the Victory Savings Week, also included an article surveying the alarming spread of Bolshevism in Europe, and hoping, nervously, that the Spartacus Group in Germany and the militants around Dr Troelstra in Holland would not find their equivalents here: 'The Bolshevist, by all the canons of British politics, is mad.'[15]

If the members of Glasgow Corporation were exceptionally keen to bring a second Tank bank to their city, this may partly have been because they hoped to impose a crushing dose of tank patriotism on a disorder bearing its own unmistakable resemblance to Bolshevism that was represented even in their own ranks. As the Victory Week went ahead, the city's newspapers also had to attend to the challenging activities of an 'unofficial movement' that could claim several elected representatives on Glasgow Corporation itself, including Councillor Emmanuel Shinwell. He was now among the leaders of an association of Clyde shop stewards agitating for the introduction of a forty-hour week (the German Spartacists had also campaigned for the eight-hour day); and insisting that only by this measure would it be possible to find work for the many thousands of former soldiers and sailors who were now returning to Scotland in search of employment.

As leader of a joint workers' committee formed at the Glasgow Trades and Labour Council, Shinwell called for workers to take part in a general strike to be held on 27 January 1919. This threat was sufficient to give new direction to the *Glasgow Herald*'s continuing discussion on the subject of the city's war memorial: on 23 January, a correspondent reckoned that 'Ignorance' was behind both the war and also 'the present social unrest', and that 'new university buildings' would therefore make a doubly appropriate war memorial for Glasgow. Others, like Alexander Ratcliffe, who signed himself 'Trade unionist', wrote to condemn the 'Bolshevik agitators' and 'Scottish Sinn Feiners' as 'a scandal and disgrace to the trade union movement'. Ratcliffe was disgusted to think that the very people who had 'discouraged recruiting' and 'advised the workers to "down tools" when the soldier needed shells' could now claim 'to champion the cause of "Tommy" by shouting – "Everybody should strike because the poor soldier cannot get a job"'.

Meanwhile those cavorting tanks were straining at the National War Savings Committee's leash. On 25 January it was declared that Glasgow Victory Week had raised over £11 million, but the achievement was swamped by the rising tide of political militancy. On Thursday, 29 January a defiant Shinwell addressed his people at a mass meeting at St Andrew's Halls: 'When we leave this Hall, we are going to walk – in an orderly way – (laughter) – with bands leading – the procession to the power stations – (applause) – for the purpose of holding a meeting – (laughter). On the road, we will not permit our ranks to be broken.'

Afraid that the situation was slipping out of control, the Lord Provost of Glasgow asked the government to intervene. The Prime Minister, Lloyd George, was in Paris at this time, but the other members of the War Cabinet were assured by the Secretary of State for Scotland, the Rt. Hon. R. Munro, that leading Glasgow citizens had recommended a campaign of 'unofficial propaganda'. Beyond that, however, it was felt that the government could do nothing since the strike itself was unofficial and in breach of formally agreed trade union policy. On 30 January the Cabinet received a further telegram from the anxious Lord Provost. He had been visited by a deputation of eleven leaders of the 'unofficial movement', including Shinwell, Kirkwood and Macrae, the MP for Govan, and these men had demanded that he request government intervention to bring about the forty-hour week without any reduction in wages. Unless this was forthcoming by the following day, their protest that had hitherto been confined to constitutional methods would, so the deputation had threatened, move on to other means. The Lord Provost added that nearly all the men in the electricity department had that day been 'compelled' to join the strike, leaving only enough workers to ensure a supply for hospitals and infirmaries.

Having recently seen the shipbuilding and engineering employers agree a forty-seven-hour week with their official trade unions, the government had no intention of acceding to this brigandish demand from Clydeside. Yet the Cabinet was also well aware that it was not just in Glasgow that mutiny and industrial militancy had attended the demobilization of the forces which, before changes that were nervously introduced at the end of January 1919, had been phased to suit the interest of employers in 'key' industries rather than the rights or deserts of the men who had served.[16] A comparable disturbance was under way in Belfast, and earlier in the month the Cabinet had discussed the advisability of drawing the various departments of state together to take 'concerted action' against the spread of Bolshevism at home.

It was against this background that a nervous Chancellor of the Exchequer, Bonar Law (who was chairing the Cabinet during Lloyd George's absence), now declared it 'certain that if the movement in Glasgow grew, it would spread all over the country'. He thought it vital for the Cabinet to be satisfied that there was 'a sufficient force in Glasgow to prevent disorder and protect those volunteers or others who could be made available to take over the operation of the generating plants'. This was by no means easy, since the police force had itself been close to striking for increased pay. On 24 January the Cabinet had been informed that there was trouble with the Metropolitan Police, the Midland Railway Police and the Scottish police, and that a certain 'Ex-Inspector Syme had recently been up in the North stirring up trouble in Glasgow'. Loyalty could, and indeed soon would, be bought with a pay rise but doubts remained about the strength of the Glasgow force. Five hundred members were still in the army, and it would be practically impossible, so Churchill thought, to arrange for their demobilization to be hastened. Agreeing that it would be preferable to use Scottish rather than English troops to suppress the uprising, they counted up the nineteen infantry battalions presently in Scotland. One of these was stationed in Glasgow, but the officers were judged poor and the men by no means fit or reliable. A few soldiers had been used as guards and train drivers during one of the big pre-war railway strikes, but, as was explained by the Director of Personal Services, Major General. B. E. W. Childs: 'at that time we had a well-disciplined and ignorant army, whereas now we had an army educated and ill-disciplined'.

Some Cabinet members were unnerved by these reports but not, it appears, the Secretary of State for War, Winston Churchill, who came up with the more considered approach that was eventually adopted. He reckoned 'there would have to be a conflict in order to clear the air', but he also observed that the situation in Glasgow had been 'brewing' for a long time and that the disaffected were in a minority. The vital thing was to ensure that the government had 'plenty of provocation before taking strong measures. By going gently at first we should get the support we wanted from the nation, and the troops could be used more effectively.' He urged 'firm, but not provocative action', suggesting that, while it waited for the 'glaring excess' that would take the revolt 'over the line of a pure wage dispute' and thereby justify military intervention, the government should take advantage of the fact that the Defence of the Realm Act was still in force and seize some of the ringleaders. Meanwhile, it was announced that the strikers were also threatening to wreck the Glasgow newpapers' offices, while the strict eight-hour day already being implemented by railway workers was bound to disorganize traffic, and make it harder to get troops to the scene.

By Friday the 31st, the news from Ireland seemed to have improved: it was thought that the strike in Belfast was crumbling, despite the fact that the strikers had formed a 'Soviet' committee that was receiving applications from small traders who wished to use electricity. Glasgow, however, was seeing 'scenes unparalleled in the civil history of the city': huge crowds had assembled in George Square (in the very place where the city war memorial would soon stand, a considerable rampart raised between the City Chambers and the people) to hear the government's reply to the Provost's request for intervention against the strikers. The Glasgow police had received their demanded pay rise a week or so before, but they betrayed little understanding of the distinction Churchill had drawn between 'firm' and 'not provocative' action. Willie Gallacher mounted the plinth of the Gladstone statue to speak, and the police launched their assault with baton charges: the *Glasgow Herald* reported 'a hurricane of blows which fell indiscriminately on those actually participating in the strike and on those who had been drawn to the scheme merely through curiosity'. The City Chambers were soon full of wounded, while the police found themselves being stoned or assailed with bottles seized from a lorry and 'hurled as hand grenades'. As the *Glasgow Herald* concluded, 'The baton charges and the rushes of the mob' created 'a turmoil so strange and exotic in contrast to the ordinary atmosphere of the Square that the impression conveyed to the eye-witness was at times that of

an artificial production' – like 'a cinematograph picture which he was viewing with conscious detachment from the scenes it portrayed'. The scenes
extended up to Glasgow Green, on the way to which the crowd is said to
have smashed up tramcars, bending their electricity poles and, in one case,
roughing up the conductor too.

The confrontations in Glasgow convinced the Secretary of State for Scotland that 'it was a misnomer to call the situation in Glasgow a strike – it
was a Bolshevist rising'. The time to send in the troops had surely come.
Major General Romer, who attended the War Cabinet from the War Office,
reported that the army had been readied and that 12,000 troops could be
put into Glasgow at short notice. It was also announced that six tanks and
a hundred motor lorries were being sent north by rail that night. The First
Lord of the Admiralty, W. Long, ventured that the strike could not hold
out for long: once its vanguard had been crushed, it could be left to the
women, who would surely soon drive their men back to work.

By 3 February the battered leaders of that 'unofficial' movement, including Emmanuel Shinwell, David Kirkwood and Willie Gallacher, had been
arrested and charged with incitement to riot and assembly. It was also
noted that 'large military drafts' had arrived in the city and placed key sites
under guard – the City Chambers, railway stations, bridges and power stations too. The troops had arrived late on Friday, 1 February and set to work
with machine guns and barbed wire. On 4 February it was reported that 'a
further proof of the vigour with which the situation would be dealt with,
should occasion arise, was the arrival of a number of tanks yesterday. The
city is already familiar with the tank as a means of advertising War Loan
stock, but the presence of this latest arm of warfare has an entirely new and
awe-inspiring aspect.'[17] The tanks are said to have 'occasioned great interest
and considerable speculation' as they made their way through the city to
the Cattle Market, where a 'tankodrome' was established. Shinwell's joint
committee responded clearly enough: 'The organized workers of Scotland
put forward an orderly demand for the 40 hours. The Government's reply
is bludgeons, machine guns, bayonets and tanks – in one word, the institution of a reign of terror.'[18] By 8 February a remarkable change had occured
in the *Glasgow Herald*'s cartoon summary of the week's events. The tank
that had been a bonneted Old Mother Hubbard in the 'Heraldoscope' of
two weeks before, was now revealed in an altogether less folksy light – bearing down on fleeing rioters, one of whom is crying: 'It will be "mashed"
picketing if it comes my way!'

The tank had come home – not just as a taxing memory, a glass image, or disarmed municipal monument, but also as an intimidating war machine ferrying policemen about and applying its 'moral effect' on the streets of a British city. The last of the troops were reported to have left Glasgow on 18 February, but the thought of those English tanks would linger in that predominantly left-wing city's political memory for the rest of the century – at once proof of the reality of class war, and also shocking emblems of a British state that was prepared to crush its own people.[19] Winston Churchill would almost certainly have preferred the judgement of Clough and Amabel Williams-Ellis: 'It is infinitely more humane to appal a rioter or a savage by showing him a Tank than to shoot him down with an inoffensive looking machine-gun.'[20] No doubt the same effect was intended during the General Strike of 1926 – when tanks were to be seen further south, rolling out of the Wellington Barracks into the streets of London.

So it was, both at home and in 'Imperial Policing' operations abroad, that the deterring lesson of the tank came to be applied in those post-war months. Armoured cars were being used against Bedouins in Egypt in March 1919. They proved less effective in the Punjab a month later, when two such machines attended the notorious massacre carried out by General Dyer at Amritsar: the approaches were too narrow to allow the cars actually to enter the Jallianwala Bagh, an open area in which Dyer's forces proceeded to kill 380 people. Tanks would soon be on the move in South Africa too, where the famously 'steely-eyed' General Jan Smuts, the former Boer leader who, having served as a member of the Imperial War Cabinet during the First World War, became Prime Minister of South Africa in time to face an armed 'Red Revolt' mounted in 1922 by striking white gold miners determined to maintain the colour bar on the Witwatersrand. The rebels had established headquarters at the Market Building in the Johannesburg suburb of Fordsburg; and having fortified the square, dug trenches, and made a blockhouse out of the public lavatory, they were rumoured to be preparing to march on Johannesburg Town Hall in a column of some 1,500. After ordering the evacuation of the district, Smuts bombarded the Market Square with artillery, and then sent in his tank, accompanied by infantry who may not have been too impressed by the fact that it broke down before arriving at the centre of the crushed rebellion.[21]

Such were the requirements of those post-war years that many of the British Tank Corps's machines had been dispatched into new areas of conflict directly from France. Thus in April and May 1919 a considerable detachment of 2nd Brigade tanks headed for the Rhine. According to the reports printed for the benefit of fellow tank men in the *Tank Corps Training Centre Journal*, the men of the 12th Tank Battalion were proud to have been the first to enter 'Hunland'. Having travelled from near Arras, where the 4th Tank Battalion claimed to come under fire from the wired compound in which those long-suffering Chinese 'coolies' were kept, they detrained their machines in outlying tank parks and drove into the centre of Cologne, where the arrival of British tanks was said to have 'excited a great deal of speculation and even alarm among the inhibitants'.[22] There is no report of screaming and fainting like that claimed to have greeted the appearance of the 16th Battalion's 'fearsome beasts' near Düsseldorf, but there were 'unauthenticated stories of the German ladies bursting into tears as the machines drove along the streets'.

In one highly symbolic demonstration, two tanks led by a band and a detachment of naval troops drew up at the foot of the cathedral steps and then, 'with half the cameras in Cologne at work', proceeded around the Cathedral to the Hohenzollern Bridge. 'These were the first Tanks to trek across the celebrated bridge, with its statues of emperors and association with the past greatness of Germany,' and the show of force had the desired effect: 'The German people are very bitter about our use of tanks, regarding the latter as the chief instrument in their defeat, and this feeling, adding to their sentimental veneration for the Rhine and their pride in the finest of its bridges, dedicated especially to the Hohenzollerns, gave to this little ceremony a peculiar significance which was not lost upon the large crowds who witnessed it.' Having made their presence felt, the men of the British tank detachments – 'Tankadors' who had indeed now crossed the Rhine – fell back on more conventional activities such as trout-fishing, cricket and, in the case of the 9th Battalion, laughing at the soldier who, impressed by the style of a 'German ex-sergeant-major', had shaved off all his hair and was now compelled to wear a hat at all times.

Tanks are said to have been used to overawe 'an angry mob' at Brobeck in Silesia,[23] but there was apparently little serious challenge on the Rhine. As the 16th Battalion's scribe reported, 'the only alarm that has occurred since our arrival was when it was rumoured that the Spartacists were going to attempt to come through the outpost line in armoured cars from Düsseldorf. Nothing, however, happened.' Industrial strikes posed few serious problems: the military authorities were not bound by 'red tape or legislation' and had developed 'an excellent way of dealing with these gentry' (a lot of people were getting shot in Germany at this time). Members of the Rhine Tank Company also assisted the military police, attending their house-to-house search for arms and 'subsequently running a tank over their captures' – an activity that was said to break 'the monotony of tank work' even if it was not viewed with 'any great amount of favour by the local inhabitants'.[24]

Other British tank soldiers found themselves working alongside the murderous and war-crazed Black-and-Tans in Ireland. Such were the challenges posed by the Irish War of Independence that, within months of the Armistice in France, the British Cabinet was increasing the supply of Peerless and Rolls-Royce armoured cars just as fast as it could, cramped by a coal strike and rising demand elsewhere. Dublin had seen its first such vehicles during the Easter Rising of 1916 – improvised conveyances made of large boilers mounted on metal-plated lorries, which were used by Guinness and also by the Post Office to deliver funds, in particular the separation allowances owing to the wives of serving soldiers, to outlying post offices.[25] But the experiments were now more systematic. Armoured Ford cars were being put through trials on behalf of the British Army and the Royal Irish Constabulary, and the Woolwich Arsenal was hastily producing revolver-proof 'car cushions' and protective steel plates that could be attached to lorries.[26]

For the readers of the *Tank Corps Journal*, this was another jaunty story involving cricket matches played in unexpected places. In January 1919 the 17th Tank Battalion had been posted to Dublin with heavy tanks, light Whippets and also armoured cars, and then dispersed around the country in some twelve detachments. For the soldiers of this battalion (soon reformed as the 5th Armoured Car Company), using tanks against Republican freedom-fighters was a puzzling experience – rather like being 'sent ratting with a tame elephant'. The elusive 'rat' would be reported in the vicinity of remote barracks of the Royal Ulster Constabulary, but it had usually slipped away by the time the armoured cars arrived. Sometimes the rat was 'too quick', but often the warning telephone call was a deception, and the armoured cars would speed down a hill, only to find a tree trunk laid across the road on the blind side of a sharp bend. Or, as happened on another occasion, the vehicle would be returning through a 'decidedly hostile village' and find itself on a street 'carpeted with a mass of broken bottles and glass, and all the population out to see the fun'. The anticipated punctures failed to occur (the Peerless armoured car had solid tyres), much to the disappointment of the presumed rat – a 'truculent individual who was standing in the centre of the road on the far side of the glass, hands in pockets, smoking a pipe', and who 'only moved out of the way just in time to escape injury to himself'. Since 'the "pucca" Tank man in Ireland' had 'little or no outside excitement', he took his comic relief as he found it. There was much chortling at the memory of one training exercise in which two Mark Vs drove into a town in the west of Ireland: hundreds of people gathered around, and then the hatches suddenly opened and the machines disgorged a platoon of kilted Highlanders. 'Tremendous enthusiasm', of course, from the 'Irish colleens'.

It is a tribute to the 'moral effect' of those tanks and (in the word attributed to one Irish paper) 'frightful' armoured cars, that they are still to this day being bundled up into an awesome image of British oppression. In this guise they were recently seen in Neil Jordan's film *Michael Collins*, where a symbolic armoured car drives into the sports ground at Croke Park, Dublin and, after being playfully engaged by a single footballer, opens fire on players and crowd alike. The accuracy of that particular portrayal of Ireland's first Bloody Sunday may be questioned, and not just by the connoisseurs who insist that Jordan's machine should have been grey rather than green. The machine guns may have been real enough, but armoured cars were not actually involved in the Croke Park massacre of 1920.

Yet if Jordan's representation of the event is false in this respect, it also demonstrates that the symbolism of the British armoured vehicle in Ireland has long since slipped out of British control. Indeed, in Northern Ireland the British tank would eventually be overwhelmed by its own moral effect. The Ministry of Defence is inclined to deny that tanks have ever been used in Northern Ireland. Spokesmen will admit to employing armoured personnel carriers, known on the streets as 'pigs', and all sorts of other wheeled vehicles with the most ferocious capabilities, but the symbolic 'tank' – a tracked vehicle with a turret and a gun – has been withheld since Operation Motorman on 31 July 1972, when the British Army used Centurions to break through the blockades isolating Republican-held 'no-go areas' in Derry and Belfast. Those Centurions may have cleared the roads into 'Free Derry', but they also fired the song of the Republican prisoners interned in Long Kesh: 'Armoured cars and tanks and guns / Came to take away our sons.' And no manned tracked vehicle has been used in Northern Ireland since, owing, as one apparently knowledgeable military participant has recently asserted on a website called the Tankers' Forum, to 'the media image of "tanks" oppressing the Catholic minority'. A considerable distance from Glasgow by that time, but too close, by far, to the imagery of Prague 1968.

9

The Prophet's Creed

The man who was known as the strategic 'brain' behind Britain's tank
force, Brevet Colonel J. F. C. Fuller, came home before the end of the
Great War. He had left the Heavy Branch headquarters at Bermicourt by
the end of July 1918, one month before his fortieth birthday, and returned
to London where he was to head a new branch called Staff Duties 7 at the
War Office. Fuller was to be responsible for establishing the Tank Corps on
a permanent basis, and eventually for training throughout the entire army.
But he joined the 'ink-slinging fraternity' reluctantly, starting work on 1
August and returning to France a few days later to witness the Tank Corps
breaking through with over four hundred tanks at the Battle of Amiens –
an operation he had helped to plan, and which only increased the determination with which he now pressed for an immediate doubling in the size of
the Tank Corps and a hugely accelerated manufacturing of tanks.

The War Office was a frustrating place for a military futurist to work,
especially one of comparatively modest rank, and Fuller likened the experience to straying up on to Epsom Downs in the horse-racing season. Finding
himself in a preserve for hidebound and horse-minded men, some of
whom, so he judged, were only there to look after their own skins, while
obstructing the very developments that might have saved so many lives on
the Western Front, he started pressing for the implementation of the Tank
Corps's ultimate scenario. Convinced that tanks would win the war for Britain as 'their invincible might sank deep into the moral fibre of our enemy',
Fuller tried, in the few months that remained before the Armistice was
signed in November, to build support for an operation he had dubbed 'Plan
1919'. Projected for 1 June 1919, this would attempt to end the war at a stroke
with a new kind of tank attack, for which several thousand fast-moving
'Medium D' tanks would be required. The Medium D has since been
described as 'the prototype machine of blitzkrieg and mechanized warfare',[1]

but in 1918 it was a barely materialized concept, dreamed up to suit the doctrines that Fuller and his colleagues had developed at Bermicourt, and also, as Fuller himself later admitted, to impress the journalists who had proved so influential in determining public perceptions of the tank, and who would – even if the generals demurred – find good 'copy' in the idea of 'fifteen tons of steel that could roar along our roads at the then speed limit of a motorcar'.[2] Intended to bring about the full-scale transformation of warfare that had only been hinted at by its slow and lumbering predecessors, the Medium D would be a swifter instrument of 'movement and surprise', having a maximum speed of twenty miles per hour, and the capacity to range over a 200-mile radius of action without incurring the usual logistical problems of fuel and supply.

At Bermicourt in May 1918 Fuller had described the Medium D as 'a solution to our difficulties' and 'an absolute means of victory if we can only get our military pedants and manufacturers to move'.[3] It was the Tank Corps's own ideal machine, developed under the auspices of Captain F. Searle's workshops near Bermicourt, and created in more or less explicit opposition to the authorities that had been responsible for the design and production of tanks in Britain. In a note written in June 1918 and described as a 'serious leg pull for Searle' Fuller suggested that tank design in England was suffering from 'the Mechanical Poet Laureate system' – i.e. it was churning out machines to order, and on the existing model. This system was like a 'mediaeval gloom' presided over by a Pope and an Inquisitor; and the 'damnable heresy', of which both he and Searle were pleased to be guilty, was 'the doubting of the immaculate conception of the Mark 1 tank – upon which by a slow and certain atavism, all other marks are being modelled'. Far better, he suggested, to widen the 'orbit of thought' by drawing up a specification, and then putting it out to a competitive tender.[4] Sketched by Searle, and modelled in prototype by one of Searle's engineers, Major Philip Johnson, the Medium D set out to break the mould established by the heavy Mark I. Based on the 14-ton Whippet, a previous light tank designed by Sir William Tritton, the Medium D had a cupola above a tracked body, and was equipped with a 240-horsepower engine and an innovative system of sprung suspension intended to increase its speed and cross-country capabilities.

The culmination of many hypothetical scenarios rehearsed in Fuller's futuristic 'Brain Barn' at Bermicourt, Plan 1919 was to become famous as one of the most prophetic scenarios in the history of tank doctrine: described (and also disputed) as the ultimate source of Hitler's blitzkrieg, and also of the tactics used by the Israelis in the Arab–Israeli wars of the fifties and sixties. It had several precursors, but, as so often happens in the story of the tank, all complicated precedents tend to be obscured by a sudden flash of revelation experienced, or at least claimed, by one originating mind alone.

Fuller would later describe how the final idea for Plan 1919 had dawned on him one day in March 1918, when he was sitting on top of Mt St Quentin, a little hill not far from Peronne, watching the British Fifth Army retreat under German attack.[5] The German spring offensive was based on new tactics of infiltration, in which self-contained bands of storm troops made their way through the line to attack British positions from the flanks and rear. The result, as Fuller saw it, was a chaotic demoralization of the British forces – one that demonstrated the 'intimate connection between will and action, and that action without will loses all co-ordination; that without an active and directive brain, an army is reduced to a mob'.

With Plan 1919, Fuller set out to 'rationalize' and expand on this idea, adopting similar tactics of infiltration but using Medium D tanks rather than storm troops to bring about the required degeneration in a vast enemy force. The first step would be for the British to trick the enemy by engaging in conspicuous activities along a ninety-mile stretch of the front. Designed to resemble preparations for a large conventional attack, these would encourage the Germans to mass their reserves along the front, concentrating perhaps as many as five armies in the area. Once this force had been lured into position, the British and their allies would break through the line with heavy tanks and then unleash vast fleets of Medium Ds, which would sail out over land that had been spared preparatory artillery bombardment of the kind that had churned up the mud at Ypres and elsewhere. Rather than engaging the enemy force along the entire length of the ninety-mile front, the tanks would cut through at selected places – a 'morcellated front of attack' – and move on at unprecedented speed to destroy the enemy's supply and command headquarters behind. The operation would finally emancipate the tank from its subordination to a primitive kind of 'body warfare', in which infantry tried to 'wear down' the enemy by attacking its personnel with 'a succession of slight wounds', and release it into its destiny as the leading instrument of a new kind of 'brain warfare', which set out to destroy the enemy's power of command with a 'shot through the brain'.

Working in close co-operation with aeroplanes, which would bomb roads and supply-routes but leave signalling wires intact in order to guarantee the spread of panic and demoralization, the Medium Ds would assault the enemy's Army, Corps and Divisional Headquarters, thereby severing their links with the forces at the front. Once its 'brain' had been disconnected in this way, Fuller anticipated that the enemy would rapidly collapse into 'strategic paralysis' even without being directly attacked – a degeneration that could be hastened if 'the shot through the brain' was combined with one through the stomach, designed to dislocate the enemy's supply system at the same time. It was then that there might be a modest and entirely secondary role for the infantry. Like the cavalry, that other relic of pre-mechanized days, the infantry would quickly have been left behind by the Medium Ds as they sailed out to prove Fuller's belief that 'the earth has become as easily traversable as the sea'.[6] But the former 'Queen of the Battlefield' would now be permitted to run forward to mop up the confused and helpless enemy force. . .

Fuller himself described Plan 1919 as a 'novelette',[7] but fictions have gone a long way in the history of tank warfare, and this one is certainly no exception. Various versions were distributed in high places, and Fuller claims to have gained the acceptance of the British general staff, and also of Marshal Ferdinand Foch, the French general in overall command of the Allied forces. Yet, while there may have been support for a concerted tank attack along the suggested lines, the required Medium Ds hadn't even been built, and the war that might, in Fuller's view, have been brought to sudden victory through such an attack, was concluded by more conventional means before anything like it could be tried.

Events had rendered Plan 1919 obsolete, but by March 1919 Fuller was outlining another futuristic scenario in which many elements of his earlier scheme were conserved.[8] Mindful of recent disturbances in Glasgow and Berlin as well as Moscow and the colonies, Fuller argued that, with the Kaiser defeated, the main threat was now 'the increase of Bolshevism throughout Europe and Asia which, unless the virus is stamped out, may involve not only Germany but Italy, France and possibly ourselves'. Being so often an 'enemy within' rather than a consolidated nation or state, Bolshevism posed a new kind of military threat. Fuller anticipated that 'civilised war' would in future be replaced by 'guerilla warfare and police work for which the present army is not equipped'; and his immediate remedy was drawn up for the benefit of a War Cabinet that was indeed much concerned by the spread of communism at home and abroad.

Aiming at the centre of contagion, Fuller proposed that the British government should raise and equip a 'Tank Expeditionary Force', which would be sent to Russia to crush the Bolshevik revolution. The force would consist of nine battalions, equipped with a total of 434 tanks, which should be ready for action in the summer of 1920. Its members would be trained at the Tank Corps's training centre at Wool in Dorset, and Fuller's section at the War Office would be greatly expanded in order to raise the force and also to develop the 'very different' tactics necessary for its successful deployment.

Recruitment would be a sensitive matter so soon after the Great War: the demobilizing nation would not tolerate the reintroduction of conscription, and the government could hardly set out to raise a voluntary force, even if time allowed, without being accused of militarism. But Fuller reckoned that the expeditionary force would be better anyway, if it were staffed by highly paid mercenaries, many of them recruited on the quiet from among the men who had served with the Tank Corps during the Great War. Separate from what War Office jargon of the time described as the 'After War Army', this elite expeditionary force would combine 'tanks, aeroplanes, armoured cars, mechanically moved machine gunners and possibly naval and chemical co-operation' too. As it rolled forward, the Tank Expeditionary Force would function as 'a moving block-house line which would clear an extensive area of country (20,000–40,000 square miles in extent), pause whilst this area was being organized and then move on and repeat the experience'. It would need mobile workshops, wireless and bridging capabilities, intelligence and transport experts, and also a political section for establishing order and governance in areas that had been cleansed of 'the virus of Communism'. The force would be temporary (Fuller suggested contracts of two years, with a possible extension to three) and highly mechanized: 'weak in man-power and strong in machine power – i.e. the Medium D'.

This hypothetical proposition was to go the same way as Plan 1919. Fuller's proposal for a Tank Expeditionary Force is unlikely to have reached many desks higher than that of the exasperated senior at the War Office who scribbled that he thought the idea of Fuller's department was to get tanks into the army, not take them off in some fantastical direction of their own. Yet by the time Fuller wrote his proposal, the British government was indeed involved in the civil war then raging in Russia – committing more than £100 million to that lost cause.[9] There was no question of sending the nine battalions that Fuller had imagined, but the anti-Communist White Russian armies were provided with training and equipment. A delegation of White Russian officers attended the Tank Corps Training Centre at Bovington, and a small expeditionary force was organized, with the involvement of Fuller's branch at the War Office. Indeed, by the time Fuller wrote his grandiose proposal, some members of the Tank Corps in France had already volunteered for 'the Russian Stunt'.

The party consisted of three officers and twenty-six men, and they left the village of Erin, near Bermicourt, on 8 February 1919.[10] Equipped with six Mark V tanks and six Whippets, they proceeded to Calais and, after seeing their machines loaded into the hold of the SS *St Michael*, embarked for southern Russia from Woolwich Arsenal. They sailed via the Mediterranean, paying due respects to the thought of fallen comrades as they passed the still-littered shores of Gallipoli, and expressing robust British contempt for the Turkish Delight and strange cigarettes sampled in Constantinople. After crossing the Black Sea, they arrived at 'Nova Rossick', where they and their tanks were greeted by ecstatic crowds. A Russian company filmed every movement as the iron saviours were unloaded, and the Cossack officers and soldiers, who jostled around the new wonder weapon in their hundreds, 'did not seem to be convinced that the tanks were real unless they were allowed to touch them – many even kissed the armour-plated sides'. On Palm Sunday, Sergeant C. L. Windle and his fellows demonstrated the powers of the new machine, which symbolized long-awaited British aid and promised the resurrection of White Russia's hopes: 'the Tank climbed a small cement wall and there was breathless silence as it slowly mounted the wall and stood on its tail; as the Tank passed over the wall and crushed it, the spectators gave a series of tremendous cheers. During the whole of the show the Cossacks followed the Tank on horseback.'

After raising morale at Novorossiysk, Windle and his fellows entrained for Ekaterinodar, where they were soon billeted in a dance hall surrounded by park and meadows, and where they mounted further demonstrations – using five tanks to surmount various obstacles and to fell 'human sized trees'. Attended by various White Russian generals, including Denikin, these 'brilliant' antics were, in the words of a local paper, enough to crush 'provocationary rumours', put about by Red sympathizers at the local market, that the tanks had arrived out of order and in no condition to be sent to the line. The British 'Tank Boys' may never have acquired a taste for the lugubrious offerings of the Russian cinema, but they enjoyed 'cordial relations' with the ladies, who wore 'short dresses and short socks', and in some cases had 'cut their hair short like a man', prompting their British admirers to wonder whether this 'fashion' was caused by fear of the Turks or of the Bolsheviks.[11] The question of tactics, so dear to Fuller, was presumably also addressed in the training school that the British volunteers set up for Russian officers.

By the summer of 1919 the British Military Mission had been moved to Taganrog, along with the Tank Expeditionary Force. As for the achievement of the tanks with General Denikin's forces, contemporary reports are mixed. One of these machines was glimpsed through a shuttered bourgeois window by a plucky but justifiably apprehensive young English governess and language teacher in Rostov: 'lumbering' along a snow-covered and nocturnal street, the machine that had so impressed the Cossacks looked to her only 'like some prehistoric beast in pain'. Far more alarming, considering the mayhem and murder that was to come, it heralded not victory but 'the retreat of the Dobrovolchesky Army'.[12] For Miss Rhoda Power, who proceeded to make her own fortunate escape through Murmansk, the imported tank was an emblem of White defeat; yet, back in London, Fuller was using his publication *Weekly Tank Notes* to create the opposite impression. He reported that 'on the appearance of Tanks, the Bolsheviks have bolted, discarding their rifles and equipment, and . . . even the Whippet Tanks have not been fast enough to overtake them'.[13] Besides such incidences of tank terror, *Weekly Tank Notes* also noted the contents of an intercepted Bolshevik wireless communication in which Trotsky is said to have informed Bela Kun that the British had supplied Denikin with 150 tanks. An impressive result, since there were actually twelve tanks in South Russia at that time, only ten of which had been engaged in fighting: 'It is interesting to note that when these tanks arrived in Russia, General Denikin organized a demonstration for the Press. The Tanks and their capabilities were largely written up in the local press.'[14]

By the end of the year, Fuller had given the job of running the school at Taganrog to the former Tank Corps Major E. M. Bruce, a fearless adventurer who had lost an arm in France while rescuing damaged tanks from the battlefield as a member of the Tank Corps's Salvage Company. Having shipped out to Novorossiysk in March 1920, together with a further twelve tanks and a handful of other 'instructors', Bruce would soon be writing to Fuller about the frustrations of trying to teach scientific tactics to the average White Russian officer: 'at an examination I asked one what he would do if a certain part of his machine was broken. He answered: "I would make the sign of the Cross and get out of the tank." '[15] As for the shipment of tanks that had accompanied Bruce, they appear to have fared better than the ten British tanks that had arrived at Novorossiysk in the autumn of 1919. Having been stranded at the quayside owing to lack of railway transportation, these are said to have been caught up in a gale and, through some bizarre and scarcely credible mishap, to have slipped from the dock into the sea.[16] Some of these British machines certainly survived until June 1920, when Major Bruce, in defiance of official British policy insisting that his role was purely advisory, led a successful White assault on Tsaritsyn with two Mark V and two Whippet tanks supported by an aeroplane and also a number of bullock carts loaded with spare fuel and supplies. The city that would soon be redubbed Stalingrad may have fallen to Bruce and his six British mechanics; but their outlaw column was still a long way from the Tank Expeditionary Force of which Fuller had dreamed.

No such fleeting victory as Bruce's awaited the British tank detachment commanded by Major J. N. L. Bryan, which sailed for Archangel in August 1919, as part of the North Russian Expeditionary Force. Had the Russian civil war gone differently, these tank volunteers might have expected to work alongside the Royalist forces as they pressed south, but that advance had been broken and, with the White cause crumbling, the tanks were actually only there to cover the withdrawal of British troops – escorting them during embarkation, but also guarding their retreat from 'the low element of the town', and using their spellbinding powers to intimidate the murderous White Russian troops whose mutinous leanings had already necessitated the use of Lewis guns, mortars and firing squads.[17] In the course of their brief and nervous visit to that brutal civil war, the detachment set up a tank school at which a 'North Russian Tank Force' was formed under Colonel Kenotkenitch, with ten officers and twenty-four other ranks trained as gunners. Since the loyalty of the lower ranks could not be relied upon even in this tiny force, it was decided that officers alone would be permitted to drive the machines.[18] As for 'esprit de tank', that was built by telling 'somewhat exaggerated' tales of the valour shown by the British Tank Corps in France.

When the evacuation was all but complete, the British detachment presented two tanks (a Mark V and a Medium B) to the North Russian Tank Force, and attended a farewell dinner, given by the doomed Russians to honour their departing 'brothers in blood'. Early the next morning, on 27 September, the British tank detachment marched through Archangel's silent streets to the Subornaya Quay, boarded the Czaritza, and sailed away. Gazing at the northern lights as their retreating liner sailed round the North Cape, Major Bryan thought of the men they had abandoned to what he, like Fuller, identified as 'the virus of Bolshevism'.[19] He later received a cable, dispatched on 29 October, which revealed that the North Russian Tank Corps had gone into action with its two machines: 'Proud keep traditions, English Tank Corps, Took in glorious fight five fortified points and

Plesetskaia Station. Colonel Kenotkenitch.' Their fate after that would remain unknown, although, as Major Bryan concluded, 'one can be sure that whatever else happened, they went down with their flags flying, fighting to the last, fit brothers-in blood in the halls of Valhalla to those whose traditions they were so proud to maintain'.

Fuller's futuristic scenarios rose and fell in uncertain relation to the practical realities of their time; and so too did the trials of the Medium D prototype, which by now had been made amphibious on Fuller's instructions. Presided over by Lieutenant Colonel Philip Johnson, a Tank Corps engineer who had been appointed head of the government's Tank Design Department, these continued until 1922, when the new tank, which had not overcome teething problems despite having achieved a speed of 30 m.p.h., was scrapped from on high – the victim, according not just to Fuller but also his Marxist admirer Tom Wintringham, of a 'conspiracy of profit'[20] that handed tank design and production over to private manufacturers. Yet Fuller's years at the War Office were not without practical results. Aided by the rising demand for its services, whether in Glasgow, Ireland, Germany, India or Iraq, Fuller and his colleagues managed to prevent the Royal Tank Corps from being split or scaled right down by a military old guard inclined to believe that the tank was either a mere eccentricity justified by the passing aberration of trench warfare, or a modestly useful gadget that could be added, without major revision of organization or tactics, to existing cavalry and infantry regiments. It was partly (if not, as Fuller would later claim, entirely)[21] as a result of his efforts that the Royal Tank Corps was established as a separate arm of five corps on 1 September 1923. It had been equipped with a flawed Medium tank, a mobile but thinly armoured model equipped with the first revolving turret, which had been commissioned from Vickers without Fuller's knowledge as replacement for the Medium D; and its ability to develop new tactical doctrine may not have been assisted by the fact that, against Fuller's advice, many senior posts in the corps were filled by otherwise redundant officers transferred from other branches. But at least this much-reduced force still existed – unlike the disbanded American Tank Corps, or the mobile tank army advocated by General Estienne in France, for which there was no future under General Pétain's policy of prioritizing defence above all in the form of the Maginot Line.

The post-war Tank Corps was imperfect, as Fuller never tired of pointing out, but it was sufficient at least to ensure that, over the next ten years or so, the cause of mechanization would be pursued with greater ardour and consequence in Britain than anywhere else. The Royal Tank Corps Centre at Bovington, Dorset, became a site of experimentation under its first Chief Instructor, Colonel George Lindsay, who had previously commanded an armoured car company in Iraq, and was convinced that the future lay in establishing an 'entirely mechanized force'. Vigorously opposed to a policy that would merely rearm infantry or cavalry regiments with mechanized vehicles, Lindsay wanted to see all mechanization concentrated in the Royal Tank Corps and pressed for the establishment of an Experimental Mechanized Force, which would begin to demonstrate how the army might work once it had been reconfigured around the possibilities opened up by the tank.

Fuller assisted Lindsay and his fellow 'RTC radicals'[22] as much as he could: first from the staff college at Camberley, which he joined as an instructor in January 1923, and, after February 1926, as military assistant to General Sir George Milne, the new Chief of the Imperial General Staff, who took steps, on Fuller's advice, to establish Colonel Lindsay's Experimental Mechanical Force – a combination of Medium tanks, armoured cars, tankettes and also a motorized machine gun battalion, which was based at Tidworth in Wiltshire, where it would be well placed to manoeuvre on Salisbury Plain. As the army's most prominent expert on tanks, Fuller was expected to command the new armoured force. When his appointment was announced in the House of Commons, he was in India assessing the possible use of tanks along the North-west Frontier and advising senior officials in Delhi that they could avoid disasters like the Amritsar massacre of 1919, if they added 'lachrymary gas' to their arsenal of scientific weapons.[23] But on returning to Britain he found that the commission would also have placed him in command of 7th Infantry Brigade and, indeed, the entire Tidworth Garrison. Refusing to accept the appointment on these terms, he threatened his resignation from the army – a decision that, whatever Fuller's calculations may have been, is said to have marked 'the virtual end of his military career'.[24] The armoured force was placed under the command of Brigadier R. J. Collins, an infantryman with no previous experience of armoured vehicles, who failed to impress the Royal Tank Corps officers under him. Fuller had moved to Aldershot as General Staff Officer to General Ironside by the time of the summer manoeuvres of 1927 and 1928, in which the armoured force was tried out against conventional cavalry and infantry. Given the command structure, Fuller would have expected little of these exercises. He was familiar with previous trials in which potentially fast Medium tanks had been obliged to crawl along singly at the speed of the marching infantryman, while the enemy killed them off merely by raising a green anti-tank flag endowed with powers far greater than any actually existing anti-tank gun could claim.[25] A disconnected onlooker, he was content to deride the manoeuvres, observing that, without direction, training and tactics (to say nothing of its chaotically diverse collection of vehicles), the 'Armoured Force' had proved itself to be the 'Armoured Farce'.[26]

The Experimental Mechanized Force may have attracted interested observers from the German Army, but in Britain it appeared to go nowhere. Indeed, it was closed down at the end of the 1928 training season, much to the satisfaction of the General Officer Commanding Southern Command, General Sir Archibald Amar Montgomery-Massingberd, who was firmly of the view that, rather than setting up an independent armoured force, the wise strategy would have been gradual mechanization of the cavalry and the infantry. Some experiments in this direction were conducted on Salisbury Plain, including the exercise that Rudyard Kipling observed in 1930, remarking (at least according to Fuller), 'It smells like a garage and looks like a circus.'[27] But the RTC avant-garde's frustrated vision of an independent armoured brigade was only to find expression in military journals or as literary fantasy in a book called *The Battle of Dora*, written by H. E. Graham, who claimed 'considerable experience' of the mechanized force.[28] The scenario was set in Jugurthia, an imaginary country rather like Poland, which had been 'reconstituted' in 1919 after 'many centuries of bondage', and then promptly sank into decadence, lulled by the sirens of pacifism and even preferring violins to guns. Seeing their opportunity, the government of neighbouring Martia issued an 'outrageous ultimatum' and then invaded. The defence of Jugurthia was mounted with the help of another neighbour 'Anglia', which, being prescient as well as good, could field an army that was not just the same size as that of Martia, but also motorized, mechanized, and equipped with an Armoured Brigade capable of independent operations of just the sort that Fuller and the RTC radicals had aspired to. Comprised of a headquarters, artillery, a signals company, medium and light tanks, and a squadron of fighter planes trained to co-operate with it, this mobile force won the day, true to the spirit if not the letter of Fuller's Plan 1919. In the words of its major: 'We went through the blighters like a hot knife going through butter. First of all we pushed their faces for them, then we turned round and kicked their backsides. And then they lay down and said they had had enough.'[29]

Fuller's refusal to take over the Experimental Mechanized Force on the terms offered might have marked the end of his influence over military affairs, were it not for the power of his pen, which remained unfettered – sufficiently at least to ensure that he existed in a state of more or less constant tension with the military establishment. As Britain's first tank intellectual, Fuller wrote books and deliberately provocative lectures and essays for the military press, promoting 'tank-mindedness' and mechanization and pitching his proposed 'reformation of war' against the 'mineralized intellect'[30] he saw passing for thought in high army circles. In one lecture, delivered at the Royal United Services Institution (RUSI) in February 1920, he had taken up the position of a future-gazing clairvoyant who could actually see the 'New Model Army' that was to come: motorized, fully mechanized, professional, smaller but also infinitely more mobile than the vast conscript armies of the Great War.[31]

In Fuller's perception, the revolutionary shift represented by the tank and plane was both inevitable and in the vital interests of the nation. Yet, it was also impeded everywhere by convention, vested interests and the bovine stupidity of the red-tabbed hierarchy. The enemy at home consisted of dim-witted politicians whose primary concern was to keep costs down, commentators who mistook ossified mental habit for the truth of any given situation and, within the military's commanding circles, the purblind advocates of the bayonet and the horse whose rallying cry was: 'Back to 1914.' Fuller wrapped all these opponents up as exemplars of 'the Haig-mind', which, in his bovine metaphor, could chew on the cud of habit, but never in a million years digest or convert it into new forms. The Haig-mind had presided over endless unnecessary slaughter during the Great War, and now Fuller and his fellow mechanizers confronted the same thick-headed positivism as a 'military dictatorship' cramping all their post-war endeavours.[32] As Fuller wrote in the opening pages of his book *The Reformation of War* (1923), 'the man who never changes his mind has mineralized his intellect. He is but a walking stone . . . he will shatter with dynamite – and it is with dynamite I intend to work.'

Fuller could claim certain licence as the former 'brain' of Bermicourt, but it was still provocatively abstract of him to insist, so soon after the end of that most bloody conflict, that modern wars were 'in the main, progressive in value, for they sweep aside obsolete laws and customs which have lost their meaning'.[33] The tank may have started out modestly, as a bullet-proof wire-crushing machine, or a 'mobile trench', but Fuller used his pen to lift it away from the carnage that had attended its progress through the war, and to relaunch it as a tried and tested strategic concept. In order to establish this radical break in the history of warfare, he gathered evidence proving that it had indeed been the tank that finally demoralized the German Army in 1918. He would cite General von Zwehl, who had said: 'It was not the genius of Marshal Foch that defeated us, but "General Tank".'[34] He would eventually also make similar use of a passage from the German veteran Erich Maria Remarque's book, *All Quiet on the Western Front*:

From a mockery the tanks have become a terrible weapon. Armoured, they come rolling on in long lines, and more than anything else embody for us the horror of war. We do not see the guns that bombard us; the attacking lines of enemy infantry are men like ourselves; but these tanks are machines, their caterpillars run on as endless as the war, they are annihilation, they roll without feeling into craters and climb up again without stopping, a fleet of roaring, smoke-belching, armour-clad, invulnerable steel beasts squashing the dead and the wounded – we shrink up in our thin skin before them, against their colossal weight our arms are sticks of straw and our hand-grenades matches.[35]

No longer a vile blood-smeared metal box floundering about in the mud like 'Mac' Francis's Enchantress (or, for that matter, the machine that Fuller once saw upended in a trench system called 'The Harp' near Vimy Ridge, with its decapitated driver still in his seat[36]), the tank became a sleek justification for the revolutionary new theory of warfare that Fuller went on to derive from the famous 'moral effect' of the new weapon. The tank's ability to strike terror into the heart of the civilian rioter or the enemy soldier, was indicative of a more general fact, namely that 'the ultimate foundations of a nation's strength are to be sought in the morale of its people, their self-sacrifice and willingness to see the war through'. This morale, as Fuller would write in the early thirties, is 'the soul of government, and when a government is deprived of it, it becomes a corpse'.

The war of morale was to be fought with new 'scientific' weapons – the aeroplane, which would fly over armies and naval fleets to 'attack the civil nerve and will directly',[37] poison gas, and tanks, which should be large 'armoured batteries' rather than light 'tankettes' of the cheap and nasty kind that cost-cutting politicians might prefer. The military of the future would seek to compel by 'terror' rather than 'destruction', an altogether less bloody prospect since Fuller was convinced that few civil populations would have the will to withstand even the thought of its new weapons. This was the abiding and hygienic lesson of Cambrai: 'To attack the nerves of an army, and through its nerves the will of its commander, is more profitable than battering to pieces the bodies of its men.'[38] Indeed, 'we may predict that the power to effect physical destruction, which reached its zenith during the World

War, will gradually and increasingly be replaced by attempts to demoralize the will of the enemy in its several forms, and so not only disorganize his armies but unnerve his people'.

By championing new weapons of the sort that pacifists and disarmers were so keen to get banned by the new League of Nations, Fuller insisted that he was actually trying to cleanse war, to raise it 'little by little, from the cock-pit of the physical struggle into the spheres of intellectual and moral conflict'.[39] In the new 'scientific' era heralded by the battles of Cambrai and Amiens, war could be purged of the 'destructive mania' exemplified by the carnage of the Western Front and carried over in the punitive approach to Germany demanded under the Treaty of Versailles: 'the idea that an enemy must be destroyed is only legitimate when it leads to a profitable state of peacefulness. Thus, should the enemy be an uncultured barbarian, his removal may in certain circumstances be a benefit to mankind; should he, however, belong to a cultured race, that is should he be useful to the world, then his slaughter, even if unavoidable, must be considered unfortunate, and if avoidable – criminal.'[40] As an engine of demoralization rather than outright destruction, the tank was perfectly adjusted to what Fuller took to be the defining virtue of the British Empire, namely its proven ability to 'establish domestic peace by the threat rather than the application of armed force'.[41]

Fuller was not alone in arguing that the scientific reformation of warfare was on the side of humanity, and, in particular, of the common soldier who had been so lucky to survive the carnage of the Western Front. On 4 February 1923, the members of a society called 'The Heretics' at Cambridge University were addressed by J. B. S. Haldane, the rising Marxist scientist who was then Sir William Dunn Reader in Bio-Chemistry. Haldane's topic was 'Science and the Future'. In his opening words, Haldane drew on his own experience of the recent war to indicate how that cataclysm had converted science into a terrifying 'DemoGorgon' that seemed, in the public mind, to turn man into its victim and servant. The blurred but representative 'scene' that Haldane evoked from the war (in which he himself had been wounded) was filled with fumes, shell bursts and great 'black and yellow masses of smoke which seem to be tearing up the surface of the earth and disintegrating the works of man with an almost visible hatred'. The few men who still appeared in the middle distance scurried about looking 'irrelevant' and impossibly frail or could be seen 'running, with mad terror in their eyes, from gigantic steel slugs, which were deliberately, relentlessly, and successfully pursuing them'.[42]

It was against this perception that Haldane set out to rehabilitate the idea of science as the means whereby man would extend his dominion over nature. He insisted, as Fuller himself was doing, that scientific weapons were far less murderous than supposedly 'humane' weapons such as bayonets, shells, and incendiary bombs; and claimed, in the course of defending chemical warfare, that 'lachrymatory gas' was actually 'the most humane weapon ever invented'.[43] Haldane's faith in the scientific future would be questioned by Bertrand Russell, the former conscientious objector who argued that, without the emergence of some kind of 'world government', science actually threatened 'to cause the destruction of our civilization'.[44] But Haldane had different opponents in mind. He struck out against pacifists and the 'complete and shameful ignorance' of politicians and the 'less competent' soldiers who supported the banning of poisonous gas. He also denounced 'one of the most hideous forms of sentimentalism which has ever supported evil upon earth – the attachment of the professional soldier to cruel and obsolete killing machines'; and lampooned the hidebound mentality that lay behind the British Army's recent decision to cease instructing every soldier in defence against hostile gas – allegedly because the fitting of respirators 'did not form the basis of a satisfactory drill, like those curious relics of eighteenth-century musketry which still occupy so much of the time of our recruits'.[45]

Fuller, who was far from a university man, chose a different ally. He pursued his version of the scientific 'Reformation of War' in correspondence with Captain Basil Liddell Hart, whom he quickly won over to the cause of mechanization, which the two of them would promote so tirelessly over the years to come. Liddell Hart, who was later to be enormously influential as a journalist with the *Daily Telegraph* and *The Times,* opened the correspondence in June 1920, having read Fuller's prize-winning essay on 'The Application of Recent Developments in Mechanics and Other Scientific Knowledge to Preparation and Training for Future War on Land', published, to the considerable dismay of many military readers, in that May's issue of the *Journal of the Royal United Services Institution.* Liddell Hart was then employed with the Army Education Scheme and preparing a new version of the manual on infantry training. Having previously trained infantrymen for the Western Front, he was as keen as Fuller on restoring mobility to the battlefield but, before he absorbed Fuller's influence, his idea of infiltration was to be implemented by infantry rather than tanks.

Fuller and Liddell Hart began their correspondence with an argument about the density of Clausewitz's notorious 'Fog of War'. Liddell Hart had sent Fuller a couple of articles, to which he answered: 'I think you have made rather too much of "the Fog of War", by converting it into a pitch darkness. The "Fog of War" very frequently does not exist at all or is, at most, but a thin mist.'[46] It could be dispersed by an effective intelligence service and also, as Fuller would argue repeatedly over the years, by the application of the properly conceived 'principles of war' – as defined in a lecture on 'The Science of War' that Fuller enclosed with his letter.

Having read Fuller's creed, Liddell Hart fell at the master's feet: 'If you will permit me to say so, it is the forerunner of the dawn of a new age in military thought – the product of an "organized" brain which has hitherto been entirely lacking in all British military writing and more even abroad.'[47] Fuller was the prophet of a new approach: 'All past students of war seem to have lost themselves in the complexities of war, and tried to work downwards from the complex, instead of upwards from, the simple and elemental.' And so they went on, with Liddell Hart hardly daring 'to couple my humble self with you', but doing so nonetheless and converting to the tank after Fuller had questioned his idea of 'expanding the torrent' with infantry on the grounds that, for as long as supplies were tied to roads, it would remain 'practically impossible to exploit penetration'. Fuller affirmed, for the benefit of his new follower, that the recent war had indeed shown that the new scientific weapons worked as much by moral effect as by actual destruction, with 'the fear of tanks upsetting the enemy as much as their killing power'. Welcoming his young convert to join him in the battle against military bureaucracy, he warned him that he should not expect to win any military essay prizes for his efforts. ('You should have proved that men on donkeys armed with bows and arrows will win the next war.')[48]

Fuller and Liddell Hart made a formidable duo over the years to come. As outriding spokesmen for the radical mechanizing wing of the Royal Tank Corps, they became, as even a hostile and debunking historian has acknowledged, 'the two most influential British military writers of the twentieth century'.[49] They pressed the case for mechanization using the pages of diverse newspapers as well as personal connections with senior generals, politicians and civil servants. As partisan historians of Britain's tank effort, they were also responsible for writing the accounts that came to be widely accepted as the impartial record of their own endeavours.

Liddell Hart would later exaggerate such differences as may have existed between them in order to present himself as the most influential advocate of mechanization[50], but Fuller was the first and most thoroughgoing exponent of the new vision. Contemptuous of the military conservatives who would only concede that tanks could be a useful adjunct to existing cavalry and infantry units, he insisted that the new weapons actually heralded the death of both cavalry and infantry, or at best their relegation to subsidiary roles. Petrol would replace muscle-power as the motive force, and the old warfare of attrition would give way to one founded on speed and mobility. The old army founded on the idea of mass would give way to a smaller but infinitely more forceful one based on power, and the war of the line would be succeeded by one in which 'area' was all-important – perhaps not a 'Cubist' war in Picasso's sense, but certainly one that required three-dimensional rather than linear tactics that would, as Fuller later put it, be 'developed in cubic spaces'.[51] This reformed approach to warfare was 'rooted in respect for the common man as soldier'.[52] There would be no room for frontal attacks of the sort still so fatally and stupidly advocated in Britain's Field Service Regulations.

Such was Fuller's contribution. He may have balked at the idea of actually commanding the Experimental Mechanized Force, but as the leading advocate of its cause, Fuller gazed out at the troublespots of the post-war world, and prescribed fleets of hypothetical tanks as their remedy: tanks in the event of another continental war breaking out; tanks to dissolve communism, and overawe rioters and strikers at home; tanks maintaining order throughout the Empire, securing defiles along the North-west Frontier and terrifying troublesome natives so effectively that there would be neither need nor excuse for primitive massacres like the one committed with Indian troops at Amritsar in 1919. He, more than anyone else, also established the tone in which the cause of mechanization was debated in the twenties and thirties, casting it in curiously futuristic and theoretical terms and identifying it with an often violently expressed assault on the attitudes of a military establishment whose idiocy he never ceased to excoriate. Fuller once explained his rhetorical purpose by remarking that, while his ideas might indeed turn out to have been exaggerated and wrong, they would at least 'cast doubt upon many of our present certainties, and so establish problems which cannot be shelved'.[53]

Fuller was the tank's first philosopher, a determined transgressor of habituated assumption whose writing seems disconcerting to this day – an unstable amalgam of wisdom and folly, of prescience, eccentricity and sheer wickedness. This is a man who imagined a great future for tracked vehicles in the colonies, which he apparently expected to remain roadless for all time;[54] and who, as a would-be arms trader in the mid-nineteen-thirties, got quite carried away by the idea of tanks that would dazzle their enemies with powerful Canal Defence lights.[55] Some of his enthusiasms are easily cited as proof of eccentricity, but real insights are threaded through even his most hare-brained speculations. Long before anyone dreamed up 'smart' munitions, Fuller insisted that wireless technology would eventually extend to the the transmission of power rather than just words, thereby making it possible to achieve the apparently magical outcome of operating machines from a distance. By eliminating time and space, wireless would open the way to 'a kind of metaphysical war' in which man-controlled weapons might well be replaced by 'the wireless controlled robot'.[56] Gazing, scientifically or just crazily, into the future, Fuller insisted that 'the vision of a fleet of tanks based on the Kent and Sussex coasts and operating in France or Belgium without first having to be transported by ship is by no means a fantastic one'.[57] As for the persistent difficulty of landing British forces on the European continent, Fuller solved that by picking up a whaling ship and twisting it about until it would work as a disgorger of equally notional landing craft – 'a self-propelled vessel, not exactly a tank, but a hybrid between a tank and a boat, that is to say a vessel which can propel itself through the water and move on land. Such a machine would look, I expect, like a small tracked submarine . . .'[58]

Fuller also provided a blueprint of the 'New Model Army' he imagined being built up around the scientific weapons of the future. Mechanization might destroy work in factories but the military authorities, if they followed his advice, could turn this sow's ear into a silk purse that was nicely fitted to post-war economic and political realities: 'The only way to attain both smallness and power combined is through mechanization.'[59] Unlike the 'conscript hordes' of the Great War, the new mechanized army would be an elite body that relied primarily on voluntary and professional soldiers. It would encourage long service, from three to thirty years, and give its soldiers greater responsibility and freedom. A technological army of leaders rather than followers, it would demand individual initiative at all levels and certainly not just the obedient application of predetermined method: 'What does a power-war, a war of machines demand of the fighting man? High intelligence in understanding the machines; self-reliance in their use, and freedom to obtain from them, in all the uncertain circumstances of war, the highest output of tactical effort.'[60] None of this would be achieved by the traditional methods of enforced 'close-order drill' or obligatory attendance at Church.[61] A liberal in matters of morale and training, Fuller wanted the army of the future to provide more education for its soldiers, recommending service schools and the provision of married quarters too. Smaller and yet more forceful than a conventional army, the mechanized army of the future could also be expected to suffer lower casualties: during the Great War casualty rates among infantry had been fractionally under 20 per cent but, so Fuller asserted, the Tank Corps had the lowest ratio of all at 12.58 per cent.

Fuller insisted repeatedly on the 'common sense' of his arguments, but he was peddling strange and hypothetical stuff and it is hardly surprising that it should have met strong opposition from soldiers who preferred to keep their boots on muddy ground. A full-scale assault on the arguments advanced by Fuller and his junior follower Liddell Hart was mounted in 1927 by Victor Wallace Germains, a former infantryman who normally wrote under the pen-name 'A Rifleman'. In a book called The "Mechanization" of War, Germains condemned Fuller for his 'absorption in technique', and for trying to pass off what was actually no more than a 'smoke cloud of verbiage' as a 'science of war'.[62] Mocking his 'ludicrous' suggestion that a new era of warfare was opened by the tank advance at Amiens on 8 August 1918, he suggested that the all-powerful tanks of Fuller's description were actually as imaginary as the Behemoths of the 1916 war correspondents: 'How many readers of the press accounts of these actions, picturing the tank as a swiftly moving steel-clad monster, itself invulnerable to the enemy's shot and shell, mowing down German infantry and gunners like corn, have any conception of the frightful truth: that the percentage of loss sustained by the tanks themselves exceeded the percentage of loss sustained by the infantry and artillery who accompanied them, and far exceeded the percentage of losses which they inflicted upon the enemy!'[63]

Admitting nothing but contempt for Fuller's claims that the pre-scientific generals of the Great War indulged in 'Witches' Sabbaths' and 'Black Masses' and 'saw things as cows see them',[64] Germains repudiated his suggestion that it was the 'moral effect' of Allied tanks that had broken the German enemy. He provided detailed rebuttals of the victories Fuller claimed for the tank – Cambrai ended in disaster as the Germans struck back, and the so-called tank victory at Amiens was, he insisted, won by infantry and artillery. Indeed, 'it is a fact commonly overlooked, that the greatest service of the tank at the Battle of Amiens, was less direct than indirect: so soon as it appeared it acted as a magnet, drawing upon itself the hostile fire, and thus covering the attacking infantry.' As an advocate of the infantry that these 'Arch-Pontiffs of the tank'[65] sought to abolish, Germains scoffed at the 'fetish' that Fuller and other mechanizers had made of the naval analogy. Their idea of bringing naval tactics on to land was as ridiculous as taking a great warship like the *Royal Sovereign* and mounting her on caterpillar tracks: 'Our Royal Sovereign, once ashore, is going to present a target which no gunner can possibly miss. It is much the same thing as if St. Paul's Cathedral were to come rolling down upon you. Keep your head and you can't help hitting it.'[66]

These hostilities, which raged right up into the late thirties, quite overwhelmed the possibility of rational debate. In the words of Barton C. Hacker, who has reviewed this battle as it raged and spluttered through the pages of British military journals, 'the whole tenor of the arguments both for and against mechanization confirms that a good deal more was at stake than merely how tanks should be used in a future war'.[67] The advocates of mechanization pursued their crusade with a quasi-religious ardour. Describing themselves as 'prophets' and 'apostles', they promulgated a 'doctrine' which knew no half measures, and which assumed that their opponents were blinkered donkeys stuck in the 'agricultural' phase of warfare. The opponents of mechanization were equally inclined to denunciation – deploring the 'mad outpourings', fanaticism and 'communistic tendencies' of the mechanizers and resenting their 'intrusive machines'.

Marked by the strong emotional investment of its advocates, the cause of mechanization was an intoxicating distillate of 'esprit de tank' as it had become manifest in the Great War. Its futuristic vision was sourced partly in the outlaw camaraderie of the young and irregular new corps and partly in the glamour and impersonal power of the new machine, with its apparently inexorable movement and its promise of a radical new tactics. Barton C. Hacker is probably right to insist that the doctrine of mechanization was also shaped by the unstable juxtaposition of sex and violence in the symbolism of the tank: a curiously ambivalent, even androgynous machine which combined male attributes like hardness, thrust and penetration with the feminine security to be found within Old Mother Hubbard's protective metal skirts.

The weird theoretical brew that was mechanization between the wars may seem strange enough to justify the suspicions of those military historians who have recently taken up the battle against the leading 'Apostles of Mobility': hunting down their errors and deceptions, trying to minimize their influence over subsequent history, and generally condemning them in the harshest terms. Liddell Hart has been revealed as a dishonest historian who cooked the books (especially those written by defeated German generals), partly in order to exaggerate his influence as the founder of the blitzkrieg, and partly to cover up his own responsibility for Britain's failure to arm against Hitler in the late nineteen-thirties.[68] Fuller has also been condemned as a self-aggrandizing wild man – wholly unjustified in his assaults on the Allied generals of the Great War, culpably detached from practical reality in his futuristic dogmas and speculations, and probably a coward too.[69] His Plan 1919 has been rubbished as an irresponsible fantasy and his insistence on the naval analogy is claimed to have bound the Royal Tank Corps to the 'ill-advised' course of trying to perfect shooting on the move: a 'pernicious' tactic that made accuracy 'virtually impossible' but which British armoured forces are said to have carried into the Second World War to their cost.[70] Fuller's project invites criticism, but the vehemence of some recent condemnations suggests a process closer to denial.

There may certainly have been a 'dark side' to Fuller's character,[71] but his story also casts a disconcertingly revealing light on the roots of modern warfare. In its doctrinal zeal, its invocations of 'science' and its unmixed contempt for convention and tradition, Fuller's mechanizing vision reaches back through the Great War and into an Edwardian past that, though dislocated by events and tactfully (or perhaps tactically) buried by Fuller himself, continued to shape his thinking for the rest of his life. To the extent that it owes anything to this lineage, the rise of the tank and its transformative tactics speak less of 'science' than of magic, and the malign fall of an early-twentieth-century dream of a new world order founded on reason. Having seen Egbert raising funds in Trafalgar Square, the American poet John Gould Fletcher, described the tank as the 'new God' for which the age had been craving.[72] Yet in J. F. C. Fuller's mental world it was the whole philosophy of mechanized warfare, rather than just the machine itself, that had been foreshadowed by the eccentric divinity of a noisily proclaimed 'New Religion'.

The Secret Imprint of the Great Beast

One day in 1921 a grubby and crumpled envelope arrived on Fuller's desk at the War Office. This missive had been brought by hand from Sicily, and Fuller may be imagined opening it with the apprehensive curiosity of one who already suspected he was facing the return of a repressed and perhaps inconvenient past. Scrawled under a heraldic letterhead reading *Collegium ad Spiritum Sanctum*, this communication invited Fuller to take up arms in a battle of altogether greater significance than the ongoing struggle for mechanization.

My dear Fuller,
   Do what thou wilt shall be the whole of the Law.
   Your friendship stands out as the best thing in my life of that kind.
   We were mules to let envious monkeys manoeuvre us into dissension. I know it was mostly the fault of my silly pride.
   The Crowned Child needs a Warrior to command the armies of Liberty: thou art the man.
   Love is the law, love under will.

The letter was signed: 'Your old friend and comrade. The Beast 666 9=2 A∴ A∴.'[1]
   Fuller may have held this curiously encrypted document at arm's length, but he knew how to decode its smallest detail. 'The Beast' was Aleister Crowley, the notorious occultist, traitor and perverted Behemoth of popular legend. The numbers 666 identified him with the anti-Christ, while 9=2 indicated that he had by now awarded himself the superhuman grade of Magus as defined by the spiritual hierarchies of the Argentum Astrum, a hermetic order signified by the letters A∴ A∴. 'The Crowned Child' was Horus, the Egyptian god of war; and Cefalu, whence the letter had been carried, was the place in Sicily where Crowley had his 'Abbey of Thelema' – actually a filthy, box-like house with an improvised altar and sexually explicit paintings on the wall. Fuller will have recognized 'Do what thou wilt shall be the whole of the law' as the founding principle of Thelema, according to

which Crowley engaged in unconventional acts of 'sex magic' involving himself, a male goat and his priestess, the 'Scarlet Woman'. He may not have known that, while feeding his doped acolytes 'cakes of light' made with human excrement, Crowley was by now also insisting that, in order to suppress petty egoism and to reach the deeper principle of 'Will' beneath, they must cut their own forearms with a razor every time they uttered the word 'I'.[2]

Fuller filed this letter away unanswered, and returned to his tanks. The next advance from this esoteric recruitment officer was dated 18 April 1922. Marked 'Private and Personal', it arrived at the War Office by conventional post from Paris: 'Demanding an oracle concerning you I received: "Before! Hold! Raise the spell of Ra . . ."' After trying an implausible appeal to Fuller's patriotism ('It is time for those who love England . . .'), Crowley returned to the oracle: 'Now, it says "I will give you a war engine . . . For you have been picked out long since as C-in-C of the armies of Ra Hoor Khuit."'

Though frustrated at the War Office, Fuller was tempted neither by this promise of an occult replacement for the cancelled Medium D, nor by the offer of a new posting as chief of staff to the ancient Egyptian god of war. Eventually, in May 1922, Crowley called at the War Office in person, but Fuller kept his distance, sending a messenger to the door with a scrap of paper on which he had scribbled: 'Nothing Doing!' Crowley's last letter is dated 13 May 1922: 'True: NOTHING is doing. That is why I am here.' He had been summoned to Fuller as 'a great man wasted', and their personal quarrel should be set aside: 'The world demands that her most important minds should co-operate at this crisis . . . You cannot avoid your destiny any more than I could mine. You must ride the wave, or be swept away by it.'

Crowley saw the world through a bewildering haze of heroin, occult science and megalomania, but he had a precise operation in mind for Colonel Fuller. He wanted the world's leading tank theorist to walk with him to Egypt, where they would 'abstract' an ancient wooden stele of the twenty-sixth dynasty from the Cairo Museum and then carry it off to Scotland. This 'Stele of Revealing' had been a central prop in the 'Great Revelation' Crowley claimed to have experienced in 1904, a mystical enlightenment that had, so he believed, ushered in the new Aeon of Horus and established Crowley as its esoteric governor and prophet. Having pinched the stele, the pair would take it to Boleskine House, near Loch Ness. Many years previously, Crowley had withdrawn here in order to carry out magical ceremonies, and he was apparently convinced that both he and the aeon could be put back on course if only Fuller would co-operate in this bizarre act of cosmic engineering. As he noted, 'Fuller's main task is to bring me back to health by means of this journey.'[3]

Starting out as a rationalist

Fuller was not to join Aleister Crowley or the crazed remnants of his esoteric band of followers, preferring instead to confine his powers of clairvoyance to descrying the mechanized army of the future. Yet before the Great War in which he became known as a tank theorist and prophet of mechanization, Fuller had been Crowley's first disciple – an incontrovertible fact that, even though it was an admitted source of Fuller's reputation as a 'brain' at Bermicourt, has since stood as a something of a poser for the historians of armoured warfare.

Fuller first came into contact with Crowley in 1905, when he was a twenty-six-year-old lieutenant with the 1st Battalion of the Oxfordshire Light Infantry. He had grown up in a clerical family (his father was the rector of Ichenor, near Chichester) and, after quitting public school for a London crammer, managed to squeeze into Sandhurst, despite his diminutive physical stature. He had fought in South Africa during the Boer War, but in 1903 his regiment had been posted to India – Ambala, the Simla Hills and then Lucknow, where he had time on his hands. Housed in a bungalow with five other officers whose needs were serviced by a total of fifty-four servants, Fuller was free to pursue his own interests.[4] His fellow officers preferred sport and carousing, but Fuller had higher concerns. He pored over the Bible, although not in the spirit of a believer; and he also explored Eastern philosophy and religions. Fuller would eventually conclude: 'All foreigners are niggers to the English,' but that was not his position in those early days.[5] He studied the Vedas and Upanishads, developing what was to become a lifelong interest in Yoga, and prevailed upon his native language tutor to introduce him to various yogis, holy men and 'advanced radicals' connected with religious movements that were then encouraging a break with medievalism, and thereby also stimulating Indian nationalism. In this way Fuller came into contact with the Hindu Arya Samaj, a religious and national movement inspired by the Vedas, and also with the Muslim Ahmidayyah movement.[6] As a budding man of letters he also found time to write florid poems on spiritual themes.

Fuller had been identified as a heretic and probable atheist by his fellows while still at Sandhurst and his new studies were grafted on to a well-established stock of militantly anti-Christian rationalism. Persuaded that the new twentieth century promised an enlightened break with tradition, he read freethinking publications like the *Agnostic Journal and Eclectic Review*, a weekly periodical edited from a house in Brixton by a certain 'Saladin' (actually W. Stewart Ross), which sustained a relentless assault on 'J. Christ' and the whole edifice of Christianity – condemned as the irrational child of a remote and ancient era of 'Ignorance, Credulity and Superstition'.[7] 'By persistent chicanery', so Saladin wrote, 'the clerics can still make an easy and dishonest living out of it; and the State is still under the impression that, to keep the people governable, it is well to keep them superstitious and ignorant.'[8] There was no quarter for the Salvation Army either – indeed, 'Saladin' held 'General Booth's Army Manoeuvres' in special contempt.[9]

By the beginning of 1905 Fuller had joined Saladin's iconoclastic assault on the religion in which he had been raised. In the issue for 21 January, Saladin included a message for 'J. F. C. F., Lucknow' in his 'To Correspondents' column: 'Your cordial letter cheers us. We feel deeply grateful to you for your enthusiastic and disinterested hostility to Priestcraft.' In April Saladin published an article by the twenty-six-year-old soldier; entitled 'Divine and other Carnage', it quoted repeatedly from the Old Testament prophets in order to reveal Jahweh to have been a bloody and brutal God, and then carried the accusation forward to the New Testament ('generally speaking, less Christ, less cruelty, less redemption, less bloodshed'). Fuller links his assault on 'Jehovah, the bloody', with an apparently vegetarian blast against the evils of meat-eating – exemplified by the Chicago stockyards, where millions of cattle, sheep and hogs were slaughtered every year in the cruellest manner. All this was the fault of the Christian deity: 'Oh lord, thou didst redeem the world by the blood of thine only son, when a little more bread-and-butter was all the world needed.'[10]

'Deep have we drunk of the cup of thy fury; it is time to dash it to the ground' – along with all the other 'symbols of an untutored age'. That was Fuller's defiant message to the God of his father and, even at this early stage, his tutorial against the sedimented ignorance of the Christian era was delivered in the name of science as well as reason. Later that year, Fuller began a series of articles under the title of 'Bible Science'. Having spent many hours combing the Bible for choice examples of superstitious idiocy, he now exhibited these, carefully citing chapter and verse as he pegged them out along the straightening line of his own contempt. With its wandering stars and blood-red moons, Bible astronomy was 'a mass of myth, fable and fiction'.[11] Bible biology and physiology were utterly ludicrous, starting with the story of how God, having scraped Adam together out of a few handfuls of dust, then extracted a rib and '"Abracadabra!" a woman stood smiling by his side'.[12] 'Sancto simplicas!' mutters Fuller before going on to expose the follies of Bible pathology and medicine, dismissed as 'quackery of the most absurd kind'.[13] There could be no doubt that 'where Ignorance reigns, her subjects grovel in the fantastic, and wallow deep in the grotesque . . .'

Such were the already sharply polarized attitudes of the young subaltern who one day that year had picked up the March issue of the *Literary Guide and Rationalist Review*. Like the *Agnostic Journal*, this publication served a network of freethinking organizations that revolved around the Rationalist Press Association. These included comparatively well-established entities such as the South Place Ethical Society at Conway Hall in London, and also many more fugitive projects like the library for rationalist and 'simple life' publications opened that year at a private house at 10 Cazenove Road, North Hackney. Much influenced by Ernst Haeckel's evolutionary conception of humanity, the *Literary Guide* hoped that the twentieth century would see the dawning of a 'new social order', a secular enlightenment in which credulous faith would be replaced by the 'free exercise of individual intellect', in which women would be emancipated and co-operation would triumph over primitive competition.

In its battles with the Church, the *Literary Guide* was firmly on the side of heresy yet, in that issue of 1 March 1905, it still expressed reservations about Aleister Crowley's privately published booklet *Why Jesus Wept*. The anonymous reviewer declared that 'this strange mingling of ribaldry, indecency, poetry, and wit could be perpetrated by no other but Mr Crowley; and certainly no other author would issue, under his own name, such a ruthless violation of conventionality'.[14] It was conceivable that 'electric shocks of this nature may prove beneficial in some cases' but 'Mr Crowley's rampant virility' did not always 'take a commendable turn' and, quite frankly, 'the manner in which he advertises his wares is to be deprecated'.

All this may have confirmed Crowley's growing suspicion that the freethinking rationalism with which he had so far been happy to go along was 'narrow-minded', 'suburban' and 'prudishly exclusive' too.[15] It certainly intrigued Fuller, who read this 'short notice' at Lucknow and wrote for a copy of the offending pamphlet. When it arrived, he found more self-advertisement inside – a leaflet in which Crowley offered the considerable sum of £100 for the best essay on his own poetical works, as they were published in a new 'Traveller's Edition'. As a young officer without significant private means, Fuller had already engaged in diverse adventures in order to augment his military salary, from gambling to cattle dealing in South Africa. He wrote for the necessary books and, in late June 1905, received a reply from the Drum Druid Hotel in Darjeeling, where Crowley was preparing to lead his disastrous climbing expedition to the previously unscaled Himalayan peak of Kangchenjunga. The books arrived not long afterwards and Fuller was soon submitting his own literary endeavours for the master's comment, elaborately structured and mellifluous affairs, on which Crowley was happy to bestow every benefit of the doubt: 'I like your poem & essay very much, though in the former you have attempted the impossible. At least nobody so far has even mastered that metre, which (to my ear) genuinely requires a genuine dactyl in the first part of each line . . .'[16]

In April 1906 Fuller, who had been suffering from enteric fever, was ordered back to London for a year's sick leave; and it was that August, at the Hotel Cecil on the Strand, that he and Crowley met for the first time. Years later, Crowley described the outlook they shared. They felt nothing but contempt for the Christian status quo but were 'absolutely opposed' to the idea of social revolution: 'we deplored the fact that our militant atheists were not aristocrats like Bolinbroke. We had no use for the sordid slum writers and Hyde Park ranters who had replaced the aristocratic infidel of the past.' Their friendship and growing collaboration have left an often bizarre correspondence to puzzle the military historians. The pair sometimes discussed literary matters, but their letters also pull the reader into an unfamiliar world of spells and incantations, of hallucinations and seances in which swastikas are seen flying through the air, of hermetic conspiracies and rituals of a most disconcerting kind. On 8 November 1906, Crowley wrote to warn Fuller: 'You must be careful – you left a devil behind you last Sunday that came within an ace of killing me! It had a sharp pointed beak (curved) no eyes, no arms or wings, no legs but a single tapering tail, balanced on a rounded piece of its own excrement . . . for some minutes I really thought as if it was all over for me.' Could this mean, as Fuller's military biographer has conjectured rather nervously, that the young captain had left a drawing behind? Fuller was certainly adept with a pencil and, as an adept of a different kind, would contribute many symbolic drawings to the literature of 'Crowleyanity'. But the cause of mechanization is not so easily saved from its esoteric background.

New era Mark I

Completed not long after that meeting at the Hotel Cecil, Captain Fuller's essay on the works of Aleister Crowley was written in close collaboration with its hero and subject. Crowley reviewed the possible titles ('"The Sphinx of the West" would do. So would "Thelema". But I think the Star is best . . .'), and sketched out the hermetically lettered design he considered appropriate for the cover. Crowley would later recall that his young admirer was 'not in the least inclined to accept any theories that might invoke belief of any kind in a spiritual hierarchy'.[17] But despite this reluctance ('He fought with me, hand to hand, week after week, about the question of Magick'), Crowley still managed to persuade Fuller to include a final chapter on his magical doctrines. Fuller won the prize, although it is by no means certain either that there were any other applicants or that Crowley, who was already approaching the end of the considerable personal fortune he had spent sampling the world's esoteric traditions and promoting himself as a flamboyant practitioner of magick, ever quite got round to handing over the promised £100. He did, however, secure the essay's publication as *The Star in the West*.

Fuller's biographer may prefer to describe it as a 'slender pamphlet'[18], but *The Star in the West* is actually a substantial 327–page book in which Fuller sets out to expound the master's philosophy under the name of 'Crowleyanity' – partly 'leg-pull', as Fuller would claim somewhat defensively sixty years later, 'but the greater part a serious attempt to fathom it'.[19] Surviving letters go some way towards justifying Fuller's claim to scepticism. On 25 May 1908 Crowley wrote to chide him for doubting 'true occultism' and insisting that, while in the future Fuller could 'always say you were pulling my leg and go to church', for him, Crowley, it was 'Crowleyanity or nothing'. Yet at the time of writing, some two years earlier, Fuller had been enthusiastic about providing other questing acolytes with 'a twisted clue of silk and hemp to guide them safely through labyrinthine mysteries of poetry and magic'. The 'leg-pull' was not forceful; indeed, earnest readers could hardly be blamed for missing it entirely, even when Fuller observes: 'It has taken 100,000,000 years to produce Aleister Crowley.'[20]

Fuller opens by commending Crowley's concentrated assault on Christianity. He gladly reiterates the diabolical inversion through which Crowley declared Satan to be the true God, condemning Christianity as a life-denying creed guilty of 'emparadising the cavernous depths of Hell'. A philosopher might recognize this reversal as a 'radicalization of evil' and place it in the tradition of Nietzsche; but Crowley had first opted for Satan against the 'Christ' of his Plymouth Brethren parents, and he had since gathered diverse esoteric precedents around this juvenile gesture, including the example of the fifteenth-century Kabbalist Pico Della Mirandola. Fuller may well have learned of other examples of this kind of inversion in India where, in the decades before Independence, the British government was often denounced as 'Satanic' by its Moslem opponents.[21] However, it was Crowley's anti-Christian version that he followed. Priests, as Fuller wrote, had only 'cramped the human mind' and the prayers uttered in England's churches were nothing but 'the misdirected energy of idiots'. The soul had to be won back from this dismal gibberish: 'by soul we naturally do not mean a haloed fowl, strumming dithyrambs on a harp, or the mere doppelganger of the living: but that inner power of good and evil, which lies latent in self . . .'[22]

Although 'Crowleyanity' was actually a superior morality, it was bound to appear fundamentally immoral to those whose minds were infected with Christianity. As Captain Fuller argued, the historical 'law of all form' commits the majority view to outdated attitudes and conventions: 'Man being inherently Lazy, and hence conservative, this power is forever reacting on him, and binding him down to a government unsuited to his times, and it is this power that he has chosen to call – the Moral Code.'[23] Born free, man 'conceived law and solicitors'. He dug 'deep trenches around his joys', and then proceeded to fill them with 'tears of exasperation'.

Against the sickening hypocrisy of bourgeois Christendom, Crowley is raised up as the genius whose 'war against poetic form'[24] makes him the true inheritor of the rebellion of Shelley and Swinburne. Fuller would insist on this until the end of his life – that Crowley was a great lyric poet even if he had also written some 'swill'.[25] In this early book, however, the swill remained undiagnosed and the Crowleyan poem is celebrated as an instrument of manoeuvre in a battle that went far beyond conventional matters of literary form: 'A poetic iconoclast to the very back bone, we find Crowley, especially in his later works, breaking away from every poetic convention and constraint.'[26] In emerging Modernist circles, poets would soon be throwing off rhyme and strict metre, dismissing that kind of verse as tinkling stuff that would eventually find appropriate refuge in children's books and tank poems ('Clankity Clankity Clankity Clank! / Ankylosaurus was built like a Tank . . .').[27] But the poems with which Crowley set out to engineer 'sudden reversals' in conventional and habituated thought were not in the least bit inclined in that direction. To be considered as poetry all verse 'must be musical', insists Fuller. In praising Crowley's 'Sword of Song', 'in which our ears are assailed by the most monstrous diversity of noises', he treats the ornate and mellifluously rhyming stanza as if it were an advancing war machine breaking up mediocre settlements of thought, clattering over those dismal 'trenches' behind which man has isolated his joys and, in its eroticism, restoring a certain warm-blooded mobility to 'this ice-bound age of frozen phalli'.

Coming to this book in the knowledge of Fuller's later concerns, it is scarcely possible not to see the Crowleyan poem as a prefigurative, tank-like apparatus. The adept who is initiated into the secret wisdom of 'Crowleyanity' is similarly charged with bringing movement back into an immobilized world. Aided by soul-loosening narcotics, which seem to conquer time and space, and esoteric traditions that rise up from the ancient past to challenge a present lost to the congealed 'realities' of the 'Moral Code', the adept presses on against all obstacles. In Fuller's rhetoric, the struggle to break through the confines of Christianity, bourgeois morality and mass thought is already halfway between a Pilgrim's Progress and a military advance. The adept straddles trenches, overthows bunkered citadels, and makes his admittedly still unmotorized way through the putrid mire of a degenerate world: 'On, on we plod, through life's byways and alleys, through mud and slime, onward we must go if we are ever to win the gates of Wisdom and Understanding and enter the Kingdom of the Holy Crown.'

Ordeals of a silver star

Having written the approved commentary on the master's poetical works, Fuller overcame his initial misgivings and entered into the closely related world of ceremonial magic. Crowley had started out as Frater Perdurabo, a neophyte in the Hermetic Order of the Golden Dawn. The Golden Dawn's most famous member was W. B. Yeats, the Irish poet who ran the London lodge, but it had been founded by a man called Samuel Liddell Mathers, who based its doctrines on an old alchemical text found at a second-hand book stall in London's Farringdon Road. By the time Fuller met him, Crowley had fallen out with both Mathers and Yeats, who thought he was a maniac ('a quite unspeakable person'), and had founded his own rival assembly, the Argentum Astrum (or Silver Star). Borrowed from the Golden Dawn, the spiritual hierarchy espoused by the A∴ A∴ consisted of a series of grades to be attained by members, the more exalted separated from the lower ones by an ethereal trench known as 'The Abyss'. The whole hierarchy was identified with a fruity mixture of hermetic sources: the Tarot, Rosicrucianism, the Sephirotic tree of life, the magic of Abra-Melin . . . Since the A∴ A∴ required a quiet oratory, Crowley had also rented Boleskine House, near Foyers by Loch Ness. He went there to work on the rituals, while putting his acolytes through gruelling initiations. It is said that Victor Neuburg, a young poet whom Crowley had recruited from a freethinking student circle at Trinity College, Cambridge, had to sleep naked on a bed of gorse for ten freezing winter nights in a row.

Despite his reservations about the 'priestcraft' of Crowley's assembly, Fuller joined this world of strangely coloured robes, ritual invocations and ordeals. Crowley's acolytes would go to church and secretly convert the service into an invocation of Adonai. They would sit motionless for long periods in almost impossible Yoga positions ('Sit: left heel pressing up anus, right foot poised on its toes, the heel covering the phallus, arms stretched out over the knees: head and back straight . . .')[28] They chanted mantras and breathed rigorously through alternate nostrils according to the precepts of Pranayama. They experimented with Crowley's considerable pharmacopeia of soul-loosening drugs: cannabis, opium, angelica and anhalonium Lewinii, the latter being a derivative of the peyotl plant, which Crowley had first come across in Mexico and then, so he asserted, introduced into Europe. Fuller later claimed to have destroyed his papers from this time. However, a sense of the atmosphere is conveyed by the surviving diary of his lifelong friend Meredith Starr, a mystical poet who is unlikely to be rediscovered for his verse ('Oh, the sedges by the river, / How they quiver, quiver quiver'). As Starr writes of a fairly routine night: 'What appeared to be ecstacy. Immunity from physical pain (I stuck pins through the lobes of both ears without feeling any noticeable discomfort). Out of Time and Space . . . Could twist (bend) a penny with thumbs and forefingers. Mesmerised a cat . . . I have passed into the Silence . . . I am immortal . . . omniscient . . . I was Christ . . . I am . . . I will do all I can for humanity . . .'[29]

The Beast had appointed Fuller his principal lieutenant by the time he decided to launch the *Equinox*, a journal that first appeared in March 1909 and was presented as opening 'a completely new adventure in the history of mankind'. Published as 'The Official Organ of the A∴ A∴', this 'Review of Scientific Illuminism' would take the esoteric truth previously known only by 'the Society of the Elect' and release it in leavening doses small enough to be ingested by the dough-like masses. Crowley packaged this esoteric project with countless pages of ranting assault: 'to the greasy bourgeois I preach discontent; I shock him, I stagger him, I cut away earth from under his feet, I turn him upside down, I give him hashish and make him run amok . . .'[30] A massive act of self-publicity on Crowley's part, the *Equinox* enabled him to present himself as the prophet of a new order, and also to continue railing against Mathers and the Golden Dawn, whose most secret ceremonies were now printed for all to see.

The *Equinox* was published from offices near Victoria Station, but its cosmic premises were less modest. By this time, Crowley had reorganized his magical theories around the 'Great Revelation' he claimed to have experienced in Cairo in 1904. He had gone there from Ceylon, taken a flat near the Boulak Museum and started putting himself about as Prince Chio Khan. On 18 March, his wife Rose is said suddenly to have sunk into a cosmic swoon and informed her prince that 'Horus' awaited him. On the next day she had taken Crowley to a nearby museum and gestured at a distant glass case, saying, 'There He is.' Approaching, they found the object that Crowley would, much later, want Fuller to help him carry off to Scotland: a twenty-sixth-dynasty wooden stele, bearing the painted image of Horus as Ra-Hoor-Khuit. This had been proof enough for Crowley, who retreated to the 'temple' prepared in his flat, and with Rose now speaking as Ouarda the Seeress, learned that 'The Equinox of the Gods' had arrived: a new aeon was dawning and he had been chosen as its initiator and necromantic engineer. Then his holy guardian angel appeared and, over three days, dictated the text that Crowley wrote down as 'The Book of the Law', an esoteric operator's manual to the cosmos, which has been aptly described as 'a series of dithyrambic verses with more exclamation marks than any other work of similar length'.[31]

This 'Great Revelation' had not even been mentioned two years previously in Fuller's *The Star in the West*, but Crowley was now quite sure that it had actually inaugurated the third aeon in the history of the world, the Aeon of Horus the Child, and at the same time empowered Crowley as the link between mankind and the 'discarnate intelligence' of the 'solar-spiritual force'. Since Horus was the ancient Egyptian god of war, his aeon would be impulsive and cruel, stripped of conscience, pity or altruism. It would be acutely sensitive to pain, and subject to 'spasms of transitory passion'. As Crowley explained in his *Confessions,* 'the New Aeon implied the breaking up of the civilization existing at the time; obviously to change the Magical Formula of the planet is to change all moral sanctions and the result is bound to appear disastrous.'[32] He claimed to have foreseen the violence of the twentieth century – both the 'collapse of humanitarianism', and the 'huge and ruthless war' with which the new aeon was inaugurated. Crowley was adamant that, long before the Great War, Fuller and he had 'clearly understood the imminence of the world catastrophe', even if they hadn't known exactly when 'civilization would begin to crack, or where'.[33]

The duty of the *Equinox* was to 'publish the Secret Wisdom of the Ages in such a form that, after the wreck of civilization, the scholars of subsequent generations would be able to restore the traditions'. He explained this apocalyptic mission with the help of an image quoted from Lord Macaulay who, in 1840, had suggested that the Roman Catholic Church would still be going strong when imperial London was a vast and ruined solitude sketched from a broken arch of London Bridge by a traveller from New Zealand.[34] Crowley and Fuller could have done without the longevity of the Catholic Church, 'but we saw the New Zealander sitting on the ruined arch of London Bridge quite clearly'. Pleased to imagine 'the Professor of Archaeology in the University of Lhasa excavating the ruins of the British Museum', they printed the *Equinox* on the best quality paper to ensure that its truth endured for these future prehistorians to find in the rubble. Such things were easily said long after the event, but even in 1908 Crowley was declaring himself pleased to know that a copy of Fuller's *The Star in the West* was lodged in the British Museum.[35]

Fuller may have argued with Crowley about magick, but he was to prove indispensable to the *Equinox*. He answered correspondents, and tried to interest mystically inclined figures like Lord Dunsany in the project. He reviewed books, including T. F. Powys's *An Interpretation of Genesis*, the meditation of a remote Dorset hermit in which Fuller claimed to detect 'Qabalah influence'. His written contributions include a savage lampoon of a rival guru, and a story in which physical blindness is ameliorated with mescalin and inner vision. He also penned 'The Treasure House of Images', a text that Crowley would later praise as 'the most remarkable prose that has ever been written', and which consists of numerologically defined incantations intended to be chanted at stars or called out at dawn to the accompaniment of pounding tom-toms. Devised in accordance with Kabbalistic principles, every chapter consists of thirty sections, each of which contains the same number of syllables. They are elaborate and windy constructions in which a god can expect to be equipped not just with an 'amethyst Phallus' but also, if the syllable count demands it, an 'adamantine' one of 'Gold and Ivory' too.

It was Crowley's contention that the scattered members of the Society of the Elect had been involved from the earliest ages in building, through 'the evolution of humanity', the grand temple through which the reign of the divine being would finally become manifest. A primary aim of the *Equinox* was to reconfigure this cosmic evolution as the heroic story of Crowley's own life. With this in mind, Fuller was appointed to take Crowley's magical diaries and convert them into the vast narrative of 'Frater P's' magical journey towards attainment – a story entitled 'The Temple of Solomon the King', which was duly serialized, chapter after chapter after chapter, in successive issues.

Captain Fuller's text is heavy with symbolic weaponry: swords, helmets, shields, even 'the glittering armour of mirth' with which the adepts shield themselves against Christian sentimentality. In the Aeon of Horus, the War of the Freedom of Souls meant setting aside pity: 'Life must be held in contempt – the life of self and the life of others. Here there must be no weakness, no sentiment, no reason, no mercy. All must taste of the desolation of the war, and partake of the blood of the cup of death . . .' After pouring contempt on the masses with their 'swinish itchings' and 'unbridled fornications', Fuller yearns for a catastrophe to sweep the Christian era away: 'The maniac's vision of horror is better than this, and even the shambles clotted with blood.'

As the child of zealous Christians, 'Frater P' was no sooner borne than 'swaddled in the rags of custom' and 'nursed on the soured milk of creed'. Yet he rose up to snap 'like rotten twigs, the worm-eaten conventionalities of the effete and hypocritical civilization in which he had been nurtured'. With apocalyptic trumpets blasting, he tore off 'the shroud of a corrupted faith as if it had been the rotten cerement of a mummy . . . He cursed the name of Christ and strode on to seek the gate of Hell . . .' Fuller has his hero rolling on unstoppably, sweeping aside sundry veils of illusion, and overturning desks and stools before 'the stuffy cloisters of mildewed learning, and the colleges of dialectical dogmatics'. Having punched his way through the world's religious traditions, Crowley realized that the suprarational could not be rationalized, and that to try expressing it in language was merely to drag it down into the words of a particular culture – the mere toys of life. Crowley's acts of ceremonial magic were intended to come closer to that vitally inarticulate truth, and so were Captain Fuller's symbolic images which remain abstract, even if they are described as showing a Lingam resting in a Yoni.

Fuller would later describe Crowley as having been altogether too churchy and sacerdotal – guilty of setting up his own spiritual bureaucracy and bogus priestcraft. But he soldiered on more or less loyally in those early years, drilling 'turnip-headed recruits'[36] in his official capacity, and sharing in Crowley's less practical exploits in the apparently large tracts of time that remained his own. One of the more ambitious operations that Crowley mounted in these years concerned the nineteen 'Calls of the Thirty Aethyrs' recorded by Queen Elizabeth's alchemist, John Dee (they were dictated by the seer Edward Kelley, who 'skryed' them from the ether and then relayed them to Dee in numbers correlated to the 'Enochian' language of angels). Crowley had dug these 'keys' out of manuscripts in the Bodleian Library at Oxford, directing Fuller to follow up such clues as might also be found in the British Museum. And then, at the end of 1909, Crowley and his poor hunchbacked understudy, Victor Neuburg, set off for Algeria, where they would use the calls to get into contact with the thirty 'Aethyrs' – each one to be imagined, apparently, as a cosmic and ever-widening circle governed by its own, usually monstrous angel. Fuller remained in London, receiving the record of the journey in letters scribbled by Neuberg at Crowley's dictation. The pair tramped through Spain and, once in Algeria, walked great distances, scaling peaks and enacting the ceremonies they had prepared to accompany the calls. They suffered minor disasters as they toiled through gorges and over desert plains – broken penknives and the water bottle falling from its slings and 'breaking all to buggery'.

Presumably this was the fault of Victor Neuburg, who had suffered much since 1905 when, as a dreamy young freethinker at Cambridge, he had been content to submit lullabies to the *Agnostic Journal*. As Crowley's 'chela', he now occupied a position that Fuller would eventually describe as 'a cross between a disciple and maid of all works'. In the record of the Algerian odyssey, Crowley reported that he had shaved Neuburg's head, leaving only two hornlike tufts at the front, which he apparently also dyed red, so as to persuade the Arabs that his slave was a demon he had captured and forced into service. He also informed Fuller: 'I have had an awful job keeping him off the Arab boys. He has a frightful lust for brown bottoms, because when he was at school he was kicked by a man with brown shoes.'[37]

The truth of this chaotic journey remains uncertain, but the pair did call the Aethyrs, including the fourteenth, which was invoked on the summit of a mountain called Dal'leh Addin near Bou Saada. In his report to Fuller, Crowley only remarked that 'of the further ceremony that I accomplished . . . it is not lawful to write'. The unlawfulness of full description seems to confirm the account later provided by members of Crowley's circle. Having built a circle of small stones and inscribed magic words in the sand,

Crowley and Neuburg are said to have mounted first their altar, and then one another in an act of 'sex magic' that confirmed Crowley's view of himself as personally embodying the hermaphroditic nature of the Aeon of Horus, and which, as a polite mid-century biographer put it, featured 'Victor taking the masculine role'.[38]

There was more such stuff to come – including a Paris 'working' in which Neuburg struggled to keep up the performance over many nights in a row. But Fuller had severed relations by then. The decisive split came in November 1910, when Crowley wrote a series of 'Rites of Eleusis' and then publicly enacted them in a series of performances at Caxton Hall in London. Crowley was now the showman, seeking to raise money, and the performance was quickly engulfed in accusations of obscenity. Fuller had earlier disagreed with Crowley over the Rites of Eleusis – his objections had prompted Crowley to write: 'You ought to remember that the Rites as now performed are only a beginning. When we can get all the world's great artists to cooperate we can have Rites a thousand times superior to Rome's.'[39] People attending these rites are said to have been primed with strongly opiated libations, but Fuller remained adamant that they had been far from obscene: 'so innocent were they that I took my mother to one of them'. However, 'Innocence is no shield against the vomitings of the gutter press,' in particular a racing paper called the Looking Glass, which pronounced the Argentum Astrum 'a blasphemous sect, whose proceedings conceivably lend themselves to immorality of the most revolting character'.

Fuller and others urged Crowley to sue for libel, but he chose hastily to quit the country for Algeria, thus prompting the Looking Glass to further articles: 'We have to congratulate ourselves on having temporarily extinguished one of the most blasphemous and cold-blooded villains of modern times.' A writ was eventually issued by one Cecil Jones, who had performed in Crowley's rites and been implicated in the same article. The case came up in 1911 and Jones lost, not least because Crowley, who attended the hearing, had himself refused to sue. Fuller broke off, unimpressed by Crowley's claim that he had withheld for 'mystical reasons' and, as may be imagined, merely irritated by Crowley's puerile insistence in rearranging letters in order to find putrefying female sex organs in the name of the presiding judge, Mr Justice Scrutton. Fuller's standing in the army can hardly have been helped by his association with Crowley at this point – a fact to which Crowley referred in a letter written after Jones lost his libel case: 'it's jolly serious for you and me as well as for Jones. I heard some ass talk about the W. O. getting angry with you – I hope not.'[40]

Crowley would later claim that his 'swollen-headed' military collaborator had offered to continue the relationship 'on condition that I refrain from mentioning his name in public or private under penalty of paying £100 each time of the offence'.[41] Fuller, however, saw the break differently. Likening Crowley to the Corsican outsider who was to be his own lifelong military hero, he replied: 'Your Waterloo took place the day you dropped their prosecution, but you differ from Napoleon in that you ran away directly the first gun was pointed at you . . . Through your own folly you now find yourself at St. Helena; it may be a serious thing for you but your friends are perhaps to be congratulated. I am extremely sorry that Jones so be the sufferer for your want of pluck.'[42] Years later, he told an enquirer: 'I broke with him because he let a friend of mine down . . . George Cecil Jones had a peculiarity, which was that he told the truth.'[43]

So they had parted, three years before the outbreak of the First World War. Crowley wrote to Fuller pleading that 'The *Equinox* without Fuller is nothing to anybody.'[44] If the relationship could not be mended, Fuller should at least complete the symbolic drawings he had been doing for the journal. But Fuller had retreated, and Crowley was left sniping at him across a growing distance. He wrote mocking poems about his broken-off collaborator, introduced jokes about Fuller's florid, excessively adjectival prose style into the index of the *Equinox,* and expressed contempt for his ongoing career in the wrong army. Having taught Fuller how to write he was, or so he would eventually declare in his *Confessions*, disappointed to find this former acolyte, who could have been scribe to the new aeon, content to 'employ his talents to no better purpose than to win prizes in competitions organized by the Army Council'.[45]

Action at a distance

By the time Fuller joined the Tank Corps in Bermicourt, Crowley had shifted his operations to America. His diaries show this sleazy transgressor of bourgeois norms being sodomized by strangers in a New York Turkish bath, and engaging in more or less daily acts of sex-magic with an array of female consorts, both hired and voluntary. Having lodged his Lingam in the Yoni of the day, The Beast would start invoking the powers of the aeon. By this time he apparently believed that cheques and other desirable offerings could be lured in through his letter box if he imagined showers of golden coins at the moment of climax.[46]

When not so indisposed, the man who had previously presented himself as a kilted Highlander, a Russian count and an oriental prince, assumed the persona of an Irish patriot and wrote the pro-German articles he would later explain as an elaborate patriotic deception – as if by advocating unlimited German submarine warfare he had really only aimed to work the normally restrained German propaganda up to the stupidly distorted pitch of insanity adopted by the British, and thereby to shock the Americans into alliance with Britain. He also found time to produce the novel that reveals his opinion of the 'wonder weapon' that in October 1917 had rolled through Manhattan at the forefront of a Liberty Loan parade.[47]

Writing *Moonchild* in New Orleans during 1917, the Great Beast saw no connection between the tank and his theory of the magical breakthrough, or of the violent Aeon of Horus. He might have seen the tank as a mythological entity, like the ancient Hindu Juggernaut of Puri, a vast wheeled cart, supposedly bearing the ashes of Krishna, which once slid forward in annual procession crushing pilgrims and even babies hurled into its path as sacrifice. In the event, however, the grandiose prophet of 'Will' rated the new weapon even lower than the unhealthily self-effacing spiritualists he mocked for gathering at seances to engage spirits in 'Telekinesis', or 'The art of Moving Objects at a Distance'. Indeed, he used the tank to illustrate the idiocy of 'Edward Arthwaite' – a character modelled on the Golden Dawn occultist Arthur Edward Waite, who was content 'to blunder pedantically along with the classical methods of magical assault, partly on the chance of a hit . . . and possibly to lead him to believe that the main attack lay there'. Arthwaite 'had not become known as the most voluminous of modern pedants without perseverance. His literary method was that of the "tank". It was not agile, it was not versatile, it was exposed to artillery attack; but it proceeded'.[48] In Crowley's conception, the tank was a poor grinding contrivance: blind, locked in a groove, unstoppable but oblivious. Less an instrument of intelligent manoeuvre than an unyielding form of stupidity, it was a pitiful thing, especially when compared to the spellbinding war engine Crowley would offer Fuller, five years later, when he tried to recruit him from the War Office to lead the army of Horus.

Yet the misjudgement was actually on the Beast's side. If the tank as Crowley here describes it finds any equivalent in Fuller's account of the Great War, it resembles nothing so much as the hidebound mental apparatus of the field marshal who had commanded the British forces on the Western Front and, in Fuller's view, been so blind to the winning and also life-saving capabilities of the tank. This was the trundling stupidity that, so Fuller believed, had brought about the unnecessary death of millions of soldiers:

'Sir Douglas Haig was not a man to abandon anything he had begun. He possessed a stereotyped mind, and, like a deluge or an avalanche, once set in motion, he could not stop, because, in my opinion, he considered this particular form of stupidity to be the one test of a good general.'[49] Having failed to grasp the significance of those first lumbering tank movements, Crowley was no more inclined to recognize, over the years to come, how the imprint of his own magical theories persisted in Fuller's vision of mechanized warfare: a vision in which the idea of 'action at a distance' would be liberated from the eccentric world of seances, magic spells and Ouija boards. Had he attended more closely to the post-war impact of Fuller's thinking, even a man as self-obsessed as Crowley might occasionally have wondered whether it was not actually he, rather than his former acolyte, who had been left behind.

There can be little doubt that Fuller had his break with Crowley in mind when he identified 1910 as the year in which he shifted from 'destructive' to 'constructive' iconoclasm. He claims that the 'philosophical and scientific' works he had read during his youthful war with Christianity had 'unconsciously taught him to think clearly'.[50] Having done his learning outside schools and against the dogmas of established religion, Fuller had, so he reasoned, converted his mind into 'a self-made threshing machine', which really came into its own when he started 'threshing the grist from the chaff of conventional theories of war'.

Though he could be circumspect about his earlier devotion to 'Crowleyanity', Fuller never abandoned his esoteric interests. In the twenties and thirties, he would return to themes he had first explored in the *Equinox*, recycling them, without any acknowledgement of their earlier incarnation, in later books such as *Yoga: A Study of the Mystical Philosophy of the Brahmins and Buddhists* (1925), in which he insisted that yoga and magic were but different routes to the same goal, and also *The Secret Wisdom of the Qabala* (1937). He maintained his correspondence with Meredith Starr, commenting that 'it has been raining works on initiation lately' and, in a letter written from the War Office on the last day of 1919, even insisting on the name Crowley had given him in the A∴ A∴: 'Normally I am P. . A . . to you.'[51]

Crowley's post-war overtures to Fuller may well have been inadvertently prompted by Captain F. H. E. Townshend, the clairvoyant sapper who had seen the need for tanks in 'The Manuscript in Red Ink', and who visited Crowley at his 'Abbey' of Thelema in Sicily in April 1921.[52] Fuller rejected them, and plainly regretted Townshend's indiscretion in letting the Beast know that his former acolyte could now be reached at the War Office. Yet he was intrigued to read Townshend's detailed description of Crowley and his Abbey, notwithstanding the Beast's insistence that both Fuller and Townshend were failing to live in accordance with their 'real will'. He also remained sufficiently interested in his pre-war adventures to fictionalize his first meeting with Crowley in an incomplete and unpublished novel called 'The Hidden Wisdom of the Illuminati'.[53] Written in the mid-twenties, and incorporating material from Townshend's letters from Sicily, the manuscript includes a detailed recreation of the former master's London rooms – full of books, ash, and shockingly erotic pictures. It even hints at a connection between Fuller's esoteric and military interests: the Crowleyan creed of 'Will' is first heard in words emanating from a fakir sitting in a 'little tank' in an Indian garden, albeit at this stage one filled only with holy water.

Some of the similarities between magic and mechanization as they exist in Fuller's writings may be relatively superficial consequences of the rhetoric that Fuller applied across both fields: the promise of power restored and of a transvaluation of all values, for example, or his habit of likening both magic and mechanized warfare to quick, surgical operations.[54] And yet in their deeper structure, 'Crowleyanity' and mechanization have so much in common that they appear to be different registrations of the same iconoclastic impulse: to compare them is like holding two accidentally superimposed negatives up to the light and finding the same pattern revealed in both.

The Crowleyan poem or magical ceremony is a transgressive engine of ecstasy and movement, and so too is the tank. Both the adept and the tank soldier are pitted against the sedimented illusions of a powerfully established majority mentality, whether these be the conventions of Christianity, the prevailing illusions of the Upanishads, or the fossilized 'realities of war' propounded by elderly generals and 'shell-shocked war correspondents'.[55] Fuller claims the status of 'science' in mechanization just as he had previously in Crowleyanity; and he places a similar emphasis on 'Will' too. In Crowley's Abbey of Thelema, the motto 'Do what you will' meant cutting through 'the haphazard wishes and desires of the conscious mind' to disclose the 'unchangeable will' of the inner self. In the doctrine of mechanization, 'an old model based on destruction will be replaced by a new military ideal, the imposition of will at the least possible general loss.'[56]

Like Crowley's magic, Fuller's theory of mechanized warfare is presented as a total philosophy, a systematic truth revealed in worldly events that the uninitiated cannot read. Both enquiries are prophetic and strongly susceptible to conspiracy theories. They are governed by 'principles' that are abstract but nonetheless accessible to the true seer: the magic formulae of the world as perceived in Crowleyanity; and the 'principles of war', such as Mass, Surprise and Movement, which Fuller remembers 'working like magic' when he first used them to clear the illogicality and fog of actual combat.[57] As a young captain, Fuller had joined Crowley in opting for Satan over the evil Christ of his father, and as a senior proponent of mechanization he repeats the same diabolical inversion: 'Condensed to its upmost . . . the bottom is top. The material has been exalted above the spiritual; the canaille has ousted the nobility; the truth is exorcized and lies are revered, the world is standing on its head.'[58]

'Crowleyanity' represented an uncompromising assault on tradition; and so too did the training protocols that Fuller organized for the new Tank Corps at Bermicourt: the tank was 'a new weapon suddenly emerging out of an idea',[59] and the search for a new tactic entailed a period of 'unending struggle against the present, and unending striving towards the future'. Both Crowleyanity and mechanization were conceived as vanguard doctrines of a new epoch or aeon. Crowley dated his Aeon of Horus to the so-called 'Great Revelation' of 1904, whereas Fuller's tank-driven equivalent began at Cambrai, described as 'the birth of a new epoch in the history of war'.[60]

Such pseudo-evolutionary clockwork thinking, in which the complexities of history are collapsed into a mechanics of Destiny, is one of the most persistent features of Fuller's thought. In *The Star in the West*, world history was said to be composed of three periods, each embracing three cycles: Renaissance, Decadence and Slime.[61] By the time of the *Equinox,* the cyclical movement of history is described with reference to the arcane symbolism of the swastika ('It shows the Initiation of a whirling force').[62] After the war, Fuller continued to think of history in terms of cycles, epochs, and catastrophic breaks. Writing from the Staff College at Camberley on 14 October 1923, Fuller told Meredith Starr: 'You are right as regards Germany & France, ultimately black magic never pays. The end of present day democracy is in sight. Today is the travail which will give birth to a new idea & the world will have completed another lap. We are approaching the end of the Roman Empire.' Writing from Catterick Camp in Yorkshire on 30 January 1930, he informs Starr: 'History is like a vast organ, the keys are fixed but according to the genius of man can the tune be varied. Nothing actually repeats itself, but there is a relationship, just as between father and son. Historical relationships are in form spirals.' On this basis, Fuller fore-saw the current machine age culminating in a massive war between East and West – 'the West being somewhat tired of the machine & the East spellbound by it' – and prophesied that, unless the seeds of a new spiritual-ity were sown, a second Dark Age would 'engulf mankind'.

This esoteric idea of history as a cross between a cosmic Wurlitzer and a vast spiralling seashell, closely informs Fuller's military thinking. Here the grand theory of history is based on the evolving technology of battle, with petrol replacing muscle as motive power, and 'shock cycles' interchanging with 'projectile cycles'. Above all, however, Fuller's cranky dialectics encour-aged a positive appetite for catastrophe. Crowley had argued that the Aeon of Horus would be born in a necessary period of chaos as the magical for-mulae of the world were changed; and twenty years later his former acolyte still yearned for chaos, the worse the better. In a letter dated 7 August 1930, Fuller informed Meredith Starr that

Chaos must precede Creation, & The God can only manifest out of night . . .True the Abyss is very close to us, & I am not at all certain that it will be a bad thing in the end if we all enter it. The problems to-day are too big & the problem solvers too small. Possibly the best way out is the simultaneous destruction of both & a chaos out of which a new cosmos can emerge.

Fuller did not confine his appetite for derangement to his private corres-pondence with former Adepts. In *The Dragon's Teeth*, a 'study of War and Peace' published in 1932, he opined that 'present-day civilization will not do: it has got to crash or decay away before the Empire of Alexander can be founded'.[63] Contemptuous of democracy with its small incremental changes, he was content not just to 'creep onwards' but 'if needs be crash our way towards the next great sunrise'.[64]

Fuller wasn't really free to pledge his political allegiance to that lurid new dawn until after the end of his army career, which finally fizzled out seven years after he refused to take command of the Experimental Mechanized Force at Tidworth in 1926. Promoted to Major General in September 1930, he had been put on half pay a few weeks later. He outmanoeuvred an attempt to post him to Bombay, and continued to irritate the military authorities with his writings – notably with *Generalship, Its Diseases and their Cure*, which recommended the abolition of the General Staff, and the formation of small mechanized armies that a proper general would want to lead from the front: i.e. in a tank.[65] The end came when Fuller's long-suffering protector General Sir George Milne retired as Chief of the Imperial General Staff and his successor, General Sir Archibald Montgomery-Massingberd, who is said to have loathed Fuller and all his unconventional works, confirmed his retirement at the earliest possible opportunity. Fuller was gone by the end of December 1933 – fifty-five years old, pensioned and already looking for another band of redemptive warriors to join.

Disarmament and Fascism

The curtain is tugged back and the audience finds itself staring into the interior of a male Mark IV tank called Titus, just about to roll forward into the Battle of Cambrai. Seen from the rear, this motorized chasm is lit only by a few small electric bulbs along the roof and the glow of a Primus stove, although, once the tank is in motion, the French countryside can also be glimpsed sweeping past through the portholes in front. The eight-man crew composes a microcosm of British life: the commander is a medical student; one gunlayer is a Scottish publican, the other a cockney; the loader is a tailor and there are also a Welsh miner, a motor mechanic and an Ulster stevedore. Lest the white colonial contribution be forgotten, the company captain is a Canadian Mountie, who will shortly guide his three tanks forward by walking into battle in front of them.

Public perception of the tank took a definite turn for the worse in the nineteen-thirties. The patriotic 'wonder weapon' of the Great War could still be found rolling forward unstoppably, but it was no longer an irresistible 'Tanko' staged by glamorous dancing girls in a famous West End theatre. Instead, it had retreated into amateur productions of the appropriately named 'Over the Top', a hideously enthusiastic drama written by the Tank Corps veteran Captain D. E. Hickey, and published as one of the best one-act plays of 1934.[66] After frying up sausages in a bantering display of esprit de tank, the self-sufficient members of this citizens' force express their far from 'scientific' faith in the horseshoe hanging on the front of the tank, and then, with spanners in hand, go clanking off 'to get the Boche out of Morris Bank'. They plough through hedges to the sound of cheering tommies and sing 'John Brown's Body' as they scatter the enemy like rabbits (Voices off: *'Kamerad! Kamerad!'*). 'We'll crush the dogs out of existence,' they yell as they roll towards the inevitable climax:

CORPORAL (*yelling*): See that bloke with the goggles? In front of us, with a machine-gun? Look at his eyes, sir.
LIEUTENANT: They seem to be sticking out of his head. Frightened to death!

CORPORAL: And that chap covering his face with his hands!

LIEUTENANT: We are on them – thirty tons of metal.

CORPORAL (*screaming*): My Gawd! It's 'orrible, 'orrible!

LIEUTENANT (*pulling himself together*): Their agony is over. Swing right at once.

Fuller might have judged this play 'a reminder of how we should rearm our land forces' – that was certainly how he introduced Captain Hickey's memoirs a year or two later.[67] By the mid-thirties, however, such clichéd tank heroics no longer captured the mood of the times. The tank was turning into something vile, as had been revealed a few years earlier in Walter Owen's allegorical novel, *The Cross of Carl*. Based on the infamous wartime propaganda myth claiming that the Germans were gathering corpses from the battlefield and boiling them down to produce fat and other useful by-products, this book tells the story of an injured British infantryman named Carl who wakes to find himself wired into a bundle of corpses ready for reprocessing at 'The Utilisation Factory of the Tenth Army Section'. Before that, Owen had shown Carl advancing across no man's land with the rest of his reluctant company. The soldier in front explodes 'like a puff-ball'; and then, as he crouches in a hole in the ground, Carl hears a confused roar coming from behind: 'It grows and disintegrates into the chugging of many feet that plough the mud. It is the attack, re-formed and reinforced, coming back upon its dreadful tracks to batter at Hill 50's gates.'[68] Here was the tank stripped of the patriotic character with which it had been so carefully endowed through the last years of the war, and ploughing on as the unameliorated engine of destruction many people now considered it to be.

J. F. C. Fuller may not have followed the literature that testifies to this shift in civilian perceptions of the tank, but he knew very well that something was happening to the British public's attitude to war. In 1916 it may only have been a few poets or harried Quakers at the *Ploughshare* who condemned the tank as an emblem of bloodthirsty brutalism. But by the early thirties, a multitude of British people had been gripped by the idea that disarmament was the route to collective security.[69] The League of Nations' Disarmament Conference opened in Geneva in February 1932, and support for the cause was demonstrated not just by the Oxford Union debate of February 1933, which resolved that 'this house will not fight for King and Country', but also by the so-called 'Peace Ballot' organized by the League of Nations Union in 1935, in which over 10 million British householders signed up for the League of Nations' approach to 'Collective Security'.

Sir Philip Gibbs, the former war correspondent who had first reported

on 'the Coming of the Tanks', was among the members of the Royal Commission on the Private Manufacture of and Trade in Arms, set up in 1935 to
consider alleged abuses by the arms industry. The commission did not
recommend nationalization of the arms industry, as many hoped, but
Gibbs found himself convinced by the case presented against firms like
Vickers. These 'merchants of death' were accused of prolonging wars to
keep their dividends up, of stimulating trade by playing one side off against
the other, of sabotaging League of Nations attempts to control the arms
trade, and – since 'steel has no fatherland' – of selling arms even to the
nations most likely to attack their own country. The arms manufacturers
craved war even though, as one of their critics told the commission, they
knew better than to 'invite us with picture postcards "to say it with tanks
. . ."'[70] According to Fenner Brockway, who addressed the commission on
behalf of the Independent Labour Party, Vickers was part of a 'Bloody
International,' which had supplied Turkey with the superior shells fired
with such devastating effect on British and Allied troops at Gallipoli, and
was already engaged in the business of arming Nazi Germany.[71]

This climate of opinion was registered by many Tank Corps veterans in
their new walks of life. For Basil Henriques, it only stiffened the moral
armour with which he tried to shield his Jewish settlement and boys' clubs
in London: the dangerous attractions of the East End street now included
the heckling agitators of the Anti-War League and the Young Communists
League, who broke up Henriques' improving discussions at Toynbee Hall
by peddling an idea of 'Peace' that knew nothing about the place of 'duty
before self-indulgence and self-satisfaction'.[72] Clough Williams-Ellis was
quite turned around by the change. In the decade of disarmament (in
which both he and his wife Amabel became ardent admirers of the Soviet
Union), he came to see the tank, which he had previously praised as a
mechanical reflection of the British character, as an offensive blot on the
national landscape. By 1937, Williams-Ellis opposed the Royal Tank Corps's
gunnery range at Lulworth on the Dorset coast as yet another example of
'the Beast' encroaching on the English countryside.[73]

Historians dispute the extent to which this rising anti-war feeling affected
government procurement programmes in the nineteen-thirties, yet there
can be little doubt that it proved too much for many of the old First World
War tanks mounted as anti-revolutionary memorials in the nation's municipal parks and squares. These may not have appeared quite as grotesque to
the pacifist eye as the trophy cannon found in Bedford by a Co-operative

Party activist (a brass plate on one side noted that it had been presented to the town by the 5th Bedfordshire Regiment, which had captured it from the enemy in Gaza, while larger letters on the other side read: 'Made by Sir George Armstrong Whitworth & Co.).[74] Yet the moral effect of the National War Savings Committee's 'presentation' tanks in parks and town squares around the country was certainly going awry. 'Old Ironsides' may have been rusting by now, but he had also become a hideous representative of war. Aylesbury Borough Council made £22 from their tank: they sold it for scrap in 1929, although two of the men who came to dismantle the hulk with oxyacetylene cutters, are said to have been injured when the fuel tank exploded.[75] The tank that had stood by the north entrance of the British Museum was cut up and removed in February 1931.[76] Remembering Turner's famous picture of an antiquated war-galleon being towed off for demolition, Major General Sir Ernest D. Swinton, raiser of the original Heavy Section, dubbed this corroded relic: 'The Last of the Fighting Temeraires'. Less sentimentally inclined veterans of the Tank Corps confessed to having been dismayed to see these 'steel brutes' set up as 'memorials of probity and patriotism' in the first place. According to one of these 'tinned soldiers', Alec Dixon, it had been a 'misguided government' that had distributed old tanks all over 'England's green and pleasant land', leaving them to brood in shrubberies or 'squat complacently' and 'begirt with flowers' in public squares.[77] He was delighted to see them removed as 'communal good sense' started to triumph over 'civic pride'. There were even ripples of discontent in the Cambridgeshire village of Swaffham Prior. Mrs Violet Betts, who moved there in 1939 when her husband was appointed station master, remembers being dismayed to see a tank and other deadly weapons in the windows of the church: 'I was much against them,' she told me. 'I was horrified. I'd had enough of war and I didn't think they should be in church.'

Fuller opposed the new mood and, of course, fulminated against all its manifestations. Condemning the idea of 'peace' as an inane and effectively pro-Soviet fantasy, he insisted that war, far from being an unnatural evil, had its roots deep in the social and economic organization of the world and could therefore be both 'a moral force, or deeper still, a spiritual force' and a 'rightful instrument of progress'.[78] He dismissed the League of Nations as a Bolshevik front and 'a Judaic-Masonic Ideal'[79] and its Geneva disarmament conference as 'an immense hypocritical swindle'.[80] Deploring the new pacifism and its apparently baleful impact on the government's determination to modernize and re-equip the British Army, he presented his own conclusions before the readers of the *Daily Mail*: 'Today the greater part of the world is still armed to the teeth; it is greedy, truculent and volcanic. What are we doing? We are meandering about with a cage of cooing doves in one hand and a blunderbuss in the other.'[81]

Many of the senior tank veterans had certainly settled down nicely by the nineteen-thirties. Sir Ernest Swinton had become a famously immobile professor of the History of War at Oxford University. Even Evan Charteris, the exotic author of *H.Q. Tanks,* had found his niche in the London arts establishment – he was Chairman of both the Tate Gallery and the National Portrait Gallery. But Fuller had always had a soft spot for renegades: his career can be measured as a succession of new orders glimpsed in the transgressive antics of one band of outlaws after another, from the acolytes of the A∴ A∴ who relished disrupting the activities of rival occultists, to the Tank Corps, which had certainly been all the better for starting out as a rabble, quite untamed by military convention. As Fuller once wrote, 'new ideas . . . originate in piratical exploits outside the existing military organization'.[82]

This sentiment was now transferred to Oswald Mosley's British Union of Fascists (formerly known as 'the New Party'), which Fuller joined within six months of his retirement, just after the notorious rally at Olympia in Earls Court on 7 June 1934, where Mosley's stewards had fallen on hecklers with a degree of violence that dismayed many of his supporters in the Conservative Party. As Fuller explained in his letter to Mosley, 'the time to join a man is at his worst moment'.[83] He had long considered himself adept at distinguishing the 'esoteric' truth of a movement or situation from the 'exoteric' trappings of its imperfect manifestation. So, while he eventually apologized for the 'roughness' that had attended the party's rise, he also insisted that it was no worse than had attended 'all new movements including Christianity', and implied that the fault lay elsewhere.[84] Things might well have taken a more polite route if the supine British middle classes had accepted their duty to history and taken an active role in the new party: in their absence, the first supporters had come from the wilder fringes and 'among the down-and-out, words are frequently accentuated by fists'.

As for the wider political vision, in a BUF pamphlet published in 1938, Fuller explained that 'a new cosmos' had emerged out of the Great War. In the 'turbulently divided' post-war years, 'those nations that had suffered least' promptly went back to 1914; and were now squared off against 'those who had suffered most'. The latter had lost everything that 1914 stood for, and it was they who had struggled forward, and eventually found the new leaders who alone could usher in the future. Unfortunately, however, the first group had triumphed, and as victors 'they formed themselves into the League of Nations, which is certainly not a British invention.' Now the enemy was not just 'Haig-mind' or the cavalry or Christian sentimentality, but the 'despotism of the money power', communism and 'the lethargy of the great middle classes'. So that is where Fuller ended up in the thirties: denouncing the Jews as 'the Cancer of Europe',[85] calling for a combination of 'Scientific Weapons' and 'Political Authority', and snarling that 'Parliamentary Democracy is utterly worn-out: today it is nothing more than a pluto-mobocracy'.[86] Perhaps that was why it would be more easily conquered by the red militants who had brought the threat of revolution, and also British tanks, to the streets of Glasgow in 1919. William Gallacher distinguished himself as the Communist MP who, in 1938, contested Chamberlain's appeasement of Hitler in the Commons (looking across at the Tory benches, he yelled: 'There are as many fascists opposite as in Germany . . . ')[87] The ship-building trade unionist David Kirkwood became the long-serving Labour MP for Dumbarton, and eventually presided over the government's involvement in building the *Queen Mary* and *Queen Elizabeth* ocean liners. As for the former conscientious objector and pacifist Emmanuel Shinwell, he became Secretary of State for War in 1947 and, like Kirkwood, ended his life as a Baron.

The Mission Overseas

When he joined the British Union of Fascists, Fuller broke the last trailing threads of influence he may still have had over military policy in his own 'comatose' country.[1] Philosophically and as a writer, however, he was well equipped for the wilderness. 'Crowleyanity' had been a matter of winnowing the kernel of esoteric 'truth' from the husk of its imperfect worldly manifestation in the various religions of the world: a 'Great Attainment', as Fuller had written in the *Equinox*, that was 'identical in all systems irrespective of the symbol man sought it under'.[2] And so it was now with the grail of mechanization. Each nation would wrap its quest in patriotic colours, but no true 'scientist' of modern warfare could afford to be overly detained by such trappings or the loyalties they implied. Once retired, Fuller converted himself into a roving military correspondent for papers such as the *Evening Standard* and the *Daily Mail*. In this capacity he travelled widely through the thirties, sallying out from the flat he shared with his famously rude wife Sonia at 37 Cheyne Court Mansions, Chelsea, to conduct his own audit of the nations and their armies, attending manoeuvres and treating such 'small wars' as broke out as valuable experiments in which the vision could be tested before the great cataclysm that was surely soon to come.

Peering out through the fiercely stained glass of his own 'tank-mindedness', Fuller saw small bands of prescient men, struggling to change the tactical formulae of their armies and, almost everywhere, coming up against the inertia of engrained habit and convention. He saw tanks forcing the gyre of history from one country to the next and counted many different ways of crashing towards the sunrise. Each nation was like an emblematic light in a vast War Window dedicated to Fuller's own creed, every one a variation in which the same basic forms appeared: ingenious engineers, prototype machines of different nationalities, wilful young disciples clutching the gospel of Mobility, great fields full of redundant bayonets and horses, purblind generals, and mediocre politicians who stood about getting in the way.

Light 1 Britain

'One of Major Clifton's tanks having a rest', postcard of tank overturned at Harper Hill, Nayland, Suffolk, 14 September 1928

Had Mosley triumphed, Fuller would have become his Minister of Defence and, no doubt, presided over a radical mechanization of the British Army. In the meantime, however, he could only watch through distanced and vengeful eyes as his former colleagues in the Royal Tank Corps struggled along against the odds. General Sir Archibald Montgomery-Massingberd may have been pleased to retire Fuller, but he had also set up a permanent Tank Brigade in November 1933, and put it under the command of Percy Hobart, recently described as 'the most ardent and radical member of the RTC avant-garde'.[3] Hobart wanted to see the development of an all-tank force, and his Tank Brigade was a pioneering, even world-leading, initiative that seemed full of promise. However, its humiliation came soon enough.

The occasion was a training manoeuvre carried out on and around Salisbury Plain in September 1934. Hobart's Tank Brigade was combined with the experimentally motorized 7th Infantry Brigade and a motorized field artillery brigade to form a 'Mobile Force' under the command of Major General George Lindsay, which was then pitched into mock battle against a larger conventional force. The Commander-in-Chief of Southern Region, General Sir John Burnett-Stuart, is said to have been determined to guarantee a victory for the conventional forces, which had been seriously demoralized by the success of the mobile force in previous exercises. So it was, at least as Liddell Hart tells the story, that Burnett-Stuart and his equally biased umpire, Major General A. P. Wavell, ordered the mobile force, dubbed 'Westland', to attack some 'Eastland' positions near Amesbury. The Eastland force included a horse-mounted cavalry brigade, a non-mechanized infantry division, some air support and a modest supply of armoured cars. Their positions were closely grouped to compensate for their lack of mobility; and the mobile force was obliged to start from over seventy miles away, west of the River Severn near Gloucester. There was only one good route for the advance, which would consequently be canalized, and since the mobile force was not allowed to start until 2 a.m., it had no choice but to advance in broad daylight.

Fuller was busy at that time drawing up a defence policy for the British Union of Fascists, exploring a possible future for himself as a 'national arms salesman' specializing in growing Asian markets, and writing yet another book in which he would denounce 'the Haig-Mind' and claim to have saved the Tank Corps from being 'scrapped, lock, stock and barrel' after the Great War.[4] However, he found time to visit the manoeuvres, or at least to 'glance through' their final exercises on Tuesday, 18 September, and to produce a harshly tinted picture of what he saw for the *Evening Standard*. Entitled 'Wolf into Poodle: the Farce of this week's Manoeuvres', his portrait opened with a contemptuous allusion designed to entertain his London readers. 'If you were in charge of, say, a hundred nursemaids wheeling their infants up and down Rotten Row and you were suddenly informed that a pack of hungry wolves had escaped from the zoo, and was rapidly making for the Marble Arch entrance to the park, what would you do?'[5] In all likelihood, he opined, you would head for 'such impregnable positions as the neighbourhood afforded' – perhaps the bandstand, where your nursemaids 'could open and close their umbrellas and make aggressive noises when the enemy approached'. But this, alas, was not how things had gone in the 'Battle of Hungerford'.

Designed to 'challenge the old idea of fighting with the new', the exercise had initially impressed Fuller as 'exceptionally interesting'. Fundamentally, what the operation demanded of the mobile force was a raid behind enemy lines, and 'with a raid speed is of the essence'. Indeed, Fuller considered that the whole operation should have been conducted like 'lightning', and declared himself unable to grasp how it was ever intended to drag the thing out over the four days allowed in the schedule. Lindsay had pushed his motorized infantry out towards Hungerford with 'commendable celerity'. But instead of dividing his force into two and dispatching Hobart's 200-machine tank brigade towards Devizes, from whence it could mount speedy attacks on the Eastland positions around Amesbury, he left it standing at the starting place for fourteen hours, and then ordered it to follow the infantry into Hungerford, which had by this time 'already become a bomb trap'. While the mobile force was stuck near Hungerford – immobilized, quarrelling, and under attack from the air – the supposedly 'immobile' Eastland force (the nursemaids who should, by this time, have been cowering behind umbrellas in their bandstand) started to become mobile. Not content with blowing up bridges and thereby cutting off the mobile force's lines of retreat, it then started rounding up the wolves, which promptly turned into poodles and fled. At one point the situation 'had become so ludicrous' that Eastland's horsed cavalry could be found 'picketing a wood in which an enemy tank battalion had sought shelter'.

As far as the Tank Corps radicals were concerned, the 'Battle of Hungerford' was a 'frame-up' by the military establishment. But Fuller, who evidently had more precise scores to settle, declared that the defender 'thoroughly deserved his gains': he could be commended for having rightly 'applied the pedestrian idea to infantry', unlike Lindsay who had foolishly 'applied the same idea to tanks'. The challenge facing the mobile force had been to get to the objective 'in the shortest possible time, and, directly the dumps, etc., were destroyed, to get home like lightning'. It had failed for the predictable reasons. The 'headquarters paraphernalia' of the mobile force, which, according to Fuller, 'resembled a travelling circus', should certainly have been cut right down in the name of mobility, but the fiasco also proved the more general point that 'tanks are not infantry, and will never become infantry; tanks are tanks and require a field strategy of their own'. As Fuller emphasized, 'our supreme military problem today is one of change of idea', and until that change took place, Britain's mobile force would indeed remain a farce. His point was amply underlined by the photographs printed in the same issue of the *Evening Standard*, which showed children scrutinising some of Hobart's awesome tanks in their final position. One of these exotic attractions, a 16-tonner, was said to have slid backwards down a hill at Wanborough near Swindon, 'with burning petrol shooting in the air and ammunition exploding' before 'embedding itself in a bank'; the second was a lighter model that, in a hasty attempt to get out of the way, had somersaulted and ended up waving its equally useless tracks in the air.

In Royal Tank Corps circles, the Battle of Hungerford, was long remembered as the event that discredited mechanization and set back the modernization of the British Army for years. As Liddell Hart described it in his history of the Royal Tank Corps, the manoeuvre was watched by 'a host of highly placed officers' who had not seen the mobile force in earlier exercises, and these men 'jumped to the superficial conclusion that as this operation had ended in frustration, any such operations would be impracticable in war'.[6]

More recently, it has been suggested that this conspiracy theory was seriously detached from reality: that British armament production did not plunge in the thirties, and, indeed, that in its policy paper of September

1935, the British General Staff remained somewhat ahead of its military competitors in commitment to mechanization.[7] However, there can be no reasonable doubt that Britain lost its lead in the thirties. Instead of reducing or even scrapping the cavalry as an anachronism and expanding the Royal Tank Corps in order to create the all-tank New Model Army favoured by Hobart and others, the General Staff resolved to mechanize the cavalry regiments, and to harness the Royal Tank Corps and its HQ at Bovington, Dorset to this end. The place that Fuller had once imagined as the crucible of an epoch-making 'Reformation of War' found itself reduced to a mere training centre where that altogether more modest conversion was to be carried out.

The Royal Tank Corps's experts were dispersed, including Lindsay, who was posted to India shortly after the Battle of Hungerford. Meanwhile, the 'scientific' tactics that had been advocated in the name of mechanization were dumped and replaced by half measures congenial to the cavalry regiments which, having embraced the tank reluctantly as a means of ensuring their own survival, promptly converted it into a useless folly – abandoning the breakthrough role for so long advocated by Fuller, and refitting the machine to fulfil redundant cavalry roles such as reconnaissance, flanking manoeuvre and pursuit. The Medium tank was spurned for light models of the kind that Fuller had always dismissed as 'mobile coffins' quite inadequate to the modern battlefield.[8] From 1937, when Chamberlain became Prime Minister, priority was given to anti-aircraft, navy and other arms that could be justified in the name of home and imperial defence. The tank budget was heavily cut, especially under the 'New Army Policy' adopted in early 1938. Britain had no tank divisions by the end of 1937, and only two by the time the Second World War broke out. Tanks were commissioned by the British government in the thirties, but they would impress Fuller only as a string of 'duds' – clanking redundancies that could never demonstrate the truth of tank philosophy, and which bestowed few favours on the soldiers who would soon enough confront a superior German Army in machines that were, as one senior General Staff officer would confirm in 1939, 'not assets but death traps'.[9] As for the British Army's field service manuals, that same year it fell to Fuller's unacknowledged Marxist follower, Tom Wintringham, to point out that the *Cavalry Training (Mechanized) Pamphlet No. 1*, issued in 1937, still contained advice on 'the use of the sword in war' and insisted that armour should be used like cavalry: 'It is not stated whether armoured cars should be given lumps of sugar after a good gallop.'[10]

Light 2 France

Juvenile interest in a Citroen-Kegresse
P28 taking part in French army
manoeuvres in the Champagne district,
6 September 1935

France had been early into tanks, thanks to General Estienne, who had
fought a tireless battle against the 'thinkers in bayonets and sabres' to build
and equip the French tank force that came into its own during the last year
of the Great War.[11] According to the post-war German government's official report on the defeat, it was the French above all who had established
the tank as 'a new and very effective weapon'.[12] Fuller's view was different
once again.

Estienne's Artillerie d'Assaut had fought three battles by January 1918,
when Fuller visited their headquarters at Chamlieu in the forest of Compiègne and recorded his contemptuous impressions in his private journal:
'Their big tanks are like kitchen ranges on tracks – quite useless';[13] and
their light Renaults were merely 'very cleverly made mountings for battalion machine guns' – good for 'local protection', but 'useless for a breakthrough'. By May 1918, when the French and British tank forces were
training together, Fuller would concede that the French men were 'most
intelligent'. But he had not changed his view of General Estienne, whom he
described as 'an ignorant and amusing little dud', who knew 'nothing of
the science of war' and only wanted to 'fill his billets with chorus girls'.

Fuller's negative impressions had been reinforced by the British Tank
Corps liaison officers who, in June 1918, visited some of Estienne's units on
the Aisne front and reported 'a complete lack of control from Corps HQ
downwards'. The HQ didn't know the whereabouts of one of its own regiments, or even of a company that was due to go into action imminently.
There was no indication of infantry working with tanks, and the only tactic
in sight was 'purely one of opportunity'. In his later books Fuller would
admit and commend the 'great victory' secured by French tanks in the Battle of Soissons, in July 1918; but his opinion at the time was less generous.
According to the note he made as he incorporated this liaison officer's

report into his private journal: 'The French Tank Corps did not distinguish itself. It never will under such a "dud" as General Estienne.' Perhaps the poor man should have been a waiter.

There was to be precious little forward movement for France's tanks in the decade following the war. General Estienne pressed the case for mechanization as best he could. In lectures given soon after the Armistice, he argued for the development of an armoured force that might eventually comprise 100,000 men, 4,000 tanks and 8,000 trucks, and which would be capable of conducting independent operations. Estienne was well aware of the limitations of the 3,000 or so light Renault tanks that France retained from the war, and in 1921 he drew up plans for a larger Medium tank, the Char B.

But Estienne's vision was not to be pursued. Under General Pétain, who remained in command until his retirement in 1930, the French Army was tied to the opposite course – its tactics predicated on the spirit of dogged defence, as epitomized by Verdun, the tank confined as a light adjunct to infantry, and all hope and resources concentrated on building the rigid system of defence represented by the supposedly unbreachable Maginot Line on France's eastern border.

It was not until the 1930s that Charles de Gaulle, a former advocate of Pétain's concept of defence, woke up to the powers of the tank while based at the Higher Council for National Defence and responsible for reviewing France's military strategy. In his book *Vers l'armée de métier*, published in 1934, De Gaulle opened his case by reviewing the beloved landscape of France – deep, but desperately vulnerable to attack – and, in unspoken acknowledgement of the Maginot Line, granted the case for 'a good hedge around the estate'.[14] His real interest, however, lay in the future evolution of warfare and the dawning but irresistible 'spirit of the times' that was mechanization. In a somewhat gilded reprise of Fuller's steely vision, De Gaulle hailed the tank as the revolutionary herald of a new epoch of warfare: 'Crawling along on its caterpillars, carrying light guns and machine guns, it advances into the front line, climbs over mounds and ditches, and beats down trenches and barbed-wire entanglements. However faltering and awkward it may have appeared at first, the tank completely upset the science of tactics. Through the tank was reborne the art of surprise, to which it added the relentlessness of machinery. Through it the art of manoeuvring was restored.'[15] De Gaulle envisioned the tank soldiers as youthful 'aristocrats of war'. Supple of mind as well as muscle and unfettered by ties of family, interest or habit, these were the young heroes of the future as foreseen by the poet Paul Valéry, who had predicted 'the development of undertakings by a few chosen men, acting in crews and producing, in a few moments or in an hour, the most shattering results in the most unexpected places'.[16]

Persuaded that the age of the mass army was coming to an end, De Gaulle urged that France should establish a small and professional mechanized force of 100,000 young men to operate alongside its conscript army, an elite force consisting of six motorized and partly armoured divisions, which would be capable of rapid indendependent operations. Such was the mechanized onslaught De Gaulle saw coming: 'a heavily armoured brigade moving across country as fast as a horse at the gallop, armed with 500 guns of medium calibre, 400 smaller pieces, and 600 machine-guns, crossing ditches three yards wide, climbing mounds thirty feet high, felling 40-year-old trees, knocking down walls twelve bricks wide, crushing all obstacles, barriers, and hedgerows . . .'

Yet whose side would this coming Juggernaut be on? The French Army shifted in this direction in the thirties, but too little and also far too late. The first motorized cavalry division, the Division Légère Mécanique was formed in 1934, and the Char B that Estienne had suggested in 1921 was finally put into slow production in 1936. Tactics were cramped by a governing framework that prioritized defence over offence, and by the fact that the only available vehicle for their implementation remained the light, infantry-supporting Renault tanks left over from the Great War.

By the late thirties, however, it was the old guard who dominated the field. The ideas of Estienne, De Gaulle and others were defeated by reactionaries like General Narcisse Chauvineau. An expert on fortification, Chauvineau was entirely convinced that 'passive defence, in positions supported by artillery fire, was superior to offense'.[17] In a book called *Is an Invasion still Possible?*, published in 1939, he ridiculed the idea of deep tank operations as 'grand tours' dreamed up by 'imaginative minds', follies that 'seem to belong to the realm of dreams rather than to the realities of future war', and insisted that the modern French division was a defensive force that 'could successfully attack only blacks' – i.e. in the colonies. For Chauvineau the tank lacked native French intelligence and 'cannot be something to fear'. It was 'a machine forced to go on relentlessly, like the wandering Jew, until it runs out of fuel'. Chauvineau would soon enough be exposed in his chauvinistic blindness, along with General Georges, who declared Germany's panzer tactics to be a dreadful blunder. But, in 1939 he had the support of Marshal Pétain, who contributed an introduction to Chauvineau's book, describing it as 'full of wisdom' and applauding its derision of mechanized armies as 'Sancho Panzas too weighted down with equipment to fight'. For Fuller this was just a pompous French version of the Haig-mind – two unknowing duffers blathering on as they teetered at the edge of the abyss. He had anticipated that the Maginot Line would be broken by German tanks, and remarked that the French were 'not preparing for the next war but for the last war but one'.[18] Fuller would have approved of De Gaulle, even without the acknowledgement De Gaulle eventually provided in 1943, when he remarked that he derived his ideas from Britain's 'best soldier' – J. F. C. Fuller: 'He was the prophet, we only followed him . . . You will find prophesied in his books everything that the Germans did with tanks. I have often wondered why he is never used.'[19]

Light 3 America

J. W. Christie in an experimental armoured vehicle.

France shrank from the idea of raising an independent armoured force, but the situation in which his American followers found themselves is likely to have impressed Fuller as equally dismal. Here too he will have seen the innovative champions of mechanization coming up against formidable forces of reaction: not just the well-entrenched prejudices of the military establishment and the cost-cutting aspirations of purblind politicians, but the isolationist thinking that was strong enough to prevent President Woodrow Wilson from taking America into the League of Nations as a leading world power and also, as time went on, the argument, advanced by President Hoover at the 1932 disarmament conference, that the tank should be banned along with all other offensive weapons.[20]

Fuller had known about the American Tank Corps since the war, when it first appeared as little more than a comic proposition to superior British eyes. The United States of America had declared war against Germany on 2 April 1917, but it was not until early August that enquiring officers from General Pershing's American Expeditionary Force made the journey from

Paris to Bermicourt, where they received the 'fairly comprehensive tactical paper' that Fuller had written 'for their education'.[21]

A little later, on 24 August 1917, an American colonel and major travelled from Paris to visit the British Tank Corps's Advanced Headquarters at Lovie. Arriving late in the evening, the pair had no sooner sat down in Brigadier General Elles's tent than the colonel was violently sick and then lapsed into unconsciousness. Having been removed to a spare tent (and, as British Tank Corps raconteurs liked to emphasize, accidentally dropped into a puddle in the process), the fellow rallied sufficiently to provide Elles with a welcome reassurance: 'You may take it from me, General, that the President intends to make this war a personal matter.' Captain the Hon. Evan Charteris judged the two well-meaning despite being 'rough and uncouth, without any manners'.[22] In the morning, the major showed Fuller a paper he had written on tanks, said to have been marked 'Very Secret' and 'Shown to No-one'. Fuller was not to read this 'remarkable effort' until a few weeks later, when it was sent on to Bermicourt having been found in an 'estaminet' near Arras. The document, which revealed the major to be 'a veritable he-man', outlined a 'tactical concept' in which planes would clear the skies and drop bombs 'just in front' of the advancing line of tanks. There were to be artillery barrages and mobile machine guns driving in to 'widen the breach' behind the tanks; and then the US cavalry would pour through the gap and swing outwards – 'Sacrificed? Of course; but winning results worth the sacrifice.' General Elles might have likened tank warfare to rugger,[23] but here it was recast as 'the flying wedge' of American football.

This document, which Fuller later mocked as 'virile but sound',[24] was actually written by Lieutenant Colonel John H. Parker, and the amusement it caused in the British Tank Corps reflected resentment at the 'millionaire spirit' of the new allies, who seemed so cocksure despite their lack of experience with tanks. Soon enough that resentment would be increased by Pershing's insistence that the American Expeditionary Force be kept intact as an independent force, and its men certainly not poured into depleted British units. This policy would prompt Fuller, at least in his private journal, to dismiss Pershing as 'an ass', who was foolishly preventing his men from getting experience alongside other units:

This year the Americans are going to do nothing, next year they are going to buy their experience at the price of 750,000 unnecessary casualties, and in 1920 they are going to really assist in winning the war. At present, they are taking tea with everyone, touring and looking for the best. Instead they should take their coats off and earn their experience by work.[25]

The British Tank Corps's American visitors came from the American Expeditionary Force's Tank Department, which Pershing had made responsible for manufacturing and fielding a force of some four hundred tanks, half of them modelled on the British heavy tank, and the other half on the French light Renault. The initiative was approved in September 1917, and the man who would lead the American Tank Corps through the remaining months of the war, Colonel S. D. Rockenbach, was appointed in December 1917.

Rockenbach's main frustration had been a lack of tanks with which to get to work. In the early months, when American production was supposedly getting under way, neither the British nor the French found machines to spare for their new allies. So training had been organized at two different centres. The Heavy battalions were trained at the British Tank Corps Centre at Bovington; while the Light Tank Service became the responsibility of the first soldier to be assigned to the new force – a man who also happened to hate the British habit of drinking tea, which he described as 'a most hellish and wasteful practice'.[26] George S. Patton was a well-connected thirty-two-year-old cavalry lieutenant who had achieved some notoriety as a 'bandit-killer' in 1916. Having used three Dodge touring cars to track down and kill the Villista commander Julio Cárdenas while serving in Pershing's 'punitive raid' against Pancho Villa's forces in Mexico, Patton had claimed, in his eagerness to move into tanks, to be 'the only American who has ever made an attack in a motor vehicle'.[27]

After joining the new force in November 1917, Patton spent two weeks at the French training centre in the forest of Compiègne. Here he fired and drove a Renault tank: 'It is easy to do after an auto and quite comfortable though you can see nothing at all . . . It is funny to hit small trees and see them go down . . . They are noisy [and] rear up like a horse or stand on the head with perfect immunity . . . The thing will do the damdest things imaginable.'[28] In December he had visited the British front near Amiens to meet Fuller, said to have provided 'interesting data'. Fuller had no recollection of the meeting. When asked, four decades later, whether George Patton was 'the one who got gin soaked and fell in an estaminet', he would deny ever having met this particular American hero.[29]

Patton's light tank school at Bourg, near Langres, bristled with salutes and haircuts and other strict procedures intended to ensure that the men 'look like soldiers and not like poets'.[30] The American Tank Corps was to have 'discipline if nothing', and perhaps that was just as well, since for many weeks it had not a single tank to practise with. So Patton's men set to work drilling, designing shoulder insignia, competing in games and polishing themselves up to a shine. In the same orderly manner, they converted stables, dug latrines and synchronized their watches against the day when their longed-for machines would finally arrive. As Patton wrote in January 1918, 'Unless I get some Tanks soon I will go crazy.' The first ten Renaults had eventually arrived late in March, but the problem remained intense. On 25 May Colonel S. D. Rockenbach wrote to General Elles of the British Tank Corps, lamenting the fact that there were still so few tanks for his men, both the heavy battalions trained in Wool, and those at Patton's centre at Bourg: 'If I don't get the machines to get in with pretty soon I don't know how I will hold them.'[31]

Patton developed an American tactics that was less ambitious for the tank than the one that Fuller and Elles had contrived for the heavy machines used at Cambrai – he planned to run his light two-man tanks alongside infantry, but without confining them all to the rear, as was the French custom. These theories were tested in the last months of the war. In September, Patton's 1st Tank Brigade participated in the American Expeditionary Force's attack on the St Mihiel Salient. Rain ensured that this was another case of swamp warfare. But Patton was there to prime his troops with an American variation on the order that Elles had issued just before Cambrai: insisting that 'AMERICAN TANKS DO NOT SURRENDER', he commended the operation as our 'BIG CHANCE; WHAT WE HAVE WORKED FOR . . . MAKE IT WORTHWHILE'. He also followed Elles's example by leading his force from the front, riding into the town of Pannes on a tank. This flourish aside, however, the tanks were of limited use, owing to lack of petrol as much as ground conditions: Fuller registered the attack as disappointing 'from the tank point of view'. The light tanks also fought in the Meuse-Argonne offensive in September, in which Patton was wounded as he marched forward into a hail of bullets, urged on by a vision of his ancestors gazing down on him from a cloud above the German line.[32] That was the end of the war for Patton, but the light tanks had pressed on with the advancing American forces until the fighting came to an end on 11 November 1918.

Having trained at Bovington in England, the 301st Heavy Tank Battalion arrived in France in August 1918, and for an initial month or so formed part of the 1st British Tank Brigade under General Baker-Carr. He was as much impressed by the American's technical proficiency as he was surprised by their habit of addressing him as 'gen' and by 'the astounding lack of uniformity of their "turn-out"'.[33] Soon enough these Americans, referred to as 'the Barbarians' by a neighbouring British general, had moved south to participate in the closing advance. They had suffered a disaster on 29 September, running into an old British minefield as they advanced on the Hindenburg Line near the Bellicourt tunnel, and losing ten tanks along with most of their crews. But there were more successful engagements in October, which had led Fuller to commend the battalion's contribution as 'brief but conspicuously gallant'.[34]

After the war the American Tank Corps returned to its base at Fort Meade in Maryland, still commanded by Brigadier General Samuel D. Rockenbach, a man who hoped to see the corps established on a permanent basis, even if he lacked the tactical vision to explain quite why. Patton was there too, commanding the 304th Tank Brigade and convinced, as an enthusiastic reader of Fuller's *Tanks in the Great War*, that even though the mechanized army of Fuller's unrestrained vision would cost more than any Western government could be expected to tolerate, the US Tank Corps should nevertheless be developed as an independent force if it was to fulfil 'the destiny' of its new weapon.[35] In January 1919 a tank service of just this kind was proposed in the March-Baker Army Reorganization Bill, but it was not to be. As Commanding General of the American Expeditionary Force, General John Pershing had already conducted a review of the lessons of the recent war, with the help of a board convinced that the future of the tank lay in infantry support and that 'there is no such thing as an independent tank attack'.[36] Aware of the political climate in those post-war years, Pershing was also of the view that in the immediate term America only needed an army capable of repulsing 'sudden invasion', and that it would have been 'militarism of a pronounced and objectionable type' to go beyond that.[37] So the National Defence Act of 1920 had scrapped the Tank Corps and placed all tanks under the control of infantry. Patton and Captain Dwight D. Eisenhower, who had been wartime commander of the tank training centre at Camp Colt, Pennsylvania, continued to argue the case against such a step but, as Eisenhower later recorded, they were threatened with court martial unless they desisted.

The decision that dissolved the American Tank Corps also used the power of the law to subordinate the new weapon to infantry tactics, in which the archaic virtue of closing with the enemy featured prominently, and in which the purpose of the tank was, as General Staff insisted, to 'facilitate the uninterrupted advance of the rifleman'. The tank was an adjunct once again and preferably a light one at that. The contrary view was heard from Fuller and Liddell Hart, whose articles were printed in American service journals, but the opposition was unyielding. In May 1927, the *Infantry Journal* published Fuller's 'Tactics and Mechanization', in which he pressed for the establishment of a separate tank arm that could serve as a 'rapid strike force'. But the rebuttal was immediate. Colonel Frank Cocheu, Assistant Commandant of the Infantry School was quite adamant that 'only through the use of rifle fire power and the bayonet attack could a battle be drawn to a successful conclusion'. The cult of the bayonet was also defended by Lieutenant Colonel W. R. Burtt, an instructor at the Army War College, who objected that 'we cannot subscribe to the view of a tank or a mechanical army . . . The Army of the future will depend upon the mobility and enlightened personnel who represent the Queen of Battle' (i.e. the infantry). From Fuller's point of view, there would have been little point in distinguishing these arguments from those of the American cavalry officer who visited Britain in 1925 to see the manoeuvres of Colonel Lindsay's Experimental Mechanized Force, and managed to conclude that their real lesson was that, with air power developing as it was, the horse-mounted cavalry would become more and more important as time went on.

A brief flicker of light passed across this dismal scene in 1928, when the US Secretary for War, Dwight F. Davies, who had attended the 1927 trials of Britain's Experimental Mechanized Force, ordered that a similar initiative be set up at Fort Leonard Wood, Fort Meade, in Maryland in July 1928. Tried over three months, it greatly impressed Major Adna R. Chaffee, who, along with the War Department Mechanized Development Board, was soon arguing that the American military should mechanize. General Charles Summerall, the Chief of Staff, was also convinced and, in October 1930, a permanent mechanized force was established at Fort Eustis, Virginia, commanded by Colonel Daniel Van Voorhis, with Chaffee joining as his lieutenant shortly afterwards. However, the military budget was under acute financial pressure following the Wall Street Crash, and the next Chief of Staff, General Douglas MacArthur, closed down the mechanized force in 1931, and ordered the various arms to mechanize at whatever pace they could achieve. Its tanks were transferred to the cavalry, having been renamed 'combat cars' in order to avoid breaking the law as pronounced by the 1920 Act, which specified that all tanks should be with the infantry.

By the mid-thirties, the American tank effort would have appeared to

Fuller as a forlorn antique rally. In a political climate where financial stringency served as the convenient consort of isolationism and disarmament, there was still no immediate prospect of replacing the ageing Renaults and British Mark VIIIs acquired in 1918. Work had been initiated on two new tanks in 1919 – one based on Fuller's Medium D, and the other being a convertible model with tracks and wheels that was to be designed by J. Walter Christie, a private engineer, who had worked both with the automobile industry and with the US Army's ordnance department during the Great War. But these had subsequently been cancelled, or the specifications scaled right down in accordance with the infantry's preference for light tanks. Christie had soldiered on privately through these years of inconstancy and, by 1928, had produced a promising prototype medium tank, equipped with both tracks and wheels for use on different surfaces, an innovative suspension system, and also an aircraft engine that made it capable of travelling at unprecedented speeds. The US Army bought seven of these machines in 1931 (five commissioned by itself, and two that had first been contracted by a Polish government that defaulted),[38] but eventually decided that they were too expensive to put into production. By 1936 the US Army had only accepted sixteen of the new T4 Christie-based medium tanks into service, and after that its development programme was refocused on light tanks.[39]

Light 4 Russia

Red Army manoeuvres near Moscow,
24 October 1935

Neither Britain, nor France, nor the United States persisted with the idea of the independent mechanized force, choosing instead to mechanize the cavalry – a half-hearted and doctrinally inane measure, as Fuller saw it, for which they would pay soon enough. To begin with, the creed of mechanization had seemed to go little better in Russia, the world of Fuller's most alarming window, packed with hideous devils masquerading as angels.

Fuller deplored the 'Red slug of Bolshevism' that had, as he once put it in unmistakably Crowleyan terms, 'slimed Russia' so successfully.[40] And one of the first manifestations of that Red slug was to be found outside the Finland Station in Petrograd on 3 April 1917, the day Lenin returned to Russia by sealed train after many years of exile in Switzerland. Said to have been remote and withdrawn on the train, Lenin arrived a little before midnight. Stepping out into a 'surging sea' of workers, soldiers, sailors, and old comrades, Lenin was not immediately on top of the situation. He was apparently so taken aback by his reception that when a captain approached him on the platform, stood to attention and saluted, Lenin himself promptly did likewise.[41] He was given a wreath by Alexandra Kollontai, which he is said to have carried awkwardly;[42] and then, having been led past a guard of honour on the platform, he was encouraged to step up into one of the Revolution's most epoch-making images. Standing on an armoured car adorned with the red party banner, he hailed the masses and the Revolution with which they had 'opened a new epoch'. He was then driven through the Petrovska district in that same armoured car, down roads lit up by searchlights and lined by files of working men and women, to the palace that served as the Bolshevik headquarters. That armoured car was to become the symbol not just of the leader's return, but also of the unyielding and steely determination with which he proceeded to smash through gradualist social democratic ideas (accepted by the Mensheviks and also many Bolsheviks at that time), about the necessity of parliamentary democracy and a 'bourgeois stage' in Russia's transition to socialism. He started the very next day, when he presented his April Theses before a 'stunned' assembly of the Social Democrats at the Tauride Palace, arguing the case for proceeding directly to full-scale revolution and what soon enough became the dictatorship of the proletariat.[43]

The symbolic affinity between armoured cars and Leninist revolution would be reaffirmed a few months later. Armoured car units stationed in Petrograd defected to the Revolution on the night of 24 October, and their machines were soon cruising the streets for the Red Guards, helping to take control of the railways stations and banks, and preparing for 'The Great October Socialist Revolution' ushered in the following day.[44] For the revolutionary American journalist, John Reed, these wild and careening vehicles were symbolic both of the brutality of the old regime, and, once appropriated, of the 'iron will' of the proletariat. One machine that remained loyal to the Tsar came 'rolling up from the Admiralty, on its way to the Telephone Exchange' and, having stalled right in front of Reed's comrade Louise Bryant as she was walking along St Isaac's Square, put on its own demonstration of the immoral effect of government power:

Some sailors ambushed behind wood piles began shooting. The machine-gun in the turret of the thing slewed around and spat a hail of bullets indiscriminately into the wood-piles and the crowd. In the archway where Miss Bryant stood seven people were shot dead, among them two little boys. Suddenly with a shout, the sailors leapt up and rushed into the flaming open, closing around the monster, they thrust their bayonets into the loopholes again and again, yelling . . . The chauffeur pretended to be wounded, and they let him go free to run to the Duma and swell the tale of Bolshevik atrocities . . . Among the dead was a British officer. [45]

One vehicle of indeterminate loyalty was to be seen passing slowly up and down the street, its siren wailing madly. [46] Others, which had been named after early Russian Tsars – Oleg, Rwik, Svietoslav – were now daubed over with huge red letters announcing their conversion to the Revolution. [47] One by the Marinsky Palace, where the council of the Russian Republic met, displayed a vast red flag, and was newly lettered in red paint. Another lurked beneath a flickering street light on the corner of the Nevsky: 'a big armoured automobile, with racing engine and oil-smoke pouring out of it. A small boy had climbed up one side of the thing and was looking down the barrel of a machine gun. Soldiers and sailors stood around, evidently waiting for something.' [48] The tactics would not have impressed Fuller, but the moral effect of these liberated machines was considerable.

Lenin was back on an armoured car on 1 January 1918, using it as the podium from which to launch the Red Army. The American journalist and revolutionary sympathizer Albert Rhys Williams met him at the first Socialist Army meeting, where he addressed the Red Guards whose newly formed armoured-car battalion was entraining for the south. [49] The event was held at a vast and freezing factory called the Mikhailovsky Manège; and by this time the attendant armoured cars were adorned with fresh evergreens as well as red banners, including the one that served as a stage – first for the balalaika and accordion players who tried to keep the waiting men warm with country dances, and then for Lenin who arrived hours late and failed to deliver a speech of the expected stiffening kind. Instead of dispatching the young soldiers to the front with the promise that the international proletariat was marching irreversibly forward, he had disappointed them by observing that, while things had been going very well up to now, they should also be prepared for occasional setbacks. With Lenin's contribution 'misfiring', it remained for his excited young American admirer to seize a moment of glory. Stepping up in the name of international solidarity, he braced the comrades by reciting the expected slogans in his own faltering and comic Russian, and then, with Lenin acting as his interpreter, offering to enlist himself if the going got that bad.

The image of Lenin on his armoured car was quickly lifted into the emerging iconography of the Russian Revolution. Soviet sculptors and artists portrayed the great leader not just passing through the Vyborg district in an atmosphere of nervous jubilation but gazing up into a great red future as his machine mounted the incline of history. This is how it was for Natwey Mannisser, whose 1924 sculpture, 'Lenin on an armoured car during the October Revolution 1917', shows Lenin on a wheeled armoured car, his head held high, and his long coat flowing over cold steel, as he is thrust into his destiny.[50] The heroic image recurs in *October*, the film made by Sergei Eisenstein in 1927 to mark the tenth anniversary of the Revolution. First the searchlights play over expectant faces in the massive crowds waiting outside the Finland Station, and then Lenin steps up on to the almost equally famous armoured car to be fêted as the redeeming saviour ('It's him!'), who has come to end the forlorn age of Hunger and War. With the banners of history unfolding all around him this man of destiny rallies the crowds from the top of his metal machine, punching the air and betraying no hint of the hesitation that attended his actual arrival. By 1927 that symbolic vehicle had already given way to the armoured limousines favoured by Joseph Stalin, but in Eisenstein's image Lenin is still the great liberator, his revolution guaranteed by the iron will of the people.

The liberated armoured car may have signified revolution, but not so the first tanks, which arrived during the post-Revolutionary civil wars of 1918–21. They too appear in Eisenstein's *October* – British and French models rolling towards Petrograd as hated engines of Western imperialism and reaction bent on crushing the Revolution. Eisenstein's capitalist tanks were attached to the forces of General Nikolai Iudenich, Commander-in-Chief of the North-western army of White Russia, which was supported by the British Navy in the Gulf of Finland. Petrograd seemed as good as lost, when Trotsky arrived in his armoured train and started mobilizing the entire population, raising a new force of worker-soldiers, and using them to bolster a demoralized military.

Those White Russian tanks exercised considerable moral effect on both sides. As Iudenich's soldiers awaited the long delayed arrival of the British tanks (which came late and in inadequate quantities), they used the mere thought of these wonder weapons to stave off the Red propaganda that was corroding morale in their ranks: 'talk among both officers and men turned upon what would be accomplished when these monsters should arrive'.[51]

Iudenich's tanks also played on the nerves of Petrograd's defenders, who heard rumours that the White army was equipped with 'the latest technical devices'. As Trotsky communicated to the Kremlin on 20 October 1919, 'The position is deteriorating. The enemy is pressing on towards Carskoe, reportedly with tanks.'[52]

In reality Iudenich's army had a total of only six British tanks, considerably fewer than were shown advancing on St Petersburg in *October*. Manned by British volunteers, these machines are said – at least when they were not out of commission because of a broken bridge at Yamburg – to have 'totally demoralized the Red troops unfortunate enough to encounter them'.[53] Tank terror played on the nerves of revolutionary Petrograd, but Trotsky improvised his own crash programme of remoralization. As Victor Serge reports, 'It was rumoured that the Whites had tanks. Trotsky had it proclaimed that the infantry was well able to knock tanks out.'[54] In some versions, Trotsky ordered a Petrograd foundry, the Putilov factory, which had been a cradle of the Revolution, to prepare some heavily armoured cars, in order to prove to his soldiers that they too had the magical weapon. Aware of the desperate situation, Lenin advised Trotsky to add ten thousand or so members of Petrograd's bourgeoisie to the city's defenders, and then to shoot a few hundred of them with machine guns placed to their rear: a measure that would surely produce a mass assault on General Iudenich's approaching forces.[55] But, if Serge is to be believed, Trotsky had other ideas of psychological motivation in mind: 'Certain mysterious but ingenious agitators spread the rumour, which may even have been true, that Iudenich's tanks were made of painted wood.'

Whether or not his fighters were successfully duped in this way, Trotsky would later record impressive results – especially in the defence of the Pulkovo heights, which took place over 21 October and the next few days. As he later wrote, 'Young workers and peasants, military students from Moscow and Petrograd, were utterly reckless with their lives. They advanced against machine-gun fire and attacked tanks with revolvers in their hands. The general staff of the Whites wrote of the "heroic frenzy" of the Reds.'[56] According to one White Russian, Trotsky's detachments of worker-communists certainly fought like lions: 'They attacked the tanks with their bayonets, and, although they were mowed down in rows by the devastating fire of the steel monsters, they continued to defend their positions.'[57] The Whites, whose victory had seemed assured only a few days previously, were routed and driven back to the Estonian frontier in two weeks. Abject and disintegrating, they could only blame the British who, according to General Rodzyanko, 'should have provided more tanks'.[58] Fuller, as we know from his proposed 'Tank Expeditionary Force', would have agreed.

The tank entered the Russian Revolution as a spellbinding contraption exercising a 'moral effect' that was the military equivalent of commodity fetishism. However, another view started to emerge once the advance of this supposedly unstoppable imperialist monster had been blocked by the even more irresistible will of the Soviet people. The question then was how the Red Army might itself make effective use of the considerable number of tanks it had captured from the defeated White forces: British Mark Vs and also French Renaults, one of which was sent to Moscow as a gift for Lenin, who is said to have been decidedly keen on tanks and even to have devised the tactics for the Red Army's first use of these White trophies in 1919.

That was also the concern of G. Sokolnikov, who wrote to Lenin and Trotsky on 5 May 1920, making the case for 'more efficient use of technical military resources in the Red Army now a campaign is to be opened on the western front'.[59] Written as the Red Army prepared for war against Pilsudski's Poland, Sokolnikov's memo was partly concerned with the 'utilization of tanks', urging that the machines captured from White forces should be quickly refitted and transferred to assist in 'the formation of tank squadrons'. Fuller would immediately have suspected that the essential point was based on the example of Cambrai and Amiens: 'Until now tanks have not been taken into account, and have not been concentrated as they ought; and their refitting has been done by primitive, local methods.'

The Soviet Union's first truly communist tank is said to have been manufactured that same year at the Krasno-Sormova factory.[60] Modelled on Renault FT tanks captured from White Russian forces, this light 'KS' tank was dubbed 'Freedom Fighter Comrade Lenin'. Fifteen more were then commissioned on Lenin's order and duly named – Red Champion, Proletariat, Victory, The Paris Commune . . . On 23 February 1922 the Soviet fleet was paraded in Moscow to commemorate the Red Army's fourth anniversary.

Over the same years, a 'Revolution in Military Affairs' was being prepared by young Red commanders recruited as the 'military specialists', with whose help Trotsky set out to build the Red Army. These pioneers of the Marxist-Leninist approach to warfare were exponents of a communist rather than 'magical' break with the past, but they were at least as futurist and theoretical in orientation as Fuller was in Britain, and they were just as ardent in their advocacy of mechanization as a means of breaking through the hypnosis of bourgeois convention.

Mikhail Tukhachevsky was to be the most influential of these battle-hardened military specialists. Many years later, J. F. C. Fuller would paint him as 'a romantic barbarian who abhorred Western civilization. He had the soul of Genghis Khan [and] loved the open plains and the thud of a thousand hoofs.'[61] However, there was considerably more to this 'apocalyptic Slav' than that. Having commanded forces on several fronts during the civil war, and suffered devastating and unexpected defeat against Pilsudski's Poland in the 1920 Battle of Warsaw, Tukhachevsky had joined the Red Army's General Staff in May of that year, but was soon back in the field, securing Communist power against popular revolt. In March 1921, he crushed the insurrection at Kronstadt naval base – led by a Kronstadt revolutionary committee, which was pressing for free elections and freedom of speech and assembly, and which condemned the 'Communist usurpers' who had turned the Revolution into 'an even greater enslavement of human beings'.[62] Trotsky warned the mutineers that they would be 'shot like partridges' and it was Tukhachevsky who placed Cheka machine guns behind his own conscript army to ensured that his threat was carried out.[63] Having presided over the operation that proved to the world that the Revolution was taking a monstrous direction under Lenin, Tukhachevsky went on to Tambov province, this time assisted by Vladimir Kiriakovich Triandafillov (a fellow 'military specialist' at the Military Academy of the Workers' and Peasants' Red Army), where he terrorized and suppressed a peasant revolt: using aeroplanes and poisonous gas, burning villages and forcing their populations into concentration camps.

As they set out to establish a theory capable of guiding the future development of the Red Army, Tukhachevsky and his fellow soldier-revolutionaries at the Military Academy learned from the doctrines of the old Tsarist army. But they did so sceptically, as Bolshevik warriors who were prepared to take nothing for granted and felt no deference towards the classical authorities of Tsarist military science.[64] Reflecting on the Red Army's unexpected defeat by Pilsudski and its experience of the Eastern Front in the First World War (a front that was never fully immobilized, unlike the Western one on which tanks first appeared), they went beyond the idea of restoring manoeuvre to open up a new area of military doctrine. In a lecture given in 1923, Tukhachevsky announced that, since it was impossible 'with the extended fronts of modern times, to destroy the enemy's army at a single blow' the army of the future should be prepared to pursue a series of linked and often simultaneous 'destructive operations'.[65] This was the 'operational art' that Alexander Svechin, one of the academy's senior professors, had first interposed between the traditional fields of tactics and strategy – a new domain conceived as 'the totality of manoeuvres and battles in a given part of a theatre of military action directed towards the achievement of the common goal'.[66] It was on this 'operational' foundation that Tukhachevsky, Triandafillov, G. S. Isserson and others built the theory of 'Deep Battle': successive operations, organized through the entire depth (perhaps as much as 250 kilometres) of the enemy's position. Traditional military doctrine prioritized the 'frontal attack', but the advocates of Deep Battle viewed the offensive as a series of 'echelons' or successive waves: the first would break the enemy's lines, the second would carry out consecutive deeper actions, and the third would pursue and rout the defender beyond his operational depth.[67]

The mechanization of 'operational' warfare came somewhat later. Tukhachevsky and other Red commanders at the Military Academy had disputed Svechin's insistence that the Soviet army was in no condition to prepare for anything but a defensive war of attrition; but even Triandafillov, who was a committed exponent of both motorization and mechanization, had assumed that the development of the Red Army would long be hindered by its 'peasant rear'. In a 1929 meeting of the Communist Academy a ruthlessly dogmatic Tukhachevsky had unmasked the 'bourgeois ideology' in Svechin's position, and also criticized his comrade Triandafillov for underestimating the extent to which the Soviet Union would be transformed by the industrialization drive of Stalin's first Five Year Plan. By 1931, when Triandafillov was killed in an air crash, Tukhachevsky was pressing for a 'complete militarization'[68] of the Soviet economy, in order to convert the Red Army into a fully mechanized force capable of implementing an altogether more offensive and destructive mode of 'operational' warfare than had been anticipated in the early twenties.

Planes, parachutists and artillery pieces would be central to 'Deep' warfare as Tukhachevsky envisaged it, but so too were tanks; and the Soviet advocates of 'operational art' were well aware of J. F. C. Fuller's contribution in this area. Having studied the tank battles of 1918 with the help of Fuller's *Tanks in the Great War* (published in Russian translation in 1923), Triandafillov knew that tanks would play an important part in future wars. He had looked beyond the primitive prototypes of his own time and into a future in which the tank would be converted 'from a tactical resource to a resource of great operational significance' – faster, more powerful, and with a much greater radius of action.[69] As an exponent of a motorized, mechanized, but also greatly expanded conscript army, Triandafillov was critical of older thinkers, like A. I. Verskhovsky, the Professor of Tactics at the Military Academy, who appeared to have been seduced by Fuller's portrayal of the mechanized but also miniaturized professional army of the future.

In his book *The Nature of the Operations of Modern Armies* (1929), Triandafillov observed that it was 'barely possible to take seriously' the arguments of foreign writers like Fuller, for whom 'defense of the idea of massive "ghastly" armies is conservatism'.[70] Describing Fuller as little more than the stooge of a fearful bourgeoisie, Triandafillov repudiated his suggestion that the mechanized New Model Army of the future would be small but fully professional, arguing that this scenario, in which conscripts were replaced by technology, reflected 'exceptional distrust of the masses, who have now become more class conscious than prior to and during the World War'.[71]

For the capitalist countries 'quality and quantity have become a contradiction to each other in the epoch of the proletarian revolution'. Like that of Zol'dan and Seeckt in Germany, Fuller's thinking was influenced by 'fear of the inevitable proletarian revolution' and reflected 'the difficulties capitalism is now encountering in its relations with the masses'. It was to be hoped that capitalist statesmen would soon follow the advice of their 'armchair warriors' and 'abandon the idea of massive armies'. But the Soviet Union should understand that 'one cannot meet the demands for quantity without . . . massive, virtually universal, mobilization of the entire able-bodied population' – including that part of the population that was responsible for supplying the million-man army at the front.[72] The Red Army should recognize that 'The best conditions for free maneuver, for extensive tactical and operational art, will be achieved . . . by the corresponding increase in the mobility of modern million-man armies by improving the technology of transportation . . . A country forced by political considerations, owing to distrust of the masses, to return to small armies of professionals cannot count upon conducting a large war.'[73] Triandafillov's version of the New Model Army was to combine motorization and mass conscription, quality and quantity.

Tukhachevsky, who added greater mechanization to the desired mix, had read Fuller too. In 1931, he wrote an introduction to a truncated Russian translation of Fuller's *Reformation of War* (it can safely be assumed that the passage about the 'Red slug' of Bolshevism had been left out).[74] He scorned the Englishman's 'incredibly muddled' reasoning, his 'high-falutin' Fuller-ian rhetoric', his brazen fascist demagogy, and his oppressive attitude to the colonies ('Like any average Englishman, he divides mankind into two categories – Englishmen and "niggers"; and this second group is by no means confined to those with black skins'). Like his colleague Triandafillov, this advocate of Deep Battle ridiculed Fuller for assuming that victory could be brought about by quick armoured strikes, and asked his readers to imagine what would happen if the British Army, mechanized and miniaturized as Fuller proposed, was to find itself at war with the USA across the Canadian border. The British would have 'Fuller's cadres of 18 divisions', whereas the US Army would have 180: 'The small English Army would be simply crushed. Is it not already clear that talk about small, but mobile, mechanized armies in major wars is a cock-and-bull story? Only frivolous people can take them seriously.'[75]

All this had to be said before Tukhachevsky, who already had good reason to cover his own rear, could safely insist that, despite the 'crust of fantasising', a 'progressive' avant-garde kernel was to be found inside the nut of this bourgeois anti-Communist's writings. French military thought was 'simply held together by the past', but Fuller had at least ensured that British thinking was orientated far more towards the future. He was to be commended for his attention to military technology and for insisting that tactics needed to be rethought in the light of mechanization. Fuller was 'a dyed-in-the-wool British imperialist' and doubtless a capitalist lackey too, but he also had 'many interesting ideas about tank actions', especially manoeuvres that might be carried out against the enemy's rear. Though intended to crush revolutionary disorder at home and ensure the 'enslavement of India', Fuller's recommendations on the subject of 'small wars' were of 'exceptional interest' to the Red Army as it faced unrest 'within our own frontiers' or, perhaps, in the Islamic regions towards Kabul.

While Tukhachevsky and his battle-hardened comrades in the Soviet Military Academy refined the theory of Deep Battle, practical steps were also being taken to build and equip the mass mechanized Red Army to come. In 1927, and with secret German co-operation, experiments began at the Kazan Tank School. The emerging 'Correct Line for the War Doctrine of Tanks' was tested by an experimental mechanized unit, which, by 1929, had the use of some 100 tanks, the majority of which were still French and British models captured in the civil war. The first mechanized brigade was founded in Moscow in May 1931. Commanded by Colonel K. V. Kalinovski, and allegedly based on the experimental armoured force established earlier by the British Army on Salisbury Plain, this brigade, which was to be expanded into a mechanized corps in 1932, was intended to work as an independent force in which various different arms were combined (two tank battalions, two motor-rifle battalions, reconnaissance, artillery, etc.).

In accordance with the first Five Year Plan, much new industrial capacity had been created by 1931, when Tukhachevsky was appointed head of the army's Technology and Armament Department: new or upgraded car and tractor factories, steel works, and also armaments factories. Initiated that same year, 'The Great Tank Programme' involved over thirty factories and produced tanks by the thousand.[76] The models were based on imported prototypes that had been tested at the Voronezh Tank Centre – the Vickers Medium from Britain, and a fast prototype bought from the American engineer J. W. Christie. By 1932, the Brigade Kalinowski had been enlarged again to form the mechanized Corps Kalinowski, equipped with 500 tanks, 200 armoured cars and 60 motorized artillery pieces.

The 1936 manoeuvres, which were designed to test the principles of Deep Battle as spelt out in new Field Regulations published that year, drew apprehensive praise from French and British visitors, including Lieutenant General Sir Gifford Martel – the man known as 'Slosher' in the early days of the Tank Corps – and General Lord Wavell. Familiar with relentless problems of supply in their own country, these observers saw a Red Army in which quality had indeed been combined with quantity – albeit at a terrible price that the British voter would never tolerate. At the final parade Martel saw over 1,000 tanks drive past in a single procession, and he noticed the promise of the Soviet BT tank, which incorporated a suspension system developed from Christie's prototype and was evidently a machine of impressive speed and versatility.[77] He was interested by the composition of Tukhachevsky's 'mechanized brigades', each of which included three tank battalions equipped largely with BTs, a machine-gun battalion, and reconnaissance battalion equipped with lighter tanks; and he was astonished to see an airborne infantry brigade drop 2,000 feet from the wings of passing planes without casualties. Martel was flattered to discover that his book *In The Wake of the Tank* had been translated into Russian and issued to the army on 'a large scale'. Even so, tactics seemed weak (the tanks appeared 'just to bump into one another'), radio was under-exploited, and the continued use of horsed cavalry on the same mechanized battlefield 'seemed quite impossible'. Martel was not much impressed by Voroshilov, effectively the Commissar for Defence, or by his Chief of Staff, Yegorov. He judged Marshal Tukhachevsky to be 'by far the ablest officer' he met: the two of them dined together several times, with Tukhachevsky converting yards into metres on the menu, as he tried to get Martel to divulge the muzzle velocity achieved by British tanks.

Sixty years later, those 1936 manoeuvres would find oblique testimony in *Burnt by the Sun*, a film released in 1994 in which the Russian director Nikita Mikhalkov plays the part of Colonel Sergei Kotov, a famous hero of the 1917 Revolution whose brief sojourn at his country dacha is abruptly threatened by a practising company of Red Army tanks. The machines line up at the edge of a ripe wheatfield nearby, and prepare to advance over the crops of outraged peasants who are powerless to stop this military exercise going ahead ('You can crush me but not the wheat,' as one furious old woman says, having taken up a post-Tiananmen Square position in front of a tank). The accompanying planes zoom overhead, albeit without parachutists standing on their wings, but Kotov is able to stop the tanks, a measure of the charismatic authority of this heroic Red commander who is himself about to go under in Stalin's purge. Mikhalkov's tanks stand as perfect symbols of that crushing regime, even if there is no sign of operational art in the way he lines them up like combine harvesters – a dozen or so disconnected adjuncts in a collectivized wheatfield.

Tukhachevsky's mechanized brigades were more forceful than that, and better co-ordinated with aircraft too. Yet they were no match for Stalin. His dislike of Tukhachevsky has been traced back to the 1920 war against Poland: a defeat for which some blamed Tukhachevsky, who had fought on the Red Army's western front, but for which he himself had blamed the south-western front, where Stalin had served as a political officer, along with his future lackeys Voroshilov, Budenny and Timoshenko. The animosity was certainly persistent. In 1930 Stalin had dismissed a memorandum in which Tukhachevsky outlined the case for mechanizing the Red Army as 'nonsense' and inappropriate for a Marxist.[78] He had expressed similar objections a few years earlier, when Tukhachevsky proposed that he offer the American engineer J. Walter Christie a large sum of money to come and design a tank for the Soviet Union – a suggestion that is said to have led the great leader to condemn his marshal for 'succumbing to western bourgeois teachings and ideas'.[79] Stalin distrusted the concentration of doctrine and force development in Tukhachevsky's hands, and the course in 'strategic theory' was dropped from the curriculum of Tukhachevsky's Faculty of Military History and Strategic Studies – reportedly because 'strategic thinking was an occupation reserved exclusively for Stalin'.[80]

The tank may have joined the red tractor as an icon within the official art of socialist realism – it would be shown rolling down the progressive road of history, through a kulak-free countryside where peasant women raised their eyes from the plough to gaze at the metallic future while the apple trees of spring blossomed prodigiously all around.[81] But the doctrine of Deep Battle was less welcome. The 'operational art' of warfare was effectively killed off during Stalin's 'Great Purge' of 1937. Denounced as a Trotskyist and fascist who was plotting Stalin's downfall, Tukhachevsky was tried at a military tribunal on 11 June 1937, in which his contacts with the pre-Nazi Reichswehr were condemned and his call for 'rapid formation of tank and mechanized units at the expense of the cavalry' was cited as an example of his wrecking strategies.[82] Tukhachevsky was executed the next day along with other 'plotters', and the purge was then extended downwards through the officers' corps until the Red Army was reduced to a petrified desert in which only the correct Stalinist line could flourish. The writings of Tukhachevsky, Svechin and other purged advocates of 'operational' warfare were suppressed and the British mechanizers such as Fuller, Martel and Liddell Hart (who had by this time been marginalized in British military circles), were denounced as 'effete spokesmen for a decadent capitalism, which dared not place its trust in the masses, and so hid behind mechanical contrivances'.[83] Under Stalin's Commissar for Defence, Voroshilov, who had overseen the purging of his rival Tukhachevsky, it was announced that independent armoured operations were out of the question, tanks were to be subordinated to infantry and tactics were focused, once again, on frontal attack rather than deep infiltration. Deep Battle was discredited, although the factories continued to build machines ordered from existing fast tank designs. The BT tank would eventually evolve into the T-34, but the officers who might have guided its early deployment were gone.

Light 5 Italy

Benito Mussolini stands atop a Fiat-Ansaldo L3-33 tankette.

The Soviet Union was the Satanic Empire that finally convinced Fuller that a 'diabolical inversion' of the kind he had first espoused when he joined Aleister Crowley's assault on bourgeois Christendom and later turned against the 'Stone Age' assumptions of the British military establishment was not always for the better. Fuller saw the Leninist dialectic as a monstrous conjuring trick that had plunged Russia into a nightmare in which 'things appear to be firmly planted on their feet, but actually are standing on their heads'.[84] As a vehement anti-Communist, he had little to say about the attempts of Tukhachevsky, Triandafillov and other pioneers of the new 'operational' art. And it would not be until long after the Second World War that Fuller learned of, or at least acknowledged, their charge that his vision of an army in which mechanization was combined with miniaturization and the end of conscription, was born of fear of the proletariat. 'Such Marxian silliness was to cost the Russians dear,'[85] he gloated, failing to grasp the extent to which Tukhachevsky had advanced beyond his own prophesies or to realize that, if the Red Army was able to re-establish itself after its initial defeat by Nazi Germany, this was precisely because, contrary to Fuller's early prescriptions, it was a mass army with a huge industrial mobilization behind it.

Fuller kept a more sympathetic eye on the various European dictators of the right who were showing considerable interest in tanks by the mid-thirties. In his books, he would argue that, along with other 'scientific' weapons, the tank demanded a new kind of totalitarian war that was irreconcilable with democracy. The fine detail of this argument may have been lost on some of the fascist dictators who embraced the tank as a theatrical prop for their strutting ambitions, a spectacular accessory that could be advantageously displayed on public occasions. But, as Fuller knew, it was one thing to infect the populace with tank miasma by parading this rolling metal object as the embodied soul of state power, and quite another to train and equip an army that was genuinely capable of realizing the promise of mechanization.

Patriotic historians may claim that Italy was the first country to use armoured vehicles, back in 1912 when primitive armoured cars were deployed against the Turks in the Battle of Zanzur in what is now Libya, but it was to be no easy road from those mythical beginnings to the Corpo d'Armata Corazzato, an armoured strike force dedicated to high-speed mobile warfare (*la guerra di rapido corso*) that was founded in 1938 as part of a wider mechanization drive.[86] Tanks first came to Italy during the Great War, when an Italian officer, Count Alfredo Bennicelli, saw French models at work and convinced the army that it would be worth importing a French Schneider tank for experimental purposes. The 1st Independent Battery of Assault Cars (*Batteria autonoma carri d'assalto*), had been formed in 1918 and used the following year in Libya.

Here as elsewhere, the struggle to beat ploughshares into swords entailed the conversion of car factories as well as military units. Italy's first native tanks were built by Fiat, a car manufacturer controlled by Giovanni Agnelli, which had expanded into arms production during the war: first, in 1918, the cumbersome 40-ton Fiat 2000 and then, in collaboration with the ship-building company Ansaldo, the 5.5-ton Fiat 3000, which was modelled on the Renault FT 17.

Yet Italy's progress towards mechanization was also constrained by cultural factors. Mindful of a long history of invasions, military planners gave priority to defending often mountainous routes of possible enemy attack, an activity in which tanks did not appear to be crucial. And even if the tank did not seem like the bourgeois deviation it was claimed to be by some Stalinist cadres in the Red Army, it was not instantly reconcilable with a military tradition that emphasized individual heroism or, for that matter, with Mussolini's vision of the fascist soldier as the Roman legionary reborne. Yet the really defining difficulties, however, were more infra-structural. As one historian writes, 'Italy had neither the industrial base nor the raw materials to be a major power in modern industrial war.'[87] The difficulty this fact represented for the army's would-be mechanizers was aggravated by Mussolini's policy of national economic independence or 'autarchy', and insufficiently alleviated by his late announcement, in February 1939, of a policy intended to 'motorize the nation', and thereby to boost the industrial capacity available for the production of arms.

In the field of tactics, the Italian Army found its own way of subordinating the tank to cavalry and infantry. Fuller's vision of an all-mechanized army of the future was dismissed by Italian tank thinkers like Manlio Gabrielli, whose book *I Carri Armati* (1923) found no application for this scenario in Italy. Indeed, when a new idea of manoeuvre was eventually introduced in the early thirties, it came with horses still attached. As advocated by General Ottavio Zoppi, the *celeri*, or 'fast ones', were to be a combined force of cavalry and sharp-shooting light infantry units, with supporting tanks organized under Colonel Gervasio Bitossi as part of the Guide Light Horse Regiment at Parma. Bitossi's introductory address to the regiment reveals that in Italy as much as in the Soviet Union (although for different reasons) the advocates of the tank found it advisable to distance themselves from the arguments of a radical British mechanizer like Fuller: certain 'extremists' may have suggested that the motor spelt the end for the cavalry, but, as Bitossi reassured the officers of the Light Horse Regiment, the tank units of the *celeri* would prove the folly of such thinking. Far from interfering with the traditional tactics and spirit of the cavalry, he promised that Italy's tanks would be content to support the horsed cavalry when its men dismounted.[88]

Such was the state of play in October 1935, when Fuller visited Italy as special correspondent for Lord Northcliffe's *Daily Mail*. He met Mussolini in Rome and informed him that the hostility with which the British press had responded to Italy's invasion of Abyssinia was the result of Jewish influence. *Il Duce* then arranged for his British admirer to travel on a troopship to Abyssinia, where he spent two and a half months observing the war then being fought under General Emilio de Bono.[89]

For the propagandists whose account of Mussolini's conquest of Abyssinia was being used in Italy's elementary schools by 1938, the 'Italian legionnaire's' triumph was the result of faith, valour and the native 'Italian genius', which had invented 'mighty and modern instruments of war'.[90] The internal combustion engine was 'first constructed by Eugenio Barsanti', and the radio by Guglielmo Marconi. The plane was first imagined by 'the Italian Leonardo da Vinci', and the tanks, which Fiat-Ansaldo actually derived from British and French examples, were 'conceived and designed' by the same native genius: 'Thus, Italy truly did everything alone; she conquered her Empire not only with her heroism, but also with her genius.'

Fuller was one of the few Englishman who really appreciated Mussolini's savage conquest of Abyssinia, but he did so without retrospectively applying Mussolini's principle of autarchy to the technology of modern warfare. While in Abyssinia, he met General de Bono, and also Marshal Pietro Badoglio, who replaced De Bono as commander in mid-November 1935, and he was not disconcerted to discover that Mussolini's army was grouped not as a tactical instrument but with every conceivable kind of unit drawn together as in 'a fascist demonstration' or 'a Lord Mayor's show'.[91] The Blackshirt militia, to which Fuller was briefly attached at the captured town of Adigrat, impressed him as another exuberant rabble in the spearhead of a new order. Indeed, the sight of these bearded desperadoes brought one of Sir Oswald Mosley's East London locations to Fuller's mind: 'They look like the "Pirates of Penzance", after having sacked Petticoat Lane.'[92] Fuller noted their 'slovenly, flamboyant dress', their badges ornamented with death's heads and thunderbolts, their war cries and violent mottoes, their carbines, bayonets and daggers, and concluded that the world had probably not seen such a force since the time of the Crusades. Celebrating this murderous bunch as 'the war chorus of the Duce, and the troubadours of his cult',[93] he insisted that it 'bore along with it the ark of a military covenant'. This 'huge melodramatic troupe'[94] was more than a patriotic horde. It was the prototypical force of a new kind of 'totalitarian attack' in which everything depended on the assault – the charge of the aeroplane or the rush of 'the military horde'.[95] And as Fuller informed readers of the *Daily Mail*, 'a kinder, more considerate, and more generous-minded body of men I have yet to meet'.[96] Dictatorships, as Fuller concluded, demanded a new kind of general: 'a man of extreme daring, of extreme energy and of extreme ruthlessness . . . in fact, a veritable scientist of war. He must not only think but strike like lightning, putting the maximum weight and velocity into his first blows.'[97]

Hearing that the Abyssinian forces had acquired, or at least been offered, modern weapons including tanks, armoured cars and radio, Fuller was confident that the Emperor's forces would only be unhinged by the scientific arsenal: 'The sudden influx of complicated arms to a weak tactical stomach may be compared to the introduction of hard-boiled macaroni to a delicate physical one.'[98] But what of the Italians? While appreciating the thrusting power of Mussolini's brutal motorized phalanx, Fuller was disappointed to find that 'As regards the theory and practice of tank warfare, we have nothing to learn from the Italians.' Many press photographs of the Abyssinian war gave prominence to Italian tanks, but Fuller's low opinion of their worth was not based on the realization that, far from convincing the world of the modernity of the Italian Army, this boastful imagery actually revealed a barbarity that 'appalled world opinion'.[99] As a 'scientist' of war, Fuller had nothing but contempt for world opinion, and he was quite capable of detecting 'a useful simplifier of tactics' in Badoglio's undeniably barbaric use of mustard gas against barefooted Abyssinians even as he mused about the 'appalling' things this blistering vapour must have done to their bare feet – 'as if by an act of magic, their *moral* collapsed'.[100]

Fuller was irritated by the ridiculous Italian officer who, on gathering that this visiting 'special correspondent' was indeed the general who had tried to mechanize the British Army, announced that he was wrong and that 'the mule is superior to the lorry'.[101] But what really clinched his judgement was the discovery that the tank battalions deployed to Ethiopia were equipped with inadequate light Fiat tanks governed by a foolish doctrine that insisted that they should be used to support infantry in offensive

operations even when the terrain was wildly inappropriate. Such incompetence resulted in the fiasco that occurred near Adowa in December 1935,
when Fuller was still in Abyssinia. Finding itself cut off by irregular troops
occupying Dembeguina Pass, a platoon of six unturreted two-man CV35
tanks tried to retreat through the pass without infantry cover. Deprived of
speed and orientation, they were attacked from the rear by Ethiopian warriors who disabled their tracks, bent their machine gun barrels with bare
hands, and then destroyed the entire platoon.[102] In part, Fuller attributed
such humiliating incidents to the fact that the Fiat light tank lacked all-
round vision and was therefore defenceless against anyone who chose to
interrupt its tracks with iron bars or incinerate its crew with a petrol
bomb.[103] But he also condemned the tactical ineptitude of the Italians, who
often confined their tanks to advancing in the rear of infantry units even
though the enemy had no serious anti-tank capabilities: 'the tank idea had
not yet begun to sink home'.[104]

Light 6 Spain

Soviet T-26 in Spain, 1939

The record would not be improved by the tank force that, two years later,
Mussolini sent to assist Franco's Nationalist forces in the Spanish Civil
War. Once again, the Italian tanks drew a lot of press attention, but their
first major engagement was a humiliating disaster. Advancing towards
Madrid as part of a larger infantry column, they were roundly defeated in
the Battle of Guadalajara in April 1937. After that experience army policy, in
Italy as elsewhere, was adjusted and concentrated more on anti-tank capacities; indeed, the 3rd *celeri* division even abandoned its inadequate tanks
and returned to horses.[105]

Fuller's assessment of the Spanish Civil War is to be found in the reports
he submitted to the British War Office, one after each of the three visits he
made to Franco's forces during the Spanish Civil War. At that time Britain

had no military attaché accredited to Franco, and the men at the War Office found their own fascist general's despatches 'very interesting', especially since 'reliable information from trained observers is hard to come by'.[106] In at least one case they informed Fuller of the things they would like to hear about (the list including anti-aircraft techniques and 'modern weapons' especially German and Italian ones).[107] Fuller discussed the war with Franco and his General Quiepo de Llano and his reports are unwavering in their support for the Nationalist cause. He insisted that the stories about Franco's forces slaughtering prisoners were 'pure inventions', and prophesied that Franco would win because he had discipline and humanity on his side and 'does not scorn national traditions'. As for the causes of the war, Spain had been destabilized by 'a large pinkish element' created by left-wing intellectuals of the type who were now doing exactly the same thing in Britain. These ludicrous figures hadn't been able to handle the crash when it came, and it was the hardened Reds alone who proved capable of taking a lead.

The Spanish war was quite unlike any that Fuller himself had taken part in – indeed, his use of inverted commas suggests a reluctance to define it as a 'war' at all. The front was enormously long but primitive, discontinuous and in places even 'hard to discover'. In Madrid he walked down a shallow communication trench, only to find himself strolling across an unwired garden 'in full view of the Reds some 800 yards away'. And while driving near Talavera, he discovered that the front line was actually the road he was travelling along. Primarily, he decided, this was 'a city war'. The rural areas were pro-Franco, and the 'militarily incompetent' Reds, had taken to the cities partly because they were inept at fighting in the open and needed bricks and mortar to hide behind, and partly because they relied on the support of the degenerate urban 'rabble'.

Fuller saw the work of Spain's internationally assisted Red army as he travelled from Irun to Malaga in March 1937. It had, he reported, been so busy pillaging and destroying churches and the houses of class enemies, that it had left bridges and other obviously 'military objectives' quite undamaged. The Reds' only military measure was to 'assassinate their class opponents' and then 'through their violent propaganda to terrify the civilian inhabitants into believing that Franco would do likewise wherever he advanced'. Atrocities were part of this primitive arsenal, as Fuller argued with reference to a ransacked cemetery near Huesca, where he had seen crosses smashed and corpses pulled out of their resting places and left lying about with shiny black jackboots rammed on to their disintegrating feet.[108]

Fuller insisted that it was only Franco's decency that had prevented him from finishing the war quickly. This had brought him into dispute with Mussolini who, no doubt humiliated by the failure of his own forces in the Battle of Guadalajara, was urging Franco to the speedy annihilation of his enemy. But then, as Fuller put it, Franco wanted to win the peace as well as the war. Fuller was dismissive of the Italian troops fighting alongside Franco's forces – describing them as little better than the fascist militia he had observed in Abyssinia. He was scathing about the Italian light tank, calling it variously 'an indifferent and blind machine' (March 1937) and 'a wretched little machine' (April 1938). He came across two derelict light tanks, one of which he reported in close detail: 'This machine I judged by eye carried 12.5 mm of armour which had been easily and cleanly penetrated by A.P. rifle or M.G. bullets, which I think proves that its armour is defective. It was claimed that these machines, like others, were put out of action by throwing bottles of petrol on them followed by a hand grenade.' Fuller didn't believe this, remarking that they had obviously been 'put out of action by A.P. bullets, and then quite possibly the petrol attack followed', and reckoning that 'this petrol tactics had been purposely exaggerated to give confidence to the troops. It is a possible means of attack against an Italian tank, but scarcely against a Russian unless it is moving through a jungle.' Other observers, including Liddell Hart, would draw excessively general conclusions from the mediocre performance of tanks during the Spanish Civil War, but Fuller advised against this: 'I do not think that we have much to learn from either tanks or anti-tank weapons in this "war", because the basis of tactics is training, and this is mainly a war of untrained men with a sprinkling of foreign mercenaries who naturally think of their own skins first.'

He returned to this question after his third visit in April 1938. The Nationalists were equipped with Italian, German and captured Russian tanks, whereas the Reds were using Renaults of Great War vintage, a number of American tractor tanks, and also some Russian medium or heavy tanks, dubbed 'formidable' by the apprehensive Nationalists, but employed only as 'mobile pill-boxes'. The official German Army report on the Civil War claims that the romance of the tank was initially such that even members of Franco's family volunteered to serve in them. They soon changed their mind 'when it became known what the inside of a burned-out tank looked like', and by the end of the war captured Russian tanks were crewed by desperate men who had been given a choice between a prison sentence or 'one attack trip in a tank'.[109] Fuller conceded that the tone of tank warfare had been badly lowered in Spain: 'the petrol-bottle-hand-grenade trick has grown into a legend. It is, of course a feasible operation against blind tanks and tanks moving through a jungle, but it should not be possible against well-designed tanks working in sections.'

The Soviet tank may have impressed Fuller as better than the dismal Italian model, but he saw little indication of any communist tactics. He had been informed that the Reds had tried a more coherent use of tanks at Brunete, deploying some 100 (the number had risen to 250 by the time this episode was mentioned in the later report of October 1937) in front of their infantry 'in Cambrai style'. But this had been a 'badly planned' assault in which most of the tanks were lost, and it confirmed Fuller's belief that the light tank, while it may be 'a fairly good scout . . . is not suitable to attack operations'. [110]

Fuller judged the Republican army to be almost inconceivably incompetent. In a series of articles written for the *Chicago Tribune*, he alleged that where Franco's army marched to the tune of discipline ('He hits, terrifies and his enemy retires. Then he *penetrates* by *going round*' [111]), the Reds had tried to overthrow all authority in their own ranks, replacing their command structure with 'utopian experiments'.

Travelling through territory recently won back by the Nationalists, Fuller found his 'most extreme' evidence of this Republican incompetence in a hundredweight or so of paper that had 'either been thrust or blown into a culvert' at Belchite. [112] Here, in the form of endless exhortations that 'might have been written by a Labour MP', was the literature of the International Brigade: banging on about 'crushing the head of the fascist cobra'; insisting that every situation could be won with the help of an appropriate slogan; and advocating, in the words of one Bill Lawrence, 'comradeship and fraternity with commanders'. As Fuller saw it, the Spanish Civil War proved the insanity of replacing discipline and strategy with slogans; and in doing so demonstrated 'the utter incapacity of the Soviet system to wage warfare successfully in a foreign country'. [113]

Tanks did badly in the Spanish Civil War. Even Fuller's anti-fascist British follower, Tom Wintringham, a former editor of the Marxist cultural journal *Left Review*, who had commanded a force in the International Brigade, reckoned that the tank had been decisively overtaken by the new generation of anti-tank weapons, and that 'there seems therefore to be no reason whatever for the British reliance on Tanks'. [114] A more influential version of that argument – i.e. that recent developments in military technology had greatly increased powers of defence over those of the offensive – was propounded by Liddell Hart, both in books like *The Defence of Britain* and also through his personal influence as friend and adviser to Leslie Hore-Belisha, the Liberal politician who served as Secretary of Defence in Chamberlain's National and War Cabinets from 1935 to 1940. Fuller, however, tried to persuade the War Office that this was a deluded line argument. Far from showing that the tank idea had been surpassed, the Spanish Civil War only demonstrated what happened when inadequately designed 'cheap mass produced' machines were used ignorantly.

Light 7 Germany

German bicycle tanks, 1920s

By that time Fuller knew it was in Germany that the really effective mechanization of fascism's primitive thrust was being prepared. He had visited the country many times and felt none of the dismay expressed by other British travellers who observed the rise of Nazism in the thirties. By now virulently anti-Semitic, this admirer of armoured divisions would merely have been irritated by Christopher Isherwood's story about the Landauers, a wealthy Jewish family who refused to sell toy soldiers or guns in their enormous glass-and-steel department store near Berlin's Potsdamer Platz. Isherwood described being taken round the store by Bernhard Landaeur, who explained that 'there had recently been a heated argument about toy tanks at a director's meeting. Bernhard had succeeded in maintaining the ban: "But this is really the thin end of the wedge," he added, sadly, picking up a toy tractor with caterpillar wheels.'[115]

To begin with, at least, the ban on tanks had not just applied in one of Berlin's largest department stores. Like other technological weapons such as poison gas, submarines and bomber planes, tanks and armoured cars had been forbidden to Germany under Article 169 of the Treaty of Versailles. Besides insisting that starving Germany hand over 140,000 milk cows,[116] that settlement also stipulated that Germany's post-war army be reduced to a negligible force of 100,000 men (of whom only 4,000 could be officers), capable of little more than policing borders and, with help from the Freikorps, crushing internal insurrection of the sort promoted by the Spartacus League. For General Hans von Seeckt, who was to command this much-reduced *Reichswehr* until October 1926, this meant reforming the general staff as a mere 'Troop Office', and accepting that the idea of a mass army or, in Clausewitz's phrase, the 'nation at arms' was effectively dead.[117] These constraints were humiliating for Von Seeckt, but they also spared him the burden of hidebound military tradition, and freed him to reconceive the entire organization, tactics and doctrine of the German Army.

After carrying out a review of the *Reichswehr*'s recent defeat, Von Seeckt set out to rebuild it as a small, elite force based on volunteers rather than conscripts. Drawing on his experience of Germany's Eastern Front, von Seeckt derived a new tactics that assumed a war of manoeuvre rather than attrition, emphasizing mobility and speed and anticipating, from the very beginning, the possibility of independent operations carried out by a combined arms force.[118] Von Seeckt was quick to see that a small but professional army could be provided with more intelligent and technically adept leadership. It might be chronically under-equipped, but at least it would not be lumbered with obsolete weaponry like the French Army, with its fleet of Renault light tanks. As von Seeckt concluded, 'the smaller the army, the easier it will be to equip it with modern weapons, whereas the provision of a constant supply for armies of millions is an impossibility'.[119]

This approach disconcerted some of the young lieutenants and captains in the officer corps, men whose experience of the war made them sceptical of Von Seeckt's theory of a small, technological army.[120] One such was Ernst Jünger, the much-decorated former storm trooper, who was already well known as the author of a novelized memoir, *The Storm of Steel* (1920). An unrepentant killer but also an entomologist fascinated by bugs with exo-skeletons, Jünger had encountered British tanks in the German Army's spring offensive of 1918, and dismissed them as witless 'cockchafers' scurrying forward 'as though drawn by strings' into the German artillery that would soon tread them into the ground.[121] Yet the machines had kept coming, and in his articles in the *Militär Wochenblatt* Jünger himself now came to terms with the mechanized arsenal that threatened to reduce his Prussian warrior-hero to an abject wretch, scurrying around in the hope of self-preservation. For the aristocratic, nationalist soldiers who had found themselves pulped into a lumpen, technologically produced mass, every new mechanical device was 'a new molestation'.[122] Yet 'if a tank, spiked with machine guns and cannon, is worth a company', Jünger anticipated that in future wars vast technological resources might still be commanded by a small elite of storm-troop-style warriors – be they tank commanders, machine gunners or pilots.[123]

As a novelist, Jünger would go on to apply the principles of 'art for art's sake' to war itself, producing the celebration of violence and hardness that Walter Benjamin condemned as 'sinister runic humbug'.[124] The *Reichswehr* had more practical ambitions. Under Von Seeckt, it set out to develop a new generation of mechanized weapons suited to its new doctrines of man-oeuvre. It would do so by bending and evading the Treaty of Versailles's restrictions, monitored as these were, at least up until 1927, by the Interallied Military Control Commission. Revolutionary insurgency helped in the early years. The socialist uprisings of 1918–19 enabled Germany's stealthy rearmers to gain a concession in July 1920: the 'Boulogne Note' conceded 150 armoured cars to the security police, and permitted the *Reichswehr* to acquire 105 armoured personnel carriers too.

The *Reichswehr*'s lust for tanks was less easy to satisfy. To begin with Von Seeckt's men had to make do with 'tactical representations' constructed out of wood and painted canvas and mounted on cars or three-wheel bicycles. These mimic machines were used, as Von Seeckt demanded in an order of 1923, to ensure that, even though actual tanks were proscribed, 'troops could learn to cooperate with them in attacks and practice anti-tank defense'.[125]

The production of the first real tanks demanded guile and deception. The 'heavy tractors' designed by Professor Ferdinand Porsche emerged as tanks from the Daimler factory. Other companies developed weapons through overseas subsidiaries: Krupp took control of the Bofors Corporation in Sweden, while Rheinmetall Corporation acquired a Swiss watch factory and used it to produce machine guns. After 1922, when Germany and the Soviet Union signed a collaborative treaty at Rapallo, more systematic experiments would also take place under cover in the Soviet Union – particularly at the Kazan Tank School on the Volga, where German officers (ostensibly ' tourists') who would go on to form tank units attended courses that could run for as long as three years. By the late twenties, prototype tanks, 'heavy', 'light' and eventually also 'medium tractors', were secretly imported for testing from German manufacturers.

General Von Seeckt had the help of a number of experienced officers. Lieutenant Ernst Volckheim, who had served in the recent war as a member of Germany's First Heavy Tank Company, was among the members of the German officer corps who promoted the tank as an offensive weapon, favouring heavy machines over light ones, and reprising Fuller's suggestion that tanks should have radios mounted in them, to facilitate communication with other units.[126] Seeckt's men studied developments in other countries: tank design but also tactics, as displayed at closely observed manoeuvres in France and Britain (1924–5). Many senior officers in the Inspectorate of Motor Troops contributed to the development of armoured vehicles, including Alfred von Vollard-Bockelberg, who directed the *Reichswehr*'s motorization progamme; Oswald Lutz, whose concepts underlay the 1925 specification for the first German Tank programme; and Heinz Guderian who, as a captain under Lutz, was free to pursue his interest in tank tactics without having to drag a reluctant infantry and cavalry establishment after him.

Produced in the late twenties, Germany's first prototype tanks where designed to specifications that had emerged directly from the new tactics. The British and American armies maintained separate ordnance design bureaus, but the German tank drive is said to have benefited from sharp competition between rival manufacturers.[127] One model was based on the example of a light amphibious tank produced for the US Marines by J. W. Christie, and another, which improved on the British Vickers Medium design, was designed to be able to fire in all directions. There were armoured cars with steering wheels at both front and back, which could be driven in either direction. Another experimental design from Krupps followed Christie's idea of a tank equipped with tracks to be used on rough terrain, and retractable wheels for speedy travel on roads. The first tank training unit was formed at Zossen in November 1933, ten months after Hitler came to power. It had only fourteen machines in all, and yet, thanks to the work done by Von Seeckt and his colleagues, it was well placed to develop into Germany's first experimental armoured division: a combined arms force founded around two armoured regiments in 1934, which was equipped with 481 tanks by the time it was assembled in the summer manoeuvres of 1935.

Fuller's theory of tank warfare was a considerable inspiration to the founders of Germany's tank force. His work was followed closely by Ernst Volckheim and the Austrian Ludwig Ritter von Eimannesberger, both of whom wrote books on the tank. Heinz Guderian also acknowledged the debt. *Tanks in the Great War* was widely studied, and Fuller's later writings appeared in German Army journals such as the *Militär Wochenblatt*; indeed, in 1926 *The Reformation of War* was excerpted over three issues of the General Staff's journal of foreign military news.

While the founders of Germany's new tank force studied Fuller's writings, he reciprocated by following their progress with close interest. He had

opposed the Treaty of Versailles as 'the handiwork of old men',[128] unnecessarily punitive and misguided in its ban on 'scientific' weapons. However,
he was quick to see that the ban had effectively turned Germany into a
laboratory in which new and hypothetical systems of warfare could be
tested. No doubt encouraged by his wife Sonia, who had been brought up
in Hamburg, Fuller had visited Germany repeatedly in the years immediately after the First World War. In 1929 he spent three months at Wiesba-
den as a brigade commander with the British Army on the Rhine; and he
was in Cologne in March 1933 at the time when Hitler secured absolute
power through the vote of an intimidated Reichstag. He met Hitler in the
winter of 1934, and was impressed by his views on race, destiny and democracy. As Hitler told this eminent member of the British Union of Fascists:
'The people are impotent, they cannot rule themselves; yet I cannot rule
the people unless I am the soul of the people.'[129] And Hitler was just that,
according to this recycled occultist, who commended the 'soulfulness' of
the Nazi project, and noted that the Germans were 'a profoundly mystical
race'.

This sympathetic observer returned in 1935 to attend Hitler's summer
army manoeuvres at Luneberg, and report on them for the *Daily Mail*.
Fuller had mocked the farcical battle between Eastland and Westland in the
British Army's Wessex exercise of the year before, but no nursemaids, per-
ambulators or Hyde Park bandstands came to mind as he now watched a
'Red army' defend the line of the river Elbe against a 'Blue army' advancing
from Lübeck. Fuller saw motorized units and armoured cars, which left
him 'in no doubt that the German Army well recognizes the value of mobility'; and he was also impressed to see Hitler spending time among his
troops: 'I saw him in the hamlet of Emminger, and he looked exceedingly
fit.'[130]

Familiar with the problems of tank supply in Britain, Fuller reported
that the German Army had been placed in 'the most advantageous position'
by the limitations imposed by the Treaty of Versailles: 'in other words it
has nothing material to scrap' and was free to build on 'the accumulated
experience' of other nations.[131] Guderian may have had to practise with
mimic tanks, but at least 'no old machines hang round the German military
neck – as, for example, our 1923 model Vickers tanks hung round our military neck'. Hitler's army was actually better off for being deprived of inadequate rust-buckets like those that had displaced the Medium Ds of Plan
1919, especially since 'old weapons means old tactics'. In order to exploit
this accidental advantage, the German general staff must also be prepared

to scrap past tactical theories: 'Should it possess the courage and also the humility to go back to school again and begin from a new beginning, then the tactical possibilities of the German Army are overwhelming.'

By the last day of those fateful 1935 manoeuvres, Fuller was informing readers of the *Daily Mail* that the importance of what he had seen could not be exaggerated. Superficially, the manoeuvres may have been a military test, but they were also 'a great national demonstration', and 'Herr Hitler was present throughout the last two days, moving from point to point and taking the keenest interest in what he saw'.[132] Fuller listed the members of Hitler's senior staff he met: General von Blomberg, the Minister for War who, as Chief of the German General Staff in the late twenties, had played a considerable part in the development of the Kazan Tank School in Russia; and also Generals Von Fritsch, Von Beck and Liebman, the head of the Berlin Staff College. At the final parade, General Von Blomberg concluded the speeches by thanking Herr Hitler for having restored to Germany her martial spirit, and there was then a ceremonial march-past involving an entire army corps and an audience of probably 100,000 enraptured onlookers who cared nothing for the rain. 'The bearing of the men was remarkable as they went by at the goose-step,' but Fuller was also much taken by the virility of the crowd, evidently quite untouched by the pacifism plaguing the British public of that time: 'Never do I remember having seen so keen a delight in soldiering, or so keen an appreciation of things military, as was displayed by these thousands of spectators.' He meant nothing but praise when he concluded that the parade demonstrated 'the invincible will of an entire nation to regain its former supremacy'.

When it came to military doctrine and tactics, those manoeuvres brought Fuller back to the essential questions of mechanization and its reformation of war. He may not have seen Germany's first tank division experimenting with radio communication, brigade structure, or the width of its front of operations, but he could already imagine the mobile anti-tank weapons that would soon enough be rolling along just behind the breakthrough tanks in Hitler's armoured spearheads. The key question for the German Army, as he defined it in the *Daily Mail*, was 'how to base offensive action on defensive power. That is how to combine the new mechanized weapons, tanks and anti-tanks, so that the second becomes the base of action of the first, and not merely the escort of an obsolescent infantry.' The British had failed, and it was now for the German Army to rise to the challenge : 'Whether it will do so depends on the General Staff and its ability not only to understand the past, but to foresee the future.'

Fuller kept up his German contacts until that question was finally answered. In September 1936 he was sponsored by the German government to visit Hitler's second autumn manoeuvres in Bad Neuheim in Hesse, reporting for the *Daily Mail* as usual.[133] And in 1939 the German military attaché at the London embassy engineered a meeting between Fuller and Guderian. Fuller may not have been the only Englishman trusted by Hitler, as one cranky website claims to this day, but he was found useful both by the German military and by senior Nazis. The political articles he now wrote as a member of the British Union of Fascists, were translated – including his piece condemning the Jews as 'the Cancer of Europe', which appeared in the British *Fascist Quarterly* at the beginning of 1935, and was printed in *Weltpost* under the title 'General Fuller über die Juden' in September of the same year.[134] His standing in Germany was sufficient to secure him an invitation, apparently sent on behalf of Ribbentrop, to Hitler's fiftieth birthday celebrations, held in Berlin on 20 April 1939. The night before he left for Germany, Fuller was called by an official of the Foreign Office. Having reported to the War Office after his tours of the Spanish Civil War, Fuller expected to be asked to note 'what kinds of tanks etc., were shown in the great military parade'. But the official had a different message: 'I understand you are attending Hitler's birthday, and so thought it as well to tell you that Sir Ian Hamilton was also asked; but that we have warned him against going as it might prove dangerous.' Fuller's claimed answer was characteristic: 'So far as I am concerned I rather enjoy a rough house.'[135]

And off he went, together with the only other Briton who attended the ceremony, the Nazi-sympathizing brewer and barrister Lord Brockett. He stayed at the Hotel Adlon, just inside the Brandenburg Gate, where he discussed the international situation with Hitler's other foreign guests. Tension had been rising between Germany and Poland since March that year, when the Polish government refused to accede to Hitler's demand for the reabsorption of the formerly German city of Danzig into Germany, and when, at least according to the War Diary of the German Armed Forces Supreme Command Headquarters, Hitler informed his generals that a military settlement of the problem seemed inevitable'.[136] Fuller learned that 'Hitler intended to have Danzig, war or no war, and that, if it came to war, Poland would be over-run in a minimum of three weeks or a maximum of six.' He asked one 'unusually well informed American' what he thought of Britain's guarantee to Poland – an assurance that bound Britain and France to intervene on Poland's behalf if she was attacked, which had been issued by Chamberlain on 30 March, and accepted by the Polish Foreign Minister, Joseph Beck, reputedly between 'two flicks of the ash off his cigarette'.[137] The American's answer, which almost certainly concurred with Fuller's own thoughts on the matter, was direct enough: 'Well, I guess your Prime Minister has made the biggest blunder in your history since you passed the Stamp Act.'

Hitler's birthday parade took place on the morning of 20 April, and the British newspaper correspondents did not overlook the presence of Britain's fascist general among the guests of honour standing 'face to face with the Fuhrer' across the Avenue of Triumph. They noted his 'cosmopolitan collection of decorations' (the British DSO, but also the French Légion d'Honneur and the Order of Leopold of Belgium), his Poona moustache and his plain top hat; and also that he looked 'like a cheeky mouse on a gaudy-hued patchwork quilt', standing there in civilian dress among all the resplendent uniforms.[138]

In his own description of the parade Fuller left no doubt that what he saw that day was an exact incarnation of the irresistible mobile force prefigured at Cambrai: 'For some three hours a completely mechanized and motorized army roared past the Führer along the Charlottenburger Strasse. Never before or since have I watched such a formidable mass of moving metal.' That afternoon the seventy foreign guests were lined up to meet Hitler in the new Chancellery, and Fuller had one of the proudest encounters of his life: 'He walked down the line and when he came opposite to me he shook me by the hand and said: "I hope you were pleased with your children?" To which I answered: "Your Excellency, they have grown up so quickly that I no longer recognize them," which was true.' Fuller was keen on that story, and would repeat it many times in later life – even to the book dealer through whom he eventually sold his collection of *Crowleyana* in the nineteen-sixties.

It was in the same reverent spirit that Britain's fascist tank general contributed an article about his visit to the *Westfälische Landeszeitung*, describing his many visits to the Führer's Germany, and telling how he had arrived in Berlin on 19 April full of the idea (tactfully attributed to Thomas Carlyle rather than Aleister Crowley) that 'all things that we see standing accomplished in the world are properly the outer material result, the practical realization and embodiment of Thoughts that dwell in the Great Men sent into the world'.[139] This sense of stepping into 'the soul of the whole world's history' hung over his visit: 'I could feel it in the streets, in the buildings in the crowds, in the rush of aeroplanes overhead and in the roaring of tanks below.' It was a story of 'Great leadership' and the 'great followership' that it created in return; and the strength it revealed in Germany did not make this Englishman envious or fearful: 'throughout life I have held that what is strong and not what is weak is best. Therefore, I believe in the strong man, strong physically, mentally and culturally. Also I believe that strong nations, like strong men, respect each other and that mutual respect is the foundation of peace.' On that basis, he had been happy to see the Union Jack fluttering from a window at the Hotel Adlon: 'Frankly, it always fills me with a sense of pride to see my national flag flying peacefully in a foreign city.'

Endtime – an admirer's guide

Had Fuller ever visited Saint Mary's church at Swaffham Prior in Cambridgeshire, he would have discovered that Squire Allix provided a written 'Explanation' spelling out the lesson of the memorial war windows he had installed in St Mary's church.[140] Marked 'For public use', this document describes how the windows open with God's call to war, typified by an Italian bugler and a phrase from Handel's oratorio *Israel in Egypt*, and then goes on to categorize the tanks, howitzers and planes of the two war windows. Allix justifies the biblical quotations that struggle to contain this parade of spectacular hardware, and explains that the de-mechanized post-war pastoralism of the final Peace window marks the point where pain and sorrow pass away, and 'God wipes away all tears'.

There was to be no such redemption to round off the pulsating views in the lights of Fuller's exploded and multinational Church of Mechanization. Yet, in his own way, Fuller did go on to provide some explanatory notes. Unlike other prominent British fascists, he was not interned during the Second World War. Yet when General Ironside, who was appointed Commander of the Imperial General Staff once war broke out, tried to appoint Fuller his deputy, the suggestion was turned down by the government on what Liddell Hart cutely describes as 'other than military grounds'.[141] So Fuller scribbled on in his usual unofficial capacity. He resumed his correspondence with a politically distanced Liddell Hart, then living in Devon, where he apparently terrified Walter Gropius, Paul Hindemith, Kurt Joos and other refugees from Germany by predicting that Hitler's English blitzkrieg would start with a landing on the Devon coast and then sweep up past the grounds of Dartington Hall, the arts centre and estate where these expatriates from the Bauhaus and elsewhere had found temporary haven,

and which they quit for America not long after hearing this dire prediction.[142]

Fuller also kept writing in the pages of the *Evening Standard,* the *New
English Weekly,* the *Leader,* the *Spectator* and other papers. He ran a more
or less continuous analysis of the events of the war, reminiscing about previous engagements, rummaging through history for precedents, and taking
time out to repudiate the arguments of those who proclaimed him a 'false
prophet' because he had advocated 'a small army in place of the mass
armies of 1914–18'.[143] Fuller claimed a big place for himself in the history
that was unfolding in Europe and North Africa, insisting that the 'secret of
blitzkrieg', ran back through modern victories such as Patton's Normandy
campaign and the Battle of El Alamein, to his own Plan 1919; and suggesting that the German strikes against Poland and France in the early stages of
the war were reprises of his own achievements at Cambrai.[144]

He was also proudly gathering evidence to prove that, from one national
theatre to the next, it was his creed that had inspired modern tank warfare.
Guderian's tribute to the influence of Fuller's writings on the blitzkrieg
may have been passed to a military attaché in Berlin,[145] but confirmation
also reached Fuller directly, thanks to a certain Captain John Crossby, who
wrote to inform him: 'your book was the standard work on which mechanized warfare was taught at the Czech Staff College', and to report that a
high Czech officer had remarked: 'How lucky you are to have a man like
Fuller. The Germans regard his book on Mechanized Warfare as their
Bible, and the entire attack in France and Flanders was based on his teaching.'[146]

Fuller gathered in such testimonials and then selected 'Extracts' which,
at some point during the Second World War, he had typed up as proof of
the way his doctrine had spread through the major armies of the world.[147]
Fuller's version of Squire Allix's 'Explanation' includes a passage from a
book by Major Malcolm Wheeler-Nicholson claiming that Fuller had outlined how the next war would go in 1926 and that, while British Army
chiefs had refused to act on his prophesy, 'The Nazis saw the value and
used his theories as a blueprint.' His predictions with regard to the disastrously 'defensive' military policy pursued by France are acknowledged in a
passage from a book by Arnold Lunn: 'In 1938, General Fuller told me that
the Maginot Line would be the tomb of France.'[148] Fuller also extracted a
letter from Mr Peter Howard who, on 3 July 1940, wrote to apologize for
once doubting this prophet: 'I suddenly remembered the last occasion we
met (1938) at the Empire Crusade Club. You then told the audience that

the French Army was not much good and that the German Army was very good indeed. I disagreed with you utterly. Events have since shown how entirely right you were and how completely wrong I was.'

When it came to the Red Army, one of Fuller's choicest 'extracts' came from a letter he received in June 1943 from an American, Lieutenant Colonel S. L. A. Marshall, who was then serving in the 'Orientation and Publications Section' of the War Department in Washington and preparing an American edition of Fuller's *Lectures on F.S.R. III*. Three years previously, Marshall had published a book on the blitzkrieg in which he insisted that 'Fuller, and not Heinz Guderian, the German tank General, or Seeckt, the father of the first lightning army, or Ludendorff, the creator of infiltration, is the unsung prophet of the new age of warfare';[149] and he now wrote to report that the Russian Attaché on Air, with whom he had recently lunched, had informed him that three months before the German attack on the USSR, Marshal Timoschenko had issued an order to the Red Army making Fuller's *Lectures on F.S.R. III* a 'table book' that every officer should have at his elbow, along with Clausewitz's *On War* and Douhet's *Command of the Air*.

Fuller received further confirmation of his influence over Soviet policy in response to an article he wrote for the *Evening Standard* in October 1940. In this, he had insisted that, as proven by Germany's victorious invasion of Poland in September 1939, the war would be decided 'not by masses of men, but instead by machines – tanks on the ground and aircraft in the air. Advances were made in seven league boots, and though casualties were comparatively light, the collapse of the defeated side was catastrophic.' Unfortunately, 'these shrieking realities of war' had yet to be noticed by the British War Office, which was so obsessed with 'masses and numbers that it could only think of calling up reinforcements quarter million by quarter million'. Next had come 'the inundation of France', the second Nazi blitzkrieg, which Fuller described as a 'rapid sword thrust of a highly shielded army of 1940 form against a brave army' that still 'belonged to 1918'. But still the message didn't sink in, and the blockheads at Britain's War Office had just kept counting as they stuffed two million men into the 'bulging' sack of Britain's army. They were, said Fuller, merely adding 'ton on ton to our human tank-fodder', when what was really needed was an army of 20,000 modern machines manned by 120,000 fighting men and maintained by another 100,000 or so – i.e. a mechanized force that, in manpower, needed to be no more than the size of the pre-war Regular Army.[150]

Tukhachevsky and Triandafillov would have snorted with contempt had they lived to read this article. But Fuller was happy to settle for the testimony of Major A. S. Hooper who wrote in response: 'You are probably aware that . . . in actual practice the Red Army looked on you as the greatest expert on tank handling. Their present practice is not so much to discard your teaching but to build even higher on that base from the study of warfare today.' This 'extract' provided Fuller with further proof that he was the founder of modern tank tactics; indeed, there can be little doubt that Fuller would be talking about himself when he acknowledged Stalin's eventual astuteness in 'adopting non-Bolshevik tactics'.[151]

Perhaps Fuller sometimes woke in the middle of the night, and mused on the curious route he had followed since those distant days in India, when he had admired Aleister Crowley's poems and gone along with the somewhat feminist secular democracy advocated by 'Saladin' and the Rationalist Press Association. Yet if he ever entertained fleeting doubts about his graduation from magic to fascism via tanks, he certainly wasn't going to march them past the readers of a little magazine called the *Occult Review*. He chose instead to inform these initiates that magic, which was like war in being 'coercive, propitiatory and dynamic', remained a 'formidable weapon under the name of "propaganda"', and to ask: 'Is not Dr. Goebbels a magician?'[152]

So Fuller found his own way back into the cranky margins, twenty years after he spurned Aleister Crowley's offer of an esoteric war machine that would guarantee him victory as commander-in-chief to the armies of Horus. He can be left there standing in the ruins of his glassy temple while bombs crashed down on Europe, finding unmistakable resonances in the closing line of a poem called 'The Doom of a City', written by James Thompson in 1857: 'Their Aeon is fulfilled.'[153]

PART III

Blitzkrieg

Drawing of lancer charging a metal machine by Leonardo da Vinci.

12

The Lancer and the Panzer

. . . today horses have to be exchanged for cars or tanks, and before the war we cavalrymen were fervent opponents of this modern ideology.

General K. S. Rudnicko, DSO

The platform at Dresden main station had recently been heightened in anticipation of the high-speed Eurotrains that promised one day to arrive here; but my eastbound transport was unmodernized, the numbered carriage attended by a guard wearing the burgundy-coloured uniform of Poland's national railway company. Having guided his few passengers to their berths, this silver-braided fellow, who looked as much like a fallen duke as a state functionary, withdrew to his galley where he would sit through the freezing night, morosely scrutinizing tickets and boiling up red kettles on an old gas ring.

I was travelling with one of the century's most abiding tank images folded up in my mind. Closer to a comic strip than a photograph, it shows a Nazi tank advancing steadily across a wooded plain: unstoppable, adorned with the appropriate black-and-white insignia, bristling with cannon and machine guns, and looking just like something out of *Tanks and How to Draw Them*,[1] a boyish primer by the British wartime illustrator Terence Cuneo. And yet charging towards this bullet-spitting monster comes a Polish lancer, helmeted and crouching in the saddle on a bay horse with a lance or curved sabre held high: a terrifically valiant figure, quite reckless of his own chances of survival. The picture shows a clash between worlds rather than just armies: on one side, a symbol of what J. F. Kennedy and many other commentators of the time would call Hitler's 'mechanized Juggernaut';[2] on the other an obsolete figure of great personal courage and élan, and also a hint of ridiculously misplaced trust – whether it be in the promises of French and British allies, whose intervention is certainly nowhere to be seen, or in the adequacy of traditional means of warfare when pitched against this terrifying modern machine.

This detached and stylized image is what time seems to have made of the catastrophic events of September 1939, when Hitler's panzer divisions 'rolled off the autobahns',[3] as one historian has put it, to launch their 'lightning war' against a Polish nation that, in the words of a *New York Times* reporter, still 'clung to eighteenth century war methods'.[4] Though dressed in the trappings of actual history, the image converts the opening weeks of the Second World War into a collision between eras: petrol against muscle, faceless mechanized power against personal valour. It shows the charge of ancient against modern, of virtue against might, of Christian faith against secular mechanics, and the outcome is never even slightly in question. A generalized visual cliché, to be sure, and yet for many years this image would also serve as an icon, sacred both to exiled Polish patriots and to the tank-worshippers of various nationalities who followed Mechanization as an epoch-making creed.

On the victorious German side, the image served as evidence of Polish primitivism, brave or just stupid depending on how many German losses had to be acknowledged. In his autobiography, Hitler's tank general, Heinz Guderian, claimed that the Polish lancers took this desperate step 'in ignorance of the nature of our tanks', and suffered 'tremendous losses' as a consequence. This assertion was repeated by Basil Liddell Hart, who wrote of 'gallant but fantastic charges with sword and lance',[5] and the poor deluded Polish cavalry have been kept charging ever since. Shortly after the collapse of the Soviet empire, one Hungarian former dissident invoked them to explain how his countrymen had felt about the rise of Poland's Solidarity movement under Lech Walesa: with its 'stodgy, proletarian' leader and its old-fashioned style of trade unionism, Solidarity seemed 'obsolete, backward' and altogether 'like a Polish cavalry charge. For a few it is quite touching, but for others something laughable, quite ridiculous.'[6] Margaret Thatcher was not inclined to snigger at Polish opposition to Communism, yet the same trope is deployed in her autobiography. 'I had realized by now that I was not dealing with Polish cavalrymen'[7] – so she (or her ghost writer) remarks of the moment, just before she was deposed as Prime Minister and Leader of the Conservative Party, when it became apparent that her own cabinet ministers were not going to rally bravely to her side in the conviction that it was 'better to go out in a blaze of glorious defeat than to go gentle into that good night'. Thatcher counted herself among the gallant lancers, unlike her senior colleagues who sneaked up with their apologies one by one, and then stole away with all the timidity of realists who knew that their abandoned 'Iron Lady' was really a tank. Such are the confusions in which the myth lives on. Even in the late nineties, a Polish emigré only had to publish a book in Britain, and those tireless lancers would be launched across the literary review pages once again. So it was when Radek Sikorski, an ardent right-wing patriot, produced an account of his purchase of a run-down manor house at Chobielin and its symbolic restoration after fifty years of Communism.[8] One London reviewer knew enough about Poland to declare the project touched with 'a cavalryman's élan';[9] another observed that, had the author come of age during the war years, 'he would, no doubt, have dug his cavalry officer's spurs into the flank of his horse and galloped heroically at an invading division of Nazi tanks'.[10]

Having talked with Denis Hills, a Briton who was in Poland in September 1939, I knew that a less trivial version of that doomed cavalry charge had been sacred to Polish soldiers who survived the débâcle. Hills dismissed 'the Balaclava stuff' as 'a bit of fantasy', but he reckoned there probably had been skirmishes in which Polish cavalry came up against Nazi tanks. He had heard of such engagements in 1940, whilst serving alongside a Carpathian Brigade of Polish lancers in Egypt. These proud men had been reconstituted as a fighting force in France after fleeing their defeated country, and Hills remembers being told off for demoralizing them by doubting their romantic stories of lancers charging against panzers. He went on to say that the Polish character seems to thrive on 'disasters'. What those dispossessed Polish soldiers had admired about the British was the Charge of the Light Brigade – mistaken, doomed but also brave and, perhaps above all considering the low social status of the infantry making up the bulk of the Polish Army in September 1939, 'carried out by gentleman, not just horrid men in heavy boots marching through the mud'.

For some Poles who settled in the West after the end of the Second World War, those heroic lancers were to become as emblematic of the Polish spirit as nineteenth-century romantic exiles like Chopin and the poet Mickiewicz, who sustained the memory of Poland from Paris even though the country had been wholly extinguished in the eighteenth century (its territory was divided between Prussia, Russia and Austria) and would only be re-established at the end of the First World War. This was how they were remembered by General K. S. Rudnicki, DSO, then a Colonel with Poland's 9th Lancers, who had watched his dog-tired but fearless men attack Nazi tanks with nothing more than bayonets and a ferocious roar.[11] It was also how they appeared to M. Kamil Dziewanowski, who served in September 1939 as a platoon commander with the Suwalki Cavalry Brigade, and who remembered his own participation in 'what may rank in the history of warfare as the last Great Charge of the Polish Cavalry'. Grossly under-equipped, the brigade had struggled to prevent the German forces advancing on Warsaw from East Prussia. Having only a few anti-tank guns and light armoured scout cars, they could only meet the crushing weight of German armour with an improvised 'technique of pursuit, of ambush, and of ruses'. Over a few brilliant autumn days, this 'proud cavalry brigade' turned itself into 'an outfit of tank hunters' but, even at desperate moments, the sabre charge was no part of its strategy. The Nazi tank may have 'looked formidable at a distance', but 'it began to show, especially at night, its impotence against daredevils who had the nerve to approach the tanks and throw gasoline-filled bottles' or who 'crept up to wreck the caterpillar treads of these tanks with bunches of hand grenades'. By 9 September, the men of the Third Light Horse Regiment of the Suwalki Cavalry Brigade were hungry and exhausted, and even their horses – 'those beautiful chestnut horses of which we were so proud' – had been constantly saddled for days and were becoming 'dispirited and vicious, sheer skeletons'. Already deposed by the new forces of mechanized warfare, they were determined to make their 'dignified exit' with 'just one more glorious charge at the enemy in the glorious tradition of our cavalry'.

That grand finale came at dawn, when those proud horsemen found an enemy infantry battalion marching along the road about a mile and a half away along the northern edge of the Zambrow Forest, accompanied by a column of transport trucks. Dziewanowski remembered stepping out into the rising sun of Poland's last clear day:

The picture of the regiment emerging from the woods was so enchanting that it seemed unreal. What a perfect model for a battle painter! Where is our Vernet or Gericault!

First we proceeded at a slow trot. The Germans still marched on, apparently unconcerned. Then suddenly our heavy machine-guns, hidden in the woods, gave tongue with a well-timed salvo. It went straight into the enemy column. The great adventure was on!

The command 'Draw sabres, gallop, march!' flew down the lines. Reins were gripped tighter. The riders bent forward in the saddles and they rushed forward like a mad whirlwind.[12]

For Dziewanowski, who survived the war to become a professor of history at the University of Boston, Poland's last cavalry charge was a symbolic triumph gleaming in the darkness of a much greater defeat. He left no doubt as to the terror it struck into the German forces, who collapsed into 'a frantic mob' and were quickly defeated with negligible Polish losses: 'The morning sun was high when our bugler blew assembly. We came up slowly, driving our prisoners ahead of us. We took about 200 men, most of them insane from fright.'

However, not all veterans of Poland's doomed defence were prepared to embrace the thought of that fabled cavalry charge against Nazi tanks as proof of the heroic 'lancer mentality'.[13] The London-based historian Józef Garlinski served in the 1st Regiment of the Polish Guard, the only regiment of lancers garrisoned in Warsaw in September 1939; and when I asked him about these mythological images, Garlinski immediately referred to the way the Nazis had engineered a 'Polish' attack on a radio station in the Silesian town of Gleiwitz (now Gliwice), as justification for their already planned invasion of Poland (which Hitler called 'meeting force with force'). The raid and subsequent broadcast urging Silesian Poles to rise up against Germany were carried out by SS soldiers dressed in Polish uniform and, as was confirmed in the Nuremburg trials, the 'Polish' corpses shown to foreign journalists were actually the bodies of murdered concentration camp prisoners. There was nothing the Nazis wouldn't do with propaganda, snorted Garlinski; and he was in no doubt that the picture of the ignorant Polish lancer charging tanks had been cooked up in exactly the same way. There may have been some situations in which Polish lancers took desperate steps: 'You can charge a tank with your bare hands, or a house for that matter – there are all sorts of ways of committing suicide.' But the image was 'a lot of nonsense' from the military point of view. Garlinski remembered the horse not as a flying steed or an elegant mount trained in elaborate rituals of dressage, but as a means of transport: 'How else could it be, considering that, in September 1939, Poland had three and a half million horses and still not one factory producing cars?' As for methods of fighting, here too the sabre charge of romantic imagination was hopelessly detached from reality. It was customary, so Garlinski recalled, for one third of the soldiers in a cavalry regiment to stay with the horses while the other two thirds fought on the ground or in trenches, just like infantrymen. Garlinski himself had been wounded and taken prisoner in exactly that kind of fighting.

Impossible, then, to sort fact from propaganda and fiction. Or so it seemed as the train rumbled through the freezing night, halting at nameless stations to allow border guards as well as occasional passengers to step in and out of the darkness.

Before leaving London, I had viewed Andrzej Wajda's film *Lotna*. Made in 1959, at the end of a brief period of liberalization introduced in 1956 when the Polish Communist leader Wladyslaw Gomulka won his country a little distance from Moscow, Wajda's first colour film follows a squadron of Polish lancers over their last few days and nights in September 1939. Lotna, which means 'Swift', is the name of a magnificent white Arabian mare, seen walking through the empty rooms of a deserted and partly shattered country mansion. This superior and heraldic creature – certainly no plodding packhorse – is first adopted by the lancers' commander and then, as he and the other officers are killed off, passed down the hierarchy of their disintegrating squad. Encircled, the lancers try to break out with sabre charges that eventually bring them up against the Nazi tank, one of which rides symbolically over a horse.

Wajda portrayed his cavalry squadron as a bastion of non-socialist values, but he did so with considerable ambiguity of meaning. Indeed, in places Lotna seems to mock its doomed members for their anachronistic, class-based outlook. As the Nazi pincer closes around them, these quixotic and apparently reckless lancers demonstrate their equestrian skills and propound the heroically complacent view that it only takes one grenade in the turret to turn a Nazi tank into an oven. When a romantic young cadet falls in love and decides to get married there and then, the squadron celebrates with fireworks, regardless of the fact that 'the Germans will know where we are tomorrow'. Throughout the film, the lancers' fate is presaged by heavy symbolism: they are likened to ripe autumnal apples ready to fall; to an ever more shattered classical statue in a ruined aristocratic garden; to a collection of fish gasping their last on a kitchen slab. They die more abject than heroic: the superb horse shot, the sword of command broken and hurled down in chaotic defeat. Lotna was appreciated for its 'surrealist' touches in France, but it was not a popular success in Poland, and it is not among the many of Wajda's films that have since been reissued on video.

Has the end of Communism finally revealed the truth of September 1939, or has it just produced a different ideological context for those doomed lancers to keep on charging through? This was the question I was taking to Warsaw. Professor Garlinski had warned me that Poland was still full of stories fabricated by people for their own interested reasons. It had even been claimed that the Nazis established a concentration camp in Warsaw, and used it to murder 200,000 people. Garlinski repudiated this furiously. As head of security in the Warsaw resistance until 1943, when he was captured and sent to Auschwitz, he would have known had any such place existed. But if you dispute with the 'bloody idiots' peddling these stories, you can expect to find yourself denounced as a spy who must be on somebody or other's payroll. In this climate, Professor Garlinski thought it all too likely that I would arrive in Poland to find the cavalry still charging into Nazi tanks, with any number of big-talking elderly bar-room heroes in the lead.

Leaving Warsaw Central station, I walked past Stalin's vast Palace of Culture – a colossal skyscraper with a huge open area in front of it, once used for military parades, political rallies and other official displays of mass loyalty, but now a metal shanty town crowded with small-scale market stalls and sex shops. The largest of the nearby billboards featured a cigarette advertisement that had scooped up Poland's cavalry charge and relocated it in Marlboro Country: a column of men wearing yellow dusters, galloping across a vast flat terrain with standing water and a freakish orange sky.

Turning left at McDonald's, I entered a courtyard and rang at the door of Tadeusz Pióro, a former general who politely wondered, over breakfast, why any writer with a choice in the matter should develop an interest in tanks – machines that, for him, represented the very opposite and probably also the end of culture. As for the fabled lancers of September 1939, General Pióro's companion Lucyna Golebiowska was immediately inclined to wonder about the Polish partiality for doomed heroics. 'What the country needs right now is constructive workers,' she said, but history had inclined Poles to prefer 'people who died in combat even through incompetence . . . we are still better at valuing self-sacrifice and dying or enduring imprisonment for the cause'.

Pióro is descended from an aristocratic family called 'Boncza Pióro', but he cut his name down to size for obvious reasons in the nineteen-forties. His father was among the Polish officers murdered on Stalin's orders at Katyn, yet as a young man he still became a committed Communist soldier and, in 1956, was appointed the First Polish Representative in the Warsaw Pact. He lived in Moscow but the command structure, which pretended to depend on representatives from the various nations within the Soviet bloc, was actually a complete 'fiction' and he had nothing to do – except enjoy his considerable salary, read papers in his office, and hope that his reputation as an anti-Stalinist 'revisionist', gained at conferences on Soviet-Polish relations and consolidated after October 1956 when Gomulka won Poland a little communist distance from Moscow, did not get taken too far. He 'resigned' from the army under pressure in 1967, just as a purge of Jewish and 'revisionist' officers was getting under way.

Pióro was in the artillery, but he knows about tanks and their pre-eminence in the Soviet arsenal. Under Stalin especially, the tank became a primary symbol of Soviet force: at once, the emblem of unstoppable state power and the embodiment of a crude idea of irresistible progress. Pióro once drove a tank down a road, and remembers feeling strangely confident: 'absolutely secure, and that nothing could happen to me'. He had no training, but the noise and the separation from the world outside gave him a feeling of invincible and irreversible momentum, strangely confirmed when he came off the road chaotically, crashing into a large concrete pole and yet rolling on unchecked. To drive a tank under Stalinism was to know what the ideologues of that regime meant by the 'cutting edge' of an irreversible history.

Throughout the Cold War, tank units provided the main attraction of official manoeuvres within the Soviet bloc. One such event, which took place in Russia in 1957, remains especially vivid in Pióro's mind. All the Warsaw Pact's chiefs of staff had been invited, together with their deputies; and Pióro was up there with a lot of Soviet generals, alongside Marshal S. Konev, then chief commander of the Warsaw Pact. One of the exhibits intended to impress everyone – the novelty of the year – was a new tank that would cross rivers not by vulnerable bridges but by travelling underwater. This would be a testing experience for the tank crew, but Soviet military planners were not inclined to let a consideration like that impede their advance. Indeed, when the designers of this new tank were considering how to dispose of engine exhaust during these underwater crossings they had seriously considered pumping it into the interior of the tank, which would presumably not be underwater for so very long anyway.

Ten of these submarine tanks had duly entered a river; and at first the display seemed successful and, indeed, very spectacular. But then something went wrong. About two metres from the far bank one of the submerged tanks got stuck, and the celebratory spectacle collapsed into a desperate scramble. The four members of the tank's crew, were down there for three hours. First, a rescue team tried to pull the submerged tank out of the water. After two hours of unsuccessful effort, the crew were told to open up the tank and swim out. Although trained to escape in this way, they were so 'psychologically devastated' by this time that they panicked and all tried to escape at once. As a consequence, they got jammed in the hatches, and all four of them drowned. What was the effect of this triumphalist demonstration going so horribly wrong? 'Someone was punished,' remembers Pióro. 'Somebody had to be punished. And, about a month later, a similar accident occurred in East Germany . . .'

In Poland, tanks are part of the debris of modern memory. Like rings in a tree, the older you are the more of these machines you are likely to have rolling around in the back of your mind.

Asked about 'Tanks in my memory', Michal Komar, the former dissident writer who was then editor of the Warsaw paper *Sztandar Mlodych* (formerly the official paper for communist youth), sat in his office and laughed. Declaring this to be 'a very funny issue', he started unravelling a frieze of remembered tanks that ran for almost the whole length of his life. Too young to recall the war, and the all but total destruction of Warsaw by the Nazis, his memories began in the early fifties, when he was growing up as the son of General Waclaw Komar, a Spanish Civil War veteran who became head of counterintelligence in the post-war period.

He remembered the parade held when the rebuilding of the old town in Warsaw was completed – a vast symbolic project, carried out while much of the population was still unhoused, which made the place 'much more elegant' than it had been before. He reckons it must have been 22 July 1953, only a few months after Stalin's death. To his surprise, he saw tanks grinding their way through those narrow and painfully reconstructed cobbled streets. And not just any old tanks. The machines Komar recalled were Jozef Stalins, the heaviest of all Soviet tanks – as if, having reconstructed the fragile heart of old Poland, the Soviet regime had to demonstrate its ability to crush it on the very first day. 'I cannot analyse the symbolic meaning of this image,' he said, still amazed at the regime that could produce such a parade.

There were more Russian tanks in the streets in October 1956, when the Soviet Union prepared to take military steps against the allegedly 'counter-revolutionary' Polish United Workers' Party, led by Wladyslaw Gomulka. Nikita Khrushchev flew into Warsaw military airport with a large and unwelcome delegation of Presidium members such as Molotov, Defence Minister Zhukov, and a dozen or so generals, including Marshal Ivan Konev. While Gomulka and the Soviets thrashed it out in the Belvedere Palace, an apprehensive Warsaw is said to have whispered that 'the ambulances started before our friends arrived'.[14] As Komar remembered, the Russians allowed tanks to move from their garrisons – 'not just to be seen, but as a signal that they were ready to attack'. Russian-commanded tank units surrounded Warsaw and entered a working-class suburb called Wola. The sight of them filled the city with 'enormous fever' – hardly subdued when Marshal Konstanty Rokossowski, the hated Soviet puppet installed as the Polish Minister of Defence, remarked that this apparent invasion was nothing more than a set of ordinary 'autumn manoeuvres'. Komar's father,

General Waclaw Komar, was head of the Polish security services, having recently been released from a spell in prison as a 'Titoist' and, for that matter, also 'an American, English, French and Italian spy'. For decades it was rumoured that, in Poland's tradition of regardless heroism, he had dispatched tanks to the Russian border and barricaded the road with tanks, thereby stopping a Russian column some sixty miles from Warsaw. But Michal Komar was inclined to play down these romantic stories – 'although they gave some weaponry to workers at SFO, a large automobile factory, and they did send a company of troops to the edge of the Warsaw'.

Komar remembered more tanks in 1968, this time loaded on to trains and being shipped in 'endless, endless transports' to Czechoslovakia where they would help to extinguish the Prague Spring. Then in 1970 he happened to be in north-east Poland, where he came across two Polish tank divisions hiding in the trees. It remained unclear exactly what they were doing there. According to one interpretation those tanks were waiting in a state of alert, prepared to attack striking workers in Gdansk, many of whom would indeed shortly be killed on the streets. Others preferred to speculate that Jaruzelski, who was Defence Minister at the time, had ordered these units to hide in the woods precisely so that they would not be used against their own citizenry.

Komar's final example dated from the imposition of martial law in 1980. Not the famous news photographs of tanks on the streets of Warsaw, or outside the 'Moscow' cinema with its posters advertising *Apocalypse Now*, but a scene glimpsed from the tiny window of a *Suka* – which, as Komar explained, means 'a dog, a bitch, and also a police car'. Arrested as a dissident, Komar was being driven through Warsaw to a prison at Bialoleka and on the way he saw tanks on both sides of the bridge across the River Vistula. When he was driven to the airport following his release three weeks later, he had looked out and seen a tank lying upside down in a ditch by the roadside. 'I asked the escorting officer what had happened. And he looked at me with enormous hatred, and told me it was all my fault – the loss of equipment, the chaos caused by the implementation of martial law.' 'So tanks are everywhere,' said Komar, having employed them to tell the story of his life.

Since so much of Poland's history has been 'made of tanks', it is not surprising that these crushing machines should have achieved a strong cultural reflection as well. They are there, rolling through books and films as well as streets – a sign of the times for much of Poland's twentieth century. Komar knew about *Lotna*, a film he suggested Wajda might have 'made with the left hand' at a time when the future looked Communist for ever. He remembered Jan Sawka's 'Car of the Year', a poster that won first prize at Warsaw's 7th International Poster Biennale in 1978 and which, in grim anticipation of martial law, showed a Soviet tank in a narrow and deserted civilian street. He also cited a hugely popular television series, called *Four Tankmen and a Dog*, based on a story written by Janusz Przymanowski, a Stalinist writer who had been a war correspondent with the newspaper of the First Polish Army, established in Russia in 1943. Przymanowski took the stories of the First Polish Tank Brigade, which served alongside the Red Army in the attack on Berlin, and built them into a propaganda epic that follows its heroic Polish soldiers as they leave Siberia (how they got there is not explained) and go on, with the help of a tank that becomes like their home, to take Berlin and win the Second World War alongside their Soviet allies. *Four Tankmen and a Dog* was filmed at prodigious cost and broadcast in episodes through the sixties – proving hugely successful in Russia and East Germany as well as Poland. The programme was very popular with the young and, as Komar's defence editor Wojciech Luczak added, almost certainly inspired many adolescent boys to become tank soldiers. It also prompted its own kind of community action. For a time in the sixties, newspapers encouraged youngsters to form themselves up into units of four, get a dog and then go out as *Pancerni* to help old ladies or do other good works for the neighbourhood – a harmless initiative, as Luczak saw it, even though it had recently been condemned as an insidious ultra-communist manoeuvre.

It wasn't just for people of Komar's generation that history was made of tanks – as I discovered when I met a class of third-year students at Warsaw University, who happily added their own more recent examples to his list. Many of the Polish towns in which they had grown up had a Soviet war memorial tank, mounted in a square or park and decked out in the rhetoric of liberation and Soviet friendship. Infants from kindergarten would customarily be brought to the tank for edification, and in the sixties many of these metal memorials had been temporarily renamed after the tanks in the TV programme. By the time these students were coming of age in the late eighties, however, these Soviet memorials were more likely to be targeted by the young: sprayed with anti-Communist graffiti, they had been converted into sites of punk protestation.

The students knew about *Four Tankmen and a Dog*. It had been repeated on television since the fall of the Soviet empire, and now enjoyed considerable success as a video series, commended for its high production values if not for its political message. They also remembered *Lucky Tony*, a flimsy but ideologically intriguing film directed by Halina Bielinska and first released in 1961. This comedy tells of a newly wed couple who, through good fortune, are handed the key to a dream house in the suburbs. Full of pastoral hopes, they set out on the train, only to find that no house awaits them – just a plot of land with a large mountain of soil on it. Setting out to shift this obstacle, they hit metal and find a Soviet T-34 left over from the Second World War. No doubt aware of the acute housing shortage of those years, Lucky Tony's wife soon fastens her washing line to the barrel and prepares to settle down. But he is less compliant and resolves to shift the metal monster. Frustrated by bureaucracy, he gets a manual on tank driving and, having accidentally bashed the thing into action, sets off chaotically down the road. Unable to stop his careering machine, he appeals for help from soldiers on the roadside or from a policeman directing traffic, but at the sight of the Russian tank, they only salute him with fearful deference and get out of his way. So Tony advances into central Warsaw. After ploughing through a street market and failing to convince a scrap merchant to take the thing off his hands, Lucky Tony eventually drives his tank home, where he and his reluctant wife learn to get along with their once unwelcome military relic. Indeed, they build their house around it, and the last shot shows them at home in their living room, the T-34 incorporated as a vast piece of utility furniture – a combined ornament rack, bookshelf and telephone stand. Adorned with plants and family portraits, it sits there as unmistakable as the Soviet Union, the guarantor of homely security and, as this covertly satirical film suggests, of domestic contentment too.

I heard more of this Polish tank lore at the University of Wroclaw in Silesia, a German-built city known for centuries as Breslau and a site of terrible fighting during the Second World War. The Nazis reconfirmed Breslau's status in a Greater Germany, but then, as the Third Reich crumbled, they drove out its largely German population (many of whom arrived in Dresden in time to be bombed by the RAF) and declared the city a fort.

The liberation of Wroclaw by the Red Army is vividly commemorated at the Russian Military Cemetery – uniform rows of identical tombstones, each one with a name and an inlaid red star, grouped behind formal hedges, and arranged within the formal, totalitarian vistas of a superpower that is no longer there to sweep up the leaves or keep the grass neatly cut. A couple of old howitzers have been incorporated into this forsaken place, but the true emblems of victory are four numbered T-34s – brutal relics, mounted on slanted concrete plinths and forever rising up in pairs at the entrances of the main avenues.

The students at Wroclaw's Institute of English knew about September 1939, and the story of charging Polish lancers. They too had been brought up on *Lotna* – not so much Wajda's film as the original novella by Wojciech Zukrowski on which it had been based, and which had been prescribed reading in schools. They recognized this as a thoroughly Communist treatment of events, but some of them seemed still to believe that the Polish cavalry had indeed conducted their war in that hopeless and decadent way. The four specimens at that deserted Russian Military Cemetery may have been left to rust in peace, but I was assured that popular lore in Poland had long been exacting its revenge on Russian tanks. If you wanted to insult someone in Silesia before 1989, you might accuse them of having lice like Russian tanks. If someone was having you on, you could reach into the corner of your eye with an index finger, pull down the lower lid and ask: 'Is there a tank driving in here?'

Wasn't the tank rather like Grendel, ventured one lecturer – a partly fabulous, partly prehistoric creature of myth? For at least one young woman, the answer was definitely in the affirmative. Born in 1968, Malgorzata Sabina grew up the daughter of teachers in the village of Goluszowice, a few kilometres from the old Czechoslovak border. This was a traditional village that, like many others in the area, had been forcibly evacuated of its largely German-born population shortly after the war, and then resettled with people from the eastern territories, who might otherwise have been removed to Siberia. She remembered one historical legend in particular. There was, she explained, a little wood or grove near the village – a tranquil, even idyllic kind of place where young lovers might be found in the spring, and where children would also go to have bonfires or gather the horse chestnuts they would take home and make into animals. In one part of this grove there stood a little shrine to the Virgin Mary. In another was a small pond, surrounded by wild raspberry bushes and so easily overlooked that it was sometimes a job to find it.

Sabina couldn't say whether this pond still fascinated the young as it had done when she was growing up in the seventies and early eighties. Perhaps children now stay in and watch television; yet for Sabina and her friends, the pond kept tugging at their imaginations. It was said to be fathomless – of quite unknown depth – and it was also said that a German tank lay at the bottom of it, having ploughed its way through the wood and not seen the danger until too late. Sabina couldn't say whether this story was a legendary invention of the childish imagination. Similar rumours clung to other ponds in the Opole region, and it did, as she volunteered, sound a little like the story of the Loch Ness Monster. And yet perhaps such a thing really had happened. The pond was small, overgrown and internally walled so that the ground rose up to its edges, making it invisible until the point at which an advancing tank would already have been sliding down into it. But there it was all the same. The Nazi tank as a legendary figure of prehistory, which in that violently cleared and resettled village was only as old as the Second World War.

What did the Polish Army think of the Soviet Union's favourite land weapon now that the Warsaw Pact was no more? The former General Tadeusz Pióro had been happy to suggest how we might find out before I left London. He got hold of the home phone number of General Julian Levinsky, then Commander of the Warsaw army region, and suggested I fax him a letter asking permission to visit a tank regiment near Warsaw. Levinsky picked up the phone himself and, with the single word 'Please', obligingly switched it over to fax mode. That was the extent of our communication, but the necessary arrangements had still been set in hand. And so the day came, at the end of November 1995, when I met up with General Pióro and his companion Lucyna Golebiowska, who kindly agreed to come along as interpreter; and we set off down Al. Jerozolimskie, walking past the military museum with its garden full of rusting tanks (I noticed a half-tracked vehicle with 'To Berlin!' emblazoned on its side), to the railway station, where we boarded a suburban train to Wesola – a place that, despite the greyness and the cold and the regimented identity of its detached houses, still aspired to the Arcadian condition of its name, which implied a 'place of joy, happiness and contentment'.

Crossing the track, we followed a winding path through woods of birch and pine, passing an abandoned children's playground and then rows of gaunt five-storey military accommodation blocks. Our destination lay beyond that, a large concrete building positioned just outside the guarded perimeter fence of the training ground. Adorned with a gilded Polish eagle and the words 'Klub Kosciuszkowska', this was the officer's club of the First Warsaw Tank Brigade – a considerable place built, so General Pióro reckoned, in the early seventies and reflecting the elite status of the tank in the Warsaw Pact's strategic thinking.

Inside, we found ourselves in a large hallway with hundreds of empty coat hooks and paintings, which also seemed to speak of busier times. General

Imagining the tank after its first engagements on the Western Front. 1. 'A few conceptions, picked up from press accounts here and there, of what "tanks" are really like', *Punch,* 27 September 1916. 2. The 'Tanko' as performed by 'speciality' dancer Regine Flory and the Palace Girls at London's Gaiety Theatre, November 1916.

3

4 / 5

6

7 / 8

'Wonder Weapon' of the First World War. 3.
An early Mark 1 British tank at Foster's works
in Lincoln, 1916. 4. Albert I, King of the
Belgians, inspecting a British tank at Tilloy-les-
Mofflaines, 17 May 1917. 5. Heavy Branch tank
and crew at Rollencourt, 18 June 1917. 6. Miss
Marie Lohr, who bought and sold war bonds,
appraising 'Egbert' at the Tank bank in
Trafalgar Square, March 1918. 7. Fuller, Uzielli,
Elles (from far left to right) and other officers of
the Heavy Branch at Bermicourt, France,
1916/7. 8. British female Mark IV tank in
Manhattan for Liberty Loan parade, October
1917.

A new kind of mobile warfare. 9. British Medium D prototype takes to the streets near Woolwich Arsenal, winter 1920/1. 10. German tanks invade Czechoslovakia, at Pohorolice in Moravia, March 1939. 11. German assault on Poland, September 1939. 12. Italian M13/40 medium tanks in Libya 1941/2. 13. Soviet T-26 medium tanks (built under licence from Vickers Armstrong) prepare to repel Nazi invaders at the opening of Operation Barbarossa, 22 June 1941. 14. Soviet T-34/76 with crew cleaning gun tube, 1943/4. 15. The Red Army's conquest of Berlin as portrayed by Pavel Sokolow-Skalja (Tass-Fenster Nr. 1236, 'On Berlin's Siegasallee Street', 1945).

12

13

ОКНО ТАСС №1236

НА БЕРЛИНСКОЙ „АЛЛЕЕ ПОБЕД"

Берлин поднял руки и крикнул „Капут!"
„Аллей побед" наши танки идут.
И Фридрих испуган и Бисмарк дрожит,
И Гитлера тень без оглядки бежит.
И даже названье сменила как будто
„Аллея побед" на „Аллею капута".

ХУДОЖНИК—П. СОКОЛОВ-СКАЛЯ   В. ЛЕБЕДЕВ-КУМАЧ

14 / 15

16

17 / 18

In the civilian eye. 16. Polish couple at home with a Soviet tank in Halina Bielinska and Wlodzimierz Haupe's film *Lucky Tony* (1961). 17. Israelis greet their victorious tanks at the end of the Six Day War, Tiberius, 9 July 1967. 18. Onlooker watching tank from hotel in

19

20

Syntagma Square, Athens, during the Colonels' Coup of April 1967. 19. Prague, August 1990: Soviet tank overturned to mark the anniversary of the Warsaw Pact invasion of 1968. 20. 'The Pink Tank 1991', a Prague war memorial recoloured by David Cerny and the Neostunners.

End of the line? 21. 'Wang Weilin' stops tanks in Changan Avenue, Peking, 5 June 1989. 22. Major General Lon E. Maggart with Abrams M1 tank at the US Army Armor Center, Fort Knox, 1996.

Pióro thought that the crudest tributes to Polish-Soviet friendship had probably been removed, but the stairs were still dominated by a large oil painting in which Russian and Polish soldiers hailed each other as comrades in the ruins of some wasted city or other. There was a spacious and well-equipped cinema and also a canteen, where we were welcomed by the officer detailed to organize our visit and then led upstairs into a rectangular room with strangely disconcerting edges. There were enough antlers mounted on the walls to support a thousand hats, civil or military. The whiskery feet of many once-darting woodland creatures were also on display – severed at the second joint and mounted on heraldic plates of wood. The tusked head of a vast boar protruded from one wall, not far from a blasted-looking hedgehog – stuffed but still running. Looking up through these spiky thickets during our conversation, I would spy a small herd of deer hanging from the ceiling in painted plywood silhouette. The aristocratic traditions of the pre-war Polish cavalry may have been surpassed long ago, but these trophies left no doubt that the modern tank officer maintains roots in the native Polish forest. It had once offered similar inspiration to Soviet officers too.

In the middle of this bony chamber sat seventeen tank soldiers, arrayed on either side of a long and exceptionally narrow table. Introductory formalities were decorous and fairly elaborate too. Chairs were thrust back as men stood suddenly to attention, and there were salutes for the former general as well as diverse handshakes and curious glances for Lucyna and me.

To begin with we talked politely about the way in which conscripts were trained, over the two stages of the Polish draft. We discussed the qualities needed by a tank soldier, who, in Poland as elsewhere, must be open-minded, personally brave, not prone to claustrophobia, and in good physical health. The three members of a tank crew were there to agree with this assessment. Sergeant Piotr Brzezinski, the tank commander, might just have been in his early twenties but the two lance corporals – the gunner and driver respectively – could hardly have been out of their teens. They emphasized the importance of teamwork, which they hoped would serve them well when the time came to find positions in civilian life; and they talked, with only a little reluctance, about the fear they had felt when confronted with a tank for the first time.

The point was briskly elaborated by Captain Jaroslaw Mojsak, an intelligent and patriotic battalion commander, who would take the lead from this moment on. He confirmed that the tank did indeed have a frightening aspect. Even as an experienced officer he could still be gripped by momentary fear when tanks suddenly came into view during a training manoeuvre.

But this admitted sense of trepidation was alloyed with something else – a reassuring 'feeling of power', which he likened to being at the Olympics when a triumphant Polish athlete is up on the podium receiving a gold medal as the Polish anthem is being played. Here, said Captain Mojsak, was the proper counterbalance to fear: a feeling of immense 'patriotic pride' that these indeed were Poland's machines.

And what of the martial law episode of 1980–1, when the Polish Army took their tanks on to the streets of Warsaw and other cities and used them to terrorize their own citizenry? I tried to sidle up on this diplomatically, by mentioning how interested the British tank pioneers of the 1920s had been in the intimidating effect that the mere appearance of tanks in the streets could have on civilian crowds – strikers, rioters or Irish Republicans. But Captain Mojsak saw immediately where we were going, and headed me off by insisting that the army had changed a lot since 1989 and, moreover, that he and his colleagues were far too young to speak with any authority about those days. Only one of the men in the room – Major Chojecki, who was now Chief of the Training Section – had been in the army during that difficult period.

As for the psychological impact of the tank, Captain Mojsak suggested that while that consideration might have been to the fore in earlier days, it was now less important. 'Tanks are getting smaller and less conspicuous,' he said. The tanks of old may have been 'big and colossal', and Soviet engineers may even, as one of Mojsak's colleagues believed, have made their tanks especially noisy in order to terrify the enemy. But the really effective modern tank no longer had any need for such primitive enhancements. Far from relying on size or noise for its effect, it would generate a more precise and realistic fear by being much more effective in combat. As a specialist, Captain Mojsak would not fear a Soviet T-34 because he knew its many inadequacies, but it would be quite another matter to face one of those American Abrams M1A1 tanks that had made such short work of Saddam Hussein's armour in the Gulf War.

Major Chojecki, who had worked with every type of Soviet tank from the T-34 to the T-80, was happy to confirm this view. He explained that 'until 1989' the Soviet idea was simply to have as many tanks as possible. There were more tanks than any other armoured vehicles, and at joint manoeuvres the tank was displayed as the main force, decked out in the claim that 'with their tanks, they could fight the whole world'. The same myth, he volunteered, had been built into the television drama *Four Tank-men and a Dog* – the mere mention of which drew affectionate laughter all round. But that was all in the past and, in the new world, quality would matter more than brute quantity. The tanks of the future would involve 'more intelligence'. The technology would be more sophisticated, and the training more demanding too. The army would no longer need so many tanks to bring off any particular engagement.

Then I asked them about tactics, referring to J. F. C. Fuller's seventy-year-old conception of the tank as a provider of 'penetration with security' and also to the more recent suggestion, which I had heard at Vickers' Challenger factory in Newcastle a couple of years previously, that the tank was still uniquely equipped for 'taking and holding ground under fire'. Coming down decisively in the defensive mode, these soldiers talked about 'holding' rather than taking ground. This has long been the Polish challenge in historical terms, and it remained so even though the capitalist West was no longer seen as the enemy. Indeed, the question now inclined those Polish soldiers to look east – into Belarus and the Ukraine, and also Kaliningrad, where the Russians were said to have as many as 100,000 soldiers.

Some mentioned the possible difficulties of trying to make a modern and specialized army with conscripts rather than self-motivated volunteers, but Captain Mojsak was defensive of the Polish way, and saw clear moral advantage in the idea of national service. American tanks may be better, but the same could not automatically be assumed for the American soldier. The Polish soldier was 'prepared to defend his country, his house, his family', and his response to threat would be superior to that of a soldier asked to risk his life in a foreign country. In this respect he would be 'unlike the American', who came from a country without experience of invasion, and might be sent to defend US interests all round the world, but who in the end was just doing a job for the sake of the salary.

I asked about the tactics of manoeuvre and surprise, of striking suddenly and then 'melting away', which had once been the pride of Poland's cavalry. It was with these offensive methods that the Polish Army had beaten the Red Army back from within striking distance of Warsaw in 1920; and yet, according to one reflective veteran at least, reliance on the same strategy rather than a more appropriate doctrine of 'endurance', had contributed to the speed with which Poland's forty overwhelmed cavalry regiments had lost to the Nazis in September 1939.[15] The tankmen at Wesola claimed to be the inheritors of those tactics, even though the horses were long gone, and there was an immediate frisson in the air when I mentioned the mythical image of the valiant Polish lancer charging the unstoppable Nazi tank, and especially when I remarked that it was still sometimes cited in Britain as proof that the Poles were brave, romantic, technically unso-phisticated and doomed.

There was a moment of tense silence, out of which Captain Mosjak stepped to speak with affronted dignity: it would be 'very unfortunate', he said, if the British had really forgotten so much that they only thought of the Polish soldier in the context of September 1939. Indeed, it was positively 'wounding' for him to think that they didn't remember the much wider involvement of Poles in the Second World War, the divisions that left the country, or the units that were reconstituted in France after the fall of Poland, and which fought with the Allies both in the air and on land. It was also 'worthwhile to stress' that even if the Poles did behave as doomed heroes, this was because the French and the British had obliged them to do so, by refusing to attack Hitler as they were bound to do by their own recently signed international agreements.

This was an interesting discussion, still suffused, as General Pióro pointed out, with a sense of unlikeliness that such an unguarded encounter between a Western writer and a former Warsaw Pact army should ever take place. Rightly or wrongly, I felt more sympathy for the patriotism of these soldiers than did some of the civilians I had met in Warsaw, who warned me that there was a long tradition of chauvinism in the Polish military, and pointed out that the army had been disorientated since the collapse of the Warsaw Pact – deprived of its traditional enemy and chronically under-equipped now that the Soviet ally had disappeared.

Tadeusz Pióro repeatedly told me that I should have come a few years earlier, when the Polish Army had the means to manoeuvre with more than brave words. The Polish Army had probably never before been so open to a Western visitor, but he was concerned that, as post-Communist austerity gripped, there was less and less to see. His doubts were confirmed when the Brigade Commander, Jerzy Michalowski, turned up halfway through the meeting, and quietly informed General Pióro that it would not be possible to show us around the training area itself. This was not, as I was later informed, because there were any sensitive secrets to protect, but because the place was simply not considered 'presentable'. I had heard about this problem elsewhere – especially from students whose drafted friends reported that the Polish Army had to struggle even to provide its conscripts with uniforms and other basic equipment. Everything was in short supply: ammunition, fuel, and perhaps also tanks themselves.

The 1st Warsaw Tank Brigade certainly had tanks: T-55s, or T-72s, made under licences bought from the Soviet Union in the sixties and mid-eighties respectively. Both designs were modernized and adjusted by Polish engineers, but such arrangements had come to a complete end in 1989 (there had previously been a T-80 that the Soviet Union wouldn't license). Polish engineers in the tank factory at Bumar Labedy have since come up with their own M91 'Twardy' (the name means 'hard'), a heavily modified T-72 with laser range-finder, computerized fire control system and Polish designed reactive armour, which explodes in order to diminish the impact of anti-tank missiles. Since 1989, the Polish government's Central Committee for Scientific Research had also considered commissioning a new main battle tank, a 50 to 55-ton specimen named 'The Gorilla', but this was never to become more than a big nationalist phantom.

Poland did have tanks, then, even though the austerity of those post-Communist times certainly fired the Polish tank soldiers' admiration for the US Abrams tank, and even lent a certain poignancy to their suggestion that the tank itself was shrinking – destined to become smaller and more intelligent, its crew already down from four to three, as the ephemeralizing army learned to do more with less. The Soviet departure was not lamented, yet even the officers' club in which we met seemed a relic from a more luxurious age. It was inconceivable, as General Pióro said, that such a luxurious officers' club would ever be built for a single tank brigade nowadays.

Further indication of the changes that have taken place since the fall of communism were provided by the solitary woman among the soldiers I met at Wesola. The exiled People's Mujahedin of Iran is reported to have female tank commanders in its force based in Iraq, albeit not out of respect for any Western-style equal opportunities policy. But Poland has not engendered such reforms, and Aleksandra Michalik wasn't a soldier at all. She had participated in the conversation throughout, picking up the thread whenever one or other soldier identified my question, perhaps a little archly, as 'one for the psychologist'. She was there to talk about the particular mental qualities required by the tank soldier, and to describe the difficulties of working with a conscript army that didn't necessarily have the motivation or the background to deal with an increasingly technical job. She commented on the fear of the tank, explaining how, as a woman, she could well imagine being frightened to death by the mere appearance of these machines. When we got to the vexed question of September 1939, she was quick to insist that Hitler himself had once remarked that, had his soldiers been as good as the Poles, he could have taken on the whole world and won.

Speaking after the soldiers had stood up and dispersed in an explosion of handshakes, salutes and respectful bows directed towards the retired general, she explained that her position as psychologist to the First Warsaw Tank Brigade was really quite new. Before March 1995, when she had assumed her new duties, she had worked as a kind of social secretary, organizing entertainment for the soldiers. The army, she explained, was conservative, and it had only been after considerable argument that she had assumed her present, truly psychological responsibilities. Her premise was simply stated: 'A soldier is just a man, and he has the right to have personal and psychological problems.' The balanced tank soldier, she added, is not burdened with machismo, which is 'the opposite of psychological sensitiveness'. The macho man wants to be something he is not, but that can be 'uncontrollable' and does not produce the 'internal equilibrium' essential to the reliable, team-working tank soldier.

It would, she says, be 'a very special kind of training' that allowed a man 'to shed normal fear' – and the Polish tank soldier is now allowed to be altogether more human than that. There is a Polish saying that calls a tank a 'moving coffin' – and not surprisingly since 'under fire, the exits can get blocked, and it is possible to be trapped'. Many soldiers have died this way, she says, adding that the fear of death is 'really about the biggest fear we have', and one that, for the tank soldier, is 'really about pain'. So the psychologist continued, talking about the curious and often very crude humour with which soldiers armour themselves against that fear, and also the ardent patriotism that enables a soldier to feel higher and more universal in his actions, elevated above the confusions and dissatisfactions of everyday life.

Repeating that 'the Polish tank soldier has a right to have problems' under the psychologically more accommodating regime that has come into being since the disintegration of the Warsaw Pact, Michalik explained that, when it came to understanding the young conscript's insecurities, her starting point had to be 'the whole society', which is presently in 'a very difficult historical position'. Poland was 'trying to join Western Europe' very quickly, and perhaps forgetting in its haste that 'our national mentality' is actually very different. The people were 'not morally prepared for the change', and most families had suffered shock and a loss of certainty. Many were under acute financial pressure too, so 'the horizons of our youth are very unsatisfactory at the moment'. The young conscript may lack understanding of the changes, yet he must still function so 'the emotional side rather than the rational takes over'. These insecurities could make the always testing experience of being closed up in a tank suddenly intolerable. So the psychologist formerly confined to booking dance bands for a Saturday night now had an expanded role helping the young tank soldier to find 'internal equilibrium' and to manage the 'emotional dissonance' that results in breakdown, depression, oversensitivity to stress. 'My job is to be there when needed, to help the young person stop thinking about the problems of life.'

Former General Pióro had listened to this disquisition in wide-eyed silence; and as we left the officer's club, with its room full of severed heads and horns, he and Lucyna Golebiowska marvelled at this new psychological creed, which had evidently gained considerable ground in the First Warsaw Tank Brigade even though Michalik admitted that she had so far still been barred from being inside a tank when it fired during the summer manoeuvres (the officer responsible had apparently been worried that she might not be able to keep her female emotions under control at that peak moment). Lucyna wondered whether this was anything but a further advance of American psycho-babble – the mothering therapeutic cliché that had been among the first Western devices to roll triumphantly over the border after the collapse of the Soviet empire in 1989, when a new age of personal liberty was ushered in with a torrent of sex shops, romantic fiction, and popular psychology books of the 'I'm OK. You're OK' variety.

We were still musing over this question when we got back to Warsaw. Comparing what he had seen with the Polish Army as he had known it in the fifties and sixties, Tadeusz Pióro declared himself encouraged by the intelligence of the younger officers, and also by the willingness of the junior men of the selected tank crew to speak up in the presence of the higher ranks. These were commendable improvements, but the psychologist was still beyond belief. In his time, the responsibility for morale had been left to a 'political officer', whose purpose was entirely ideological: 'the birth dates of Lenin and Stalin – that was all a soldier need to know to feel OK in those days'. Smiling at the thought, Pióro raised a glass: 'Let's drink to the political officers.'

Through Sixty Years of Mist

Both the soldiers of the First Warsaw Tank Regiment and their psychologist were adamant that everything we know about September 1939 is the product of propaganda. But whose propaganda? I met the film-maker Maria Kwiatkowska at the gates of the Warsaw Documentary Film Centre, a vast complex of buildings unimaginable except as the product of a command economy with a serious ideological mission to fulfil, and was taken to a viewing theatre where a canned heap of old film footage lay ready to roll.

Here, then, was the Polish cavalry, filmed at ceremonial occasions in the early thirties. Some of these symbolic manoeuvres were accompanied by orchestrated renditions of folk music, but the strong sense of archaism actually had more to do with the aristocratic demeanour of these proud, surpassed lancers. Watched by proud dignitaries wearing ornate hats and uniforms, the manoeuvres that marked the fifteenth anniversary of cavalry training at the Grudziadz garrison, showed the cavalry to be at the very heart of the independent Polish state secured under Pilsudski's leadership at the end of the First World War. Grainy, flickering pictures showed a Poland of braid, epaulettes, and little pennants fluttering at the ends of upright lances: a land of consummate horsemanship, but also of embedded and hierarchical attitudes that would have been recognized instantly by the British tank veteran who told me that, for the pioneers of the First World War tank, the horse had always also been 'the social difficulty' – an object of irrational worship on the part of those for whom cavalry is 'the high class thing to be in'.[1] Watching these impeccable horsemen, I remembered the words of General K. S. Rudnicki, who had later admitted that the pre-war cavalry had been 'fervent opponents' of the idea that the cause of mobility could best be served by exchanging horses for cars or tanks. Given Poland's scant financial and industrial resources, a greater commitment to mechanization would probably not have made a vast difference in September 1939, but it had to be admitted that 'our devotion to horses and ancient cavalry traditions were to some extent a brake on the propagation of the idea of a change of mount, and that was undoubtedly our mistake'.[2]

Yet there was a lot of finely tuned force here too – enough to lend some support at least to the claim, which I heard more than once, that, even if the Polish cavalry had charged against tanks, this might not always have been quite as stupid an action as it sounds. There was no questioning the horsemanship of the riders who surged over closely placed hurdles with astonishing speed, or came thundering down steep ramps with the same impressive mixture of force and agility. Those horses may have been emblematic of aristocratic values, but the cavalry was also demonstrating the art of manoeuvre – of materializing somewhere with sudden concentrated force and then melting away just as instantly – which had been vindicated in 1920, when Pilsudski drove the Red Army back from near Warsaw, and captured large tracts of Belarus and the Ukraine in the process. Watching some of these ghostly displays, I remembered Arnold Böcklin's painting 'War', which I had earlier seen in Dresden: mounted figures rising over a doomed city with the shocking force of the horsemen of the Apocalypse. The horse may well have been accessory to a backward-looking nationalism in Pilsudski's Poland, but it wasn't hard to imagine those cavalry units being as annihilating as anything the nineteenth-century battlefield had known.

The rest of Maria's films showed Poland trapped in the ideological pincer movement that gripped the country in September 1939. The view from the West was provided by a Nazi film called *Baptism by Fire*. Here the Poles were presented as vile aggressors, their buglers sounding the assault, while their government plotted with London, described as 'the centre of the war drive'. The film pictured people of German ancestry being burned out of their homes in Silesia and other once German places, or trudging down the road in search of refuge. As for the German soldiers who had massed along the Polish border in order to defend their threatened country from Polish invasion, they were shown stripped to the waist and lying in the autumn sun as if they were only hygienic young romantics on a woodland outing. The film enwreathed them and their war machines in filmic slush of the pastoral kind, right down to the leaves planted in their helmets.

Such were the images from the Western front, but Maria's next selection from Warsaw's repository of flickering lies was a view from the East. The first was Dovchenko's *Liberation*, a Soviet documentary made in 1940 to justify the Red Army's invasion of Poland, portraying it as a defence of 'fraternal' populations in the Ukraine and Byelorussia, which began some two weeks after the Nazi attack, on 17 September 1939. Whatever Dovchenko's qualities as a film maker, *Liberation* was undoubtedly a loathsome piece of propaganda, its crudest points hammered home with the help of a sonorous commentary. Making no reference at all to the broader context of the war, the film opened with an idyllic view of the Ukrainian and Byelorussian countryside, claiming that this had long been the land of the happy peasant, only lost to Russia when Poland beat the Red Army in the war of 1920. Rivers that had once been spiritually as wide and deep as any ocean had since been carved up by invading speculators. National languages had been forbidden and native poets spurned as the Poles set up their own statues to Mickiewicz. Overlooking the fact that the Soviet Union had already starved countless peasants to death, the film showed once-happy husbandmen struggling under the Polish yoke, forced from the land and driven into terrible factories where they were savagely exploited. The Poles, meanwhile, reclined in mansions, luxuriating in decadent comforts such as grapes, wine and ancestral portraits, while their national newspapers warned that they would be 'devoured' by the subjugated natives 'if we don't drown them in blood and impose such terror that their blood curdles in their veins'.

Having established this picture of the Poles as exploitative parasites, Dovchenko moved on to show the heroic Red Army coming to the rescue: a torrent of tanks surging unstoppable through fields and rivers, fêted and decked with flowers by grateful villagers. That metal stream was there to undo the humiliation of 1920, when the Red Army had been defeated by Pilsudski's cavalry in what is sometimes described as the last nineteenth-century war. Yet Dovchenko's army of liberation was also full of horse-borne riders, brandishing sabres and lances as they bore down on the hated enemy, and establishing that the Red Army was organically connected to the peasantry: closer to the native rhythm of Byelorussia or the Ukraine than the bloodsucking Poles could ever be – as grounded, perhaps, as the horsemen of Ghengis Khan. Towards the end of the film, the Polish overlords are wheeled out of their mansions in their bath chairs, and their land is restored to the people. Thanks to the smiling liberator, Khrushchev, who walks through Dovchenko's film in his actual function as military commander of the region, Ukrainian and Byelorussian poets and traditions are honoured once again. Indeed, Dovchenko invites his viewers to wallow in the reinstated folkloric traditions of a peasantry that was actually fated to be all but annihilated under Stalin.

Buried as it has been for so long under flagrant propaganda like this, who is to know the truth of September 1939? Professor Tadeusz Jurga is a patriotic military historian who has toiled over several decades to draw up an accurate and properly Polish account of that devastating defeat. He turned up at the appointed time, formally dressed and with the grave sense of occasion of a man convinced that there were still outstanding scores to be settled between Poland and Britain. As he talked, Professor Jurga pulled dates and details out of his own book on September 1939, a vast tome that he eventually signed and ceremoniously handed over as a gift. He started off by insisting that, contrary to those who had wanted to see nothing but an undignified rout with a few deluded lancers charging at tanks, the Poles had actually fought for longer in 1939 than the French did in 1940. Having dispensed with the myth of the two-week collapse, he emphasized that Poland had actually mobilized 200,000 soldiers in a major, and in places successful, counter-attack. The Germans had complete superiority in numbers, air and armaments, so there was never the slightest chance of a Polish victory. Even so, Hitler's Eighth Army had been forced into a tactical withdrawal. The only comparable situation was in the Ardennes in 1944.

Jurga opened his assault against insulting historical mythology by reciting some stories of extraordinary Polish heroism. He mentioned the Polish armoured brigade of 6,000 men that had so effectively held up German troops advancing into southern Poland under Field Marshall Kleist that it took him five days to get through thirty kilometres of mountains. He honoured the memory of Captain Wladyslaw Raginis, who managed to hold back Guderian, who had come through East Prussia with three divisions. Raginis had only 800 men in a line of improvised concrete bunkers, incomplete and with no ventilation. Yet he nevertheless held that line for two days. 'It wasn't just blind fanaticism,' says Jurga. Raginis knew what was coming. He had taken a vow with his deputy, Lieutenant Brykalski, never to give up; and when the German tanks finally broke through those bunkers, he had seen the wounded Brykalski carried out and then killed himself with a hand grenade in order to keep his word.

If there was defeat there was also an overwhelming sense of betrayal. The Polish had started fighting in the anticipation of relief from their allies, but the French and British dithered even after their declaration of war against the Nazis, and failed to attack Germany on its western front. Special condemnation was heaped on the British General Ironside who, when faced with desperate pleas for assistance, and when every hour counted, offered only to sell the Poles raw materials so that they could manufacture their own weapons, or suggested that they might be permitted to use the money the Polish government had in London to buy arms from neutral countries such as Belgium or Spain, or perhaps Canada – although on second thoughts that too might be in breach of international agreements.[3] With assistance from the Allies, the defence of Poland might have gone on for longer, even after the Soviet Union invaded from the east: supply lines might have been established through Rumania. But the West was pusillanimous and, as Jurga leans over to emphasize, 'Poland had to pay for this political game.'

As for the story of Polish lancers charging tanks, there was, said Jurga, never any question that the Poles did this out of ignorance. The inter-war leader Pilsudski certainly assumed a central role for the cavalry, with its proven tradition of mobility and surprise – perhaps not so foolishly, since he imagined that Poland's future wars would be against Russia, the defeated enemy of 1920, and of a kind that demanded intelligence and manoeuvre rather than head-on collision. The Polish staff had come to see things differently in the thirties, however, and were, so Jurga insisted, keen to mechanize. By September 1939 every Polish cavalry brigade had an armoured division with little tankettes and armoured cars, and they also had effective anti-tank guns, produced in Poland.

Yet the official War Diary of the German Army claims that Poland's Pomeranian Cavalry Brigade was 'shattered in a series of charges against the XIX Corps's armour, pitting mounted lancers against tanks'.[4] Were there no such episodes in which Polish lancers charged tanks? 'It was an arranged scene,' insisted Jurga. The event that underlay the myth occurred towards the end of the first day of the invasion, 1 September. It was in the Pomeranian corridor in north Poland, a strip of land that reached up to the Baltic between Germany and East Prussia. The German Fourth Army was breaking through towards East Prussia. There was a large Polish force in the corridor, and its commanders didn't know whether the Nazi ambition was to conquer all Poland or merely to cut through Pomerania and annex the free city of Danzig. As part of the German onslaught, Guderian's 19th Armoured Corps was threatening the rear of the Polish units withdrawing from the corridor. So one of the Polish cavalry regiments – the 18th Lancer Regiment – was ordered to delay the German infantry while the rest of the Pomeranian Cavalry Brigade withdrew to the south.

This, Jurga stressed, was a 'very difficult order'. And history being what it is, the real documentation of this event turned out to be in London all the time – at the Sikorski Institute, which has a collection of statements made by soldiers of the 18th Lancer Regiment who survived the débâcle of September 1939. These brief testimonials confirm that the regiment was spread out over several kilometres, covering four villages near Chojnice, charged with holding the Nazi forces back for as long as possible, and impeding their advance across the corridor towards East Prussia.

They were not well equipped. Reliant on bicycles as well as horses, they had fewer than twenty anti-tank guns, and only enough French helmets for the soldiers who would be directly involved in the fighting. Their mobilization was considerably hindered by the late arrival of carts and packhorses, for which they had to rely on German peasants and farmers living in the area. According to a number of these testimonials, the regiment's many problems were aggravated by the fact that those same local Germans had informed the Nazis about the precise location of the Polish forces.

The commander of the Pomeranian Cavalry Brigade, General S. Grzmot-Skotnicki, briefed the officers of the 18th Lancer Regiment on 30 August, informing them that the outbreak of the war was only a few hours away. The lancers' commander, Colonel Kazimierz Mastalerz, whom Jurga describes going about his duties with a pipe in his mouth, the very picture of the gallant officer, then invoked the 'glorious past' and vowed that his highly trained regiment would fulfil its task to the best of its abilities and to the glory of both fatherland and flag. News of Mastalerz's solemn oath is said to have made 'a great impression' when officers relayed it to their men.

The fighting took place in what one Polish survivor remembered as 'thick milky fog', and on the Polish side it was a bloody disaster, attended by fabulous acts of heroism. The survivors' accounts insist that the regiment behaved with great discipline and heroism throughout, and that there was hardly any panic even in the most desperate of situations. The lancers managed to destroy some German tanks, and they shot down some aircraft too. They resisted a frontal attack on the first day and, as surviving members claim, inflicted considerable losses on German forces.

But the lancers faced overwhelming defeat as the blitzkrieg gathered pace. The Polish artillery was silenced within a couple of hours. Communications within the 18th Lancer Regiment were lost on the 2nd. And by the 3rd there was said to be no trace of an organized battalion in evidence. Final capitulation came on 4 September. The suvivors told of devastation and desperate retreat, sprinkling their accounts with such 'pretty episodes' as they had come across in the fog of that chaotic war. They remember being encircled by tanks and trying to break through in a hopeless attempt to recombine with other remnants of their regiment. They tell of heroic and fatal sabre charges, perhaps aimed at the very heart of a fatal German ambush. They describe coming across the remnants of a scattered battalion, its surviving members reduced to shouting and making as much noise as possible in the attempt to create an impression of far greater numbers than

they could actually muster. One brave group is glimpsed trying to hold
back the enemy with a single damaged cannon, which they could neither
bear to leave to the Germans nor persuade to work. A desperately emblematic Polish infantryman is recorded too. This solitary fellow was found
staggering across a field with a hand grenade in his right hand, a bayonet
on his right arm, a spade in his belt and a rosary: 'thus walked our beloved
and solitary infantryman, looking for friends or enemies and dreaming of
victory – begging for it from our Queen'. Yet that Queen, the Virgin Mary,
was to be no match for Nazi tanks, either for this wandering infantryman,
or for the men of Rudnicki's 9th Lancer Regiment (which incorporated the
remnants of the Pomeranian Cavalry Brigade on 8 September), who would
also seek protection from Our Lady and, as the defeat built around them,
cling desperately to the discovery that all the decisive moments in their battle with the Nazi invaders had occurred on a Sunday.[5]

At 1 a.m. on 2 September there was another meeting with the Brigade
Commander, General Grzmot Skotnicki, who is reported to have kissed
surviving members of the 18th Lancer Regiment with tears running down
his cheeks as he congratulated them on their courage and heroism. He
declared that the story of that dreadful day would be engraved in golden
letters in the history of Poland's cavalry, and then he took off his own Military Medal and, since no senior officers remained, pinned it on to the surviving soldier who stood closest to him. The testimonials are full of stories
in which officers, often wounded, lead attacks and die heroically: one attests
that the lancers had lost every single battalion and squadron commander
by the end of that first day.

The regiment commander, Colonel Mastarlez, was certainly dead by
then. At about seven o'clock that evening, he and the survivors of two line
squadrons, who had been trying to hold back the German 20th Motorized
Infantry Division in a wooded area near Chojnice, set out to attack the German infantry from the rear. At about 7 p.m., near a place called Krajanty,
they came across a loosely formed infantry battalion in a clearing some
300–400 metres away. Judging that this force lacked both protection and
lookouts on its wings and rear, the Poles charged it successfully, taking it
by surprise and suffering few losses in the attack. As one participant, Major
Stanislaw Malecki, wrote, 'Panic ensured in the German ranks and scattering of the troops.' But then, quite suddenly, German tanks appeared from
the woods, and started a 'stormy shelling' of the lancers with machine
guns: 'our immediate withdrawal of the squadrons to the side, behind a
nearby ridge of woodland – a good anti-artillery point – did not save us

from the consequences of this attack, from terrible losses. From behind the cover of the ground, the buglers played their assembly call for a long time . . . only half of the horsemen stood up . . . Near the field upon which the charge took place, the regiment's Commander, Colonel Kazimierz Mastalerz, had fallen with almost the entirety of his troop'.

There are some variations in the accounts of this single episode in the disintegration of a regiment that had lost 80 per cent of its men in one day's fighting. Professor Jurga suggests that Mastalerz and his men had successfully carried out their sabre charge against the German infantry battalion, and were actually on their way back past some woods when they were surprised by German armoured cars rather than tanks. Other historians of this campaign observe that Mastalerz, far from being ignorant of tanks, had actually been with a company of light tankettes from the 81st Armoured Troop, and only left them behind because they were in bad mechanical condition.[6] It is said to have been this incident, more than any other, that shaped the popular image of the September campaign and which, though not seen by Guderian, underlay his account of Polish cavalry charging tanks out of 'ignorance'. On the next day, the bodies are alleged to have been shown to Italian war correspondents, who were informed that the Polish cavalrymen had died charging tanks; and from then on the story was to be endlessly recycled as an example of Poland's stupidity in the face of mechanized Nazi power: embellished with every telling, the story 'became a continual source of German propaganda'.[7] While confirming that the image of ludicrous Poles charging tanks had indeed been adopted as Nazi propaganda, Jurga had not felt it to be his job as a military historian to track down the detail of this contemptible fiction. He suggested it would probably be worth looking at a German paper called *Die Wehrmacht*, which contained just such drawings signed under the name of Matejko, presumably an insulting reference to the nineteenth-century Polish artist Jan Matejko, who was famous for his patriotic history paintings.

Jurga, however, was both more knowledgeable and more exercised about the uses to which the same imagery had been put during the Communist years. Others would speak of television documentaries produced during that time, but Jurga, when asked for an example, went straight for Wajda's film *Lotna*. The writer and editor Michal Komar had recalled how this film had been criticized in 1968, adding that Wajda had himself named it as the one film he would like to remake. But Jurga was merciless, and condemned it as outright Communist propaganda and an offence against the record of the Polish Army. The primary guilt may have belonged to Wojciech Zukrowski, the Communist author of the original novella who would later become one of the few Polish intellectuals to support Jaruzelski's imposition of martial law (an accomplished writer, Zukrowski became so hated that people used to return his books to him, leaving them piled up on his doorstep in Warsaw). But Jurga was in no doubt that the sins of Zukrowski's *Lotna* were repeated by Wajda's film, which, as Jurga stressed, didn't just show the Poles as stupid romantics. The more telling point is that the cavalry were mostly landowners and aristocrats – these were the people Wajda showed lying in bed, confusing horses with women, and demonstrating their equestrian skills while the world was burning. It had suited both the Nazis and the Communists to portray the Polish Army as foppish upper-class decadents who betrayed their people and country. As Jurga remembered it, Wajda's film was straightforwardly in the tradition.

The same ideas had dominated historiography during the Communist era, dismissing the Polish Army as weak and badly commanded, full of braid and pompous aristocratic pretension. Under the Soviet system, September 1939 was not even mentioned in the encyclopaedias – largely, Jurga suggested, because the Kremlin had no desire to reveal how much formerly Polish land had been annexed to the Soviet Union by the end of the Second World War. In 1970 Jurga had himself travelled to Moscow to participate in the 13th Congress of Historians. He remembered being approached in the corridors by an officer from the Soviet Military Historical Institute, who complained because of an article Jurga had written for the *Polish Military Historical Review*, comparing German and Polish forces in 1939. Moscow normally intervened to stop this kind of research, and the Soviet historian had been 'very aggressive' about it, demanding that Jurga tell him 'how he had managed to find evidence that the Poles had these forces, and, for that matter, that the Poles had done any fighting at all'.

Things got a lot worse when 'the whole question of historical revisionism' came up a little later, and Jurga found himself among a group of historians whose work was perceived to be flagrantly out of line with the Soviet interest. He remembers how dismayed he and his colleagues at the Polish Military Academy had been by an East German publication called *The Germans and the Second World War*: 'their hair stood on end' when they read it and saw Nazi propaganda being recycled for Communist ends. But the axe had really fallen when Leszek Moczulski (who by the mid-nineties was head of a right-wing party called KPN) wrote a journalistic book called *The Polish War*. Jurga had reviewed it for the state publishing house, suggesting some additions and corrections, and then recommending it for

publication. When the book came out, a colonel wrote to the army magazine complaining about it, and things escalated rapidly from there. Returning from holiday in Slovakia, Jurga found himself being denounced in the
papers and dismissed from his job at the Military Academy. It was, he says,
'the worst time of my life . . . people were destroyed psychologically'. Such
was the price to be paid for challenging the myth of the foolish Polish lancer riding out, like a ludicrous Don Quixote, against the Nazi tank.

The ideologies that kept those Polish lancers charging on for many years
through both Nazi and Communist eras were even-handed only in the
sense that they falsified the record on both sides of the polarized image.
Just as the supposedly ignorant Polish forces actually had tankettes and
armoured cars, albeit insufficient ones without adequate tactics or sufficient
mass behind them, so the invading German Army was hardly the 'mechanized Juggernaut' suggested by the image of an unstoppable tank.[8] According
to an analysis published in the fifties by the US Army Department, Nazi
propaganda presented the invasion as 'little more than a manoeuvre',
depicting the German armies as 'highly motorized with tank support out of
proportion to the actual number of armoured vehicles they had available'.[9]
The military historian R. L. Dinardo suggests that this idea of the Nazi
army has been sustained by film footage, some of it made under Goebbels
to show the German Army as the epitome of mobility, speed and power,
and then adopted and used by Allied film-makers: thus Frank Capra turned
Goebbels' propaganda pictures against the Nazis in *Why We Fight*, and they
have since been used in numerous television documentaries including the
influential Thames TV series *The World at War*. In reality, the German
Army was far from being the all-mechanized force that was imagined
speeding east across the Polish plain by the journalists, Italian or American,
who are also said, that September, to have coined the phrase 'blitzkrieg'.
Indeed, the Nazi war machine was heavily reliant on horses, a fact that figured in the uses to which Poland was put once conquered – a source of
slave labour and also *Lebensraum* for the Nazi Reich, a convenient location
for genocidal concentration camps, but also a factory for producing horses
for a German Army that could hardly get enough of them.

The newspaper reports that informed the world of events in Poland
proved as susceptible as any Pomeranian cavalryman to the milky fog of
war. On the day the invasion began, the *Daily Mirror*'s Cassandra opined
that, while 'Hitler believes he can cut Poland to ribbons in three weeks', the
more sanguine commentator would remember the 'tremendous signifi-

cance' of 'Liddell Hart's famous maxim, that at least three times the strength is needed by the attacker to overwhelm the attacked'.[10] Yet as the invasion continued, it knocked Basil Liddell Hart off his pedestal and left the British press denouncing one German atrocity after another – whether it be the Reichstag speech in which Hitler declared that 'profound barbarity' would long since have engulfed Danzig (Gdansk) had it not been for the German people living there, or the Luftwaffe's habit of murdering fleeing women and children from the air and, as the *Daily Telegraph* reported, dropping poisoned chocolates among the children of Lublin.[11] British papers reported Polish claims to have immobilized and destroyed German tanks, and also to have dispatched its air force into a small but successful bombing raid on Berlin. They praised Polish soldiers for 'fighting like lions' and were slow to question Polish dispatches in which chaotic retreats were presented as staged withdrawals designed to lure the foolish invader into traps that would soon snap shut on them.

For a time they awaited news of Poland's own tanks: as the *Daily Telegraph* observed on 9 September, 'nothing has yet been heard of the small Polish tanks of which the army is understood to possess several thousand'.[12] And, as things slid from bad to worse without effective intervention from Britain or France, they joined Poland's defenders in transferring their hopes for relief to 'General Rain', who might arrive in time to transform western Poland into 'a great marsh in which the German armies, dependent on their mechanized divisions, will be bogged in the mud'.[13] But it was to be the Red Army, not 'General Rain', that broke in on 17 September: 'eye-witnesses of the Russian invasion of Poland say that monster tanks formed the spearhead of a swift Russian advance . . .'[14]

The *Daily Mail*'s services correspondent took a slightly more theoretical approach, treating the war as if it were a field exercise ('Cavalry v. Tanks') mounted in order to test the argument that had been raging in British military circles since the First World War.[15] He had spoken to a Polish officer whose views demonstrated that 'The Poles think that the German mechanized divisions will be useless anyway.' This officer's conclusion was based partly on an assessment of the condition of the country's roads, which were certainly not up to the standard of Hitler's autobahns. There were many roads in the west of Poland, but they were not 'strategic' since they ran north to south, reflecting the requirements of a pre-Versailles world in which Poland had not existed as a sovereign nation. The German invaders may indeed have had thousands of tanks, but the Poles 'do not consider the tank to be a weapon which brings victory automatically to its users. Only by the power of manoeuvre is it able to triumph, and for that you must have roads.' Apparently deceived by this quaint and mistaken argument, the *Daily Mail*'s services correspondent settled back to watch the war unfold as a 'fascinating test of all military history'. Would 'the heavy lumbering, conscripted mechanized forces of the Germans prevail over the alert, mobile, audacious cavalry and infantry of the Poles'? That question had been answered by the 11th, when the *Mail* reported that Warsaw radio had been heard describing fighting around its own building and then playing Chopin's funeral march. By the 14th the German pincer had closed around a large and 'doomed' Polish Army near Kutno, west of Warsaw, and insufficient consolation was provided by the report that the cavalry units involved in Warsaw's counter-attack had captured 'ten large German tanks'.

The 'strategic problems' raised by the Nazi offensive were better traced out on the 17th, by Commodore L. E. O. Charlton, in the pacifist weekly *Reynolds News*. Cutting through the illusions of the earlier Polish reports, Charlton insisted that it was 'idle' to minimize the 'terrific impact' of the Nazi motorized formations or to pretend that Polish withdrawals had been prearranged.[16] The Poles had lost because they were 'hopelessly inferior' in air power, because they had miscalculated the power of the Nazi tank brigades and motorized divisions, and because of the 'undue preponderance of so vulnerable an arm as cavalry' in their 'little mechanized' army.

The Italian press viewed the events through a different prism, and from much closer too. Mussolini was aligned with Hitler even though he stayed out of the war at this stage, and the observations of the Italian correspondents who followed in the tracks of the German advance were reported all over the world. On 8 September, the British *Daily Mirror* had quoted the correspondent of the Rome paper, *Popolo d'Italia*, who paid tribute to the 'heroic resistance' of the Poles: 'he said the Poles even attacked tanks and machine-gun nests with cavalry'. This image of the Polish lancer as a truly magnificent loser was pursued with some ardour in the Italian press; yet if reckless heroism was one side of the medal, the other showed only the utter hopelessness of Poland's defence. As Giovanni Artiere observed in *La Nazione*, the German Army was vastly superior, not just in its technical resources, but in 'the intellect of the higher ranks'.[17] Other reports claimed that the *Luftwaffe*, elsewhere accused of mowing down civilians, was so confident of its superiority that its bombers flew without even bothering to load their machine guns, and with only sufficient petrol for eighty minutes' flight.[18] As for the Polish Army's attempts to shoot down German aircraft, 'they seem like children trying to bring down an eagle with a catapult'.[19]

For these Italian correspondents, Polish courage was a heroic and fully conscious phenomenon of the last ditch. The Poles, so they reasoned, must have known that resistance to the German attack was futile: 'For this reason we believe in the romantic spirit of the Polish people – this is confirmed by the desperate attack of the Polish "Pomeranian" cavalry at the East Prussian border – we cannot believe the naïveté of the people in charge. Many are the mistakes of the Polish High Chiefs of Staff . . .'[20] In Warsaw, I was repeatedly told that it was probably Curzio Malaparte, the flamboyant fascist intellectual and war correspondent, who launched the myth of ignorant Polish lancers charging Nazi tanks. But it was actually Indro Montanelli, later to become one of Italy's most eminent journalists and writers, who identified 'horses against armoured cars' as the *leitmotif* of the war.[21] He watched the four-sided attack closing in on the Polish cavalry near Kutno and Gabin, west of Warsaw, and described it as if it were a play enacted in a theatre full of melodramatic special effects. The night was 'as bright as day thanks to floodlights'. German tanks and armoured cars spread out on the sandy plain, while 'above the heads of the advancing columns swarms of planes draw bizarre swirls, like flocks of starlings, in a chorus of diffused and monotonous engine noises'.

On the previous day, the Polish cavalry had tried 'four furious charges with the heads down and their lances in rest like a tournament of 1,000 years ago'. The roads had been piled high with dead horses, marking 'the senseless itinerary of the Polish cavalry pushed by desperation against the wall of German armoured divisions'. The massacre of horses had been terrible, thanks partly to the German commanders, here said to have given 'the chivalrous order to the gunmen to shoot low, to avoid a pointless slaughter of brave soldiers'. Despite ceaseless bombing the trapped Polish Army mustered itself on the following day, and carried out more 'mad cavalry charges against German fire', reminding Montanelli of Waterloo and the Spanish corridas. No one, least of all the Polish lancers, could have been in any doubt that these charges would be fatal: 'For the Polish there is no hope. But their objective is neither victory nor escape. It is to die with weapons at their feet. This is their objective and they will reach it at any price.' The Italian conclusion, printed above a report by Giovanni Artiere in *La Stampa* on 14 September, was: 'The machine wins'.

The Nazi press in Germany was predictably full of self-congratulatory articles, emphasizing the youth and 'penetrating power' of Germany's armoured divisions, and the speed of their advance: 'with the same uncanny effectiveness with which our tank force had already, on the first day, secured kilometre after kilometre of this ancient German territory, it continued its advance on the second day . . .'[22] German newspapers reached around to find prehistoric ancestors of the unstoppable Nazi tank – an article in the Culture section of the Sunday *Deutsche Allgemeine Zeitung* described a horsedrawn armoured battle car that Voltaire had proposed as a miraculous weapon that France might unleash against the Prussian forces of Frederick the Great.[23] It noted the destruction of the Pomeranian Cavalry Brigade, and granted that its captive survivors had done their best against the Nazi Juggernaut: 'They are no cowards, as they stand before us now, for we at some points felt their stubborn resistance. But against the breathtakingly daring spirit of our soldiers, against the language of our tank guns and machine guns they did collapse.'[24]

German papers emphasized the shock and surprise, admitted by prisoners, when they saw 'our motorized units advanced faster through this impassable territory than the Polish cavalry'.[25] They claimed valour and even grand, self-sacrificing heroism of the Polish kind, for their own young tank officers – like the lieutenant who, by launching his tank against a Polish train, was said to have 'saved his comrades and died a military martyr'.[26] One article sought to attribute the brutality of the all-powerful tank to the Poles, citing an incident in which 'Polish tanks roll over defenceless Germans' – i.e. in which Polish soldiers were said to have turned their machines against innocent German nationals in Poland, shooting them, and then crushing their corpses under tanks.[27] Another denigrated the idea of Polish lancers' courage, converting it into credulous stupidity, by claiming that captured Polish soldiers and officers 'again and again confirm' that the Polish military leadership had set out to deceive its own soldiers about the enemy they were facing: 'The Germans, so they want them to believe, have no real tanks but only cardboard dummies, the bombs of the German air force are harmless – and this is why the Polish cavalry repeatedly attacks German tanks and is then quickly destroyed.'[28] So bravery became stupidity, and German losses could be acknowledged without confusion of purpose.

As for *Die Wehrmacht*, this turned out to be a Berlin fortnightly, the paper of the German Army. And while it did feature drawings signed by a certain 'Matejko', the name was not actually adopted in mockery of Poland's great history painter, Jan Alojzy Matejko. Named Theo rather than Jan, *Die Wehrmacht*'s Matejko was an Austrian-born illustrator, and quite well known before he threw in his lot with the Nazis. His drawings of September 1939 were violently partisan and much concerned with tanks, even if they did not feature the doomed Polish lancer I had been told to expect in Warsaw. One showed the 'cleansing' (*Säuberung*) by a tank of a Polish city of snipers: attended by a squad of watchful infantrymen, the machine is advancing along a tramline in a cobbled street that is empty except for dead or surrendering Poles.[29] Another was printed beneath a text headed: 'This is how our tanks fight', emphasizing how much the Poles had 'underestimated the power of our modern weapons' and claiming that 'irresponsible propaganda' had persuaded the Polish soldiers that 'our tanks were only tin can fakes'. For this reason 'an almost grotesque attack occurred when a Polish cavalry regiment attacked some of our tanks. You can imagine the catastrophic consequences.'[30] That picture was apparently best left to the imagination, where it has thrived ever since, for in the drawing that accompanied this crowing text Matejko actually chose to show how the German Army dealt with Polish anti-tank cannons. So there it was – a *Kampfwagen* advancing through trees to crush two such anti-tank weapons under its tracks, having already 'annihilated with one blow' their Polish crews whose scattered corpses litter the foreground. A propagandistic reconstruction, to be sure, although such events did happen: General K. S. Rudnicki describes how one of his captains had lost an anti-tank gun in just this way: 'simply run over by a tank after its crew had been machine-gunned'.[31]

In Germany as elsewhere, news reports were interspersed with articles drawing more general conclusions from the unfolding Nazi victory. These were provided by military analysts who, like their counterparts in other countries, were primarily interested in Poland as the laboratory in which different military systems and philosophies were being tested. Reviewing the first two weeks of 'The Battle in Poland', Dr Ernst Kredel praised the effectiveness of Germany's young tank force, emphasizing the modernity of its military strategies and declaring Poland's horse-mindedness to be more or less instinctive:

In accordance with the national character of the Pole, the Polish leadership before the war had trained its army for a war of mobility corresponding to the vast reaches and flat spaces in the Polish landscape. The existence of such spaces, and the fact that all roads through the country are in an unimaginably bad condition, are the reasons for the Polish preference for the cavalry and its vanguard position in the organization of the Polish Army. That horses and lances will not do to attack modern fighting vehicles is a lesson learnt – alas – too late, and to their disadvantage, by the Polish cavalry. True, the Poles also had some tank divisions, according to their own account some 600 armoured vehicles; but these have never been as highly regarded as lancers in the Polish Army.[32]

A more thoroughgoing analysis had been published two days earlier by Lieutenant G. Soldan, an officer with a long record as a tank intellectual. Like Cassandra in the *Daily Mirror*, Soldan found his point of departure in Basil Liddell Hart's theories of defence, citing that author's *Defence of Britain* in his opening paragraph.[33] Liddell Hart may have persuaded the British that increased powers of defence had all but overwhelmed the possibility of offensive action, but the Russians had always believed otherwise, and the German operation in Poland proved how right they had been. Soldan made a great deal of the mobility, speed and constancy of the modern tank. Recalling that the efficacy of this weapon had been long disputed in the literature, he observed that all that had changed with the creation of new combined units, the 'so-called fast or tank divisions' – an initiative in which Soldan declared Italy as well as Germany to have been exemplary.

Soldan emphasized that the use of 'the new technological equipment and armoured vehicles' had to be guided by new strategies that served to 'fill the dead technology with tactical spirit and life'. Marshal Pilsudski had not been able to 'free himself from old-fashioned views' about the exclusive importance of the infantry, artillery and cavalry: 'The latter had remained the predominant force in Poland, but it could hardly make a decisive showing against a German Army that had moved on.' Soldan conceived the war as a conflict between two historical epochs of warfare: one that finally resolved the heated argument that had long been raging, in Germany as elsewhere, between the advocates of mechanization and horse-minded traditionalists for whom tanks were at best mere adjuncts to the infantry: 'Today it can be clearly stated that it is the Führer himself who has put an end to these debates, and resolved the question unequivocally in favour of the tank force. That this was completely right is proved conclusively by the recent events.'

It was Michal Komar who told me with some satisfaction that 'the tanks seem to have disappeared' in recent years. The Soviet tanks have gone, although at that time, in 1995, it was sometimes still questioned precisely how far they had withdrawn. The Polish Army's tanks seem to be going in some sense too. There was a grievous lack of equipment, and the proposed new main battle tank, the high-tech monster named 'The Gorilla', lacked reality. A wooden model was said to have been produced, but the project had already been shelved for financial reasons.

Some suggested the tank was still all too present as a habit of thought: a phantom repressor, which kept overriding truth and democratic tolerance;

an instinctive reaching out for the coercive powers of the state. Tadeusz Pióro and Lucyna Golebiowska saw signs of this persistent tank-thinking in the election of a few weeks before, in which the former Communist Aleksander Kwasniewski had beaten Lech Walesa, a true popular hero who had come to seem bloated with vanity, and who had horrified his own Catholic supporters when he tried to crush a television interviewer by saying that he – that is the reporter – would certainly have been flushed down the drain had abortion been legal. Kwasniewski may have lied about his educational qualifications in an official biography, but there was surely something all too tank-like about the way Walesa and his supporters had muttered about annulling the election that had put an old Communist into power.

Poland's entry into NATO has yet to make a reality of the apparently superior Western tanks of which the men of the under-equipped 1st Warsaw Tank Brigade may still only dream. However, even in 1995 real tanks were already beginning to arrive from the West. During my visit, it was announced that the British Army would be renting use of an old tank training area in the Polygon. I came across a different manifestation of the post-Communist armoured vehicle when visiting Warsaw's old city late one morning to walk the narrow streets where Michal Komar had seen Jozef Stalin tanks manoeuvring in 1953. It was freezing, and I withdrew into a restaurant called Bazyliszek-Hortex on the Old Town Square. A stray maniac in the downstairs bar detained me briefly, ranting obscenely about Jews and the terrible capabilities of Polish women. Escaping upstairs, I found a large dining room with a beamed ceiling and a reconstructed traditional ambience reminiscent of the country house in Wajda's *Lotna* – although here the horses were strictly confined to snowy pastoral paintings on the wall. The place was almost empty, and yet completely filled by a loud English business-man, who was sitting by the window and interviewing a taciturn Pole over lunch and starched white linen. Here was the besuited Western capitalist, leaning forward like a master of the universe to fire lines like: 'I have a man in Dubai,' at a bearded fellow with a thick blanket of hair and a carpet-like sports jacket. One was enjoying a glass of mineral water; the other was making his way through a packet of Marlboro and a barrel of beer.

'Chemistry is very important,' said the confident Englishman, after establishing that the Pole thought he could probably train a dozen men in two days.

'Chemistry?' asked the Pole, with one eyebrow remaining puckered up even after his would-be employer had explained that he meant 'the chemistry between people'.

The job would entail many things. He must understand the advisability of not starting a family just yet and he would also need to know how to use a gun. This could be difficult logistically, because 'in England and Wales, guns are illegal', but if the gentleman accepted the offer, he would meet a man called George, either here or in Germany, who would be sent to bring him up to scratch.

Then, as workmen with a yellow crane carried out final adjustments on the Christmas tree they were mounting in the Old Town Square outside, this grey silhouette explained that the colonel who headed his company recruited 90 per cent of his employees from the army: 'If you are willing to learn, personally I think the opportunities are excellent.' Having sung the praises of an American software package called Roadshow, which made route-scheduling much easier than it had ever been before, this confident Englishman, whose well-known security company specialized in running 'cash in transit' through unsafe areas in the former USSR, announced: 'We have approximately forty-five armoured vehicles operating with us now.'

And yet it would be hasty to conclude that the charge of those fabled Polish lancers was finally coming to an end in a long awaited clearing of ideological mists. In January 1997 the *European* carried an article headed: 'Poland's handsome cavalry ride again'.[34] Accompanied by a picture captioned as the 'Last Hurrah' in which 'Poland's elite cavalry takes on Germany's Panzer divisions in September 1939', the article announced that 'fifty-seven years after its valiant but doomed charge against Nazi tanks, and half a century since the last regiment was disbanded, the Ministry of Defence has accepted the offer from the Cavalry Squadron of the Polish Republic Association to fund a ceremonial unit'. Edward Sieradski, a training consultant who was behind the initiative, explained: 'We are trying to create something out of nothing . . . It has been said that it is easier to make a jet aircraft now in Poland than it is to form a professional cavalry.' But it certainly wasn't just for Margaret Thatcher that gallantry defined the difference between a true Pole and a Marxist, and Sieradski was convinced that a few unmechanized cavalry officers could set a useful example in the decollectivized future: they 'knew which wine to drink with fish and how to use a knife and fork. That is what made them distinct from ordinary military men.'

14

Into Russia with Curzio Malaparte

'Brunelleschi's cupola was shimmering high above the roofs of Florence.'[1] That moonlit scene is evoked in *The Skin*, a novel written shortly after the Second World War by Curzio Malaparte, the Italian writer, cultural agitator and fascist irregular. Malaparte admired the vaulted domes of his country's great Renaissance cathedrals. For centuries those cupolas had represented the height of Europe's technical and spiritual achievements; and, in the fascist iconography of the nineteen-thirties, they served alongside the ruins of the ancient Roman Empire as symbols of the imperial tradition. Mussolini promised to revive. Yet Malaparte also knew that the modern age was made of different stuff. He was among the most conscious of the literary activists who helped to prise the word 'cupola' away from Christendom's most glorious buildings, and attach it to less redemptive modern edifices. Some shreds of the cancelled spiritual life may still have clung to 'the steel cupola of Marxism + Leninism + Stalinism'[2] that had risen in the Soviet Union. Yet, by the time Western observers had properly identified that looming structure in the East, there could be little serious doubt that the word 'cupola' really belonged to the revolving gun-turrets mounted on thousands of smoking tanks.

It was by no means ignorant of my informants in Warsaw to suggest that Malaparte might have been the Italian journalist who launched the myth of foolish Polish lancers charging German tanks. In his novel *Kaputt* (1944), Malaparte testified to the barbarity of Hitler's rule over Poland as he had observed it, a guest in the highest Nazi circles in Warsaw a year or so after the onslaught. Malaparte was also a war correspondent, and one who was predisposed to make heavy use of the horse-versus-tank motif. Yet he would not actually bring this polarized imagery to bear on Hitler's Eastern Front until 1941, when he followed the German invaders into the Ukraine.

Malaparte actually spent the fateful month of September 1939 on the island of Capri, convalescing from a rheumatic infection picked up on a recent expedition to Italy's East African colonies (about which he wrote for *Corriere della Sierra*), and overseeing the construction of the astonishing stone house he was creating on top of a remote and craggy promontory called Punta Massulo. Now recognized as one of the most original twentieth-century buildings in Italy, his 'House Like Me' (*Casa Come Me*) was to be an exemplary manifesto of the 'New Way': at once an autobiographical poem in which Malaparte could recognize 'the secret form of my soul' and a romantic thesis intended to give modern articulation to classical forms, and thereby to suggest that every Italian civilization since the Etruscans had really been an experiment in surrealist aesthetics.[3]

Built into the most spectacular views over cliff, sea and shore, Casa Mala-parte was to prove unusual enough to attract interested visitors – including Field Marshal Erwin Rommel, whom Malaparte claimed to have shown round the just-completed house when he visited Capri in the spring of 1942. During the course of this apocryphal tour, the commander of Ger-many's Afrika Korps asked whether he had designed and built the house himself. Malaparte lied and claimed that he had acquired it just as it was. He then gestured towards the distant blue coastline of Amalfi, a superb view that Malaparte had made into pictures with the help of large chestnut-framed windows, and boasted, 'I designed the scenery.' '*Ach so!*' said Rom-mel, as he marched off in the direction of North Africa, where his Afrika Korps would shortly be defeated at El Alamein. A typical Malaparte story that: glib, self-aggrandizing and of slippery status since the known facts of Rommel's life don't put him anywhere near Capri at this time. Alberto Moravia once joked: 'I do not believe Malaparte, even when he tells the truth.'[4] A disconcertingly appropriate witness, then, with whom to approach realities that can hardly be matched even by the most disordered of surrealist fantasies.

The man who took his name from Napoleon Bonaparte ('Malaparte' means 'Bad Side'), was born to German-Italian parents in Tuscany as Kurt Erich Suchert. Having fought with the Alpine Regiment on the French front in the First World War, he emerged as a radical republican, cham-pioning the exhausted Italian troops who had deserted the ranks during a combined Austro-German assault at the mountainous frontier town of Caporetto in 1917. Not content with heading for the plains in their hun-dreds of thousands, the routed Italians yelled 'Blacklegs' at reserves moving up the line, and formed columns to march eagerly into captivity.[5] The men who ran were viewed with contempt by their enemy, including Erwin Rom-mel, who had practised infiltration tactics at Caporetto as a lieutenant with the Württemburg Mountain Battalion. They were also hated by nationalists at home as cowardly renegades who had turned the Italian Army into the laughing stock it would remain for many decades to come – notorious for being full of swagger after such 'mean little victories' as it might achieve in Abyssinia or against a disorganized Republican enemy in the Spanish Civil War, but quick to surrender when the stakes were raised in the Second World War.[6] Yet Malaparte saw them as striking proletarian heroes, and celebrated their rebellion in his swiftly banned first book *Viva Caporetto!*

Soon afterwards, he emerged as a leading right-wing intellectual. In 1928 he became the editor of *La Stampa,* which he converted into a fascist paper – or as near as it could be, considering that Malaparte remained a freebooting maverick who would question Hitler's masculinity and mock Mussolini for the garish vulgarity of his neckties. In 1933 Malaparte was found guilty of 'offending a minister's office', and jailed on the island of Lipari. He was rehabilitated by the time the Second World War broke out, but it was not until 1940 that he started work as war correspondent for *Corriere della Sera.* He reported from France and then Greece and Yugoslavia from where, having announced the imminent launch of Operation Barbarossa in June 1941, he proceeded to the Soviet-Rumanian border to see the attack begin and then follow the advance into Bessarabia and the Ukraine.

Read with amazement and also considerable irritation in Italy, Malaparte's dispatches were taken up by the British, American and Scandinavian press. Hitler had crowed of the Soviet Union, 'all we have to do is kick in the door and the whole rotten structure will collapse'.[7] The Wehrmacht's Chief of Operations, General Alfred Jodl, had chosen a different metaphor, insisting that the Russian colossus was really no better than a swollen pig's bladder: prick it, and it would surely burst.[8] Yet Malaparte, who had written several books about Lenin and the Soviet Union, doubted this prediction of another 'short and easy war' and refused merely to denigrate the Soviet enemy. His articles were sufficiently at odds with Nazi expectation to ensure that he was expelled from the war zone in September 1941 at Goebbels' order, and then confined under house arrest for four months by Mussolini when he returned to Italy.[9]

Malaparte was an aesthete among war correspondents. He was capable of polishing up a closely observed description of some terrible act of carnage one minute, and then turning to write a fussy letter of instruction about the exact type of hook (chrome-plated and L-shaped) that should be used to affix blue air-raid curtains to certain carefully specified windows in his house on Capri. Yet he wasn't convinced by the Nazi propagandists who portrayed the assault against Russia as a predestined struggle between

Europe and the Asiatic horde fired by a Jewish-Bolshevik conspiracy. On the contrary, he recognized Barbarossa as a war between two polarized expressions of the European tradition. In his judgement, which was to prove more accurate than that of Hitler and Jodl, the 'steel cupola' of Soviet Marxism was not 'the mausoleum of Ghenghis Khan' but 'the *other* Parthenon of Europe'. As such, it would prove far more resistant than the Nazi leaders were prepared to imagine.

Learning on the move

By the time of that assault against Russia in 1941, the Germans had proved their mastery of tank warfare in a whole series of 'lightning' attacks, each one closely studied as an exercise in tanks and how to use them on varied terrains. After 'Case White' in Poland came 'Operation Weser Exercise', the occupation of Denmark and Norway in April 1940, where a small and widely distributed force of some fifty tanks was found to have considerable effect on enemy morale despite the difficulties imposed by wooded and mountainous terrain.[10] The commander of this force reported that his vehicles had been largely confined to roads, where their advance was often impeded by roadblocks, and that his men had often been unable to elevate their guns sufficiently to engage the enemy higher up the steep slopes. There were additional lessons to be learned about the use of smoke-shells and also tracer, which was essential if tank gunners were to have any clue what they were doing when they sprayed wooded mountainsides with machine-gun fire. The enemy habit of hiding in buildings and using anti-tank guns at short range made it advisable for a panzer force to adopt the pre-emptive policy of destroying houses overlooking crossroads before they approached. The new Mark IV panzers sent to Norway were much appreciated for their multiple turrets, which made it possible to fire to the front and sides at the same time.

By 10 May 1940 it was the turn of Belgium, Holland and Luxembourg to experience the next big blitzkrieg under the codename of 'Operation Yellow': first the air strikes, which destroyed Allied aircraft on the ground, then the networked tanks and motorized infantry, advancing in close co-ordination with mobile artillery. Ten panzer divisions were involved this time, and all three countries fell within days. First, the three panzer divisions of Germany's Army Group B broke into Belgium and Holland from the east and soon blasted their way through France's mechanized cavalry; as the commander of one panzer regiment noted in his progress report, the French tanks were easy to shoot up from the side because they were 'slow and especially sluggish when turning . . . The enemy tanks behave leaderless, aimless, badly commanded, tactically inferior, and try to get away soon.'[11] Just as anticipated in the plan drawn up by General von Manstein, the Allied forces in France had mistaken Army Group B for the main attack and advanced into Belgium to meet them. It was only then that General von Rundstedt's larger Army Group A made the decisive move. Spearheaded by Panzergruppe Kleist, it drove through Luxembourg and the Ardennes, meeting little resistance, and exploiting surprise and concentration: five panzer divisions arrived at Sedan on the River Meuse to confront a French Army that had never conceived of using its tanks in mass, preferring to sprinkle them around – 'from Swiss frontier to the English Channel', as one German tank general put it contemptuously.[12]

Sedan was taken with the help of co-ordinated Stuka attacks and after a battle in which the Germans first learned the advantage of combining armour and infantry in mixed battle groups – crossing the River Meuse and driving a wedge between the British and French armies as they thundered into central France. Erwin Rommel, who commanded the 7th Panzer Division, would later describe the view from that irresistible metal column:

the people in the houses were rudely awoken by the din of our tanks . . . Civilians and French troops, their faces distorted with terror, lay huddled in the ditches, alongside hedges and in every hollow beside the road. We passed refugee columns, the carts abandoned by their owners, who had fled in panic into the fields . . . On we went, at a steady speed, towards our objective.[13]

France's foolishly linear defences were shattered, and in days the outwitted British Expeditionary Force was forced back on to the beaches at Dunkirk, where, thanks to Hitler's mysterious decision to halt his panzer divisions, it was able to escape from the beaches.

France surrendered on 22 June and the incompetent Marshal Pétain was left muttering about the baleful influence of Marxism on the character and morale of the French people. More practical lessons were learned on the winning side. In their experience reports, Germany's panzer commanders emphasized the superior power of the 7.5 cm Kw. K. tank gun when firing armour-piercing shells and the relative uselessness of the 3.7 cm model.[14] They stressed the advisability of installing a commander's cupola on the Panzer II; the advantages gained by the German tank commander's habit of surveying the battlefield from the open hatch; the effectiveness of courageous zigzag advances and also of attacks from the flank. They outlined the best way of attacking a French Char B1 from behind, and insisted that tanks should not be used either in woods or in cities, where they proved 'practically defenceless' against anti-tank guns mounted in basement windows and rooms. The 'poor combat morale' of the French was also noted, along with their fatal habit of using tanks in small formations that were easily smashed. In the longer view of Major General von Mellenthin, the battle for France was really 'a clash of principles' between two theories of armoured warfare – one that believed in massing tanks, and the other in splitting them up in the discredited manner of the First World War.[15]

For a time it seemed that the blitzkrieg would soon be extended across the English Channel to Britain. Many commanders, including Rommel, were in favour of striking while the British Army was defeated and deprived of the arsenal it had left behind in France.[16] Operation Sealion was duly planned. Indeed, on 13 July 1940 an experimental company of submersible tanks was formed in Germany, each one proofed against water and equipped with a snorkel tube to be held above water by means of a buoy.[17] But the German Navy had been savaged in the assault on Norway and after the *Luftwaffe*'s defeat in the Battle of Britain, the proposed invasion was postponed.

After France, then, it became the turn of Greece (Operation Marita) and Yugoslavia (Weisung 25) to experience 'lightning war' in the form of six Stuka-attended panzer divisions, including those comprised in Panzergruppe Kleist, which attacked on 6 April 1941. Germany's tanks might have suffered considerable wear and tear in the terrain, but their Yugoslav enemy had no armour at all and Skopje, Nis, Belgrade, Sarajevo, Zagreb were all taken in little over a week. According to von Mellenthin, the conquest of Yugoslavia was 'little more than a military parade', whereas real lessons were learnt in Greece, where Allied forces managed to hold out for a little longer, until 23 April.[18] The terrain was punishing here too: steep slopes, hairpin bends and, as a German combat report records, roads that were actually terrible cart tracks like the one on which five tanks of General Balck's 3rd Regiment of the 2nd Panzer Division threw their tracks while advancing on Pandelejmon Castle.[19] The art of deploying tanks in mountainous terrain was further demonstrated as Balck's tanks crossed the slopes of Mount Olympus to drive back British and Australian forces, grinding their way along cart tracks and a railway, squeezing through gaps blasted in an impassable gorge and fording the Pinios river to assault the village of Tempi. With the enemy fleeing in panic, Balck's men pressed on, capturing weapons as well as prisoners, feasting off abandoned British supply trucks and taking the town of Larissa. Once the dust had settled, they could draw their own satisfaction from a captured British Intelligence report announcing that 'The German Panzer Regiment 3 knows no going difficulties and negotiates terrain which was regarded as absolutely safe against armour.'[20]

The next big German tank operation occurred in North Africa where, as Rommel wrote in his summary of 'The Rules of Desert Warfare', war would be 'waged in its most modern guise . . . It was only in the desert that the principles of armoured warfare as they were taught in theory before the war could be applied and throughly developed.'[21] To begin with, that new 'guise' of war was demonstrated by the British Seventh Armoured Division, more popularly known as the 'Desert Rats'. This force had started life before the war as a 'Mobile Division' raised by Major General Percy Hobart DSO, MC, the former member of the 'Royal Tank Corps avant-garde' whose experimental tank brigade had suffered such humiliation in the 1934 Battle of Hungerford. Hobart had arrived in Cairo in 1938 and set his tanks gliding about among petrified trees on the stony sand of the Western Desert. Since 'Hobo' had been one of the earliest advocates of radio telephones in tanks,[22] it is possible that these exercises, carried out in May 1939, also saw the beginning of the 'typically English' kind of radio communication that Keith Douglas would recall using in the battle of El Alamein in 1942: a weird banter in which formal official codes were overtaken by a more colourful kind of 'veiled talk'. Regional and class dialects were mined for their non-standard usages, and before long whole tank battles would be conducted in a confusing idiom derived from cricket, popular songs and horse-racing: a 'mysterious symbolic language in some ways like that of a wildly experimental school of poets'.[23]

Still at odds with the military establishment, Hobart was relieved of his command shortly after war broke out: he was retired to England where he would serve as corporal in the Home Guard until 1941, when Churchill was pleased to see him remobilized in time to develop his 'funnies' – specialized swimming, mine-sweeping and flame-throwing tanks for the Normandy landings. The Desert Rats had gone into action under General Sir Archibald Wavell in the winter of 1940–1, as the spearhead of the Western Desert Force that overthrew a far larger Italian army commanded by Marshal Rudolfo Graziani. This operation began in December 1940, when the Seventh Armoured Division sped across seventy miles of uncharted desert to surprise the enemy from the rear, proving their 'moral effect' against unprepared Italian units as they captured Sidi Barrani and severed the Italian line of retreat back into Libya. After sweeping into the Bardia defences (a 'glorious gallop' in the phrase of one participant[24], which apparently inspired Eden to come up with his own variation on Churchill's famous phrase about the Battle of Britain: 'never has so much been surrendered by so many to so few'), the Western Desert Force was joined by the 6th Australian Division, and set about driving the Italians out of Libya. First Tobruk was taken, and then the Italians were pushed back through Cyrenaica, to be finished off with another brilliant tank thrust that thrilled the folks back home. This time the 7th Armoured Division advanced 150 miles in thirty-three hours, much of it over rough and partly uncharted desert to cut off the retreating Egyptian Army near a landmark known as 'the Pimple', a low hill near Beda Fomm (7 February 1941). In the words of the commander, Lieutenant General Sir Richard O'Connor, it was 'a wonderful show'.[25]

By the time this operation was finished, O'Connor's corps had advanced some 700 miles and devastated a much larger (and also largely unmotorized) Italian army of nine divisions. It was a shattering defeat for General Graziani, and for those of his officers who found themselves shooting at their own demoralized soldiers as they threw down their weapons and crowded, Caparetto-style, on to any vehicle they could find in a desperate attempt to escape. It left the allies with a legacy of bad jokes about the capabilities of Italy's woefully inadequate Fiat tanks (Q: How many gears does an Italian tank have? A: Five – one forward, four reverse).

Adolf Hitler was among those who followed Wavell's ongoing victory with close interest. He would later describe Africa as one of the great mistakes of the Italian High Command. ('The Italians had no protection against the British tanks, and they were shot like rabbits. Many senior officers fell beside their guns. That's what gave them their panic terror of tanks.'[26]) However, his immediate response was to called Rommel back from his triumph in France with the 7th Panzer Division, show him some illustrated accounts of the action from British and American magazines, and order him to proceed to Tripoli, where he was to command a new 'Afrika Korps' that would strike back with such Italian assistance as could be mustered. Soon afterwards, Rommel's generalship would in turn be admired by the British, not least by mechanizers such as Fuller and Liddell Hart, for whom praising the 'desert fox's' uncanny genius was the same as commending the brilliance of their own earlier teachings on which this eager student had depended.[27]

Rommel arrived in North Africa in February 1941 to prepare for the arrival of the two divisions that would become his Afrika Korps. It was a modest force to begin with, and one that Rommel, who was anticipating further

British attack at any moment, augmented by ordering the manufacture of considerable fleets of dummy tanks mounted on Volkswagen cars. The recently victorious British force had been much weakened by now: the 6th Australian Divison had been assigned to Greece, and the 7th Armoured Brigade was back in Egypt, replaced in Libya by the inexperienced 2nd Armoured Brigade. Striking with new Mark III and IV tanks as well as his VW Panzers, Rommel took Mersa Brega, a bottleneck that had marked the westernmost point of Wavell's advance, and then proceeded, contrary to the orders of his Italian general, to attack Agedabia, breaking through to repeat, though in reverse, the same cross-desert thrust the British had recently used to cut off the retreating Italians. In two weeks he had driven the British out of Cyrenaica and back into Egypt, leaving only the besieged stronghold at Tobruk, a fortified town surrounded by a closely defended anti-tank ditch, which had foiled Rommel's first attempt to take it.

The second assault was initiated on the evening of 13 April. First a force of engineers and infantry from the 8th Machine-Gun Battalion went forward to create a bridgehead by blowing in the anti-tank ditch, and then the 5th Panzer Regiment set off for Tobruk, some 7 km to the north, with thirty-eight tanks and three self-propelled anti-tank guns. They advanced 6 km into enemy territory, but found themselves under heavy counter-attack from all sides – an 'unpleasant situation', as the commander Oberst Olbrich would later report, and one in which a whole battalion would be left in the lurch. Olbrich ordered a retreat, but the force was so heavily attacked as they went back across the anti-tank ditch, that the 200 or so prisoners they had captured managed to escape. For Rommel, this fiasco, in which seventeen out of thirty-eight panzers were lost, was further proof that the command 'had not mastered the art of concentrating its strength at one point, forcing a breakthrough, rolling up and securing the flanks on either side, and then penetrating like lightning, before the enemy has a time to react, deep into his rear'.[28]

There were other lessons to be drawn, as Rommel's memoirs make abundantly clear. To begin with, don't expect too much from your ill-trained and under-equipped Italian allies. Their officers will try to stop you bombing strategically vital coastal towns if they happen to own holiday homes there, and their soldiers, though brave and steadfast against barefooted Abyssinian tribesmen, will be found 'extremely sensitive to enemy tanks and – as in 1917 – quick to throw up the sponge'.[29] Meanwhile – and this was one of Rommel's more Fullerish precepts – note the clean economy of the new kind of mobile warfare as compared with a conventional war of

position: 'In a mobile act, what counts is material, as the essential comple-
ment to the soldier,' which means that it is far less bloody than a war of
position where the attacking infantryman rather than the tank is the target.
Understand too that 'Speed is the one thing that matters here.'[30] Rommel
spelt out this rule in a letter to his wife Lucie-Maria, but he also applied it
to his tank commanders, who had to learn not to stop unnecessarily to
refuel or restock with ammunition, or to overhaul their vehicles. Too much
thought could evidently ruin a tank operation: 'a commander's drive and
energy often count for more than his intellectual powers'. Rommel's
mechanics were also learning on the job. They reported that a number of
tanks were lost during this advance to Tobruk owing to fine dust clogging
the crankshaft, and then cutting off oil circulation.[31] A 'dry felt filter' of the
kind used by the British would reduce incidents of engine failure. As for
the trouble with auxiliary brakes, this was caused by defective shims and
tersely attributed to poor inspection by the tank manufacturers.

So there was Rommel, unable to take Tobruk, but launching elegant
metal strokes into the desert he recognized as the site of 'the pure tank battle'.[32] This was a war of abstract thrusts and pirouettes, performed against
stark desert vistas that would soon be commemorated in picture books. It
was a terrain in which military operations really seemed to have the character of those clean sweeping arrows with which military strategists have
always liked to represent the chaos of battle: a theatre in which, as Samuel
Hynes has said, a Good War is 'only a matter of space, and freedom and
the right machine'.[33]

Code-named 'Battleaxe', Wavell's counter-attack of 15–17 June 1941 was a
disaster summed up in the last recorded words of Major C. G. Miles, commander of C squadron the 4th Royal Tank Regiment, who ran into
entrenched 88 mm anti-tank guns in the Halifaya Pass and was heard on
the radio, saying: 'They are tearing my tanks apart.'[34] He was killed half an
hour later, and Battleaxe became 'a byword for blundering'.[35] Winston
Churchill certainly thought so: impatient for some decisive tank thrusts of
his own, he removed General Wavell from his post as Commander-in-
Chief of the Middle East. Rommel was more generous, noting that the real
lesson of Battleaxe concerned the British Mark II Matilda infantry tank.
This machine may have worried Rommel's panzermen, whose reports testify to their inability to penetrate its heavy frontal armour, but for Rommel
it was both undergunned and far too slow: a tank, in other words, that had
made it quite impossible for Wavell's army to seize the initiative. As for the
Italian Army, there were jokes on the German side too, which eventually

surfaced in Hitler's table conversation. On the night of 3–4 January 1942 (by which time this lover of the cinema could have ordered up a recently issued American comedy film called *Bowery Blitzkrieg*, about a street punk who goes into the boxing ring), Hitler mocked rumours that 'the expression "Blitzkrieg" is an Italian invention. We picked it up from the newspapers. I've just learnt that I owe all my successes to an attentive study of Italian military theories.'[36]

Driving east with Oberleutnant Shultz

A confident background, then, against which Hitler launched 'Barbarossa', his massive assault on the Soviet Union, which opened on 22 June 1941, with co-ordinated strikes by three distinct army groups, 3.2 million men in all, arrayed along a frontier that stretched from Murmansk to the Black Sea. Curzio Malaparte was in no position to observe the *Luftwaffe*'s opening strike against sixty-six Soviet airfields, but he did go to Jassy by the Romanian border to watch some of the tanks of Field Marshal Gerd von Rundstedt's Army Group South assemble with their unmechanized Romanian allies for a thrust into the Ukraine that would follow a week or so after the main strike led by Fourth and Third Panzer Groups to the north of the Pripet marshes.[37] Nine years previously, Malaparte had enraged the Gestapo by touring Germany and then publishing a book suggesting that Hitler, rumoured to have had a testicle bitten off by a dog when a child, had the attitudes of a woman.[38] No mention of that, however, from the rhapsodizing journalist, who now pretends to hear the music of Honegger and Hindemith in the 'continuous, uniform roar' of a thousand engines, and who notes 'blue tongues of smoke' belching out of the panzers' exhausts: 'once again the smell of men and horses gives way to the overpowering reek of petrol'.[39] He watches a mechanized division that has come directly from its recent victories in Greece: its sunburnt soldiers are clear-eyed, statuesque, coated in white dust, and in one case even clutching an owl; and they sit on open trucks that have the image of the Parthenon painted in white lead on their bonnets. When the time eventually comes, he sees these armoured columns driving east 'like thin lines drawn with a pencil on the vast green slate of the Moldavian plain'.[40]

This was just a tiny fragment of the vast force that surprised the Soviet Union, while an unbelieving Stalin was still shooting the German deserters who tried to warn him that Hitler, his ally in a non-aggression pact, was poised to attack. By the end of June, Stalin's western front had 'virtually ceased to exist as an organized force';[41] 417,000 Soviet soldiers were caught just in the initial encirclement west of Minsk. The tank tactics used against Russia may have been similar to those rehearsed in previous much smaller assaults: the same devastating co-ordination of air and land warfare, the same repertoire of metal-fingered probes, massed and speedy thrusts, pincer movements and envelopments. However, the panic among the conquered was better founded than ever before. This was a 'war of ideologies' and, on the racial front, a 'war of extermination' too. After Malaparte's glittering steel machines went not just the motorized infantry but also the SS killing squads, sent in to pursue Hitler's murderous policies of 'cleansing' against the Jewish and civilian population. Pumped full of rabid propaganda about Bolshevism and the sub-human nature of Slav, Russian, Mongol and Jew, the regular troops were ordered to execute commissars and 'partisans' on the spot, and licensed to butcher and starve prisoners of war and civilians too.

Malaparte watched as they swept the wagons and horses of their slow Romanian allies from the roads, and concluded, from a hilltop in Bessarabia, that the German force was

not an army but an immense travelling workshop, an enormous mobile foundry that stretched as far as the eye could reach in every direction. It was as if the thousands of chimneys, cranes, iron bridges and steel towers, the millions of cog-wheels, the hundreds and hundreds of blast-furnaces and rolling-mills of the whole of Westphalia, of the entire Ruhr, were advancing in a body over the vast expanse of corn-fields that is Bessarabia. It was as if an enormous Krupps Steelworks, a gigantic Essen, were preparing to launch an attack on the hills of Zaicani, of Shofroncani, of Bratosheni.[42]

And yet, as a German anti-tank gunner called 'Frank' insisted, there would be no mayhem and carnage, no burning of crops and villages on either side. 'Modern armies aim to destroy the enemy's industrial capacity, not his fields and villages. It is a case of the machine – in the literal sense of the word – destroying the machine.' So, after 'the gigantic mobile steel-works has passed', the newly Germanized birds would start to sing again, and the wind would rustle in unbroken corn. Despite the slaughter of those early weeks in which hundreds of thousands had already died, Malaparte could share that gunner's naïve belief in modern warfare as a mechanical pastorale. An armoured column, he wrote, is 'a precision instrument *par excellence*'. For in mechanized warfare, it seemed, at least to this dreamy participant, that 'only machines are vulnerable, that human life must at all costs be respected. That is why, on these battlefields, death assumes the character of an accident, of something outside the logic of events. There is something absurd about the dead in this war.'[43]

Nothing, however, even remotely as absurd as these words that come down to us from 'Frank' via Malaparte the surrealist war correspondent. That abstract idea of mechanized warfare, which we have already seen descending from Fuller to Rommel, would survive a little longer in North Africa. Indeed, in September 1943 the American writer John Steinbeck would entertain the identical thought as he wandered through 'a huge used tank yard' on the edge of an unnamed North African city. Having noted the fragments of burned shoe and fabric and the splashes of dried blood alongside the messages, phone numbers and profiles pencilled inside the turrets of blasted machines called Hun Chaser or Lucky Girl, he informed readers of the New York Herald Tribune that 'Modern war is very hard on its tools. While in this war fewer men are killed, more equipment than ever is wrecked, for it seems almost to be weapon against weapon rather than man against man.'[44] Yet in Operation Barbarossa, such tank theorizing would soon enough be silenced by the reality of a genocidal invasion that would not finally be defeated until 1,710 towns and 70,000 villages had been destroyed and the phrase 'scorched earth' filled with new meaning.[45]

In one of his Ukrainian dispatches, written from Cornolenca on 14 July 1914, and later reprinted as 'Steel Horses', Malaparte describes advancing through cornfields in just one of those 'precision instruments' as it headed out from a captured collective farm at Skuratovoi, to meet a Soviet counter-attack. Dawn is yet to break and the soldiers, who have been caught out by the sudden order to move, are still tossing soap, combs and shaving brushes at each other as they lumber into war in their anti-aircraft lorries. Malaparte is with them, squatting on a box of ammunition and talking with Oberleutnant Shultz, a university social researcher who has published a number of essays on Soviet Russia, but who now finds himself in charge of the anti-aircraft section of this mechanized column. They discuss literature and philosophy as they drive into action. Educated soldiers went into war this way on all sides. The British tankman and poet Keith Douglas would read Maeterlink's descriptions of ant communities, two days before leading a Crusader, loaded with Penguin books, into battle at El Alamein.[46] But Malaparte and Shultz chose to discuss the Communist writer Vsevelod Ivanov's *Armoured Train No. 14–69*,[47] comparing their own armoured column to the White Russian train in that play of the Russian Civil War, a terrifying and apparently unstoppable thing surrounded by 'hidden perils' – 'Woe to the man', as Shultz observes, 'who leaves the column.' While soldiers in some of the other lorries wash their jackboots with soap and water, Shultz ventures the distinctly theoretical viewpoint that 'From the social viewpoint, machines are very interesting and very dangerous characters.'[48]

The fearful metal column clatters on into the breaking day, led by heavy tanks that 'emit a delicate yet vivid radiance', their metal skins having been 'enveloped in a pink aura' by the rising sun. Larks explode out of the corn, patrols of infantrymen carry out 'mopping up operations' on the slopes of nearby hills, and the sound of artillery and anti-tank guns thunders up ahead. The enemy is eventually sighted – a distant glint of steel, which is immediately refracted through the Nazi 'Asiatic' stereotype. 'The Mongols! The Mongols!' goes the cry, for the German units have already, so Malaparte reports, learned to tell Mongolian from other units of the Red Army: 'tanks manned by Asiatic crews fight not in formation but singly, or in groups of two or three at the most (it is a tactic that recalls, in a sense, that of the cavalry-patrols).'[49]

The German soldiers called these racialized Mongol tanks *Panzerpferde*, or 'armoured horses'; and that was the point of this motorized 'gymkhana' for Malaparte too. The Soviet system had turned these horsemen into mechanics and replaced their passion for horses with 'an extraordinary passion for machines'.[50] Yet the old ways lived on, if only in the abstract way in which the forms of classical antiquity could still be detected in the modern edifice of Malaparte's house on Capri: 'They come forward not in a body but singly. They advance through the cornfields in a series of broad sweeping movements, like horsemen performing evolutions in some gigantic circus. And their audacity is reminiscent of that for which the old-time cavalry were famous.' Oberleutnant Schultz observes that these *Panzerpferde* are using 'a technique of enticement . . . One has to be very careful not to swallow the bait – not to allow oneself to be lured on to ground that has been mined or ambushed by large armoured formations . . .'[51]

As this description makes clear, the battle between the tank and the horse was not, for Malaparte, just a matter of German panzers bearing down on a primitive unmotorized enemy. Nor was it just a stylistic device for differentiating the industrialized Nazi war machine from the Soviet cavalry that would indeed soon ride out of the marshes to confront it ('Where the German motor failed, the Russian horse's legs continued to move,' as one German tank general would later write).[52] Instead, Malaparte used the tank-horse motif to characterize the astonishing Soviet mechanization in which the horses of the steppe had been replaced by machines, while their riders had been lifted up, along with millions of peasants, and processed into a Red proletariat with the help of three Five Year Plans. It was this massive industrial conversion, guided by Lenin's formula, 'Soviet + electrification = Bolshevism', that sustained the Soviet Army, making it a far more considerable enemy than Nazi denigrators would allow.

Travelling behind the advancing front line, Malaparte was initially only able to diagnose this extraordinary transformation in the condition of dead Soviet soldiers. At one point this roaming correspondent comes across a group of Soviet tanks, which has fallen victim to the German 'Pak' anti-tank gun. Interested to see examples of the special tanks used to transport assault troops, he checks over one of these burned-out machines, noting its large calibre machine gun, and the benches inside, and then moves on to inventorize the working parts of the driver: a charred spinal column resting against the back of the seat, and a scatter of limb bones piled up beneath the instrument panel.[53] Another dead Russian soldier is described as a 'new corpse' – 'delivered from the great factory of the Pyatlyetka', a 'mass produced' specimen of a new race – less a soldier who has died at war than a worker 'killed in an industrial accident'.[54] The dandy in Malaparte is brought out by the contents of a heavy Russian tank – found lying on its side in Yampol on the River Dnestr. The dead driver is still in place. Dressed in a grey tunic, with close-cropped hair that is scorched and blackened at the back of the neck, the corpse turns out to be that of a woman of about thirty: '"Brave girl," I say to myself. I stretch out my hand, gently and reverently caress her brow. "Poor dear," I mutter.'[55] A re-gendering ceremony, there, for a mechanized soul – momentarily won back from 'that industrial "morale" which is indispensable to those called upon to fight in this war'.[56]

All war correspondents are inclined to dramatize their fleeting perceptions, but Malaparte did so with hideous flair in *Kaputt!* (1944), a novel written shortly after his removal from the Ukraine.[57] In a chapter called 'Horse Kingdom', he recounts a journey he made in the Balta area not long before his expulsion from the Ukraine. Driving towards the front with the aim of viewing a Russian 'bulge' in the line, he arrives in a desolated village called Alexandrovska, and parks his car by the orchard fence with a view to resting in the prosperous-looking house beyond. A dead mare is stretched out by the gate (a dark bay with a long yellow mane, as the fastidious Malaparte notes) – and the empty house stands there in abandoned chaos. The evening is sultry, the air thick with an impending thunderstorm, and Malaparte closes the window and stretches out to sleep on a ripped-up mattress.

Unmotorized Romanian cavalrymen march by and rifle-shots crackle in the distance, but nothing disturbs his night so much as the organic stench of the decomposing mare.

In the morning he drives on through a world that smells of 'things rotten, of decomposing matter'. He passes a gang of Rumanian soldiers who have found some Jews – old men, women and children – hiding in the reeds, and are shooting at them with the cry of: 'Mice, Mice!' And then he finds the counterpart of his dead mare:

Farther along on a marshy stretch between the road and the river, a Soviet armoured car lay overturned. The gun stuck out of the conning tower, the trap door was open and twisted by the explosion; inside, amid the mud that had filled the car, was a man's arm. It was a carcass of an armoured car. It stank of oil and petrol, of burnt paint, of gutted leather and scorched iron. It was a strange odour. A new odour. The new odour of the new war. I felt sorry for that armoured car, but sorry in a different way than I had felt at the sight of the dead horse. It was a dead machine. A rotting machine. It had already begun to stink. It was iron carrion, overturned in the mud.[58]

This smell dominates the area, hanging over cornfields littered with 'overturned cars, burned trucks, disembowelled armoured cars, abandoned guns, all twisted by explosions. But nowhere a man, nothing living, not even a corpse, not even any carrion. For miles and miles around there is only dead iron. Dead bodies of machines, hundreds upon hundreds of miserable steel carcasses.' And, as he notes over the remains of a German plane: 'the smell of rotting iron won over the smell of men and horses – that smell of old wars: even the smell of grain and the penetrating, sweet scent of sunflowers vanished amid that sour stench of scorched iron, rotting steel, dead machinery'.[59]

Malaparte encounters a live specimen of the new Soviet man a little later, having entered another burned and butchered village to find an abandoned Soviet office, with a portrait of Stalin over which some Rumanian soldier has pencilled: 'Aiurea!' – meaning 'Oh Yeah!' He sits there among scattered propaganda pamphlets, remembering Tolstoy's *War and Peace*, and the Tartar horsemen, some armed with bows and arrows, who had once harried Napoleon's retreating soldiers over the same ground. The thought of those days brings him back to the dead mare: 'I thought of the poor, lonely stench of the dead mare overcome by the smell of scorched iron, petrol, rotting steel, of the new spell of this new war of machinery.'

It is in that desolated place that some Romanian soldiers turn up with a captured Tartar armoured-car driver whom Malaparte agrees to drive back, along with an escort, to army headquarters in Balta. On the way, they spend another night at the house with the dead mare, a 'ghostlike' mansion in which Malaparte surveys the Soviet tank driver, noting his 'veiled, narrow eyes, slanted like a cat's', and compressing his theory of modern Russia into a brief description of the Tartar tank man's hands:

They were the hands of a young recruit of the Piatiletka, of an *udarnik* [industrial commando] of the third Five-Year Plan, of a young Tartar who had become an engineer, a tank driver. Softened by the incessant thousand-year-long rubbing against the silky coats of horses, against manes, tendons, hocks, muscles of horses, with reins, with the smooth leather of saddles and harness, they had passed within a few years from horse to machine, from flesh to metal tendons, from reins to controls. A few years had been enough to transform young Tartars of the Don and the Volga, of the Kirghiz Steppe and the shores of the Caspian and Aral seas, from horse-breeders into qualified workers of the USSR . . . [60]

By this time the reeking dead mare has become redolent of 'the ancient law of war', which was 'human and animal', and which remains, at least in this small patch, capable of 'conquering the odour of rotting steel, dissolving iron and putrified metal', and of 'mastering the new law of mechanical war'. War stinks, but in two ways. That seems to be Malaparte's point. For two decades he himself had been straddling the division between organic tradition and machine-based modernity as these two polarized attractions coexisted in the imagination of Italian fascism;[61] and, having sniffed at both sides of the Eastern Front without ever really penetrating its surface, he now came down on the side of nostalgia: indeed, he settled into that horsey stench as if it were 'an old fatherland'.

15

The Tiger and the Mouse

'Everything is shrouded in a purple haze.'
K. Simonov, *Stalingrad Fights On* (1942)

A dead horse was among the least appalling of the sights that would be created by the German soldiers whom Malaparte had seen shaving, joking and philosophizing nervously as they ploughed east into the heat of the Ukrainian summer. In the early weeks when, as General F. W. von Mellenthin has written, 'the German blitzkrieg looked as though it would carry everything before it',[1] few of those battle-hardened panzermen would have bothered to ponder the paradoxical fact that, as Keith Douglas would shortly note in North Africa, 'the view from a moving tank is like that in a camera obscura or a silent film – in that since the engine drowns out all other voices except explosions, the whole world moves silently'.[2] Yet, with so much 'lightning' victory already behind them, they may well have yearned for the battlefield, recognizing it, again in Douglas's words, as 'the simple, central stage of the war', the place where 'the interesting things happen'.[3] Perhaps some of these young men could remember going to their tanks with a sense of relief too, as the Englishman David Holbrook would do in 1944, rejecting the desperate 'skirt clinging' of his abject personal life and his 'yearning for the tender softness of a woman's company. Now he wanted only the other directed purpose – to be a servant of the large destructive machines with men in war.'[4]

The initial romance of Barbarossa took a different form for other soldiers, including Wolfgang Schöler, who later managed to look back on June 1941 as a time of unexpected tenderness.[5] Employed on the military railroad, he followed the tanks far into the Ukraine, to places where terrified parents had forbidden their young daughters to wash, or wear any but the drabbest of clothes. Yet, in Schöler's memory, everyone relaxed once the German soldiers arrived and, far from behaving like the monsters of Communist expectation, started showing photographs of their own folks back home. Schöler himself claims to have fallen in love with a pretty nineteen-year-old village teacher. A gentler occupation may fleetingly have seemed possible to some in Byelorussia and the Ukraine, both of which had suffered great hardship under Stalin's recently enforced collectivization of agriculture. But these illusions were not to last, even if they did outlive the elderly Jew Malaparte saw, or perhaps planted, in the doorway of a fruit shop in Beltsy early that August, desperately calling out in German, '*Alles gut, alles gut!* – All's well, all's well!'[6]

Though not part of the main opening attack north of the Pripet Marshes, Malaparte's soldiers drove into a series of immense tank battles that have since been the subject of much military-operational analysis, each one weighed, measured and then accorded its place in the sequence of events that saw the overthrow of the blitzkrieg and the final defeat of the Nazis in 1945. The first breakthroughs were as overwhelming as they were unexpected, and the advances that followed were sufficiently spectacular for General Franz Halder, head of Germany's Armed Forces High Command, to imagine in his diary that 'the Russian campaign has been won in the space of two weeks'.

In those first days, Soviet forces suffered total disorientation and casualties by the hundred thousand. Whole Soviet commands disappeared along with their armies, and virtually all the Red Army's badly trained mechanized corps are said to have lost 90 per cent of their strength in the first week.[7] Ill-equipped and lacking adequate tactics or command, the Red Army was sliced to pieces in a series of vast pincer movements. Moving on from Minsk towards Moscow, the German forces were frontally assaulted as they approached the River Dnepr, but their attackers, the 5th and 7th Mechanized Corps of General Kurochkin's 20th Army, were obliterated by the anti-tank guns travelling, in the by now well-rehearsed manner, just behind the armoured spearhead. There was intense fighting at Vitebvsk, and the Red Army recovered sufficiently to mount some bitter and costly counter-attacks around Smolensk, which saw several days of hand-to-hand fighting, and also ferocious battles between the panzers and the Soviet tank force pulled together from various remnants by Marshal Rokossovsky.

The advance towards Moscow was slowed by this resistance; and by 11 August, General Franz Halder, who had considered the enemy effectively beaten in July, had woken up to the difficulties faced by his men as they hammered their way into the East. Increasingly distant from supplies and replacement weapons, they found themselves sprawled out over 'an immense front line', without any depth in which to organize themselves and subject to 'incessant attacks'.[8] By September Hitler had decided that the year's objective was not Moscow as his tank generals Guderian and Hoth had wanted, but Leningrad in the north and the Ukraine, where the better equipped armies of the Soviet Union's south-western front, under General M. P. Kirponos, had managed to delay the Nazi advance. So Guderian's Second Panzer Group turned south, to help cut off and encircle the four Soviet armies still holding out at Kiev – a victory in which the Germans are said to have taken 665,000 prisoners.

Owing to this ferocious detour, the attack on Moscow, codenamed 'Operation Typhoon', didn't actually begin until 2 October. Two panzer groups carried out a planned 'pincer' encirclement at Vyazma, cutting off five Soviet armies and opening a gap in Moscow's western defences. Meanwhile, Guderian's Second Panzer Group broke through further south to take the town of Orel with such speed that its tanks arrived on the streets before the trams had stopped running, and then moved on to Bryansk where three additional armies were trapped and destroyed.[9] By this time, nearly 3 million Soviet soldiers had been captured and marched west as slaves to be beaten, starved and, in the Nazi idiom, 'scrapped through labour'. Appointed by Stalin to take over the devastated western front, General Zukhov found the road to Moscow was as good as open. There was much panic in the city – what the historian John Erickson records as 'the Great Skedaddle' as people mobbed trains, desperate to escape.

Yet by the end of October 1941, Germany's lightning war was actually slowing into a war of attrition. Logistical problems persisted, and the advance had not been helped by Hitler's decision to divert his forces in order to take Leningrad and the Ukraine, and even to withdraw five divisions in order to re-equip them for the wars he planned to wage after the speedy resolution of Barbarossa. Many tanks and motor vehicles had been lost, both to the Red Army and, as the rains came, to the enemy known as 'Marshal Mud'. Hitler's new autobahns may have facilitated the invasion of Poland, but few roads in the Soviet Union were paved and, in the words of the commander of the Fourth and Third Panzer Armies, Generaloberst Erhard Rauss, 'the attacker, who must seek to retain the initiative, is much more affected by mud than the defender'.[10] The Second Panzer Group, fighting around Orel, had lost 60 per cent of its tanks to mud, and there could be no certainty over replacements since, as early as July 1941, Hitler had decided to concentrate his armaments industry on the production of submarines and aircraft, which would be needed once Russia had been briskly overwhelmed. With its broad tracks and high clearance, the new

Soviet Medium tank, the T-34, might have managed to 'sail over the October mud seas',[11] but Germany's floundering machines were not so blessed. It is estimated that a tenth of them had been lost to mud by November when 'Marshal Winter' put in an unusually ferocious appearance, stiffening the ground but introducing another set of problems too. Lubricants congealed in engines, and recoil liquid froze inside guns. Tanks failed to start and, even if they were successfully warmed up with the help of fires, could hardly move through the snow: as had been discovered in Poland two winters before, once frozen, Hitler's invincible tanks only had to hit a tree to crack at the seams.

Meanwhile, with a scarcity of supplies from the rear, German armies were ordered to pursue the policy of 'living off the land', an operation that meant stripping whole villages of their food reserves and shooting any objectors among those now declared 'superfluous mouths'.[12] Hitler and his cronies had been so confident in the speed of the irresistible blitzkrieg that they had seen no need to equip their forces with adequate winter uniforms, so 'living off the land' would soon enough also come to mean prising coats and felt boots off dead Russians, or stealing them, along with furs and other clothes, from captured soldiers and local inhabitants, who were then left to freeze or die by famine.[13]

In November the Germans launched the final thrusts on Moscow, planning to envelop both the city and the Soviet forces gathered to the south. Kalinin was taken and then Klin. There was desperate fighting within a few kilometres to both north and south of Moscow, and reaching into the suburbs too. But this was to be the extent of the German advance. The first significant setback came on 29 November, when SS troops were pushed out of Rostov by Soviet riflemen who fought their way into the town across the frozen river. The first of December saw Field Marshal Von Kluge's last attempt to seize the Minsk-Moscow road in preparation for a final advance, but the men of the 20th Corps could take no more: John Erickson describes them freezing in the snow and screaming that they could go no further. Perhaps it was the lucky ones who ended up back in Warsaw, where Curzio Malaparte would later claim to have seen men from the eastern front, wide-eyed, staring and unable to blink because the Russian frost had taken their eyelids.

The early weeks of Barbarossa had been a débâcle for the Red Army. Stalin had tried to improve the situation by terrorizing and, in some cases, shooting his generals. He had ordered his forces to mount a full-scale 'counter-attack', apparently unconcerned that they were everywhere overwhelmed if not in total disarray; and that, even when they had tanks to meet the German spearheads, these were inadequately armoured and, as one despairing general put it of his own T-26s, only fit 'for shooting sparrows'.[14] Stalin had also sunk out of view for a few days, apparently himself a long distance victim of the 'tank fright' that struck so many Soviet soldiers.

Yet the Soviet Union had immense human and industrial resources, and also a ruthless totalitarian state machine with which to rally both through the winter months. By reaching deep into its rear, it could raise new armies in a matter of weeks. Many armaments arrived under 'lend-lease' arrangements from allies in the West, including British tanks that were considered highly inadequate. But Stalin also oversaw a speedy and unimaginably arduous relocation of industry. Huge metallurgical plants and arms factories were lifted from the ground, whether in Leningrad, Moscow or the southern Ukraine, and carried east. By November 1941, 1,523 factories had been dismantled, loaded on to trains, and shipped to Siberia, Central Asia, or the Urals, where the city of Chelyabinsk was reborn as 'Tankograd' – its Chelyabinsk Tractor Factory vastly expanded with plant relocated from Kharkov and Kirov, and given over to accelerated production of T-34s. Thousands toiled under the most punishing conditions on sixty-four production lines, churning out T-34s, their turrets pressed rather than cast for speed.[15] Self-propelled guns poured out in this metal torrent too, as eventually did heavy 'Josef Stalin' tanks, although not until late in 1943.

Marshal Zhukov launched his counter-attack against the exhausted Germans near Moscow on the morning of 5 December, when snow lay thick on the ground and the temperature was as low as thirty degrees below zero. The assault involved twelve armies extended over a 500-mile front, and was greatly assisted by the Far Eastern divisions that Stalin had transferred from Mongolia, along with their tanks and aircraft, as soon as a reliable spy informed him that the Imperial Japanese Kwantung Army was not about to attack his eastern frontier. The first German retreat was ordered the next day, a reversal that could be slowed but not stopped by Hitler's notorious 'stand and fight' order issued shortly afterwards.

Moscow was only the beginning of an acute crisis for the German forces in Russia. Hitler's Army Group North was hit a month later, in January 1942, when troops in the Demyansk pocket were encircled and drawn into a long and desperate series of battles through which the vastly outnumbered men of the SS Death's Head Division would only hold their ground at the cost of near annihilation.[16] These reversals curtailed Hitler's early fantasy of sending his tanks south through the Soviet Union to conquer the oilfields of Iran and even the Suez Canal; yet in the summer of 1942, while the Soviet authorities still considered Moscow to be his main objective, he launched a massive southern campaign, intended to press down through Stalingrad and into the oil-rich Caucasus to the east of the Black Sea, and on as far as Baku on the Caspian Sea. In co-ordination with the Kleist Panzer Division and the Seventeenth Army, the Panzer Divisions of General Paulus's Sixth Army resisted a fierce but poorly co-ordinated Red Army assault at Kharkov, converting it into a disaster by catching four Soviet armies in a pincer movement and presiding over another week of barely imaginable carnage in which Russian infantrymen linked arms and charged into the guns, and at least one hardened Soviet general surveyed his slaughtered men and shot himself.[17] The Eleventh Army under General von Manstein was triumphant on the Crimean Front: overwhelming Kerch and driving whole Soviet armies back to the sea at the Taman Peninsula, where they were pulverized on the beach; and then turning his 'annihilation fire' on the heavily fortified Black Sea naval base at Sevastopol.[18]

While Stalin reviewed the defeats of the early summer and victimized his beaten commanders, including Timoshenko, who was among those relieved of their command, Hitler broke off his planned assault on Stalingrad, in order to mount another and, as he imagined, decisive encirclement on the lower Don at Rostov. This meant detaching the 40th Panzer Corps from Paulus's Sixth Army, which would then push on for Stalingrad, as it proceeded to do, breaking through the Soviet 4th Tank Army to threaten the city, which was already the scene of terrible aerial bombardment, and now became the site of hideous hand-to-hand fighting in which battles would be fought in drains, or between the floors of shattered industrial buildings and where tanks, always vulnerable in built-up areas, would 'burn like candles'.[19] Combined with the fall of Rostov, the threat to Stalingrad drove Stalin to issue his famous 'Not a Step Backwards' order, and to instruct his commander Yeremenko how to defend the city: 'The most important thing is not to let panic take hold, do not be afraid of the enemy thrusts and keep your faith in our ultimate success.'[20]

The propaganda pamphlets must have helped too – like the one that told of Pyotr Boloto, a 'sturdy, thick-set' anti-tank rifleman, who, together with his comrades, had crippled fifteen advancing German tanks: "'When the first tank was coming at me," he said, "I thought that the end of the world had come."'[21] But by the time this hero had settled into his stride, he was even rolling cigarettes and smoking them as he battled on – one for every three knocked-out tanks. The same red courage fired the elderly workers who, on hearing that German tanks had broken through close to their machine plant, hastened their repair of some damaged tanks, and then clattered out across the yard to hold back the onslaught until the necessary Red Army units arrived. The sheer hatred that kept Stalingrad fighting was stoked and inflamed by stories like that of a young lieutenant called Vadim Tkalenko. Having served as a scout working with partisans behind the German line, Tkalenko had seen the bestial Nazis at work during a punitive raid on the village of Khristinovka, near Uman. First, these monsters had taken the elderly father of a claimed partisan leader and, having roped him up between two light tanks, torn him to pieces while his fellow villagers were obliged to looked on. When this failed to elicit the whereabouts of 'Uncle Vanya', they had taken twenty infants from their peasant mothers' arms, tied them together and crushed them beneath a tank. Whatever the status of that atrocious story as fact or necessary fiction, the message was clear: No Mercy, and No Surrender.[22]

'Operation Uranus', the Soviet counter-attack, was launched on 19 November. Planned and implemented under the commander of the southwestern front, Colonel General N. F. Vatutin, it consisted of an armoured pincer movement that cut through the weak and extended Axis flanks to the south and north of Stalingrad, and then curved round to encircle both the Sixth Army and some units of the 4th Panzer Army too. Having achieved this, Vatutin's men proceeded to kill off their trapped, starved and frostbitten enemy in 'Operation Ring'. By the time the job of 'reducing the Stalingrad pocket' was finished in January 1943, 209,000 men had been killed, and 91,000 captured, of whom only 5,000 would ever return to Germany

As one Soviet counter-offensive followed another, the Red Army was to become increasingly skilled in its use of armoured forces. Indeed, the Soviet Union's prodigious production of tanks was accompanied by a recovery of the kind of Deep Battle doctrine that had been developed under Tukhachevsky before the war. This was achieved with the help of G. S. Isserson, a surviving member of the late Marshal Tukhachevsky's obliterated Deep Battle circle, and also of Marshal Fedorenko, chief of the Armoured Forces Administration, who revived the idea of combined arms units, and started building the tank armies that would eventually defeat the Germans. The Soviet winter offensive of early 1943 was held back and outmanoeuvred by General von Manstein's Panzer divisions in the Ukraine – the Donbas operation and the March retaking of Kharkov and Belgorod, hailed to this day as 'classics' of mobile warfare.

The turning point came in the summer, and in particular on 5 July 1943, when the Germans opened the Battle of Kursk. 'Operation Citadel' was planned as a double envelopment in which two massive panzer armies would cut the Soviet line from both north and south to close a bulge in the line some 250 km long and 160 km wide. Intended to devastate the Soviet forces in Central Russia, Citadel had been delayed partly because the Allied invasion of North Africa made the anticipated attack on France unlikely, therefore freeing up reserve divisions to be brought in from the west. Yet Hitler also held back because he wanted time to build more tanks, particularly the new heavy models, the Panthers and 60-ton Tigers in which so much hope was placed. This was another occasion where the 'idea' of the tank outran practical considerations, since the delay also assisted the Soviet Union, which was capable of producing tanks in considerably greater quantities over the same time.

Kursk has often been described as the biggest tank battle in history – for Hitler it was to be a 'beacon' signalling to the world that Germany could still triumph against the communist hordes.[23] In one recent estimate, the Germans mustered fifty divisions with 435,000 men and 3,155 tanks, to hurl against a Soviet force of over a million men and 3,275 tanks. A Titanic clash between two vast 'Tank armadas' – that is how John Erickson describes it,[24] but this sort of imagery, also used in the memoirs of German generals, is distrusted by other historians. Preferring to view these apocalyptic events from an apparently neutral military-operational perspective, they now insist that the Battle of Kursk was actually four distinct battles, not one of them 'involving a thousand tanks in one huge swirling battle'.[25] The northern assault, made by Colonel General Walter Model's Ninth Army, failed to penetrate more than 10 km, while to the south Colonel General Hermann Hoth's stronger force of panzer divisions and elite SS units advanced by some 35 km punching their way in with vast tank 'fists' of as many as two hundred massed machines, threatening the town of Oboyan, and then advancing on the railway junction of Prokhorovka in order to encircle Soviet resistance from both south and west, thereby opening the road to Kursk.

It was on 12 July, in a small triangle of ground some three square miles south of the railway junction of Prokhorovka, that the major defeat was inflicted on the Second SS Panzerkorps by the Russian 5th Guards and 5th Guards Tank Armies. Historians continue to argue about the precise number of tanks involved on that day. Soviet sources claim that 500 German tanks fought against 793 Soviet machines, mostly T-34s but also some British Churchills. The American historian of the SS Death's Head Division suggests that it was actually only 273 German tanks that went up against some 900 T-34s, in what was nevertheless still 'the largest single armored battle in the history of land warfare'.[26] Though not as numerous as the 100 estimated by the Russians, Germany's Tigers were better armoured and had a greater range than the T-34s. Their 'Elephant' tank destroyers were formidable too. Yet the Soviet force overcame this advantage with a desperate advance in which it lost half its tanks. The battle is said to have become 'an enormous armoured brawl'[27] in which every tank and crew fought on its own terms, blasting and ramming as the occasion demanded.

Others insist that Prokhorovka 'was not a battle with tanks charging on one huge field, but rather a series of attacks and counter-attacks across a stretch of countryside ranging in an ark about 20 km wide . . .'[28] As for the clouds of dust that, in some of the more vivid accounts, still rise above the cornfields to provide a scenic background for the Stukas that were effectively used against Soviet tanks for the first time at Kursk, those are now dispatched with terse reference to the fact that the fighting took place in heavy wind and rain. The tank-counting continues, but no one has yet disputed the killing or the fact that, by the end of 12 July, Prokhorovka was 'a graveyard of burned out Soviet and German tanks'.[29]

The Battle of Kursk would go down in history as the moment when Germany lost strategic control of the war, marking what the Soviet Marshal Konev called 'the swan-song of the German armoured force'.[30] At the time this was not universally recognized by the German commanders. They had seen the upset of their timetable for the Kursk assault and suffered heavy casualties too, with 20,000 killed among the three SS divisions alone.[31] And yet they had suffered a comparatively light loss of tanks overall, and inflicted considerably more damage on their enemy. Major General von Mellenthin blamed Hitler, who summoned Field Marshals von Manstein and Kluge to East Prussia on 13 July and ordered them to cancel the offensive, insisting that, with the Allied landing in Sicily, SS divisions must be withdrawn from the east and the 'Stalingrad' divisions training in France be sent to Italy instead of Russia.

The Red Army followed the German defeat by attacking on the Orel Salient, north of Kursk, and then launched an offensive from the south that struck back towards Belgorod and Kharkov. After that came the great drive west, pursued through vast, often brutal and hard-fought operations on many fronts. The onslaught was initiated in June 1944, when an enormous force assaulted the area of Hitler's Army Group Centre, north of the Pripet Marshes, burying twenty-eight German divisions as it surged forward, a fiery tide that covered 450 miles in a month. The Red Army pressed on over plains and through cities, fighting its way into the shattered remnants of Berlin to unleash an orgy of vengeful looting and rape on the 'cellar tribes' who survived in the burning ruins. The tanks were in attendance throughout, massive and unbreakable Josef Stalins and also T-34s of the sort that would soon be mounted on plinths at Soviet war cemeteries and memorials throughout the war zone.

Thick fur

'They're crawling towards us, Obab, can you see them?' – so said Captain Nizesalov, the panic-stricken White Russian commander of Armoured Train 14–69 in Vsevelod Ivanov's play of that name. He has discovered that bridges can be blown up, and that, even where the all-important tracks remain intact, the Communist enemy can find other ways of immobilizing his invincible machine. The Red leader has promised that 'the wheels shall clog with peasant meat',[32] but in the end it is actually a Chinaman who has the courage to lie down on the tracks, trusting that the driver will make the old-fashioned mistake of bringing his train to a halt when he sees a body on the line.

Looking out of their increasingly hard-pressed columns, the German soldiers of Barbarossa also came to see the advancing Soviet enemy as fearsome and barbaric: a racial creature incapable of independent thought, yet tenacious and apparently immune to suffering. Close to nature, the Red soldier was a master of camouflage: an elemental beast who thrived in darkness, swamps and fog, and could vanish into the ground in a moment. In their overwhelming assaults the Soviet soldiers seemed, according to Generaloberst Rauss, 'to grow out of the earth, and nothing would stop their advance for a while . . .'[33] This alien propensity was terrifying for the *landser* or infantryman, but by the winter of 1942–3, it was not so reassuring to be in a tank among this vividly imagined horde either. As Major General von Mellenthin put it, 'the German armoured units were like isolated rocks in a vast ocean with the Russian masses rushing past to their right, to their left, and far behind'.[34]

This was a scarifying transformation for the German soldiers, who had started the war 'sitting on our lorries and telling dirty jokes', as one wrote in his diary in September 1939, a few hours before the opening assault on Poland.[35] After the initial exhilaration of 'the hurried rush forward', came a slow Hell in which the tank, once the symbol of an unstoppable Aryan spearhead, now felt more like a hollow boulder, buffeted and scorched by a fiery deluge, and threatened by primitive and unanticipated weapons, including the unnerving 'spectre of the mine-dogs' that had been used against German tanks in the 1941 advance on Moscow.[36] Laden with explosives and with a six-inch spindle detonator sticking up from their backs, these animals were trained to crawl under approaching panzers, and caused considerable apprehension, even though the Germans adopted a policy of shooting every dog in sight, with the result that some mine-dogs are said to have taken flight and crawled under Soviet tanks for shelter. By November 1942 it was found that Hitler's tanks could even be delayed by mice, gnawing their way through vital electrical flexes.[37]

'Tank fright' may have been the predominant Soviet response in the early weeks of the German invasion, but it was the Soviet machines that now defined the war – not just the incapable T-26s or the vast 52–ton KV II, a 'lumbering mammoth' that could be immobilized with a shot to the treads,[38] but heavy Josef Stalins, which made their first appearance towards the end of 1943, and the medium T-34, which for Rauss represented 'the heart of the Russian armored force' – under-gunned but tough enough to resist German anti-tank fire and versatile too: wide-tracked, with a powerful engine, high ground clearance and a low silhouette.

Rauss recalls one such machine that had been immobilized with a direct hit in the fighting along the middle Donets in February 1943:

when German tanks approached, it suddenly reopened fire and attempted to break out. A second direct hit again brought it to a standstill, but in spite of its hopeless position it defended itself while a tank-killer team advanced on it. Finally it burst into flame from a demolition charge and only then did the turret hatch open. A woman in tanker uniform climbed out. She was the wife and co-fighter of a tank company commander who, killed by the first hit, lay beside her in the turret.[39]

A provocative find that, especially for German soldiers raised on the Nazi cult of woman as maiden and mother, guardian of race and home. Yet Rauss never doubted the lethality of the Soviet Union's female warriors nor their formidable if 'sub-human' qualities as 'political fanatics, filled with hate for every opponent, cruel, and incorruptible. The women were enthusiastic Communists – and dangerous.'

According to John Erickson, some 800,000 women and young girls – real people rather than mere creatures of Communist ideology – were mobilized in the Soviet war effort.[40] Thousands were drawn into digging anti-tank ditches in Leningrad, Moscow and elsewhere, or working under unimaginable conditions in arms factories or coal mines. Many served the Red Army as signallers or doctors and nurses, but Soviet women also distinguished themselves as warriors: fighter and bomber pilots, partisans, machine-gunners and snipers. On the front line they survived both the lack of provision, exemplified by the oversized male greatcoats in which they waddled about 'looking like hayricks', and also the derision of their male comrades who were given to shouting, 'Who's this babe?' and muttering about 'a powder-puff division'. They crawled out into no man's land with a rifle; and some proved capable even when it came to hand-to-hand combat, with its terrible sounds of crunching bone and tearing cartilage.[41]

Soviet tankmen may have disliked the thought of women joining them, but many would serve (and also die) as medical orderlies with armoured units: clinging to the side of tanks as they drove into battle, desperately trying to keep their feet clear of the tracks, while ever ready to pull men out of the turret hatches of burning tanks as circumstances required.[42] There were also women driver-mechanics, tank commanders and even platoon commanders. One of the most famous examples was Lieutenant Alexandra Boiko, who, together with her husband, wrote to Stalin offering to donate 50,000 roubles to the cost of building a tank and asking that they should both be trained at the Chelyabinsk Tank Technical School so that they could then drive the machine they had paid for into action on the front line. After a short period of training (Soviet tank drivers were routinely sent into battle after barely more than an hour's practice), Alexandra Koitos took command of a vast 45–ton Josef Stalin tank and, with her husband serving as driver-mechanic, fought her way through the Baltic states and on through Poland and Czechoslovakia into Germany.

Many women also bought and pushed their way into service with the smaller T-34 medium tanks. Maria Oktyabrskaya, a posthumous Hero of the Soviet Union, went to the tanks after her husband was killed in action. She too offered to pay for a tank with her savings, requesting that she should be trained to fight with it: her machine, in which she was to be killed in 1944, was called Amazon. Others started out as medics, like Irina Levchenko, who, after being so seriously wounded that she was registered for military retirement, pushed her way into the Stalingrad Tank School and ended the war as a Lieutenant Colonel and Hero of the Soviet Union, still only just past twenty years old. Financed by donations from her family, the public and a schoolgirl from Omsk, Yakaterina Petlyuk's tank, named The Kid, saw action at Stalingrad, Kursk and Kiev. The unstoppable Marina Lagunova fought at Kursk and in the assault on the Dnepr river; even after losing both her legs when her tank was destroyed, she learned to drive again and became an instructor with a tank training brigade.

German infantrymen, or *landsers*, became acclimatized to other monstrous sights as the expectation of a quick if not clean mechanized victory gave way to what one shocked soldier, Mielert, told his wife were 'horrible days . . . None but the participants can understand what happened here . . . I have been hunted as one would only hunt a wounded animal, have sat five hours in a swamp, in ice cold water up to my stomach, under continuous fire from a tank.'[43] Driving over bodies became part of the degenerate routine of the Eastern Front. In October 1941 dead Russians were being used to further the German advance, their corpses being laid out as logs or planks in front of Germany's motorized units to assist their passage through marshy areas.[44] But by 1943 there was nothing unusual about the sight of tanks 'driving heavily over that moving mass of human flesh', reducing bodies to 'bloody paste' and rolling on with terrible remnants clinging to their treads.[45]

To begin with, German tank men might have inspected destroyed Soviet machines with interest, like those that Malaparte saw standing over one wrecked specimen in the early days, shaking their heads to mutter victoriously, 'Yes, yes, but . . .'[46] Soon, however, it would be death and abject monstrosity, rather than just the science of mechanized warfare, that knew no sides; and then looking into a destroyed Russian tank would be a more taxing experience. Hans Werner Woltersdorf was among a group of men who peered into one such blasted machine: 'Had the first grenades not pierced it? Indeed, they had. The men looked into the tank, and were near vomiting, so they didn't look further but instead went away, embarrassed. A headless torso, bloody flesh, and intestines were sticking to the walls . . . It wasn't good to look into the tank . . . One always sees oneself sticking to the walls in a thousand pieces like that, without a head.'[47]

As the war went from bad to worse, training in the art of mechanized warfare gave way to brutal measures designed to harden soldiers up for the coming onslaught. This is how it was for Guy Sajer, a Franco-German infantryman with the Gross Deutschland Division. He underwent training in the spring of 1943, at a camp near the Ukrainian town of Romny, a hellish institution with the words: 'We are born to Die' emblazoned over its entrance.

One day we were given anti-tank exercises – defensive and counterattack. As we had already been taught to dig foxholes in record time, we had no trouble opening a trench 150 yards long, 20 inches wide, and a yard deep. We were ordered into the trench in close ranks, and forbidden to leave it, no matter what happened. Then four or five Mark-3s rolled forward at right angles to us, and crossed the trench at different speeds. The weight of these machines alone made them sink four or five inches into the crumbling ground. When their monstrous treads ploughed into the rim of the trench only a few inches from our heads, cries of terror broke from almost all of us . . . We were also taught how to handle the dangerous Panzerfaust, and how to attack tanks with magnetic mines. One had to hide in a hole and wait until the tank came close enough. Then one ran, and dropped an explosive device – unprimed during practice – between the body and the turret of the machine. We weren't allowed to leave our holes until the tank was within five yards of us. Then, with the speed of desperation, we had to run straight at the terrifying monster, grab the tow hook and pull ourselves on to the hood, place the mine at the joint of the body and turret, and drop off the tank to the right, with a decisive rolling motion. Thank God, I myself never had to mine a tank coming straight at me. Lensen, who promoted to ober, and then sergeant, partly because of his prowess in this exercise, gave us a demonstration which no suspense film could ever hope to equal. His assurance was partly responsible for his horrible end a year and a half later. [48]

Lensen may have failed, going the same way as the two machine-gunners Sajer once saw being furiously crushed under a Soviet tank: 'the treads worked over the hole for a long time, and . . . the Russian crew kept shouting, *"Kaputt, Soldat Germanksi! Kaputt!"*' But other German *landser*s described the extreme horror of trying to enact this manoeuvre, using methods of 'hand to muzzle' combat that had already been tried and tested against T-34s by the 'tank annihilation squads', set up in 1941, of Theodore Eicke's SS Death's Head Division. [49] One anonymous soldier left an account of pulling the ripcord on the magnetic mine he was trying to attach to an approaching T-34, only to discover that the machine was pasted all over with anti-adhesive concrete; the tank turned to crush him, but he had fallen back into a slit trench and was only saved by the fact that, when the machine was right on top of him, he got the thing stuck to its bare steel belly. [50] Hans Werner Wolterdorf got lucky too:

We sneaked up to it through the wood from behind . . . My heart was pounding . . . I climbed carefully on to the tank from behind and approached the hatch cover . . . Damn! How did one get the cover open? I braced myself against the turret with my thighs and tore at the cover until I realized that a bolt was fastened with a padlock. So the crew was locked in . . . They were riding in a sealed coffin.

Unable to squeeze his grenade in through the available aperture, Woltersdorf used his flare pistol instead. There were shrieks and cries from inside, and then a 'fearful thunderclap . . . I couldn't get the men from the Moscow tank brigade out of my head. What a drama must have been played out in their coffin!'[51]

Some of the most potent testimony to the monstrosity of that war came from members of Paulus's Sixth Army during their last days in the encircled Stalingrad pocket. Seven mailbags full of letters came out on the last plane to take off before the Red Army's ring of fire was closed. They were impounded by the Nazi authorities, and the names of both senders and addresses obliterated. It is thought that the Nazis imagined printing some of them as a heroic tribute to those who had died at Stalingrad, until they read them and found tormented civilians emerging from beneath the cover of their uniforms to denounce the criminal cause that was Barbarossa, in words that even Goebbels couldn't convert into props of Nazi glory. The letters, which only survive in 'transcriptions' prepared by the compiler of the original 'Stalingrad Report', Heinz Schröter, must now be counted unreliable if not entirely fictional documents, but their huge post-war impact has nevertheless given them a wishful measure of historical reality.[52] 'All around me', as one of these apocryphal correspondents writes to his Monika, 'everything is breaking up, a whole army is dying, and the days and nights are on fire.'[53] Another apologizes for the brevity of his letter, explaining: 'my thoughts keep disintegrating like those houses under gunfire'. One more described his life as a 'psychological monstrosity', and thought he would never sleep again:

On Tuesday I knocked out two T-34s . . . It was grand and impressive. Afterward I drove past the smoking remains. From a hatch there hung a body, head down, his feet caught, and his legs burning up to his knees. The body was alive, the mouth moaning. He must have suffered terrible pain. And there was no possibility of freeing him . . . I shot him, and as I did it, the tears ran down my cheeks.[54]

By the last days those soldiers' tears were freezing over everything: tears for their enemy, tears for themselves and their comrades, and tears for their shattered war-machines too. 'I have wept so much in the last few nights that even I find it unbearable. I have seen a comrade weeping, too, but he had a different reason. He was weeping over his lost tanks, of which he had been desperately proud. And incomprehensible as my weakness is, I can fully understand a man mourning over inanimate war equipment.'[55] The writer of this nameless missive from the steppe appears surprised by this peculiar form of grief. He goes on to explain to his unknown addressee that while he himself had always been easily moved to tears by the cinema and books, or by the sight of animal suffering, he has 'never been affected by the loss of material things'. As a soldier, he knows that 'no tanks are animate' and he could never have 'bewailed those tanks that were used as artillery on the open steppes when there was no more petrol left and which were shot to pieces with so little trouble'. And yet, 'the fact that a tough, uncompromising soldier, and a brave man at that, should have wept like a child sufficed to move me to tears last night'.

As defeat closed in, even the charisma of the German tank was to become dysfunctional. This may not have been the case in Normandy in the summer of 1944, where the legendary 'invincibility' of the Tiger was found 'paralysing' by the Allied soldiers who knew that their Cromwells and Shermans were, in the German phrase, mere 'Tommy-cookers' by comparison. According to one British participant, David Holbrook, the decision to call the Mark VI the Tiger was 'a subtle stroke of psychological warfare' and one that fomented an 'hysterical fear' among British soldiers, who were quickly dismayed to find that a burning Sherman would emit mocking smoke rings as well as shouts and monstrous gouts of fire.[56] There may only have been thirty-six of those superior German machines in Normandy, yet, as Holbrook recalls, the Tiger was 'the thing in our minds . . . a formidable thing'.[57] On the Eastern Front, however, there came a time when the General Inspector of Panzer Troops felt obliged to insist on a less fantastic understanding of these machines and their capabilities. In September 1944, in response to a report describing how the Soviet infantry fled at the mere sight of a Tiger tank, and claiming, optimistically, that the Red Army's heaviest tanks seemed to do the same ('When a Tiger appears, most Josef Stalin tanks turn away and attempt to avoid a firefight'), he nevertheless came out against magical thinking of the kind that had long attended the tank. He insisted that 'statements like "thick fur", "impregnable", and the "security" of the crews in the Tigers, which have become established phrases by other units and also partially within the Panzertruppen, must be wiped out and invalidated'.[58]

Many German infantrymen may well have craved the 'thick fur' of a Tiger tank during the last winter of retreat, but the men of the depleted panzer divisions found themselves endangered by the ignorance of the grenadier and infantry officers under whose command they often fell. In a report submitted in November 1944 the commander of one regiment complained that his Tiger II tanks were being 'shoved from division to division and, by inappropriate employment, given tasks that were not achievable and couldn't be carried out'.[59] They were being ordered to stand guard over battle lines without close infantry protection (lacking a machine gun, the Porsche-Tigers were particularly vulnerable to unseen attack), obliged to accompany weak infantry forces into unscouted terrain in total darkness, or dispatched down forest roads where trees made it impossible to traverse their guns. Correctly employed in concentrated mass, a Tiger force 'will always bring success', but the commands to which they were now often subordinated had no understanding of the true 'combat principles' of tank warfare.

Another report, from a battalion of Mark V Panthers sent to the Eastern Front in January 1945, also charged that senior infantry officers had reached 'a low point' in their

understanding of the needs and capabilities of the Panzerwaffe . . . The Grenadiere commander sees in the Panzer a cure for all of the difficult combat situations, because he doesn't know and can't recognize the weaknesses and limited capabilities of the Panzers. The Grenadiere commander sees in the Panzer a strong, armoured, powerful monster with a giant gun without recognizing its disadvantages such as weak side armour, limited sight capability, and lower manoeuvreability in comparison with the SPW [armoured infantry carrier].[60]

The grenadiers would desert their tanks during a battle and then come back 'to ask why the advance hasn't started again and why the battle lasted so long!' They would complain every time tanks slowed down, as if they were magical spells that could reasonably be hurled across the steppe or into forests where they would not even be able to traverse their guns for trees.

There are Grenadiere that prefer to see the Panzers only advancing forward. Every warranted halt and observation based on Panzer tactics makes them impatient. When Panzers are halted somewhat longer in front of a village that has been reported to be heavily occupied by the enemy, in order not to run into flanking fire from an enemy Paknest or dug-in enemy tanks, these actions are laid out as lack of zeal . . . The view that 'Panzers must again learn to drive forward' is sometimes voiced on the spot, where driving forward would mean massive destruction.[61]

In this way did the German tank force die, denouncing the mythologies of the wonder weapon, as it was driven back towards Germany, where eventually even the greenest training units that remained were thrown into the path of what General Rauss would dub, archaically for a panzerman, 'the super steam-roller' of the victorious Red Army.[62]

*

The last German to believe in the irresistible power of the tank may have been Hitler himself. It was he who had led his armies to destruction: coming up with the crazy and inconsistent objectives of Operation Barbarossa, deviating from plans, disrupting and sacking his generals, fatally delaying their advance at crucial moments, ordering them to stand fast against overwhelming Soviet counter-attack and thereby drastically reducing their ability to manoeuvre. And yet, to the very end, he and his Minister of Propaganda, Goebbels, were trying to inspire their defeated armies with 'talk of new miracle weapons'[63] that went far beyond the Panthers, Tigers and King Tigers.

'Technology is always opposed to mythology,' wrote Hitler's architect and wartime Minister for Armaments and Munitions, Albert Speer, in March 1952, when news reached him in Spandau prison that a Soviet T-34 had been installed in Wannsee, within the American sector of Berlin, as a monument to the victory over Nazism.[64] Informed that there were similar monuments all over Europe, he noted that this was basically a 'Hitlerite idea', and recalled how, in the summer of 1941, he had walked with Hitler through the Chancellery park, along a gravel promenade where classical sculptures were already interspersed with model tanks of Type IV – a reminder of the victory boulevard that Hitler planned to create in Berlin, in which captured weapons would be mounted on marble plinths. Being a classicist, Speer felt 'an instinctive dislike' for the project, but Hitler was convinced of 'the stunning effect that must necessarily be produced by the display of military triumphs. The fact that his – and my – architecture operated with traditional stylistic elements, with columns, arcades, cornices, pilasters, which were hardly compatible with the caterpillar treads of armoured vehicles, or with cannon barrels and gun carriages, seemed to trouble him no more than it does the Russians today.' Speer was convinced that 'the products of industry are not susceptible to monumentalization' and that, far from appearing 'mythic', Hitler's victory boulevard 'would have been an embarrassment'.

Yet he knew that even as a military commander Hitler had been 'inclined to think of the psychological rather than the military potency of a weapon'. Moreover, 'the objections of military experts meant nothing to him once he began ranting about the devastating psychological effect'. Hitler may have applied this psychological theory to the Stuka dive-bomber, for which he devised a siren capable of emitting the 'demoralizing howl' he 'regarded as having a greater effect than the explosive force of the bombs'. But such 'psychologising of all military technology became sheer grotesquery' at other times. There was the occasion when Hitler begged Rommel and Speer to construct rotating flame-throwers like vast garden sprinklers, which could be used as 'the prime defense against invasion. The idea was that nothing terrified a soldier more than a jet of flame aimed at him.'[65] But that was modest compared with Hitler's recurrent vision of a vast supertank:

I recall a characteristic episode that took place in May 1943 in the East Prussian headquarters. At the time, Hitler was being shown a full-size wooden model of a 180-ton tank that he himself had insisted on. Nobody in the tank forces displayed any interest in the production of these monsters, for each of them would have tied up the productive capacity needed to build six or seven Tiger tanks and in addition would present insoluble supply and spare-parts problems. The thing would be much too heavy, much too slow (round twelve miles an hour), and moreover could only be built from the autumn of 1944 on. We – that is Professor Porsche, General Guderian, Chief of Staff Zeitler, and I – had agreed before the beginning of the inspection to express our scepticism at least by extreme reserve.

In keeping with our arrangement, Porsche, when asked by Hitler what he thought of the vehicle, replied tersely in a noncommittal tone: 'Of course, mein Führer, we can build such tanks.' The rest of us stood silently in a circle. Otto Saur, observing Hitler's disappointment, began to rant enthusiastically about the chances for the monster and its importance in the development of military technology. Within a few minutes he and Hitler were launched on one of those euphoric raising-the-ante dialogues such as I had occasionally had with Hitler when we discussed future architectural projects. Unconfirmed reports on the building of superheavy Russian tanks whipped them up further, until the two, throwing all technical inhibitions to the wind, arrived at the overpowering battle strength of a tank weighing 1,500 tons, which would be transported in sections on railroad cars and put together just before being committed to battle.[66]

In a footnote, Speer adds that, at the suggestion of an engineer, Hitler had actually ordered such a tank to be built a year or so before. Its short-barrelled mortar would have the extraordinary calibre of eighty centimetres, and there would be twin turrets too, each one armed with a fifteen-centimeter long-barrelled cannon. The front would be armoured to a thickness of 250 millimetres, and it would be driven by four U-boat diesel motors, yielding a total of 10,000 horsepower.

At our request a much-decorated tank colonel had been brought from the front. He finally managed to say that a single hand grenade or an incendiary charge exploded anywhere near the ventilator opening could set fire to the oil vapours of these vehicles. Hitler, irritated by the disturbing remark, replied, 'Then we'll equip these tanks with machine guns that can be guided automatically in all directions from inside.' Turning to the tank colonel, he added in a lecturing tone, 'After all, I can say for myself in all modesty that I am no amateur in this field. It was I who rearmed Germany.'[67]

So far as Hitler was concerned, it was only he who had forced the Wehrmacht to equip itself with modern weapons in the first place. In 1942, while battling with his army chiefs over his disastrous strategy in the east, he had denounced his general staff as cowards whose minds were 'fossilised in obsolete habits of thought'.[68] As he told his Chief of Operations General Jodl on the evening of 16 August 1942, he had thrown money at the Wehrmacht under his Four Year Plan, only to be told repeatedly that orders were not being passed on and that 'The Wehrmacht does not want it.'[69] He had had to step in and order 'mass production, without limit'. 'Tanks, I was told, were of no value unless they were both light and fast; again after a hard struggle, I imposed my will and ordered the manufacture of heavy tanks.'[70] He also recalled how, before the war, he had himself visited Krupps and arranged for SS units to be equipped with Panzer Mark IVs – only to find, once war had been declared, the previously reluctant army 'shrieked to high heaven that these tanks be allotted to them!'

When it came to his supertank, Hitler got further towards reality than might have been expected. There was never any chance of a tank weighing 1,500 tons; yet, on Hitler's orders, Professor Ferdinand Porsche and Dr Muller of Krupp are said to have started designing a supertank in March 1942. As was the way with such projects, the brief had changed considerably by the time Hitler was shown that wooden mock-up of the 188-ton Behemoth that had started out as 'Mammoth' and since been renamed 'Mouse'. Two prototypes were built. Maus 1, was equipped with a customized Daimler-Benz aircraft engine and a Krupp turret weighing fifty tons alone. Its performance in trials is reported to have been less than impressive. The engine could hardly shift the thing and the suspension system gave up the ghost on the first day. It was realized that there was hardly a bridge in the world that would be able to support this fantastic contribution to the art of mobile warfare, so the prototype was fitted with a snorkel in the hope that it would at least be able to proceed under water to a depth of eight metres. A special fourteen-axle railway wagon was built to move it up to the battle front and, Allied bombing raids allowing, tests were still being carried out at the proving ground near Kummersdorf in the summer of 1944, when Krupp was ordered to stop work on the project. For years after the war it was rumoured that both Maus tanks had deliberately blown up before Kummersdorf fell to the Red Army, and even that Maus 2, which had been mounted with a formidable 128 mm cannon, had seen action in the unsuccessful defence of that site. Yet in the nineties, a Mouse turned up along with other gargantuan Nazi innovations including a massive 'Elephant' anti-tank gun, at the Museum of Armoured Forces at the Kulinka tank testing ground, near Moscow, where it is said to have been put through further inconclusive tests in 1951–2. The thought of this unlikely monster still polarizes opinion on the tank-enthusiasts' websites: realists insist that it was quite useless and point to the number of Panthers that could have been made with the metal, while more visionary participants in the discussion insist on the improving effect the sight of one of these things might have had on the morale of retreating German soldiers, if they saw a Maus advancing up the line to take on the Communists once and for all.

Curzio Malaparte's 'House like Me', Capri

16

Tributes: A Flag for Europe
and the True Birth of Punk

Captain Curzio Malaparte came out of the war quite well. He had some further interrogations to undergo, this time with the government that had replaced Mussolini's fascists, but nothing, really, to delay his return to Capri and to the 'House like Me', which he now painted bright red. Perhaps the shocking events he had witnessed as a war correspondent prompted him to reappraise the autobiographical edifice he had dedicated to revealing the spirituality of things. The house, which has recently been called an 'architecture-poem hybrid',[1] may still have evoked the cell on Lipari in which Malaparte had once been imprisoned. But the war had surely reduced the enigma of the 'sail', actually a low and curved white wall, with which Malaparte had ordered his builders to bisect and screen the roof terrace. There it was, as the homecoming war correspondent would have been pleased to find, perfectly placed above scale-like steps to catch the wind that was driving this hard-nosed structure, by now revealed as a symbolic landship for the twentieth-century soul, further into the rocks.

A place to write, then, and to memorialize the Second World War. Not for Malaparte an apologetic image offered in a sentimental spirit of reconciliation or cure, and certainly no classical monument either. No weeping mother or child; and no heroic citizen-soldier rising up to slay the beast. No unrendered ironstone boulder like the one that would be displayed in the United Nations building in New York, symbolically suspended between its latent uses as sword or ploughshare. And certainly not a T-34 mounted on a sculptured plinth, and left to rust over a square or war cemetery, as in Prague, Berlin, Poznan, Breslau and so many other devastated places. Malaparte's tribute was to be a surreal testimonial, at once self-aggrandizing and cruel. A truth snared in stylized lies, it would eternalize the shock of that uniquely vile war by treating it in the spirit of the communist peasant in Ivanov's *Armoured Train 14–69*: a simple man who knew that 'You can't mend steel, you have to refound it.'

The first monstrous 'novel' that Malaparte extracted from his war experiences, *Kaputt*, was to be a huge best-seller all over the world. But

Malaparte cut deeper in *The Skin* (1949),[2] a sequel that was to appal the Vatican so much that it was quickly placed on the index of books proscribed to Catholics. In these pages, the Eastern Front is a haunting memory, brought suddenly to mind during the Allied liberation of Rome in June 1944. Captain Malaparte had been a liaison officer with the American Army by that time, and he describes driving into the city just behind the jeep of 'General Cork' of the Fifth Army, which had just fought a protracted and costly battle against the First German Parachute Division garrison at Cassino. The column is spearheaded by tanks: Shermans this time, from which gum-chewing American soldiers beam out at a delighted populace. Asked to guide the liberators into the capital, Malaparte selects the picturesque route used by Sulla, Caesar, Cleopatra and Tiberius in the days of ancient Rome. So there they go along the Via Appia Antica, tanks clattering past ancient towers and cupolas, cruising over ruts and grooves dug by the wheels of Roman chariots. As they pass the tombs of Roman nobles, the sound of their tanks is augmented by a chorus of 'Gee!' and clicking Kodaks. A monument to Cleopatra causes General Cork, who is actually modelled on the Fifth Army's General Mark Clark, to shout for clarification, 'a famous signorina, wasn't she?' They roar on up to the Colosseum ('Our bombers have done a good job,' yells the general at the sight of this ancient ruin). All goes fine until the column reaches the heights of Tor di Nona. It is here that a man comes running along the road towards them waving his arms in welcome and yelling: 'Long Live America,' but then he slips and falls under the tracks of a Sherman tank. The man is flattened, reduced to a mere 'carpet of skin', and the rapture of liberation is suddenly replaced by furious accusation from the crowd. Jumping down from his vehicle to watch this scene unfolding, Malaparte manages to land, with his own grotesque but undeniable literary flair, three years back and a thousand miles to the north-east.

To begin with, it was enough for Malaparte to observe that a 'dead man' is 'just a dead man', more or less of a kind with a dead dog, and that many times over the previous years, he had seen, 'on the roads of Serbia, Bessarabia and the Ukraine', the imprint of a dog that had been killed and crushed by a tank. Repeatedly, there had been nothing left but an imprint or an 'outline', 'drawn on the slate of the road with a red pencil. A carpet made of the skin of a dog.' Pursuing this comparison further, he remembered a day in July 1941, when he had arrived in Yampol, on the River Dniester. And there lying in the dust of the street, was 'a carpet of human skin'.

It was a man who had been crushed by the caterpillars of a tank. The face had assumed a square shape, and the chest and stomach were splayed out at the sides in the form of a diamond. The outspread legs and the arms, which were a little apart from the torso, were like the trousers and sleeves of a newly-pressed suit, stretched out on the ironing-board. It was a dead man – something more, or something less, than a dead dog or cat.

Malaparte had sat on the doorstep of a ruined house opposite that flat-tened corpse with his companion and witness Lino Pellegrini. They saw 'light transparent mist' rise from the marshy bank of the River Dniester, and clouds of black smoke spiralling upwards from the burning houses of Soroca beyond that. And they watched the approach of a gang of Jews in black caftans, equipped with spades and shovels. Forced to dispose of the dead Russian soldiers, these doomed figures came up to lift that flattened outline from the dusty road. They pried at the edges of the thing, and then raised it – a 'fabric' consisting of 'a fine network of bones' that peeled off the road like 'a starched suit'. Once the dead man had been loosened in this way, one of the Jews impaled the head with the end of his spade, and the party slowly moved off, talking among themselves in soft, muffled voices. It was, according to Malaparte, the onlooking connoisseur of war and its horrors, 'an appalling and at the same time a delicate, exquisite, unreal scene': 'The standard-bearer was a young Jew with long hair that hung loosely over his shoulders. His eyes shone forth from his pale, lean face with a melancholy, unwavering stare. He walked with his head high and on the end of his spade, like a flag, he carried that human skin, which flapped and fluttered in the wind exactly as a flag does.'[3]

As this medieval figure steps slowly through the burning world, Mala-parte leans over to his friend and witness Lino Pellegrini and says: 'That's the flag of Europe. It's our flag.' Somewhat disgusted, Pellegrini rejects the thought: 'A dead man isn't the flag of a living man.' Asked to describe the inscription on the flag, Pellegrini suggests that it may be no more than 'a dead man is a dead man'. But Malaparte counters by insisting that the flag really says that 'a dead man is not a dead man', and that 'if you knew what a dead man was you would never sleep again'. Pellegrini tries again with 'the dead must bury the dead', but Malaparte concludes that the true mes-sage is that, 'this is our country's flag . . . A flag made of human skin,' for in the ruin of nations, 'our true country is our skin'. The wind ruffles the dead man's hair, which is matted with blood and dust and stands up 'like the rigid mane of a plaster saint', and the two Italians also argue about the meaning of this hideous sight.

And that is how it ends, with Malaparte and his friend, who still protests his belief in a different flag inscribed 'God, Freedom, Justice', falling in behind that procession of doomed Jews: the standard-bearer followed by gravediggers with spades on their shoulders, shuffling along to the river bank, where a pit is already full of charred and broken bodies of men and horses. Being a literary man, Malaparte thinks of Gogol, who was born in the Ukraine, and also of Taras Bulba, who died at the stake there, but not before ordering his Cossacks to flee the Poles by hurling themselves into the river. Meanwhile, the young standard-bearer marches on, head held high, eyes fixed on the distance with a glassy stare that reminds Malaparte of Pieter Bruegel's 'Dulle Griet', or 'Mad Meg' as she is more commonly known – a medieval figure stepping through the chaos with open-eyed indifference, as if guided by an archangel: 'He walked straight ahead, enveloped in his black kaftan, seemingly oblivious of the stream of vehicles, men, horses, baggage-waggons and gun-carriages that rushed in furious haste through the village.' Eventually, this procession arrives at the disposal point, where Malaparte sees 'our country's flag, the flag of the country of all peoples and all men, cast into the filth of the communal grave'.

It was this artfully frozen image of utter degradation that Malaparte superimposed on the liberation of Rome. Asked to convey American condolences to the family of the man who has been crushed by the Sherman, Malaparte and a US Army chaplain drive through the flag-decked city and down an alley to a 'mean-looking' house, where they find the flattened man stretched out on a bed and attended by a grieving woman, who is worried at the difficulty of making this object fit for burial as a human being. Her difficulty underscores Malaparte's suggestion that, in the age of the tank, a dead man is no longer really a dead man at all: he is more like a carpet or a piece of sticky paper. Malaparte suggests that it could be worth 'bathing him with a little hot water. The water might make him swell and give him a more human appearance.' There is no heating in the house, so they try a sprinkling of cold water. The 'horrible thing' swells a little, but only enough to justify a minor shift in metaphor, from the thickness of a tailor's cardboard pattern to that of felt.

Shouts of victory and the 'proud blasts' of bugles resound through the streets of the ancient Roman city outside. Yet Malaparte knows that, even though every citizen that evening may have believed himself a hero like Brutus or Cassius, none are really any different from the thing on the bed: 'skins cut to look like men, miserable human skins'. Having registered the war's redefinition of the human condition, Malaparte turns to see a classical

Renaissance building out of the window: not a dome or a cupola this time, but Michelangelo's Capitol, rising from the hill that had served as the symbolic hub of state and empire in the time of Augustus as well as Mussolini. That, he concludes, is the place for his flag – 'our flag, the true flag of us all, victors and vanquished, the only flag worthy to fly that evening from the tower of the Capitol. I laughed to myself as I thought of that flag of human skin flying from the tower of the Capitol.'

There were critical, self-searching tributes on the German side too. In his poem 'I read about tank battles', Bertolt Brecht remembered the 'Augsburg dyer's son' who as a child had tried gamely to match young Brecht's skill at marbles: 'Where are you now among the grey tanks driving / in clouds of dust to lay sweet Flanders low?'[4] And how, as would be added in the postwar years, was it possible for you to get there? Some Germans looked to the philosophy of Friedrich Nietzsche as they tried to grasp the cause of this unfathomable disaster: he, surely, had seen the 'blond beast' coming – fired up by 'the will to power', and hearing 'the roar of life' in the sound of his surging motors.[5] Others offered a more psychoanalytic explanation, including Dr Wilhelm Reich, the originally Freudian analyst who had taken up the cause of proletarian sexual politics in the nineteen-twenties, campaigning for a freer expression of children's sexuality, a greater availability of contraceptives, and the legalization of abortion.

Reich had been obliged to flee Germany when Hitler came to power in 1933 but he continued his researches in Scandinavia and America. Writing *The Mass Psychology of Fascism* during the war, he argued that the mechanization of warfare practised by the Nazis was coupled with a repressive mechanization of the human character. As the exploiter and forger of this connection, Hitler was the true father of the 'punk' personality.

Reich arrived at this conclusion with the help of an article that appeared in the *New York Times* on 24 June 1942. In this account of Rommel's early success against the British in Libya, the Afrika Korps's stunning victories were attributed to the fact that the Eighth Army had 'speed, anger, virility and toughness: as soldiers in the traditional sense, the Germans are punk, absolutely punk'.[6] Rommel and his commanders may have been scientists, 'continually experimenting with and improving the hard, mathematical formula of killing' ('war is pure physics to them'), but the soldier was a professional killer with 'the psychology of the daredevil track rider. He believes he is the toughest man on earth.' Reich declared this the best description of 'mechanical militarism' that he had ever read: 'It discloses at one blow the complete identity of mechanistic natural science, mechanical human structure, and sadistic murder.' Those German panzer men were 'mechanical automatons', and, rather than learning how to fight in the same mechanical way, those who would defeat fascism must instead come to understand: 'How does such a complete functional identity of machine, man and scientific murder come about?' Writing as the war raged on, Reich conceded that answering this question would not help to determine 'whether the mechanical monstrosity will reach the oil wells of Baku or not', but it was nonetheless the only way of really facing down the Nazi tank and its 'punk' army.

For this increasingly unconventional psychoanalyst, overthrowing fascism entailed getting back to the human orgasm. It meant reconnecting with the animal core of humanity and freeing up the stream of sexuality and relatedness to nature: the wellspring of what Reichians to this day are not afraid to call 'peace and love'. Repressed by the machine-civilization that had dulled and 'rigidified' his sense of himself, modern man had learned to think of his brain as a 'control centre' and the 'ruler' of his organs, to which it was connected by telegraphic nerves. In buying into the mechanistic view of life, he had become 'plasmatically rigid', distorting his genital function as he 'armored himself against the natural and spontaneous in himself'. Reich considered this 'biological stiffening' to be a literal tightening of the neuro-muscular tissues, and he identified it as the precondition of the 'fascist plague', with its dead hierarchies and its attempt to establish 'dominion' over nature and supposedly lesser races. The Nazis had taken the young men whose sexual energy Reich had sought to liberate in the early thirties, and rebuilt them as tanks.

Reich argued that this beaten and perverted inner 'nature' would continue to haunt the rigidified fascist personality. Such a 'return of the repressed' might take the form of a sentimental love of pets in some, but it could also put a twisted kind of soul into the armoured mind of the Führer-craving killer punk:

No matter how immobile his pelvis and back may be; no matter how rigid his neck and shoulders may be; or how tense his abdominal muscles may be; or how high he may hold his chest in pride and fear – at the innermost core of his sensations he feels that he is only a piece of living organized nature. But as he denies and suppresses every aspect of this nature, he cannot embrace it in a rational and living way. Hence, he has to experience it in a mystical, other worldly, and supernatural way, whether in the form of religious ecstasy, cosmic unification with the world soul, sadistic thirst for blood or 'cosmic seething of the blood'.

In this way, human mysticism, which represents the last twisted trace of true human vitality, 'becomes the fountainhead of mechanical sadism'.[7]

It was Reich's view that there would be no liberation from, or indeed for, the tank man without liberation of the inner core of 'nature' that lies deep within: repressed and deformed by the metal of character armour, by patriarchal social organization, and by the mechanistic metaphors that had replaced 'the self-regulatory intelligence of the body plasma' with a 'goblin in the brain'.[8] As he attempted to theorize that inner 'nature', Reich took the libido of Freud's theory, and reconceived it as a form of life-energy that actually existed – describing it first as 'bio-electricity' and then as 'orgone', the enigmatic stuff that he claimed could sometimes be seen as a blueish glow around mountains and trees, and that was also emitted by people during periods of emotional excitement and orgasm.

Convinced that this vital life-force could be accumulated, Reich came up with a curious apparatus in which the remarkable, life-enhancing effects of 'orgone' could be measured, whether in mung beans or in human beings, who are nowadays advised to disrobe before they enter an 'orgone energy accumulator' for their chosen period of time. As for the structure of an orgone box, the essential thing is that it should be entirely enclosed with metal. One expert, James DeMeo, PhD, of the Orgone Biophysical Research Laboratory in Ashland, Oregon, recommends an interior layer of steel or iron sheet (copper, lead and aluminium are to be avoided), and then goes on to advise that more orgone will be accumulated if the wall is built up of many alternating metal and non-metal layers, in which steel or iron sheeting is interspersed with soil, cork sheets or (especially recommended) beeswax. 'Thick Fur' has no place on this list, and the resulting composite is not of a kind that would impress the engineers of Chobham armour, in which ceramic materials are mixed with metal.

Reich's therapeutic answer to the tank was not to prevail, any more than his theory of the 'emotional desert', or the 'cloud buster', a disconcertingly gun-like instrument consisting of hollow metal pipes earthed in water, with which he claimed to be able to manipulate orgone in the atmosphere. Reich imagined many applications for this vital stuff: it could be used to alleviate cancer, to cure burns and hasten the growth of plants, to bring down the rains on desert areas and perhaps also to detoxify nuclear waste. But the American Food and Drug Administration insisted, with unyielding fervour, that he was a mendacious crank who had been fraudulently claiming to cure cancer patients with his orgone boxes. By the fifties, the FDA had obtained a court injunction ordering the banning and even the burning of the books and papers in which Reich expounded his orgone theory. Reich died in an American jail in November 1957. Yet for the Reichians who still pursue the unorthodox science of 'orgonomics', the metal box has certainly been regained.

PART IV

The Coming of the Merkava

The Death of God has left us with a lot of appliances.
Avital Ronell, *Finitude's Score*

Settler children celebrating the Jewish holiday of Purim while Israeli soldiers keep guard in the Palestinian Authority controlled part of Hebron, Sunday, 23 March 1997.

The Steeling of Zion

Christ and the disciples are suddenly frozen in the attitudes of Leonardo's 'Last Supper'. They are bathed in bright light 'as if a war is passing over them'; and then the following words are sung across them:

> Don't you hear Messiah coming in his tank, in his tank?
> Messiah in an armour-metalled tank?
> I can see the pillared fire, speeding on the metal tire
> Over muck and out of mire
> And the seraphim a-shooting from its flank!
> O Messiah, he stands grimy in his tank![1]

A scene from Sir Harrison Birtwistle's opera, 'The Last Supper', which had its première in April 2000 at the Deutsch Staatsoper, a much-bombed and restored building in what was once East Berlin. Far from merely dramatizing the New Testament story, the librettist Robin Blaser has imagined Christ returning after two thousand years to re-enact the founding ritual of Christianity in the knowledge of the bloody history that has since unfolded in his name. Hence that arresting stanza, quoted from a poem by the Ukrainian-born Jewish Canadian writer A. M. Klein, which comes as close as the pious Jews of East Europe ever got to having a tank with which to defend themselves against Nazi mass murder.

First published in November 1941, Klein's 'Ballad of the Days of the Messiah' has since been left to clank along more or less unregarded. 'The effect can only be called grotesque,' so one of A. M. Klein's critical admirers has said of this exceptional composition.[2] Another has declared it 'hopelessly marred' by a rhythm 'more suited to a jig than a ballad'.[3] Yet Klein's jog-trot tank is only dire in the truth it tells about the twentieth century. Here is the Messiah, the appointed of God who might be expected to travel on nothing more supercharged than a white donkey, trying to bring Justice and Redemption to a modern world that has already crashed the gates of Paradise with a technological apocalypse of its own making.

In an article called 'War: The Evolution of a Menagerie', written during the build-up to war in February 1939, Klein condemned the 'mad warriors' (among whom J. F. C. Fuller can certainly be counted), who claimed that 'methods of warfare have been the most important factors in the development of civilization'. What these dreamers called 'evolution' was actually a perverse return to savagery: 'The submarine – is not that the swordfish of battle? And the tank owes its existence mainly to the admirable example of the tortoise, which suggested a method of defence even to the great Caesar . . . What a commentary upon mankind, which instead of evolving from the ape, devolves to the beast.'[4]

Though his ballad was written before the Nazis had unleashed their 'final solution' on European Jewry, Klein knew there was nothing redemptive about the tanks that were already leading Nazi killing squads into the ghettos of Eastern Europe. A passionate Zionist, Klein was also a great denouncer of anti-Semitism, whether it be found in Nazism, which Klein had attacked from the earliest days, or in the combined 'gall and stupidity' of the Polish government in exile which, less than a year after Hitler's blitzkrieg swept over their country, chose to worry about 'surplus' Jews in Poland, and even invited Jewish organizations to help find ways of 'kicking Jews out of Poland' once the Nazis were defeated.[5] So what was this deeply concerned man doing, a year or so later, writing a ballad that comes so close to mocking the beliefs of that same imperilled minority?

'Ballad of the Days of the Messiah' is partly derived from a song by Benjamin Wolf Ehrenkranz, one of the great nineteenth-century Yiddish singers, originally from Galicia, who moved around performing and often extemporizing his songs in coffee houses, inns and at public gatherings. The ballad in question, 'Moshiachszeiten', satirizes the orthodox belief that in the coming 'days of the Messiah' the faithful will feast on roasted Leviathan (in some versions the flesh of Behemoth is served up as well) and specially preserved wine, and gloat at the sight of 'heretics' like Ehrenkranz himself choking on their own mistaken malice.[6]

In Klein's poem the Leviathan is cooked up with the help of 'powder and torpedo', and the satire is adjusted too – redirected towards the desperate circumstance of the ghetto Jews who could only defend themselves against Hitler by praying for divine intervention. Klein did not write as a believer. In a newspaper editorial written in January 1930, he had considered the false Messiahs who had imposed themselves on the Jewish people over the centuries of exile.[7] The Jews of the ghetto may have been so immersed in sorrow and despair that they valued faith more than their own survival, yet for Klein 'the Messiahs were the straws to which the drowning men clung'. If there had been an alternative by the early thirties, that was largely thanks to Theodor Herzl's Zionist vision of a Jewish national homeland, which was already being made a practical reality in Palestine:

Although we can admire the beauty and sincerity of the belief in the miraculous intervention of Divinity Itself in our affairs, still rationalism forbids us to stand with arms akimbo, stolidly awaiting the Courier of the Lord. Our aspirations towards the Homeland must be achieved by our own personal efforts, and not by a blind expectation of another's aid. The Roast Leviathan which is to be in Messiah's days, in our days shall be savoured in Palestine![8]

It was not contempt that animated Klein's apparently mocking ballad but Zionist impatience, similar to that expressed by Vladimir Jabotinsky, the Zionist visionary, youth leader and champion of armed self-defence, who travelled the ghettos of Poland and East Europe in the 1920s and 1930s, warning their Jewish population that disaster was coming, and that they must evacuate to Palestine – 'liquidate the diaspora', he had beseeched them, 'or the diaspora will surely liquidate you'.

As a fantasy of power dreamed up on behalf of the powerless, Klein's redemptive tank is in the magical tradition of the Golem, as told in the ancient Jewish legend that Klein himself kept revisiting as 'one of the brightest fables to issue out of the darkness of Jewish diaspora history'.[9] In its most popular version, the Golem was a human 'automaton' fashioned out of the mud of the Moldau river by a 'Hebrew Faust' called Rabbi Loew in sixteenth-century Prague. Conjured up and initially controlled by Kabbalistic manipulation of the tetragrammaton, the four-lettered name of God, the Golem was a mechanical man that came to the aid of its persecuted people in their hour of need: a 'clod of earth' become, miraculously, a powerful 'defender of the faith'.

The Nazi threat prompted A. M. Klein to replace the Golem with a fantasy tank, but the coming of the state of Israel, proclaimed in 1948 and secured through a bloody war of independence that Klein himself saw as the culminating synthesis of Jewish history, was to initiate more practical transformations. The roast Leviathan of Messianic prediction may not have materialized, as Klein himself joked during an ecstatic visit to the Jewish homeland in August 1949,[10] but other miracles were already under way. The creation of Israel would relegate the Golem to the museum of the diaspora, a quaint 'medieval monstrosity' that lingered on as a mere legend in a world governed by science and secular power. It would eventually also replace

Klein's useless Messianic tank with a machine that can be seen as well as believed.

Squaring the triangle

In Tel Aviv I went to the David Gate as instructed, and presented myself at a checkpoint guarded by an adult child with an automatic weapon resting in her arms. A phone call produced a lieutenant who escorted me through the Ministry of Defence compound to the building where I was to meet Major General Israel Tal, the man who presided over the design, development and also the naming of Israel's own tank: the 'Merkava', which is Hebrew for 'Chariot'.

A small man who seems quite unaffected by his enormous fame as a national warrior, Major General Israel Tal still works here, even though now in his seventies and long since retired from his famously impeccable uniform into jeans, a light blue shirt and a casual blouson jacket. Such is Tal's line of business that he has inevitably been likened to one of his own machines – a kind of human ironclad, whose 'exterior sternness cannot hide his sensitivity'.[11]

Apologizing for the lack of staffwork and explaining that the Israeli Defence Force has been too busy really to develop that side of things, Tal leads me into an office that is equally casual about the trappings of ceremony, military or otherwise. It is a scruffy, polytechnic kind of place. There were battered metal cabinets full of papers, and manuals, including, as I soon find out, the British Army publication that exalts Tal's breakthrough at Rafa in the Six Day War, treating it as a model of 'Adherence to Mission', which in Israel refers to a military operation that holds true to its fundamental aim while also allowing its units to improvise in the unpredictability of actual conflict. His office is littered with projectiles – big shells cut into cross-section; a display rack full of rod penetrators – and the wall is adorned with photographs of tanks. The Merkavas Mark I to III may look much the same to the inexpert eye. But not to Israel Tal, who can see the precise difference between life and death, as he glances from one to the next.

Israel Tal has long been known for his philosophical turn of mind. In Israel's tank literature he is celebrated as the kind of man who will pause to condemn the very idea of nationalism, even while preparing to fight tooth and nail for his own nation; who will turn on the eve of a massive war of survival, and start talking about Spinoza, whose work he studied at the

Hebrew University in Jerusalem, shortly before he was appointed Commander of Israel's Armoured Corps in the mid-sixties. So when he pauses and observes that 'the tank is a compromise', I am not immediately sure that we have actually arrived at our true subject matter. Perhaps the tank is a compromise in the philosophical sense that all material things, according to Spinoza's *Ethics*, are 'nothing but affections of the attributes of God', i.e. the finite and imperfect vehicles through which the divine substance is revealed. Perhaps it embodies a compromise between the Jewish dream of a peaceable national homeland and the practical requirements of Israel's creation and defence.

Yet Tal is actually talking about a different conundrum, closely connected to the laws of physics, which has been faced by everyone who ever designed a tank. From the earliest models to the most recent, all tanks represent a triangular reconciliation of three partly contradictory parameters: firepower, mobility and protection. A tank is inevitably a compromise because gains according to one parameter often entail losses in another, and every tank-producing nation has evolved its own 'tank triangle' as its designers and engineers have struggled to come to terms with this intractable fact. Some countries have placed more emphasis on firepower or mobility, but Israel, which produced the Merkava after the October War of 1973 in which Israeli tank crews suffered grievous losses, is famous for giving priority to protection above all.

Characteristically, however, Tal introduces his theory of the tank by rejecting the whole concept of the 'tank triangle' as logically flawed. The Merkava is unique because it is founded on the realization that 'Protection' should not be conceived as a separate parameter alongside 'Mobility' and 'Firepower'. Experience has taught the Israelis that protection actually belongs among the working systems of the tank, like the engine, automotive powers, the tracks, and everything that provides firepower. 'What we say is that the tank is a synthesis, or a compromise between firepower and mobility, and not the synthesis of the three parameters.' The point he stresses is that 'You strive to produce a machine that would provide firepower and mobility. Protection is only a by-product, like the gun and the engine and everything else.' This, says Tal, 'is our original approach' and 'the most important difference between our design and all the rest in the world'.

The Israeli reconceptualization of the tank owes much to a programme of ballistic research that, Tal insists, is second to none. Having fought six wars with its Arab neighbours since 1948, Israel has had ample opportunities to study the effects of battle, both on its own machines, and on those it has captured: 'In my view, we are leaders in tank technology. We have thousands and thousands of direct hits of Western anti-tank weapons against Soviet tanks, and of Soviet weapons against Western tanks.' As the victor in all its wars, Israel has had the additional advantage that 'the battle-ground remained with us'. Tal has filing cabinets stuffed with reports on those closely studied hits – with each incident of penetration carefully photographed, measured, and accompanied by an evaluation and a report explaining exactly what happened and at what range. This one, he says of a randomly selected example, is a Merkava that received six direct hits in the 1982 war with Lebanon and yet nobody inside was killed. Here's a tank that withstood an armoured piercing projectile, and another that was penetrated by a shaped charge from a T-62. This, he says of his inventory, is the data-base, and no other country has anything like it. If the Merkava is the best tank in the world, that is because it is the only tank to have been created by tank soldiers from within their own experience – the very dream, as it hap-pens, that Fuller had for the Medium D.

In traditional tank design, protection is largely a matter of armour-plating, used to protect both the crew and the working systems of the tank. But the Israelis found that everything looks different once protection is reconceived. For a start, you realize that protection actually contributes to mobility, enabling the tank to come closer to the enemy, and also to fire-power, since, by coming closer, the machine will be able to increase its accuracy and penetrating capability. 'So in that respect, the capability of the tank to launch a very high volume of fire is an outcome, not only of the gun but also of its protection, whether it can absorb many direct hits, and face the enemy close. Its firepower is stronger, naturally, and in the same way, its mobility is increased too. So this is the most basic thing that makes the Merkava a different tank from any other tank.'

But there is another conceptual leap in Tal's revisionist theory of the tank, and one that was of glaring importance after the October War in which so many Israeli tank soldiers were killed in their machines. Having redefined 'Protection' as belonging with the systems of the tank, Tal and his team realized that it actually consists not of one but of two distinct parameters. The first concerns the extent to which the tank gives protection to the people inside it. And the second is 'to what extent it provides protec-tion to itself, to the entire system'. And we found that 'these two para-meters are completely different from one another. We can provide protection to people inside a tank, many many times more than to the entire system we call a tank.'

So the designers of the Merkava had set out to build their new tank on this knowledge. They were convinced that the people in a tank could be protected even though the tank itself might be destroyed and immobilized. This could be done 'provided – and this was our conclusion – that the people be placed at the very centre of the tank, and all the materials of the machine be arranged around them'. So, in order to kill the people, you must first penetrate not just through armour-plate, but through all the materials of the tank. That is the story of the Merkava: the crew at the centre, and then everything else arranged around them.

Tal reckons that 75 per cent of the weight of the Merkava participates in this business of protecting the tank's crew, whereas in a conventional tank, the proportion may be only 50–55 per cent. The screens and the suspension system are made out of ballistic steel, and both the engine and the transmission are placed in the front of the tank for the same reason. Every working part has been appraised from the same point of view: 'it is not enough that it functions in the optimal way. It should be located in such a way that it also helps with the basic protection of the tank.' The men who worked the tanks of earlier generations might find it hard to believe, but the Merkava even seeks to protect its crew by surrounding them with diesel fuel. As Tal explained, the fuel tanks, which are incorporated into the wall of the Merkava, are specially designed to become 'dynamic machines' when the tank is hit. The impact of an incoming projectile creates hydrostatical pressure, which is used to turn the fuel itself into a resistant medium pushing back at the projectile. As the philosophical Tal says of this ingenious dialectical manoeuvre, 'We make the projectile commit suicide. The energy of the projectile is used to defeat it.'

Meanwhile, the Merkava's new 120 mm high-pressure gun is not bad either. Tal, who was himself a formidable tank gunner, claims that the dispersion of a group of shells fired at 1,000 metres is now less than the diameter of the gun tube. 'If you tell that to my colleagues or experts in England, they would say that it is bullshit, that it cannot be. But it is. Sometimes the dispersion of the group would be only two centimetres . . . They will tell you that is impossible, but they don't know.' He picks up a fin-stabilized rod penetrator that happens to be lying nearby in his office, and remarks that, if fired at 45 degrees from the same gun, it would fly to an altitude of 50 km and travel 200 km. Military experts in England might dismiss that as nonsense too, but 'you tell them that we killed many, many of our enemies with it'.

Over the years, the Israelis have also experimented with the technology of armour itself. In the late seventies, they produced the Blazer system of explosive reactive armour, panels of high explosive sandwiched between metal plates, which would explode outwards when hit by an incoming projectile. This was used with some success on Centurions and other tanks in the 1982 war with Lebanon, and more effective systems of reactive armour were later developed in the USSR. However, the armour on the latest Merkava is innovative in a different way: it is passive armour but attached in a modular form that ensures that the machine is 'always young, like Dorian Gray'. Move four bolts, as Tal puts it, and you can put on a new panel – the tank is always the most up to date, you don't have to design a new tank every time you want to improve the armour. This, says Tal, is unique. 'The Merkava is the only tank in the world that is modular,' although it would appear that other tank-producing nations, including the French, have since caught up.

Tal counts off other noteworthy qualities of Israel's tank. It has the capacity to carry more people than its crew: there is space for infantry, staff officers or commanders. A low entrance at the rear of the machine makes it possible to evacuate soldiers from the field under fire, while also enabling the crew to escape in case the tank is hit – including injured men who might be unable to haul themselves out through the upper hatches of a burning tank. Tal also mentions the tracking device that can lock the gun on to a target, and thanks to which it no longer matters whether the Merkava is moving or stationary or even what speed it is going when it fires: the hit probability is exactly the same . . .

However, he is most proud of the protection factor. Previous experience had taught the IDF to expect that 26 per cent of the soldiers wounded in modern battle would suffer burns. Since 1948, the Israeli Armoured Corps had seen more than enough of its men roasted alive or falling out of their tanks with their skin hanging off them in smoking shreds. Yet, as Tal insisted, of the fifty or so tank soldiers who had so far been wounded in the Merkava during the recent war with Lebanon, not one was burned by fire. This improvement was owed partly to the introduction of fireproofed munitions containers, which prevent munitions exploding even at 1,000 degrees. However, it was primarily owing to the fact that the fighting compartment in which the crew reside is entirely dry, electrically operated and quite without contact with fuel or even hydraulic oil. In short, the Merkava Mark III, is as safe as a monstrous killing machine can be: a tank for a small country of four million that, humanitarian considerations aside, must do everything it can to minimize losses among its trained tank forces.

Old iron

Israel Tal means several things at once when he describes the Merkava as 'a national asset'. There is pride in the fact that it is Israeli through and through, with each successive Mark depending less on components imported from abroad. The Merkava is a symbol of self-reliance, proof that Israel, so long obliged to make do with obsolete tanks cascaded down from retooling Western armies, can produce what it needs – at least in one branch of military technology – to command its own theatre of war. It is also, so Tal insists, 'one of the most economical products that Israel has produced'. In saying this, he is referring not to the huge American subsidy that went into its initial development, but to the more homespun calculation that enables him to claim the Merkava as 'the cheapest tank in the world'. The important thing in the Israeli economy is how much local currency you have to spend for each American dollar you save. If each dollar you save costs you less than the exchange rate, then you are making a positive contribution to the balance of payments, and it is from this point of view that the Merkava is 'the most economically worthwhile product that Israel produces'.

And yet the tank has conquered Israel's soul as well as its economy, as was forcibly demonstrated in *Tsahal*, a film about the Israeli Defence Force that Claude Lanzmann made in 1994. The tank soldiers interviewed here are utterly committed to the cause of national self-defence, and profoundly bonded with their machines. Yuval Neria, a reservist who saw many of his comrades killed around him in the October War, speaks most movingly of these excoriating experiences, and the difficulty of having been the sole survivor from his tank unit. Yet he then observes, with a helpless smile, 'I like tanks very much, I like to drive them. I like to shoot from them. A tank is a very beautiful machine. It is a very strange machine. It's not human at all, but it's very dynamic, very vital.' Yanosh Ben-Gal, who commanded the Seventh Brigade in the Golan Heights in the same war, explains what it was to join the IDF, having come to Palestine as a child from Poland via Siberia, India, Teheran and Egypt: 'I joined the army in 1955. The army was my home. I was born again. My second birth was in a tank.' Ilan Liebovich, a company commander filmed at the end of five years with a Centurion, ventures that Centurions have souls: 'if you give a tank your love, your care, it will give you everything back. There is a connection between a soldier and his tank.' He too describes his tank as

my home . . . Every one has his own tank. When you have your own tank you know it better. You have little places to put little things, in order to have your own comfort. You can be in these tanks for days. You have to build them like your second home: pictures, a place to put your little packet of cigarettes, places for your special tools . . . in order to get them as fast as you can if you have a problem.

These soldiers, who have given so much to their state, testify to the adjustments that history has imposed on the Jewish personality that now recognizes a war machine as home. In the words of one contemporary commentator, the state of Israel has converted the Jew 'from a member of a disempowered and vulnerable religious minority into an armed citizen-soldier of a sovereign state governed by a Jewish majority'.[12] In doing so it has gone far beyond the changes that A. M. Klein, the author of that Messianic tank, saw unfolding in the earliest days of the new state. 'Reconstructed Israel will its Israelis reconstruct,'[13] predicted Klein after visiting Israel in 1949, and it was already apparent the remade Jew would have little in common with the defenceless, Messiah-craving victims who had been slaughtered like 'sheep' by the Nazis.[14] Yet as a literary man sent to travel the new state in search of a new Isaiah, Klein was disconcerted by the 'hard intransigence' of the emerging *sabra* poets, who 'scoffed at all delusions intellectual, adored only the soil and the gun', and had no time for the traditions of the ghetto with its 'melting, paralysing self-pity'.[15] Noting the 'hard, clipped, guttural' Sephardic pronunciation of the Hebrew that was now lined up so aggressively against the 'soft, caressing' tones of Yiddish, he also found himself at odds with the 'crew of chauvinists' who argued so impatiently for 'the negation of the Diaspora' – a 'pernicious' and arrogant doctrine, as Klein now described it, which sought to achieve what 'all the tyrants of all the ages failed to achieve with fire and sword'.[16] Scandalized by this tendency to deny the Jewishness of the non-Israeli Jew, Klein warned that Israel should not take the route of Ireland's Sinn Fein – 'Ours Alone' was not a proper slogan for the new Jewish state.

A similarly metallic imagery, with its polarization of hard qualities and soft, turns up in *The Seventh Day,* an influential book made up from a series of reflective conversations among kibbutzniks who served with the IDF during the recently won Six Day War of 1967. The editors of *The Seventh Day* set out to capture the reactions, immediately after that astonishing victory, of the triumphant *sabras*, 'whose toughness has become a legend, but whose inner world is so hard to penetrate'.[17] Many if not all of those urgent post-war discussions show the historically toughened *sabra* to be sensitive and humane at heart, still hoping to come to peaceable terms with the defeated Arab. The participants admit that some Israeli soldiers had to be restrained from committing outrages against Arab prisoners and civilians, and they worry that the restraint may not always hold in the future. The word 'sabra' started out as the name of the prickly pear cactus, and in its application to the new native-born Israeli Jew it implies a similar compound of 'inner sweetness and hardened façade'.[18] Yet these soldiers seem to blame the displaced and defeated Arabs for this tanking of the Jewish soul. As Amos Oz asks, in words that have since been cited as proof that Israelis are capable of blaming their victims just as the Nazis once did,

> the question is how long we, as ordinary flesh and flood, can bear it . . . Can you imagine living this way and still being the same person, the same nation in a few years' time? Can it be done without our getting to the stage in which we'll quite simply hate them? Just hate them. I don't mean that we'll take a delight in killing, or turn into sadists. Simply deep bitter hatred for them for having forced such a life on us.[19]

Iron in the soul, and in the very fabric of the state too. The metal of the Merkava may be modular and strengthened with diesel fuel, but as Major General Israel Tal himself has made clear, Israeli armour has long been alloyed with more spiritual matter too. In his preface to the battle memoirs of Avigdor Kahalani, one of Israel's most honoured tank heroes, Tal commended the extraordinary courage displayed through successive wars by the men of the Israeli Armoured Corps. Writing in 1975, he noted that they 'may again be called upon to form an iron wall protecting Israel until peace shall finally prevail'.[20]

That phrase, 'Iron Wall', might resonate with the 'Iron Curtain' that the former tank pioneer, Winston Churchill, saw descending across the continent of Europe shortly after the Second World War, and first named in a speech given at Fulton, Missouri, on 5 March 1946. But in the Zionist imagination it evokes the older vision of Vladimir Jabotinsky, the revisionist Zionist (celebrated by A. M. Klein as 'the active subconscious of all Israel'),[21] who spent his life, advocating and also organizing armed Jewish self-defence. He founded the Jewish Legion to fight the Turks under British command in the First World War, and then, in Jerusalem in 1919, he reformed his force to create Haganah, the Jewish Self-Defence Corps and precursor of the Israeli Defence Force. By the 1930s Jabotinsky was also the 'spiritual father' and early commander-in-chief of the Irgun, the underground terrorist organization led by Menachen Begin, which ran numerous 'retaliatory' raids against Arabs, and mounted a violent revolt against the British mandate in Palestine.

Metal had a potent symbolism in Jabotinsky's imagination. Indeed, he projected his concern with the arming of the Jews in Palestine back into his novel of Biblical times, *Samson the Nazarite*, which is much concerned with the symbolic power of the sword. Samson gains a sword, even though 'it is forbidden by the law of the five cities to hand over iron to the people of his tribe', and his last words to the people of Israel begin with the injunction: 'They must get iron. They must give everything they have for iron – their silver and wheat, oil and wine and flocks, even their wives and daughters. All for iron! There is nothing in the world more valuable than iron.'[22]

By the time he wrote that novel, in the later 1920s, Jabotinsky had already turned the phrase 'iron wall' into one of the leading slogans of Zionist intransigence and struggle. In 1923 he had published articles acknowledging Arab objection to the Zionist Settlement as both rational and well founded. The Zionist project was indeed to build a Jewish homeland, not a mixed, democratic state that would offer equal opportunities to all inhabitants; and to await Arab agreement for that project would be tantamount to abandoning Zionism. Jewish settlement would only be able to make progress 'under the protection of a power independent of the native population – an iron wall, which will be in a position to resist the pressure of a native population'. Since, in public at least, Jabotinsky regarded the expulsion of the Arab population from Palestine as 'totally unthinkable', his iron wall was not the same as an armoured border, nor would it be as inflexibly placed as the Iron Curtain that Winston Churchill would later see stretched across Europe ('from Stettin in the Baltic to Trieste in the Adriatic'). It was to operate internally, and on an altogether more mobile basis, through the years when the Jewish majority was built. Like Tal after him, Jabotinsky imagined a future condition in which mutual concessions could be granted and peace would prevail – a peace in which the defeated, if not actually displaced, Arabs would learn to live as good neighbours with the victorious Jewish majority. In the meantime, however, 'the only way to achieve a settlement in the future, is total avoidance of attempts to arrive at a settlement in the present'. In Jabotinsky's view it was far better that the iron governing the settlement in Palestine should be Jewish than composed of British bayonets.

So besides being an economic miracle, the Merkava is an emblematic machine built in the gap between violent means and virtuously perceived ends. Its armour is symbolically connected with the essential stuff of the Zionist imagination: the iron of the empowered and no longer diasporic

Jew, of the hard-edged state, even of the character of the Zionist woman, as praised by Vladimir Jabotinsky in words that are displayed on the wall of the Jabotinsky Institute in Tel Aviv: 'of this I am certain: every woman is an archangel . . . a soul woven from silken and armoured threads . . . Unbreakable material'.

First moves

'He jumped to the head of the line, huh?' Israel Tal chuckled when I mentioned that the first tank ever to fire on an enemy had been commanded by a British Jew, Basil Henriques, who claimed only to have achieved this 'ghastly' distinction (in France on 15 September 1916), because his lumbering machine had got to the front line twenty minutes earlier than expected and he had just kept going, having no idea where he was.[23] Tal also volunteered that a British armoured vehicle had attended the formation of his own earliest memory.

It dated from August 1929, when Arabs in Jerusalem, Hebron and Safed, inflamed by the Mufti of Jerusalem, picked up swords, clubs and knives and set upon their Jewish neighbours in a series of savage attacks. Tal, who was five years old at the time of these massacres, recalls that an Arab mob, rampaging through the devout and unarmed Jewish quarter of Safed (an ancient centre of kabbalistic wisdom), tried to burn him alive, along with his mother and sister. Rescued by the Jewish underground, they were escorted into the centre of the town by British and Arab policemen. Tal was being carried on his uncle's shoulders as they passed an armoured car. Perhaps there was an altercation, for the soldier standing in the turret knocked Tal's uncle in the head with the butt of a Lee Enfield rifle, and the two of them fell to the ground. That is how the world began for Israel Tal, and after that founding moment 'we fought all the time, all along the years we fought. When I was a child I held a rifle in my hand.'

A photograph on Tal's office wall reveals that Palestinian Jews were already thickening up the metal of their vehicles by the time of that symbolic confrontation in Safed. It shows an improvised armoured truck somewhat reminiscent of the boiler-plate vehicles used by the Post Office in Ireland in 1916. Dated 1921, it was taken at Hedara, a kibbutz that was fighting for survival against Arab opposition. Under the British mandate over Palestine, Haganah, the underground Jewish defence organization, was permitted to improvise armour for some of the trucks it used to take supplies into Jewish areas, but it was not until the state of Israel was proclaimed in

November 1947 that the armouring of Zion began in earnest. Israel was attacked by neighbouring Arab states when the British mandate finally expired in May 1948, but the fighting had broken out before that, with the disengaged British military standing by as attacks and counter-attacks spiralled away right under their noses.

One Israeli chronicler has dated the beginning of the Israeli Armoured Corps to the Arab ambush of a convoy of doctors, nurses and university students making their way to the Hadassah Hospital and Hebrew University on Mount Scopus.[24] This outrage, which was actually a reprisal for the considerably more bloody massacre carried out at the Arab village of Deir Yassin by Menachem Begin's Irgun, may well have led the Haganah to intensify their search for armour, assisted by compliant British soldiers. The first acquisition, a GMC armoured car that came complete with machine guns and ammunition, was spirited out of the British base known as 'Bevingrad', and hidden under a haystack in a remote Jewish settlement. The second, which came with a two-pounder gun, was stolen from a barracks in Jerusalem. Prior to their departure from Palestine, the British destroyed many of their armoured vehicles by pushing them off a precipitous ridge. A more or less derelict Sherman tank was purloined on its way to this place of destruction, and later refitted with essential parts scavenged from vehicles abandoned at old British dumps (the vital track plates were reclaimed from the beach at Haifa Bay, where the British had used them to create a tank road across the sand).[25] Two Cromwell tanks were also stolen from a depot in Haifa with the help of sympathetic British drivers. Haganah brought these stealthily acquired machines into service alongside trucks fitted with improvised armour. Some of the latter only had 'sandwich' plates made of plywood and steel, but others were named 'butterflies' after their wing-like, armoured sides; and there were also 'roadblock breakers', fitted with special iron fixtures at their fronts. By May 1948, when the British departed and the newly proclaimed state was attacked by the better-equipped armies of Lebanon, Syria, Jordan, Iraq and Egypt, Israel's force of improvised and patched-up vehicles had been drawn together as the 8th Armoured Brigade under the *Palmach* leader Yizhak Sadeh.

This was a hybrid outfit manned by volunteers, many of them recently arrived settlers who had served with various armoured units in the Second World War. Its first tank battalion, known as the 82nd, had two companies, whose members were barely in a position to communicate at all. The 'Russian' company was commanded by Major Felix Beatus, a former Red Army tank commander, and manned by more or less experienced immigrants from East Europe: its common languages were Russian and Yiddish. The second company was predominantly English-speaking. The brigade's expanding collection of armoured vehicles was equally international. Some of its tanks arrived as they were captured from the enemy, like a Syrian Renault that was taken undamaged at Kibbutz Degania by Lake Galilee, abandoned once its horrified crew had seen what a determined kibbutznik could do to a tank with a home-made Molotov cocktail. Others were more or less obsolete imports left over from the Second World War: Hotchkiss light tanks bought in France and illegally imported under the heading of 'agricultural machinery'; old and officially scrapped US Shermans, acquired variously in Italy or the Philippines, and mounted with ancient but unused Krupp artillery guns bought from Swiss mountain ordnance dumps.

The brigade carried out its first uncertain operations during the war of independence. Among them was Operation Danny, in which Jordanian forces were pushed back from the Jerusalem road, and there was also an armoured assault in the Negev Desert – in which a formerly British and reputedly unassailable concrete fort at Iraq Suweidan, was taken. The two battalions of the 8th Armoured Brigade pushed into Sinai, defeating an Egyptian counter-attack, dislodging Egyptians from strong points and getting as far as El Arish, before being ordered to withdraw – a Sherman, immobilized by its loss of a track, was left behind at El Arish, a relic that the Armoured Corps would revisit in successive wars to come. Other actions fell to the 7th Armoured Brigade, a new unit hastily mustered in the midst of the war. Equipped with half-tracks and armoured cars, it was manned largely by just-arrived immigrants released from British detainee camps in Cyprus. This force was launched into battle against Jordanians holding the police station at Latrun, where many of its members died before their names had even been recorded. It was then regrouped and taken north to assist in the securing of Galilee.

These were makeshift operations, at least one of which (an attack on Iraq-el-Manshieh carried out on 16 October 1948) is said to have been accompanied by a Russian chorus of: 'Where's the infantry?' shouted into tank radios by Major Beatus's horrified men as their antiquated Hotchkiss machines sank into Egyptian defence ditches.[26] Israel's multilingual armoured vehicles were susceptible to mechanical breakdown, and they sometimes got lost or strayed into minefields owing to their communication difficulties. Before long Major Beatus was replaced by Colonel Shaul Yaffee, who set about refounding the Israeli Armoured Corps with experienced men of the Haganah, who would then develop more effective methods of tank warfare that prioritized assault, mobility, and surprise. Yet in part the Israel Defence Force's famously distinctive doctrine of armoured warfare originates in these early, often chaotic engagements: the use of armour in combined arms forces, and the principle of the territorial front or *Ugdah*, which disposes its brigades as it sees fit, while working within an overall operational plan – even the principle that the officer leads from the front, and that the tank commander goes into battle standing up in his hatch, a dangerous position that nonetheless ensures a far superior commanding view. Training was continued in the same improvised spirit after the victory of 1949. The emergent Israeli Armoured Corps used abandoned or forcibly cleared Palestinian villages as assault courses and is said to have drawn heavily on tank scenes in Hollywood war films, and diagrams lifted from an American manual.

Some officers visited France to undergo training at Saumur, where they worked alongside visiting Syrian officers, and learned the art of the combined tank-infantry formation known as 'Sous Groupement Blindée'.[27] Yet if Israel's tank pioneers effectively reinvented the principles of armoured warfare, this was partly because international diplomatic sensitivities obliged them to raise their force without much assistance from other more established armies. Israeli tank doctrine was influenced by the methods of the *Palmach*, the strike forces of the Haganah, which had prioritized mobility, assault, and surprise. But it was also informed by the wider operational doctrine in which Israel was conceived as 'the Few Against the Many'. The IDF must be prepared to fight a 'war of survival', which should be short and intensely destructive of the enemy's larger force and equipment. This strong orientation towards assault was necessitated by economic considerations (full-scale mobilization would bring the Israeli economy to an immediate standstill), and also by geography, for Israel was small and lacked strategic depth in which to mount sustained defence.

Some of the armoured brigade's early manoeuvres are recorded as moments of farcical embarrassment. In 1951 a live-firing demonstration intended to show what tanks could do to support infantry ended in chaos, with shells exploding only thirty yards from the tanks that had fired them and scattering the now doubly contemptuous senior infantry officers who had come to watch. Events such as these combined, with the memory of failed tank operations in the War of Independence, to delay the acceptance of armour in the Israeli Defence Force, but impressions changed as the Corps developed. By that time the deputy commander of the 7th Armoured Brigade was Lieutenant Colonel Uri Ben Ari, the son of a German First

World War hero who had lost his father and ninety-three other members of his family to the Nazis. Ben Ari is said to have 'read about the armoured battles of the Second World War', studying the operations he was soon to emulate through the memoirs of German panzer leaders. [28] Be this as it may, his methods were demonstrated in annual exercises carried out in the Negev Desert, war games in which Blue Army went up against Red, while the top men drove around in jeeps and studied the results. In the 1952 exercise, Ben Ari led a massive armoured breakthrough, surprising a more conventional infantry force, and irritating senior officers including the Chief of Staff, Yigael Yadin, who objected to this thrust as a breach of the rules of the game. In 1953 Ben Ari's tanks and supporting half-tracks penetrated 170 km into 'enemy' territory, cutting through the opposition's flank to assault an infantry brigade position and causing such panic among the defenders that they threw down their weapons and ran. IDF commanders may have been have been infuriated once more, but the event was observed by Prime Minister Ben-Gurion, who ordered an increased allocation of tanks and ammunition for the Armoured Corps. [29]

The psychological or 'moral' effect of the tank undoubtedly had its uses in the early days, but the more practical capabilities of the Israel Armoured Corps would not be proved beyond doubt until the Sinai campaign of 1956, which was preceeded by a frantic arms race. Nasser had agreed a massive arms deal with Czechoslovakia in September 1955, but Egypt had also been supporting anti-French forces in Algeria, so the French supplied Israel with some 250 Shermans and light tanks, which were secretly offloaded at Haifa. Meanwhile, Israel's ordnance experts had introduced their own improvements to the Corps's ramshackle collection of existing machines. Following the example of the British engineers who, during the Second World War, had employed a counterweight to mount a large 17-pounder gun on a Sherman hull, thereby producing the 'Firefly' which was used against heavy German Tiger and Panther tanks in Normandy, they had mounted fast-firing French CN 75–50 guns on to the desert-worthy bodies of their old Shermans.

Launched at the end of October 1956, Israel's assault against a larger but also weaker Egyptian force in the Sinai was the culmination of an escalating and, from the Israeli side, also deliberately escalated series of raids and retaliations. Decisive events in this sequence include the hanging of two Jewish saboteurs in Cairo in January 1955. The Israelis retaliated with a bloody raid on Gaza, led by the ferocious Ariel Sharon, which left many Egyptians dead, and also put an effective end to the policy of moderation espoused by the Israeli Prime Minister of that time, Moshe Sharett. After the Gaza Raid

Nasser committed Egypt to attacking Israel with fedayeen units, first from the Gaza strip and latterly from bases in Jordan, Lebanon and Syria too. From April 1956, these state-run 'terrorist infiltrators'[30] took their campaign of assassination and sabotage into Israel. Israeli units mounted provocative and equally murderous 'retaliatory' strikes; and IDF Intelligence set about killing the fedayeens' Egyptian operators with parcel bombs disguised as books: the one that blew up in the face of Lieutenant Colonel Mustafa, the Egyptian military attaché who ran the fedayeen in Jordan, contained an exploding biography of Gerd von Rundstedt, the German tank general who had led blitzkrieg assaults against France and the Soviet Union during the Second World War.

Nasser's nationalization of the Suez Canal, at the end of July, brought Britain and France into a more or less acknowledged tripartite alliance with Israel – the background against which Israel's assault on Egyptian Sinai was launched on 29 October 1956. Egypt was dug in, having opted for fixed lines of defence, despite the urgings of their German adviser, General Farmbacher, who had fought with Rommel in North Africa, and who advocated a mobile defence, in which the enemy could be allowed to break through in order to be entrapped.

Israeli tank soldiers such as Colonel Uri Ben Ari, by now Commander of Israel's 7th Armoured Brigade, and Major General Chaim Laskov, recently appointed commander of the Israeli Armoured Corps, may also have recognized Sinai as 'perfect tank country' reminiscent of the North African Desert in which the British Eighth Army had eventually defeated Rommel and the Afrika Korps. But General Moshe Dayan, who had long denigrated the idea that tanks should have any role except as adjuncts sprinkled about to support infantry operations in small packets, entered the war with other ideas.

In the initial plans, armour was to be left out of the assault or, in the case of Ben Ari's 7th Armoured Brigade, used merely as a decoy, mounting a fake offensive in order to deceive the Jordanians. Indeed, one infantry commander even suggested that Israel's Sherman tanks should be taken by transporter to Suez, once it had been captured by the infantry, and parked there as a theatrical show of force.[31] Ben Ari was among those who argued for some supporting missions to be assigned to the tanks as part of the Southern Front. But, in the event, he found these concessions insufficient. Instead of waiting according to plan at a concentration area at Nahal Ruth, some twenty-five kilometres inside Israel, he had advanced towards the border, and was ready when the commander of the Southern Front ordered him to assist the infantry advancing with some difficulty against the well-defended village of Kusseima. So it was that Major Shmuel Gonen, surged over the ridge in his Sherman, riding out of a huge cloud of dust to fire the first tank round of the war – a dramatic moment that would be much mythologized in the years to come, even though argument continues as to the part the tanks actually played in the conquest of Kusseima. The 7th Armoured Brigade then moved on through the unguarded Deika Pass to attack Egyptian positions at Abu Agheila from the rear, overwhelming the equivalent of three infantry brigades in one hour.

Moshe Dayan is said to have been furious when he tried to track down Ben Ari and his force some twelve miles west of Kusseima, and found nothing but clouds of dust on the horizon as they poured west from there. The 7th Armoured Brigade had evidently started its own war, and was now twenty-five miles into Sinai: 'I recalled my childhood days when a herd of cows, stung to frenzy by summer flies, would go wild and bolt from my hands, while I, shamefaced and utterly at a loss, would watch them disappear into the distant fields, their tails high as a final act of defiance.'[32] The breach may have been disastrous from the point of view of discipline and yet, as Dayan concluded: 'Better to be engaged in restraining the noble stallion than in prodding the reluctant mule.' So, with Dayan's blessing, the whole Sinai operation was accelerated to keep up with the speeding Armoured Corps, which advanced 250 km to the Suez Canal in 100 hours, having fought intense battles over several fortified positions (Abu Agheila, the Daika Pass, the Rauffa Dam), routed a larger and better equipped Egyptian armoured brigade, and survived accidental assault from its own air force. The Egyptian collapse was greatly assisted by the threat of Anglo-French assault on the Suez Canal (initiated on 5 November, the day Egypt and Israel agreed a ceasefire) and, indeed, by the earlier intervention of the French and British air forces, which destroyed Egypt's air force on the ground over three days from 31 October, and then helped to clear the way for the IDF's advance through Sinai.[33] It would later be suggested that Israeli armour had only triumphed because it was effectively attacking the rear of an Egyptian force that was actually orientated towards British and French forces threatening the canal zone to the south. But in Israel, the 7th Armoured Brigade's breakthrough would be remembered as 'the outstanding feat of the war', a 'perfect "Blitzkrieg" style' of operation that laid the foundations for the 'brilliant' tradition of later years.[34]

Within Israeli armour circles, the 1956 Sinai campaign is remembered as the moment when IDF doctrine woke up to the real possibilities of mechanized warfare. Moshe Dayan was converted, the IDF was reorganized as a mobile armoured force, and the tank became the undisputed king of the battlefield. A new doctrinal credo emerged too. 'Adherence to Mission' replaces the detailed, blow-by-blow 'campaign' plans of most wars, with the insistence that while Headquarters may establish a broad plan of battle and, indeed, retain the right to modify it as things go ahead (a right known as 'Optional Control'), the unit responsible for implementing the plan is left to devise the best route to its achievement. Not for the Israeli Army the ever more detailed briefs passing down the chain of command, or the confusion that follows as combat troops await instruction from officers who are in no position to grasp the immediate situation. The Soviet tanks that were crushing an uprising on the streets of Budapest that same autumn were widely recognized as monstrous emblems of Stalinist inhumanity. But in Israel it had been demonstrated, once again, that with tanks, desert war could be a clean sweep pressed home with comparatively few losses – although not for the conscripted Egyptians who died in their thousands under the Sinai sun, or for the Palestinian refugees who found themselves trapped in the soon-to-be-annexed Gaza Strip, and liable to summary execution when the IDF went in to sort out the fedayeen for good.

Masada to Tel Dan

Moshe Dayan found time for a few reflective pauses as he roared around Sinai through the swirling dust and fire of the 1956 campaign. Visiting the Egyptian town of Kusseima in search of the bolted 7th Armoured Brigade, Israel's Chief of Staff glanced down to see a flint arrowhead, exposed along with other Stone Age shards and fragments by the tracks of one of his delinquent Sherman tanks. Picking up this memento before moving on to the next arena, he wondered, momentarily, about antiquity: 'who knows what wild tribe suddenly descended on this community thousands of years ago, scaring them into such panic flight that they left behind their implements, workshop and raw materials'.[35]

Tanks and archaeology seem often to have advanced together in Israel – two different approaches to the problem of securing the territory. Sometimes the tanks have gone in first, while the archaologists have followed in their tracks to unearth evidence of ancient Israeli settlement in the flattened Palestinian land. And yet it could also work the other way around. Yigael Yadin is remembered as one of Israel's great archaeologists. Yet while still in his early thirties, Yadin had also served as the IDF's Chief of Operations to Ben-Gurion during the 1948–9 War of Independence, and even then his archaeological knowledge had proved directly useful· to the Israeli Armoured Corps. In order to open access into Sinai, the Armoured Corps had to overcome an Egyptian force at Uja El Hafir, near the old border. Yigael Yadin had previously discovered an ancient Roman road through uncharted (and apparently impassable) desert into Uja El Hafir, so Yizhak Sadeh's armoured brigade followed this unknown approach to attack the Egyptians on an unprotected flank.[36] After that Yadin returned to his civilian vocation as Professor of Archaeology at the Hebrew University in Jerusalem, and the leader of excavations at Hazor in upper Galilee (1955–8). His most famous dig, carried out in 1963–5 with the assistance of the Israeli Defence Force, was at Masada, a raised plateau by the Dead Sea, where the Israeli sense of being the few against the many found the most potent corroboration imaginable as evidence emerged of the mass suicide of the Maccabees, ancient Israelites who for years had held out on their rock against the Romans until that last night in AD 73 when they chose death rather than captivity and subjection.[37] Masada was to become a uniquely special site for Israel, and particularly for the Israeli Armoured Corps, which, when commanded by David Elazar, developed what has been described as a 'Wagnerian' commissioning ceremony for young tank lieutenants: an oath of loyalty, sworn at midnight in a ring of burning torches on top of the Masada plateau.[38]

That combination of modern tanks and ancient archaeology took a different form in the very north of Israel, as I discovered as a volunteer at Kibbutz Dan in 1970. Intensive agriculture already dominated the whole Huleh Valley as it stretched out beneath the Golan Heights, conquered in the Six Day War a few years previously; but the ancientness of the land around Dan was still palpable. There was a temple to Pan in the nearby Golan village of Banias, and beyond that the looming ruin of Castle Nimrod, a twelfth-century Crusader (actually largely Muslim) bastion, which could be seen, but at that time definitely not visited, high up on the slopes of Mount Hermon. For the kibbutzim, however, the really defining site lay in the valley just on Israel's side of the old frontier with Syria.

A low hill to the north of the kibbutz, Tel Dan sits in a wooded nature reserve, close to springs forming a head of the river Jordan; and the digging, which commenced in 1966, had already revealed a large ramparted city said to have been settled by the Israelite tribe of Dan in the twelfth century BC. According to the Old Testament, Dan marked the northernmost point of the land of the Israelites, which once stretched from here all the way south to Be'er Sheva. After the division of Solomon's kingdom in the tenth century BC, it was at Dan that Jeroboam is said to have set up a golden calf and reinstituted its worship. No trace of that idolatrous object has yet been found, but the ongoing excavations have exposed many layers of settlement going right back to the fifth millennium BC. Early digging revealed a mud-brick gate with Canaanite arches, dating back to the second millennium BC, when Dan was known as 'Laish', a city mentioned in the ancient Egyptian Execratory Texts as well as in Vladimir Jabotinsky's novel *Samson the Nazarite*. More recently, interest has been concentrated on a different find: two fragments of an inscribed tablet, which speaks of Beth David or the 'House of David'. Some cite this tablet as proof that the old 'United Monarchy' of Solomon and David – i.e. the Biblical kingdom of Israel – really did exist. Others doubt the discovery altogether, suspecting it to be a displaced claim to the territory: a fake planted in the interests of present-day Zion.

It is said that Nebuchadnezzar once razed Dan, but in 1970 it was the memory of Syrian and Palestinian attempts to do the same again that still burned in the kibbutz. As volunteers, we were taken on a tour of the Golan Heights, and shown strong points that had been captured in the Six Day War, including Tel Azzaziyat, with its commanding prospect over the whole Dan area. We saw the cleared Palestinian village of Kfar Szold where, when Moshe Dayan finally chose to assault the Golan Heights in the last stages of the Six Day War (actually the day after Syria announced its acceptance of the UN-brokered ceasefire agreement between Israel, Egypt and Jordan), heroic Israeli engineers had driven eight bulldozers into a storm of hostile fire. They had effectively sacrificed themselves to clear the way so that the Colonel Arieh Keren, an Auschwitz survivor known to his comrades as 'Biro', could lead a column of tanks from the Mendler Armoured Brigade up on to the Golan Heights via a quite unexpected route, and begin the bloody business of pushing back the Syrians, already softened up by many hours of aerial bombardment. We were also told of schoolbooks found in captured Syrian villages, in which basic mathematical procedures such as addition and multiplication were allegedly taught not by the usual childish exercises involving apples and baskets, but as a gleeful piling up of slaughtered Jews.

Meanwhile, Katyusha rockets were still falling noisily in the fields. Fired by Yasser Arafat's Palestinian guerrillas from Syria and Lebanon, they did little damage by and large, only serving to burnish the memories of war that were lodged around the kibbutz in the form of burned-out enemy tanks. One or two of these rusting hulks may have been relics from the war of independence, like the burned-out Syrian Renault preserved as a monument by the entrance to Kibbutz Degania to the south, but others were from the Six Day War – T-34s from the 2nd Syrian National Guard Tank Battalion, left in the places where they had been destroyed as they bore down on the kibbutz during a disastrously unsuccessful raid of 5 June 1967, which left 200 Syrian soldiers dead. Though immobilized, those memorial tanks were still active as war machines, compressing the altogether more complex history of Jewish-Palestinian relations into the image of a savage Nazi-like power that had to be defeated.

The memory of the Six Day War was still dominant, yet for some kibbutzim, Tel Dan had another layer of significance, marking as it did an earlier moment in the history of the Israeli Armoured Corps. Tel Dan had been a flashpoint in the conflict with Syria during the fitful 'War of the Tractors' that first broke out on 15 March 1951, when Israel initiated the massive programme of drainage and irrigation works with a view to converting the Huleh Valley from a malarial swamp – actually an area of abandoned Palestinian villages, fields, orchards and no longer very malarial swamps in which Ghawarnah Arabs had raised water buffalo during the British mandate[39] – into the intensified agricultural factory that it was by 1970. In order to achieve this, they took bulldozers into one of the three demilitarized zones created on the Israeli side of the old Palestine-Syria border in the armistice agreements of 1949, and set about rechannelling the Jordan. Affronted by this violation, the Syrians opened fire on the Israeli vehicles from their positions on the heights above. According to a document received by IDF Intelligence, that same month the Syrian Chief of Staff also ordered that 250 refugees living in the Kuneitra region should be equipped with machine guns and sent across the frontier, which Israel was not yet capable of turning into the impermeable 'iron wall' of some Zionist aspiration, to fire on Jewish workers.[40] Whether or not that alleged army of 'infiltrators' was ever raised, the pattern of continuing hostilities was set at this time. Down in the valley, Israeli tractors would go out, with or without an army patrol, to cultivate land around the disputed border areas. Meanwhile, the Syrians and displaced Palestinians surveyed the scene from the heights above, and decided whether or not to fire on them. When they did so, the Israelis would fire back, or bomb Syrian positions in fierce retaliatory strikes. Eventually a truce would be negotiated by the United Nations staff in the area.

In the early nineteen-sixties, these smouldering tensions were inflamed by Israel's establishment of a National Water Carrier, which went into service in July 1964, moving water from the Sea of Galilee down to the Negev Desert where it was used to irrigate land farmed by new Jewish settlers. It was in that second phase of the War of the Tractors, that Tel Dan became the measure of the difference that Israel Tal would make to the Israeli Armoured Corps, once he became Commanding General on 1 November 1964.

Tal was one of the officers who had been brought in from the infantry to expand and re-establish the Armoured Corps after the Sinai War, and also to help reorganize the IDF as a mobile armoured force, as suggested by that closely studied victory. New armoured brigades were formed, and a more effective platoon structure was devised as well. Known for his technical abilities, Tal presided over an upgrading programme, in which Israel's battered old tanks were retrofitted for the future; thus the 'Super Sherman' emerged from Israeli workshops – a Sherman equipped with a new diesel engine and a specially designed 105 mm gun. When it came to the acquisition of new tanks, many of Tal's colleagues may have favoured the AMX-30, a fast but lightly armoured French tank, but Tal was convinced that it would prove inadequate for the battles to come. At his insistence, 50-ton Centurion tanks, known for their heavy frontal armour, were procured from the British, although supply was delayed as the British cavilled about Israel's 'retaliatory' raids against its Arab neighbours. By 1960, when these heavy machines were brought into service, Tal was commanding the 7th Armoured Brigade, where he quickly became convinced that many of the breakdowns that had affected the brigade's vehicles as they chased across the desert in the 1956 Sinai campaign were the result of human error.

Tal may have interrupted his military service to study philosophy for three years in 1961, but he had not stopped reflecting on the kind of armoured force his country was likely to need in the future. When he took command of the Armoured Corps, he told his senior officers that the terrain on which Israel could expect to fight in the future was 'ideal tank country', suitable for the deployment of 'great masses of armour'.[41] The precondition of success, however, was that Israel should have a disciplined and technically competent force, and not just an enlarged one reliant on barely trained reservists, whose difficulties were aggravated by the curious assortment of machines that Israel had been able to procure over the years. The Armoured Corps had been greatly expanded since the Sinai campaign, but Tal believed it had also suffered a serious decline in quality. In response, he launched a disciplinary campaign, starting with his officers, who would henceforth have to pay far greater attention to their own uniforms. This battle had been initiated by Tal's predecessor as commander of the Israeli Armoured Corps, David Elazar, who had decreed that his men could no longer go about in multi-coloured ankle socks. Tal now insisted that boots be correctly tied and that officers ensure that the tops and bottoms of their uniforms matched. Throughout the force, Tal introduced rules, standing orders, a certain amount of ceremonial discipline, and precise rules governing the operation and maintenance of tanks.

Tel Dan turned out to be the place where Tal's determination was first tested. The first 'Nukheila incident' took place on 3 November 1964, two days after Tal assumed command of the Armoured Corps. At that time, the land on the Israeli side of the border was being prepared for farming from Kibbutz Dan, but the workers, who went out with tractors and road-levelling equipment, had been coming under fire from Syrian tanks, actually old German panzers, dug in at two overlooking positions: in Nukheila village just north of Tel Dan, and at Tel Azzaziat, a hill to the south-east that dominated the valley.

Tal's predecessor, General David Elazar, had been determined to demonstrate that the enemy tanks at Nukheila could be destroyed by the 105 mm gun of Israel's Centurion tanks. So a company of the 7th Armoured Brigade had been sent to Dan, and stationed near the border to await the next Syrian assault. In Shabtai Teveth's colourful account, the tank soldiers sang through the night to the accompaniment of Captain Shamai Kaplan's accordion, and by dawn they were watching as the Israel tractor and road-making equipment went out, preceded by engineers checking the path for mines. At midday the Syrians opened fire, and the Centurions moved into their positions and fired back. There followed a duel of an hour and a half, in which the Israeli tanks fired eighty-nine shells without causing any serious inconvenience to their enemies. For some, the episode confirmed that the Centurion tank, with which the Armoured Corps was then replacing its Shermans, was an over-complicated machine of limited capability; but Major General Tal, who arrived at Tel Dan shortly after the firing had ceased, was in no doubt that the fault lay with the men who had failed to use their machines effectively. After an investigation, he turned the incident into a lesson of failure: Captain Shamai Kaplan, who had commanded the Centurions, was humiliated for putting his tanks too close together, using the wrong kind of ammunition, and not ceasing fire when it became obvious that no damage was being done. Informality and disregard – swaggering or not – for the outward show of military discipline may have worked for Sharon's lethal paratroopers, but it had no place in Tal's Armoured Corps, where so much depended on technical proficiency.

Tal's reforging of the Armoured Corps was disliked by many. He was accused of 'robotizing' a force that actually owed its strength to its characteristically non-hierarchical commitment to an idea of individual freedom within a collective, and a strong idea of social justice.[42] These were residues of a left-wing culture that had entered the IDF through *Palmach* veterans and kibbutzniks who saw themselves as an elite force, and were not at all sure that officers should automatically be saluted. Tal took steps to ban bullying of the humiliating kind known in Israel as *Tirturim*, in which junior officers would order their men to bury a cigarette butt with full honours, or harness them up as horses.[43] Convinced that a technically proficient Armoured Corps could not proceed on the basis that 'There are as many doctrines as there are Jews,' Tal declared his own war on doctrinal *laissez-faire*: forbidding tank crews from zeroing their Centurion's 105 mm guns, and insisting on the method specified in the user's manual.

In Shabtai Teveth's celebratory account, Tal's difference was made manifest at Tel Dan. After the first Nukheila incident, a force of Shermans were stationed at Dan, with Centurions in support. On 13 November 1964, the road-builders' patrol went out along the track leading to the springs and, as expected, the Syrians opened fire on it. The Shermans moved forward into their planned firing positions to respond, but one of them got into difficulties as it approached, so a Centurion took its place and proceeded to destroy the two Syrian tanks on Tel Nukheila. That result marked the acceptance of the Centurion, which many Israeli tank soldiers had previously judged over-complicated, and from then on, as the water war grew, the shooting got better and better.

Syria responded to Israel's National Water Carrier by taking steps to deprive Israel of water by diverting the Golan springs feeding into the River Jordan. But Tal's Centurions were there to deal with this initiative too. As Teveth tells the story, the Syrians would open fire on tractor drivers or patrols on the road to the Dan springs, and Israel's Centurions would respond. First Tal's men blasted Syria's earthmoving machinery two kilometres away at the base of Mount Hermon. The Syrians then withdrew their water diverting equipment to a presumed safe area close to the B'not Yaakov bridge, by the old British Customs House. But the Armoured Corps's Centurions got them there too – destroying tractors and a dredger from a range of over six kilometres. So, once again, they withdrew their attempt to divert the Jordan's tributaries further south to a place east of the Israeli town of Kurazim – only to find, on 12 August 1965, that Israeli Centurions could reach them even from eleven kilometres away. For those who have written the history of the Israeli Armoured Corps as an epic journey from victimhood to nation-saving power, it is a matter of some significance that Tal himself was at the gun of a Centurion in the last-mentioned of these portentous engagements, leading his men from the front and confirming his reputation as one of the best gunners in the corps.

Jewish Blitzkrieg?

Tal had made his difference by the time the Six Day War broke out in June 1967. The Israeli Armoured Corps was technically competent, familiar with working alongside infantry and air force, and at home with its Centurion tanks. Raised on the slogan: 'Follow Me', its officers and tank commanders expected to lead the way into battle standing in their open hatches, a costly tradition but one that made it infinitely easier to see where you were. Briefing his men before they went into battle, Colonel Shmuel Gonen, by now commander of the 7th Armoured Brigade, reminded them that Israel was 'the vanguard' of the Jewish people. If anyone continued to doubt that the tanks of the Israeli Armoured Corps represented the vanguard of the IDF, it wasn't the soldiers of Egypt's Sinai Field Army, who would soon be looking up in horror from their roadside backgammon games, approaching the Israeli tanks desperate to surrender, or tearing off their boots, and fleeing into the sands where thousands would die under the sun.

Like the 1956 assault on Sinai, the Six Day War came at the end of a deliberately escalated spiral of terrorist raids and 'retaliatory' strikes, including one, in November 1966, in which Israel sent ten light tanks accompanied by a parachute battalion into Jordan's West Bank, where they destroyed a police station before moving on to wreak havoc in the town of Samua. Israel kept tanks out of its annual military parade on Independence Day (15 May) 1967. However, this gesture, which reflected the fact that the parade was held in a demilitarized zone in Jerusalem, was reported in the Egyptian press as proof that Israel's heavy weaponry was actually arrayed against the Syrian frontier, in preparation for an assault that the Soviet Union insisted would take place two days later. As for the Egyptian defence of Sinai, Nasser's General Staff had drawn up a plan, known as 'Operation Kahir', in which the Egyptians would cede ground, allowing the Israelis to penetrate deep into Sinai, where they would be enveloped and then blasted to pieces.[1] Yet this plan was never implemented. Concerned with maintaining his prestige in the Arab world, Nasser could apparently not accept the idea of yielding any ground at all to the enemy, so the Sinai Field Army adopted a Soviet system of linear defence organized in depth. Many of Egypt's supposedly superior Soviet tanks were dug in, hull-down in sand-bagged positions, the very opposite of a mobile force.

Recently described as 'a clockwork war carried out by the IDF against three relatively passive, ineffective Arab armies',[2] the Six Day War began with a concentrated series of Israeli air strikes, which in a few hours wiped out the Egyptian air force on the ground. Once the Egyptian Army had been deprived of air cover, Sinai was to be taken by Southern Command. The Israeli force, which faced seven Egyptian divisions, consisted of three division-sized task forces, or *ugdot*, respectively commanded by Generals Yoffe, Sharon and Tal. An opening feint involving dummy tanks, encouraged the Egyptian High Command to expect an assault in the wrong place, and therefore to shift forces to a position to the east of the planned assault. It then fell to the tanks of the northernmost *ugdah* under General Tal to spearhead the initial breakthrough into Sinai – projecting a succession of thrusts and enveloping manoeuvres far into the desert in an attempt to avoid 180 Egyptian artillery pieces massed on the front – and to surprise from behind a force of otherwise invincible Stalin 3 tanks.[3] Distinct from the 'head-on plunge' of subsequent reputation, Tal's more subtle 'mailed fist', began with an assault on a heavily defended crossroads near Rafa, at the base of the Gaza Strip. One division would break through from the north, while another moved in from the east to hit the Egyptian defences from behind. Launching the operation, Tal reminded his officers that the outcome of the war could well be decided by this, its first battle: 'Every objective must be taken – no matter what the cost in casualties. We must succeed or die.'[4]

It fell to Lieutenant Avigdor Kahalani to lead the assault at the head of Major Ehud Elad's Battalion 77 of the 7th Armoured Brigade. Driving out of Kibbutz Nahal Oz in their Pattons, he and his comrades crossed the frontier, and pressed on through narrow country lanes, sometimes getting wedged between the stone walls of adjacent fields. There were chaotic moments as tanks got lost in the sands, reversed on to their own jeeps, or frantically improvised as they found some positions far more heavily defended than Israeli Intelligence had suggested.

For the soldiers it was certainly never as if their tanks were simply the predestined bearers of a victorious idea of mobile warfare. Yet out of this seething confusion came a number of remembered manoeuvres – fitful and apprehensive advances that retrospective mythology would later convert into a series of superb glissades. Major Ehud Elad's Pattons had their moment after they had pushed through the frontier to assault a heavily defended position at Rafah North. As ordered, Elad directed his own tank into the fire of five Egyptian anti-tank guns, advancing alone until his two Patton companies realized that he was not merely making a reconnaissance run, and joined him in pressing home the assault. Triumphant romance would also be found in the advance of eighteen Centurions of the 7th Armoured Brigade under the brigade's deputy commander, Lieutenant Colonel Baruch 'Pinko' Harel. For a while this reserve squadron of two companies waited on the road north of Rafah; but Harel tired of waiting for an order that seemed never to be coming so, in accordance with the principle of Adherence to Mission, they simply headed south towards Rafa, clearing Egyptian guardsmen out of the village of Umm el-Kalb without even leaving the road, and then retreating into an orchard so that 'Pinko' Harel, who was without a map of the terrain, could take to the radio in order to find out where they might be. Then on they rolled, blasting concrete dragon's teeth out of the road in order to join the assault on the Egyptian defences at Rafah North.

After Rafah Junction had been won in a ferocious and costly battle that would later be claimed as the most important operation of the Six Day War, 'Pinko' Harel and his Centurions moved on to the Jirardi Pass, on which the 7th Armoured Brigade intended to mount an enveloping attack. Ordered by Brigade Commander Shmulik to continue advancing only if resistance was light, Harel's Tank Battalion 82 had set off with three Centurion companies, and a collection of jeeps and half-tracks. Shmulik had assumed that he would be obliged to halt before the Jiradi Pass, which was heavily defended by the 112th Egyptian Infantry Brigade. But the Egyptian soldiers apparently believed what their radios told them: namely that the Sinai Field Army was advancing steadily on Tel Aviv, and that their air force was only absent because it was conducting devastating bombing raids on Israel. So Harel's tanks kept coming while the Egyptians looked on and did almost nothing. They advanced through the entire 14 km length of the pass, with Harel still unconvinced that he had encountered more than light resistance. He radioed for instructions when he found himself not far from El Arish, and Tal and his senior officers refused to believe his reported position: the column had penetrated so far into enemy territory that they were in great danger, cut off behind enemy lines with fuel and ammunition running out.

Many other victorious Israeli tank fables would emerge from these concentrated thrusts into Sinai. Colonel Rafael Eitan's ferocious 202nd Parachute Brigade was led by Pattons as it advanced on Rafah from the south along a disused road from Nitzana. The tanks of Ugdah Sharon advanced on the Egyptian stronghold of Abu Agheila, paving the way for an infantry brigade that followed in mud-smeared civilian buses and other vehicles that Israeli pilots claimed easily to have told as their own: hot-dog vans, milk trucks and ice-cream wagons. As for Lieutenant 'Ein Gil', commander of an Armour School company of nine Pattons, he received a radio order intended for somebody else, and charged deep into the Egyptian rear, disappearing into the desert where he would blast about on his own initiative. Other stories paid tribute to the *ugda* of reservists commanded by Brigadier General Avraham Yoffee, a man of considerable age who normally worked as Israel's Head of Nature Conservation. One of Yoffee's two armoured brigades, commanded by Colonel Isaachar 'Yiska' Shadmi, crossed the frontier and then followed a dry stream bed, crawling in low gear across 50 km of desert to arrive at the road junction at Bir Lahfan, where it would stand in the way of Egyptian attempts to reinforce positions that Tal's forces were attacking at El Arish, and commit merciless slaughter on the 4th Egyptian Tank Division.

Combined with the assaults of the Israeli Air Force, these thrusting manoeuvres soon broke the Egyptians; and the tanks then entered a race intended to prevent their retreat – not just a pursuit, which would have enabled the Egyptian army to escape over the Suez Canal, but an attempt to devastate it before it could do so. There was chaos as the Israeli tanks advanced on the same roads as the retreating Egyptians; indeed, the two forces got so mixed up together that at one point Yoffee ordered his tanks to move sharply to the right of the road and then shoot up any machines that had stayed where they were. Yoffee's tanks inflicted ferocious slaughter at the Mitla Pass. Israel Tal's forces trapped and destroyed an Egyptian brigade near Bir Gifgafa. Sharon's tanks unleashed their inferno at Nakhl. 'This was a Valley of Death,' as Sharon later said. 'I came out of it like an old man. Hundreds were killed: there were burning tanks everywhere. One had the feeling that man was nothing.'[5] The Sinai was won in less than four days: an Egyptian Army of some 100,000 men had been routed, and some thousand tanks had been either destroyed or captured. In the speedily published and breathless words of Winston Churchill's son and grandson, the victory represented 'one of the swiftest and most decisive victories the world has ever seen'.[6]

The pious Jews of the European ghetto may have waited in vain for the roasted Leviathan that would attend the coming of the Days of the Messiah, but celebrations of Israel's more earthly 'miracle of arms'[7] were certainly tempered by a knowledge of smoking flesh. Many retreating Egyptian tank crewmen were 'fried' in their machines by the napalm assaults of the Israeli Air Force. Israeli tank soldiers had suffered too. Major Ehud Elad of Tank Battalion 77 died while gazing through binoculars in an attempt to find a way round anti-tank guns commanding the approach to the Jirardi Pass. His crew reported to have heard the order: 'Drive faster,' and then nothing as his body fell out of the cupola, decapitated by a passing shell. Lieutenant Avigdor Kahalani of the 7th Armoured Brigade, was the first across the line into Egypt, but he too was hit a few hours later as he led a company of Pattons down the road towards El-Arish. Leaving the road and mounting a ridge to search out enemy tanks for his company to attack, he was engulfed in flames when his command tank was hit. For a moment, as Kahalani later recorded, he burned in his turret – '"What's happening to me?" I screamed. "I'm coming apart!"' He eventually managed to haul himself up and out of the cupola: 'Everything was burnt except my boots, a few tattered remnants of my blouse and a strip of underpants hanging from my body.'[8]

The Israeli Armoured Corps's victories in 1956 and 1967 had significant repercussions in the literary sphere. The wishful Messianic vehicle of A. M. Klein's 'Ballad of the Days of the Messiah' had never been widely admired in Israel, and it was now displaced by a different kind of fantasy tank. In 1970 Amos Oz wrote a story called 'Late Love', concerned with the obsessions of an elderly Russian Jew and former Bolshevik called Shraga Unger, who has worked for many years as a lecturer, travelling from one kibbutz to another to warn of the threat facing the people of Israel.[9] Unger is convinced that the extermination of Jewry is being plotted once again, this time in Moscow. He detects signs of the coming assault everywhere – even the sea is full of darkness and danger. The Soviet Union was indeed supporting the Arab states in their dream of wiping Israel off the map. But Unger's Communist plot is, nevertheless, the jumpy, mind-blown vision of a damaged man, cooked up in a tight little room in Tel Aviv. Unger tries to warn Israel's Defence Minister, Moshe Dayan, but his letters remain unanswered. At his lectures, it is only the elderly kibbutzim who are prepared to hear him argue that the Jews must mount a global counterplot to outdo the murderous one being hatched in Moscow.

Many fervid visions burn in the mind of this ageing man, but none more powerful than the one that forms when he picks up a book called *The History of Israeli Tank Warfare.* Unger knows nothing about the subject, but as he studies a photograph of one of Israel's armoured columns pouring into battle 'in a great cloud of dust', he imagines 'this roaring Jewish onslaught' suddenly manifesting itself at another time and in another place. The picture might have shown Ben Ari's tanks bursting through Sinai in 1956, or Shamai Kaplan in the Six Day War, driving forward at the head of his company of Centurions and shouting that they would be the first to the Suez Canal. But in Unger's imagination that dusty column was transported back into the East European world of A. M. Klein's ballad. There it was, suddenly bursting through the forests of Poland towards the Warsaw ghetto: 'The image, I cannot deny, aroused a surging excitement inside me which I have not experienced for years. Can you possibly share this grim fantasy with me: hundreds of furious Jewish tanks crossing the length and breadth of Poland, brutally trampling our murderers underfoot, inscribing a savage Hebrew message across the scorched earth with their tracks in letters of fire and smoke.'[10]

The ghetto is liberated. The Nazi troops are scattered, pursued down every street by these 'fists of fury', and mowed down as the survivors emerge to 'clasp the tanks to their breasts. With delirious fingers they explore the Jewish steel. What savage rejoicing. It is as if the heavens have opened and the vengeance of the martyrs has hurtled to earth with horrific rage.' And then this vengeful Jewish blitzkrieg speeds on, through Poland, Lithuania and the Ukraine, following in the tracks of Hitler's tanks as it rips up fields of snow, flaying 'the cursed Slavic lands', and routing the Red armies from Minsk to Smolensk. The onslaught is felt throughout Russia: 'a blind, white-hot anger is piercing her flesh like a knife to the very depths of the plains and drives everything into submission'. And, at the end of it all, here comes Moshe Dayan, hero of the 1956 Sinai War and Minister of Defence through the Six Day War, standing in the main square of Kishinev to receive the surrender of the Governor-General. It's a great dream of vengeance, but it doesn't last. Shraga Unger finds himself looking at another photograph, and concluding: 'Tanks. Na! Such clumsy machines. And for the time being all we are facing is miserable Arabs.'

Any irony intended by that phrase 'miserable Arabs' is likely to have been lost on a lot of Israelis who fought in the Six Day War. The Arabs were seen as deadbeats, ready to murder and rape defenceless Israelis, but pathetic as soldiers, barely worthy of the Israeli warriors who proceeded to kill them in large numbers. One variety of this contempt can be heard in the voice of the paratrooper who came out of the war on the Golan Heights to report that Syrian camps were both vile and stuffed with luxurious and effeminate accessories: 'The Syrian camps were all filthy. We could find no food – nothing but chocolate and perfume, masses of eau de Cologne. Even in their tanks they had chocolate and eau de Cologne.'[11] Another dwelt on the incompetence of the officers behind the Egyptian rout – ridiculous fools who led from behind, thought it beneath them even to speak to their men, and, indeed, thought nothing of just abandoning them in the Sinai Desert. One derided senior commander from the Sinai Field Army, Brigadier Ahmen Abd El-Naby, even abandoned his brigade of intact Stalin tanks, and fled. Asked later why he hadn't at least destroyed the tanks, this captive told the *New York Times*: 'I had orders to withdraw. My orders did not say to destroy my tanks . . . If I had blown up the tanks the Jews would have heard me. It makes a lot of noise to destroy a tank.'[12]

Real Nazis, but only fantasy Jewish tanks – that's how it had been for A. M. Klein. By the time Amos Oz wrote 'Late Love', however, it was the Holocaust rather than the tank that was operating as a thing of the mind. The Holocaust was explicitly invoked by commanders as they prepared their men for battle, yet many of Israel's combatants can hardly have needed the reminder – including Colonel Arieh Keren, known as 'Biro', who led the Mendler Armoured Brigade's Super Shermans up on to the Golan Heights to attack Kuneitra. Having survived Auschwitz, he dismissed the shell splinters that cut into his face by saying: 'Stalin and Hitler couldn't do me in. You think these Syrians can?'[13] The same point is made even more strongly in the story of the final rehabilitation of Shamai Kaplan, the man whom Tal had humiliated a few years earlier after the failure of his Centurion tanks in the first Nukheila incident. He spent much of the Six Day War standing tall in the hatch of his Centurion, ordering his men this way and that, as they cleared trenches and blasted at dug-in tanks or anti-tank positions. 'We will be the first to the canal,' he had shouted, before driving into an ambush set by Egyptian T-55s. He was killed by shrapnel, and a carefully transcribed poem was later found in his pocket: 'Never again shall our necks be offered like sheep to the slaughterer. If we must die, then let us die in battle.'[14]

By 1970, the year of Amos Oz's story, the transformation of the Jew from the cowering ghetto victim to the victorious armed citizen was complete. The victorious tank had been made Israel's own. Indeed, work had just begun on the development of the Merkava, promising an end to the Armoured Corps's long history of getting by with such hand-me-down weapons as could be procured from unreliably committed Western governments. The memory of the Holocaust was becoming an effective appliance too. As Peter Novick has demonstrated, the memory of that slaughter was not invoked as uniquely Jewish in 1948 or even 1956, but by 1970 it too had been incorporated into Israel's 'iron wall', a form of reactive armour likely to explode in the face of any Western liberal who questioned Israeli power.[15]

The Six Day War was quickly recognized as a miraculous new scene in the military drama that had opened with the Crowley-shadowed prologue at Cambrai. That was certainly how Basil Liddell Hart saw it from his armchair in England. Writing in 1968, he applauded the Six Day War as 'a perfect blitzkrieg', a 'superb' and 'subtle' operation that provided the best yet vindication of the theories he had formulated at the beginning of the century.[16] The self-appointed 'father' of the blitzkrieg commended Israel's Chief of Staff, Major General Yitzhak Rabin as an even better student than Guderian or Rommel ('generous as they were in acknowledgement'), and one who had provided 'the best demonstration yet' of Liddell Hart's own epoch-making theory of the 'indirect approach'. In support of his claims, he cited a personal letter from Yigael Yadin, claiming that his works had been 'carefully studied for "lessons" ', which 'were, thank God for us, not learnt by the Arabs, including the British-conceived Arab legion'.

Israeli historians may be more inclined to emphasize the extent to which their Palestinian enemies relied on the Nazis – whether it be the Mufti of Jerusalem asking Hitler to extend his genocide to Palestine, or the terrorists who were trained in murder by Nazi experts. Yet the blitzkrieg lineage suggests that Israel, not content with using the biographies of German tank generals as bombs to kill Arabs, had inherited a whole method of warfare from the Nazis. Interested to know how Major General Israel Tal saw this line of descent, I asked him about J. F. C. Fuller, and whether he had indeed studied the British pioneers of tank warfare. 'Yes, of course,' he replied, quickly adding General de Gaulle to the list, and then reaffirming: 'I am familiar with the literature, with Fuller's teaching and Liddell Hart's, and Tukhachevsky.' He had been a friend of Richard Simpkin, the British editor of Tukhachevsky's *Deep Battle*, and he was satisfied to note that his breakthrough at Rafa had long been studied in British military academies, his successful 'selection and maintenance of the aim' being contrasted with the negative example of Hitler's advance on Moscow.

There were other similarities that placed Israel's tank general in the same line as Fuller. Following the triumph of the Six Day War, Tal came up with his own version of the 'all-tank concept', arguing that Israel required an

army that would operate by fast breakthroughs carried out by 'all-tank' brigades, supported by air but not hindered by armoured infantry in their
half-tracks, which should be relegated to 'mopping-up' operations. Aware
that funds were short, Tal argued that priority should be given to building
an army of tanks rather than armoured personnel carriers.

His view that the tank was 'the decisive strategic weapon',[17] was hotly
contested within the IDF, and there were further arguments about the
future defence of Sinai. In the event Israel established the Bar Lev line, a
rigid system of heavily fortified strongholds evenly spaced along the east
bank of the Suez Canal. Together with Ariel Sharon, Israel Tal had opposed
this from the start, insisting that rigid defence went against the Israeli doctrine of mobile warfare. They advocated a different system in which
armoured forces would be held at some 10 km distance from the canal,
ready to sally out to destroy Egyptian forces if they crossed – a suggestion
that confirmed the suspicions of those who considered Tal guilty of, what
one champion of the Bar Lev line, Major General Avraham Adan, called
'tankomania'.[18]

These Bar Lev bunkers would be overrun by the Egyptians in the first
days of the October War in 1973. But for many months before that, during
the War of Attrition that followed the Six Day War, Israeli soldiers garrisoned on the Bar Lev line endured terrible bombardment. Far from operating as a mailed fist against the Egyptians, the tank soldiers stationed to the
rear of the line found themselves running an ambulance and delivery service. According to one, Pinchas Kenan: 'we would arrive in the position
with the tank to take out the wounded. [Other] soldiers would hang on to
the tank and beg to be taken out also. We had to throw them off the tank.
They were like wild animals. They were white with fear, dirty and stinking,
and the worst of it was their bulging eyes. This was something I saw often
during the War of Attrition.'[19] It was not what Tal and his colleagues
thought armoured warfare should be about.

Asked about his alleged 'tankomania', Tal insists that, though he was
much criticized at the time, 'even today, I hold the same idea'. Since the
early seventies, there may have been many innovations in the field of firepower and precision munitions. With the development of ground-to-
ground munitions, 'it will be necessary to rely on other means of deterrence, and to have the means to bomb Teheran, to bomb Baghdad, to
bomb other countries, in order to destroy their capitals and towns in the
event that they try to render war against Israel into a total war'. Israel needs
to remain far ahead of its potential enemies in military technology, yet the

basic force on land is the mobile armoured formation. And that will remain true 'in the future even more than in the past', despite those people who object that the tank is increasingly obsolescent. That, scoffs Tal, is a futile objection, which has been stalking the tank from the very beginning – 'they used to say this when the tank appeared for the very first time'.

Tal and his fellows were well aware of 'the literature' as they designed the operations for which the Israeli Armoured Corps would become famous; yet theirs was not simply a reprise of Fuller's idea as it may since have been refracted through German, American and Soviet experience. Indeed, Tal described Fuller's thought as full of limitations. Fuller and his fellow pioneers 'compared tank formations to fleets on the sea, but in that respect they were wrong, for the medium of the ground is not like air or water'. On sea, it may be possible to move in all directions with the same speed, but on land that is quite impossible. Clausewitz understood that land is 'a stopping and disturbing medium': with terrain comes 'friction', and that changes the picture completely. As for Fuller's idea of sending a fleet of British tanks into Russia, to extinguish Bolshevism with tanks, that too was hopelessly idealistic. Russia at that time was a huge region, with the civil war reaching from the Black Sea up to Archangel – 'If they had intended to capture Moscow or St Petersburg, all right, but just to go into Russia . . .'

Having raised his eyebrows at the folly of that proposal, Tal cites these examples as proving that 'theories on paper' only have limited influence on 'military thinking in the future'. What matters is the example drawn from 'the practice of this theory'. From this point of view, Tukhachevsky was not doing the same as Liddell Hart and Fuller might have imagined. His Deep Battle consisted of advancing and encircling the enemy, 'which is exactly what the Red Army did in the Second World War'. It may have looked like another blitzkrieg on paper, but in practice it was vitally different. So Tukhachevsky's teaching was very modern and original, just as had been that of Fuller and Liddell Hart before him. Above all, however, it was the implementation that counted, and 'the lessons gained out of reality'. That difference had to be stressed before Tal would admit to being in the tradition that comes down from Fuller: a line that is 'based more upon practice, what came out of these theories, rather than the theories themselves'.

Tal had never planned his operations by sitting down and thinking that the time had come for another blitzkrieg. He and his fellow officers in the Armoured Corps had made their decisions out of 'the basic situation'. And the fundamental fact was that 'we were the few against the many'. Israel's military methods had emerged from this necessity. 'There was no room for the question how much is enough. The entire nation had to fight.' Before the War of Independence, the Jewish defence of Palestine had taken the shape of the area defence system, which was maintained all around the country and manned by everyone: 'old people, women and children'. This was not the partisan tradition, in which fighters could move around and hide and use the ground. Instead, it demanded the defence of 'stationary positions' such as villages: 'So the whole nation was fighting, maintaining rigid defence all around the country – strong points, spread all over the country.'

That tradition of compulsory national service has continued ever since, with all young girls and boys going into the forces. But to be the few against the many had other aspects. Israel had been few not just in people but in resources and 'economical staying power'. If it is to win conventional wars, says Tal, a country needs both economic might and assault power. Tal and his fellow generals knew that wars are usually wars of attrition rather than of assault, and that as such they are won by the party with economic superiority. That was how Russia defeated the Germans in the Second World War; and it was abundantly clear that victory would have gone to the Arabs, had Israel allowed its wars to become wars of attrition.

So Israeli military doctrine was formed in the knowledge of the new state's national situation after the War of Independence. 'We knew we wouldn't stand a chance if the thing attained the shape of an attrition war, because we are the few and they are the many.' The alternative was to adopt a strategy that relied only on assault power, 'namely, by assault power to decide wars very quickly and fast . . . So you see when the Arabs made their operational plans, they tried to force us into a defensive war of attrition. Whilst our interest was to wage a war of decision, by assault power. And to gain the decision, not by overwhelming resources, but by deciding battles and campaigns in the field, open fighting.' Defensive war means attrition, and for Israel, that was just another name for inevitable defeat. 'So that is why we gave the priority to the offensive.' And 'the tool on land, the tool to wage an offensive war on land, especially in the Middle East, which is ideal tank country, is the armoured mobile formation. So by nature we had to act in the manner, along the lines of the blitzkrieg, you see. So even if there were no theories of the blitzkrieg, we would do it, because the situation forced us to do it, you see.'

As for his own place in the history of tank warfare, Tal, in the course of reviewing the Israeli Armoured Corps's past victories, refers to the Battle of

Kursk of July 1943. The history books describe this as 'the greatest tank battle in history', but this, he says is 'absolutely not true' – or at least, it is only true if you remember that the books making this claim were written before the Six Day War or the October War. The Battle of Kursk was indeed huge, but Tal is soon breaking it down into its constituent parts on a piece of paper. He mentions the fatal delays as Hitler vacillated, waiting for the delivery of the Tigers, of which so few in the end would be used. Having sketched out the points where the German pincer movement tried to cut into the Kursk salient from the north and south, Tal then remarks that Israel is, geographically, 'an exact replica of the salient of Kursk'. One and a half million soldiers may have taken part in the fighting at Kursk, but the tanks only fought in the north and south corners, just as Israel's tank battles had been concentrated in the Golan Heights and Sinai. Tal has conducted extensive researches with the help of a German colleague, and concludes that, even including tank destroyers and self-propelled artillery pieces, there were at most 4,000 tanks involved. In the October and Six Day Wars, the number was '5,000, 6,000 or even more'.

Atonement – the Golan Heights

If the October War of 1973 is sometimes called the War of Atonement, that is partly because it awakened the Israelis to the fact that their enemy could no longer be complacently dismissed as a bunch of 'miserable Arabs' and that their own tank operations would not always consist of elegant and invincible thrusts attended by vast clouds of dust. Caught out by the combined assaults of Syria and Egypt, the Israelis mobilized late and found themselves fighting desperate defensive battles in which their outnumbered tank units were obliged to mount what Tal later described as 'piecemeal counter-attacks against large, well organized forces – in direct contradiction to the principles of armoured warfare'.[20]

Before assaulting the Golan Heights, the Syrians had assembled a massive force right under the eyes of Israeli observers on Mount Hermon, deceiving those soon to be silenced onlookers by employing their tanks hull-down as if for defensive purposes. Both Syria and Egypt launched synchronized assaults at 14.00 on 6 October, choosing that day because it was Yom Kippur, and Israel would be at its least prepared for war. After initial airstrikes and an artillery barrage, three Syrian mechanized divisions launched a carefully designed series of attacks along the length of the 'purple line' marking the border agreed after the Six Day War. An Australian UN observer watched hundreds of Syrian tanks participate in the northern attack near Kuneitra. Advancing four abreast and rolling past either side of this astonished man's bunker, Syria's tanks surged on towards the Golan with their tank commanders standing upright in their hatches: not so much an attack, thought the Australian, but more 'like a parade ground demonstration'.[21] One Israeli officer is recorded as saying: 'They flowed in like water, finding their way wherever they had the chance.'[22] An Israeli tank commander would later observe, 'I never knew there were so many tanks in all the world.'[23]

The Syrians came with a formidable arsenal of Soviet hardware – T-54s, T-55s and also brand new T-62s, which were later found to have been driven into battle with only a few kilometres on the clock. Well aware of the obstacles that lay in their path, the Syrians had incorporated armoured engineer units with bulldozer tanks, flail tanks for disarming minefields, and bridge-laying tanks into the head of their column. Shielded from the Israeli Air Force by a surface-to-air missile system, the advance of this Soviet style steamroller went smoothly enough until the head of the Syrian column reached the anti-tank ditch north of Kuneitra. The bulldozer tanks and bridge-laying vehicles came under devastating fire from well-placed Israeli tanks on the ridge above, and Syria's massive military 'parade' was quickly reconfigured as a monstrous traffic jam.

By 22.00 on the 6th, the Syrians were breaking through the anti-tank ditch, to begin their assault on the fifty or so Israeli Centurions of Colonel 'Yanosh' Ben Gal's greatly outnumbered 7th Brigade. Fighting raged for four days, while Israeli ministers in Jerusalem feared the worst and discussed the possible use of nuclear weapons.[24] The Golan Heights provided the Israelis with no room for manoeuvre, and the 7th Brigade's four dozen Centurions had been ordered by Moshe Dayan, by now Israel's Defence Minister, to hold their ground and fight to the last in the spirit of the Maccabees on Masada. As that plain north of Kuneitra filled with shattered and burning Syrian tanks, the Israeli tank crews on the ridge above renamed it variously 'the Graveyard', 'the Vale of Tears' and, perhaps more finally, 'the Valley of Death'. Meanwhile, the Syrians kept coming in apparently endless numbers. By 9 October the exhausted Israeli units were reduced to a few tanks, fighting at almost point-blank range with Syrian machines. The brigade commander 'Yanosh' Ben Gal had just about given up – he would later describe himself as having already picked up his radio-telephone to give the order to withdraw – but at exactly that moment the final reserve force of seventeen tanks arrived, with fortuitous Hollywood-like timing, and the Syrians started to retreat.[25]

It was on that desperate last day that Avigdor Kahalani achieved mythical status as the Lieutenant Colonel in command of the Seventh Brigade's lead 77th Battalion. In his best-selling book of the battle, *The Heights of Courage*, Kahalani tells of the hours in which he and his band of heroes rose into the epic moment when Israel was saved. Pulled away from the contingencies of ordinary life with its petty ordeals, they are swept up into the days of pure martial spirit. On the way, the women personnel are evacuated, including 'Shlomit', who disconcerted Kahalani by asking him, in front of his subordinates, if he wasn't frightened to think of going into another war considering the 60 per cent burns he had suffered in the last one. This was a difficult question for a tank hero who had spent an agonizing year undergoing skin grafts in hospital, but Kahalani tells of snuffing it out by replying that it was his body that had been injured, certainly not his spirit.[26] There follows a briefing in which Colonel 'Janosh' Ben Gal informs his senior men that they will be going to war that day, and then, just as they get up to leave, the Syrian planes sweep overhead to bomb the base. The cry: 'To your tanks,' prompts a hasty donning of fireproof coveralls and Kahalani's 'battalion of lions' roars into its great engagement: a tiny band of scruffy, long-haired heroes drawing a much-needed sense of power from the clatter of their Centurions' tracks as they head out through the Syrian artillery barrage (using the tarred road but still trying to avoid damaging irrigation pipes) to engage the 'tidal wave' of Soviet steel from earthen ramps on 'Booster Ridge' north of Kuneitra.

The Syrians experienced major difficulties at the anti-tank ditch, but they got moving by night, using infra-red sighting systems that gave them additional advantage over the Israelis. Aware that the fate of Israel depended on their stand, Colonel Ben Gal's vastly outnumbered men blasted away, at long range and short, suffering dire losses as enemy tanks broke right into their own formation. Kahalani presided over events in his battalion, rallying his companies and narrating the war over the radio: urging a late-coming major and former deputy battalion commander to 'Grab a tank and come along,' or reporting back to Ben Gal on progress so far: 'We've stopped them. It's quite a sight. The valley is full of burning and abandoned hardware.'[27] The Syrians poured in apparently limitless reserves, and the Israelis kept blasting away at all comers, including the new T-62, happy, as Kahalani boasts, to prove that 'this newest ghost in the Soviet-Syrian arsenal was as destroyable as the T-54 and T-55 which preceded it'.[28]

The 7th Brigade kept at it for four days, with brief periods of comparative calm, in which the dead and wounded were retrieved and shattered tanks were brought down from the ramps for repair or replacement. Its battalions suffered dreadful losses, and were almost dislodged from their positions. But on the last day, 9 October, Kahalani rallied his reduced and flagging force. Incorporating remnants of another battalion and receiving the last available reinforcements, he led them on to reoccupy the ramps overlooking the Vale of Tears, and then proceeded to wreak havoc on the Syrian forces massed below, only pausing when, in Kahalani's words, 'the valley was a mass of "bonfires"'. Kahalani later heard that 'we had that morning saved Israel. It sounded exaggerated to me . . .'[29]

If the 7th Brigade had to fight it out alone to the north, that was because the commander of the Israeli forces in the Golan, Brigadier General Rafael Eitan, had been obliged to commit his reserves to the southern Golan, where the Syrian attack had been far more successful. Here they had advanced over flatter terrain to devastate the Israeli 188th Barak Brigade, which faced ten Syrian tanks to each of its own, and was largely wiped out as its men tried, more or less suicidally,[30] to hold positions in order to gain Israel time in which to mobilize reserve forces and get more of its ill-prepared armoured force (20 per cent of its tanks were apparently being serviced at the time of the attack)[31] ready for action. Such was the contempt in which the Syrian Army had been held since the Six Day War that Israeli settlers on the Golan were only evacuated after the attack had begun. The feeling among them now, however, was that 'there was going to be a holocaust'.[32] The man in charge of Israel's Northern Command, General Yitshak Hofi, may have commanded the assault on the Golan Heights in the Six Day War, but he is said to have been so overthrown by the opening events of this Syrian counter-attack that he was to be found lying on his camp bed muttering in despair, 'All is lost, all is lost.'[33] The Syrians reached as far as Nafakh, advancing on to the slopes overlooking the Jordan Valley, and were only pushed out of the headquarters of IDF's Northern Command by a desperate rallying in which the commander of the Barak Brigade, Colonel Ben-Shoham, died fighting in his tank, along with most of his staff officers. For a while much depended on a single tank commanded by an armoured corpsman named Zvika. By this time, however, and 'as if by miracle', some reserve tank brigades had advanced chaotically up the escarpment of the Golan Heights. Over the next two days, the Syrians were pushed back, or surrounded at Hushniye, where another Valley of Death was created. The Israeli Armoured Corps then broke into Syria to engage the 3rd Iraqi Armoured Division, which was advancing without maps or any apparent co-ordination with the Syrian forces, and was soon shot to bits. After that, Syria was savaged from the air, a systematic destruction of its industrial base, factories, oil plants, and the military command centres, including the Ministry of Defence, destroyed along with 200 people, many of them residents of the diplomatic quarter surrounding it.

Atonement – Sinai and Suez

When the tanks on the Golan were reckoned up, it emerged that 177 Israeli tanks had defeated a force of 1,400 Syrian machines. The Egyptian Army that had attacked Israel from across the Suez Canal was much larger – forty-two brigades in all, 1,700 tanks, 2,500 armoured vehicles, 2,000 artillery pieces – and it too had been massed in preparation for war without Israeli Intelligence noticing. As with the Syrians, the Egyptian Army was no longer a chaotic horde led by incompetent, politically appointed officers who considered contact with their men beneath them. Indeed, the Chief of Staff, Saad el Shazly, had rebuilt and also remoralized the force by means of briefings, pamphlets written by himself, outward bound training, sports and personal contact. Egypt had also received considerable foreign aid. Korean pilots had helped reform the twice-blasted air force, but relations with Soviet advisers had been difficult. 'The Russians have many qualities, but concern for human feelings is not among them'[34] – so wrote Shazly, explaining that these advisers had viewed the Egyptians with contempt, resenting their luxurious cars and jewels, and chiding them for failing to produce a total mobilization of the savage kind with which Stalin had turned the course of the Second World War. The Soviet advisers were eventually sent packing, but the all-important equipment remained: surface-to-air missiles, planes, tanks, including T-62s with their formidable 115 mm guns, and infantry anti-tank weapons too – rocket-propelled grenades, and wire-guided 'Sagger' missiles. The Israelis might find ways of looking back on it differently, but if the October War was an 'historic encounter' in Shazly's book, that is because it was 'the first combat between the essentially World War Two concept of armor and the infantry weapons of the next generation'.[35]

Egypt's preliminary aim was to cross the Suez Canal on the widest possible front, set up five divisional bridgeheads, and overwhelm the Bar Lev line: an ambition that entailed not just subduing two lines of strongly fortified bunkers, but defeating the mobile tank force guarding the space between them. Before that, however, they had to cross the canal, and then make their way over or through a huge rampart on the eastern bank, a formidable thing of sand containing a fabled secret weapon as bizarre and psychologically potent as the vast flame-throwers Hitler asked Albert Speer to consider modelling on garden sprinklers. Buried in the sand rampart were tanks filled with oil that in the event of an attack would, so the Egyptians understood, be pumped into the Suez Canal just below the water line and then ignited to turn the whole thing into a blazing inferno. The Israelis considered the canal impassable, especially by the Egyptian Army, at which Israeli soldiers were inclined to laugh even as they watched its men practising for the crossing. Bar Lev and the associated defences were Israel's Maginot Line. Even Moshe Dayan had scoffed that the Egyptians would never be able to cross the canal unless they somehow managed to enlist the combined assistance of both American and Soviet engineers.[36]

The attack was launched on the night of 5–6 October. Commando units crossed the canal just before the commencement of a huge artillery barrage, and prepared to ambush the Israeli tanks at their intended firing positions. The next afternoon, wave after wave of men started crossing the canal at selected places between the Bar Lev forts: using hundreds of inflatable dinghies, they chanted: 'Allah is the greatest, Allah is the greatest,' as they paddled through covering clouds of smoke. Ten brigades crossed in a couple of hours, and while twelve bridges were assembled and put in place and thirty-one ferries brought into service, other engineers used powerful water cannon to blast sixty breaches in the raised sand rampart on Israel's side of the canal – choosing that number so that the bridges could be moved from one place to another to avoid concentrated attack. By the end of the 7th the Egyptians had landed 100,000 men, 13,500 vehicles and over 1,000 tanks. Meanwhile, the three Israeli armoured brigades committed to guarding and relieving the Bar Lev outposts had been shattered, losing two-thirds of their tanks – some to Egyptian tanks firing from the far side of the Suez Canal, but many also to tank-killing infantry units, which ambushed them with rocket-propelled grenades and missiles.

The Israelis had gathered sufficient resources by the 8th to commit two tank divisions, under Generals Adan and Sharon, to a counter-attack on the Egyptian bridgeheads, convinced of what an Israeli historian calls 'the near miraculous power of the concentrated armored punch'.[37] But here again they failed horribly: hindered by lack of reconnaissance, and confused by Egyptian jamming of communications, the attack collapsed into what Sharon called 'a tankman's nightmare'.[38] According to Shazly, who would deride Israel's conduct of the war as mediocre 'staff college stuff', they failed to concentrate their tanks and instead 'persisted in throwing away the lives of their tank crews. They have assaulted in "penny packet" groupings and their sole tactic remains the cavalry charge.' Through these 'kamikaze' charges, the Israelis lost another 260 tanks in two days.

Some of the blame for the disasters of the first few days would later be placed on the commander of Israel's Southern Front, Major General Shmuel Gonen, but Egypt's use of new infantry anti-tank weapons was also a major factor. One Israeli tank commander described noticing little specks in the dunes ahead of him as he drove forward. To begin with he thought they were old tree trunks, but as he closed on them he realized they were actually men. He wondered what they were doing standing there, quite still and solitary, as hostile tanks bore down on them, but 'suddenly all hell broke loose. A barrage of missiles was being fired at us. Many of our tanks were hit. We had never come up against anything like this before . . .'[39] That was how many Israeli tank commanders were introduced to the Sagger, a Soviet-built, wire-guided 'suitcase missile' that could be fired by a single infantryman and directed to its target with a joystick, somewhat in the manner of a model plane.

But Egypt was to snatch defeat from the jaws of its own initial victory – thanks largely to Anwar Sadat's War Minister, Ahmed Ismail, who directed the campaign with the unerring rigidity of a man who insisted on implementing a preconceived plan, and who was said to have insisted that 'Wars are a dialogue between one plan and another . . .'[40] Chief of Staff Shazly had been opposed to any deeper second-stage assault into Sinai, arguing that it would take the Egyptian tank divisions out of range of their SAM umbrella, thereby exposing them to the Israeli Air Force, which was ready and waiting once again to prove the truth of Shazly's dictum that 'Tanks without air cover are sitting ducks.'[41] The Egyptian Army was heavily concentrated at the front already, and the idea of a 'quick thrust', especially one that actually consisted of several thrusts scattered over a 100-mile-long front, was bound to be fatal. Yet the order came, a political decision motivated partly by Sadat's agreement with the Syrians. Almost the entire force was committed, and 250 tanks were lost in a few hours; this time it was an Egyptian commander, General Mamoun of the Second Army, who retreated to his bed in a state of mental collapse.

As an American reconnaissance plane soon noticed, the Egyptian drive into Sinai left the west bank of Suez unguarded. So the Israelis crossed, led by Ariel Sharon. There was fierce fighting but the Egyptian infantry was without its anti-tank guided weapons battalion, stuck on the east bank doing nothing but not allowed to retreat. Sharon's carve-up was performed on men who, owing to Sadat's lying news reports, had no idea what was coming down on them. As Shazly remarked drily, 'swift armoured thrusts with close air-support against unprepared men was the sort of war at which the Israelis excelled'.[42] By the time Sadat managed to secure a ceasefire, his entire Third Army had been encircled, and was being used as a bargaining chip to free Israeli prisoners. The Israelis were also advancing north to cut off Egypt's Second Army.

The October War represented another victory for Israel, but certainly not a short and decisive 'miracle' like the Six Day War. This was a costly and destabilizing outcome, which landed the country in a period of pro-tracted economic and also political difficulty. Surviving soldiers mounted a vigil outside the Ministry of Defence and demanded the resignation of Moshe Dayan, the Minister of Defence. A judicial inquiry by the Agranat Commission revealed the failure of IDF Intelligence, which sent Israelis into war without night sights, or any remotely adequate conception of the infantry weapons they were facing. The commission also confirmed that the army leadership had been incompetent, condemning both the Chief of Staff, David Elazar, and the commander of Southern Command, General Shmuel Gonen, for failing to prepare for war, or to conduct it adequately. Golda Meir resigned a year later, and Menachem Begin came to power at the head of the right-wing Likud alliance not long afterwards.

Meanwhile General Tal and his engineers pressed on with their ballistical tests for the Merkava, taking their pick of the wrecked tanks scattered around the battlefields and all the more determined to put protection of the crew above any other consideration in their emerging design. Their tribute to the many Israeli tank soldiers who died in the October War would be that innovative 'spaced armour concept', the low silhouette of the machine, the removal of the normal commander's cupola (made possible by the introduction of a panoramic periscope), and also the dry, low-slung fighting compartment in which even the driver, isolated in most previous models, was at last able to take up his position as part of the team. The IDF received its first Merkavas in 1979, in time for further improvements to have been introduced before they spearheaded Begin's invasion of Lebanon in June 1982.

Getting out of the tank?

'Yes, they use our guns.' That was all Tal said about Wang Weilin and the column of tanks he stopped in Tiananmen Square. The Chinese, he explained, had usually mounted Soviet 100 mm guns on their tanks, but the guns on the tanks in the picture from Tiananmen Square looked to him suspiciously like the British 105 mm L7, which had been licensed to America, relaunched with a round breech as the M68, and then sold on to Israel. Apart from that, however, the image only proved that the 'moral effect' of the tank was now mostly a matter of impressing civilians, who only know that they are facing a powerful machine that threatens to kill them. Having himself seen the 'shock effect' of the tank work on the battle-field, Tal could understand how the mere sight of a tank 'really created panic' in the First World War. Yet he reckoned it was no longer much of an issue when tanks engaged in fire-fighting, which nowadays often occurs at such a distance that the machines can hardly even be seen.

However, the morale of your fighters is another thing altogether. And what is unique about the Israeli nation at arms is the fact that ' we are the only country in the world which has lived for fifty years until now, even today, with many countries around the globe, and all our neighbours, doubting our very right to exist . . . We are the only country that has been fighting for fifty years.' And against this background, the young of Israel have developed a 'national pattern of behaviour of warriors'.

Reaching back into his past, Tal recalls the years he spent serving with the British Eighth Army in Italy. There, in the mountains, he fought along-side the Italian Cremona Regiment, and found the men mediocre and quite uninterested in assaulting the enemy because they had no 'national interest' in it: 'No morale and no motivation. They used to shout and cry "Madonna! Madonna!" when somebody had a scratch: "Madonna! Madonna!" . . .' This sounds like another post-Caporetto slur against the Italians, but Tal's point is that 'in the time of Garibaldi, when they waged their war of liberation, they fought like giants'. And so it was with Israel. What matters is not just that it has acquired the military equipment, or that its tank commanders lead from the front, but rather the whole mental-ity of the nation: 'So I say, what is unique to us, even today, and it doesn't matter to what extent we are a divided people, we are even more a demo-cracy than a classical democracy, because we are divided up to the very end. But still we are united very much when it comes to our existence. That's why our young generation has never left this pattern of behaviour.

And we can rely on our fighters and our commanders and our young girls, that they will fight until the end, even beyond the end.' To prove this point about morale, Tal produced the transcript of a talk he had recently given at the US Armor Center at Fort Knox:

The place of armour in the art of land warfare is not only a physical matter but also to a great extent a matter of state of mind. In this connection I once told our armoured warriors the following: 'Be proud of your corps, whose fighting thrust never falters from start to finish, and whose men surge forward without respite though their tanks burn and explode all around them . . .'

I never went to look over the Merkava Mark III or to see it being put through its paces either in the Lebanon or at the Armoured Corps head-quarters at Be'er Sheva to the south. 'We are at your disposal,' Israel Tal had said, but the video he gave me was enough. It shows the Merkava behaving as tanks tend to do on promotional videos: an irresistible hunk of destiny flying through the air to the accompaniment of relentless pounding music, squirting clouds of smoke and fire in all directions, rushing through swamps and over the most impassable Golan-like boulders, blasting heli-copters out of the sky, and destroying enemy positions on the ground with-out even slowing to take aim. Looking at this terrifying appliance, which needed no attendant seraphim to help it burn up the night, I wondered what A. M. Klein would have made of the deadly machine that Major Gen-eral Tal and his men have engineered in the place of the desperate Messi-anic phantom he imagined in 'Ballad of the Days of the Messiah'.

A 'questionable amalgam between Hollywood and Holy Writ'[43] – that is how Klein described the new state of Israel after his enraptured visit of 1949. He was reluctant to dwell on the place of force in the establishment of the Jewish homeland; and although he observed that the Arabs had disappeared from many towns and villages in the new state, he was not inclined to worry over the extent to which their 'miraculous' flight (387,000 Arabs are esti-mated to have fled in the first half of the 1948 War of Independence) had been deliberately prompted by Jewish expulsions and atrocities carried out under the Haganah's Plan D 'for gaining control of the territory of the Jewish state and for the defence of its borders'.[44] Klein would not face that truth, but the history that has since produced the Merkava might still have reminded him of the dark side of the legend of the Golem. Formed out of mud by a rabbi's incantations, the Golem came to the aid of the beleaguered Jewish faithful. Yet in many versions of the tale, this ferocious automaton also slips out of its maker's control, escaping into the world as a blind but terrible force: in the words of one of Klein's poems, 'The golem ran amok!'[45] Klein identified the warning buried in the legend – 'one realizes that an artifact, a mere mechanical man, is no substitute for the truly human in the image of God created'.[46] Once it has broken away, the Golem becomes the emblem of exactly the kind of faithless brutality it is created to oppose, a Jewish Frankenstein's monster recoiling on its erstwhile controllers. In a poem called 'Talisman in Seven Shreds', Klein imagines it swallowing the divine parchment, the name of God become so much monstrous spit.[47]

Is a similar reversal implicit in Israel's progression from the Messianic tank of Klein's 'Ballad of the Days of the Messiah' to the actually existing Merkava Mark IV, as it is shortly to be? Yaron Ezrahi, an Israeli political writer associated with the Israel Democracy Institute has recently described the Golem as perhaps 'the most instructive expression of Jewish fantasy in the face of danger'.[48] As a fantasy of the ghetto Jews, who really did live as the few against the many, the Golem demonstrated Jewish faith in the power of sacred words over conventional worldly force. But, as Ezrahi asks, what happens when the Jewish people cease to be a powerless minority, and are no longer obliged to defend themselves with fantasy, irony, and mere jokes? In his account, the legend of the Golem comes into its own at this very moment: an allegory warning that power can easily develop a destructive momentum of its own.

With the establishment of the state of Israel, the East European ghetto Jew's helpless dream of the Golem was replaced by a different imaginary apparatus that converted military force into an expression of the Jewish will. In the new Israeli mythology, the Jews came to think of themselves as heroic freedom fighters – paratroopers, tank commanders and, in Ehrazi's phrase, 'virtuosos in military strategy'. Yet this heroic imagery remained fundamentally defensive: sustained by actively managed memories of the Holocaust; so closely welded to the idea of Jewish victimhood as to be unable to grasp the sufferings of its own Palestinian victims; and, indeed, so forcefully collectivized that it could hardly even register the individuality of the Israelis who were to fight and die in the national cause. Israeli power was itself armoured by a mentality that predisposed the Israelis to see themselves as 'the few against the many' even when they were actually massively empowered, the strong against the weak.

Ezrahi suggests that it was victory that made possible a reappraisal of this defensive predisposition: the triumph of the Six Day War 'mitigated the sense of victimhood and vulnerability in which Jewish orientations to the use of physical force had been encoded in the past'.[49] As an indication of this awakening, he cites an observation made by a tank soldier shortly after that victory. On hearing an artillery man describe how shocked he was to find that the enemy he had killed turned out to be a local Arab peasant, this soldier remarked that it was easier in a tank because you couldn't see what happened inside the tanks you hit: 'it is only when you get out of the tank that you start having problems'.[50]

In the years to come, many Israelis would find ways of not 'getting out of the tank' in that way. Right-wing nationalists carried on, pushing Jabotinsky's Iron Wall out into the occupied territories and wrapping it around their expropriating settlements. Orthodox immigrants hailed the Israeli tank as a piece of rolling theodicy, God's word on tracks, piling up redemptive theocratic visions of the kind that eventually motivated the assassination of Yitzhak Rabin. Yet at the same time as Tal's engineers were forging the Merkava out of the ballistical lessons of the battlefield, other Israelis were developing a different view of Israeli power. And as Ezrahi writes, they've been doing so ever since, spurred on by the perceived incompetence of the government and military leadership. The desire to 'get out of the tank' was increased after the October War of 1973, when it emerged that Golda Meir might conceivably have avoided conflict with Sadat, and had actually endangered the lives of her own soldiers during the conflict by making inappropriate public announcements (according to Shazly it was through one of her statements to the media that the Egyptians first realized that the Israelis had crossed the Suez Canal). It found further fuel in 1982, provoked first by Menachem Begin and Ariel Sharon's hawkish invasion of Lebanon in 1982 and by the discovery that, once the IDF had occupied West Beirut, Ariel Sharon had stood by – indeed the IDF even provided requested illumination – as Israel's Lebanese Christian allies engaged in a protracted slaughter of Palestinians in the refugee camps of Sabra and Shatilla. After these events, 'the Israeli willingness to accept unqualified redemptive versions of Zionism has begun to erode'.[51] Begin repeatedly described the PLO as a reincarnation of the Nazis, but other Jews were thinking differently, including the London writer Emanuel Litvinoff, who produced a novel in which it is the good Israeli Jew who finally turns out to be a former Nazi.[52] More atrocities followed the Palestinian uprising, or intifada, of the late eighties when Yitzhak Rabin oversaw a period when Israeli soldiers turned their guns on stone-throwing Palestinian youths. For Ezrahi, this was the most corrupt moment in the history of the IDF, and one that demanded a breaking up of the Israeli armour in which victimhood, military force and the Holocaust were so lethally combined.

It was the success of this counter-stream that made it possible for Ezrahi to suggest that, by the late 1990s 'the most revealing icon of contemporary Israeli civilization' was not the ultra-protective Merkava tank but the rubber bullet, which the Israeli Army had adopted some ten years previously, perhaps to protect Palestinian demonstrators or maybe just to save the 'tender souls' of the Israeli soldiers who were expected to fire on these youths. In Ezrahi's hopeful account, this softening marks a disengagement from the whole Israeli epic of the few against the many, and represents the first step on 'the long and arduous path to a peace agreement with the Palestinians'.

Getting out of the tank means throwing off the parentalism that made it possible for Golda Meir to refer to Israeli soldiers as 'her children'. It involves changing the kinds of stories that fathers tell their sons, and questioning what Ezrahi describes as 'the convergence between the state and the family'. It necessitates thinking of Israel as a democracy rather than a Jewish state, and recognizing that the significant lost archaeology of the Holy Land includes the relics of the recently obliterated Palestinian landscape and not just the ideologically convenient residues of the ancient Kingdom of Solomon. It also demands a considerable struggle to bring some real individual subjectivity to the state's collectivized rituals of remembrance. Ezrahi exemplifies this by describing the life and work of a photographer. 'Erez H' grew up on a kibbutz and was told as a seven-year-old that his father had been killed serving as a paratrooper in the Six Day War.[53] There was no personal expression of grief, and the state moved in to the orphaned boy's life. The Department of Rehabilitation and Immortalization supported the family. The Ministry of Education sent books. There were pictures of monuments to fallen soldiers, stories of heroism and also birthday cards in which the army was presented as mother to the nation's war orphans. Erez H's father was remembered, but his unique personality was quite lost in the collectivity of state-led public commemoration.

Following the heroic path that the authorities opened up ahead of him, Erez H eventually became a paratrooper like his father; and in 1982 he found himself being shipped to the north to take part in an assault in Lebanon. It was at this point that he broke away, declaring himself afraid and not prepared to die for the cause. For some, Erez H was a coward who had betrayed his father's memory; but not according to Ezrahi, who remarks that Erez H became an individual at exactly the moment when he rejected the hero's path, albeit an individual with a short jail sentence to serve. Once released he sought out the individuality of his father, finding signs of it not in the letters of an official stone monument, but in some old photographs his father had taken, especially one showing a flowering cactus in a broken terracotta pot.

Erez H became a photographer, and in 1990 mounted an installation in which he and a fellow artist invoked the forms and rituals of national remembrance in order to call them into question. To do this, Ezrahi argues, was to break through the armour of the heroic self, redraw the lines between self and state, and restore the space for subjectivity and privacy that had been squeezed out of Israeli life. For their efforts, Erez and his collaborator found themselves being denounced as 'traitors' by right-wing nationalists on a television programme. One of their critics was the hero of the Golan Heights, at that time a Labour member of the Knesset, Avigdor Kahalani. He was outraged by their tampering with 'sacred' military symbols: 'Why do you stay in the country?' he asked Erez. 'Get up and leave.'[54] Erez's answer was that he would stay, precisely because 'there are people like you who think critics cannot be patriotic'.

This was an important argument, Ezrahi suggests, because it helped to consolidate 'alternative psychological and cultural facts, the kind of orientations that have come to be associated in late-twentieth-century Israel with the rise of individualism, the decline of military values, and the readiness to make hard concessions to the enemy in order to reach a settlement'. The man who is on the front line as far as those concessions go, Israel's present leader Ehud Barak, was a tank man before he became Israel's Chief of Staff, and one who distinguished himself west of the Suez Canal in the October War. His apparent willingness to consider returning the Golan Heights to Syria has brought him up against strong resistance from the Golan residents, many of whom are recent immigrants from Russia, and who find a strong champion of their cause in Avigdor Kahalani. And yet some of Israel's tank heroes are less intransigent, including Yuval Neria, the Colonel who appeared speaking about his paradoxical love of tanks in Claude Lanzmann's film *Tsahal*. Neria spent twelve days holding out against the Egyptians in 1973, the only survivor of his tank unit; but his anger at the political and military leadership responsible for the failures of that bloody war led him to combine with other officers and form the 'Peace Now' movement in 1977, and to press Begin to accept the peace initiative outlined by Anwar Sadat, when he visited Israel to address the Knesset in November 1977.[55]

General Tal had not been surprised by this polarization among tank veterans. The Israelis are, as he remarked, democratic to the limit. They will disagree about everything, right up to the wire. At the time of our meeting in

January 1999, his tanks were still rolling in southern Lebanon – still firing and coming under attack from Hezbollah guerrillas, who claim to have proved that the legendary Merkava is actually far from invincible, and can be destroyed by firing two anti-tank guided missiles at once into the narrow gap between its turret and body. As for the future, Tal seemed to oscillate between two views. Speaking from deep within his own historical experience, he cited the League of Nations Conference at Evian in July 1938, at which no country agreed to accept Jews who might then have been rescued from Nazi Germany. In Tal's view this refusal made the European nations partly responsible for the coming Holocaust and, as he said with terrifying intransigence, it meant that Israel was on its own, and must ensure that it has the capability to destroy the entire world if its own survival demands it. It would not be until May 2000 that Israel's tanks were hastily pulled out of Lebanon, but Tal, who shared many of the values of the Labour Party under Yitzhak Rabin, had himself been working for a more orderly kind of settlement, especially since the 1993 Oslo Agreement between Israel and the PLO. Having done so much to create Israel's doctrines of armoured warfare he had since founded a different kind of tank, a think-tank devoted to defining 'the doctrine of peace'.

Many mistakes had indeed been made, he volunteered of the past, before recalling the moment when Sadat addressed the Knesset, acknowledging, much to the disgust of his former Chief of Staff Shazly, that the state of Israel was 'a fait accompli', and suggesting that the time had come to build 'a durable peace based on justice'.[56] As Tal observed, 'when we established the military, we never envisaged that in our days peace would prevail. But now there is peace with Egypt, with Jordan, and also with the Palestinians. So eventually we hope that a comprehensive peace will prevail. Until then, you see I think President Sadat of Egypt was right, when he came to Israel to make peace with us, and he said that in the end everything would depend on whether there was a comprehensive peace, or only a specific peace with individual Arab countries. As long as it is not comprehensive, it is not secure. So we are now in a very, very delicate chapter of our history. Once a comprehensive peace prevails, then Israel will become a normal country.'

In the course of our discussion I presented Tal with a copy of Klein's 'Ballad of the Days of the Messiah'. I would not have been surprised had this war-toughened tank soldier dismissed it as an irrelevance; but General Tal appeared genuinely interested as he read the poem, gathered in from the diaspora. He wanted to know about Klein, and whether the ballad had been written in Yiddish, Hebrew or English. He paused to recite two lines from the fourth verse, in which the Messiah descends by parachute, and Klein then puts a question that would never be asked of Tal's tanks: 'O I see him falling! Will he shoot? Will he shoot? / Will Messiah's falling herald aim and shoot?' When he reached the word 'seraphim', Tal looked up to ask if I knew that it meant 'angel', and had etymological roots connecting it with fire.

This was not the first time I had heard Holy Writ cited in connection with the tank. When I visited the Vickers Challenger factory in Newcastle, I found a public affairs manager who tried to dispatch all thought of disarmament with the help of a few lines from St Luke: 'When a strong man armed keepeth his peace, his goods are in peace. But when a stronger than he shall come upon him, and overcome him, he taketh from him all his armour wherein he trusted, and divideth his spoils.' But Tal's interest went far deeper than that. Descended from a deeply religious family, he knows the scriptures well. He cited chapter and verse to support his claim that Jewish warriors have been leading their men into battle with the cry of 'Follow me!' since long before the beginnings of Western civilization. And he knew too much not to realize that the 'pillared fire' of Klein's tank was not just a blazing gun tube but a reference to Chapter XIV of the Book of Exodus. After dividing the Red Sea so that Moses could lead the people of Israel out of captivity in Egypt, the Lord looks down through a 'pillar of fire' to see the Egyptians following in hot pursuit. He then causes the wheels to fall from their chariots, and instructs Moses to stretch out his hand and close up the sea over their heads. It was hardly those unwheeled chariots that Tal had in mind when naming Israel's tank the Merkava, but the scriptures had been a source there too.

Encouraged to find such interest, I mentioned the fact that the tank had so often been called a 'Behemoth', after the monstrous creature mentioned in the Book of Job. Tal was surprised to hear this, pointing out that in Hebrew this word referred to many far from frightening beasts, including the cow and even the modest sheep. In English, he guessed, it had become inflated to imply a larger creature, not clever but big and frightening. And then he turned to his shelves and started rooting around among the military manuals until he found a concordance to the Bible. We looked up the word, and as the mystery thickened, Tal's assistant, an officer who was shortly to become director of the Merkava factory, was detailed to hunt out some bilingual editions of the scriptures. We searched up all the instances, and when we found inconsistencies between the King James and another

English translation, Tal phoned his wife and asked her to get out the steps and consult yet another edition stored high up on his shelves at home. For a long time the Hebrew root for the word 'Behemoth' remained stubbornly modest, merely a generic name for the beasts of the field. And yet as we followed the thread through various translations of Israel's oldest book of doctrine, it finally emerged that there was a second version, this one possibly derived from a Hebraistic form of the Egyptian word for 'water-ox'. Two names then, as Tal pointed out with some satisfaction, and one considerably more monstrous than the other.

Such rarefied etymological considerations would soon be brutally set aside. During the Palestinian uprising that broke out on 29 September 2000 (after Ariel Sharon's inflammatory visit to Jerusalem's Temple Mount), sheer monstrosity would once again obliterate the thought of peaceable de-escalation. Having withdrawn chaotically from Lebanon earlier in the year, Israel's humiliated tanks were now to be seen lined up unambiguously against unarmed Palestinian civilians. That, as the London-based Islamic Human Rights Commission proclaimed, was the revealed truth about Israel; and, once again, there was a press picture to encapsulate the point. Taken on 29 October near the Gaza Strip's Karni crossing, Ahmed Jadallah's photograph showed an approaching Israeli tank with a Palestinian boy standing in front of it, dwarfed by this massive opponent but still defiantly raising his arm to hurl a stone into the metal beast's reactive armour. The Chairman of the IHRC, Massoud Shadjareh, confirms that his organisation selected this emblematic image of Israel's ruthless 'iron wall' in conscious memory of Wang Weilin's stand in Tiananmen Square. Yet in this case, as he adds, the unnamed youth was reported killed by Israeli fire a few weeks later.[57]

PART V

After the Cold War

Poliscar in New York's Lower East Side, 1991.

Conversion: Pink Tank and Poliscar

'Tough Limo' is the name of a multi-media installation by the New York-based Catalonian artist, Francesc Torres. Created in 1983 and intended to explore the place of 'military behaviour in human culture', it was inspired by a hand-made model tank given to Torres's grandfather when he was imprisoned in Franco's jails – a birthday present from a fellow inmate. Torres converted this little metal replica into a vast wooden structure, painted in crude camouflage colours, and placed as if it were bearing down on an already half-crushed collection of chairs – the latter being inspired by the jumbled heap of empty chairs left in the wake of Anwar Sadat's assassination at a 1981 military parade in Egypt, and representing 'an unprotected, horizontal, open social forum, its people conspicuous by their absence'.[1] Torres cut five little windows into the tank, one for each member of the crew, and then placed a live iguana in a glass box behind each. Like a number of his works of this period, 'Tough Limo' reflected the artist's interest in the neurologist Paul MacLean's theory of 'the Reptilian Complex' – deep-seated behaviour such as 'territoriality, aggression, ritual display', which MacLean associated with the oldest of three evolutionary layers in the human brain.[2] People who viewed the work, either at the University of Virginia's Anderson Gallery or in the version that Torres took to Tokyo in 1987, will have been able to judge the artist's claim that 'the reptilian nature of the tank is evident on many levels; it is a territorial weapon, it intimidates by appearance, it crawls on the terrain, and it is camouflaged for concealment . . .'[3]

A decade earlier, one of London's rising avant-gardists went so far as to imagine himself as a tank. That was how the television producer Michael Kustow starred in *Tank*, his 'autobiographical fiction' about the three years in the late sixties when he was director of the Institute of Contemporary Arts. Naming himself 'k' (sounded as the last syllable – the 'guttural glottal' – in the word 'tank'), Kustow projected himself as a 'blunt tank muscling in on a point of vantage, claiming it on behalf of legions of unruly bandits armed with paintbrushes, cameras, musical instruments, amplifiers, projectors, jokes'.[4] 'K' was both an 'affable tank' and a merciless transgressor of bourgeois norms and 'Britishry'. Adequately boxed up by a few years at Oxford, here he was ploughing his way through a succession of unsatisfactory lovers while scanning developments on the exotic avant-garde horizon in Warsaw or in Prague, where, after 1968, no rolled-over arts administrator, however overheated, would ever have identified himself with a tank. Aware of the risks he was taking with his reputation, Kustow allowed an imaginary reader to make a new contribution to the growing inventory of tank rhymes – 'clank', 'rank', but now also 'wanker': 'thousands die and you use the vehicle of their death as an image for your puerile soul-searching'.[5]

Since the tank was so strongly prefigured in the cultural imagination before it was ever engineered into practical existence, it is consistent that so many artists have more recently tried to repossess it. In 1980 the West German artist Anselm Kiefer portrayed Second World War tanks as the enemies of art and spirituality, showing them as emblems of abstract power and aggressive forgetfulness in a work called 'Iconoclastic Controversy'.[6] In England, Liliane Lijn projects lights through old Centurion sighting prisms in works such as 'The Woman of War'; while David Hepher, known for his intensely realistic paintings of council flats and tower blocks, uses little tanks to suggest the military aspect of the perplexing street maps placed at the entries to vast housing estates in London. In Scotland, Ian Hamilton Finlay has produced a whole series of pastoral tanks, drawn or cut in stone, wreathed in foliage and driven back into a classical context.[7] A tank covered in camouflage paint is entitled 'Classic Landscape', while another figures in a 'heroic emblem' alongside a fragmentary saying of the pre-Socratic philosopher Heraclitus ('Thunderbolt steers all'). Finlay places others in leafy Arcadian settings, symbols of death in Arcadia that refer back through Poussin to Virgil and Theocritus. He has also coined a number of lapidary 'camouflage sentences' such as: 'To camouflage a tank is to add what Shenstone calls "the amiable to the severe" – the beautiful to the sublime, flutes to drums.'

Some of the artists who seized on the tank in the last two decades of the twentieth century were no better than the tacky heavy-metal bands or film producers – from 'Tank Girl' to James Bond – who noisily exploit the miasma of this heavy war machine. But others, more like exorcists than celebrants, did rather better during the promising interval that followed the end of the Cold War. Peace, or perhaps just Western victory, was proclaimed as the Berlin Wall came down in 1989 and the tank seemed historically redundant once again. Many thousands were to be destroyed or converted into civilian use under international agreements such as the Conventional Armed Forces in Europe Treaty, signed in 1990, which reduced the Warsaw Pact's tank fleet from 60,000 to 13,000 distributed between eight successor states; while Nato's allowance went from 25,000 to 20,000.[8] Within Nato, there was a 'cascade' of more or less obsolete tanks to less advanced countries like Greece and Turkey; and, as happens after every major war, there were attempts to stave off the closure of armaments factories by converting them to civil use. Artists may have been utterly irrelevant to the ill-fated 'groundnuts scheme' of the late nineteen-forties, in which agricultural machines made by former British armaments firms such as Vickers (where Sherman tanks were replaced by unsuccessful 'Shervik' caterpillar tractors) would be used to improve colonial economies in Africa. Yet the Cold War, which had dominated Europe and much of the world's industrial base for many decades, was an 'imaginary war'[9] waged between two polarized blocs. It had undeniably real effects, but was sustained symbolically – by political rhetoric, epic military scenarios, and terrifying images of nuclear apocalypse, mutually assured destruction, and tanks pouring through the Fulda Gap. For this reason, the climate of 'conversion' that attended the initial disintegration of the Eastern bloc was indeed a moment to be seized by artists as well as scrap merchants and Western business consultants. Briefly, before the next round of wars got started and the monster hardened up again in Yugoslavia or Kuwait, it was possible to dream of taking the tank to pieces, of stripping it of its symbolic power, and even returning it to the art gallery.

Painting it pink in Prague

For nearly fifty years a Soviet Stalin II tank stood on a three-metre-high stone plinth in a square in the Smíchov district of Prague. Dedicated to the memory of the Soviet soldiers killed during the liberation of Prague in May 1945, this wartime relic, still identified as Tank No. 23, was an established part of the scene. Its gun barrel pointed westward, past cars and passers-by; and it was surrounded by trees, herbaceous borders and a couple of flag poles used on those regular occasions when the Communist authorities celebrated the Soviet liberation of their city.

On 28 April 1991 Prague woke to find its memorial tank converted into a very different kind of icon. At five o'clock that morning David Cerny, a student at Prague's Academy of Applied Arts, turned up with a number of accomplices and a film crew, climbed the plinth and set about painting the

tank bright pink. The police came along at 5.45 a.m., but Cerny had anticipated their arrival, and was able to fob them off with fake documents of
permission from the Mayor's Office and Charles University Film Academy.
The artists continued their work, proving that their gesture had nothing to
do with good taste by adding a smirking boy's appendage that poked
upwards from the cupola, an extended finger borrowed from America's
best-known rude gesture. Having finished, they daubed their signatures in
white along the bottom of the grey stone plinth: 'David Cerny' and 'The
Neostunners'.

Cerny and his fellows had completed their work by 6 a.m., and uproar
broke out a few hours later. Photographers poured into the square and telephone lines burned between City Hall, the Foreign Ministry and the offices
of State Security. Mindful of the sensitive economic negotiations then
under way between the Soviet and Czechoslovak governments, the Minister
for National Defence, Mr Dobrovsky, denounced the pinking of the tank as
an act of vandalism, and official apologies were hastily carried to the Soviet
Embassy. Aware that the forty-sixth anniversary of the Red Army's liberation of Prague on 9 May 1945 was only days away, he also dispatched the
soldiers who went along the next day to cover the stone plinth with sheets
of protective plastic and then repaint the tank in proper military green. By
8 May, the General Prosecutor had charged David Cerny under an infamous article of law concerned with 'public disturbances': Paragraph 202 is
remembered as the 'rubber paragraph' because the Communist authorities
used to stretch it out to suppress every kind of dissident activity (including
Václav Havel's own endeavour to place a floral tribute to Jan Palach in
Wenceslas Square) under the general rubric of riot.

Unreformed Communists may have been consoled by this uncompromising response; although not sufficiently to restrain the nocturnal vigilantes
who would later express their opposition to Cerny's action by smearing
white paint over Prague's memorial to Jan Palach and also a monument in
West Bohemia commemorating the American soldiers who had fallen in the
liberation of that part of Czechoslovakia. There were others, however, who
judged the re-greening of the tank to be the real provocation. An appeal was
launched by a weekly classified-ads magazine called *Annonce*, and a special
Pink Tank account was opened at a nearby bank so that supporters could
make donations towards the cost of Cerny's anticipated fine. The members
of a Society of Friends for the Restoration of the Pink Tank took up cardboard and scissors, turned themselves into an agit-prop column of pink
tanks and marched on the memorial to demonstrate against the restoration

of this 'symbol of violence'. On 9 May, the twice-daubed Tank No. 23 was surrounded by clamorous disputation, with political insults echoing from its sides. As one champion of the pink tank remarked, 'When they started to shout "Fascists", we yelled back "Communists", and they stopped.'

By 16 May, a group of fifteen deputies from the Czechoslovak federal parliament, all of them connected either with Civic Forum or its sister movement in Slovakia, Public Against Violence, had resolved to take the matter into their own hands. Led by Jiri Ruml, and with David Cerny standing by as 'artistic adviser', this group of former dissidents converged on the newly greened monument. Dressed in blue boiler suits with letters on their backs identifying them as deputies, and therefore as immune from prosecution (despite their own attempts to get their special status waived), they took up their brushes and, encouraged by a large and supportive crowd, set about re-pinking the tank in protest, as Ruml declared, 'that paragraph 202 could ever again be abused'. On a poster taped to the tank's plinth the deputies announced that they would gladly pinken 'the rest of the tanks in Czechoslovakia', but one was more than enough for the Soviet Foreign Minister, who condemned this 'vile act of political hooliganism'.[10] Ironically, the man chosen to fly to Moscow to make a televised apology to the Kremlin was Alexander Dubcek, Chairman of the National Parliament and former leader of the reform communist government that, in the phrase of one of its members, had been 'steam-rollered' by Soviet tanks in 1968.[11]

President Václav Havel expressed misgivings too, and not just because the gesture threatened ongoing negotiations with the Soviet Union. Speaking on 19 May in his regular Sunday radio address to the nation, he conceded that 'an ugly tank' is not 'the best memento of war victims', yet he also insisted on the respect that should be accorded to the feelings of those people in the USSR for whom this tank was a symbol, 'a memory of all the Soviet victims of World War II'.[12] Cerny's initial action may have been 'an understandable expression' of youth, but Havel condemned the deputies' repeat performance as an irresponsible expression of 'powerlessness, of frustration with their own parliament'. Noting that partygoers at the tank site had already wrecked 'a star made from some pretty flowers', he wondered where it would all end: 'Will we have the St Wenceslas statue painted red, St Vitus Cathedral in blue, all the paintings in the galleries spray painted?' By this time, Prague's pink tank had given rise to a whole industry of models, postcards, toy replicas, and T-shirts, some of which were said to be selling for one sixth of the average Czech monthly salary.

*

The controversy over the memorial tank in Prague 5 had actually begun a year or so before David Cerny's unexpected intervention, when the local council first proposed that this emblem of Soviet power be dismantled, thereby provoking the Communist Party to raise a 40,000-strong petition demanding its retention. Politicians in the new parliament had discussed the proposition, with President Václav Havel taking a moderately pro-tank line as he warned of the dangers of rewriting history to suit present moods, while others, including the Foreign Minister, Jiri Dienstebier, favoured replacing the tank with a less provocative memorial. Caught in this embarrassing battle between remembrance and its deliberate negation, Tank No. 23 was removed from its plinth on 14 June, and shifted to a military airfield north of Prague, destined to be painted green yet again, and then settled back into the obscurity of a military museum. Cerny's signed and 'authorised' series of postcards documenting the mutation of Prague's contentious tank appeared at about the same time, financed by a tour agency called Souvenir Satin, the owner of which had also promised to cover Cerny's legal fees. One, entitled 'The Pink Tank (1991)', showed the crudely pinkened machine in its full glory, its finger thrusting upwards with jaunty confidence. Another was taken after the authorities had flattened this offensive digit and tried to cover the humiliated memorial with a suitably green but undersized military tarpaulin: this variation was entitled 'The Covered Pink Tank (1991)'.

Outside Czechoslovakia the tale of the pink tank could be relished as a beguiling anecdote that proved that Prague had not lost its dissident sense of humour. It offered teasing consolation to a world that, as the Iron Curtain came crashing down eighteen months previously, had been rash enough to imagine its armoured fighting vehicles consigned to the fairground and museum, and its arms factories converted to civil use. Here, at least, was a break from the apparently endless column of tanks that would 'roll' across the fields of that pastoral delusion in 1991 – crushing civilians in Lithuania, bursting through improvised barricades along shattered roads in Slovenia and Croatia, adorned with the corpses of butchered Shiites in a propagandized image of Saddam Hussein's tanks from southern Iraq, or advancing towards Kuwait with breathless television reporters perched on them, all dressed up in military camouflage, and babbling excitedly into the camera as they peered into the coming dust of Desert Storm. Faced with this gruesome column, it was a relief to find that 'magical Prague' had retained its playful quality.

Within Czechoslovakia, however, the story of the pink tank had different ramifications. Though born in 1968, Cerny turned out to be a conventional 'happenings' man working twenty-three years after his time. When Cerny claimed to have painted Tank No. 23 because he wanted to give it 'a more human face', he placed his action in the same line of descent as the posters that went up on Prague walls in the summer of 1990 to advertise an impending concert by the Rolling Stones: 'When the tanks roll out, the Stones roll in'.[13] A trainee transgressor who believed that 'art should consist of conflict', Cerny expressed his wish to confront people – to break through their stereotyped ideas, to mystify and provoke them, to force them to question their own complacent assumptions.

First among the sedimented ideas targeted by Cerny and his accomplices was the Communist symbolism of the tank. The first Soviet tanks entered Prague in May 1945. Hailed by crowds and adorned with seasonal lilac as they advanced, the post-war Communist state worked hard to ensure that their memory would be for ever wreathed in the rhetoric of liberation. The Soviet tank became an emblem of state power. Here, as in the West, the tank was customarily portrayed as a 'peacemaker', deterring enemy aggression. In Communist iconography it was up there with the patriotic mother holding a child in one hand and a wholesome loaf of bread in the other, gazing out after her husband as he marched off heroically to defend the homeland. The Soviet tank was central to the formal May Day processions, which in later decades at least were only staged on a grand scale every five years because they were expensive and the armoured columns did such damage to the roads. It was also part of Communism's song-and-dance routine: the Russian Alexandrov ensemble, which visited Czechoslovakia repeatedly during those years, is still remembered for its singing and dancing tank commanders, strutting about in their characteristic helmets and being covered with flowers by enraptured crowds as they re-enacted the liberation of Eastern Europe. Communism created and insisted upon its own myth of 1945, but it was not just unreformed Party members – 'tankies', as their pro-Soviet equivalents were known in Britain – who felt that the difference between Nazism and the Communism of 1945 was still worth marking, and that the memory of those Soviet soldiers deserved better than the blithe kind of 'disruption' that could be achieved with a few tins of pink paint.

The pink tank also revealed that different generations had very different ideas of this symbolic machine. The younger generation was mindful of Soviet tanks, but for them the heroic meaning of Tank No. 23 had been thoroughly corrupted by the experience of more recent years. As Prague's Academy of Fine Art explained in a statement justifying student Cerny's antics, the tank had become an altogether different kind of symbol after the Soviet invasion of 1968. This time the flowers weren't draped over the advancing machines as garlands of welcome; instead, they had been placed in gun barrels as symbols of helpless protest.

One of Cerny's 'Neostunners', told the magazine *Reflex* that Tank No. 23 had been pinkened in order to insist on historical truth after decades of official distortion. There were all sorts of conjectures about the inauthenticity of Tank No. 23: it was apparently not the original 'first' Soviet tank into Prague, as the Communist cult had encouraged people to assume (that one, actually numbered I-24, was said to have been destroyed, along with its commander, and then removed by the Red Army as 'scrap' that could not possibly be left as a historic monument).[14] It also emerged that the Red Army had never fought in the immediate area of the tank memorial, a zone that had actually been 'liberated' by a division of 'Armed Forces for the Committee for the Liberation of the Peoples of Russia,' a maverick force raised from among Soviet prisoners in Germany by the captured Red Army commander General Andrej Vlasov. This doomed force had gone into battle first against the advancing Soviet troops and latterly, as they battered their way into Prague, against the Waffen SS (with whom they actually soon combined in a desperate attempt to escape the Red Army). For this 'Neostunner', the pinkened tank was really a tribute to Vlasov and his soldiers, who had been hideously liquidated by Stalin after American forces refused to help them evade Soviet capture.

Like the best Prague fables, however, the story of the pink tank also has a darker side, as I found in Slovakia, then still the eastern province of Czechoslovakia, but filled with nationalist and separatist ambitions since November 1989, and standing in increasingly troubled relationship with Prague. Here too, the pink tank was quickly caught up into a web of arcane speculation of the sort that used to proliferate under Communism, where it was difficult to establish that anything was quite what it seemed. To begin with, Slovakia seemed to share Prague's joke. Some objected that Cerny's prank was derivative, a mere copy of the pink weapons produced years earlier by the Slovak artist, Stano Filko. A Slovak photographer cleaned up by selling postcards of the pink tank, and there was amusement in the Slovak National Assembly, in Bratislava, when Communist deputies tried to pass a motion of censure against those of their fellow deputies who had gone out to repinken the tank. They were promptly asked to specify what law insisted that a tank should always be green. It was surely a basic principle of military camouflage that a tank should take the colour of its environment: green in woodland and fields; sand-coloured in desert; white in snowy terrain; and pink, surely, when among flowers in a Prague square.

Meanwhile, the well-known Bratislavan activist Jan Budaj had a different way of identifying the pinkness of Tank No. 23 with the colour of Václav Havel's insufficiently post-Communist regime. For many years, Budaj had lived under acute pressure from the state, a dissident – or in the phrase of a Slovak sociologist, 'an island of positive deviance' – he was at once a stoker, an environmentalist and a happenings artist whose disruptive acts of street theatre took considerably more risks than David Cerny ever needed to. In 1989 he was among those who took the Velvet Revolution to the streets of Bratislava; indeed, he emerged as leader of Public Against Violence and a national hero. But a few minutes before the polls closed in the first democratic elections, he was obliged to resign his candidature with the party he had just led to victory. Budaj had failed to pass the controversial 'lustration' process, designed by the federal government to prevent former secret police agents from establishing themselves in political office. As critics said of this procedure, it absolved former Communists on the basis that they were simply doing their job, and then used old secret police files to come down especially hard on their former victims. It was also, as Budaj had himself found out, subject to political manipulation.

As a former avant-gardist, Budaj appreciated David Cerny's action, but he had serious reservations about the fifteen deputies from Civic Forum and Public Against Violence who had gone out to repeat it. The action may have seemed like a mere gambol, a light-hearted moment of release from the grind of government, but it was far from this. To begin with, the time for dissident 'happenings' had surely passed, and rather than indulging in a nostalgic reprise of the days when the powerless dissident would enact Lennonist gestures against the corrupted Leninist state, these deputies should have hesitated before breaking the law. As Budaj put it, reprising an objection that Havel himself had expressed, 'it is a serious matter when the state refuses to obey its own law'. Indeed, those deputies should have recognized that their responsibility now was to change the law, not mock it or flout it for the sake of dramatic effect. Rather than resorting to easy gestures, they would have done better to bring about the repeal of Article 202.

But Budaj wasn't going to let the matter rest there. Indeed, he ventured that the real achievement of the deputies who had repinked Tank No. 23 had been to transform this machine into 'a political weapon rather than a weapon of war' – one that was only too good at reflecting the ambiguities of Václav Havel's regime. The pink tank served as diverting camouflage; it put a joke where there was actually another government setting itself above the law. Budaj pointed out that Jiri Ruml, leader of the deputies who repainted the tank, had been prominent in the Communist Party in the fifties. He had later become a reform communist and then a dissident, but he was now playing a central role in the lustration process; indeed, he was chairman of a committee that stood in judgement over people who had been rotting in prison, or slaving in uranium mines while Ruml himself was still a loyal Party man. Meanwhile, a law was soon to be enacted that would extend the lustration procedure into new spheres. It would prohibit those who had had any connection with the secret police from working in the media, a development that, as Budaj saw it, contravened natural justice, and would certainly, given the unusual degree of pressure that the Communist authorities used to exert in this area, assist those who now wanted to limit the independence of the press. For Budaj, who still didn't know when he would get a chance to clear his name, the pink tank was indeed a story of 'magical Prague'. It suggested an alarming convergence between the Prague of Kafka and that of Václav Havel – a city of doors behind doors, unanswerable accusations, and of authority that, even if it was no longer entirely inscrutable, was apparently still prepared to play games with the law.

Yet in Slovakia tanks were not just symbols to be loved, reviled and abused; they also constituted the livings of tens of thousands of people. From the late forties, Stalin turned Slovakia into a logistical zone dedicated to the supply and equipment of his expanding war machine. Vast steel and aluminium works were developed, along with a massive heavy armaments industry that manufactured Soviet-designed tanks and other weapons, both for the Warsaw Pact and also for export to liberation struggles, terrorist groups and pro-Soviet forces throughout the world.

When Václav Havel became President he announced that the new Czechoslovakia would be beating its swords into ploughshares, calling for an end to tank manufacture, and committing his government to programmes of 'conversion', that would diversify this chain of centralized factories into a wide range of civil engineering projects carried out in partnership with Western companies. Tank production stopped for a number of months but, faced with the prospect of mass unemployment in central Slovakia together with an alarming upsurge of nationalist sentiment in the area, the vision of 'conversion' was proving hard to sustain.

In March 1991 President Havel had visited Slovakia and, when not being cursed and spat upon by demonstrators in Bratislava, warned officers at the Trencin army base against allowing military forces in Slovakia to be abused by nationalists in support of their demands for independence. He stressed that 'the picture of tanks in the streets' was truly horrifying, but there was apparently little that could done to prevent the stricken armaments industry from clinging to its old ways.[15] A factory in Detva had broken away under new non-communist management, converting most of its capacity to civil production and marketing itself in the West, but this was a rare exception. Over in Martin, a heavy-metal town right down to its graffiti ('Iron Maiden', 'Slayer', etc.), pragmatism had already triumphed over Havel's symbolic promise, and 200 tanks were being made for export to Syria. This reversion to old ways was on a small scale and quite insufficient to stop the industry's decline, but it had filled many with a sense of shame and the air was bristling with accusing fingers. It was said that, even though the first conversion schemes predated the revolution of 1989, the old Communists who still controlled the majority of these factories had been deliberately sabotaging attempts to make progress in this direction.

I visited Martin early in July 1991, travelling east through a land of cherry trees, ruined crag-top castles and roadside scrapyards that were already filled with old tanks, to find a vast industrial zone, which still clattered with the antique sound of typewriters. The gargantuan ZTS tank factory had the word 'Welcome' written over its door in a suggestive assortment of languages. There was no question, however, of a foreign observer being received without special permission from the Director, and it didn't take long to discover that Mr Segla was at that moment sequestered with his senior managers and trade union leaders in a nearby hotel. They were in a meeting with the Slovak Minister for the Economy and members of the three parties forming the coalition government; and the question on the table was whether Mr Segla and his colleagues were really as responsible for the failure of conversion as had recently been suggested by Martin Krajkovic, a deputy in the Slovak National Assembly, who had denounced 'the rotation of the pink *nomenklatura*' in and around the tank factories at Martin.

The Hotel Grandis stood triangular and out of season in rising woods at the foot of mountains that had yet to experience the full impact of winter sports as it was hoped Western visitors would soon come to know them. Somewhere outside, a party was singing folk songs, but the sound was beaten back by raised voices from the conference room: 'If we value politics more than knowledge we shall fall back . . .'

Some left as quickly as possible when the meeting broke up, but others gathered in the wooden dining room for a late lunch that dwindled through the afternoon, finally leaving Mr Segla alone with his shiny-faced colleagues, their corner table straining under a formidable weight of elbows and sticky liqueur glasses. Mr Segla had busied himself throughout the meal, a large man striding in and out of the kitchen, ordering more rounds of drinks, winking at a waitress, and stroking his goatee at more pensive moments. It was a comfortable performance from a man who had just been given two months to prepare a detailed analysis of the present situation in his troubled factory and to clarify precisely who had been responsible for the failure of previous attempts at conversion. The future may have promised little but redundancy and disintegration; yet Mr Segla still seemed secure in the habits of the previous era – the time in the late fifties, when, as his Director of Conversion would soon be telling a consultant from the West, the general manager of the ZTS *kombinat* presided over a chain of ninety-eight armament factories employing 85,000 people, and was as powerful as any government minister.[16]

In the absence of hard information, rumours had been coiling up around the factory. Critics may not have understood much about the technicalities of tank production, but they had kept an intricate tally of suspicions. Newspaper articles had alleged that 100 tanks had been manufactured and then 'lost' from the official record, and that fifty-seven had been made even though the state had cancelled the order. There had been further speculation that 82 T-72 tanks had been sold to the Czechoslovak Army only to be returned secretly to Martin so that they could be sold a second time to Syria.

Deputy Martin Krajkovic was careful to differentiate mere suspicion from proven fact, but he had little doubt that ZTS was controlled by members of an unreformed Communist network – an 'octopus', as he called it, that had tentacles in every branch of the factory, and also in Slovakia's new Ministry for the Economy, where many former members of the Communist regime at Martin had found employment as 'experts'. There was talk of intermediary bank accounts in Switzerland, of secretive visits to Russia, of terms struck during secret nocturnal meetings with the politician Vladimir Meciar (then out of office but gathering his nationalist forces for his approaching return to power), and of a new ZTS joint-stock company that had been set up in the name of privatization, but was, so the claim went, being manipulated to ensure that the old guard were more and more in control of their ailing factory. It was even suggested that, under the command economy, component parts for tanks had been ordered in excessive quantities to create an impression of high productivity, and then bulldozed into the ground at secret sites around Martin. I was told that the Communist mafia had worked tirelessly to discredit every conversion plan that arose, including a potentially encouraging programme to make safari and cross-country vehicles for Chrysler, while claiming to implement them in order to secure state funds that could then be used, contrary to the expectations on which it was granted, to buy the loyalty of the workforce by providing bonuses and pay-rises, even while the factory was producing almost nothing. The loyalty of the trade unions was certainly not in doubt, for their representatives had written to the regional paper mocking ZTS's critics as ignorant fools who, now that the scheme involving safari jeeps had failed, would doubtless save the many thousand workers in ZTS Martin by replacing tanks with 'safari ironing boards'.

This story would drag on for years to come. The factory's problems may have seemed to decrease considerably when Vladimir Meciar and his Movement for a Democratic Slovakia came to power in 1992; but the ensuing resumption of subsidies would prove quite insufficient to stem the decline in ZTS's unconverted and desperately obsolete business. One order of T-72 tanks was shipped to Syria, despite considerable diplomatic difficulties and the blocking of shipments in German and Polish ports. But such was the pressure exerted on Israel's behalf by America that, by September 1993, the director, Mr. Segla, had to cancel a contract to provide Syria with a further 300 tanks, already largely paid for with Saudi backing, saying: 'conflictive relations between Slovak and Czech military industries and a backlog of problems make it uncertain whether the factory can respect its agreements'.[17] The workers, meanwhile, were being laid off in batches of a thousand at a time.

After listening to a torrent of allegations, plausible but also paranoid in the measure of corruption they suggested, I asked Krajcovic what he thought about the pink tank in Prague. He laughed at the mere mention of it, replying that, of course, he liked David Cerny's work, and promptly describing it as a perfect illustration for his thesis about the ongoing 'rotation of the pink *nomenklatura*'. For him there could be no doubt: the pinkness of the tank reflected the persistence and continued immunity of Communist power within Václav Havel's Czechoslovakia. The General Prosecutor's decision to charge Cerny so quickly proved that, within the Prague legal establishment just as in the Slovakian armaments industry, the 'pink *nomenklatura*' held on to power. While he proposed to throw the book at David Cerny, the Prosecutor had failed to act against the countless, far more serious offences of the old Communist regime.

It had all gone very differently for Josef Kneifel, the famous 'tank bomber' of East Germany who stepped out into the cold and rainy evening of Sunday, 9 March 1980, having chosen a time when he knew most of his fellow citizens were at home watching a popular TV thriller, and placed an explosive charge beneath a Soviet war memorial tank in the central square of Karl-Marx-Stadt (since renamed Chemnitz). Kneifel detonated this symbol of the 'hated power' that had just invaded Afghanistan and watched chunks of metal come clattering down in the courtyard of an adjacent police station. He then drove home in jubilation, singing the 'Ode to Joy' from Beethoven's Ninth Symphony. Eventually betrayed by a garrulous priest, he spent seven years in the notoriously severe Bautzen prison before being expelled to the West.[18]

Eleven years later, Soviet war memorials were under pressure all over Eastern Europe and, even though the old Communist law had been invoked, David Cerny's gesture was allowed to pass away unprosecuted as an artful prank. By that time, indeed, the Soviet tank was suffering an apparently terminal identity crisis even in its own disintegrating homeland. The limitations of Gorbachev's reforms were made dismally clear on 13 January 1991, when Soviet tanks were unleashed against secessionists in Lithuania. Perestroika froze into a terrible image of resistant demonstrators pushing back against a tank that had crushed one of their compatriots, a booted foot sticking out from under the tracks. Gorbachev denied giving the order, but his words were never a match for those uttered by the partly crushed victim, who later spoke to the press from a hospital bed in Vilnius. And then, in August, with the coup against Gorbachev, the Soviet Union's much-travelled tanks rolled into Moscow and other Russian cities, sent in under the mistaken assumption that the mere sight of them would prove as compelling as it had previously been found in diverse East European cities.

It was Boris Yeltsin, then President of a resurgent Russian nation, who emerged, at least in his own estimate, as the man who could finally bring those trundling machines to a halt. Looking back in his memoirs, he would declare that, by June of that year, many Russians had been filled with 'a sense of the end of Soviet history'.[19] The image of the USSR was 'inseparably linked with the image of a military power', so much so that the very word 'Soviet' had been turned into an unutterable piece of metal: '"Soviet man" and "Soviet tank" were both concepts that were inextricably and mysteriously joined.' Gorbachev may have reformed the world's image of the USSR by 'silencing the tanks' but he was still 'babbling' on about the Soviet way of life, not realizing that 'the Soviet Union could not exist without the image of the empire'.

Yeltsin found his own symbolic moment on the morning of 19 August. Looking out from the beleaguered White House in Moscow, he saw a tank parked outside, with the driver sticking his head out of the hatch only to find himself in the midst of a crowd of citizens quite 'unafraid of the tank treads'. Seeing this odd reprise of the Prague Spring, the Russian President 'felt a jolt inside' and resolved to go out and 'stand with those people'. So shortly afterwards, 'I clambered on to a tank, and straightened myself up tall.' Then, feeling a sense of 'utter clarity, complete unity with the people standing around me', he spoke out into the television cameras – declaiming against 'the eternal night' and reciting his famous appeal to the Russian people. Yeltsin had broken the spell of the Soviet tank and, consciously or not, he had also reprised one of the Soviet Union's most cherished founding images – the one that Lenin gave to the world when, returning to Russia from exile in 1917, he climbed on to an armoured car outside the Finland Station in Petrograd, to hail the masses and inaugurate the Revolution.

That lineage may have been in Yeltsin's mind when he described the failed August coup as 'the end of the twentieth century'. But the kind of history that is written with tanks was not to be terminated so easily; and even if the image of Yeltsin on his machine was embraced by many justly frightened Russians as 'an icon to ward off the darkness closing in', this was not to say that it would prove efficacious.[20] Within weeks of the Soviet Union's final expiration at the end of 1991, tanks were falling out of the disintegrating Red Army, and turning up in the 'small wars' that broke out along Russia's periphery. Early in 1992, Russian tanks, together with their blond-haired (i.e. northern) crews, were claimed to be engaged on both sides of the murderous conflict between Azeris and the Armenians in Nagorno Karabakh. And by the autumn of that year, they were also to be found furthering Russian ends against the nationalist aspirations of Eduard Shevardnadze's Georgia. In October 1993 Yeltsin turned his tanks on the rebel Russian Parliament, shelling the White House from the banks of the Moskva River; and in 1994 he ordered them into their first, brutal and disastrous engagement in Chechnya. Like Clinton's visit to Tiananmen Square, this story was all too easily wrapped up by distant cartoonists, one of whom dutifully showed Yeltsin's return to old form: standing on a subdued Soviet tank to pronounce democracy in 1991; and driving it with grim-faced and apparently quite orthodox zeal in 1994. In reality, it was only the prelude to the bloody onslaught of 1999, in the midst of which Yeltsin handed his deeply corrupted office over to Vladimir Putin.

Not content with forcing David Cerny's Prague gesture back into history, this remobilization would also challenge those American artists who have persisted in drawing up designs for the redundant Communist tank. In 1998, the New York artist Jerilea Zempel organized a group of women to create a crocheted pink and floral net – a 'tank tea cosy', which was fitted over an old Soviet tank at a military museum in Poznan, Poland, converting an instrument that once symbolized oppression into a ridiculous, fuzzy dinosaur: 'mighty, awesome, stopped dead in its tracks'. Joe Davies had been less fortunate in getting access to redundant tanks in Berlin a few years earlier. His plan was to create a motorized 'armoured garden' – taking decommissioned tanks, filling their turrets with soil, trees, rocks and other materials associated with traditional Japanese gardens, and then installing them 'in urban contexts where the threat to natural environments has significant urban origins'. But that was an overtaken project too.

The Poliscar (a war machine for people without apartments)

1991, the year of Desert Storm was a time of acute crisis in New York too. The city's first black mayor, the Democrat David Dinkins, had apparently fallen at the first post, unable to finance the progressive social policies of his 1990 election campaign; and a worried State Governor, Mario M. Cuomo, had stepped into the void with plans to prime the city's slumped economy with $7 billion worth of public works. Meanwhile, the twentieth century's great metropolis continued to fall apart. Celebrated streets such as Fifth Avenue and the Avenue of the Americas were cratered with potholes, and some of the poorer areas looked as if they had been bombed. Buildings stood burned out, barricaded and abandoned, while a similarly damaged population was living on the streets or in filthy plastic shanties among the ruins. There were said to be at least 100,000 homeless people in New York, and perhaps the same number again living as squatters, many of them in semi-derelict buildings that had come into City ownership during the seventies when private landlords walked away, blaming their troubles on a system of rent control that had made their properties a financial liability. These outcasts were everywhere to be seen. They shuffled along, loaded up with greasy plastic bundles or pushing improvised vehicles filled with salvaged bottles and tin cans. They crouched weeping in doorways, and stood on the corner ranting insanely or begging: sometimes obscenely, sometimes with an exaggerated and unreliable politeness. The whole city seemed under invasion from Skid Row, so much so that visitors who found themselves with no choice but to ask for directions on the street were advised to deck their question in reactive armour: 'Can you tell me the way to —— or should I just go f— myself?'

Many solutions were wished upon New York's homeless population during that critical year, but it was not until Krzysztof Wodiczko came along that anyone appeared to offer these outcasts a tank with which to defend themselves. Wodiczko called his invention a 'Poliscar' in acid tribute to the democratic ideals of the ancient Greek city state, but it had no sooner gone on show at the Josh Baer Gallery than the *Village Voice* art critic went along to set the record straight. Noticing that the device came to a sharp point, this observer declared herself in no doubt that the Poliscar had been 'designed by, if not for, men'.[21] She ran through a quick succession of metaphors, calling the Poliscar 'a cop from another planet', a 'souped-up tin man' and 'a war toy for the homeless', before settling for the idea that it was 'a robot with a tank-shaped body geared to survival in a police state' or, more simply, a 'mobile tank'.

Alerted by this account, I went down to the Josh Baer Gallery to find that the Poliscar was indeed a strangely theatrical contrivance: unlike anything that had existed before and yet deliberately engineered out of resemblances to things familiar. Isolated in an art gallery, it conjured up a hectic rehearsal of precedents. Wodiczko had built in allusions to Kafka, Goya, Aldo-Rossi, Tatlin's famous tower; and the drawings displayed alongside the device invoked the visionary machines sketched by Leonardo da Vinci. The Poliscar could look menacing in one frame of reference, while at the same time appearing flimsy and comical in another. It was at once a mechanized Ku Klux Klansman and, as some of the homeless people who had seen it were apparently quick to recognize, an automated and electronically wired wigwam. Exuding counterfactual energy, this utopian contrivance challenged the viewer to recognize that the world might be different, and to consider the host of possibilities excluded by the machines to which modern history had granted practical reality.

The Poliscar was certainly rich in associations, but was it a tank? Its sides were made of black fabric rather than armour, but in its symbolic aspect this thing certainly played with the idea of the tank: the carefully produced impression of solidity and bulkiness, for example; or the narrow siting slit and the guarded relationship it implied between the interior of the machine and its monolithic exterior appearance; even the curiously paradoxical impression of an archaic apparatus only realized in modern times. But Wodiczko's contraption was considerably more specific than this. Rather than evoking modern machines like the Abrams M1A1s used in the Desert Storm operation against Iraq earlier that same year, it had a strangely anti-quarian affinity with the first tanks that ever existed: the dream-laden, slow-moving British prototypes that went into action as little more than monstrous symbols on the Western Front in 1916.

The exhibition included some small models showing how this peculiar vehicle would look assembled in all three of its available positions. The driving position was suggestive, but it was only when adjusted to the flatter sleeping position that the Poliscar settled into the rhomboid or 'lozenge-like' shape that had earned the first tanks the nick-name of 'Cubist slugs'. This was not a matter of abstract resemblance alone. While taking the shape of those early tanks, the Poliscar also revived the curious symbolic excess that was one of their defining characteristics. Like the first tanks, Wodiczko's paradoxical vehicle seemed at once a rational mechanical struc-ture and a ludicrous cultural fantasy, a modern throwback that made a point of deriving its novelty from ancient times. It looked both menacing and comic, a war-machine, but one that had nothing to compel with except its surprising visual appearance. The Gulf War had demonstrated how much more brutally effective tanks had become since those experimental days, but it had also opened the way for Wodiczko, whose Poliscar recov-ered the symbolic materials of the early tank, and used them to suggest other potentialities.

The Poliscar was exhibited alongside a sequence of photographs showing it on the street against a background of devastated buildings and derelict lots covered with the improvised plastic shelters of the homeless. But if the memory of the Western Front was fleetingly stirred by this shattered back-ground, this was only in order to emphasize the shattered state of New York's Lower East Side. Wodiczko had put his machine on the pavement just around the corner from Tompkins Square Park. This had been a coun-ter-cultural playground in the sixties when bands such as the Grateful Dead, the Jimi Hendrix Experience and the Fugs played there, but in 1991 it was notorious as the battlefield on which the police had repeatedly assaulted the host of homeless people who had taken up residence there. Skirmishes had given way to full-scale street battles, with punks and anar-chist squatters joining the homeless in resisting the police, who came to evict them, tooled up as if for a full-scale military operation. The park had finally been cleared on the night of 23 June 1991, and then closed off – a piece of no man's land isolated behind a hurricane fence.

The shanty town against which Wodiczko had photographed his Poliscar had been erected by some of the park's evicted population on derelict lots just round the corner from Tompkins Square. The residents of one such settlement had stuck up a rough wooden sign, naming their place 'Dinkinsville' in bitter tribute to David M. Dinkins, New York City's first black mayor. Before his election, Dinkins had been highly critical of the City's policy of shovelling the homeless into 'dehumanizing' night-shelters. But here he was, after only a short time in office, unable to finance his progressive social policies and himself resorting to police violence as a means of driving his city's vast homeless population into those same, much-hated facilities. Dinkinsville was no sooner named after him than it became famous as the symbol of his failure and humiliation. It also foreshadowed the coming of Rudy Giuliani, who was elected mayor on a law and order ticket in 1993, and set out to sweep the homeless off the streets. But it was in the brief preceding interval that Wodiczko launched his Poliscar.

I had met Krzyzstof Wodiczko in Vancouver in the late seventies. A recent immigrant from Poland, where he had trained as an industrial designer, he was already known for his curious allegorical vehicles. He showed me sketches for a machine designed to demonstrate the repetitious futility of labour under the Communist regime that gloried in its name: an actor would push upwards like Sisyphus, only to find his burden crashing back down on him at the moment of achievement. There were also drawings of a pivoted contrivance, a kind of minimalist see-saw, which did the same for the artist or intellectual. A man, perhaps Wodiczko himself, would walk slowly along a metal platform until it tilted slightly, then turn and repeat the action *ad infinitum* while the whole vehicle, minutely propelled by this see-sawing movement, gradually crept along in one direction. I couldn't see much future for these devices in that famously unlaborious West Coast city, where 'The Western Front' was a venue for rock concerts and poetry readings, and where design, even in those distant days, was an overpriced metal restaurant called Eye Scream. Wodiczko seemed fastidious, aloof and very European.

This time I found myself sitting in a Greenwich Village coffee house full of ancient European busts, while Wodiczko expounded on his work in precisely engineered sentences, many of which came with bibliography and footnotes attached. The Poliscar was only the latest in a series of vehicles

Wodiczko had designed with the help of 'consultants' drawn from the homeless population. An earlier 'Homeless Vehicle Project', widely exhibited as 'a strategy of survival for urban nomads', had produced successive variations on the supermarket shopping trolley, a vehicle that is frequently appropriated by the homeless and used for transporting possessions, staking out tiny patches of territory, and storing scavenged items such as the empty bottles and drink cans for which New York stores were legally obliged to pay a small deposit on return. With the first of these 'homeless vehicles' Wodiczko had set out to customize the shopping trolley, redesigning it so that it would fit the needs of the homeless more precisely. He had introduced a lockable area, appropriate storage containers, and much enlarged rear wheels for negotiating kerbs and pavements. His fourth variant even unfolded telescopically to offer the user rudimentary sleeping and washing facilities, along with the cover under which private bodily functions could be carried out. If the Poliscar resembled a tank, this earlier vehicle resembled nothing so much as a 'smart' Cruise missile that had landed on a surprised shopper's Baskart.

I asked this self-appointed designer to Dinkinsville how he answered the accusation that he was just a joker playing games with the homeless. He laughed and suggested we begin by recognizing that the homeless did not really exist. Of course, there were many people living on the streets, but this was not what he meant. What he denied was the idea of 'the Homeless' – a unifying concept that suited everybody except the people to whom it was so easily applied. Charities might use this term to raise dollars, but it also enabled politicians, public administrators and unyielding passers-by to lump all the unhoused together with a single distancing gesture, thereby reinforcing their dispossession.

Many of the conventional arguments of the Left, including those that sloganized about the 'common interest' of the homeless, also served to perpetuate this fixed idea, treating the homeless as a uniformly needy and helpless mass who need to be spoken for, when in reality there are actually different groups, people with very different histories, cultures and outlooks, who should be helped to speak for themselves. Anyway, as Wodiczko insisted, this population does not just consist of passive, externally determined victims: they fight back, leaving their own mark on the urban environment, and making what they can of the situation that obliges them to live their lives as outcasts in other people's public space.

Yet if the prevailing idea of the 'homeless' reinforced the exclusion of the people it was used to describe, it was hardly better, surely, to romanticize these urban outcasts as 'nomads'. What, after all, had these urban dispossessed in common with the marauding 'peoples of the steppe' to whom Wodiczko has likened them?[22] After pointing out that it was homeless people, not he, who had first identified the Poliscar as a tent, Wodiczko suggests that they were perhaps only like nomads 'in the sense that nomads, contrary to popular belief, want to attach themselves to a place'. He insisted that the homeless were 'the true public of the city'. They had been 'expelled from society into public space' but were confined to living within it as 'silent, voiceless actors'; they were in the world but outside it – visibly present and yet deprived of both voice and vote.

These 'people-without-apartments' were the 'evicts' of a city that was being carved up to produce exclusive 'real estate citadels'. The refurbishment of old buildings and the restoration of historical façades and statues provided the civilized cover under which the displacement of the city's most vulnerable inhabitants continued. This combination of eviction and conservation could be at its most intense in public squares and parks, where the restoration of previously disregarded statues helped to 'delegitimize' the homeless who had clustered around them, thus making it acceptable for the police to move them on as feckless and unsightly loiterers. Eviction and beauty run together, said Wodiczko.[23]

Asked how the design world had responded to his various homeless vehicles, Wodiczko declared himself amazed to see how pervasive the myth of modern design remains: 'The minute you present a proposal, people think you must be offering a grand vision for a better future.' They can't see a thing like the homeless vehicle or the Poliscar as the 'concretization' of a present problem, a makeshift transitional device, or an aesthetic experiment. Instead, 'they think it must have been designed for mass production, and instantly imagine 100,000 Poliscars taking over the cities'. People were so dazzled by 'evangelical utopias' that they could hardly recognize practical measures devised on the realistic assumption that it would probably take thirty years to get beyond all this misery and to reintegrate the great mass of homeless people into the city.

As Wodiczko saw it, design was a quality that had been stripped from the homeless as part of their dispossession. When the police evicted the homeless from temporary settlements like the one in Tompkins Square Park, they simply mashed up their possessions as so much rubbish, thereby proving that part of their deprivation was to be bereft of designed equipment and the status it bestows. The homeless had 'no architecture', and were reduced to 'statusless non-persons' as they wandered about pushing a shopping cart originally designed for middle-class use. Since his machines were intended to battle against this deprivation Wodiczko liked them to be ostentatiously designed, and trials of the customized shopping trolley had already revealed something of the confusion this could engender among passers-by. Some only had to see the vehicles to conclude that they must be intended for their own use, and that their homeless users were really demonstrators offering the devices for sale. People would go up and start touching and inspecting the vehicles, betraying the unconscious assumption that, as non-persons, the homeless have no claims to privacy or property. Some entered the spirit of the occasion and recommended various improvements in the design, but the machines had induced resentment in others, who reacted angrily – presumably, so Wodiczko suggested, because as specially designed objects the homeless vehicles demand a kind of respect for their users, which is not normally granted to members of an outcast population. These onlookers tried to strip the designer element away, like the affronted businessman who had castigated the homeless vehicle as 'a barrel for bums', thereby tossing both it and its potential users back into the conceptual dustbin to which the homeless are customarily confined.[24] As for the 'people-without-apartments' themselves, they were often too needy to assess Wodiczko's inventions except in terms of their immediate use value. In 1989, when the homeless vehicle was tested on the streets of Philadelphia, a man had approached Wodiczko saying, 'Thank you, thank you. Me and my brother live in a box over there. We need something like this real bad.'

The Poliscar threatened to go into action more forcefully than a converted shopping trolley could ever do. At one point, Wodiczko had considered fitting his vehicle with caterpillar tracks, which would have emphasized the deteriorating condition of New York City and its pot-holed roads in particular. It had proved difficult to find a sufficiently light set of caterpillar tracks, but it was primarily for another reason that Wodiczko had discarded the idea. Caterpillar tracks would have made the Poliscar altogether too much like a tank, reducing the sense of visual ambiguity that he wanted to retain. So Wodiczko opted for little wheels, which served to undermine the tank impression and which also paid quiet tribute to the Russian Constructivist Vladimir Tatlin, whose 'tower' of 1920 – actually a repeatedly modelled proposal for a Monument to the Third International – was sometimes exhibited on wheels.

It was when I asked him to say more about the difference between his

Poliscar and a tank that Wodiczko first referred to his Polish background. He explained that the Polish language was without a word for weapon: the word *Broń* denoting a means of defence rather than an instrument of aggression. The tank had a bloody and terrible history as an instrument of force, but the Poliscar was not like that. Unlike the tank, it was a war machine that did not have war as its aim: in Clausewitz's language, it was an instrument of 'manoeuvre' as opposed to 'battle', of mobility and displacement, of sudden disappearance and reappearance rather than of steady and unstoppable advance. Closer to the Polish cavalry than to the German panzers of September 1939, the Poliscar was actually the very opposite of a tank. Designed as an instrument of 'speed' – a notion that Wodiczko referred to Paul Virilio rather than its earlier advocate J. F. C Fuller – it was a 'nomadic war machine' and as such an intelligent instrument devoted to the avoidance of engagement rather than to battle itself.[25] Indeed, its objectives were peace, survival and an increase in communication, not the death and destruction that stood as the aim of 'state war machines' such as the tank. If the Poliscar attacked anything, Wodiczko volunteered, it would probably be the earth, digging itself into the ground in the tradition of popular resistance movements or guerrilla warfare, or even in the manner of a hunted animal – for the Poliscar was closer to the hunted animal that learns to reckon with enemies than to the hunter who goes out to destroy and kill. As the homeless had already found out, it was the police cars, not the Poliscars, that functioned like tanks.

As much a tool as a weapon, the Poliscar would work by speaking rather than shooting. It was equipped to talk back (and down) at the onlooker, through the television monitor installed in its shiny conical point. Indeed, it was designed to reverse the customary relationship between people with and without apartments – concealing the normally all-too-visible homeless person from view, while at the same time using its cameras to submit respectable passers-by to surveillance of the kind that normally runs the other way.

The full extent of the Poliscar's communicative mission was revealed by the videotape running on the TV monitor of the prototype on show at the Josh Baer Gallery. A succession of homeless people spoke out from the pavements around Tompkins Square Park. They revealed the miseries of their condition and the difficulties of ever getting out of it, but they also looked ahead to the improvements that could be brought by a fleet of Poliscars and the Homeless Communication Network they would establish throughout Manhattan. As one man promised, 'it's gonna be a completely different video' once the homeless get their hands on the camera.

Others pointed to the barriers and schisms that hinder even rudimentary organization within this drifting population: 'You've got a group of Haitians over there; you have Spanish-orientated people over there, Cubans and all that; and then you've got this group here, which is a mix of blacks and whites and Indians and all that.' Without communication of the kind that might be provided by a fleet of Poliscars, 'it would be very hard to organize all those people'. Another man explained that while New York was a computer-age city, the people who lived in its parks and streets might as well be in 'the Stone Age or the Tin Age': the challenge for the Homeless Communication Network was 'to link the most primitive forms of communication to the computer age'. It should also provide an early warning system, giving the homeless time to mass in opposition to impending evictions and other police actions. One of Wodiczko's evicts recalled how, at 5 a.m. on 3 June when the police turned up to drive the homeless out of Tompkins Square Park, Father George Kuhn at the Catholic church of St Bridgid's rang his bell for half an hour: 'He woke up numbers of people, you know, and the ringing of the bell was an expected signal. Everyone knew that if the bell was ringing, that meant the police were coming in.' It would, as this fellow suggested, be 'quite an achievement' if the Homeless Communication Network could function across Manhattan as 'an extended form of that bell'.

Elsewhere in his exhibition Wodiczko showed how his Homeless Communication Network might work in practice. As 'mobile communications and living units', the Poliscars would be equipped with CB radios, and also a microwave system that would provide a video link between the individual vehicles. A parabolic antenna mounted on the top of a Poliscar in one community would enable it to transmit video material to those in other areas, via repeaters attached to the Empire State Building. A link to public access and cable systems would be available through receivers planted on that same emblematic building.

The Homeless Communication Network would certainly 'increase the sense of security among those who live outside' by transmitting early warning of planned evictions; but the Poliscars would also 'establish links between various encampments', each one functioning as a 'mobile speech-act machine for homeless self-representation and expression'. The network would increase understanding of 'antagonisms and differences' among the homeless, thereby decreasing tensions and creating 'social and cultural bonds' between the various homeless groups, while at the same time challenging prevailing images of their condition. It would enable the homeless population to participate properly in local and national elections, while providing essential information on matters such as health and legal aid, assisting with the 'formulation of political, educational and aesthetic strategies' and also creating new links between the homeless and the city that had evicted them – advertising events, for example, or notifying potential employers of the skills available within this outcast group.

Back in the real world, meanwhile, Wodiczko regretted that he had not yet been able to mount a proper 'social experiment' with the Poliscar. He was not looking for mass production or implementation, but he denied that the claimed practicality of his Poliscars was just part of their rhetorical effect. The communications equipment proposed was very accessible – and if the microwave system could not be established, it would always be possible to distribute tapes by hand. A fourth wheel would certainly have to be added, since the pavements had put too much pressure on the existing three-wheeled prototype. It would, as Wodiczko speculated, only take one of the charities concerned with assisting the homeless to raise its focus from the immediate emergency of food, shelter and heating . . . As few as four or five Poliscars would begin to put a new network into the externally defined mass of the homeless, and if a workshop was established with basic production facilities, some of the more educated and capable people among the homeless would surely step forward to take the initiative. It even seemed possible that a certain amount of income might be generated by selling information and programme material to established television channels. In the meantime, however, Wodiczko's Poliscar was stuck in the Josh Baer Gallery, where it provoked sarcastic and unusually irritated comments suggesting that the homeless would probably find more use for the large and well-heated exhibition space than for the exhibit that was, anyway, only to be had for $60,000.

Even if some entrepreneur of impossible projects had come along with the idea of putting the Poliscars into production, there was no possibility of saving the symbolic shanty town of Dinkinsville. Ten days after Wodiczko's exhibition closed, in the early hours of 15 October 1991, the bulldozers moved in, accompanied by a posse of evicting police wearing riot gear. Some of the people of Dinkinsville set fire to their own shelters in helpless defiance, but there was no possibility of resistance. The right-wing tabloid *New York Post* took a pastoral view of the clearance, showing an obliging policewoman holding a cat as its owner gathered up a few things.[26] After promising that there had been 'outreach', Mayor Dinkins's office insisted that, with winter approaching and despite all its problems, the hated and notoriously brutalizing shelter system offered 'a better way'.

A man named Mohamed Ali was among the evicts of Dinkinsville who refused to go into the shelters. Before wandering off into the rain, he gave the *New York Times* a very different account of the police operation, describing how the bulldozers had 'rolled in around sunrise' and adding that 'it was like an army . . . like the one that went to Saudi Arabia'.[27] Many local residents, and certainly not just the derided yuppies of the Lower East Side's conservationist citadels, were relieved to see the end of Dinkinsville. They didn't mean harm to the homeless, but they were tired of the noise, the fires, the rats and the drugs. They'd had enough of people shitting in the street and using the fire hydrants as showers. Wodiczko, who had lived nearby on the Lower East Side since the early eighties, would have understood their response, but by this time he had moved to Paris, where he was already drawing up plans for a telematic shepherd's crook – an 'Alien Staff' – for Europe's migrant population. As a designer of lifestyle accessories for people-without-apartments, he would have felt for the evicted Pixie Louise Moore who went off in her wheelchair telling reporters that 'there was nothing shoddy about where we lived'. He would also have been touched by Mohamed Ali, who described how happy he had been in the New Stone Age settlement of Dinkinsville, concluding sadly: 'I feel like I lost my apartment.'

Wodiczko was pursuing the 'demilitarization of technology' as a professor at MIT by the time Rudolph Giuliani was elected Mayor of New York in 1993. His Poliscars found no place in the arsenal that this celebrated hard-liner brought to bear on New York's disorders. Nor was his Homeless Communication Network favoured by Giuliani's police commissioner, William Bratton, the advocate of 'zero tolerance' who walked into a precinct police station in Queens shortly after his appointment and told his men, 'I said when I took this job that we would take this city back for the good people who live here, neighborhood by neighborhood, block by block, house by house. But I'm going to need all of you in the game.'[28]

Punishing it in Turkey

The tank compels partly by symbolic power, and yet, even in the name of conversion to civil use, it was never to be treated merely as a heavy kind of sign. In June 1992 I travelled to Ankara to give a lecture as part of a series organized by a group of Turkish art historians. The venue was distinctive. As one of the public buildings commissioned to establish Ankara as the capital city of the secular Turkish Republic founded by Atatürk in 1923, the

State Museum of Painting and Sculpture was built in a style that mixed operatic tradition with a more forceful assertion of total political power. The event was not well attended, but there was still a pack of wolves in the house, their golden heads gazing back at the stage from ornately gilded walls.

After my talk, in which I showed slides of Tiananmen Square, the Poliscar and Prague's pink tank, I was introduced to a man called Vahap Avsar, an artist who said he wanted to add an image to my collection. At first I was puzzled, since Vahap was quite empty-handed. But he proceeded to paint his picture in words. Having conjured up a tank without any difficulty, he placed it in a reclining position on a hillside. He then put a symbolic barrier around it, leaving me to decide whether this was a picket fence, a thread of wire or a low chain of the sort that might surround a monument in a municipal park. The tank was soon attended by a uniformed soldier, standing guard with a rifle in his hand; and a little notice appeared too: mounted on a board by the sentry box, it announced that the tank was being punished. It was here that Vahap Avsar paused. He could no longer remember the details of the machine's offence, but he was in no doubt that it had failed in some way, and possibly caused serious harm to its own crew.

I was surprised by this fragmentary and disconnected image, which seemed quite invalidated by the faltering English with which Vahap Avsar goaded it into view. Modern Turkish history is full of tanks, and it was all too easy to imagine them crushing Kurdish separatists or rolling on to the streets in one of the military coups that have been such a persistent feature of post-war Turkish history. But even in a country where military hardware has so often been used to replace history with state-imposed order, it was hard to imagine a tank undergoing punishment on a hillside.

To begin with, it seemed possible that Vahap Avsar was describing one of his own imaginative works: an installation, perhaps, concerned with the military state and its irrational powers of enchantment. But the punished tank was no such thing. Vahap couldn't offer a precise date or location, but he insisted that the tank had existed somewhere in Turkey, and that it really was being punished. He had seen it as a child, but he thought he probably still had a photograph, which he promised to hunt up the next time he went home to Izmir.

Vahap wrote a few weeks later, but his enclosures were not as I had expected. He sent three picture postcards that showed tanks as revered icons of Turkey's secular state: all-powerful guardians of the principles of

Atatürk, and of the nation he had forged from the ruins of the Ottoman Empire. On two of these specimens, the venerated machines were drawn against red skies of scudding glory, with barrels raised high and their heroic young commanders painted in behind them. Although still an adorational object draped in a stately red flag bearing Turkey's white crescent and star, the third tank was a more worldly machine – photographed, rather than painted, advancing along an urban street with a decidedly modern building behind it and a passive civilian crowd lining the route of its procession.

Vahap also included a photocopy of an article called 'Carpets of Bombs' by the German theorist Friedrich Kittler.[29] Kittler had noticed new motifs appearing in the rugs woven by Afghan refugees settled in Pakistan since the Soviet invasion of their country. The blossoms and gazelles of tradition were giving way to Russian tanks, helicopters and hand grenades in carpets that were being sold in Western cities in aid of Afghan Relief. This transformation, which may actually have been fostered by traders and charity promoters who knew what would sell in the West, now seems only to prefigure the emergence of the Taliban from those same US-aided refugee settlements in Pakistan. Woollen tanks would soon give way to real ones, reconquering Afghanistan and then serving as instruments of hideous fundamentalist punishment – a report issued by the Afghan Islamic Press agency in 1998, announced that the Taliban supreme leader, Mullah Mohammed Omar, had decreed that three Afghan men found guilty of sodomy were to be left for half an hour under a stone wall that had been knocked over on top of them by a tank, and then spared (as they were duly said to have been) if they survived the ordeal.[30] But for Professor Kittler in 1990 those woven tanks were still no more than fluffy demonstrations of nomadic resilience: a tent-dweller's punning riposte to Soviet carpet-bombing that proved the truth of Nietzsche's observation that beauty results 'when power becomes gracious and descends into the visible'.

Vahap had not forgotten the punished tank, but he had not been able to find the remembered photograph. However, one of his friends had insisted that there was indeed a tradition in the Turkish military of punishing inanimate objects. The idea seemed to be that if a soldier committed suicide by hanging himself from a tree, then the tree was guilty of 'letting the soldier die', and should be punished by confinement. So a fence and a sentry box would be erected around the tree, and a watchman installed. Similarly, if a tank was responsible for the death of a soldier ('in other than war conditions, I suppose') it would be confined at the scene of its crime, with a shaming fence or barbed wire and a sentry standing guard.

It was possible that these curious ceremonies of humiliation dated back to the days of the Ottoman Empire, when Turkish warriors would punish their horses for failing in battle. But Vahap also ventured a more far-reaching theory. The Turkish people were of middle-Asian origin, and it was conceivable that this habit of punishing objects stemmed from ancient shamanistic tradition. It was, he suggested, a consequence of thinking that everything, both creatures and objects, was equal in spirituality and intelligence – 'therefore a piece of stone, a tree, a tank(!) can be guilty and should be punished. This is what we get as a result of examining all the clues.'

I tried to clarify this mysterious story on subsequent visits to Turkey. In October 1992 I attended a large international symposium in Ankara – one that took place under the title: 'Identity-Marginality-Space'– just after Serbian tanks broke into Croatia, crushing any remaining illusions about the end of the Cold War and its consequences in Europe. As speakers sounded off against the 'global lobotomy' that ideologies had wrought on the world, and cursed post-modernism as 'a new marketing device for the rapid production of Western intellectuals', I tested Vahap Avsar's punished tank on various interpreters. The writer Orhan Pamuk (whose novel *The White Castle*, concerns a symbolic machine that stands between East and West) warily conceded that the image was 'very Turkish', and suggested that Turkey was such a diverse country that it could not be made to cohere except by means of fables and myths, whether these concerned punished tanks or the insidious power of Turkey's frequently claimed 'state within the state'. The former child prodigy artist and manic anti-Islamist Bedri Baykam thought about it over breakfast in the Ankara Hilton, and recalled that similar things were said to have been done to a warplane in the seventies. He had heard that one that had 'refused to take off' during the Turkish invasion of Cyprus had been punished in a similarly weird way.

I also met an architect and academic, Professor M. Yildirim Yavuz, who thought he might even have seen the punished tank, or something like it, during his military training several decades previously. He remembered a machine on a hillside near a place called Dumlu, north of the eastern Turkish city of Erzurum. It was left over, so he imagined, from the disastrous offensive against Russia launched by Enver Pasha in the early months of the First World War. The Turks had expected the Russian enemy to come from one direction, but they suddenly materialized from the mountains on skis, and the whole 51st Division had been eradicated. There had been a terrible retreat through the mountains, in which many soldiers froze to death, having abandoned their coats, as ordered, in order to carry more weapons and ammunition. The armoured vehicle that Professor Yavuz remembered only vaguely was probably, he thought, a relic from those times. Perhaps it had failed to work, and was still there, rusting in the name of its crime.

The dates being what they were, that dimly recalled machine near Dumlu could hardly have been a tank, but I, who knew no more of Enver Pasha's assault on Russia than I could dimly recall from John Buchan's jingoistic First World War novel *Greenmantle*, was in no position to establish whether it was entirely mythical. The actual tank that came into view shortly afterwards was hardly a perfect candidate for the part either. Some British visitors returned with a snapshot of a battle-scarred Turkish tank they had come across while visiting in Cyprus. There it was on its hillside with steps leading down to it and a large notice, written in very formal and official Turkish, which declaimed:

This tank is a symbolic example of, and a monument to, the audacious daring of Turks. It belongs to a special force whose orders on 2 August 1974 were to attack the enemy from the side and rear. Above and beyond the call of duty, the tank was brought to its place through an impossibly steep and slippery terrain, but under heavy enemy fire it was crippled and burnt out and has stayed here ever since.

Nearly a personified tank, then, but not one that was undergoing punishment as a guilty renegade – except at the hands of the protester, of Greek-Cypriot sympathies, who had splattered this grisly monument with red paint.

By this time I was largely convinced that the punished tank was a fiction, another stretched and exoticized tank image of the kind that has proliferated in post-war paintings and films. It may have been less ominous than the tanks in Ingmar Bergman's *The Silence* (1963), eerie presences glimpsed through a train window or grinding, like the end of the God-forsaken world itself, into a deserted middle-European square. But Vahap Avshar's image nevertheless seemed to belong in the same imaginary category as Sam Fuller's *The Big Red One* (1980), in which a North African tribeswoman gives birth inside an American tank using ammunition belts as stirrups, and also Emil Kusturica's *Underground* (1995), in which an improvised Serbian tank is loaded and fired, all too prophetically, by a monkey. The punished tank was surely no more real than the tanks that some have claimed, none too convincingly, to hear in Igor Stravinsky's Symphony in Three Movements, said to have forced their way in from wartime newsreels viewed during the years of its composition.

Yet in 1995 I was able to pursue this curious image further in Istanbul. I discussed it with a variety of people while viewing the equally strange and paradoxical installations exhibited by artists from around the world in the 4th International Istanbul Biennial. And as I did so, I heard more stories of bizarre punishments applied to inanimate bits of equipment. I was told, once again, about the plane that wouldn't fly during Turkey's invasion of Cyprus, although in this version, it was a recalcitrant engine that had been taken off the failed machine for humiliation and punishment. I heard of a horse that had been put in prison after throwing its rider, and of a battalion in which something bad had happened, which had reputedly been sent to Izmir, where it remained for years long after the responsible officers had moved on. In another example, it was said that a soldier had died after falling from an obstacle on an assault course, so the guilty apparatus was submitted to punishment. One woman went home to check the experience of her husband and came back the next day to confirm that, during his military service, he had known trees and even park benches to be punished.

Keen to be seen as a modern and, indeed, reasonable, force, the Turkish military is reluctant to discuss these stories about tanks, planes and benches being punished. And yet, as I was told by the journalist and writer Murat Belge, one did not have to resort to the ancient shamanistic past to understand this image. The point to remember is that, on the bottom line, the military is 'both the only organization in the country and the reason why there are no other organizations'. There is, as Belge pointed out, a huge culture of crime and punishment in the army. In part, this may reflect the background of many conscripts, who have grown up in a society where 'beating' is institutionalized. Personal violence is certainly said to be tolerated in the Turkish Army even though defined as a statutory crime under the Law of the Armed Services. Victims of beatings may be entitled to complain, but in practice many don't, often preferring a quick beating to the protracted official punishment – an informal system that has been described as central to the Turkish Army's way of establishing discipline.[31]

Seen from this perspective, the main purpose of military training in the Turkish style is not to prepare for war but to break conscripts down before raising them up again in a 'steel shirt' of externally applied discipline; and that is how it is for the soldier detailed to punish a park bench or tank. As with the soldiers of the Israeli Armoured Corps, who, before Israel Tal came along and banned the kind of bullying known as *Tirturim*, were forced to bury cigarette butts with full military honours, the message conveyed by these acts of surrealistic humiliation is, quite literally, that there is no logic here except that of power. As Belge puts it, 'You must abandon your reason on entering the army – leave it in the cloakroom.' And if a tank or park bench can be humanized, then how much easier it must be to dehumanize the enemies of the republic, whether they be seen as Kurdish separatists, communists, or Islamic fundamentalists. We'll leave the punished tank there: a heavy metal reality falling out of the back of an unreliable arabesque image, having survived its ordeal by artists and never once lost its demeanour as a working war machine.

Fort Knox: Cybertanks and the Army After Next

On the fifth day of my visit to the US Army Armor Center at Fort Knox, Kentucky, I was taken to a motor pool to inspect America's latest tank. Made by General Dynamics Land Systems, the 69-ton Abrams M1A2 was attended by little noticeboards identifying its various parts, and also by Sergeant Moreno, who took me inside the machine and showed me some of its unique capabilities. He pointed out the independent thermal viewer, which enables the tank commander to scan the battlefield and 'acquire' targets, which can then be passed on to the gunner, and also the Inter-Vehicular Information System – a digital positioning and navigation system that informs the tank commander not just exactly where he is on the battlefield, but the position of his own forces too.

I only saw a small computer screen with a few tank icons on it, but for Sergeant Moreno, a gunner who knows the advantage of Total Asset Visibility, this satellite-linked gadget called IVIS made the M1A2 unique – a 'digitized' tank that relegated all its precursors and rivals to prehistory. We were an evolutionary leap ahead of the Abrams M1A1, the tank that had triumphed in Desert Storm, and was then brought home to Fort Hood, where Dolly Parton climbed up on to a representative specimen to perch there, lewd and triumphant among battle-hardened men, for the cover of *Vanity Fair*. It was a primitive image: desert-coloured steel behind, a rudely protruding gun tube and then Dolly in the midst of her admiring throng, wearing scarlet lipstick and a lubricious smile, her body adorned with white fur and a swooping dress of silvery sequins that only slightly limited the visibility of her own total assets ('I *do* have big tits. Always had 'em – pushed 'em up, whacked 'em around. Why not make fun of 'em? I've made a fortune with 'em.').[1] That had been the M1A1 in full victory rig: another round of shiny projectiles for Saddam and trashy jokes for the homecoming soldiers who, five years later at Fort Knox, would still smile at the memory of Dolly's pose – commending 'the wonders of modern technology' and speculating that, even in the digital era, silicon was not just a matter of motherboards and chips.

The M1A2 was an imposing monster even without such provocative trimmings, but it also seemed strangely diminished by the very fact of its existence. By this time I had become accustomed to floating around in virtual reality, where so much of the downsized US Army now lives, and, however smart or 'leap-ahead' its gadgets might be, no mere object plonked down on a tarmac square was going to seem anything but disappointing. Since this heavy machine was meant to be all about mobility, what about starting it up and going for a run? The suggestion made Sergeant Moreno apprehensive, and perhaps not surprisingly, since the M1A2 still suffered from a design fault. Until 1998, when a driver safety interlock switch was retroactively fitted into all models, it was possible for the Abrams' turret to be rotated while the driver's head was sticking out. General Dynamics Land Systems admit to one nasty accident in a maintenance area, but lurid rumours had more than one head, perhaps even seven or eight, rolling as the lowered gun tube swung round.

Despite that interruption of old-fashioned reality, my launch into the virtual world of America's latest tank had been well planned. My first hands-on experience had been in the driving school. To begin with, an instructor had sat me down and punched home some well-rehearsed points about the Abrams M1 Tank Driver Simulator. It cost $75 to take a driver a mile in the real tank, whereas the simulator only cost $5.44 per mile. Having offered this consolation to the absent American taxpayer, the sergeant went on to emphasize that his simulators also helped to create 'faster people – faster thinking people'. 'I was trained to be dangerous,' said the sergeant of his own primitive instruction in a bygone world without simulators. In those days, the trainee driver had to make do with driving twelve to eighteen miles in a real tank, which he would never be allowed to crash or turn over for the sake of a lesson. Nowadays, he does fifty to sixty miles in simulation before starting on the real thing. The driver simulator was designed to be 'a little more difficult to drive than the real thing', so there was no doubt at all that 'If you can drive my simulator you can drive a tank.'

The driver simulator turned out to be a large box mounted on a set of hydraulic lifts. The interior, in which you lie on your back, more or less horizontal with feet forward, while viewing the world through three sighting blocks around your head, may be identical to that of the real Abrams M1A1, but driving the US Army's main battle tank was also strangely reminiscent of riding an old-fashioned moped. You steer with a small handle-bar-like thing, and accelerate with a grip throttle at one end.

Like all beginners, I started on an autobahn that threads its way through a gently undulating Central European landscape, empty except for a thin scattering of trees. With a little urging from Sergeant Gaillard, I realized that, when you're driving a tank, it doesn't really matter if you don't stick to the road. So I veered over to the right, skidding into a spin, which the Sergeant promised would never happen in real life, and then began to glide over grass – a landship sailing over a frictionless ocean of virtual turf. Despite the internal accuracy of the simulator, it was hard to reconcile this sledging sensation with anything that I knew about tanks – with their heavy way of crushing bodies, tearing up tramlines and breaking roads.

As the necromancer of this simulated world, Sergeant Gaillard sat at his console, throwing up special effects such as night and day, lightning, snow and rain. He launched smoke, and incoming shells that exploded nearby, and the whole world disappeared, momentarily, when he fired the gun over my head. Trees posed little problem, but eventually I drove into a hill, travelling too fast and at the wrong angle, and everything went dark. I was a dead tank driver by now, but the green world was soon resurrected in front of me, and I sailed on through deserted suburbs towards the distant towers of a large city. Is that Dresden or Warsaw? I wondered before a rising sense of seasickness took over. Sergeant Gaillard, who knew there was nothing virtual about this particular threat to his simulator, closed everything down as soon as I mentioned it: 'OK,' he said speedily, 'I'm coming to get you out.'

Next stop was the gunnery simulator, or more precisely, the 'M1 Abrams Unit Conduct of Fire Trainer', where a couple of elderly ex-tankers were leading a group of national guardsmen from New York state through an exercise. Peering into the sights, I saw another green world with houses, shrubs and other pastoral features. Having got a parked helicopter lined up in the sights, I was shown how to 'lase' – pressing a button that, in a real tank, would be connected to a laser system that calculated the range of the target and lined up the gun automatically. There was a great thud as I squeezed the trigger, and the helicopter collapsed into a sparkling plume of fire and smoke.

I turned the machine gun on to a collection of advancing infantrymen, but their demise was disappointingly abstract, quite without the splatter and gore of the average computer game. Even so, it was the video arcade and computer game that kept coming to mind. When I mentioned this, everyone agreed. 'Sure,' they said. 'The kids who have done a lot of video games have exactly the right kind of hand-eye co-ordination.' As Chief of Staff of the Armor School, Colonel Lenze, put it, 'Nintendo has done great things for this generation.'

By the time I reached the Mounted Warfare Simulation Training Centre, the simulation was opening up into a completely virtual world, where 'connectivity' rather than the single machine was the creed. This, as some of the Armor Center's consultants in 'distributed interactive simulation' have claimed, was the military version of 'cyberspace' as envisaged by William Gibson in his 1986 novel *Neuromancer*: 'a global artifical reality that can be visited simultaneously by many people via networked computers'.[2] Major Leppert, who guided me through this particular hall of wired and thudding boxes, explained that it was the home of the Simulation Network (SIMNET), the largest simulation facility in the world for mounted warfare. Leppert had sufficient simulators here to field forty-one M1 tanks at once along with nine Bradley infantry fighting vehicles. These machines could see and hear each other on a common terrain, and they could engage a common computer-generated enemy too. 'We're going to put you out into the Mojave Desert,' said Leppert, loading up a stretch of digitally replicated terrain from the US Army's 650,000 acre National Training Center at Fort Irwin, California. And that was more or less exactly what he did, having appointed a driver and loader to complete our crew. So there we were, four grown men climbing into a plastic box made by Jacuzzi to drive out into high desert terrain that had once been home to the Pinta Indians: a land of igneous rocks, dry lake beds called *playas*, creosote bushes and, in reality if not simulation, the endangered desert tortoises that, owing to a rigidly enforced ecological edict, seem to be the one thing that America's practising tanks still have to stop for.[3] As the commander of our simulator, Major Leppert was soon sighting distant targets and shouting 'lase' and 'fire' as I, the gunner, fumbled around with the requisite buttons, trying to suspend my disbelief and making a poor show of blasting a distant enemy tank. Soon enough all was darkness again – no fire and no pain, but virtual death all the same. We had been hit by an entirely different tank that I, the speedily diagnosed victim of a condition called 'target fixation', hadn't even noticed.

There is a strange atmosphere in these places – a surreal mixture of play and the actual consideration known as 'lethality' in the pervasive jargon. The US Army has been training with simulators for some time, but its experiments with virtual reality are still at an early stage. The tank that destroyed mine in the Mojave Desert may have been computer generated – part of a 'semi-automated force' constructed from within the software – but the SIMNET people are also capable of 'networking with remote locations'. This 'distributed 3D virtual environment' enables men in tank simulators from Fort Knox to engage on the same battlefield as, say, helicopters operated by more men in plastic boxes at Fort Rucker in Louisiana: 'They see my tanks. I see their helicopters.' There were already highly accurate virtual geographies modelled on real landscapes and, by the time of my visit in April 1996, 'dynamic terrain' – virtual ground you can actually dig into – was thought to be only just around the corner. 'We're catching up with Disney,' as one of SIMNET's exponents joked, and the cyberconsult-ants, who are never far away from the US military these days, thrive as the struggle continues.

Simulations come in various shapes and sizes in the digitizing US Army. Virtual simulations create worlds in order to get 'man in the loop at item of equipment level', whereas 'constructive' ones like those used to model large deployments of soldiers and equipment are 'just an interaction with a computer'. Both these types may be incorporated into 'live' simulations too – like the Advanced Warfighting Exercises held at the National Training Centre at Fort Irwin, where digitally equipped experimental forces go into combat with a conventional force trained in a Cold War tactics that 'likes kicking butt', and where the Nintendo connection is said to break down: 'Unlike Gameboy, we make the game harder as you get better at it.'

'Everything short of actual war is simulation,' explained one senior offi-cer, but even that line is becoming hard to hold. Far from being mere mimics of combat, the simulators have entered into the actuality of warfare, and are dragging it into a 'seamless' future in which simulation and reality will slide in and out of each other with no detectable joins. As the stretch of the Mojave Desert used in SIMNET demonstrates, it is already possible to create accurate 3D virtual terrains from satellite data. This sort of 'terrain visualization' promises that the American forces of the future will arrive in distant and previously unvisited terrains that they already know better than the locals – as is already said to have happened in Iraq in 1991. Meanwhile, with infra-red sighting systems, the experience of driving a tank into war is visually identical to that of practising in a simulator. Repeatedly I was told not just that the new generation of digitized weapons bear an increasing resemblance to simulators, but that with virtual simulators it is possible to train soldiers to use weapons that don't yet exist, and to commission manu-facturers too. As Bruce Sterling wrote in an article for *Wired* magazine that was soon adopted as another army hand-out, the US military's migration into cyberspace offers an eerie prospect of twenty-first-century America as a peaceful place, with 'amber waves of grain and all that' and hardly any visible military presence to disrupt its pastoral aspect until the moment requires.

Then the whole massive, lethal superpower infrastructure comes unfolding out of 21st-century cyberspace like some impossible fluid origami trick. The Reserve guys from the bowling leagues suddenly reveal themselves to be digitally assisted Top Gun veterans from a hundred weekend cyberspace campaigns. And they go to some godforsaken place that doesn't possess Virtual Reality As A Strategic Asset, and they bracket that army in their rangefinder screens, and then they cut if off, and then they kill it. Blood and burning flesh splashes the far side of the glass. But it can't get through the screen.[4]

Not bad as a vision statement – except that, as the men at Fort Knox were quick to point out, the weapons had better be designed and built before the next call comes.

New wave warfare

Meanwhile, how smart is a smart munition? The people who apply IQ tests to weapons will concede that there was some serious intelligence in the Tomahawk Cruise missiles used in the Gulf War – the ones that steered their way past surprised television reporters in Baghdad before landing on selected electronic installations and destroying them with electromagnetic pulse warheads. But the weapons that the whole onlooking world saw going into bunkers through ventilator shafts no longer seem so bright at all. They turn out to have been nothing more than 'dumb' bombs guided with the help of adjustable tailfins and a laser designating system controlled from the plane.

That was in 1991, an aeon ago in this story, and a new generation of missiles has arrived since. In this frantic evolution, the technology that was to be found in the cockpit of the plane twenty years ago, is steadily being transferred to the unmanned missile. During the Gulf War, piloted planes had to fly over their targets – the RAF lost a number of Tornadoes that way. No one would want to do that nowadays. As Serbia found out, the new 'stand off' missiles can be fired from way beyond the range of enemy ground defence systems. They promise an 'over the horizon capability' that makes it possible to hit your enemy without exposing your own force to any danger at all. Give or take a few accidents (and a heavily controlled press), they are said to be kinder on the enemy too, making it possible to 'take out' your target without causing 'collateral damage'.

There is something else in the American arsenal too – a new kind of instrument known as the 'non-lethal weapon', which comes in many varieties.[5] You might be driving along in a tank and find that your fuel has suddenly been turned to jelly, transformed by a 'fuel viscosifier' released into the atmosphere around you. Maybe your weapon is suddenly sealed up with an unimaginably adhesive layer of glue, or the road beneath you turns out to be coated with an impossibly slippery Teflon-like material. The rubber parts in your vehicles may abruptly decompose on you, or the wheels of your plane crystallize on contact with the runway.

Rioters already face quite a range of 'non-lethal' weapons: electric batons, rubber bullets, stun guns, or shotguns that fire doughnut shaped beanbags, like those used by the US Marines in Somalia in February 1995. Thanks to recent advances in this technology (which the US Marines prefer to call 'less than lethal'), they can now also look forward to 'blunt-object trauma' after being hit by acoustic pulse 'bullets', and to being blinded, temporarily or not, by laser rifles. Future insurrectionists advancing on an American embassy may find themselves suddenly tied up in thick, spaghetti-like stuff fired from a glue gun. If the ground starts flaming at their feet, that will be because it has been covered with fire gravel, which combusts on contact.

In 1989 the soldiers of Operation Just Cause forced General Noriega in Panama to listen to endless rock music all day and night. But many other 'non-lethal' capabilities are being talked about too. Carbon fibres are already being used to short out electricity grids and power stations, and computer systems can be destroyed by means of a massive electro-magnetic pulse. Future hostage takers and, for that matter, future cult members like the Branch Davidians of Waco, might find the room they're in suddenly filling up with foaming bubbles that leave them immobilized rather than dead, able to breathe but not to see or even hear. They might also succumb to a 'sleep agent', fired as a chemical pellet and mixed with dimethyl sulphoxide to ensure quick absorption through the skin. If the prophets of non-lethal weaponry are to be believed, even the most fundamentalist of anti-American zealots will find their thoughts melting away, tranquillized and 'psycho-corrected' by subliminal stimuli they can't even remember receiving.

Wherever you are, the entire world will start to fall apart all around you. The rubber parts in your machinery may suddenly perish while metals begin to crack up, their molecular structure undermined by embrittlement agents. Nearby walls may start crumbling thanks to the same low-frequency 'infra-sound' that causes you vomiting, loss of bowel control, and perhaps the odd epileptic seizure too. Everyone knows about agent orange, the defoliant that was used so ruinously in Vietnam. But nowadays you can also expect to be deluged by unseasonal rain falling from chemically seeded

clouds, and to find your roads blocked by landslides induced by soil destabilizing agents.

New weapons are being dreamed up all the time. Some military research-
ers talk of robotic vehicles, probes and fighting machines. They speculate
about ant-sized micro-robots, which might be marched into a radar or
computer system, or far smaller nano-robots that would enter the bloodstream and start fooling around with your molecules. Others have been
more interested in reinventing the suit of armour. Not so long ago, some
hopeful developer was punting the Soldier Integrative Protective Ensemble:
an exo-skeletal suit that would protect the individual soldier against biological and nuclear weapons, automatically take aim at whatever the soldier
looked at, and, even do the walking for him. It made the fantastic 'warrior
suits' in John Steakley's science fiction story *Armor* seem lame.

For Alvin and Heidi Toffler, this is all part of 'Third Wave' warfare – a
description that, like Bruce Sterling's reflections on the new virtual warfare,
has been enthusiastically adopted by the American military and its think-
tanks.[6] According to the Tofflers' scenario, Second Wave warfare, which
belonged to the industrial age, involved indiscriminate killing, area bombing, a massing of forces, centralized command structures, and a front line
on which fighting was concentrated. Third Wave warfare is a product of
the information age, and therefore of a revolution 'as deep in its way as the
neolithic and industrial revolutions'. First demonstrated by the American-
led coalition force in Desert Storm, it features precision strikes and virtual
realities – a dispersed front, and a massing of simultaneous effects rather
than forces. It belongs to an age of widely distributed threats in which
'niche wars' are to be expected at least as much as massed confrontations
between states or nations.

General Sullivan's revolution

Colonel Jerry Veach, Chief of Staff at the US Army Armor Center,
explained the changing shape of the US military with the help of a device
he calls 'the rubber Russian'. Before 1989 it was a relatively simple matter to
work out what sort of force you needed. You took a latex toy Russian soldier, and stretched it out as far as it would go. When it was at breaking
point, you would design your own force to meet it and then let the thing
go. Since 1989, however, the rubber Russian had been no more, and there
was even a piece of the Berlin Wall in the Armor Center's Patton Museum
to prove it. Yet, as Veach added quickly, this was not to say that the world

was a safe place – only that the dangers were different. In his view, the end of the Cold War boiled down to a saying, much cited in military brochures and presentations, by the then director of the CIA, James Woolsey: a large dragon had been slain, but we now lived in a jungle filled with 'a bewildering variety of poisonous snakes'.

The army was led through this period of change by General Gordon R. Sullivan, a former Assistant Commandant of the Armor School in Kentucky, who was President Bush's Chief Of Staff of the US Army from 1991–95. General Sullivan later became head of the Association of the United States Army, but when I met him, in 1996, he was a civilian sitting in a gleaming corporate headquarters in Washington, DC, a Vice-President of Coleman Research Corporation who also worked as a consultant to corporate leaders, and a director of various companies including the Shell Oil Company, General Dynamics Corporation and a number of charitable agencies too.

Faced with 'the real world constraints of a decreasing budget', General Sullivan had, as he explained, been obliged to oversee a 'downsizing' operation that reduced the army to 500,000, dumping nearly 300,000 people, and leaving it only the ninth largest in the world. At the same time, he also had to reconfigure the force, converting it from a 'threat-based' Cold War organization with a major forward base in Europe, to a 'Force Projection' army based largely in the Continental United States. This smaller, post-1989 force had to be ready to fight high intensity wars if need be, but it must also be capable of foraying out into the farflung jungles of the world to launch short sharp strikes against the bewildering variety of poisonous snakes that might threaten American interests – tin-pot military regimes, terrorists, even drug cartels capable of acquiring formidable military technology in the age of free silicon. On top of that, it needed to be prepared for an increase in 'Operations Other Than War' (UN peace-keeping, disaster relief, protecting US citizens in trouble spots around the world, or 'securing democracy' in places like Haiti or Panama), which may be carried out in collaboration with other states or aid agencies.

Sullivan also had to bear American public opinion in mind – in particular a growing feeling that the post-Cold War world could be ruled from a fiery distance, using precision strikes of the new 'over the horizon' variety and 'smart munitions', which could, so the story went, find their way down a street and go straight in through the letter box at No. 18 to 'take out' enemies without incurring American losses.

Sullivan confirmed that this 'no body bags' theory of war, had become a powerful influence in recent years. He first noticed it in 1989, during the Just

Cause operation against General Noriega in Panama. Yet this 'fondness for technology' probably went back to the atomic bomb: 'it's clearly not blood-less, but it is a technological solution to warfare, which suggests, "Right. Thank you very much. Boom. Enough." ' The dream of a distanced precision war had obvious attractions for civilian politicians, both Democrat and Republican, who wanted neither their electoral standing nor their encour-agement of the arms industry complicated by too many American deaths. It was also nourished by the example of Desert Storm, which quickly came to be seen as the model of future American wars: speedy, overwhelmingly suc-cessful, and with few home casualties.

Sullivan himself stood back from this vision of bloodless US power and off-screen enemy death that no longer even seems real. 'I don't see it,' he said, getting up to fetch a framed piece of khaki parachute silk embroidered with columns of names in black thread. 'There's forty-three of them,' he said with growing emphasis. 'These are the men who were killed in action while I was the chief. We're talking 1991 to 1995. . . People tell me the world is OK. But we're ending this century the way we began it. And it is very unstable, very dangerous, and we have to accept certain realities, harsh as they may be. We must leverage our people with the best technology, but don't kid yourself. We can't kid ourselves. There is no bloodless war.' He wanted to be quite clear that he was not arguing for bloody wars, but he cautioned against the techno-idolatry that might encourage some military reformers to think that the US forces could safely be downsized some more. It was likely to be the marines and the army – 'the people that take the fight to the enemy' – who suffered the large number of casualties, and 'we must not burden them with unrealistic expectations'. Technology may certainly be part of the answer, but there was never going to be 'a silver bullet that you can just put out there and that's going to be the end of the conflict'.

As for the digitization of the battlefield, the primary technological inno-vation with which his name is associated, when Sullivan suggested that it was deaths in the Gulf War that 'got us focused', he was referring not to the obscure terminations suffered by 100,000 or so Iraqi enemies, but to what he calls 'blue on blue casualties'. 'Immediately after the Gulf War, immediately the shooting stopped, we sent a team to the Gulf to ascertain how the engagements took place, and we tried to learn what we could about the tank engagements, the direct fire tank engagements . . . and lo and behold, what the team found out, what the world now knows, is that in some cases we killed ourselves.' That was obviously 'a distressing piece of news' and, after taking a 'very introspective look' at the problem, it was plain that these unintended acts of fratricide resulted from a lack of 'situational awareness' aggravated by the long ranges over which the military could now fire. And 'as we started down that road, we realized that with digital technology, we could have almost perfect situational awareness'.

Using his own style of management talk, Sullivan announced that the challenge had been 'to get out of the stovepipes'. The tanks were talking vertically with each other, as were the artillery, the aviators, and the infantry too. But there was a serious lack of horizontal integration between them, and the technology was now there to make that possible: 'the artillery already had this digital equipment, but what wasn't there was the horizontalization, that really was the full digitization of the battlefield'. People now commend Sullivan for launching the army in this direction, but he took no credit, saying that 'there was no other decision' to be made: 'Intellectually, we started looking at it and boom! – there it was.' He remembered 'a bunch of things that came together – one was the global positional system used in the Gulf War; the other was JSTARS, an airborne radar system that looks at the ground and can pick up moving target indicators. So essentially what you have is the phenomenon where you know where you are, global positioning, and you know where the enemy is – so you're starting to get precision on to the battlefield.'

Digitization was the key to the smaller but more effective army of the future, and to get there it would be necessary to break many deeply embedded traditions and habits. As Sullivan put it, 'Training to fight is not the same as training to do the things you know how to do,' and the digitized force of the future could only be brought about by experimentation. Doctrine would have to be reviewed at all levels, and the force restructured throughout. Also required was a new and much more collaborative relationship between military planners and commercial developers of software and weapons. If horizontal integration was to become a reality, training procedures would have to be redesigned to encourage far greater initiative at fairly low levels within the force: 'What you are trying to create is men and women who can improvise during battlefield situations.' As for the difficulties of embarking on such a demanding course at the same time as downsizing, Sullivan insisted: 'Only a world class organization could do this without disintegrating.' Thanks to digitization, downsizing could coincide both with tooling up and also a deliberate remoralization of the force. Part of a wider transformation that followed on the abandonment of the draft and the recruitment of women soldiers, it marked the US Army's recovery from much of its post-war history: the first engagements of the Korean War, in which inexperienced soldiers of the 24th Infantry Division were routed by Korean T-34s that they hadn't even been trained to recognize (in the ensuing shambles, one North Korean tank crew is even said to have borrowed a ten-gallon can of petrol from an American officer);[7] and more particularly, as Sullivan conceded, the Vietnam War, in which the US Army was widely seen to have degenerated into an ill-commanded rabble of drug-crazed conscripts, more or less as shown in *Apocalypse Now*.

So it was that, urged on by Sullivan and his carefully chosen slogans (he promised to 'change the way the army thinks about change' and insisted, in a precautionary strike against the downsizers, that 'small is not better, better is better'), America's warriors climbed into their simulators and set out for the future. The first of Sullivan's experimental exercises was named after the Louisiana Maneuvers with which the US Army had prepared for entry into the Second World War. The original exercises had put 400,000 troops into the field, but the 1992 reprise, in which digitally linked tanks, infantry and helicopters shared a common picture of the battlefield, used simulations rather than vast troop movements and set about 'experimenting with new technologies before prototypes are built'. Considerable pay-offs were being reported before the end of the first year. There were new systems of force tracking – partly inspired, it seems, by those already employed by Federal Express, and advances in 'telemedicine' made it possible for remote field hospitals to relay digital images of injuries back to the US for specialist medical advice. As for simulated 'terrain databases', agencies such as the Defence Mapping Agency and the Topographic Engineering Centre were soon producing digitized real terrains – stretches of Bosnia or Somalia, say, for the use of troops that could expect to be going into operation in these places.

By the beginning of 1995 the digital crusade had acquired the name of 'Force XXI' – a campaign intended to 'leverage superior American technology', thereby creating the Army of the twenty-first century. A series of six battle labs were established at different bases around the US, each one concerned with defining concepts and 'materiel' requirements in selected areas of military activity. They also conducted a rolling series of advanced war-fighting exercises, designed to show how brigades, divisions and corps should be restructured to make the most of digital technology. Force XXI was still more of a goal than a reality, but the many military leaflets issued to promote it were confident that digitization would finally disperse what Clausewitz called the 'fog of war'. Combine horizontal integration and increased 'situational awareness' with long-range precision strikes and the availability of a common view of the battlefield, and you have major increments in each of Force XXI's three key outcome zones: 'lethality, survivability and tempo' – nothing less, as these military futurists claim, than an unbeatable 'quantum leap in capability'.

Divergent thinkers at work

To visit the Armor Center in Fort Knox, you fly to Louisville and then follow the highway past thin, road-stretched towns you can drive through without ever reaching. This is dry Bible country with a mall or two, a few stranded-looking Bavarian restaurants and a dismal brick bungalow called the Endtime House of Prayer Church. It's a land where the radio pumps out country songs that rhyme 'negligée' with 'walk away', while tele-evangelists rhapsodize about 'going all the way with Jesus', and tank soldiers sit behind their wire, reading magazines with names like *Full Strut* and looking forward to the weekend, when they will hunt wild turkeys in the Kentucky woods.

There is nothing to match the Federal gold depository, which stands on ground rented from the military, just off Bullion Boulevard and only a narrow golf course away from America's tanks. The first military notice at the main entrance notifies drivers that, under Federal law, it is illegal to carry firearms beyond this point. Immediately beyond that stand two massive tanks, mounted on plinths on each side of the road, and adorned with letters welcoming you to the US Army Armor Center – 'Home of Cavalry and Armor'.

The focus never slips within this 170-square-mile installation. The post newspaper is called *Inside the Turret*. Bumper stickers on civilian cars say: 'Drive Defensively. Drive a Tank', and senior tank officers punctuate their deliberations with little phrases like 'boom boom' and express appropriate personal philosophies too: 'If you shoot straight with people, they'll probably shoot straight with you.'

The Commanding General, Major General Lon E. Maggart, had even named his meeting room 'The Tank'. It was a small room, with a table, low-slung chairs and the usual trophies and memorabilia on the walls – pictures and drawings from the glorious past, the swagger stick of the captured commander of Iraq's 110th Brigade, and a slightly sultry photograph of Princess Diana – an icon of alliance presented by the British liaison officer and displayed by more than one senior officer at Fort Knox.

General Maggart was, in Sullivan's phrase, 'first through the wire' into Iraq during Desert Storm. As commander of the First Brigade of 1st Mechanized Infantry Division – 'The Big Red One' – he had also taken part in a carefully rehearsed manoeuvre new to tank warfare. Having attached teeth-like ploughs to their Abrams M1A1s, his men had driven along the Iraqi trenches, one tank on either side and each pair preceded by a Bradley infantry fighting vehicle that straddled the three-and-a-half-foot-wide trench and fired into the Iraqi soldiers as the sand was pressed down on them. The 1st Division buried an estimated 650 Iraqi conscripts alive. Designed to 'terrorize' the Iraqis into surrendering, the manoeuvre was later condemned as contrary to US Army doctrine, which calls for troops to leave their armoured vehicles to clear out trenches. Shortly after the war, Maggart was reported as observing that, though it sounded 'pretty nasty', burying the Iraqis that way had been better than endangering American troops.[8] The International Red Cross raised questions and the Iraqis demanded that these 'repugnant' war crimes be investigated by the UN. When I asked Maggart about these objections, he dismissed them with a few words: 'Much ado about nothing,' he said tersely, explaining that the Iraqis had been warned, and adding that if being squashed in a collapsing trench is bad, 'What about being burned in a tank?'

By naming his meeting room 'The Tank' Maggart had designated it a place of close teamwork, mentoring and leader-development. He had also declared it a future-oriented 'think-tank' dedicated to breaking through into the digitized future. Maggart knew that, as an intrinsically conservative organization, the US Army had in the past spent too long learning to fight the last war; and it was here that he and his battle-tested senior staff – the 'heavy hitters' as he calls them – gathered in order to suspend convention and, in that most characteristic of Force XXI phrases, 'think outside the box'.

Like the training protocol that J. F. C. Fuller had devised for the British Tank Corps at Bermicourt during the First World War, the point of this new dispensation was to pitch intellect against obsolete military habit, and project yourself far into the future. Maggart's preferred destination was the year 2015, which put him neatly between Force XXI and a shadowy formation known as 'the Army After Next'. Having propelled themselves forward to that year, his officers were encouraged to look back at the twentieth century, primitive, cramped and prehistoric as it would already seem, and ask themselves: how do we get here from there?

Such is the new kind of officer at Fort Knox. The word 'visionary' is frequently used, and not just by those who excuse themselves from the new climate, by claiming to be 'plain earthy' and more concerned with the nuts and bolts of basic training. The tank officer of the digital age is a man of 'concepts', a paradigm-shifter whose kit includes a theory of history that would make the most grandiose of Hegelian philosophers seem cramped and unimaginative. These men reach back into the mists of time to talk about the still evolving 'dialectic of the arrow and the shield'. They will expound enthusiastically about Heinz Guderian's achievements, and pay tribute, far more handsomely than their colleagues in the British Army, to Basil Liddell Hart, J. F. C. Fuller and Percy Hobart, the pre-war British 'apostles of mobility' who informed Guderian's thinking. They will cite the *Communist Manifesto* to suggest the improvements that can follow when workers apply critical thinking to their own enterprises; and they will also break off in mid-flight, as General Maggart does, to announce himself convinced that 'digitization will change the doctrinal base' or to suggest that 'Third Wave warfare' is only really suited to the armies of America and the free world (it will push initiative and decision way down the line, in a manner that could not be tolerated by despotic or totalitarian regimes). As for the undeniable possibility that, in the world of 'free silicon', some of the technology of digitized warfare may be acquired by rogue states and other such poisonous snakes, Maggart is confident that 'nobody will be able to match our training, even if they get the technology . . .'

The method being used at Fort Knox was simple enough, as Maggart explained. First you develop 'a concept, a theoretical or intellectual base'. Then you experiment with it, initially 'using models and simulations', and later 'under field conditions with real men and equipment'. After that, you produce 'a piece of doctrine or doctrinal literature'. As part of his attempt to establish 'the intellectual basis' of this new situation, Maggart had set up an Advanced Warfighting Working Group, an unofficial army gathering that retained close contacts with the Armor Center. The AWWG was joined by a variety of out-of-the-box thinkers – military people, technology experts and also Pamela Jaye Smith of MYTHWORKS, a consultancy that provides 'mythic tools' and 'archepaths' for Hollywood actors and screenwriters, and advises would-be 'Alpha-Babes' how to become 'women of mythic Significance'. Maggart had met Smith in 1994, when her company was involved in filming digital army exercises in California, and he brought this exponent of 'applied mythology' into the AWWG to help promote 'divergent thinking' about the instantaneous interconnectivity offered by digitization, and to produce a new angle on the problem of 'form' and its resistance to change.

In her presentations to the AWWG Pamela Jaye Smith also introduced certain principles of the 'Ancient Wisdom', likening the connectivity of the digitized world to the 'net of gems' in oriental philosophy, and outlining an archetypal context for the personality patterns that could be found among present-day warriors. Concerned to 'realign our modern warfighters to their noble heritage', she started in December 1995 with a talk called 'WISE HEART, SHARP SWORD: Warriors, Weapons, and the Battlespace of Tomorrow', in which she announced that 'the world as we know it is falling apart', and then teased out the positive implications of that apocalyptic fact. She also theorized the 'battle space blob' ('a graphic interpretation of how the entities in a battle space form and shape themselves around intent and can be altered by same'). Having linked digital technology to a new and still evolving kind of 'group consciousness', Smith traced war back to the Heavens with the help of Lucifer and the Dead Sea Scrolls, and suggested that conflict enters the world through the tension between the Solar Plexus and the Astral Field. Her description of the 'Warrior Path' drew heavily on notions such as karma, Mission ('Protect the Weak and the Innocent', which was not to say the lazy and the stupid), chivalric love, and warrior bonding, the latter being defined as a higher form of love. Her examples of 'the Worthy Opponent' included Patton and Rommel, but also Darth Vader and Luke Skywalker; and she probed the possibility of 'transferring battle intensity to everyday life' before suggesting the future warrior would be like a magician, turning spirit into matter with sudden force, and also battling on Mental Planes for the cause of Divine Law and Order.

Whether or not he ever derived new doctrine from this redefinition of the 'intellectual base' of warfare, Maggart was sufficiently impressed to issue a testimonial describing Smith as 'the George S. Patton of modern military esoteric thinking', adding that 'her thoughtful commentary on leading and leadership is incisive, brilliant and strikes like a spear in the heart of those who claim to be leaders but who remain intellectually bound to age-old concepts which no longer apply to the information age world of high technology military operations'.[9] J. F. C Fuller may have belonged to the age of the motorized force rather than the 'distributed-network' model made possible by radio,[10] but he would have understood Maggart's commendation. So too, perhaps, would Aleister Crowley – even though he apparently never considered the possibility, proposed by Pamela Jaye Smith, that a weapon-system like a tank might be an 'incredible entity', or, to use the Sanskrit word, a *deva* or 'shining one'; and that as such it might be further empowered by the application of sacred geometry, sound, markings and symbols of precisely the sort that 'Magick' had gone in for.

Maggart's senior officers certainly seem to have got the point. As 'notionalizing' futurists, they were likely to pick up a standard piece of military equipment at any moment, and twist it into the strangest of shapes. Take the minefield. For most residents of the late twentieth century, a mine was a dumb explosive device that may be stuck in the ground and then all too easily forgotten until it blows the foot off a passing child. But this is not how it looked to a future-oriented, out-of-the-box, Army After Next Major like William H. Parry III. As Chief of the Battlefield Synchronization Division at Fort Knox, Parry gazed out from his hypothetical observation post in the future and saw the minefield as a discriminating and highly intelligent instrument. 'We played around with that,' he said. 'We played around with it in simulation only. It was not a fielded capability. We gave the mines the capability of being an intelligence collector, which is in fact what these intelligent mines will be able to do. They will have settings on them that will allow them to be intelligence collectors and report information back to you.' And what might that information be? Major Parry ventured that the message might go as follows: 'I'm a mine, and there is something with the following seismic activity that is occurring out here that leads me to believe, based upon the artificial intelligence circuitry built into me, that it's a T-80 tank. Do you wish for me to fire a top attack munition and kill that tank, or just sit here in a passive mode and report that to you?' He added, almost as an afterthought, that the smart minefield will also 'have the capability' of being switched on and off: 'I put it out there, I turn it on. All of a sudden, I turn the minefield off and I drive through the damn thing.'

Or take the business of 'Focused Dispatch', the subject of an experimental advanced warfighting exercise conducted by the Armor Center's Mounted Warfighting Battle Space Battle Lab. Parry explained the point of this experiment as follows: 'I've got a digital tank and I've got a digital artillery piece, and the way that I currently do a call for fire to the artillery, to the gunners, is that I've got the guy out here and he's sitting on a piece of dominating terrain, or whatever, and he's looking down into a kill zone. And he sees a target and he says that meets the commander's intent for me using indirect fire and so on. What he does is, this observer calls his company commander on the radio and says, "I've got ten tanks at this grid". The platoon leader calls his company commander on the radio and says, "I've got ten tanks at this grid." The company commander says, "OK, I'm going to shoot artillery at this in accordance with my current plan. Fire Support Officer, fire artillery at that target." The Fire Support Officer then sends that back to the field artillery battalion fire direction centre. And he says, "I've got ten tanks at this grid," and they compute the mission based upon elevation, altitude, deflection, gun target line, fuse, shell and some other stuff, which is technical stuff to them. That is then sent to a firing battery operations centre, which then passes it off to a platoon that is physically going to do the shooting. The guns are laid, the rounds come out.' The best artillery guys, from start to finish, would have a round in the air in three to five minutes, and that delay, said Parry, was why no army had ever been much good at firing artillery at moving targets.

All this would change, however, with the horizontal integration allowed by digitization. 'Well wait a minute, you know, if I've got a tank with a digital system and an artillery piece with a digital system, then why do I need to fiddle fart around with all these intermediate steps? Why can't I go from this guy to this guy?' The answer, said Parry, was that he could – although there were still some software limitations, including one that made it impossible to disentangle multiple sightings of the same target – so ten tanks could quickly become twenty, thirty, forty, fifty and sixty as the information poured in.

Colonel Pat Ritter, who was among the most intellectual of Maggart's tankers, has two degrees in English literature. 'I can think of no better background for this kind of work than the study of humanity,' he explained, before launching into an account of the transformations digitization is bringing to the military's concept of battle space. Starting in ancient times with the closely massed Macedonian phalanxes and the less tightly packed squares of the Roman legions, he then marched up through the Napoleonic Wars, the American Civil War and the Somme to demonstrate the 'empty battlefield syndrome', in which increases in the range and accuracy of weaponry make battle space progressively more lethal and empty at the same time: 'the more lethal the battlefield gets, the more empty it gets, the more dispersion you get . . .' Digitization was set to continue this transformation. In future, battle space would be a non-linear, partly electromagnetic domain, which no longer demanded a massing of combat power at 'the Forward Line of Troops'. Operations would be decentralized and distributed throughout the depth of battle space, and a new emphasis would fall on the idea of Simultaneity. With digitization, it became possible to plan, co-ordinate and execute synchronized actions while remaining dispersed – so you could get a massing of effects without taking the risk of massing forces for a single concentrated attack. Future strategy would be of a 'holistic' kind – co-ordinated across army, navy and air force, and full of pre-emptive strikes that 'defeat enemy attacks even before they occur'. The enemy would find themselves in a situation like that faced by a former Iraqi officer of the Gulf War, who had since visited the Armor Center to describe how his tanks had started blowing up all around him before he even knew he was under attack.

Desert Storm is both a model and inspiration to the prophets of digitization, who proclaim it as the first time an Information Age force met a force trained in the Cold War tactics of the Soviet Union. But the soldiers at Fort Knox wore it with special pride – the 100-hour engagement that had vindicated years of talk and preparation, leaving them and their machines 'tried and tested', and also saving the Armor Center from reforming politicians who might otherwise have sought to abolish or 'restructure' it. Ritter had commanded the 1st Battalion of the Third Army in Desert Storm, and the memory served as the anchor of his recitation. Indeed, there came a point where this hermeneut of future warfare interrupted his futuristic monologue and got up to talk about a picture hanging on his office wall. He looked like any other man walking across his office towards a photograph, but he was actually wading through the thermal imaging system and digitized screens towards a non-virtual world that seemed as obscure as the dark side of the moon. The photograph offered a glimpse of things that happen beyond the brightly simulated virtualities of techno-Christendom. It revealed a primitive place where hardware impacts on wetware (i.e., people), and where death is not just the going down of a simulator's lights. The picture showed Ritter's own kill – an Iraqi armoured vehicle, reduced to twisted hunks of metal in the sand, with triumphant American soldiers looking back at the camera.

Basic humanity

With his background in literary studies, Ritter knew that, like mechanization before it, digitization is a metaphor that can easily be taken too far. As he explained, the military is a highly conservative organization. As an advocate of change, he found this frustrating. Yet he understood that it was also right, since the nation's youth would pay the price for any critical mistake. As a characteristic of most if not all armies, this instinctive conservatism obliged the proponent of military reform to behave like a 'capitalist marketeer', picking out 'a symbol, a vision, a logo, a saying', and promoting it ceaselessly in writings and presentations. Mechanization had been just such a concept in its time, and the slogans of digitization were the same – 'Strike at a Distance', 'Over the Horizon', 'Information Warfare'. . . As a tanker, Ritter went out of his way to hold the old-fashioned humanist ground that was likely to be overwhelmed by this tide of overstatements. Even in the midst of rapid technological change, he insisted on the pre-digital human qualities that cause a man to bond with his tank. In Desert Storm Ritter's own M1A1 had been called Demon's Den, and he had effectively lived in or on it for six months. The men were flown home shortly after the Gulf War, but it was three months later that the tanks arrived back at Fort Riley: 'We got it off the train, off the flat car, and I got up on the tank and got into my cupola, honest to God, I felt like I was going home. I felt like it was home.'

An irrational sense of attachment, to be sure; but also proof that simulators and computers can't do everything. Having carried out his own 'deep reconnaissance of concepts', Ritter insisted: 'What you really need to be successful in combat is a system that is innovative, that exercises judgement, that solves problems, that can build cohesion in human beings and groups of human beings. And the last time I checked the list of technologies and systems, there was only one system out on the battlefield that could do that. And that is the human being with the most advanced computer ever known to man, which is the one between your ears.' As part of his advocacy of human rather than technological values, Ritter insisted that training was everything, and questioned the tendency of tank designers all over the world to reduce the crew to perhaps only two men – such a step would inevitably erode the warm-blooded sense of solidarity that had traditionally sustained the courage and morale of tankers. Exercises at the National Training Center had demonstrated that tankers equipped with the latest systems of tactical-email were inclined to stop using the keyboard or the mouse as soon as contact was made, and to revert instinctively to the radio. This demonstrated that human, and if possible face-to-face contact remained an essential part of tank warfare, especially between commanders and their officers. 'There is a need to look a soldier in the eye, to talk to a comrade,' said Ritter, doubting that any good officer would be prepared to send his tanks into battle with nothing more than an email message. Ritter preferred radio as a medium through which you can sense a subordinate's mental state; and he wanted to see video-conferencing facilities introduced into the tanks of the future. Technology should not be used in a manner that undermines 'the moral responsibility of commanding'. Used badly, digitization could serve to stifle initiative, by burying the soldier in data overload and providing senior commanders with all the information they needed to interfere from a previously unimaginable distance. The essential thing was to introduce it in accordance with the spirit of 'maneuver warfare', to equip the more junior commander to make speedier and far more accurate decisions at the point of combat.

This insistence on the human qualities of leadership is a Fort Knox truism, a down-home truth intoned in the midst of a technological storm. Among its most ardent exponents was Colonel Fritz Treyz, the commander of the 1st Armor Training Brigade. When he recommended Robert A. Heinlein's science fiction novel *Starship Trooper*, it was not for its fantastic gadgetry, but because he considered its account of the training of young entrants into the 'Federal Service of the Terran Federation' to be pinsharp on 'the ethics and morality' of soldiers in the future. For Treyz and his men, 'training' means taking sloppy young civilians, inviting them to sling any drugs they may still have on them down an anonymous chute, and then rebuilding them as proper American soldiers. Since this was obviously a gruelling process for the new recruit, I asked Treyz whether he would ever condone the Turkish method of forcing a young entrant to punish a tank. But for Treyz that story was only an opportunity to point out how much the US Army has changed since the sixties: 'What you are actually talking about is creating stress,' he says. It used to be, in the past, that 'the stress was created between the drill sergeant and the soldier. And the drill sergeant in the past would humiliate him, make fun of him, treat him like dog meat.' But not any more. 'Tough training' was still the order of the day, but the stress was only put on the soldier accomplishing the task he has set out to do. 'You've got to put the stress in the right place – not just on the soldier, but between the soldier and the task.' There is 'a great deal of human dignity' in this, says Treyz, handing me yet another paper in which he writes: 'Soldierization is far more than a transition; it is a remarkable transformation that has no parallel in the larger society.'

The tank dissolved

As for the main battle tank, what transformations are necessary to ensure a future for this heavy metal machine in the coming epoch of 'intangible assets'? Many have expressed doubts, suggesting that the main battle tank is a cumbersome anachronism that should have died with the twentieth century – a logistical nightmare, which is increasingly threatened by advances in helicopter and missile technology. Yet Colonel Ritter had an immediate answer to this. 'I've heard that before,' he said, going on to expound another law that emerges 'when you check the history of it'. His point was that, whenever it is demonstrated that a new technology can have a 'negative impact on a weapons system, then there's always a hue and cry that the weapon system is no good and that it is now the time of this new system'. After World War Two it was the aircraft that made the tank irrelevant. After Israel's October War of 1973 it was the hand-held anti-tank guided missile. But, as Ritter remarked, 'the fallacy of all of those arguments is based on an ignorance of what I call "the context of combat"'. He went on to stress the fallacy of comparing 'system on system', since this contest very seldom occurred in combat: 'Combat is a lot of things, but it is not one particular technology against another. Combat is chaos. Combat is confusion. Combat is very complex. Part of the complexity is that there are many systems in competition with each other.'

'An artificial lake, homeless trees and substantial returns from a summer colony . . .'[11] That is what the great post-war German novelist Uwe Johnson wrote of the once more wooded place north of New York where General Patton trained some of the soldiers he took to Europe in the later stages of the Second World War. By the time they left in 1944, Patton and his tankers had devastated the landscape with their Shermans: churning up the ground, smashing trees and leaving a derelict wasteland that would, so Johnson found, prove good for nothing but flooding and subsequent conversion to affluent tranquillity as Patton Lake. History has not been so erased at the Armor Center. Here historical tanks are mounted on roundabouts or isolated behind little box hedges by the roadside. These antiques are drawn from the wider collection at the Armor Center's George S. Patton Museum, where the story of the tank is told from a strongly American angle (starting with the caterpillar-tracked Holt Tractor, rather than the British prototypes of the First World War), where Israel Tal is honoured alongside Generals MacArthur and Patton; and where the 'historical luncheons' series is named after J. F. C. Fuller. Every one of these hedged and mounted tanks was once the latest machine of the moment, and each now challenged the men at Fort Knox to protect their more recent model from the ever-advancing museum. An Abrams M1A1 had already been sucked into those halls of monstrous redundancy; and the just-fielded M1A2 was already beginning to look like 'The Last Main Battle Tank' – soon to be written up in the Armor Center's *Armor* magazine as a superb system that was, nonetheless, invalidated by a new generation of anti-tank missiles: no longer just the primitive, wire-guided Sagger, but longer-distance 'fire and forget' weapons such as the self-guided Longbow Hellfire or the Indian NAG, which could kill at a range of six kilometres.[12] A few weeks earlier, I had heard a similar point of view from an employee of the Missiles Division of Aerospatiale, the French producer of the Eryx, a light hand-held anti-tank missile which, unlike earlier models, could be fired from within enclosed spaces. 'I wouldn't want to be in a tank,' this man told me at a company conference near Paris: it was 'not a very nice place to be' any longer – 'better outside'.

The tank had been engineered out of the cultural imagination in the second decade of the twentieth century; and it was apparent, eighty years later, that if it was to survive into the twenty-first century as anything other than an obsolete hunk of old steel, it must now be turned back into a 'concept'. So it was that the paradigm-shifting heavy hitters at Fort Knox had dissolved their machine back into its idea and were busily projecting it into the future on billows of speculation that outstripped all but the most far-reaching science fiction. General Sullivan had informed me that, far from being just a heavy metal object, the tank was actually a 'concept' – 'mobile protected space with a direct fire weapon' – that would be needed far into the conceivable future. Colonel Ritter agreed: 'maybe it won't even touch the ground – maybe it will ride on an electro-magnetic cushion; maybe it will have no turret; maybe its gun will be a laser beam . . .' But there would always be 'one platform providing direct and indirect force defence power'.

The future of this theoretical weapon was in the hands of the Directorate of Force Development – the director of which, Colonel Bryla, was just handing over to Colonel Kalb at the time of my visit. Bryla was known for holding his meetings on a balcony, in order to escape prophylactic Federal rules about smoking, which he did profusely. And it was there, with the garbage trucks roaring around us, that he explained how his own future-gazing had started. About three years ago, the then commander of the Armor Center had announced that, since it had been decided to build 1,079 M1A2 tanks, it was time to ask about Tank 1,080. What would its 'configuration' be? 'Digitization is great,' said Bryla, 'but you can't shoot digits and kill people with them. And that's what we're about. We're supposed to figure out how best to kill people, or to achieve our objective by scaring them to death in terms of what we could be able to do.'

To begin with, as Bryla remembered, they decided that they weren't after a mere variant on the M1A2: 'we want something radical . . . we definitely want something that might be classified "leap ahead" or "breakthrough"'. Not just another gradual evolutionary variation, then, but a total mutation: 'Maybe we don't even call it a tank.' Perhaps, as a previous commander of the Armor Center, General Paul Funk, had suggested in order to maintain the break with convention, we should call it 'a crank'. 'Maybe it flies. We don't know.' A new kind of power pack would have to be considered if the Abrams's all too familiar 'logistical tail' of fuel trucks was to be shed. But since the traditional mission of the tank wasn't about to go away, it would definitely be something that 'provides continuous firepower, that takes and holds ground'. Having got together with the Abrams programme manager and other experts, they reluctantly concluded that the technology needed for the Future Main Battle Tank (FMBT) of their dreams would probably not be available for some time. So they fell back into the real world and, with a sadly pragmatic eye on what they could expect to get funded, started thinking in terms of merely evolutionary progression – a new upgrade of the Abrams, which they called the M1A3.

That was how things had stood when General Maggart took command in summer 1995, and pushed his fallen Directorate of Force Development back up into the clouds. The digitized and horizontally integrated army known as Force XXI would come on stream in 1999–2000, and last for maybe ten or fifteen years. But the time had come to think seriously about 'the Army After Next'. What would that look like, and would the proposed M1A3 meet the doctrine of that time? Maggart was reluctant to accept that the technology would not be there to support a more 'leap ahead' scenario; and, after a meeting with the generals of the Armor Caucus, it was decided that, 'if ever there was a time in recent memory when the US Army's Armored Force can take a risk in terms of modernization, it's now'. They resolved to put 'a mark on the wall, and make that 2015, and let's go get a new tank'.

So they 'stood down the normal bureaucracy', got together with scientists, manufacturers and academics, and formed Integrated Concept Teams to elaborate concepts in four areas. The Main Battle Tank of the Future fell to Major Monroe Harden, who urged his team to 'think outside the box', using 'creative thought and logical extensions of reality'. They were to assume both that Force XXI was in place, along with the doctrines that it had substituted for the previous Air Land Battle scenario, and that digitization was delivering on its promises – enough to give the commander 'dominating situational awareness' and 'informational supremacy over the bad guys'. They also presumed that this situational awareness would allow the commander to disperse the force so that every tank could have its own route of march, and that there would be a capacity both to 'mass effects' without necessarily massing forces and also to launch precision strikes of extraordinary accuracy. As Harden said, 'You saw that on CNN this morning, where the Israelis took out one parked car in a busy street, destroying just that one parked car. The attendant traffic accidents were, I'm sure, not inconsequential.' By linking 'sensors to shooters', it would be possible to attack simultaneously in depth. The enemy facing this kind of fast-tempo 'maneuver strike pulse' would be getting it everywhere at once – 'supply trucks, headquarters, all getting taken out before he has even figured out where the force is . . . He doesn't know what the hell is going on, and oh by the way he just got an armored brigade screaming right through where his battle position used to be.' The point of these 'quick high tempo operations' is to do everything so speedily that you're 'inside the enemy's decision cycle all the time'. You mass your effects, kill him, and then disperse in one location after another, until his command and control system collapses. Obviously, you couldn't do this, if your tanks had to stop every six or eight hours to be refuelled from a hundred supply trucks wandering around the battlefield, or if your scouting vehicle was the old and all too visible Humvee ('Arnold Schwarzenegger kind of stuff, that ain't very good'). Likewise, there was no question of producing machines that would necessitate establishing a logistics port and then building up the force over months, as had been done before Desert Storm. Under the new system tailored for a world full of poisonous snakes, it must be possible to be sitting in some army post in Texas one day, and then be going into battle in some far-off place the following morning.

The Directorate of Force Development took a lot of ideas from the 'far out thinking' of an army group called Revolution in Military Affairs. They went up to Detroit where the Tank Automotive Research Development Engineering Center was based, and consulted electro-magnetic gun experts among other 'people working on conceptual stuff'. A key concern was 'shrinking the logistical tail'. As the saying went, 'Without a revolution in logistics, there will not be a Revolution in Military Affairs.' So they interested themselves in 'exotic fuel – lots of ways of doing that'. Using scenarios to help focus the thinking, these 'notionalizing' futurists set out to 'break with tradition' by pushing even the most familiar scenarios to new extremes, including the old track-versus-wheel argument, which by the early nineties had become a battle between the US Army and the Marines whose preference for wheeled vehicles has been confirmed by the success of their new LAV, which first proved itself in Panama in 1989. Even the normally confining 'laws of physics' were not safe from these men, who would suddenly turn round and mention the television series *Star Trek* – saying that the perfect scout vehicle would be like a Klingon bird of prey – something that 'goes in unseen, and only uncloaks if he has to kill something'.

Just as General Funk had advised his mould-breaking men to think in terms of the 'crank' rather than the 'tank', the Future Main Battle Tank was soon relabelled the Future Combat System. It was likely to have completely new capabilities, like being able to shoot accurately over hills. It might well have its own air defence systems too, and it might be equipped with multiple missiles rather than wasting time with a traversable turret and a single gun tube. As for the traditional qualities of the tank, Major Harden had a list of enduring attributes ready to pull out when anybody said that the tank was dead: protected sensors and leadership, combat intelligence forward on the battlefield; offensive mobility with combat power; lethality, survivability; versatility ('you can revise your mission'). There are, of course, other systems that can do some of this, but 'it is only the tank that can do them all simultaneously, and over a sustained period of time'.

The 'shock effect' was also on that list. In the early years of the tank, this symbolic capability might have been expected to fade once the improved machine became genuinely effective as a weapon. But no such development has taken place to date. High technology was all very well, but General Maggart was happy to retain the civilian's impression of tanks as 'ponderous machines that will squash you', saying there was 'enormous emotional potential in these things'. Indeed, the shock effect of the tank as it might be engaged in 'Operations Other Than War' was much cited in defence of the weapon. Major Mike Campbell of the Marine Corps had been in Somalia a few years previously, and he remembered offloading the first Abrams M1A1 and driving into Mogadishu: 'Do you know what happened? Nothing. That's the point.' If fifty-six Pakistani peacekeepers died after the Marines pulled out, that was, as the Pakistani commander had himself said, because they had no armour. The tank, said General Maggart, was 'really a statement . . . When the US puts a tank on the ground, it means business, OK? And so when we went to Bosnia to do Operations Other Than War, the first thing that rolled across the bridge . . . wasn't a doggone water purification unit. It was a tank . . . And let me tell you, if you want to get somebody's attention, just put an M1A1 tank on the ground.'

Colonel Ritter was especially well equipped to comment on the symbolic aspect of tank warfare. The very name, he said, was originally 'a codename for a water tank'. And anyone who doubted 'the moral effect' of the tank's appearance on tax-paying civilians only had to visit one of the military's combined arms live fire exercises, where non-military onlookers were overawed by what they saw – 'and they're lying back in bleachers, watching it in front of them shoot out that way. And they are just amazed.' As far as Ritter was concerned, the 'shock effect' remained central to the tank's power as a weapon. When he was commanding his battalion in Desert Storm, he designed a formation on the aircraft. He advanced in a 'combat diamond' that enabled forty-four of his fifty-eight tanks to fire simultaneously. Riding with the lead platoon, he too remembered turning round and seeing, for the first time even after twenty years in the army, a 'fully deployed tank battalion': 'I turned and looked and – look at my arms now, the goose bumps have come up. I mean I can still see that sight, I cannot imagine what it must be like on the other side, seeing all that come at you, with many of those tanks with mine ploughs on the front of them – rugged, almost like shark's teeth.' And when they did fire in synchrony, the first thing Ritter saw as the dust cleared was white flags everywhere: 'I do not believe it was the fact that the people that were surrendering saw the destruction, but rather that they saw us shoot, and saw the potential for the destruction to occur on their body.'

If soldiers fear the tank, this may, Ritter opined, be connected with their wider distaste for robotic warfare. 'You feel confident that as long as you're fighting another human being, somehow, you can find a way to trick him, to beat him, but it's the fact that there's this cold uncaring, unemotional machine out there, coming towards you. Because, you see, you don't see the crewman in an attack. All you see is the tank. And it's: "Oh my God, what am I going to do now?"' As for civilian fear, this was no less effective for being a primitive feeling born partly of ignorance. Experienced tankers might feel irritated every time a maintenance M113 personnel carrier appeared on the news and the broadcaster said: 'And the tanks rolled in today.' But that, as Ritter knew, was exactly the point when it came to over-awing civilians: 'If it has a track it's a tank in many people's eyes.' And even though a tank can easily be destroyed under the right circumstances, it still looks invincible to civilians who know nothing else about it. That, said Ritter, was why the Russians sent them into Czechoslovakia in 1968.

No place for a woman

I was exhausted by the time I got to the airport at Louisville, leaving behind the tanks, the bullion depository and also the men of the Ku Klux Klan, who had paraded through that Kentucky town the Sunday before, their racism all dressed up in prim Sunday school language. After five days of military presentations, I had lost the ability to tell a soldier from a stargazing intellectual or, for that matter, a civil software consultant. The officers at the Armor Center had been diligent in their explanations, but I still felt as if I'd had my brain sucked out through my ears, and replaced by acronyms, abbreviations and a million little arrows beamed in with the help of overhead slides. I had seen much to confirm Jean Baudrillard's observation that 'war drifts slowly into technological mannerism',[13] even though I had not met a single soldier who didn't know the difference between simulated and actual combat.

On the plane I wondered vaguely which of the many Integrated Concept Teams connected to Force XXI had come up with the doctrine that the best way to keep a secret was actually to bury it underneath a flagrant display of openness. This is not the British way, as I had been reminded when I met the British liaison officer at the Armor Center, Lieutenant Colonel O'Reilly. He had informed me that I was seeing considerably more than had been shown to Britain's General Sir Michael Rose, when he had passed through a few weeks previously. My visit had been cleared through the Pentagon, but somebody at the British Embassy in Washington was apparently still wondering how I had managed to 'slip through the cracks'.

Unmixed official secrecy is certainly not the order of the day at Fort Knox, and the 'cracks', if such they were, seemed as wide as the Grand Canyon. There had indeed been occasions when voluble soldiers drew the line, as Major Monroe Harden had when I asked him to be a little more precise about his concept for the Future Main Battle Tank ('I've pretty much reached the wall, as far as what I can say now'). But in general the Armor Center had seemed unusually dedicated to demonstration and display. The presentations had been polished and well rehearsed, and the soldiers were plainly used to adorning their parked M1A2 tanks with explanatory notices and then standing by to answer questions. At times, it had seemed as if the whole place only existed to receive visitors, give them a ride on a simulator, and pack them off with a head full of swirling futuristic jargon about Total Asset Visibility and other tricks of the warfare to come.

In part this showmanship may have been aimed at convincing the American taxpayer that downsizing had gone quite far enough. But when Colonel Pat Ritter remarked that there was 'great benefit in letting people see things', he was also connecting the tanker's old argument about 'shock effect' with a wider theory of deterrence of the kind that characterized the Cold War. 'We demonstrated for fifty years that we could kick their butt,' Ritter said of the manoeuvres that were carried out in Europe before the collapse of the Warsaw Pact, and the principle lives on in the less predictable age of poisonous snakes. Yet there was another motivation behind this openness, a commercial one that would receive its sharpest confirmation in

General Sullivan's office in Washington, DC. At the end of our conversation, the former Chief of Staff drew my attention to a picture on his office wall. It portrayed a robed Saudi monarch, painted in stylized and heroic mode, with an Abrams M1A2 surging up beneath him. Sullivan observed that the Saudis were 'very pleased' with the tanks and simulators they had recently bought. He also confirmed that as a director of General Dynamics, which produced the Abrams tank, he had indeed been able to help out a little with the contract. No doubt the simulator-trained drivers who had demonstrated the Abrams had also performed better than the poor man whom the disgraced former British cabinet minister Jonathan Aitken blamed for the failure of his post-Gulf War attempt to sell Challenger 2s to Kuwait: this fellow was said to have brought his 'roaring monster' to a chaotic halt just yards from the royal box with his gun pointing 'directly into the stomach of the visibly shaken emir'.[14]

Of all the questions I had taken to Fort Knox, there was only one that seemed disconcerting and positively unwelcome. Far from being about hardware, the digital qualities of the future battlefield, or the offscreen nature of Iraqi death, it concerned the role of women soldiers in America's tank force. I had been interested to know whether, by the time we got to Force XXI, or even the Army After Next, women soldiers would have penetrated the last remaining bastion of male comradeship, and be serving in the tank – or in whatever 'platform' will then embody the concept of Mobile Protected Firepower. There had already been women tank mechanics at Fort Knox, and some Canadian women soldiers were said to have been through simulator training there too. But no women had yet served inside an American tank, although it was apparently more than a senior officer's career prospects were worth to come out and describe that tight and dangerous space as an all-male zone.

General Sullivan had spoken positively about the expansion in the number of women in America's armed forces: a transformation that had followed the cancellation of the draft in 1973 and helped lift the now 'all-volunteer' army out of a seriously demoralized period. Nearly all the women who joined were high-school graduates, and they helped set new standards at the beginning of the all-volunteer army, raising the army's expectations of male recruits and encouraging it to 'incentivize' high-school graduates all round. But there were still clear demarcations in Sullivan's mind: 'I think it best that we do not assign women to combat battalions,' he said, adding that there seemed to be 'general agreement' on that point.

As a retired chief of staff Sullivan could say what he wanted. But officers at Fort Knox had fielded this question with palpable reluctance. I might have expected a certain amount of innuendo along the lines of: 'What kind of woman wants to get inside a tank?' But the officers I had spoken to were not at all inclined to speculate in this degenerate manner, and confined their remarks to more neutral matters such as upper body strength, and what it takes to load 75-pound shells into a gun tube successively and at speed, or to get out into the mud to haul hawsers about when a tank breaks down and needs towing. As Commanding General Maggart's special assistant, Colonel Jeanette S. James came to one meeting prepared to address this question, but so decisively did Maggart set the topic aside as really 'not an issue', that I never heard her view.

The place of women in the military was a politically sensitive issue in America at that time, and the practice of excluding women soldiers from combat units was certainly not unanimously accepted by those concerned to push on with this 'unfinished revolution'.[15] Meanwhile, it was also abundantly clear that, with digitization bringing about fundamental changes in both doctrine and battle space, the difference between combat and support services was going to be increasingly hard to sustain. The tactical silence I encountered on this question testified to military sensitivities about the Clinton administration – those 'White House Commissars of Political Correctness', who, if right-wing Republican commentators were to be believed, had hated the military ever since their draft-evading days in the sixties, and were now gleefully cashiering senior officers who spoke their minds. In May 1996, this 'relentless lynch mob' is said to have driven the chief of naval operations, Admiral Mike Boorda, to suicide by questioning his right to wear certain valorous combat pins on his medal ribbons.[16] Yet the army had other critics too. It was no advocate of equal opportunities who had urged me, before I visited the Armor Center, to understand that I was visiting 'a bastion of reaction'.

Tank thinking in Washington, DC

William S. Lind had suggested we met at a restaurant in Union Station – a place called Sfuzzi's, which he reckoned was one of the few remaining places on Capitol Hill where the muzak, and perhaps also the customers, were sufficiently under control to allow a proper conversation. Arriving in that vast classical building at the appointed time, I found that even this last resort had closed down three months earlier. William S. Lind, however, was quite unmistakable. Tall and wearing a classically cut greatcoat and a grey fedora, he had the profile of a man who uses a previous age's idea of elegance to armour himself against the sliding spirit of his times.

Lind directs the Center for Cultural Conservatism at the Free Congress Association in Washington. He also played a major part in driving the case for military reform in the last years of the Cold War. He served as President of the Military Reform Institute and later joined forces with Senator Gary Hart, the leading candidate for the Democratic Presidential nomination in 1988, to co-author a book called *America Can Win*, which promised to turn military reform into a major programme of government. Senator Hart gave way to Mike Dukakis when his presidential campaign came to a sticky end thanks to a photograph involving a yacht and a young woman called Donna Rice. Lind, however, has pressed on with his assault on the US military establishment, condemning the bloated and bureaucratic officer corps, the defence industries and procurement system that have developed monstrously expensive and inappropriate weapons, and the entrenched doctrinal ideas that committed America's forces to fighting firepower/attrition wars rather than manoeuvre warfare of the far superior kind pioneered by the Germans in the twentieth century's two World Wars. As a result of these faults, the US military had scarcely carried out a successful operation since the Korean War. Indeed, Lind has argued that this decadent monolith was so bad at fighting that for years every conflict had faced America with a choice between 'national humiliation' and 'nuclear war'.

As we strode out of Union Station, Lind gestured at the nearby Federal Judiciary Building. This edifice was so new that contractors were still unrolling the turf in front of it, but Lind had already consigned it to Hell as a lesser edifice that merely occupied its space rather than commanding it. 'There', he said, 'is a sign of how we are passing from an age of gold to an age of silver.' Basically, he observed, we were talking about the decline of Western civilization. The British had peaked in the 1860s, and America had been sliding down hill since about 1910. The final blow for both had come with the First World War. Lind paused to tie an unravelling shoelace, unassailed by the normally persistent African-American beggars who plainly registered the shock effect of his formidable appearance without necessarily knowing that this was a man who, apart from not being sentimental with his small change, was quite prepared to argue publicly that America would be a better place had the South not been defeated in the Civil War. I mentioned the burgeoning cherry blossom all around, but Lind soon yanked us back on to more serious ground. Multiculturalism had been a disaster, he said, even though few people in a position of public influence had the courage to say so. Telling the Republicans from the Democrats nowadays was like having to choose between Donald Trump and Madonna – 'take your pick of the trash'. He had dispatched the entire American political establishment by the time we arrived at the Red River Grill, where he ordered a Jamaican spiced jerk chicken burrito and turned his fire on the army.

Though interested in military strategy and doctrine since boyhood, Lind has not seen active military service. This fact did not inhibit him from criticizing the army's ideas of manoeuvre in an influential article published in the *Military Review* back in the late seventies; and he has since written much on the subject, including his *Maneuver Warfare Handbook* (1985), which set out to introduce members of the US Marine Corps to the art of manoeuvre in simple language.[17] Mocking the official 'how to' primers and true/false multiple-choice questions of the marine's official training, Lind defines manoeuvre as an open form of combat that relies on the initiative of junior commanders and is inherently disorderly. Inspired by the infiltration tactics developed by the Germans in 1918, manoeuvre warfare is the opposite of set-piece scenarios or the mere piling up of resources demanded by the war of attrition. It is intelligent, mobile, improvisational, and more dependent on trust and a 'shared way of thinking' than on high-tech gadgets. It demands a lean and decentralized force, rather than a bureaucratic monolith; and its officers must be educated 'in terms of how rather than what to think' – certainly not just instructed in techniques and the acquisition of facts. When it comes to military education, Lind makes classical claims – the adept of manoeuvre warfare needs to be capable of 'questioning and creative thinking' and of putting 'immediate situations into a larger context built of history, philosophy, and an understanding of the nature of the man'. Field exercises are essential if participants are to learn to live with 'friction' and develop the power of 'critique' that is so essential to successful manoeuvre warfare. Wary of the military appetite for technology, Lind warns that 'computerized games where the computer attempts to decide "who won" are worse than useless: the computer can only reward "kills", which means the game compels fire-power/attrition warfare'. Lind's book has become an 'undergound' manual within the US Marines. His ideas have been taken up by forward-looking marines stationed at Fort Knox, who needed no prompting to place Lind in the line of J. F. C. Fuller. On the army side, Colonel Ritter had also declared the book 'useful', even though he felt obliged to follow his commendation with a barbed question about its opinionated author, 'When was the last time he served in combat?'

Sitting in that Washington restaurant, Lind might reasonably have commended himself for having already made some difference. However, a little was not enough, and he was scathing about the US Army's recent record. In his view, every war the USA had fought since the Second World War had been a cabinet war, and the US Army, which gave up thinking strategically when nuclear weapons effectively put warfare under civilian control, had resorted to all sorts of dishonesty in the endeavour to present themselves as victors. Vietnam was a fiasco, with the military saving face with the help of its own 'stab in the back' theory. The 1980 attempt to free US hostages in the Iranian Embassy had been bungled, and the successful invasion of Grenada in October 1983 did not make up for the 241 marines lost in a Beirut bomb attack that same month. As for the Gulf War, that was hardly the out-and-out victory claimed by the heroes of Desert Storm. Here, says Lind, were three great world powers combining to take on a regional power which, in the event, didn't even fight. If one remembered the operational objective, which was 'to encircle and destroy the Republican Guard', then it was actually a failure. 'And yet we proclaim it as a great victory.'

According to Lind, who was just warming up, the US Army was stuck in the anachronistic French tradition of attrition warfare. The Marines were somewhat better disposed towards the idea of manoeuvre, thanks to their traditional involvement in amphibious and littoral warfare. But here too there seemed to be ample room for improvement. Lind named a couple of the young marines I had met at Fort Knox and suggested that they represented almost the whole of the armoured community's serious thinking on the matter. The interesting thing now, he said, was the development of light armoured forces, using vehicles such as the Marine Corps's LAV, which, as those marines had also told me, the army had refused to take seriously because it had wheels rather than tracks.

'The US military has reached the point of corruption,' said Lind, 'where the product is the programme and the budget.' This was 'a military where the whole world is internal' – budget, equipment and research – and which reads very little history and thinks only about its equipment: techno-idolatry instead of proper strategy. Lind railed against the cybercolonels in the spirit of a latter-day Ernst Jünger determined to rescue the soul of the warrior hero from the mechanical devices that threatened to displace it. 'What you saw', he said of Fort Knox, 'is an institution designed not to train in armor, but to sell armor and to train officers to sell armor.' You can spend hours getting an American military presentation and at the end of it not be able to say one thing that it meant: 'Whenever I get a briefing, I say throw the slides away and let's talk.'

The US Army's system of basic training 'wouldn't look any different if it had been designed by the KGB' – what kind of basic training is it, he asked, that creates unit-cohesion and then immediately breaks it up by dispersing its new soldiers to different posts all around the world? Despite its futurist battle labs and talk of a Revolution in Military Affairs, the US Army Training and Doctrine Command (TRADOC) was really just 'the Soviet refrigerator industry in uniform, producing a great many very bad refrigerators'. As for the Abrams main battle tank, Lind denied that it was a tank at all: 'it looks like a tank but it is not a tank because it doesn't have operational mobility'. At just under seventy tons, this latest addition to America's baroque arsenal is too vast and cumbersome to cross bridges, while its massive fuel consumption makes it far too dependent on supply trucks really to move. This accusation is quickly brushed aside by the military ('Noted,' said General Sullivan drily when I mentioned it to him), but Lind was adamant, reiterating a point that I had also heard from the marines who had been unable to get the army interested in developing a new version of their wheeled Light Armoured Vehicle: like ignorant civilians, 'they define a tank by what it looks like, not by what it does'. As for the emphasis that the men at Fort Knox had placed on the shock effect of the tank, I anticipated that Lind might have some regard for this traditional capability, which continues to prove useful for peace-keepers as well as murderous warlords. The crude and often sexualized potency of the tank's appearance explains why the late Serbian thug known as 'Arkan' liked to pose in front of one – holding a young tiger while the masked killers and rapists who formed his own army of 'Tigers' clustered menacingly around the gun-tube behind him. It also suggests that the truly representative tank of the late twentieth century may actually have been not a state-of-the-art digitized machine like the Abrams, but rather a 'scarred and cruddy ancient' such as the 'old Soviet T-34' that provides the apocalyptic final image of Don Delillo's novel *Mao II* (1991). Seen grinding its way through the cratered streets of Beirut at the head of a carousing wedding party, this 'heavy presence' has been 'sold and stolen two dozen times, changing sides and systems and religions. The only markings are graffiti, many years of spritzed paint.'[18] For Lind, however, talk of the shock effect was just primitive nonsense: at that point you're back at 'the Chinese war junk floating down the river banging gongs and waving flags at a British frigate. It all looks fine until the frigate wakes up and puts an end to the matter with 24-pounders.'

According to this critic, 'the furthest thing from any unit in the American army now is war'. The main priority has become 'force protection' and when an army reaches the point where the whole focus is placed on protecting its strength, then 'it has reached the phase of complete uselessness – the final rococo stage of development'. So the agenda of political correctness now loomed over the whole downsized edifice. Fair-mindedness had replaced martial excellence as the guiding value, and officers were careful to hold their tongues on sensitive issues and not to drive at more than twenty miles an hour on post. Describing such preoccupations as so many 'rococo cherubs, the last baroque embellishments' on a decadent structure, Lind stressed that officers now get promoted on their record in exactly this sort of area – with preferment going to those who have not caused complaints on the equal opportunities front.

No such muzzle constricted Lind, who went on to denounce the presence of women in the army as absurd, and to suggest that their moral effect on this supposedly fighting force was probably worse than that of the serving homosexuals whose rights President Clinton had supported. But the US Army was 'Stalinist' on this issue and a male officer who voiced any misgivings would not be advancing his career: it would be like being in Moscow in the 1930s and saying that this man Trotsky might have a point or two. Asked to elaborate, Lind resorted to an archaic anthropological scenario. The traditional duty of women was the passing on of culture, while the second great responsibility in the history of mankind, which was defence, went to men. Mix the first up with the second, and what is there left to defend? Duties had gone down the plughole, mused Lind, and we were living in a world where there were only rights. Enter, then, the risk-averse 'checklist army', which, as one of Lind's followers had argued, had prioritized the manager over the warrior and produced soldiers who, when they finally went into action at the National Training Center, revealed themselves to be more concerned with 'crossing the line of departure in correct formation' than in moving out rapidly in order to exploit enemy weakness.[19]

In the end, it was the continuing collapse of Western civilization that necessitated Lind's proposed reformation of war. The point, he said, was that nation state was no longer going to fight nation state: 'Look at Bosnia, Somalia, Liberia.' The wars of the future would be sectional, and within states – 'issues of race, culture, ideology will be what wars are about'. This observation brought us back to the culturally divided American city. Tanks had been used against rioters in Detroit in 1967, and I was also reminded of the words of Captain Lynch, the marine at Fort Knox who had described surging up Interstate Five in an armoured column towards Los Angeles during the riots of early May 1992. The marines were filmed from the moment the gates came off at Camp Pendleton, and the LAVs surged out to fill all six lanes of the highway, a battalion of 1,500 men driving north to relieve the beleaguered police and National Guard. Cheered on by crowds gathered on the overpasses, they paused at the since closed El Toro Air Station in Tustin, just south of Los Angeles. After some final riot-control training they were ready to head into the burning war zone in their LAVs and were disappointed when, in the interests of moderation, it was decided that the 600 or so who went into Los Angeles would travel on five-ton trucks ('not a sexy thing to take into the battle'). Perhaps someone had remembered the Posse Comitatus Act, which outlawed the use of Federal troops in internal policing operations. Perhaps, as Captain Lynch preferred to think, the sight on CNN of those marines and their LAVs rolling up the road had already helped to calm the worst riots in American history. In spirit, William S. Lind had been out there with Lynch. Indeed, writing in the *Marine Corps Journal* in December 1994, this spooky commentator had predicted: 'The next real war we fight is likely to be on American soil.'[20]

End of the road?

What has actually happened since then? The Marines have not been sent in with their LAVs to discipline the city, and reimpose American values on its diverse inhabitants. The Abrams M1A2 has been commissioned, but in small numbers – seventy-seven were built in the mid-nineties, but by the year 2000 the commitment was for 1,174 further M1A2s, made from upgraded M1A1s. These new models would have certain enhancements, bigger computer memory, improved armour, second generation FLIR viewing systems, and the IVIS readied to operate with the wider battlefield management system due to be introduced across all platforms. These machines will be in service for the next two decades at least; and that is the likely prospect for other tank-producing countries too. Though procured in comparatively small numbers, French Leclercs, British Challenger 2s, German Leopards, Japan's Type 90s and India's new Arjun tanks will roll on through the first quarter of the twenty-first century, upgraded as they go by various 'Technology Insertion Programmes'. The British firm Vickers may even be commissioned to produce a light 'plastic' tank, like the 'E-glass' armoured prototype that was rolled out in front of the press cameras in March 2000. Yet in February 2001, Britain's Master General of the Ordnance announced that the 70-ton main battle tank will have had its day by 2025.[21]

As for the outcome of the Fort Knox Directorate of Force Development's deliberations, in January 2000, the US Army committed some $2 billion for the research and development of a range of 'Future Combat Systems', explaining that the new defence scenario would demand replacement of current battlefield platforms sooner than planned, and anticipating that the first fielded systems could be expected in 2010 rather than 2015. 'We can no longer be 'risk-averse', said the US Army acquisition official Lieutenant General Paul Kern: 'we don't have twenty years to do it'.[22] The search is now on for the technologies that will equip the new vehicle. The key considerations include 'robotics, networked sensors, and active armour protection'. The word is that this 'system of systems' will be 'fly light and fight heavy'. It will weigh twenty tons or so and be easily transported in a Lockheed Martin C-130 aircraft. Less than a third as heavy and far more manoeuvrable than an Abrams tank, its ability to avoid being hit will depend partly on its successful horizontal integration with other forces, including air and navy. Its armour may be modular, and consist not of heavy metal or even plastics, but of 'active systems' that pre-empt incoming projectiles, or of heavy magnetic fields. Systems of 'signature management' will doubtless be used too – the idea being, as a spokesman for General Dynamics remarks, 'to avoid detection, to prevent the enemy locking on to you and, in the event of failure, to destroy his missile before it reaches you'. Once it has arrived at its destination, the Future Combat System may turn out to be a lightly manned ground platform equipped with a variety of robotically controlled systems capable of defeating any number of threats – from a 70-ton main battle tank to a soldier with a laser blinder. As for the cannon, electromagnetic gun systems are to be considered, along with lasers, particle beams, pulsed weapons, and the hypervelocity Compact Kinetic Energy Missile. Indeed, it may be that a single gun is dispensed with for a more accurate system of missiles, which can be fired simultaneously, and without the laborious and time-consuming business of reloading, or rotating the turret to take aim. Fuel consumption will be drastically reduced. If the technology doesn't yet enable solar power to be beamed down in the form of microwaves from a satellite, then the answer may be to use a hybrid-electric system in which a small and comparatively lightweight engine feeds fuel storage cells from which the power for surges can be drawn.

Lieutenant General Kern acknowledged that this prospect represented a 'big gulp' for the army. Whether or not the Future Combat System emerges as a tank, it is to be expected that, no sooner are its features outlined, than another Toffler-like 'wave' will come crashing through to invalidate it with mind-blowing billion-dollar consequences. Indeed some members of America's defence establishment are already speculating about the Army after the

Army After Next. Professor Martin Lipicki, who is surely the Salvador Dali of the National Defense University in Washington DC, has estimated that the next quantum leap in the world of 'free silicon' will follow from the integration of biotechnology with miniaturization and information processing.[23] Stargazing military academics foresee a new kind of 'fire ant warfare' in which areas will be dominated not by high-tech Behemoths but by hosts of tiny, semi-autonomous insect-machines, and surveyed by 'long-loiter high altitude drones' and clouds of 'surveillance dust' made up of microscopic winged things carrying sensors.[24] Powered by photosynthesis rather than diesel fuel, these 'hybrid biomechanical devices' will open a 'microscopic theater of combat' and, in all likelihood, bring the human bloodstream into battle space. Whatever the shape or form of the Future Combat System, any old-fashioned enemy tank that survives long enough to stray into this new kind of 'mesh war' will find itself on a terrain 'littered with sensors and emitters backed by hidden projectiles'. Its nemesis may be a tiny sensor-bearing robot that jumps on to it and sits there, like a flea on a dog, giving its position away, and then moving on to eat its way through the tank's gaskets or fuse its moveable parts.

For that hypothetical machine, the story of the tank closes just as it began: in a cloud of frantic period fantasy. Yet armoured vehicles really were cruising America's city streets by the end of the twentieth century. In the event, however, they were not LAVs of the kind in which US Marines advanced on Los Angeles during the 1992 riots, but examples of a new type of civilian platform known as the SUV, or 'sports utility vehicle'. A formidable monster, which is often way too big to be squeezed into a conventional garage, the SUV is a considerable improvement on the old Ford Edsel, a cumbersome gas guzzler that came to be known as the 'Yank Tank' in the 1950s. It is equipped with crumple zones, bull bars and special body side reinforcements. Its users enjoy a luxurious interior described, at least in the marketing blurb that accompanies the Ford Explorer, as 'a very civilized sanctuary'; and its high ground clearance elevates them far above the urban loiterer, gang-member or instantly crushable mere car owner. These four-wheel-drive machines are designed to appeal to the 'urban gentry', and not least to women, who value a sense of security and of conquering rugged terrain even while on the school run or driving to the suburban shopping mall. According to a medical anthropologist who has carried out 'archetype research' with potential consumers, the booming SUV market is powered by a straightforward story: 'It's a jungle out there. It's Mad Max. People want to kill me, rape me. Give me a big thing like a tank'.[25]

Notes

CHAPTER 1. The Heaviness of an Age

1 See my 'Icon of the Revolution', *Guardian*, 4 June 1992.

2 T. D. Allman, 'The Crushing Wheel of China', *Vanity Fair*, October 1989, pp. 224–61.

3 *Tabloid World News*, 8 April 1998.

4 Deng's address was recorded via Beijing Domestic Television Service, 27 June 1989.

5 Quoted from *The Gate of Heavenly Peace*, a documentary film of 1995 directed by Richard Gordon and Carma Hinton. For the transcript see the associated website at http://www.nmis,org/Gate.

6 The phrase is quoted from Patrick Ryan, the US naval attaché whose 'Department of Defense, US Milgroup, Situation Report #2, Oct 1, 1973' is to be found in National Security Archive, Electronic Briefing Book No. 8: Chile and the United States Declassified Documents Relating to the Military Coup, Sept 11, 1973. (www.gwu.edu/~nsarchiv).

7 Broadcast on *Twenty Four Hours*, a radio programme on BBC World Service (Eastern Service), Sunday, 23 February 1986.

8 See James Hamilton Paterson, *America's Boy: The Marcoses and the Philippines*, London: Granta, 1998, pp. 389–90. Also James Fenton, 'The Snap Revolution', *Granta* 18, Spring 1986, pp. 33–169.

9 Bohumil Hrabal, *A Close Watch on the Trains*, London: Cape, 1968, pp. 11–12.

10 Uwe Johnson, *Two Views* (1965), Harmondsworth: Penguin, 1971, p. 102.

11 See Timothy Garton Ash, *The File: A Personal History*, London: HarperCollins, 1997, pp. 66–7.

12 The photograph floats alongside other icons of anti-spectacular struggle in Len Bracken's, *Guy Debord: Revolutionary*, Venice, California: Feral House, 1997, p. 223.

13 Giorgio Agamben, 'Tiananmen' in *The Coming Community*, Minneapolis: University of Minnesota Press, 1993, pp. 85–7.

14 Wu Hung, 'Tiananmen Square: A Political History of Monuments', *Representations* 35, Summer 1991, p. 85.

15 Frances Fitzgerald, *Fire in the Lake: The Vietnamese and the Americans in Vietnam*, New York: Vintage, 1972, p. 26.

16 Martyn Harris, 'A Chinese puzzle personified', *Sunday Telegraph*, 3 June 1990, p. xxii.

17 Robbie Barnett, 'Symbols and Protest: The Iconography of Demonstrations in Tibet 1987–90' in R. Barnett (ed.), *Resistance and Reform in Tibet*, London: Hurst, 1994. This observation, which does not appear in the final version as printed, is quoted from a draft sent to the author by Barnett and dated March 1990.

18 Robert Barnett, 'Symbols and Protest . . . ', p. 240.

19 The documentary *Waco: The Rules of Engagement* was directed by William Gazecki and released by Somford Entertainment in 1997. See also www. waco93.com.

20 Senate Vol. 143, Washington, 4 June 1997, No. 75.

21 John Leicester, 'British object to immediate deployment of army', *Houston Chronicle Interactive*, 27 June 1997.

22 Simon Winchester, 'You will learn to love China', *Sunday Times*, 29 June 1997.

23 Pico Iyer, 'The Unknown Rebel', *Time Asia*, 13 April 1998, vol. 151, no. 14.

24 *Guardian*, 26 June 1998, p. 20.

25 See Benedict Anderson, 'James Fenton's Slideshow', *New Left Review*, no. 158, July/August 1986, pp. 81–90.

26 Rajesh Ramachandran, 'A Tank with No Teeth', *The Week*, 12 October 1997.

27 Tony Heath, 'Is this what he died for?', *Guardian*, 6 December 1996.

28 'Memorial ads anger veterans', *Guardian*, 9 September 1997.

29 'Bush says Rival Can't Fool Voters on Defence . . .' *Washington Post*, 17 September 1988.

30 For a transcript see 'The first Bush Dukakis Debate: September 25, 1988', http://www.netcapitol.com/Debates/88 1st.htm

31 David Hoffman, 'Bush Pushes "Peace through Strength"', *Washington Post*, 19 October 1988.

CHAPTER 2. A Monster is Evolved

1 'A petition to the House of Commons from John George and Son of Saint Blazey in the County of Cornwall', 20 March 1838, National Army Museum, 7202–12.

2 Major Clough Williams-Ellis, MC, and A. Williams-Ellis, *The Tank Corps*, London: Country Life, 1919, p. 6.

3 Winston S. Churchill, *The World Crisis 1915*, London: Thornton Butterworth, 1923, p. 74.

4 Brevet Colonel J. F. C. Fuller, *Tanks in the Great War*, London: John Murray, 1920, p. 15.

5 'Tanks and the Royal Commission on Awards to Inventors', *Tank Corps Journal*, Wool, vol. 1, no. 7, November 1919, pp. 198–9. Continued in *Tank Corps Journal*, vol. 1, no. 9, January 1920, pp. 252–4.

6 Fuller, *Tanks in the Great War*, p. 9.

7 See Major General Sir Ernest D. Swinton, KBE, CB, DSO, RE (Retired), *Eyewitness: Being Personal Reminiscences of Certain Phases of the Great War, Including the Genesis of the Tank*, London: Hodder and Stoughton, 1932, p. 102.

8 Fuller, *Tanks in the Great War*, p. 9.

9 Quoted in Brian Holden Reid, *J.F.C. Fuller: Military Thinker*, Basingstoke: Macmillan, 1987, p. 35.

10 Swinton, *Eyewitness*, p. 5.

11 Williams-Ellis, *The Tank Corps*, p. 6.

12 H. G. Wells, 'The Land Ironclads', *Strand Magazine*, December 1903, vol. 26, pp. 751–64. The story was reprinted with the added introduction in the *Strand Magazine*, November 1916, vol., 52, pp. 501–13. The story is here quoted from the *Tank Corps Journal*, vol. 1, no. 2, May 1919, pp. 44–8.

13 Swinton, *Eyewitness*, p. 140.

14 Sir Albert G. Stern, KBE, CMG, *Tanks 1914–1918: The Logbook of a Pioneer*, London: Hodder and Stoughton, 1919, p. 8.

15 See, for example, Ole-Luk-Oie, *The Great Tab Dope*, London: Blackwood and Son, 1915.

16 Swinton, *Eyewitness*, pp. 135–6.

17 Rear Admiral Sir Murray Sueter, *The Evolution of the Tank: A Record of Royal Naval Air Service Caterpillar Experiments*, London & Melbourne: Hutchinson & Co., Revised Edition, 1941, p. 61.

18 Swinton, *Eyewitness*, p. 10.

19 Ibid., p. 149.

20 Ibid., p. 162.

21 Williams Ellis, *The Tank Corps*, p. 10.

22 For a summary of this history see David Fletcher, *Landships: British Tanks in the First World War*, London: HMSO, 1984.

23 Swinton, *Eyewitness*, p. 174.

24 A. G. Stern, *Tanks 1914–1918*, p. 46.

25 Swinton, *Eyewitness*, p. 190.

26 Ibid., p. 194.

27 Ibid., p. 196.

28 Ibid., p. 221.

29 Basil L. Q. Henriques, *The Indiscretions of a Warden*, London: Methuen & Co., 1937, pp. 113–14.

30 See R. E. Beall, 'The Green Fields Beyond', Imperial War Museum, 82/22/1.

31 Swinton, *Eyewitness*, p. 242.

32 Williams-Ellis, *The Tank Corps*, p. 18.

33 Captain D. G. Browne, MC, *The Tank in Action*, Edinburgh and London: Blackwood, 1920, p. 25.

34 Anon., 'A Tank Officer Looks Back', in E. D. Swinton (ed.), *Twenty Years After, the Battlefields of 1914–1918: Then and Now,* London: Newnes, 1936–8, vol. 2, pp. 835.

35 Swinton, *Eyewitness*, p. 253.

36 'Tank Major' and Eric Wood, *Tank Tales*, London: Cassell and Co., 1919, p. 12.

37 Henriques, *Indiscretions of a Warden*, pp. 134–5.

38 Imperial War Museum film archive, IWM 116/01.

39 Henriques, *Indiscretions of a Warden*, p. 115.

40 See the passages from Solomon's diary printed in Olga Somech Phillips, *Solomon J. Solomon: A Memoir of Peace and War*, London: Herbert Joseph, 1933, p. 194.

41 See John S. Sargent's painting 'Camouflaged Tanks, Berles-au-Bois', Imperial War Museum, 1618.

42 O. S. Phillips, *Solomon J. Solomon*, p. 166.

43 Ibid., p. 167.

44 Ibid., p. 172.

45 Ibid., p. 171.

46 Ibid., p. 172.

47 Ibid., p. 174.

48 Swinton, *Eyewitness*, p. 264.

49 Ibid., p. 254.

50 Ibid., p. 248. There were actually many women among the loyal workers at William Foster and Co.

51 Ernest D. Swinton, *The Tanks*, reprinted from the *Strand Magazine* (where it appeared in September 1917) London: L.U. Gill and Son, *circa* 1917, p.4.

52 Swinton, *Eyewitness*, p. 227.

53 B. Henriques, *Indiscretions of a Warden*, p. 114.

54 Swinton, *Eyewitness*, pp. 272–3.

55 Ibid., pp. 256–7.

56 D. G. Browne, *The Tank in Action*, p. 29.

57 Brigadier General C. D. Baker-Carr CMG, DSO, *From Chauffeur to Brigadier*, London: Ernest Benn, p. 204.

58 Swinton, *Eyewitness*, p. 281.

59 Ibid., p. 277.

60 Donald A. Mackenzie, *From All the Fronts,* Glasgow & Bombay: Blackie & Son Ltd., 1917, p. 94.

61 Williams-Ellis, *The Tank Corps*, p. 25.

62 Henriques, *Indiscretions of a Warden*, p. 115.

CHAPTER 3. Big Joke

1 Paul Fussell, *The Great War and Modern Memory*, Oxford: Oxford University Press, 1975, p. 115.

2 Captain B. H. Liddell Hart, *The Tanks: The History of the Royal Tank Regiment and its*

Predecessors Heavy Branch-Machine Gun Corps, Tank Corps and Royal Tank Corps, Vol. I, 1914–45, London: Cassell, 1959, p. 70.

3 Ibid., p. 69. Writing shortly after the war, J. F. C. Fuller states that it was only thirty-two of the forty-nine tanks that reached their starting point (*Tanks in the Great War*, p. 56).

4 Quoted in B. H. Liddell Hart, *The Tanks*, vol. I, p. 74.

5 See David Fletcher, *Landships*. Also 'The Coming of the Tanks', in Philip Gibbs, *The Battles of the Somme*, London: Heinemann, 1917, pp. 253–66.

6 Lieut. Geoffrey H. Malins, OBE, *How I Filmed the War: A Record of the Extraordinary Experience of the Man who Filmed the Great Somme Battle etc.*, London: Jenkins, 1920, pp. 230–1.

7 Stephen Foot, *Three Lives: An Autobiography*, London: Heinemann, 1934, p. 153.

8 William Foster & Company, *The Tank: Its Birth and Development*, Lincoln, *circa* 1919, p. 42.

9 Williams-Ellis, *The Tank Corps*, p. 29.

10 John Buchan, *A History of the Great War* (4 vols), London, Edinburgh and New York: Thomas Nelson and Sons Ltd., 1922, vol. 3, p. 196.

11 D. G. Browne, *The Tank in Action*, pp. 34–5.

12 Captain J. T. Foxell, Imperial War Museum, 91/24/1.

13 Captain D. H. Pegler, 106 Brigade, RFA (24th Division), Imperial War Museum, 82/7/1.

14 The Revd Canon C. Lomax, Imperial War Memorial, 87/13/1.

15 Details about the withdrawal of Swinton as official 'Eyewitness' in the summer of 1915 are held in the Public Record Office (HO 139/22/95). The Press Association was sorry to see him go, stressing the inspiring qualities of his 'vivid stories of the great deeds of valour now being performed by our gallant troops in Flanders'. The new arrangement, organized by the Newspaper Proprietors Association, is described by correspondent Valentine Williams in his autobiography, *The World of Action*, London: Hamish Hamilton, 1938. For details of the correspondents on the Front in September 1916 see p. 298. Philip Gibbs supported the newspaper that declared Swinton an 'Eyewitness' who only wrote Eyewash (*Realities of War*, p. 7).

16 William Beach Thomas, *With the British on the Somme*, London: William Heinemann, 1917, p. 260.

17 Philip Gibbs, *Battles of the Somme*, London: William Heinemann, 1917, p. 260. Gibbs also reports a Cockney soldier, 'covered in blood' and with a broken arm, exclaiming, 'It was like a fairy tale! . . . I can't help laughing every time I think of it' (p. 261). Gibbs had been a reporter for the *Daily Chronicle* before the war; his novel *Intellectual Mansions S.W.* (London: Chapman & Hall, 1910) had given gratefully received support to the Women's Suffrage movement.

18 Philip Gibbs, *Realities of War*, London: William Heinemann, 1920, p. 321.

19 Wilhelm Reich, *Passion of Youth: An Autobiography, 1897–1922*, New York: Farrar, Strauss, Giroux, 1988, pp. 61 and 62.

20 Paul Fussell, *The Great War and Modern Memory*, pp. 36–74.

21 Quoted in L. Day, *The Life and Art of William Heath Robinson*, London: Herbert Joseph, 1947, p. 169. A reproduction of Heath Robinson's three-wheeler 'tank' is to be found in Barbara Jones and Bill Howell, *Popular Arts of the First World War*, London: Studio Vista, 1972, p. 69.

22 Quoted from A. G. Stern, *Tanks 1914–18*, p. 99. Stern doesn't name Dukes but Basil Henriques' collection of press cuttings, now at the Tank Museum in Bovington, includes a clipping which does so.

23 P. Gibbs, *Realities of War*, p. 6.

24 Brigadier General C. D. Baker-Carr, CMG, DSO, *From Chauffeur to Brigadier*, London: Ernest Benn, 1930, p. 198.

25 Williams-Ellis, *The Tank Corps*, p. 30.

26 The *Weekly Dispatch* for 24 September 1916 printed tank cartoons by a variety of cartoonists, including Bateman, Hassal and Fred Buchanan.

27 This postcard is reproduced alongside Heath Robinson's tank in Barbara Jones and Bill Howell, *Popular Arts of the First World War*, London: Studio Vista, 1972, p. 69.

28 *Illustrated London News*, 21 October 1916, pp. 474–5.

29 *Illustrated London News*, 25 November 1916, p. 628. See also *ILN*, 2 December 1916, pp. 666–7.

30 Quoted from Helen Bettinson's television documentary *Tanks: The Wonder Weapon of World War One*, BBC2 Timewatch, 12 November 1995.

31 W. Beach Thomas, *With the British on the Somme*, pp. 220–1.

32 Ibid., p. 219.

33 P. Gibbs, 'The Coming of the Tank', in *The Battles of the Somme*, pp. 255–6.

34 Philip Gibbs, *Open Warfare: The Way to Victory*, London: William Heinemann, 1919, p. 99.

35 Christine Kühlenthal, letter to John Nash, quoted in Ronald Blythe, *First Friends*, London: Viking, 1999, p. 126.

36 P. Gibbs, *Realities of War*, p. 6.

37 P. Gibbs, 'Northward from Thiépval', in *The Battles of the Somme*, p. 322.

38 C. D. Baker-Carr, *From Chauffeur to Brigadier*, p. 193.

39 See the testimony of G. E. V. Thompson, Imperial War Museum, 75/36/1.

40 R. E. Beall, 'The Green Fields Beyond', Imperial War Museum, 82/22/1.

41 The phrase 'pocket hell' is quoted from a poem by C.E.B., printed in the programme of Harry Tate's Matinée for the Tank Corps Prisoner of War Fund, London Hippodrome, Thursday, 7 November 1918. A copy is saved in Brigadier General Hugh Elles's scrap-book in the Tank Museum Library, Bovington, Dorset.

42 Major R. F. G. Maurice, *Tank Corps Book of Honour*, London: Spottiswoode, Ballantyne and Co., 1919.

43 G. E. V. Thompson, Imperial War Museum, 75/36/1.

44 B. Henriques, *The Indiscretions of a Warden*, p. 120.

45 D. G. Browne, *The Tank in Action*, p. 36.

46 Fred Curran's 'The Tanks that Broke the Ranks' was advertised by the Star Music Company as available at an unusually high cost to pantomimes playing theatres rather than music halls (the latter were ordered to stop featuring the song forthwith). Advertisements appeared in *The Era*, (25 October and 1 November 1916) and *The Stage* (16 and 23 November 1916). The words here are quoted from the perhaps different version performed by Peter Dawson in 1916, which survives in the BBC archives and was used in Helen Bettinson's Timewatch film *Tanks: The Wonder Weapon of World War One*, BBC2, 12 November 1995.

47 *Vanity Fair* was staged by Alfred Butts at the Gaiety Theatre from 6 November 1916. Lyrics were by Arthur Wimperis and Percy Greenbank and the music by Herman Finck. On 9 November 1916, *The Stage* described the sequence involving Herman Darewski's song 'The Tanko' as an 'illustration of the Somme "tanks"'. See also the *Play Pictorial* , vol. XXX, no. 178, 1917, p. 16. The picture, also printed in the *Sketch*, 29 November 1916, was captioned: 'At last released for publication by the Censor! H.M.L.S. Tanko'. Kurt Ganzl describes Regine Flory as 'a febrile and highly sexual performer, something of a "special taste" with that part of the public which championed her'. She eventually shot herself in the office of the impresario Alfred Butts at the Threatre Royal in Drury Lane. Kurt Ganzl, *The Encyclopedia of the Musical Theatre*, Oxford: Blackwell, 1994.

48 Quoted in P. Fussell, *The Great War in Modern Memory*, p. 89.

49 P. Gibbs, *The Battles of the Somme*, p. 19.

50 D. G. Browne, *The Tank in Action*, p. 42.

51 Ibid., p. 501.

52 Williams-Ellis, *The Tank Corps*, p. 48.

53 Swinton, *Eyewitness*, p. 9.

54 'Tank Major' and Eric Wood, *Tank Tales*, London: Cassell & Co., 1919, p. 2.

55 W. Beach Thomas, *With the British on the Somme*, p. 225.

56 P. Gibbs, *The Battles of the Somme*, p. 322.

57 P. Gibbs, *Open Warfare: The Way to Victory*, p. 102.

CHAPTER 4. Breaking the Line (the War Artist's Dilemma)

1 D. G. Browne, *The Tank in Action*, p. 250.

2 Williams-Ellis, *The Tank Corps*, p. 41.

3 'Tanks in Action' in Donald A. Mackenzie, *From All Fronts*, pp. 94–102.

4 Captain F. S. Brereton, *The Armoured-car Scouts: A Tale of the Campaign in the Caucasus*, London, Glasgow and Bombay: Blackie & Son, 1918, pp. 351–69.

5 J. F. C. Fuller, *Tanks in the Great War*, quoted in D. G. Browne, *The Tank in Action*, p. 507.

6 First published in 1916, *Sea Garden* was reprinted in H.D., *Collected Poems*, New York: Boni and Liveright, 1925. The early poems mentioned here are 'Storm' and 'Oread', the latter being collected in H. D., *Heliodora and other poems*, London: Cape, 1924, p. 31.

7 Quoted in Stephen Kern, *The Culture of Time and Space 1880–1918*, Cambridge (Massachussetts): Harvard University Press, pp. 287–8 and 302.

8 'The Cubist War' in S. Kern, pp. 287–312.

9 Solomon J. Solomon, *The Practice of Painting*, London: Seeley & Co., 1910, p. 267.

10 Olga Somech Phillips, *Solomon J. Solomon: A Memoir of Peace and War*, London: Herbert Joseph, 1933, p. 175.

11 Solomon J. Solomon, *Strategic Camouflage*, London: John Murray, 1920, p. 1.

12 Ibid., p. 52.

13 O. S. Phillips, *Solomon J. Solomon*, p. 181.

14 S. J. Solomon, *Strategic Camouflage*, p. 16.

15 Ibid., p. 28.

16 Filippo Tommaso Marinetti, 'The Futurist Manifesto' quoted from Adriam Lyttelton (ed.), *Italian Fascisms: From Pareto to Gentile*, New York: Harper Torchbooks, 1975, pp. 209–15.

17 'Inferior Religions', in Wyndham Lewis, *The Wild Body: A Soldier of Humour and Other Stories*, London: Chatto & Windus, 1927, p. 238.

18 Wyndham Lewis, 'One Way Song' (1933) in Alan Munton (ed.), *Wyndham Lewis: Collected Poems and Plays*, Manchester: Carcanet, 1979, p. 22.

19 Swinton, *Eyewitness*, p. 196.

20 The 'Futurist' ode appeared alongside 'Classic' and 'Swinburnian' variants. See *Tank Corps Journal*, no. 13, May 1920, p. 7.

21 P. Westerman, *To the Fore with the Tanks!*, p. 103.

22 Quoted by A. G. Stern, *Tanks 1914–1918*, pp. 100–1. Stern remarks that Wells's description fell victim to censorship, but it was printed as part of Wells' 'Land Ironclads and their function in War and a Permanent Peace', in the *Daily Chronicle*, 18 December 1916.

23 P. G. Konody, 'Mr Nevinson's new pictures', *Observer*, 1 October 1916. Quoted from Nevinson's own press cuttings collection in the Archive of Modern British Art at Tate Britain. See also *C.R.W. Nevinson, Retrospective Exhibition of Paintings, Drawings and Prints 1889–1946*, Cambridge: Kettle's Yard Gallery, 1988.

24 *Evening Standard*, 7 June 1916.

25 *Daily Telegraph*, 13 June 1916.

26 *Daily Chronicle*, 30 September 1916.

27 William Loftus Hare, 'Art and the Tank: A Review of C. R. W. Nevinson's Pictures', in *The Ploughshare: A Quaker Organ of Social Reconstruction*, vol. 1, no. 11, December 1916, pp. 352–3. The earlier correspondent's remarks on Nevinson's exhibition appeared in *The Ploughshare*, vol. 1, no. 10, November 1916, p. 324.

28 *Times Literary Supplement,* 18 January 1917. This article is a review of the following item.

29 *The Western Front: Drawings by Muirhead Bone, with Commentary by C.E. Montague,* London: Country Life, 1917, vol. 1. Quoted from Montague's description of Plate XLII.

30 John Cournos, 'The War in the New English Art', *Welsh Outlook,* May 1917.

31 Eric Kennington, *Tanks and Tank Folk,* London: Country Life, 1942, p. 11.

32 Ibid., p. 8.

33 Entitled 'A Tank', the picture is now in the Imperial War Museum. See also Samuel Hynes, *A War Imagined: the First World War and English Culture,* London: Bodley Head, 1990, opposite p. 178.

CHAPTER 5. Raising the Heavy Branch at Bermicourt

1 Anon (Capt. the Hon. Evan Charteris), *H.Q. Tanks,* privately printed, 1920, p. 1.

2 Major General J. F. C. Fuller CB, CBE, DSO, *Memoirs of an Unconventional Soldier,* London: Nicholson and Watson, 1936, pp. 192–3.

3 A cutting of this photograph is held among the Sir Leslie Shane papers, held at Lavinger Library Special Collections, Georgetown University, Washington (Box 79; Folder 24).

4 Captain D. E. Hickey, *Rolling into Action: Memoirs of a Tank Corps Section Commander,* London: Hutchinson, 1936, p. 41.

5 D. G. Browne, *The Tank in Action,* p. 51.

6 Charteris, *H.Q. Tanks,* p. 24.

7 'At the end of three months I was the Timber King, carrying on trade far beyond the borders of my own Kingdom'. Stephen Foot, *Three Lives – And Now,* London: Heinemann, 1937, p. 162.

8 D. G. Browne, *The Tank in Action,* p. 52.

9 Charteris, *H.Q. Tanks,* p. 33.

10 J. F. C. Fuller, *Memoirs of an Unconventional Soldier,* p. 87.

11 Charteris, *H.Q. Tanks,* p. 15.

12 J. F. C. Fuller, *Memoirs of an Unconventional Soldier,* p. 88.

13 C. D. Baker-Carr, *From Chauffeur to Brigadier,* p. 205.

14 J. F. C. Fuller, *Tanks in the Great War,* 1920, p. xiv.

15 Ibid., p. xiii.

16 E. Charteris, *H.Q. Tanks,* p. 7.

17 Ibid., p. 6.

18 Ibid., p. 87.

19 Major General F. E. Hotblack DSO, MC, quoted from his war memoir in the Imperial War Museum, 76/136/1.T.

20 E. Charteris, *H.Q. Tanks,* p. 87.

21 J. F. C. Fuller, *Memoirs of an Unconventional Soldier,* p. 47.

22 Ibid., p. 67.

23 Ibid., pp. 74 and 76.

24 Ibid., p. 78.

25 Ibid., p. 79.

26 Ibid., pp. 83–4.

27 J. F. C. Fuller, *Tanks in the Great War,* p. xv. Also *Memoirs of an Unconventional Soldier,* p. 193.

28 E. Charteris, *H.Q. Tanks,* p. 33.

29 Quoted from a letter to Major N. W. Dundas, written by Frank MacDonald, from the Dublin Registry of Deeds, on January 20, 1920, and kept with Dundas's copy of *H.Q. Tanks* at the Tank Museum Library, Bovington, Dorset.

30 S. Foot, *Three Lives,* p. 169.

31 E. Charteris, *H.Q. Tanks,* p. 27. Widely held in the Tank Corps, this view of the staff at GHQ as fossilized public school boys, who couldn't see the future in tanks, or bear their dirtiness, was shared by C. E. Montague, a journalist with the *Manchester Guardian* who volunteered for the

trenches and also served as an officer escort for war correspondents. He described the Generals at GHQ as 'poor custom-ridden souls', whose instinct was to veto 'an engine of war so far from "smart" as the tank'. See his *Disenchantment*, London: Chatto & Windus, 1922, p. 159.

32 C. D. Baker-Carr, *From Chauffeur to Brigadier*, p. 204.

33 E. Charteris, *H.Q. Tanks*, p. 38.

34 Telephone conversation with Colonel Mark Dillon (who joined the Heavy Branch as a Reconnaissance Officer at Christmas 1916), 12/9/95.

35 S. Foot, *Three Lives*, p. 203.

36 E. Charteris, *H.Q. Tanks*, p. 4.

37 J. F. C. Fuller, *Memoirs of an Unconventional Soldier*, p. 87.

38 Major General F. E. Hotblack, 'Notes of Appreciation of Hugh Elles', Tank Museum Library, Bovington, BTM 069.02 (41).

39 J. F. C. Fuller, *Memoirs of an Unconventional Soldier*, p. 89.

40 The phrase is quoted from a Sergeant Littledale. See C. and A. Williams-Ellis, *The Tank Corps*, p. 40.

41 Ibid., pp. 89–90.

42 C. D. Baker-Carr, *From Chauffeur to Brigadier*, pp. 206–7.

43 E. Charteris, *H.Q. Tanks*, p. 37.

44 Hugh Elles, 'Introduction', to C. and A. Williams-Ellis, *The Tank Corps*, pp. ix–x.

45 C. D. Baker-Carr, *From Chauffeur to Brigadier*, p. 240.

46 J. F. C. Fuller, *Memoirs of an Unconventional Soldier*, p. 95.

47 Ibid., p. 91.

48 Ibid., p. 92. The naming of tanks was soon regulated, and not just by the rule that names had to begin with the letter of the Battalion to which they belonged (although this prompted one section commander to name his two male tanks Grouse and Grumble and the female consorts, Giggle and Gossip). See 'A Tank Corps Officer Looks Back', in Ernest D. Swinton (ed.), *Twenty Years After, the Battlefields of 1914–18*, London: Newnes, vol. 2, p. 840.

49 J. F. C. Fuller, *Memoirs of an Unconventional Soldier*, p. 96.

50 B. H. Liddell Hart, *The Tanks, Vol. I 1914–39*, pp. 93–4.

51 J. F. C. Fuller, *Memoirs of an Unconventional Soldier*, p. 110.

52 C.D. Baker-Carr, *From Chauffeur to Brigadier*, p. 212.

53 Liddell Hart, *The Tanks, Vol. I 1914–1918*, pp. 95–6.

54 Ibid., pp. 101–3.

55 J. F. C. Fuller, *Memoirs of an Unconventional Soldier*, p. 113.

56 Ibid., p. 119.

57 C. D. Baker-Carr, *From Chauffeur to Brigadier*, p. 227.

58 Major General J. F. C. Fuller, CB, CBE, DSO, 'Introduction' to Leon Wolff, *In Flanders Fields: The 1917 Campaign*, London: Longmans, 1959, p. xvi.

59 D. G. Browne, *The Tank in Action*, p. 103.

60 R. E. Beall, 'The Green Fields Beyond', Imperial War Museum, 82/22/1. By the time Beall was thinking of him, Robert Blatchford, the popular socialist prophet of 'Merrie England', had become a fervent supporter of the war against Germany. See his *General Von Sneak: A Little Study of the War*, London: Hodder and Stoughton, 1918.

61 D. G. Browne, *The Tank in Action*, p. 193.

62 J. F. C. Fuller, *Tanks in the Great War*, p. 124.

63 C. D. Baker-Carr, *From Chauffeur to Brigadier*, p. 254.

64 Ibid., p. 228.

65 D. G. Browne, *The Tank in Action*, p. 234.

66 Ibid., p. 255.

67 Quoted from R. E. Beall's memoir, 'The Green Fields Beyond', Imperial War Museum, 82/22/1.

68 D. G. Browne, *The Tank in Action*, p. 185.

69 C. D. Baker-Carr, *From Chauffeur to Brigadier*, p. 255.

70 D. G. Browne, *The Tank in Action*, p. 249.

71 J. F. C . Fuller, *Memoirs of an Unconventional Soldier*, pp. 170–1.

72 Brigadier General H. Elles, 'Introduction' in Williams-Ellis, *The Tank Corps*, p. v.

73 See J. P. Harris, *Men, Ideas and Tanks*, Manchester: Manchester University Press, 1995, pp. 108–13.

74 Capt. Geoffrey Dugdale, MC, '*Langemarck*' and ' *Cambrai*': A War Narrative 1914–1918, Shrewsbury, 1932, p. 102.

75 Williams Ellis, *The Tank Corps*, p. 109.

76 D. G. Browne, *The Tank in Action*, p. 276.

77 D. E. Hickey, *Rolling into Action*, p. 104.

78 D. G. Browne, *The Tank in Action*, p. 278.

79 J. F. C. Fuller, *Tanks in the Great War*, p. 153.

80 *The Tatler*, 5 December, 1917.

81 Quoted from Major General F.E. Hotblack's 'Notes of Appreciation of Hugh Elles', Tank Museum Library, Bovington, BTM 069.02(41).

82 D. G. Browne, *The Tank in Action*, p. 271.

83 C. & A. Williams-Ellis, *The Tank Corps*, p. 108.

84 This excerpt from the *Balkan News* is among the Fuller papers at the Liddell Hart Centre for Military Archives, King's College. London, 1/2/82.

85 D. G. Browne, *The Tank in Action*, p. 278.

86 Ibid., p. 278.

87 C. D. Baker-Carr, *From Chauffeur to Brigadier*, pp. 271–2.

88 Major General F. E. Hotblack DSO, MC, recollections in Imperial War Museum, 76/136/1.

CHAPTER 6. Banking on the Tank

1 *Wolverhampton Chronicle*, 6 February 1918.

2 Quoted in Rear Admiral Sir Murray Sueter, *The Evolution of the Tank: A Record of Royal Naval Air Service Caterpillar Experiments*, London & Melbourne: Hutchinson, 1941, p. 182.

3 George A. Sutton, 'How Britain raised £6,000,000,000 for the War', in H. W. Wilson and J. A. Hammerton (eds.), *The Great War: The Standard History of the World-wide Conflict*, London: Amalgamated Press, n.d., volume XI, p. 268.

4 George A. Sutton's special responsibility for 'selling campaigns' is stated in a memorandum entitled 'The National War Savings Committee' in Public Record Office, *National Savings Committee: Origin, History, Development 1917–19*, NSC 7 2.

5 Bonar Law's comment is made in a letter dated 11 January and issued to the National War Savings Committee, presumably for publicity purposes. See Public Record Office, NSC7 38. Sutton's reiteration of the point is quoted from his 'How Britain raised £6,000,000,000 for the War', p. 268.

6 *War Savings*, September 1916.

7 See 'Report of War Savings Work undertaken by Women's Auxiliary Committee for War Savings, 20 February 1918', in *National Savings Committee: Origin, History, Development 1917–19*, Public Record Office, NSC 7 2 .

8 G. A. Sutton, 'How Britain raised £6,000,000,000 for the War', p. 276.

9 H. Holford Bottomley, CBE, 'How Tanks Sold War Bonds', *Tank Corps Journal*, May 1919, no. 2, p. 53. Before the war Bottomley had published a couple of text books on business technique: *The Clark's College System of Typewriting* (London, 1910) and *Successful Salesmanship for All Engaged in Business* (London, Clarks College Book Department, London 1908).

10 A report on the London tank bank and its organization is to be found in 'National Savings Committee: Report on Special Activities during October, November, December 1917'. See *National Savings Committee: Origin, History, Development 1917–19*, Public Record Office, NSC 7 2.

11 *The Times*, 28 November 1917.

12 As Barbara Jones and Bill Howells have written of these souvenirs, 'The basic steel lozenge of the British tank was translated into a remarkable variety of forms. Angular or rounded, dumpy or elongated, hump-backed, tall or short, they were made both plain and fancy. They were churned out by do-it-yourselfers and by industry in brass, copper, lead, aluminium, silver-plate, tin-plate, wood and china, and even in bone in the manner of French prisoner of war work in the Napoleonic wars.' See Barbara Jones and Bill Howells, *Popular Arts of the First World War*, London: Studio Vista, 1972, p. 67.

13 *The Times*, 6 December 1917, p. 4.

14 *The Times*, 4 December 1917, p. 3.

15 Imperial War Museum Film Archive, IWM 193.

16 *The Times*, 4 December 1917.

17 *The Times*, 20 November 1918.

18 *The Times*, 30 November 1917.

19 *The Times*, 4 December 1917, p. 3.

20 *Evening News* (Portsmouth), 18 December 1917.

21 H. Holford Bottomley, 'How Tanks Sold War Bonds', p. 53.

22 *Glasgow Herald*, 18 January 1918, p. 3.

23 'The Tank Campaigns: Notes and Suggestions', Public Record Office NSC 7 38.

24 The Newcastle Tank organizer's report is in National Savings Committee, 'Report on Special Activities during October, November, December 1917', Public Record Office, NSC 7 2.

25 'Report on Special Activities during October, November, December, 1917', *National Savings Committee: Origin, History, Development 1917–19*, Public Record Office, NSC. 7 2.

26 H. Holford Bottomley, 'How Tanks Sold War Bond's, p. 53.

27 *Wolverhampton Chronicle*, 6 February 1918.

28 *Wolverhampton Chronicle*, 12 February 1918.

29 Once again, the military authorities tried to place a limit on the symbolic exuberance of the tank. Some way through the Tank Bank campaign, a 'military decree' forebade moving demonstrations, and also put an end to the procession from the goods yard to the barricaded enclosure. The war-damaged conditions of the tanks was cited as the reason for these adjustments.

30 George Bernard Shaw, letter to Ellen Terry, 7 January 1918. Quoted in Stanley Weintraub, *Journey to Heartbreak: Tthe Crucible Years of Bernard Shaw 1914–1918*, New York: Weybright and Talley, 1971, p. 259.

31 John Gould Fletcher, 'New God', the *Egoist: An Individualist Review*, 5. 3 (March 1918), pp. 45–6. I owe this reference to Trudi Tate, *Modernism, History and the First World War*, Manchester: Manchester University Press, 1998, p. 121.

32 *The Times*, 29 November 1917.

33 *The Times*, 30 November 1917.

34 *War Savings*, vol. II, no. 5, January 1918, p. 53.

35 *Glamorgan Free Press*, 23 May 1918.

36 *The Times*, 1 December 1917.

37 *The Times*, 3 December 1917.

38 *Glamorgan Free Press*, 23 May 1918.

39 *Caerphilly Journal*, 6 June 1918.

40 *Evening News* (Portsmouth), 18 December 1917.

41 This is the figure provided by H. Holford Bottomley in 'How Tanks Sold War Bonds', p. 53.

42 *South Wales Evening Press*, 1 June 1918.

43 H. Holford Bottomley, 'How Tanks Sold War Bonds', p. 53.

44 Mrs C. R. Buxton (editor), 'The Mechanism of Publicity', *Cambridge Magazine*, 6 April 1918.

45 *Cambridge Magazine*, 1 December, 1917, p. 179.

46 *War Savings*, vol. II, no. 7, March–April 1918.

47 *War Savings*, vol. II, no. 4, December 1917.

48 See the leading article in *The Times*, 21 January 1918.

49 Reported in *War Savings*, vol. II, no. 3, November 1917.

50 *The Times*, 8 December 1917.

51 *War Savings*, vol. II, no. 5, January 1918.

52 *The Times*, 15 February 1918.

53 *Great Thoughts of Horatio Bottomley*, London: Holden and Hardinghem, 1917. Bottomley had his own answer to Britain's heavy losses. The country needed another 'Cromwell in Parliament' who would 'call up 5,000,000 coloured men from the Empire, and not drain Britain of her wealth producing mechanics' (p. 38). See also Julian Symons, *Horatio Bottomley*, London: Cresset Press, 1955. For a condemnation of Bottomley's oratorical style by an advocate of 'clear thinking', see A. Clutter Brock, 'Demagogue's Art', in *The Times*, 11 July 1922, p. 13.

54 *John Bull*, 8 December 1917, p. 1.

55 'Tank Tosh', *John Bull*, 16 March 1918, p. 1. The same issue includes a cartoon of a 'War Bond Tank' collecting 'unclaimed millions' from a horrified banker.

56 'Tank Tosh', *John Bull*, 23 March 1918.

57 A year previously, on 14 November 1916, Lansdowne had circulated a paper to the cabinet arguing that the war was destroying civilization, and that a peace should be negotiated on the basis of returning to the status quo as it had been before the war. Vigorously contested, the proposal was instrumental in advancing Lloyd George towards the premiership, since he could promise victory through his relations with labour, which enabled him to secure a steady supply of munitions. See A. J. P. Taylor, *English History 1914–45*, Oxford: Oxford University Press, 1965, pp. 65–6. In cartoons of 1916/17, Lloyd George was often presented as a tank riding over the 'Pacifist Palisade'.

58 See J. F. C. Fuller's ' Introduction', to Leon Wolff, *In Flanders Fields*, London: Longmans, 1959, p. xii.

59 *The Times*, 6 December 1917.

60 *Glasgow Herald*, 11 January 1918, p. 8.

61 *Cardiff Times and South Wales Weekly News*, June 15 1918, p. 3.

62 Quoted from 'The Tanks Afield', in *The Silver Bullet: The Official Bulletin of the National War Savings Committee*, 5 June 1918.

63 *Caerphilly Journal*, 13 June 1918.

64 For a picture of Sergeant Collins see 'Citizens of Merthyr acclaim their V.C.', *Cardiff Times & South Wales Weekly News*, 8 June 1918.

65 *Exchange Telegraph*, 16 September 1918, quoted in Sueter, *Evolution of the Tank*, p. 207.

66 A. J. P. Taylor suggests that just such a combination of militancy and patriotism was to be found in South Wales and Clydeside: in both areas a pacifist and allegedly 'Bolshevik' radicalism coexisted with the highest levels of volunteer recruitment in the country. See A. J. P. Taylor, *English History 1914–1945*, p. 39.

CHAPTER 7. Moral Victory

1 J. F. C. Fuller, *Memoirs of an Unconventional Soldier*, p. 162.

2 C. D. Baker-Carr, *From Chauffeur to Brigadier*, pp. 209–10. It was on the afternoon of 1

February 1917 that Shaw drove to inspect tanks in 'an immense closed Rolls Royce', having lunched with General Sir Douglas Haig who had 'made me feel that the war would last thirty years, and that he would carry it on irreproachably until he was superannuated'. After riding in a new tank, Shaw noted that 'the terrible clatter' suggested 'a speed far higher than the turgid crawling they were actually doing'. They also examined a new type of incendiary shell and a malfunctioning flame-thrower. Shaw judged Haig to be 'disconcerted and distressed' by new weapons like tanks. See Stanley Weintraub, *Journey to Heartbreak: The Crucible Years of Bernard Shaw, 1914–18*, New York: Weybright and Talley, 1971, p. 221.

3 E. Charteris, *H.Q. Tanks*, p. 25.

4 John Singer Sargent, letter to Evan Charteris (24 July 1918) in the Hon. Evan Charteris, KC, *John Sargent*, London: Heinemann, 1927, p. 212.

5 E. Charteris, *H.Q. Tanks*, p. 26.

6 B. H. Liddell-Hart, *The Tanks*, vol. 1, pp. 108–9.

7 E. Charteris, *H.Q. Tanks*, p. 25.

8 The remark is recorded in 'The Private Journal of Lt. Colonel J. F. C. Fuller Relative to the Expansion and Employment of the Tank Corps, December 1917 to July 26 1918', held at the Liddell Hart Centre for Military Archives at King's College, London. Charteris also refers to the incident in *H.Q. Tanks*, pp. 26–7.

9 Quoted in A. G. Stern, *Tanks 1914–1918*, pp. 100–3.

10 Ibid., p. 38.

11 Ibid., p. 69.

12 Escott Lynn, *Tommy of the Tanks*, London: W. and R. Chambers Ltd, 1919.

13 P. Westerman, *To the Fore with the Tanks!*, p. 88.

14 Major W. H. L. Watson, *A Company of Tanks*, Edinburgh, 1920, p. 11.

15 Richard Haigh, *Life in a Tank*, Boston and New York: Houghton Mifflin, 1918, pp. 1–2.

16 Ibid., p. 5.

17 Samuel Hynes, *The Soldier's Tale: Bearing Witness to Modern War*, London: Pimlico, 1998.

18 P. Fussell, *The Great War in Modern Memory*, Oxford: Oxford University Press, p. 89.

19 The remark is quoted from Buchan's review of C. and A. Williams-Ellis's *The Tank Corps*. See *Tank Corps Journal*, January 1920, p. 251.

20 John Buchan (ed.), *The Long Road to Victory*, John Buchan's Annual, London: Thomas Nelson and Sons, 1920.

21 Major F. E. Hotblack, DSO, MC, 'The Call: the tale of a tank', in J. Buchan (ed.), *The Long Road to Victory*, p. 160.

22 C. E. Montague, *Disenchantment*, London: Chatto & Windus, 1922, p. 98.

23 Brigadier General Mathew-Lannowe, Commander of the Tank Corps Training Centre, writes of 'esprit de tank' in his introductory notice to the first issue of the *Tank Corps Journal* (vol. 1, April 1919, p. 5).

24 See J. P. Gallagher, *Fred Karno: Master of Mirth and Tears*, London: Robert Hale, 1971, p. 123.

25 'A Tank Corps officer looks back', E. D. Swinton (ed.), *Twenty Years After*, p. 837.

26 Williams-Ellis, *The Tank Corps*, pp. 110–11.

27 'A Tank Corps officer looks back', p. 837.

28 'The Return of Samuel Pepys', the *Whippet*, vol. 1, no. 1, December 1918.

29 F. S. Brereton, *The Armoured-car Scouts*, pp. 11 and 105.

30 Swinton, *Eyewitness*, p. 149.

31 D. G. Browne, *The Tank in Action*, p. 34.

32 Williams-Ellis, *The Tank Corps*, p. 281.

33 Swinton, *Eyewitness*, p. 131.

34 Swinton reprints 'Tank Tips', in *Eyewitness*, pp. 272–4.

35 Williams-Ellis, *The Tank Corps*, pp. 106 and 65.

36 A. G. Stern, *Tanks 1914–1918*, p. 128.
37 Swinton, *Eyewitness*, p. 307.
38 R. H. Lutz (Selector), *The Cause of the German Collapse in 1918* (Sections of the official report of the Commission of the German Constituent Assembly of the German Reichstag, 1919–1928), Stanford University Press, 1934, pp. 68–72.
39 *Weekly Tank Notes*, 31 August 1918.
40 *Weekly Tank Notes*, 24 August 1918.
41 Arnold Zweig, *The Case of Sergeant Grischa* (1927), London: Secker, 1930, p. 177.

CHAPTER 8. Bringing it All Back Home

1 See, for example, Jay Winter, *Sites of Memory, Sites of Mourning: The Great War in European Cultural History*, Cambridge University Press, 1995. See also Adrian Gregory, *The Silence of Memory: Armistice Day 1919–1946*, Oxford: Berg, 1994.
2 This account of Swaffham Prior's war memorial windows is assembled with the help of press cuttings and copies of the *Swaffham Prior and Reach Parish Magazine,* currently in the possession of Mrs E. J. Preston at Burwell; and also of C. P. Allix's papers and scrapbook, held at the County Records Office, Shire Hall, Cambridge.
3 In this view, the Britishness of the tank stemmed from the fact that it was 'the weapon for men who, if they must fight like to fight like intelligent beings, still subjecting the material world to their will, and who are most unwillingly reduced to the roles of mere marching automata, bearers of burdens and diggers of the soil; roles for which the patient German did not seem averse. . .' Major Clough Williams-Ellis and A. Williams-Ellis, *The Tank Corps*, London: Country Life, 1919, pp. 281–2. For Williams-Ellis's defence of the landscape see, *England and the Octopus*, London, Geoffrey Bles, 1928.
4 Basil L. Q. Henriques, *The Indiscretions of a Warden*, London: Methuen, 1937. Henriques discusses the continuing temptation of the street to boys who, for want of an alternative, have grown up in this dangerous zone in his later book, *Club Leadership* (London, 1949).
5 For Wilfred Bion's account of his years in the Tank Corps, see his *The Long Week-End 1897–1919*, Abingdon: Fleetwood Press, 1982. For his psychoanalytic use of the idea of the container and the contained, see Gérard Bléandonu, *Wilfred Bion: His Life and Works, 1897–1979*, London: Free Association Books, 1994.
6 This may have been the same 'ghastly incident' described by D. G. Browne, whose tank crew were on guard duty when a battalion of Northumberland Fusiliers encamped in Oosthoek Wood, showed lights at 3 a.m. and suffered over 100 dead or wounded in the subsequent bombing. See D. G. Browne, *The Tank in Action*, Edinburgh & London: Blackwood, 1930, p. 135.
7 See 'The Tanks Come Home' and 'War Tanks for Towns', in the *Silver Bullet: The Official Bulletin of the National War Savings Committee*, 16 April 1919.
8 *Silver Bullet*, 16 April 1919, p. 85.
9 The National War Savings Committee's 'Memorandum of Suggestions for the Reception of a Presentation Tank' and also the modifying letter of 22 December 1919 are held at the Public Record Office, NSC 7/38.
10 See 'General Swinton on his Tanks', *Silver Bullet*, 3 September 1919.
11 *Tank Corps Journal*, Sept/Oct 1919, reprinted from the *Observer*, 31 August 1919.
12 Quoted from the aims of the National War Savings Committee as spelt out in the first issue of the *Silver Bullet*, 15 May 1918.
13 *Glasgow Herald*, 14 January 1919.
14 A photograph of a 'captured' British tank being used by the German Army against the revolution in Berlin is printed in Capt. D. G. Browne, *The Tank in Action*, Edinburgh and London: Blackwood, 1920, opposite p. 500.

15 *Glasgow Herald*, 14 January 1919.
16 This system of demobilization according to 'industrial priority' was abolished by an Army Order of 29 January 1919, and replaced with one in which release was determined by age and length of service. J. F. C. Fuller was of the opinion that, had this 'flagrantly unjust' system not been replaced, the mutinies it provoked would have led to revolution, 'for I doubt whether there was a soldier in the country who, if called upon to do so, would have fired on the rebels'. See Major General J. F. C. Fuller, *The Army in My Time*, London: Rich and Cowan, 1935, pp. 157–8. According to the Christian socialist George Lansbury, the delay in demobilization was caused by government fear of 'Red Flags' rather than 'Red Tape' (*Daily Herald*, 11 January 1919).
17 *Glasgow Herald*, 4 February 1919.
18 *Glasgow Herald*, 10 February 1919. Photographs of the Glasgow 'tankodrome' appear in *The Bulletin*, 4 February 1919.
19 For a retrospective novel on these events see Russell Galbraith, *George Square 1919*, Edinburgh: Mainstream, 1988.
20 Williams-Ellis, *The Tank Corps*, p. 281.
21 Lewis Sowden, *The Land of Afternoon: The Story of a White South African*, London: Elek, 1968, pp. 66–71.
22 See the various battalion reports from the 'Army of the Rhine' in 'Battalion News from Home and Abroad', *The Tank Corps Journal*, vol. 1, no. 4, August 1919, pp. 109–11. The report for the 4th Tank Battalion jokes about fire from the Chinese compound asserting that 'according to Chinese theology the greatest favour you can confer on your friend is to help him to get to Allah or to whosoever it is that holds his place [for Chinamen]. John Chinaman regards Tommy as his ally and friend and hence many of the dangers and diversions of our life . . . Bullets have been known on more than once occasion to whistle through our camp, and it is told of our then brigadier that when riding on horseback near the old trenches, he was treated in so friendly a fashion by the Chinese that half a dozen "tracer" bullets only just missed their targets. History goes on to record that the said brigadier dismounted, and finding the culprit, proceeded to administer "stern" justice of the only kind which John really understands.' If this was carried out in the spirit of the events of later months, this may mean that 'John' was shot on the spot. It appears that the Chinese grew more restive in the months to come. By June they were looting French provision trains, and coming under fire from British troops. For an account of this officially suppressed story, see Robert Fisk, 'The Search for my Father', *Independent on Sunday (Sunday Review)*, 21 February 1999, pp. 12–18.
23 Captain B. H. Liddell Hart, *The Tanks*, London: Cassell, 1959, vol. 1, p. 205. The commander in question, Sir William Robertson, was an early champion of tanks, as he insisted when visiting tank detachments in Germany. He informed them that he was proud to have been 'personally responsible for the ordering of the first hundred tanks to France' (reported in *Tank Corps Journal*, vol. 1, no. 4. August 1919, p. 119).
24 See report headed 'Rhine Tank Company', *Tank Corps Journal*, vol. 2, no. 17, September 1920, p. 106.
25 These 'boiler armoured cars' are pictured and described by the wife of the Secretary for the Post Office in former Mrs Archibald Hamilton Norway, *The Sinn Fein Rebellion as I Saw It*, London: Smith, Elder & Co., 1916, pp. 85–7.
26 Cabinet paper on 'Mechanical Transport, Armoured Cars and other forms of Protection for Troops in Ireland' (7 December 1920), Public Record Office, Wo/32/9541.

CHAPTER 9. The Prophet's Creed

1 Anthony John Trythall, *'Boney' Fuller: The Intellectual General*, London: Cassell, 1977, p. 81.
2 Major General J. F. C. Fuller, *The Army in My Time*, London: Rich and Cowan, 1935, p. 179.

3 Fuller's note on the Medium D, made on 24/5/18 in *The Private Journal of Lt. Colonel J. F. C. Fuller Relative to the Expansion and Employment of the Tank Corps, December 1917 to July 26 1918*, the Fuller Collection, Liddell Hart Centre for Military Archives, King's College, London.

4 Colonel J. F. C. Fuller, 'Tank Design with Reference to Orbit of Thought and Selection by Concentration a serious leg pull for Searle', 19/6/18. Item B. 79 in *The Private Journal of Lt. Colonel J. F. C. Fuller Relative to the Expansion and Employment of the Tank Corps, December 1917 to July 26 1918*, the Fuller Collection, Liddell Hart Centre for Military Archives, King's College, London, B.79.

5 J. F. C. Fuller, letter to Basil Liddell Hart, 22 September 1922. This correspondence is held at the Liddell Hart Centre for Military Archives, King's College, London.

6 Major General J. F. C. Fuller, *Memoirs of an Unconventional Soldier*, London: Nicholson and Watson, 1936, p. 323.

7 Ibid., p. 322.

8 Fuller's 'Proposals towards the formation of a Tank Expeditionary Force', are to be found in a file named 'Employment of Tanks against Bolshevists in Russia', Public Record Office, WO/32/5685.

9 See Douglas Goldring, *The Nineteen Twenties*, London: Nicholson & Watson, 1945, p. 7.

10 Sergeant. C. L. Windle and 'Ranger', 'With the Tanks in Bolshevik Russia', *Tank Corps Journal*, vol. 1, no. 3, July 1919, pp. 80–1.

11 On the sorrowful nature of the Russian cinema, see F. E. Hotblack's comment in 'The Tank Corps in Russia: An Appeal', *Tank Corps Journal*, vol. 1. no. 3, July 1919.

12 Rhoda Power, *Under Cossack and Bolshevik*, London: Methuen, 1919, p. 173.

13 *Weekly Tank Notes*, no. 45, 21 June 1919.

14 *Weekly Tank Notes*, no. 48, 12 July 1919.

15 Fuller quotes from Bruce's letter in 'The First Battle of Tsaritsin (Stalingrad).' See Major General J. F. C. Fuller, *Watchwords*, London: Skeffington, 1944, p. 22.

16 Ibid., p. 334.

17 Major J. N. L. Bryan, 'With the Tanks in North Russia', Chapters VII-IX, *Tank Corps Journal*, vol. 1, no. 10, February 1920, pp. 274–7; Chapter X, *Tank Corps Journal*, vol. 1, no. 11, March 1920, p. 303.

18 Major J. N. L. Bryan, 'With the Tanks in North Russia', Chapter XVII, *Tank Corps Journal*, vol. 2, no. 15, July 1920, pp. 74–5.

19 Major J. N. L. Bryan, 'With the Tanks in North Russia', Chapter XIX, *Tank Corps Journal*, vol. 2, no. 16, July 1920, pp. 96–8.

20 Tom Wintringham, *How to Reform the Army*, a special issue of *Fact*, April 1939, p. 68. It was, Wintringham affirmed, culpably stupid for the Cavalry Training (Mechanized) Pamphlet No. 1, issued in 1937, to insist on 'the use of the sword in war' or to suggest that armour should be used like cavalry: 'It is not stated whether armoured cars should be given lumps of sugar after a good gallop'.

21 Major General J. F. C. Fuller, *The Army in My Time*, p. 176.

22 J. P. Harris uses the phrase 'RTC radicals' to describe a group of progressive officers based at the Royal Tank Corps headquarters at Bovington in the early twenties primarily, George Lindsay, Charles Broad, Percy Hobart and Frederick Pile who were trying to implement ideas similar if not identical to those of J. F. C. Fuller. See J. P. Harris, *Men, Ideas and Tanks: British military thought and armoured forces, 1903–1939*, Manchester: Manchester University Press, 1995, pp. 198–201.

23 Major General J. F. C. Fuller CB, CBE, DSO, *India in Revolt*, London: Eyre and Spottiswoode, 1931, p. 141.

24 Trythall, *'Boney' Fuller*, p. 144.

25 Fuller, *The Army in My Time*, p. 179.
26 Fuller, letter to Liddell Hart (27 August 1928), quoted in Brian Holden Reid, *J. F. C. Fuller: Military Thinker*, London: Macmillan, 1987, p. 185.
27 Fuller, *The Army in My Time*, p. 188.
28 H. E. Graham, *The Battle of Dora*, London: Clowes and Sons, 1931.
29 Ibid, p. 63.
30 J. F. C. Fuller, *The Reformation of War*, London: Hutchinson, 1923, p. x.
31 J. F. C. Fuller, 'The Development of Sea Warfare on Land . . .', *Royal United Service Institution Journal*, vol. LXV, pp. 281–98. Quoted in A. J. Trythall, *'Boney' Fuller*, p. 83.
32 Fuller, *The Army in My Time*, p. 188.
33 Ibid., p. 20.
34 Ibid., p. 115.
35 Erich Maria Remarque, *All Quiet on the Western Front*, London: Putnam, 1929, p. 306. Quoted in J. F. C. Fuller, *The First of the League Wars: Its Lessons and Omens*, London: Eyre and Spottiswoode, 1936, pp. 212–13.
36 Fuller, *Memoirs of an Unconventional Soldier*, p. 107.
37 Ibid., p. 129.
38 Major General J. F. C. Fuller, *Lectures on F.S.R. III: Operations between Mechanized Forces*, London: Sifton Praed & Co., Ltd., 1932, p. 7.
39 Ibid., p. 38.
40 Ibid., p. 37.
41 J. F. C. Fuller, *Imperial Defence, 1588–1914*, London: Sifton Praed, 1926, p.5.
42 J. B. S. Haldane, *Daedalus or Science and the Future*, London: Kegan Paul, Trench, Trubner & Co., 1924, p. 1–2.
43 J. B. S. Haldane, *Callinicus: A Defence of Chemical Warfare*, London: Kegan Paul, Trench, Trubner, 1925, pp. 27 and 7.
44 Bertrand Russell, *Icarus or The Future of Science*, London: Kegan Paul, Trench, Trubner & Co., 1924.
45 J. B. S. Haldane, *Callinicus*, p. 35.
46 Fuller, letter to Basil Liddell Hart, 10 June 1920.
47 Basil Liddell Hart, letter to Fuller, 14 June 1920.
48 Fuller, letter to Basil Liddell Hart, 8 February 1923.
49 J. P. Harris, *Men, Ideas and Tanks*, p. 242.
50 John J. Mearsheimer, *Liddell Hart and the Weight of History*, London: Brassey's Defence Publishers, 1988.
51 Fuller, *The Army in My Time*, p. 172.
52 Fuller, *Reformation of War*, p. ix.
53 Fuller, *Lectures on FSR III*, p. vii.
54 Colonel J. F. C. Fuller, *Pegasus: Problems of Transportation*, London: Kegan Paul, Trench, Trubner, 1925, p. 55.
55 Trythall, *'Boney' Fuller*, p. 183.
56 J. F. C. Fuller, *Towards Armageddon: The Defence Problem and its Solution*, London: Lovat Dickson, 1937, p. 132.
57 J. F. C. Fuller, *Machine Warfare: An Enquiry into the Influence of Mechanics on the Art of Warfare*, London: Hutchinson, 1942, p. 120.
58 Fuller, *Lectures on F.S.R. II*, p. 32.
59 Fuller, *Towards Armageddon*, p. 214.
60 Ibid., p. 125.
61 Ibid., pp. 97–102.
62 Victor Wallace Germains ('A Rifleman'), *The "Mechanization" of War*, London: Sifton Praed &

Co., Ltd, 1927. These remarks are quoted from the 'Foreword' by Major General Sir Frederick Maurice.

63 Ibid., p. 22.

64 Ibid., p. 103.

65 Ibid., p. 228.

66 Ibid., p. 56.

67 Barton C. Hacker, 'Imagination in Thrall: The Social Psychology of Military Mechanization 1919–1939', *Parameters, Journal of the US Army War College*, vol. XII, no. 1, March 1982, p. 56.

68 See J. J. Mearsheimer, *Liddell Hart and the Weight of History*, London: Brassey's, 1988.

69 See J. P. Harris, *Men, Ideas and Tanks, passim*.

70 Ibid., p. 204.

71 Ibid., p. 83.

72 John Gould Fletcher, *Egoist*, 5, 3 (March 1918), pp. 45–6.

CHAPTER 10. The Secret Imprint of the Great Beast

1 Aleister Crowley's letters to Fuller are held in the Fuller Collection at the Liddell Hart Centre for Military Archives, King's College, London (Fuller IV/11–16. V).

2 For an account of Crowley's activities at Cefalu in 1921, see Nathalie Blondel, *Mary Butts: Scenes from the Life*, New York: MacPherson & Co., 1998, pp. 102–6.

3 John Symonds, *The Great Beast: A Life of Aleister Crowley*, London: Rider & Co, 1951, p. 226.

4 Fuller, letter to his mother, 17 May 1905.

5 J. F. C. Fuller, 'The Hidden Wisdom of the Illuminati', an incomplete manuscript, dated 1926, and held in the Liddell Hart Centre for the Study of Military Archives, King's College, London (Fuller IV/14).

6 Fuller, *Memoirs of an Unconventional Soldier*, p. 17. See also A. J. Trythall, *'Boney' Fuller*, p. 20. In his book, *India in Revolt* (London: Eyre & Spottiswoode, 1931) Fuller describes encountering the Arya Samaj while he was in the Punjab in 1903–4, and being 'amazed at the efficiency of its organization and system of self-help and social welfare' (p. 75). He likened the Arya Samaj to the Protestant movement in Europe, seeing it as part of a wider religious renaissance that helped to throw off medieval fundamentalism in India and to inspire the national anti-colonial idea. While he plainly understood the concern of Sir Valentine Chirol, who in 1907, described the Arya Samaj as a serious threat to British rule, he accepted its claim for the profundity of India's religious traditions and also that 'Indian wisdom can solve Europe's social problems' (pp. 74–5). The Ahmadiyyah movement was founded in 1889 by Mirza Ghulam Ahmad, whom Fuller met in Lahore in 1904 and, much later, described as a pacifist and advocate of universal brotherhood who had been influenced by the Arya Samaj as well as by Madam Blavatsky's Theosophical Society (pp. 63–4). The Ahmadiyyah movement remains committed to a tolerant and rational expression of Islam to this day, and is violently opposed by fundamentalists.

7 *The Agnostic Journal and Eclectic Review*, 21 January 1905, p. 41.

8 Saladin in the *Agnostic Journal and Eclectic Review*, 27 May 1905, p. 330.

9 *Agnostic Journal and Eclectic Review*, October 21, 1905, p. 269.

10 J. F. C. Fuller, 'Divine and Other Carnage', *Agnostic Journal and Eclectic Review*, 15 April 1905, pp. 229–30.

11 J. F. C. Fuller, 'Bible Science',*The Agnostic Journal and Eclectic Review*, 21 October 1905, p. 269.

12 J. F. C. Fuller, 'Bible Science continued: Biology and Phsyiology', *The Agnostic Journal and Eclectic Review*, 28 October 1905, pp. 276–7.

13 J. F. C. Fuller, 'Bible Science: Pathology and Medicine', *The Agnostic Journal and Eclectic Review*, 4 November 1905, pp. 300–1.

14 'Short Notice' of Aleister Crowley's *Why Jesus Wept* in the *Literary Guide & Rationalist Review*, 1 March 1905, p. 41.

15 John Symonds and Kenneth Grant, *The Confessions of Aleister Crowley: An Autohagiography*, London: Routledge and Kegan Paul, 1979, p. 446.

16 Crowley to Fuller, 3 August 1906.

17 Crowley, *Confessions*, p. 541.

18 See Trythall, *'Boney' Fuller*, p. 25.

19 J. F. C. Fuller, 'Aleister Crowley 1898–1911: An Introductory Essay by Major General J. F. C. Fuller', in *666, Bibliotheca Crowleyana: Catalogue of a unique Collection of Books, Pamphlets, Proof Copies, MSS., etc. by, about, or connected with Aleister Crowley*, Keith Hogg (82 High St., Tenterden, Kent), 1966, p. 5.

20 Captain J. F. C. Fuller, *The Star in the West: A Critical Essay upon the Works of Aleister Crowley*, London and Felling-on-Tyne: the Walter Scott Publishing Co. Ltd., 1907, p. 126.

21 On the Moplah version of 'Satanic' British government, see Major General Sir Charles W. Gwynn, *Imperial Policing*, London: Macmillan, 1939.

22 Fuller, *The Star in the West*, p. 18.

23 Ibid., p. 67.

24 Ibid., p. 42.

25 Fuller, 'Aleister Crowley 1898–1911', *666, Bibliotheca Crowleyana*.

26 Fuller, *The Star in the West*, p. 35.

27 Jack Prelutsky, *Tyrannosaurus Was a Beast*, London: Walker Books, 1989, p. 14.

28 *Equinox*, vol.1, no. 1, p. 28.

29 Meredith Starr's 'Diary of S.S. Probationer to the A∴ A∴' is among the Fuller papers held at the Liddell Hart Centre for Military Archives, King's College, London.

30 Aleister Crowley, *Equinox*, vol. 1, no. 1, March 1909, p. 133.

31 John Symonds, *The Great Beast: A Life of Aleister Crowley*, London: Rider & Co., 1951, p. 64. For an account of Crowley's 'Great Revelation' see pp. 61–3.

32 Crowley, *Confessions*, p. 404.

33 Ibid., p. 618.

34 Tobias Döring, 'Discovering the Mother Country', *Journal for the Study of British Cultures*, Tubingen, no. 1/2, vol. 4., 1997, p. 181.

35 Crowley, letter to Fuller, 25 May 1908.

36 Fuller uses this phrase in a letter to Meredith Starr written in January 1913. Fuller's letters to Meredith Starr are in the possession of Miss J. Grey, Clayton, Douro Road, Cheltenham.

37 Crowley, letter to Fuller (18 December 1909), quoted in Jean Overton Fuller, *The Magical Dilemma of Victor Neuburg*, London: W. H. Allen, 1965, p. 159.

38 Ibid., p. 155.

39 Crowley, letter to Fuller, 28 November 1909.

40 Crowley, letter to Fuller, 1 May 1911.

41 Crowley, *Confessions*, p. 636.

42 Fuller, letter to Crowley, 2 May 1911.

43 Jean Overton Fuller, *The Magical Dilemma of Victor Neuburg*, p. 184.

44 Crowley, letters to Fuller, 5 May 1911 and 17 August 1911.

45 Crowley, *Confessions*, p. 544.

46 S. Skinner, (ed.), *The Magical Diaries of Aleister Crowley*, 1923, Jersey, Nevill Spearman, 1979, p. 6.

47 Aleister Crowley, *Moonchild*, London: Sphere, 1972, p. 18.

48 Ibid., pp. 144 and 151.

49 Ibid., p. 102.

50 Fuller, *Memoirs of an Unconventional Soldier*, pp. 27 and 460.

51 Fuller, Letter to Meredith Starr, 31 December 1919.

52 Townshend's letters are held in the Harry Ransom Humanities Research Center, the University of Texas at Austin.

53 'The Hidden Wisdom of the Illuminati' is with the Fuller papers at the Liddell Hart Centre for Military Archives, King's College, London. This uncompleted novel tells the story of a wealthy young bachelor, who has grown up in Allahabad, the son of an English civil servant and student of Oriental religions and philosophy. Having inherited his late father's fortune, the narrator indulges himself as Fuller was never able to do. He finds a blue-eyed Pathan girl in a bazaar and takes her as his mistress, and then embarks on the search for a suitable guru, who eventually materializes as a voice emanating from a 'little tank' in the garden. In this book the tank is no more than an innocent water container, a pool in which a naked fakir sits reciting the creed of Thelema ('Do what thou wilt is the whole of the Law'), and setting Fuller's narrator on the path that will soon enough lead him to Althothas.

54 Writing in 1926, Fuller has his Crowley figure, Althothas, claim that his methods 'are perhaps those of a surgical operation. It is better so, better than weeks of gradual treatment' ('Hidden Wisdom of the Illuminati').

55 Fuller, *Memoirs of an Unconventional Soldier*, p. 9.

56 Ibid., p. 29.

57 Ibid., p. 27.

58 Fuller, *Machine Warfare*, p. 7.

59 Fuller, *Memoirs of an Unconventional Soldier*, p. vii.

60 Ibid., p. 202. One chapter of Fuller's, *The Reformation of War* (1923) is entitled 'The Last Lap of the Physical Epoch'. Fuller was thinking of history as a cycle of eras long before the mid-thirties, when he found further confirmation of this tendency in the work of Lewis Mumford.

61 Fuller, *The Star in the West*, p. 287.

62 *Equinox*, 1. III, p. 229.

63 Major General J. F. C. Fuller, *The Dragon's Teeth: A Study of War and Peace*, London: Constable 1932, p. 8.

64 Ibid., p. 8.

65 J. F. C. Fuller, *Generalship: Its Diseases and their Cure: a Study of the Personal Factor in Command*, London: Faber & Faber, 1933. See also A. J. Trythall, *'Boney' Fuller*, p. 177.

66 E. and D. E. Hickey, 'Over the Top', in J. W. Marriott, *The Best One-Act Plays of 1934*, London: George C. Harrap and Co. Ltd., 1935. pp. 191–220.

67 Quoted from Fuller's 'Introduction' to Captain D. E. Hickey's memoirs, *Rolling into Action*, London: Hutchinson, 1936, p. 13.

68 Walter Owen, *The Cross of Carl: An Allegory*, London: Grant Richards, 1931, p. 42.

69 A. J. P. Taylor ascribed this change partly to the appearance through the twenties of a number of novels and memoirs that provided a far from glorifying account of the Great War works by Sassoon, Graves, Owen, Aldington, and also E. M. Remarque's *All Quiet on the Western Front*. The unmentioned exception is Ernst Jünger's *The Storm of Steel*, a decidedly unpacifist work, which appeared in English translation in 1929. See A. J. P. Taylor, *English History 1914–1945*, Oxford: Oxford University Press, 1965, pp. 361.

70 Sir Philip Gibbs, 'Arms and the Man', in *Ordeal in England*, London: Heinemann, 1937, p. 47.

71 Fenner Brockway, *Profits from Blood: The War-Makers Exposed*, London: Independent Labour Party, 1935.

72 Basil Henriques, *Indiscretions of a Warden*, p. 41.

73 See Clough Williams-Ellis (ed.), *Britain and the Beast* (London: J. M. Dent, 1937), which features a picture of the Royal Tank Corps's gunnery range on its end papers – emblematic of the English landscape at its most precious and threatened.

74 In May 1935 this gun was described by S. F. Perry in his evidence before the Royal Commission on the Private Manufacture of and Trading in Arms. See Fenner Brockway and Frederic Mullally, *Death Pays a Dividend*, London: Victor Gollancz, 1944, pp. 23–4.

75 Reported in the *Bucks Herald*, 8 September 1999.

76 Major General Sir Ernest D. Swinton, *Eyewitness: Being Personal Reminiscences of Certain Phases of the Great War, Including the Genesis of the Tank*, London: Hodder and Stoughton, 1932, photograph opposite p. 318.

77 Alec Dixon, *Tinned Soldier: A Personal Record. 1919–1926*, London: Jonathan Cape, 1941, p. 273.

78 Fuller, *First of the League Wars*, pp. 301 and 295.

79 Fuller, *Towards Armageddon*, p. 17.

80 Fuller, *First of the League Wars*, p. 242.

81 Major General J. F. C. Fuller, 'Britain's out-of-date Defence Force', *Daily Mail*, 6 December 1933.

82 Fuller, *Reformation of War*, p. 73.

83 Trythall, *'Boney' Fuller*, p. 181.

84 J. F. C. Fuller, *March to Sanity: What the British Union has to Offer Britain*, London: British Union of Fascists, 1938.

85 Fuller's article of this title was first published in the *Fascist Quarterly*, vol. 1. no. 1, 1935, and later reprinted in *Weltpost*. See Trythall, *'Boney' Fuller*, p. 184.

86 J. F. C. Fuller, 'Our Strategic Position in September', *New Pioneer*, vol 1. no. 1, 1938.

87 Quoted in Douglas Goldring, *Marching with the Times 1931–46*, London: Nicholson & Watson, p. 96.

CHAPTER 11. The Mission Overseas

1 Fuller dated the commencement of this 'coma' to autumn 1926, when General Milne, the Commander of the Imperial General Staff, announced the formation of the Experimental Mobile Force (in 'an exceptionally able address', which Fuller, who was then Milne's military assistant, almost certainly had a hand in writing), and then 'fell into a stony silence which would have done credit to the Sphinx'. See Fuller's *The Army in My Time*, p. 187.

2 J. F. C. Fuller, 'The Temple of Solomon The King', *Equinox*, no. 1, vol. IV (September 1910), p. 139.

3 Harris, *Men, Ideas and Tanks*, p. 244.

4 Fuller, *The Army in My Time*, p. 176. Fuller's interest in a possible career as a national arms salesman is mentioned in Trythall, *'Boney' Fuller*, p. 183.

5 Major General J. F. C. Fuller, 'Wolf into Poodle: the farce of this week's manoeuvres', *Evening Standard*, 21 September 1934, p. 7.

6 B.H. Liddell Hart, *The Tanks*, vol. 1, p. 335.

7 Harris, *Men, Ideas and Tanks*, pp. 251–3.

8 Fuller, *Machine Warfare*, p. 12. Fuller was inclined to blame his former Bermicourt colleague, 'Slosher' Martel, who had constructed a 'one man tank' that gave 'an impetus to cheapness' and contributed to the situation in which 'the tactical value of Medium and Heavy machines was lost sight of in the idea of the Light tank'. See Fuller, *The Army in My Time*, p. 185.

9 Harris, *Men, Ideas and Tanks*, p. 301.

10 Tom Wintringham, *How to Reform the Army*, a special issue of *Fact*, April 1939, p. 33.

11 Fuller, *Tanks in the Great War*, p. 186.

12 R. H. Lutz (Selector), *The Cause of the German Collapse in 1918 (Sections of the officially authorized report of the Commission of the German Constituent Assembly of the German Reichstag, 1919–1928)*, Stanford: Stanford University Press, p. 68.

13 Quoted from *The Private Journal of Lt. Colonel J. F. C. Fuller Relative to the Expansion and Employment of the Tank Corps, December 1917 to July 26, 1918*. LHCMA, King's College. London.

14 Gen. Charles de Gaulle, *The Army of the Future*, London: Hutchinson, 1940, p. 13.

15 Ibid., p. 57.

16 Ibid., p. 59.

17 Chauvineau is here quoted from Alvin D. Coox, 'General Narcisse Chauvineau: False Apostle of Prewar French Military Doctrine', *Military Affairs*, 37, February 1973, pp. 15–19.

18 Fuller, *The Dragon's Teeth*, p. vii.

19 Trythall, '*Boney*' *Fuller*, pp. 209–10.

20 Charles Messenger, *The Art of Blitzkrieg*, London: Ian Allan, 1991 (Second Edition), p. 95.

21 Fuller, *Memoirs of an Unconventional Soldier*, pp. 157–8.

22 Charteris, *H.Q. Tanks*, p. 12.

23 Hugh Elles, 'Introduction', to C. and A. Williams-Ellis, *The Tank Corps*, p. xi.

24 Fuller, *Tanks in the Great War*, p. 277.

25 Note dated 25/5/18 in *The Private Journal of Lt. Colonel J. F. C. Fuller Relative to the Expansion and Employment of the Tank Corps, December 1917 to July 26 1918*, LHCMA

26 Carlo D'Este, *A Genius for War: A Life of General George S. Patton*, London: HarperCollins, 1995, p. 228.

27 Ibid., p. 204.

28 Ibid., p. 207.

29 J. F. C. Fuller, letter to John Welldon, 15 December 1959, Tank Museum Library, Bovington, Dorset.

30 Ibid., p. 214.

31 Col. S. D. Rockenbach, letter to General Hugh Elles, 25 May 1918, copy in *The Private Journal of Lt. Colonel J. F. C. Fuller. . .* LHCMA.

32 D'Este, *A Genius for War*, p. 263.

33 Brigadier General C. D. Baker-Carr, *From Chauffeur to Brigadier*, pp. 305–9.

34 Fuller, *Tanks in the Great War*, p. 282.

35 Charles Messenger, *The Art of Blitzkrieg*, p. 50.

36 See George F. Hofmann, 'The Demise of the US Tank Corps and Medium Tank Development Programme', *Military Affairs*, 37, February 1975, pp. 20–5.

37 John J. Pershing, 'Our National Military Policy', *Scientific American*, August 1922, p. 83. Quoted in Hoffman (Ibid.).

38 Richard M. Ogorkiewicz, *Armour: The Development of Mechanized Forces and their Equipment*, London: Atlantic Books, 1960, p. 266.

39 Ibid., p. 192.

40 Fuller, *Reformation of War*, p. 268.

41 N. K. Krupskjaya, *Memories of Lenin*, Moscow: Foreign Languages Publishing House, 1959, 347.

42 E. H. Carr, *The Bolshevik Revolution 1917–1923*, London: Macmillan, 1950, vol. 1, p. 78.

43 Orlando Figes, *A People's Tragedy: The Russian Revolution, 1891–1924*, London: Cape, 1996, p. 387.

44 John Reed, *Ten Days that Shook the World*, London: Lawrence & Wishart, 1961, p. 31.

45 Ibid., p. 161.

46 Ibid., p. 49.

47 Ibid., p. 70.

48 Ibid., p. 69.

49 Albert Rhys Williams, *Journey into Revolution: Petrograd, 1917–18*, Chicago: Quadrangle Books, 1969, pp. 179–82.

50 Owned by the State Historical Museum in Moscow, Natwey Manniser's sculpture was exhibited at the 'Kunst und Diktatur' exhibition at the Kunstlerhaus, Vienna, May 1994.

51 George Stewart, *The White Armies of Russia*, New York: Macmillan, 1933, p. 225.

52 J. M. Meier (ed.), *The Trotsky Papers*, vol. 1, 1917–1919, The Hague: Mouton, 1971, p. 707.

53 Richard Luckett, *The White Generals: An Account of the White Movement and the Russian Civil War*, London: Longman, 1971, p. 318. For the broken bridge at Yamburg see Stewart, *The White Armies of Russia*, p. 230.

54 Victor Serge, *Memoirs of a Revolutionary, 1901–41*, Oxford: Oxford University Press, 1963, p. 93.

55 Lenin, letter to Trotsky, 22 October 1919, in J. M. Meier (ed.), *The Trotsky Papers*, vol. 1, pp. 717–19.

56 Leon Trotsky, *My Life*, Goucester, Mass.: Peter Smith, 1970, p. 431.

57 Kirdetzov, as quoted in Leon Trotsky, *My Life*, pp. 434–5.

58 Luckett, *The White Generals*, p. 321.

59 *Trotsky Papers*, II, p. 6.

60 See J. Milsom, *Russian Tanks*, pp. 20–7.

61 Major General J. F. C. Fuller, *The Decisive Battles of the Western World (and their influence upon history)*, London: Eyre & Spottiswoode, 1956, vol. III, p. 339.

62 O. Figes, *A People's Tragedy*, pp. 761 and 763.

63 Ibid., pp. 762–3.

64 See Jacob W. Kipp, 'Foreword' to V. K. Triandafillov, *The Nature of the Operations of Modern Armies (1929)*, Ilford & Portland: Frank Cass, 1994, p. x.

65 Quoted in James J. Schneider, 'Introduction: The Legacy of V. K. Triandafillov', in V. K. Triandafillov, *The Nature of the Operations of Modern Armies*, p. xxx.

66 Jacob W. Kipp, 'General-Major A. A. Svechin and Modern Warfare', in A. A. Svechin, *Strategy*, Minneapolis: East View Press, 1992, pp. 23–56.

67 See Richard Simpkin, *Deep Battle: The Brainchild of Marshal Tuckachevaskii*, London: Brassey's, pp. 40–4. See also Frederick Kagan, 'Army Doctrine and Modern War', *Parameters*, Spring 1997, pp. 135–51.

68 Jacob W. Kipp, 'General-Major A. A. Svechin and Modern Warfare', p. 47.

69 V. K. Triandafillov, *The Nature of the Operations of Modern Armies*, p. 21.

70 Ibid., p. 27.

71 Ibid., p. 28.

72 Ibid., p. 26.

73 Ibid., p. 29.

74 Tuckhachevsky's 'Preface to J. F. C. Fuller's *Reformation of War*' is translated in Richard Simpkin, *Deep Battle*, pp. 125–34.

75 Tukhachevsky, 'Preface to J. F. C. Fuller's *Reformation of War*', quoted in Dr Jacob Kipps, 'Mass, Mobility, and the Red Army's Road to Operational Art 1918–36, which is available on the website of the Foreign Military Studies Office at Fort Leavenworth, Kansas, USA (http://leav-www.army mil/fmso).

76 J. Milsom, *Russian Tanks*, p. 38.

77 Lieut.-Gen. Sir Gifford Martel, *An Outspoken Soldier*, London: Sifton Praed, 1949, pp. 135–52.

78 Shimon Naveh, 'Michail Nikolayevich Tukhachevsky', in H. Shukman (ed.), *Stalin's Generals*, London: Weidenfeld & Nicolson, 1993, p. 265.

79 J. Milsom, *Russian Tanks*, p. 41.

80 Shimon Naveh, 'Michail Nikolayevich Tukhachevsky', p. 266.

81 This is how it is seen in Alexander Deineka's 'Das Volk während der Großen Vaterlöndischen Krieges', 1944, Staatliches Russisches Museum, St Petersburg.

82 Dmitri Volkogonov, *Stalin*, London: Weidenfeld & Nicolson, 1991, p. 322.

83 J. Wheldon, *Machine Age Armies*, London: Abelard-Schuman, 1968. Quoted in J. Milsom, *Russian Tanks*, p. 51.

84 Ibid., p. 211.

85 Major General J. F. C. Fuller, *The Conduct of War, 1789–1961: A Study of the Impact of the*

French, Industrial and Russian Revolutions on War and Its Conduct, London: Eyre and Spottiswoode, 1961, p. 247.

86 This account of the mechanization of Italy's army is drawn from John J. T. Sweet, *Iron Arm: The Mechanization of Mussolini's Army, 1930–1940*, Westport, Conn.: Greenwood, 1980.

87 Ibid., p. 181.

88 Ibid., pp. 83–4.

89 Trythall, *'Boney' Fuller*, p. 188.

90 Tim Parks, *An Italian Education*, London: Minerva, 1997, pp. 276–7.

91 Fuller, *The First of the League Wars*, London: Eyre and Spottiswoode, 1936, p. 57.

92 Ibid., p. 60.

93 Ibid., p. 62.

94 Ibid., p. 58.

95 Ibid., p. 57.

96 Fuller in *Daily Mail*, 4 December 1935. Quoted in Trythall, *'Boney' Fuller*, p. 189.

97 Fuller, *First of the League Wars*, p. 54.

98 Major General J. F. C. Fuller, 'Abyssinians Marching on Makale', *Daily Mail*, 5 December 1935.

99 J. J. T. Sweet, *Iron Arm*, p. 110.

100 Fuller, *First of the League Wars*, pp. 39 and 85.

101 Ibid., p. 65.

102 J. J. T. Sweet, *Iron Arm*, p. 110.

103 Ibid., p. 68.

104 Fuller, *First of the League Wars*, p. 69.

105 Sweet, p. 160.

106 These remarks are quoted from the assessment by War Office officials that accompanies Fuller's report on his first visit to General Franco's Army in March 1937, Public Record Office. WO. 106/1578.

107 C. J. Deverall's letter to Fuller is held alongside the latter's 'Report on a Visit to Nationalist Spain, October 1937', Public Record Office, WO 106/1579. Fuller reported on rising friction between Mussolini, who wanted to see 'total annihilation' of the Reds, and Franco, whose more moderate (and intelligent) aim was, as an admiring Fuller claims, 'to win the peace whilst he is winning the war'.

108 Major General J. F. C. Fuller, 'Along the Red Trail in Aragon'. Fuller submitted this article, which includes a reference to its own publication in the *Chicago Tribune*, along with the report of his visit of April 1938, Public Record Office, WO 106/1585.

109 Dated 30 March 1939, this Report of the Generalstab des Heeres, is quoted in T. R. Jentz (ed.), *Panzer Truppen 1: The Complete Guide to the Creation & Combat Employment of Germany's Tank Force, 1933–1942*, Atglen: Schiffer, 1996, pp. 46–7.

110 Major General J. F. C. Fuller, 'Report on a Visit to Nationalist Spain, October 1937', Public Record Office, WO 106/1579.

111 Major General J. F. C. Fuller, 'The Red Collapse in Spain'. Public Record Office, WO 106/1585.

112 The typescript of Major General J. F. C. Fuller's article 'Rag-picking on the Spanish Battlefields' is in the Public Record Office, Public Record Office, WO 106/1585.

113 Major General J. F. C. Fuller, 'With Franco's Victorious Armies', Public Record Office, WO. 106/1585.

114 Tom Wintringham, *How to Reform the Army*, p. 38.

115 Christopher Isherwood, 'The Landauers', in *Goodbye to Berlin*, Harmondsworth: Penguin, 1969, p. 156.

116 See Irene Cooper Willis, *England's Holy War: A Study of English Liberal Idealism During the Great War*, New York: Knopf, 1928, p. 371.

117 See Larry H. Addington, *The Blitzkrieg Era and the German General Staff, 1865–1941*, New Brunswick, Rutgers University Press, 1971, pp. 28–9.
118 James S. Corum, *The Roots of Blitzkrieg: Hans Von Seeckt and German Military Reform*, University of Kansas Press, 1992, pp. 29–32.
119 General Hans von Seeckt, quoted in J. S. Corum, *The Roots of the Blitzkrieg*, p. 100.
120 J. S. Corum, *The Roots of the Blitzkrieg*, pp. 57–8.
121 Ernst Jünger, *The Storm of Steel*, London: Chatto & Windus, 1929, pp. 286–7 and 310.
122 For Jünger's observation that 'every new mechanical device is a new molestation.' see Thomas Nevin, *Ernst Jünger and Germany: Into the Abyss, 1914–1945*, London: Constable, 1997, p. 92.
123 For an account of Jünger's military writings see Thomas Nevin, *Ernst Jünger and Germany*, pp. 77–94. Also Marcus Paul Bullock, *The Violent Eye: Ernst Jünger's Visions and Revisions on the European Right*, Detroit: Wayne State University Press, 1992.
124 Walter Benjamin, 'Theories of German Fascism: On the Collection of Essays *War and Warrior*, edited by Ernst Jünger' (1930), *New German Critique*, 17, Spring 1979, p. 128.
125 J. S. Corum, *The Roots of the Blitzkrieg*, p. 133.
126 Ibid., pp. 127–9.
127 Ibid., p. 101.
128 Fuller, *Dragon's Teeth*, p. 42.
129 Fuller, *Towards Armageddon*, p. 43.
130 J. F. C. Fuller, 'Armoured Cars' Feat in German "War"', *Daily Mail*, 7 September 1935.
131 J. F. C. Fuller, 'British General and German Army Test: power of using new weapons', *Daily Mail*, 5 September 1935.
132 J. F. C. Fuller, 'Great German Army March Past', *Daily Mail*, 9 September 1935.
133 For the suspicions of the German generals who resented Hitler's admiration for Fuller, and suspected that this visitor might be a spy, see Trythall, p. 192.
134 Trythall, *'Boney' Fuller*, p. 184.
135 Fuller, *Machine Warfare*, p. 13.
136 World War II German Military Studies, *War Diary of German Armed Forces Supreme Command Headquarters*, vol. 7, part IV, Helmuth Greiner, The OKW War Diary Series, The Polish campaign in 1939, C-065c, 30pp.
137 A. J. P. Taylor, *The Origins of the Second World War*, London: Heinemann, 1961, p. 211.
138 *News Review*, quoted in A. J. Trythall, *'Boney' Fuller*, p. 204.
139 *Westfälische Landeszeitung*, 30 April 1939. Quoted in Trythall, pp. 205–7.
140 A copy of C. P. Allix's 'Explanation of the War Memorial Windows in St. Mary's Church Swaffham Prior' is held among the Allix papers at the County Records Office, Shire Hall, Cambridge.
141 Basil Liddell Hart, *The Tanks*, vol. 1, p. 391.
142 Liddell Hart's prophesies are remembered by Peter Cox, who for a long time ran the art college at Dartington. Recorded in an interview with the author broadcast in *Dollars, Conifers, Sperm Banks and the Edge of Time*, BBC Radio Three, 26 May 1996.
143 Major General J. F. C. Fuller, 'After the tank, what?', first printed in *Evening Standard*, 5 April 1944, and collected in *Thunderbolts* (London: Skeffington, 1946), p. 58.
144 See 'The Secret of Blitzkrieg', in *Thunderbolts*, pp. 100–1. Also 'Cambrai to El Alamein', in Major General J. F. C. Fuller, *Watchwords*, London: Skeffington, 1944, pp. 15–17.
145 Trythall, *'Boney' Fuller*, p. 211.
146 John Crossby, letter to Fuller (4 August 1940), Liddell Hart Centre for Military Archives, King's College, London, IV/7/5.
147 For this collection of 'Extracts' see Liddell Hart Centre for Military Archives, King's College, London, IV/7/15.+24.
148 Quotation from Arnold Lunn, *Come what May*, London: Eyre and Spottiswoode, 1940.

149 S. L. A. Marshall, *Blitzkrieg, the History, Strategy, Economics and the Challenge to America*, 1940.
150 Major General J. F. C. Fuller, 'Why keep two million men in khaki', *Evening Standard*, October 1919, 1940.
151 Major General J. F. C. Fuller, *Russia is Not Invincible*, London: Eyre and Spottiswoode, 1951, p. 7.
152 Major General J. F. C. Fuller, 'The Attack by Magic', *Occult Review*, vol. LXIX., no. 4 October 1942, pp. 123–4.
153 Major General J. F. C. Fuller, 'The City and Bomb', *Occult Review*, vol. LXXI, no. 1, January 1944, p.11.

CHAPTER 12. The Lancer and the Panzer

1 Terence Cuneo, *Tanks and How to Draw Them*, London and New York: Studio, 1943, p. 20.
2 J. F. Kennedy, *Why England Slept* (1940), London: Sidgwick & Jackson, 1962, p. 7.
3 Nicholas Bethell, *The War Hitler Won: September 1939*, London: Allen Lane, 1972.
4 *New York Times*, 12 September 1939.
5 Basil Liddell Hart, *The Tanks: Volume II, 1939–1945*, London: Cassell, 1959, p. 4.
6 Gaspar Tamas, quoted in David Selbourne, *Death of a Dark Hero*, London: Cape, 1990, p. 31.
7 Margaret Thatcher, *The Downing Street Years*, London: HarperCollins, 1993, p. 854.
8 Radek Sikorski, *The Polish House*, London: Weidenfeld & Nicolson, 1997.
9 Roger Boyes, 'The Laird of Chobielin', *Times Literary Supplement*, 26 September 1997.
10 Natasha Fairweather, 'Poles before swine', *Observer*, 15 September 1997.
11 General K. S. Rudnicki, DSO, *The Last of the War Horses*, London: Bachman & Turner, 1974. p. 38.
12 M. Kamil Dziewanowski, 'Last Great Charge of the Polish Cavalry', *Army* (published by the Association of the US Army), vol. 20, no. 4, April 1970.
13 Rudnicki, p. 15.
14 Flora Lewis, *The Polish Volcano: A Case History of Hope*, London, 1959, p. 215.
15 Rudnicki, pp. 62–3.

CHAPTER 13. Through Sixty Years of Mist

1 Colonel Mark Dillon, former reconnaissance officer with the British Tank Corps, telephone conversation 12/9/95.
2 Rudnicki, p. 65.
3 Tadeusz Jurga, *Obrona Polski 1939*, Warsaw: 1990, p. 630
4 War Diary of German Armed Forces Supreme Command Headquarters, D. Detwiler (ed.), *Vol 15. Part VII, The Eastern Theatre*, World War II German Military Studies, New York and London: Garland, p. 82.
5 Rudnicki, p. 45.
6 Steven Zaloga and Victor Madej, *The Polish Campaign 1939*, New York: Hippocrene, 1991, p. 110.
7 Ibid., p. 110.
8 See R. L. DiNardo, *Mechanized Juggernaut or Military Anachronism?*, New York & London: Greenwood Press, 1991.
9 Robert M. Kennedy, *The German Campaign in Poland (1939)*, Washington, Department of the Army Pamphlet 20–255, 1956, p. 130.
10 Cassandra, 'Chessboard for War', *Daily Mirror*, 1 September 1939.
11 *Daily Telegraph*, 6 September 1939.
12 This is a grossly inaccurate report. Zaloga and Madej claim that, while Poland's armoured force

was actually larger than that of the United States of America in September 1939, it consisted only of some 100 armoured cars and just under 900 tanks. Most of the latter were light two-man tankettes armed only with machine guns, but some were more effective modified versions of British Vickers E light tank. See *The Polish Campaign*, pp. 88–92.

13 'Rain Aids Poles', *Daily Mirror*, 13 September 1939.

14 *Daily Mirror*, 18 September 1939.

15 The phrase 'Cavalry v. Tanks' is used as a subheading in 'Time is helping Poland . . .' *Daily Mail*, 2 September 1998.

16 Commodore L. E. O. Charlton, 'Poland at Bay: Strategic problems that Nazi offensive raises', *Reynolds News*, 17 September 1939.

17 Giovanni Artieri, 'La battaglia di varsavia, duecentomila polacchi nella morsa delle colonne motorizzate Germaniche', *La Nazione*, 12 September 1939.

18 *Corriere della Sera*, 3 September 1939.

19 *Corriere della Sera*, 5 September 1939.

20 Alceo Valcini, 'Come é avvenuto il collasso militare Polacco', *Corriere della Sera*, 10 September 1939.

21 Indro Montanelli, 'Cavalli contro Autoblinde', *Corriere della Sera*, 12 September 1939.

22 *Völkischer Beobachter*, 4 September 1939, p.3.

23 *Deutsche Allgemeine Zeitung*, 16 September 1939.

24 *Deutsche Allgemeine Zeitung*, 13 September 1939, p. 3.

25 *Deutsche Allgemeine Zeitung*, 15 September 1939, p.3.

26 *Deutsche Allgemeine Zeitung*, 11 September, 1939, p. 4.

27 *Völkischer Beobachter*, 21 September 1939, p. 7.

28 *Der Führer*, 16 September 1939, p. 2.

29 *Die Wehrmacht: Herausgegeben Vom Oberkommando der Wehrmacht* (Berlin), no. 20, 27 September 1939.

30 *Die Wehrmacht*, no. 19, 13 September 1939.

31 K. S. Rudnicki, *The Last of the War Horses*, p. 36.

32 Dr Ernst Kredel, 'Die Schlacht in Polen',*Völkischer Beobachter*, September 15, 1939

33 G. Soldan, 'Der Feldzug in Westpolen', *Deutsche Allgemeine Zeitung*, 13 September 1939. I take this to be the same G. Soldan who published articles about mechanization in German military journals during the early years of von Seeckt's Reichswehr. See for example, George Soldan, 'Bewegungskrieg oder Stellungskrieg', *Militär Wochenblatt* 20 (1922). Soldan, whose study *Der Mensch und die Schlacht der Zukunft* was published in 1925, is cited alongside Seeckt by Tukhachevsky in his preface to Fuller's *Reformation of War*.

34 Anna Tyczynska, 'Poland's handsome cavalrymen ride again', *The European*, 2–8 January, 1997.

CHAPTER 14. Into Russia with Curzio Malaparte

1 Curzio Malaparte, *The Skin* (1949), London: Redman, 1952, p. 357.

2 Curzio Malaparte, *The Volga Rises in Europe*, London: Redman, 1957, p. 12.

3 See Marida Talamono, *Casa Malaparte*, Princeton Architectural Press, 1992.

4 Raffaele La Capria, 'On the Way to Villa Lysis / On the Way to Villa Malaparte', in Michael McDonough (ed.), *MALAPARTE: A House Like Me*, New York: Clarkson Potter, 1999, p. 87.

5 See John Keegan, *The First World War*, London: Hutchinson, 1998, pp. 370–6.

6 Alan Moorehead, *Eclipse*, London: Hamish Hamilton, 1945, p. 105.

7 Alexandra Riçhie, *Faust's Metropolis*, London: HarperCollins, 1998, p. 499.

8 Quoted from Peter G. Tsouras, 'Introduction' to Peter G. Tsouras (ed.), *Fighting in Hell*, New York: Ballantine, 1995, p. 41.

9 See Malaparte's 'Foreword' to *The Volga Rises in Europe* (op. cit.).

10 Excerpts from this report, dated 18 July 1940, are reprinted in Thomas L. Jentz, *Panzer Truppen: The Complete Guide to the Creation & Combat Employment of Germany's Tank Force*, vol. 1, 1933–1942, Atglen: Schiffer Military History, 1996, pp. 110–14.

11 These are the words of Oberst Eberbach, commander of Panzer-Regiment 35, quoted from Jentz, *Panzer Truppen*, vol. 1, p. 118.

12 Major General F. W. von Mellenthin, *Panzer Battles: A Study of the Employment of Armour in the Second World War* (1956), Ballantine, 1971, p. 16.

13 B. H. Liddell Hart (ed.), *The Rommel Papers*, London: Collins, 1953, p. 19.

14 Jentz, *Panzer Truppen*, vol. I, pp. 116–41.

15 Von Mellenthin, *Panzer Battles*, p. 28.

16 Liddell Hart, *The Rommel Papers*, p. 106.

17 Jentz, *PanzerTruppen*, vol. 1, p. 142.

18 Von Mellenthin, *Panzer Battles*, p. 38.

19 Jentz, *Panzer Truppen*, p.153.

20 Von Mellenthin, *Panzer Battles*, p. 44.

21 B. H. Liddell Hart *The Rommel Papers*, p. 197.

22 See Trevor J. Constable, 'They Called Him "Hobo"', first published in Constable's *Hidden Heroes* (London, 1971), and available in revised form on the Tankers Forum.

23 See Keith Douglas, *Alamein to Zem Zem*, London: Editions Poetry, 1946, pp. 97–9.

24 Basil Liddell Hart, *The Tanks*, vol. 2, p. 52.

25 Ibid., p. 54.

26 Hitler made this remark on 4 Jan 1942. See *Hitler's Table Talk 1941–44: His Private Conversations*, London: Weidenfeld and Nicolson, 1953, p. 175.

27 As Liddell Hart wrote, 'His family and staff have related how assiduously he then studied the theory of mobile armoured warfare, and particularly the books of its British advocates, as comparatively little had been written on the subject elsewhere'. Rommel's triumph in France 1940 is cited as proof of 'The quickness with which he grasped the idea'. Liddell Hart, *The Tanks*, vol. II, p. 65. The Blitzkrieg is really just a re-enactment of Lidell Hart's doctrine of the 'indirect approach' and 'expanding the torrent'.

28 *Rommel Papers*, p. 28.

29 Ibid., p. 131.

30 Ibid., p. 104.

31 See the experience report of the Werkstatt-Kompanie of Panzer-Regiment 5 in Jentz, *Panzer Truppen*, vol. I, p. 160.

32 *Rommel Papers*, p. 197.

33 Samuel Hynes, *The Soldier's Tale: Bearing Witness to Modern War*, London: Pimlico, 1998, p. 145.

34 Robin Nielland, *The Desert Rats: 7th Armoured Division 1940–45*, London: Orion, 1991, p. 73.

35 Liddell Hart, *The Tanks*, vol. II, p. 92.

36 *Hitler's Table Talk*, p. 172.

37 See John Erickson, *The Road to Stalingrad: Stalin's War with Germany*, vol. 1, London: Weidenfeld and Nicolson, p. 167.

38 See the chronology of Malaparte's life in M. McDonough, *MALAPARTE: A House Like Me*, New York: Clarkson Potter, 1999, p. 81.

39 Curzio Malaparte, *The Volga Rises in Europe*, p. 26.

40 Ibid., p. 27.

41 David M. Glantz and Jonathan House, *When Titans Clashed: How the Red Army Stopped Hitler*, Lawrence: University of Kansas Press, 1995, p. 53.

42 Curzio Malaparte, *The Volga Rises in Europe*, p. 47.

43 Ibid., p. 58.

44 John Steinbeck, *Once There Was a War*, London: Heinemann, 1959, p. 138.

45 The figures for towns and villages are quoted from Omer Bartov, *The Eastern Front, 1941–45: German Troops and the Barbarisation of Warfare*, London: Macmillan, 1985, p. 153.

46 K. Douglas, *Alamein to Zem Zem*, p. 9.

47 Malaparte attributes it to 'Leonev', but the Armoured Train he cites is surely that of Vsevelod Ivanov's play set in the Russian civil war. See Vsevelod Ivanov, *Armoured Train 14–69: a play in eight scenes*, translated by Gibson Cowan, London: Lawrence, 1933.

48 Curzio Malaparte, *The Volga Rises in Europe*, p. 76.

49 Ibid., p. 77.

50 Ibid., p. 89.

51 Ibid., p. 81.

52 Generaloberst Erhard Rauss, 'Russian Combat Methods in World War II', in Peter G. Tsouras (ed.), *Fighting in Hell*, New York: Ballantine, 1995, p. 41.

53 Curzio Malaparte, *The Volga Rises in Europe*, p. 88.

54 Ibid., p. 61.

55 Ibid., p. 117.

56 Ibid., p. 60.

57 Curzio Malaparte, *Kaputt* (1944), London: Redman, 1948, pp. 37–53.

58 Ibid., pp. 41–2.

59 Ibid., p. 43.

60 Ibid., pp. 51–2.

61 'In 1926, true to his taste for controversy, Malaparte single-handedly fabricated a polemic within the Italian literary world between two opposed cultural movements *strapaese,* which extolled nature and rural values and glorified an heroic and mythical past, and *stracittà,* which championed progress, technology and the urban environment by regularly contributing to the strapaese journal *Il Selvaggio* while founding the first stracittà journal *900*'. See Vittoria Di Palma, 'Preface' in M. Talamono, *Casa Malaparte*, p.18.

CHAPTER 15. The Tiger and the Mouse

1 Von Mellenthin, *Panzer Battles*, p. 185.

2 K. Douglas, *Alamein to Zem Zem*, London: Editions Poetry, 1946, p. 19.

3 Ibid., p. 7.

4 David Holbrook, *Flesh Wounds*, London: Methuen, 1966, p. 91.

5 Schöler's testimony is to be found in Johannes Steinhoff *et al.* (eds), *Voices from the Third Reich: An Oral History*, London: Grafton, 1995, p. 120.

6 Curzio Malaparte, *The Volga Rises in Europe*, p. 86.

7 D. M. Glantz and J. M. House, *When Titans Clashed*, p. 51.

8 Ibid., p. 74.

9 J. Erickson, *Road to Stalingrad*, p. 215.

10 See Generaloberst Erhard Rauss, 'Effects of Climate on Combat in Russia', in Peter G. Tsouras (ed.), *Fighting in Hell: The German Ordeal on the Eastern Front*, New York, Ivy, 1995, p. 199.

11 J. Erickson, *Road to Stalingrad*, p. 250.

12 See Rolf-Dieter Müller & Gerd. R. Uberschär, *Hitler's War in the East 1941–1945*, Oxford: Berghahn Books, 1997, p. 300.

13 For the 18th Panzer Division's plundering of civilian boots and furs in that winter, see Omer Bartov, *The Eastern Front, 1941–45, German Troops and the Barbarisation of Warfare*, London: Macmillan, 1985, p. 135.

14 These are the words of Major General Golubev of the 10th Army. See Erickson, *The Road to Stalingrad*, p. 130.

15 Ibid., pp. 78–9.

16 See Charles W. Sydnor, Jr., *Soldiers of Destruction: The SS Death's Head Division 1933–45*, Princeton: Princeton University Press, 1990, pp. 208–54.

17 This was General Gorodnyanskii, see Erickson, *Road to Stalingrad*, p. 347.

18 Ibid., p. 350.

19 Ibid., p. 406.

20 Ibid., p. 370.

21 K. Simonov, *Stalingrad Fights On* (trans: D. L. Fromberg), Moscow: Foreign Languages Publishing House, 1942, p.15.

22 Ibid., pp. 19–20.

23 Walter S. Dunn Jr., *Kursk: Hitler's Gamble, 1943*, London: Praeger, 1997, p. xi.

24 J. Erickson, *The Road to Berlin: Stalin's War with Germany*, vol. 2, London: Weidenfeld and Nicolson, 1983, p. 101.

25 Dunn, *Kursk*, p. xiii.

26 C. W. Sydnor, *Soldiers of Destruction*, p. 288.

27 Ibid., p. 289.

28 W. S. Dunn, Jr., *Kursk*, p. 154.

29 Glantz and House, *When Titans Clashed*. See also Glantz and House, *The Battle of Kursk*, University of Kansas, 1999, p. 167.

30 Quoted in von Mellenthin, *Panzer Battles*, p. 278.

31 W. S. Dunn, Jr., *Kursk*, p. 188.

32 V. Ivanov, *Armoured Train 14–69*, p. 45.

33 Rauss, 'Russian Combat Methods in World War II', *Fighting in Hell*, p. 44–5.

34 Von Mellenthin, *Panzer Battles*, pp. 208–9.

35 Stephen Fritz, *Frontsoldaten: The German Soldier in World War II*, University of Kentucky Press, 1995, p. 33.

36 Rauss, 'Russian Combat Methods in World War II', *Fighting in Hell*, p. 87.

37 Von Mellenthin records that this happened to the tanks of General Heim, commander of the 13th Panzer Division, whom Hitler promptly sacked for 'indecision'. See *Panzer Battles*, p. 205.

38 C. W. Sydnor, *Soldiers of Destruction*, p. 167.

39 Rauss, *Russian Combat Methods*, p. 33.

40 This overall figure, like the individual examples that follow, is quoted from John Erickson, 'Soviet Women at War', J. and C. Garrard (eds.), *World War 2 and the Soviet People*, London: Macmillan, 1993, pp. 50–76.

41 See the accounts in Katharine Hodgson, 'The Other Veterans: Soviet Women's Poetry of World War 2', in J. and C. Garrard (eds,) *World War 2 and the Soviet People*, p. 93.

42 This was the experience of Nina Vishnevskaia, as quoted in Reina Pennington, 'Women in combat in the Red Army', in Alexander Calder (ed.), *Wars*, London: Penguin, pp. 350–1.

43 Stephen Fritz, *Frontsoldaten*, p. 38.

44 Antony Beevor, *Stalingrad*, London: Viking, 1998, p. 36. A photograph of fallen Russian soldiers used this way is reprinted in J. and C. Garrard (eds), *World War 2 and the Soviet People*, New York, St Martin's Press, opposite p. 130.

45 Guy Sajer, *The Forgotten Soldier* (1971), London: Orion, 1973, pp. 227 and 232.

46 Malaparte, *The Volga Rises in Europe*, p. 42.

47 Fritz, *Frontsoldaten*, p. 48.

48 Guy Sajer, *The Forgotten Soldier*, pp. 206–7.

49 C. W. Sydnor, Jr., *Soldiers of Destruction: The SS Death's Head Division, 1933–45*, Princeton: Princeton University Press, 1990, p. 192.

50 This anonymous *landser*'s account is quoted from Lucas's *War on the Eastern Front* in Stephen G. Fritz, *Frontsoldaten*, p. 41.

51 Ibid., p. 44.

52 I owe this information to Antony Beevor, who categorizes the letters among the 'fictional' sources in his *Stalingrad* on the grounds that their authenticity is 'very much in doubt' (p. 485). For Heinz Schröter's account, see his *Stalingrad*, pp. 192–3.

53 Anthony Powell (tr.), *Last Letters from Stalingrad*, London: Methuen, 1956, p. 10.

54 Anonymous soldier, quoted from Schneider and Gullans, *Last Letters*, in Fritz, *Frontsoldaten*, p. 89.

55 Anthony Powell (tr.), *Last Letters from Stalingrad*, pp. 61–2.

56 D. Holbrook, *Flesh Wounds*, pp. 186–7 and 130–1.

57 David Holbrook, conversation with author 18/7/98.

58 Jentz, *Panzer Truppen*, II, p. 219.

59 Quoted from a report dated 25 November 1944, by Hauptmann Fromme, commander of schwere Panzer-Abteilung 503. See Jentz, *Panzer Truppen*, II, p. 220.

60 Report of 1. Abteilung/Panzer-Regiment 24, Jentz, *Panzer Truppen*, II, p. 229.

61 Ibid., p. 230.

62 Rauss, 'Russian Combat Methods in World War II', *Fighting in Hell*, p. 59.

63 Von Mellenthin, *Panzer Battles* , p. 383.

64 Quoted from Peter Conrad, *Modern Times, Modern Places*, London: Thames and Hudson, 1998, p. 481. See also Albert Speer, *Spandau: The Secret Diaries*, London: Collins, 1976, p. 189.

65 A. Speer, *Spandau: The Secret Diaries*, p. 188.

66 Ibid., pp. 38–9.

67 Ibid., p. 39.

68 H. R. Trevor-Roper, *The Mind of Adolf Hitler*, p. xviii.

69 *Hitler's Table Talk 1941–44: His Private Conversations*, London: Weidenfeld and Nicolson, 1953, p. 633.

70 Ibid., p. 634.

CHAPTER 16. Tributes: A Flag for Europe and the True Birth of Punk

1 Michael McDonough, *MALAPARTE: House Like Me*, p. 27.

2 Curzio Malaparte, *The Skin*, London: Redman, 1952, pp. 299–336.

3 Ibid., p. 329.

4 J. Willett and Ralph Manheim, *Bertolt Brecht: Poems, Part Three 1938–1956*, London: Eyre Methuen, 1976, pp.352–3.

5 Hermann Glaser, *The Cultural Roots of National Socialism*, London: Croom Helm, 1978, p. 138.

6 Quoted in Wilhelm Reich, *The Mass Psychology of Fascism* (1946), New York: Pocket Books, 1970, p. 315.

7 Ibid., pp. 326–7.

8 Ibid., p. 326.

CHAPTER 17. The Steeling of Zion

1 First published in the *Hebrew Union College Monthly*, 29, 1 November 1941, A. M. Klein's 'Ballad of the Days of the Messiah' is here quoted from *The Collected Poems of A. M. Klein*, Toronto: McGraw-Hill Ryerson Ltd, 1974, p. 243.

2 Zailig Pollock, *A. M. Klein: The Story of the Poet*, Toronto: University of Toronto, 1994, p. 110.

3 Miriam Waddington, *A. M. Klein*, Toronto: Copp Clark, 1970, p. 70.

4 A. M. Klein, 'War: the Evolution of a Menagerie' (10 February 1939), collected in M. W. Steinberg and Usher Caplon (eds) *Beyond Sambation: Selected Essays and Editorials, 1928–1955*, University of Toronto Press, 1982, pp. 44–5.

5 A. M. Klein, 'The Shadows Move' (10 May 1940), in *Beyond Sambation*, pp. 71–2. In May 1944,

Klein would also comment on the Polish court-martial in England of thirty Jewish 'deserters', who had refused to 'bear arms under officers and among troops who shared and uttered the anti-semitic notions of the very enemy whom they were supposed to fight'. See 'The Three-Fold Exile', in *Beyond Sambation*, p. 214.

6 S. Spiro, *Tapestry for Designs*, Vancouver: University of British Columbia, 1984, p. 104. On Ehrenkranz, see A. Z. Idelsohn, *Jewish Music*, New York: Schocken Books, 1956, pp. 441–3.

7 A. M. Klein, 'Messiah in Our Days' (January 1930) in *Beyond Sambation*, pp. 11–12.

8 A. M. Klein, 'The Shadows Move' (10 May 1940), *Beyond Sambation*, pp. 71–2.

9 A. M. Klein, 'The Golems of Prague', *Canadian Jewish Chronicle*, 28 November 1952. Collected in *Beyond Sambation*, pp. 423–5.

10 A. M. Klein, *Beyond Sambation*, p. 345.

11 Shabtai Teveth, *The Tanks of Tammuz*, London: Weidenfeld & Nicolson, 1968, p. 193.

12 Yaron Ezrahi, *Rubber Bullets: Power and Conscience in Modern Israel*, New York: Farrar, Straus and Giroux, 1997, p. 175.

13 Klein, *Beyond Sambation*, p. 363.

14 Ibid., p. 353.

15 A. M. Klein, *The Second Scroll* (1951), Toronto: McClelland and Stewart, 1994, p. 73.

16 A. M. Klein, 'The Dangers of Success' (18 March 1949), *Beyond Sambation*, pp. 333–5.

17 Avraham Shapira (ed.), *The Seventh Day: Soldiers Talk about the Six-Day War*, London: Deutsch, 1970, p. 1.

18 Ezrahi, *Rubber Bullets*, p. 5.

19 Shapira, *The Seventh Day*, p. 135–6. These words are spoken in a discussion of the difficulty of living in the knowledge that the problem is irreconcilable, and can only lead to one war after another. Norman G. Finkelstein quotes them, in this much truncated form, as proof that Israelis have indulged in blaming the victim, just as the Nazis used to do with the Jews. See his *Image and Reality of the Israel-Palestine Conflict*, London: Verso, 1995, p. 116.

20 Israel Tal, 'Preface', to Avigdor Kahalani, *The Heights of Courage: A Tank Leader's War on the Golan*, Westport: Greenwood Press, 1984, p. xiii.

21 A. M. Klein, *Beyond Sambation*, p. 76.

22 Vladimir Jabotinsky, *Samson the Nazarite*, London: Secker, 1930, pp. 24 and 297–8.

23 Basil Henriques, *The Indiscretions of a Warden*, London: Methuen, 1937, pp. 118–19.

24 David Eshel, *Chariots of the Desert: The Story of the Israeli Armoured Corps*, London: Brassey, 1989, p. 2.

25 Ibid., p. 5.

26 Shabtai Teveth, *The Tanks of Tammuz*, pp. 41–2.

27 Eshel, *Chariots of the Desert*, pp. 25–6.

28 Eric Hammel, *Six Days in June: How Israel Won the 1967 Arab-Israeli War*, New York: Scribner, 1992, p. 24.

29 Eshel, *Chariots of the Desert*, p. 26.

30 Benny Morris, *Israel's Border Wars, 1949–56: Arab Infiltration, Israeli Retaliation and the Countdown to the Suez War*, Oxford: Clarendon, p. 381.

31 Eshel, *Chariots of the Desert*, p. 36.

32 Major General Moshe Dayan, *The Diary of the Sinai Campaign*, Jerusalem: Steimatzky, 1966, p. 92.

33 See Benny Morris, *Righteous Victims: A History of the Zionist-Arab Conflict 1881–1999*, London: John Murray, 1999, pp. 289–92.

34 Eshel, *Chariots of the Desert*, p. 45.

35 Dayan, *Diary of the Sinai Campaign*, p. 95.

36 Eshel, *Chariots of the Desert*, p. 19.

37 See Yigael Yadin, *Masada: Herod's Fortress and the Zealot's Last Stand*, London: Weidenfeld

and Nicolson, 1966. Also Yigael Yadin, *Hazor: The Rediscovery of a Great Citadel of the Bible*, London: Weidenfeld and Nicolson, 1975.

38 Insight Team of the *Sunday Times*, *Insight on the Middle East War*, London: Deutsch, 1974, p. 126.

39 See Meron Benvenisti, *Sacred Landscape: The Buried History of the Holy Land since 1948*, University of California Press, 2000, p. 128.

40 Morris, *Israel's Border Wars 1949–1956*, p. 95.

41 Teveth, *Tanks of Tammuz*, p. 60.

42 Ibid., p. 63.

43 Ibid., p. 70.

CHAPTER 18. Jewish Blitzkrieg?

1 Hammel, *Six Days in June*, p. 144.

2 Benny Morris, *Righteous Victims*, p. 313.

3 Israel Tal described this at a conference reported in Abraham Rabinovitch, 'The War Nobody Wanted', *Jerusalem Post*, 15 June 1997.

4 Ibid., p. 173.

5 Randolph S. and Winston S. Churchill, *The Six Day War*, London: Heinemann, 1967, pp. 171.

6 Ibid., p. 177.

7 Colin Legum used this phrase in the *Observer*. Quoted in R. S. and W. S. Churchill, *The Six Day War*, p. 195.

8 Avigdor Kahalani, *The Heights of Courage*, p. 55.

9 Amos Oz, 'Late Love', in *Unto Death* (1971), London: Vintage, 1992, pp. 93–175.

10 Ibid., p. 162.

11 R. S. and W. S. Churchill, *The Six Day War*, p. 189.

12 Ibid., pp. 167–8.

13 Teveth, *The Tanks of Tammuz*, p. 267.

14 Ibid., p. 246.

15 See Peter Novick, *The Holocaust in American Life*, London: Bloomsbury, 2000. Also Norman Finkelstein's review 'How the Arab-Israeli War of 1967 gave birth to a memorial industry', *London Review of Books*, 6 January, 2000, pp. 33–6.

16 B. H. Liddell Hart, 'Strategy of a War', *Encounter*, February 1968, pp. 16–20. In staking his claim, Liddell Hart also mentions the 'lengthy discussions, some on the map', he had held with Generals Laskov and Rabin, while visiting Israel in 1960.

17 Eshel, *Chariots of the Desert*, pp. 88–9.

18 Interview with Major General Avraham Adan in David A. Korn, *Stalemate: The War of Attrition and Great Power Diplomacy in the Middle East 1967–1970*, p. 104.

19 Interview with Pinchas Kenan, *Hadashot*, 9 April 1990. Quoted in Korn, p. 207.

20 Israel Tal, Preface in Avigdor Kahalani, *The Heights of Courage*, p. xi.

21 See *Insight on the Middle East War*, p. 63.

22 Ibid., p. 77.

23 Ibid., p. 63.

24 Morris, *Righteous Victims*, p. 404.

25 Ibid., p. 495.

26 Kahalani, *The Heights of Courage*, p. 31.

27 Ibid., pp. 84 and 70.

28 Ibid., p. 98.

29 Ibid., p. 120.

30 Eshel, *Chariots of the Desert*, p. 105.

31 *Insight on the Middle East War*, p. 76.

32 Morris, *Righteous Victims*, p. 406.

33 Ibid., p. 406.

34 Lt. General Saad el Shazly, *The Crossing of the Suez*, San Francisco: American Mideast Research, 1980, p. 101.

35 Ibid., p. 226.

36 Ibid., p. 53.

37 Morris, *Righteous Victims*, p. 417.

38 Ibid., p. 419.

39 *Insight on the Middle East War*, p. 107.

40 Ibid., p. 112.

41 Shazly, *The Crossing of the Suez*, p. 237.

42 Ibid., p.262.

43 A. M. Klein, *The Second Scroll*, p. 21.

44 In 1951, Klein wrote 'Kindness and humanitarianism are commendable qualities; but, here, let the facts be put straight. Not a single Palestinian Arab was ever expelled from the country by Jews! It was to be, so thought the refugees, no more than a strategic withdrawal from the area of battle, maintained until such a time as the invading forces drove the Israelis into the sea.' 'The Arab Refugees', *Beyond Sambation*, p. 409. For the true story, see Benvenisti, *Sacred Landscape*, pp. 108–92.

45 A. M. Klein 'The Golem', *Collected Poems*, p. 284.

46 A. M. Klein, 1952 editorial, quoted in R. F. Brenner, *A. M. Klein, the Father of Canadian Jewish Literature: Essays in the Poetics of Humanistic Passion*, Lewiston: Edwin Mellon Press, 1990, p. 49. See also Klein's *Beyond Sambation*, p. 424.

47 A. M. Klein, 'Tetragrammaton', in 'Talisman in Seven Shreds'. *Collected Poems*, p. 134.

48 Yaron Ezrahi, *Rubber Bullets*, p. 176.

49 Ibid., p. 193.

50 Ibid., p. 195.

51 Ibid., p. 126.

52 See Emanuel Litvinoff, *Falls the Shadow*, London: Michael Joseph, 1983.

53 Yaron Ezrahi, 'Father's Milk: Father's Tales that Feed and Kill', *Rubber Bullets*, pp. 117–42.

54 Ezrahi, *Rubber Bullets*, p. 141.

55 Ibid., pp. 230–1.

56 Morris, *Righteous Victims*, p. 453.

57 Ahmed Jadallah's picture was displayed on the Islamic Human Rights Commission's website (www.ihrc.org) and used on leaflets too. For a variant, see 'Anti-Israel demo targets M&S', *Independent*, 10 December, 2000, p. 8. A few weeks later, Jadallah's photograph would also appear on the cover of a fiercely anti-Israeli issue of the American Trotskyist publication, *The Internationalist*, No 9, January–February 2001.

CHAPTER 19. Conversion: Pink Tank and Poliscar

1 Dating from 1983, 'Tough Limo' was installed at the Anderson Gallery, Virginia Commonwealth University, Richmond. It is pictured in John G. Hanhardt (ed.), *Francesc Torres: La Cabeza Del Dragón*, Museo Nacional Centre de Arte Reina Sofia, 1991, pp. 166–9.

2 John G. Hanhardt (ed.), *Francesc Torres: The Head of the Dragon* (anthology), Ministerio de Cultura, Museo Nacional Centro de Arte Reina Sofia, 1991, p. 51.

3 Ibid., p. 61.

4 Michael Kustow, *Tank*, London: Jonathan Cape, 1975, pp. 21–2.

5 Ibid., p. 203.

6   See Nan Rosenthal, *Anselm Kiefer, Works on Paper in the Metropolitan Museum of Modern Art*, New York: Metropolitan Museum of Art, 1998, pp. 92–3.

7   Yves Abrioux, *Ian Hamilton Finlay: A Visual Primer*, Edinburgh: Reaktion Books, 1985.

8   Richard Ogorkiewicz, 'The Present and Future of Armour', Institute for Security Studies (Cape Town), *Monograph No. 2: Mailed Fist*, March 1996, Cape Town.

9   Mary Kaldor, *The Imaginary War: Understanding the East-West Conflict*, Oxford: Blackwell, 1990.

10 Vitaly Churkin, quoted in Matt Welch, 'The Politics of Pink: A Memorial Defaced, Controversy Hatched', *Prognosis* (Prague), issue 3, vol. 1, June 1991, p. 3.

11 See Zdenek Mlynár, *Night Frost in Prague: The End of Humane Socialism*, London: Hurst, 1980, p. 77.

12 Václav Havel's address is quoted from 'The Return of the Pink Tank', *Prognosis*, issue 3, vol. 1, June 1991, p. 8.

13 Matthew J. Reisz, 'Back to the future in Bratislava', *Independent on Sunday*, 17 March 1991.

14 Vera Krincvajová, 'The Last Great Tank Battle', *SL International* (Prague), July 1991, p. 11.

15 'Slovaks rough up "Judas" Havel', *Guardian*, 15 March 1991.

16 Yahia Said, 'Defence conversion: regional and international aspects: a case study of Martin, Slovakia' in M. Kaldor, U. Albrecht, G. Schméder (eds.), *Restructuring the Global Military Sector: Vol II, The End of Military Fordism*, London & Washington: Pinter, 1998, pp. 264–85.

17 See 'Breaking a Contract for 300 T-72s', *Intelligence Newsletter*, no. 224, 15/9/93.

18 Walter Wüllenweber, 'Kein Zeremoniell für der Panzersprenger', *Berliner Zeitung*, February 15/16, 1992, p. 33.

19 Boris Yeltsin, *The View from the Kremlin*, London: HarperCollins, 1994, p. 35.

20 Vanora Bennett, *Crying Wolf: The Return of War to Chechnya*, London: Picador, 1998, p. 22.

21 Elizabeth Hess, 'Secret (Homeless) Agent Man', *The Village Voice*, 24 September 1991.

22 Wodiczko's concept of nomadism and of the war machine that does not have war as its purpose was derived partly from Gilles Deleuze and Félix Guattari, *Mille Plateaux*, Paris: Les Éditions de Minuit, 1980.

23 For this argument about gentrification and Wodiczko's relation to it see Rosalyn Deutsche, 'Uneven Development: Public Art in New York City', *October*, No. 47, Winter 1988, pp. 3–58. Also Rosalyn Deutsche, 'Architecture of the Evicted,' in *Krzysztof Wodiczko, New York City Tableaux*, New York: Exit Art, pp. 28–37. See also Sharon Zukin's books, *Loft Living: Culture and Capital in Urban Change*, Johns Hopkins University Press, 1988 and *Landscapes of Power: From Detroit to Disney World*, University of California Press, 1991.

24 For an account of the Philadelphia trials see Julie Courtney, 'The Homeless Vehicle Project: Philadelphia', in *Krzysztof Wodiczko, New York City Tableaux*, New York: Exit Art, 1989, pp. 40–1.

25 Paul Virilio, *Vitesse et politique*, Paris: Edition Galilée, 1977. See also *Pure War*, New York: Semiotext(e), 1983.

26 Miguel Garcilazo, 'Tompkins II: Riot cops & Shantytown', *New York Post*, 16 October 1991.

27 Thomas Morgan, 'New York City Bulldozes Squatters' Shantytowns', *New York Times*, 16 October 1991.

28 William Bratton, *Turnaround: How America's Top Cop Reversed the Crime Epidemic*, as excerpted in the *Sunday Times*, News Review, 22 March 1998, p. 1.

29 Friedrich Kittler, 'Carpets of Bombs', *Parkett*, 24, 1990, p. 108.

30 'Resurrection for Sodomites', *Guardian*, 26 February 1998.

31 Mehmet Ali Birand, *Shirts of Steel: An Anatomy of the Turkish Armed Forces*, London and New York: I. B. Tauris, 1991, p. 118.

CHAPTER 20. Fort Knox: Cybertanks and the Army After Next

1 See Kevin Sessums, 'Good Golly, Miss Dolly!', *Vanity Fair*, June 1991. Cover picture and other photographs by Annie Liebovitz.

2 Julia Loughran and Marcy Stahl, 'New Technology Brings 3D Cyberspace to Defense Applications', *Defense Daily* (http://www.defensedaily.com/reports/vrml.htm).

3 On the National Training Center and its establishment after the Vietnam War, see Daniel P. Bolger, *Dragons at War: 2–34th Infantry in the Mojave*, Novato: Presidio Press, 1986, pp. 1–14.

4 Bruce Sterling, 'War is Virtual Hell', *Wired*, 1, 1, 1993. For the military's use of this article, see James Der Derian's report on his visit to the National Training Center, 'Cyber-Deterrence', *Wired*, 1 September 1994.

5 See, for example, Nick Lewer, 'Non-Lethal Weapons', *Medicine and War*, vol. 11, 1995, pp. 78–90.

6 Alvin and Heidi Toffler, *War and Anti-War: Survival at the Dawn of the 21st Century*, New York: Little, Brown and Company, 1993. See also the Tofflers' Preface to John Arquilla and David Ronfeldt (eds), *In Athene's Camp: Preparing for Conflict in the Information Age*, Rand Corporation, 1997. For a critical assessment of the Tofflers' wave theory, see R. I. Dinardo and Daniel J. Hughes, 'Some Cautionary Thoughts on Information Warfare', *Airpower Journal*, 9 (Winter 1995), pp. 69–79.

7 Michael Hickey, *The Korean War: The West Confronts Communism 1950–1953*, London: John Murray, 1999, p. 50.

8 Patrick J. Sloyan, 'Buried Alive: US Troops Used Plows to Kill Thousands in Gulf War Trenches', *Newsday*, 12 September 1991.

9 Maggart's testimony is quoted from the Mythworks website (www.mythworks.net). Pamela Jaye Smith's contributions to the AWWG are described with the help of tapes and notes from her talks forwarded to the author.

10 Manuel De Landa, *War in the Age of Intelligent Machines*, New York: Zone Books, 1991, p. 74.

11 Uwe Johnson, *Anniversaries II: From the Life of Gesine Cresspahl*, New York: Harcourt Brace Jovanovich, 1987, p. 154

12 Stanley C. Crist, 'The M1A2 Abrams: The Last Main Battle Tank?', *Armor*, July–August 1997, pp. 14–16.

13 Jean Baudrillard, *The Gulf War Did Not Take Place*, Sydney: Power Publications, 1995, p. 34.

14 Quoted from Jonathan Aitken's memoirs, *Pride and Perjury*, in the *Sunday Times News Review*, 19 March 2000, p. 2.

15 See Maj. Gen. Jeanne Holm, USAF (Ret.), *Women in the Military: An Unfinished Revolution*, Novato: Presidio Press, 1993.

16 See Martin Walker, 'Suicide "caused by snotty Clintonoids" ', *Guardian*, 22 May 1996, p. 10.

17 William S. Lind, *Maneuver Warfare Handbook*, Boulder, Westview, 1985.

18 Don Delillo, *Mao II*, London: Vintage, 1992, p. 239.

19 Major Donald E. Vandergriff, 'Without the Proper Culture: Why Our Army Cannot Practice Maneuver Warfare', *Armor*, January–February 1998, pp. 20–4.

20 William S. Lind, quoted from Thomas E. Ricks, 'The Widening Gap between the Military and Society', *Atlantic Monthly*, July 1997.

21 Major General Peter Gilchrist's remark, made at the Seventh European Armoured Fighting Vehicle Symposium, is reported in *Jane's International Defence Digest*, April 2001, p. 3.

22 B. Bender and A. Koch, 'US Army to accelerate Future Combat Systems', *Jane's Defence Weekly*, 26 January, 2000, p. 4. For a view of possible Future Combat System technologies from inside the defense company Western Design Howden, see Asher H. Sharoni and Lawrence D. Bacon, 'The Future Combat System', Parts 1–3, *Armor*, July–August 1997, pp. 7–13; September–October 1997, pp. 29–33; January–February 1998, pp. 37–42.

23 Martin Libicki, *The Mesh and the Net: Speculations on Armed Conflict in a Time of Free Silicon*,

National Defense University, March 1994. (www.ndu.edu/ndu/inss/macnair/macnair28/m028copy.html)

24 Lonnie D. Henley, 'The RMA after the Next', *Parameters*, Winter 1999–2000, pp. 46–57.

25 See Jack Hitt, 'The Hidden Life of SUVs', *Mother Jones*, July/August 1999.

Acknowledgements

While writing this book, I developed a persistent desire to escape into a world that was innocent of heavy terrestial machinery. One day, I typed the word 'gite' into a search engine, and found a picture of an isolated stone farm building perched above woods in a high mountain meadow that might have been stolen from *The Sound of Music*. This dreamy pre-modern clearing is reached by driving to Lourdes and then heading into the Pyrenees for the town of Cauterets, a now bankrupt nineteenth-century spa town in a deep valley, where visitors still take the waters and suck locally produced aromatic sweets to counteract the sulphurous taste. From there an unsurfaced dirt road rises up the side of a steep and wooded valley. The prospect of a terrible fall looms at every hairpin bend but motorized vehicles don't have to be abandoned until the track shrinks to a narrow footpath snaking on up through the trees. After twenty minutes or so, the climber is delivered onto a gently sloping hay meadow with abundant alpine flowers and exhilarating views of distant snow-covered peaks. By now, the presence of metal is reduced to a few easily negotiated strands of wire fence and a sporadic clanking of cowbells attached to senior members of a scattered fudge-coloured herd.

The grassy slope known as Espoune is only an interval between soaring peaks above and a vertiginous ravine that plunges down from its lower edge. Yet near this wooded drop are three summer farms, traditional buildings that originally combined a hayloft with housing for animals as well as a cowman or shepherd. One is still used by a morose farmer but the others belong to members of the Meillon family and turn out to be relics of a considerable Pyrenean dynasty. The first great Meillon built and ran the Grand Hôtel d'Angleterre in Cauterets, an opulent establishment that had its heyday in the 1900s, when Edward VII and Sarah Bernhardt were among its celebrated guests. His son, Alphonse Meillon, is remembered as a great 'Pyreneist', a self-taught historian, naturalist and surveyor who made the first detailed maps of the peaks and valleys around Cauterets. By the end of the twentieth century that extravagant age had quite shrunk away, and the

Meillons were left with these rude places of candle light, woodsmoke and memory.

Among the many striking features of Espoune's sublimely disconcerting geography was a large boulder lying in a damp stretch of meadow a few yards from a dashing stream. Having spent some time reading on this erratic sun-warmed rock, I asked Jacques Meillon to tell me about it. Sizing it up at a glance, he declared it to be a slab of hardened and silicified sandstone. It might conceivably have been dragged to its present location by a glacier in some distant age, but he thought it far more likely to have tumbled down the steep slopes of 'Le Tuque de la Courbe', which rose to a weirdly twisted and disintegrated peak high above. After studying this boulder, on which lichen had superimposed yellow and green explosions and also scratchy creeping barrages of brown and grey, he recalled that for several generations the Meillon children had known it as the tank and incorporated it into their improvised war games.

My thanks, then, to Jacques Meillon, for providing me with an appropriate place to disengage from the story of the tank – a spectral twentieth-century machine, which will not really have gone down into history until that free-standing boulder is once again just a piece of silicified limestone on a mountainside.

I first tried to come to terms with the symbolic dimensions of the tank while writing *The Village that Died for England*, an account of the eighty-year feud that started when, under the cover of the First World War, a supposedly 'temporary' tank gunnery range was set up in the depths of Thomas Hardy's Wessex. If this book retains any connection with Dorset, that is primarily thanks to the existence of the Royal Armoured Corps' Tank Museum at Bovington, where I am much indebted to David Fletcher. As Keeper of the Archive and Reference Library at that unlikely tourist attraction, he has been generous with his assistance over many years now.

If one could dedicate a book about tanks to anybody, this one would be for Robin Blaser, who introduced me to the works of A. M. Klein and, years ago in Vancouver, helped me to appreciate that the poetics of the twentieth century extended far beyond the literary page.

I owe my awareness of the war memorial windows at St Mary's, Swaffham Prior, and elsewhere to Peter Cormack of the William Morris Gallery in East London. I am also indebted to Neil Trevithik and Sarah Bowen, with whom I made a radio programme about Swaffham Prior's windows, broadcast as 'Through a Glass Darkly' in BBC Radio 4's *Document* series on 14 September 1995.

My understanding of post-war Polish experience was generously informed by Neal Ascherson, Malgosia Pioro and Andrzej Krauze, and I would have got nowhere in Poland without the help of Tadeusz Pioro, Lucyna Golebiowska, Emma Harris, Maria Kwiatkowska and Ania Kowalcyck. Similarly, Mark Urban pointed me in useful directions in Israel, and was tolerant of my initial ignorance.

I was greatly assisted by Tobias Döring, who reviewed and translated the relevant German newspaper coverage of September 1939, and also by Marina Nordera, who searched the Italian press of the same month. Malgosia Pioro, Lore Windemuth and Roberta Cremoncini have assisted me with translations from Polish, German and Italian. For a translation from Yiddish, I am grateful to Emanuel Litvinoff and an anonymous volunteer at The Wiener Library in London.

I am indebted to Jürgen Kamm, Jürgen Schlaeger, Peter Drexler and also Manfred Pfister of the Free University in Berlin, who invited me to give lectures on some of the book's themes in Dresden, Berlin and Potsdam. Also to Benoit Junod, who invited me to lecture in Turkey on behalf of Sanart.

I am greatly obliged to David Hayes and Chris Mitchell, who read a draft of the manuscript and made many improving suggestions. Others who have helped, often over particular points in the text, are Robert Bud, David Edgerton, David Edgar, Veronica Horwell, Heinze Kosok, Neil Belton, Jürgen Kamm, Indira Ghose, Claire Pajaczkowska, John Brewer, Ian Patterson, Helen Bettinson, Kurt Ganzl, Iain Sinclair, Grahame Thompson, John Goudie, Paul Gilroy, Alison Grubb, John Allison, Mick Dillon, Juraj and Tania Mihalik, David A. Mellor, Edna Longley, Tony Gould, Angela Weight, Christopher Martin, David Hare, James Cornford, Orlando Figes, Antony Beevor, Murray Grigor, Andrew Barry and Brian Edwards.

Some of the research behind this book would have been impossible without the involvement of newspapers and magazines. I am grateful to Rosie Boycott, who commissioned me to visit the US Army Armor Center at Fort Knox for the British edition of *Esquire*. The visit took place in April 1996, and the article appeared as 'Future Wars' in *Esquire*, September 1996. I owe thanks to the *Guardian*, for which I explored both Prague's pink tank (25

July 1991) and the imagery of Tiananmen Square (4 June 1992); and also to be *Independent on Sunday Review*, which published my account of Krzysztof Wodiczko's Poliscar, (12 January, 1992). Other versions appeared as 'The Poliscar' in Z. Aktüre and Benoit Junod (eds), *Identity, Marginality, Space*, Ankara, 1992, pp. 54–60; 'The Poliscar: not a tank but a war machine for people without apartments', in Manuel J. Borja-Villel (ed.), *Krzysztof Wodiczko; Instruments, Projeccions, Vehicles*, Barcelona: Fundació Antoni Tàpies, 1992, pp. 259–85. Thanks also to Ian Jack, who published my first account of the British development of the tank in the First World War, 'Here come the Tanks', *Granta* 53, Spring 1996, pp. 123–39.

I am grateful to the Authors' Foundation for an award and also to the British Council for various travel grants that have enabled me to lecture and attend conferences in Germany, Poland and Turkey. In one case, I got off the plane to be met by representatives who seemed to be expecting a different 'Patrick Wright' who was, I believe, head of the British Civil Service under Margaret Thatcher. However, everyone behaved well as the realization dawned, and the dinner and hotel were both splendid.

PW

Fulbourn, July 2000
www.patrickwright.co.uk

Index

Malaparte, Curzio 270–3, 308; in First World
War 271–2; on German invasion of Russia
272–3, 280–6, 287, 288, 290, 299, 309–11;
house 271, 307, 308; on invasion of Poland
264, 270; novels 270, 272, 284–6, 308–12
male and female tanks 35
Malecki, Stanislaw 258
Malins, Geoffrey 38–9
Mamoun, General 363
Manchester: tank bank in 86, 87, 89
Manchester Guardian 89
Manisser, Natwey 199
manoeuvre warfare 440
Manstein, Field Marshal Eric von 274, 292,
293, 295
Mao Zedong 11, 12, 16
Marconi, Guglielmo 211
Marcos, Ferdinand 8–9
Marinetti, Filippo 57, 58
Mark I tank 28–9, 30, 31; first deployment
35–7, 38–53
Mark II Matilda infantry tank 279
Mark IV tank 74, 102, 122, 176
Mark V tank 109
Marshall, S. L. A. 227
Martel, Gifford Le Q. 65, 73, 78, 206–7, 208
Masada 339
Mastalerz, Kazimierz 257, 258, 259
Matejko, Jan 259, 265
Matejko, Thèo 259, 265–6
Mathers, Samuel Liddell 163, 165
Matthew-Lannowe, G. B. 62, 68
Maus tank 306–7
mechanization 25, 185–6, 427; in France 187–90;
Fuller's ideas on 142–54, 173–4; German
invasion of Russia and 282; Germany 217–25;
Italy 208, 209–13; in Russia 196–208; Spanish
Civil War 213–17; in USA 190–6
Meciar, Vladimir 389
media *see* film; journalism; television
Medium D tank 134–5, 136, 142, 324
Meir, Golda 364, 368, 369
Mellenthin, F. W. von 275, 287, 295, 296
memorials and monuments: British 122–4,
178–9; East Germany 390; Friends of War
Memorials 18; Israel 341; Poland 241, 242–3,
392; in Prague 379–90; Russian 304; stained
glass 113–17, 179; Swaffham Prior church
113–14, 115–17, 179, 225; USA 430
Merkava tank 17, 322–30, 352, 364, 366, 368,
369, 371, 372
Merson, Billy 86, 107
Merthyr: tank bank in 99, 100
Messines Ridge 75
Metropolitan Carriage, Wagon and Finance
Co 34, 102

Michalik, Alexandra 249–51
Middlesbrough: tank bank in 90
Mielert, Harry 299
Mikhalkov, Nikita 207
Miles, C. G. 279
Militär Wochenblatt 219, 221
Military Review 440
military service: Israel 356; Poland 245, 247;
Russia 204; United Kingdom 82, 98
Milne, A. A. 107
Milne, George 143, 175
mines 425; mine-dogs 297
Mitsubishi Type 90 tank 18
Mitterrand, François 8
Moczulski, Leszek 260
Model, Walter 294
Mojsak, Jaroslaw 245–6, 247, 248
Molesworth, Lietenant Colonel 71
Molotov, Vyacheslav 239
Montague, C. E. 60
Montanelli, Indro 264
Montgomery-Massingberd, Archibald Amar
144, 176, 183
monuments *see* memorials and monuments
Moore, Louise 402
moral effect of the tank 107–10, 130, 133, 146,
434; Russian civil war 199–200, 201; Russian
revolution 198; Tiananmen Square 365
Moravia, Alberto 271
Moreno, Sergeant 409, 410
Mosley, Oswald 180, 183, 211
'Mother' 28–9, 30, 31, 57
Motor Cycle 29
Moynihan, Daniel 15
Muller, Dr 306
Munro, R. 126
Murray, Gideon 90
music hall songs 50–1, 105
Mussolini, Benito 208, 210, 211, 215, 263, 270,
272
Mustafa, Lieutenant Colonel 336
myths 423–4

NAG missile 430
Nagorno Karabakh 391
name of the tank 34–5, 45, 46, 434
Napoleon I 24, 170
Nasser, Gamal Abdul 335–6, 346–7
National Army Museum (London) 23
National War Bonds campaign 81–100
National War Savings Committee: trophy
tanks and 122–3, 179; War Bonds campaign
81–100
NATO 379
naval imagery 54
navigation 48, 409